# Jamaica

## THE ROUGH GUIDE

There are more than one hundred Rough Guide titles
covering destinations from Amsterdam to Zimbabwe

### Forthcoming titles include
Bangkok • Barbados • Edinburgh
Japan • Jordan • Syria

### Rough Guide Reference Series
Classical Music • The Internet • Jazz • Opera
Reggae • Rock Music • World Music

### Rough Guide Phrasebooks
Czech • French • German • Greek • Hindi & Urdu • Indonesian
Italian • Mandarin Chinese • Mexican Spanish • Polish • Portuguese
Russian • Spanish • Thai • Turkish • Vietnamese

### Rough Guides on the Internet
http://www.roughguides.com/
http://www.hotwired.com/rough

**Rough Guide Credits**

Text Editor:            Ann-Marie Shaw
Series Editor:          Mark Ellingham
Editorial:              Martin Dunford, Jonathan Buckley, Samantha Cook, Jo Mead, Amanda Tomlin,
                        Kate Berens, Paul Gray, Vivienne Heller, Sarah Dallas, Chris Schüler, Helena Smith,
                        Julia Kelly, Caroline Osborne, Judith Bamber, Kieran Falconer (UK), Andrew
                        Rosenberg (US)
Online editors:         Alan Spicer (Online UK), Geronimo Madrid (Online US)
Production:             Susanne Hillen, Andy Hilliard, Judy Pang, Link Hall, Nicola Williamson, Helen Ostick
Cartography:            Melissa Flack, David Callier, Maxine Burke
Finance:                John Fisher, Celia Crowley, Catherine Gillespie
Marketing & Publicity:  Richard Trillo, Simon Carloss, Niki Smith (UK), Jean-Marie Kelly, SoRelle Braun (US)
Administration:         Tania Hummel, Alexander Mark Rogers

**Acknowledgements**

The authors would like to thank the entire Jamaica Tourist Board for fantastic support during our time on the island; Annie Shaw for long-suffering editing; and an unknown security guard at the Edge Hill Hotel in Kingston for inspiration. Thanks also to Samantha Cook for guidance, Susanne Hillen for patience, Link Hall for typesetting, David Callier (and MicroMap, Romsey, Hants) for cartographic excellence, Susannah Walker for proofreading, Nicola Williamson and Ian Cummings for painstaking photo research, Alison Cowan and Nick Thomson for help with Basics, and Steve Barrow and Greg Salter for contributions to the music piece. Individually, the authors would like to acknowledge the following:

Adam: Hugh Crosskill for the overview, Yvonne Walters for the sights of Kingston, Simon Crosskill for a bird's-eye view at Sabina Park and all the city's bars, Mutabaruka for the intro to Rasta, the Simpsons for the MoBay angle, Donahue Jarrett for a miraculous recovery, Seb and Alice for the Jamaica Support Team, Colin and Georgii for a stone dog in Spanish Town, and Jason Henzell for larks and Red Stripe on the south coast.

Polly: Big up everyone who gave insight into sweet Jamaica, especially Michele and Trevor Williams, Victoria Bate, Simone Eschmeier, Andrea Lewis and family, Horatio Spencer, Claude, Ricardo, Super Herb, Aubrey, Mayron, Chris Sharp, Vana Taylor, Jan Pauel, Alton Smith, Gibbs, Byron Murray, Ian Robinson, Mike Schwartz, Lynette Wilks, Walter Elmore, African Symbol, Steve Barrow, Congo Ashante Roy, Headley Bennett, Miss Ena, Jennifer Lyn, Ken Boothe, Bozra, Dermot Hussey, Prince Alla, Miguel Lorne, Strangejah Cole, Robert Kerr, Leroy Sibbles, Bridget Anderson, Jahmali, Natty Remo, Janet Davidson, Mikie Bennett, Gussie Clarke, Lynda Lee Burkes, Jah Stitch, Peter Bentley, Gaylene Martin and Roger Williams; to Pat Hannan, Dawn Smith, Judith Thompson, Dan Hammond, Miss Monty, Iva Walters and Juliet Tyson at the JTB and Colin Levy, Claire Griffin and Jane Jervis at Barclay Stratton. Extra special thanks and love to the family: Celia, Matt, Granny, Jean, Imogen, Emma and all the west London crew.

This first edition published October 1997 by Rough Guides Ltd, 1 Mercer Street, London WC2H 9QJ.
Distributed by the Penguin Group:

Penguin Books Ltd, 27 Wrights Lane, London W8 5TZ.
Penguin Books USA Inc, 375 Hudson Street, New York 10014, USA.
Penguin Books Australia Ltd, 487 Maroondah Highway, PO Box 257, Ringwood, Victoria 3134, Australia.
Penguin Books Canada Ltd, 10 Alcorn Avenue, Toronto, Ontario, Canada M4V 1E4.
Penguin Books (NZ) Ltd, 182–190 Wairau Road, Auckland 10, New Zealand.

Printed in England by Clays Ltd, St Ives PLC.
**Typography** and **original design** by Jonathan Dear and The Crowd Roars.
**Illustrations** throughout by Edward Briant.

# Jamaica

## THE ROUGH GUIDE

Written and researched by
Polly Thomas and Adam Vaitilingam

THE ROUGH GUIDES

## Help Us Update

We've gone to a lot of trouble to ensure that this first edition of *The Rough Guide to Jamaica* is accurate and up-to-date. However, things inevitably change, and if you feel we've got it wrong or left something out, we'd like to know: any suggestions, comments or corrections would be much appreciated. We'll credit all contributions and send a copy of the next edition (or any other Rough Guide if you prefer) for the best correspondence.

Please mark letters "Rough Guide to Jamaica" and send to:
Rough Guides, 1 Mercer St, London, WC2H 9QJ,
or Rough Guides, 375 Hudson St, 9th floor, New York, NY 10014.

Or send email to: mail@roughguides.co.uk

Online updates about this book can be found on Rough Guides' website at http://www.roughguides.com/

## Rough Guides

Travel Guides • Phrasebooks • Music and Reference Guides

We set out to do something different when the first Rough Guide was published in 1982. Mark Ellingham, just out of University, was travelling in Greece. He brought along the popular guides of the day, but found they were all lacking in some way. They were either strong on ruins and museums but went on for pages without mentioning a beach or taverna. Or they were so conscious of the need to save money that they lost sight of Greece's cultural and historical significance. Also, none of the books told him anything about Greece's contemporary life – its politics, its culture, its people, and how they lived.

So with no job in prospect, Mark decided to write his own guidebook, one which aimed to provide practical information that was second to none, detailing the best beaches and the hottest clubs and restaurants, while also giving hard hitting accounts of every sight, both famous and obscure, and providing up-to-the-minute information on contemporary culture. It was a guide that encouraged independent travellers to find the best of Greece, and was a great success, getting shortlisted for the Thomas Cook travel guide award, and encouraging Mark, along with three friends, to expand the series.

The Rough Guide list grew rapidly and the letters flooded in, indicating a much broader readership than had been anticipated, but one which uniformly appreciated the Rough Guides' mix of practical detail and humour, irreverence and enthusiasm. Things haven't changed. The same four friends who began the series are still the caretakers of the Rough Guide mission today: to provide the most reliable, up-to-date and entertaining information to independent-minded travellers of all ages, on all budgets.

We now publish 100 titles and have offices in London and New York. The travel guides are written and researched by a dedicated team of more than 100 authors, based in Britain, Europe, the USA and Australia. We have also created a unique series of phrasebooks to accompany the travel series, along with the acclaimed series of music guides, and a best-selling pocket guide to the Internet and World Wide Web. We also publish comprehensive travel information on our two web sites: http://www.hotwired.com/rough and http://www.roughguides.com/

## The authors

Polly Thomas is a freelance writer and unwilling florist/market-researcher whose Jamaica addiction began in her teens and shows little sign of abating. She is also co-author of the new Rough Guide to Trinidad and Tobago.

Adam Vaitilingam is a barrister, freelance writer and occasional sax player who lived in the West Indies from 1989 to 1993. He has contributed to several other Rough Guides, and is presently working on our forthcoming guides to Barbados and Antigua.

# Contents

# Chapter 3: Ocho Rios and the north coast

# Chapter 4: Montego Bay and Cockpit Country

# Chapter 5: Negril and the west

# Chapter 6: The south

# Part Three: Contexts

# Index

# List of Maps

---

**MAP SYMBOLS**

| | | | |
|---|---|---|---|
| - - - | Chapter division boundary | ✈ | Airfield |
| ═══ | Road | ✝ | Church |
| ━∙━ | Railway | ⊠ | Post office |
| ══ | River/canal | ⓘ | Jamaica Tourist Board office |
| ▓ | Urban area | ⌐ | Beach |
| ▒ | Park | ⎀ | Waterfall |
| ◠ | Cave | ◉ | Hotel |
| ♦ | Site of interest | ■ | Restaurant |
| ∴ | Ruin | | |

---

# Introduction

**R**ightly famous for its beaches and music, beautiful, brash **Jamaica** is much more besides. There's certainly plenty of enchanting white sand, turquoise sea and swaying palm trees but, less expectedly, there's lots to see away from the coast: spectacular mountains and rivers, tumbling waterfalls, and cactus-strewn savannah plains. The cities, meanwhile, provide a reminder that the island is more than just a tourist attraction, particularly Kingston – the dynamic, sprawling and unrepentantly Jamaican metropolis which helped to inspire the music of **Bob Marley** and countless other home-grown **reggae** superstars.

Despite the island's immense natural allure, it's not just the physical aspect that makes the country so absorbing and, to many visitors, so utterly addictive. Notwithstanding the invasion of tourists and American satellite tv, Jamaica retains an attitude – a personality – that's more resonant and distinctive than you'll find in any other Caribbean nation. It's a country with a swagger in its step – proud of its history, sporting success and musical genius – but also a weight upon its shoulders. For Jamaica has not avoided the familiar problems of a developing country – serious poverty, dramatic inequality of wealth, and social tensions that occasionally spill over into localized violence and worldwide headlines. The mixture is potent, and has produced a people renowned for being sharp, sassy and straight-talking. Don't expect anyone to beat around the bush here; Jamaicans get on with life, and this can sometimes make them appear rude, uncompromising, even aggressive. Particularly around the big resorts, this direct approach is often taken to extremes, with harassment (including sexual harassment) sometimes reaching infuriating levels.

But there's absolutely no reason to be put off. As a foreign visitor, the chances of encountering any trouble are minuscule, and the Jamaican authorities have spent millions making sure the island treats its tourists right. As the birthplace of the **"all-inclusive"** hotel, Jamaica has become well-suited for those who (like many people) want to head straight from plane to beach, never leaving their hotel compound. But to get any sense of the country at all you'll need to

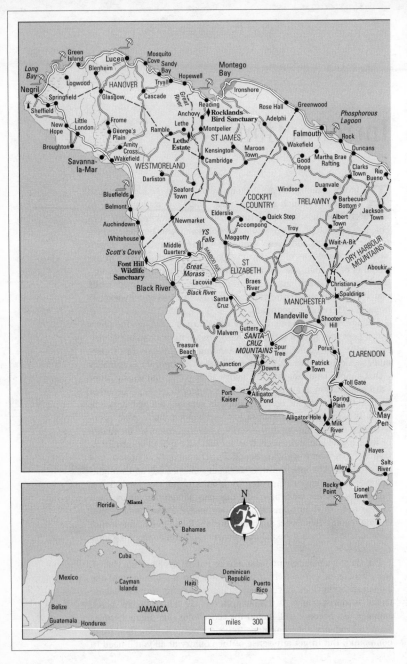

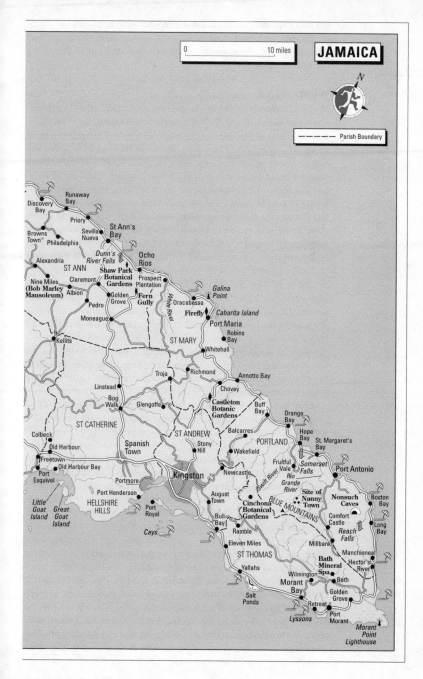

JAMAICA

0            10 miles

N

- - - - - Parish Boundary

Discovery Bay
Runaway Bay
Priory
Browns Town
Philadelphia
Sevilla Nueva
St Ann's Bay
Dunn's River Falls
Ocho Rios
Alexandria
ST ANN
Shaw Park Botanical Gardens
Prospect Plantation
Nine Miles (Bob Marley Mausoleum)
Claremont
Fern Gully
Golden Grove
Albion
Oracabessa
Galina Point
Pedro
Firefly
Cabarita Island
Moneague
Port Maria
Kellits
ST MARY
Robins Bay
Whitehall
Troja
Richmond
Annotto Bay
Linstead
Chovey
Bog Walk
Glengoffe
Castleton Botanic Gardens
Buff Bay
Orange Bay
ST CATHERINE
ST ANDREW
Balcarres
PORTLAND
Hope Bay
St. Margaret's Bay
Colbeck
Spanish Town
Stony Hill
Old Harbour
Wakefield
Freetown
Fruitful Vale
Somerset Falls
Port Antonio
Old Harbour Bay
Newcastle
Swift River
Port Esquivel
Portmore
Kingston
Rio Grande River
Site of Nanny Town
Nonsuch Caves
Boston Bay
Little Goat Island
Port Henderson
HELLSHIRE HILLS
Port Royal
August Town
Cinchona Botanical Gardens
BLUE MOUNTAINS
Comfort Castle
Long Bay
Great Goat Island
Cays
Bull Bay
Ramble
Reach Falls
Millbank
Manchioneal
Eleven Miles
ST THOMAS
Hector's River
Yallahs
Bath Mineral Spa
Wilmington
Bath
Morant Bay
Golden Grove
Salt Ponds
Retreat
Port Morant
Lyssons
Morant Point Lighthouse

White River

get into exploring mode. It's undoubtedly worth it, as this is a country packed with first-class attractions, oozing with character, and pumping with the irrepressible strains of dancehall music, Jamaica's current obsession.

## Where to go

Most of Jamaica's tourist business is concentrated in the "**big three**" resorts of Montego Bay, Ocho Rios and Negril which, between them, pull hundreds of thousands of visitors every year. Probably the most evocative name in the Caribbean, **Montego Bay** is a busy, commercial city with hotels lined up along its main strip, a stone's throw from a couple of Jamaica's most famous beaches. Though "MoBay" has lost some of its old lustre, the place retains a gritty vitality, with a busy street life and a great entertainment scene, most obvious during the annual **Reggae Sumfest**. West of here, its low-rise hotels slung along seven miles of fantastic white sand and two miles of dramatic cliffs, **Negril** is a different type of resort – younger, more laid-back, and with a long-standing reputation for unbridled hedonism that still carries a hint of the truth.

East of MoBay, and the least individualistic of the big three, **Ocho Rios** embodies high-impact tourism – purpose-built in the 1960s to provide the ultimate package of sun, sand and sea. It's not an overly attractive place, and the beaches don't compare favourably with Negril and MoBay, but tourist infrastructure is undeniably strong – the place is packed with shops, restaurants, bars and watersports – and you're right by some of Jamaica's leading attractions, including the famous **Dunn's River** waterfall, dramatic **Fern Gully** and the lovely **botanical gardens** at Shaw Park.

Away from these resorts, you'll have to look a bit harder to find your entertainment – Jamaica's quieter **south** and **east** coasts offer a far less packaged product – but there are plenty of real gems worth hunting out, particularly if you're keen to escape the crowds. In the island's lush, rain-fed northeast, sleepy **Port Antonio** provides a gateway to some of Jamaica's greatest natural attractions, like the cascading **waterfalls** at Reach and Somerset, and outdoor activities; **rafting** on the majestic Rio Grande, and **hiking** through the dense rainforest of the John Crow Mountains. The south coast offers different pleasures, from gentle beach action at the terminally easygoing **Treasure Beach** – a useful base for exploring local delights like the **YS waterfalls** and the gorgeous lagoon at Gut River – to boat safaris in search of local wildlife on the Black River.

Last, but in no way least, **Kingston** is the true heart of Jamaica, a thrilling place, pulsating with energy and spirit, that is home to more than a third of the island's 2.5 million population. This is not just the nation's political capital but its art, theatre and music centre, with top-class hotels, restaurants and shopping, and a clubbing scene that is second to none. A stunning backdrop to the city, the **Blue**

**Mountains** offer more cool hiking possibilities, while the nearby fishing village of **Port Royal**, once a great pirate city, and the former capital of **Spanish Town**, with its grand Georgian buildings, provide more historic diversions.

## When to go

For many visitors, Jamaica's tropical **climate** is its leading attraction – hot and sunny all year. The weather is at its most appealing during the peak tourist season, which runs from mid-December to mid-April, when rainfall is lowest and the heat is tempered by cooling trade winds. Things can get noticeably hotter during the summer and, particularly in September and October, the humidity can become oppressively intense. September is also the most threatening month of the annual hurricane season, which runs officially from June 1 to October 31, though it's worth bearing in mind that, on average, the big blows only hit about once a decade.

As you'd expect, prices and crowds are at their highest during peak season, when the main attractions and beaches can get pretty packed. Outside this period – from Easter to early December – everywhere is quieter and, though the main resorts throb with life pretty much year-round, quieter tourist areas like Port Antonio and Treasure Beach can feel a little lifeless. The good news is that hotel prices everywhere fall by up to 25 percent, there are more bargains to be had in every field of activity, and a number of **festivals** – including the massive annual Reggae Sumfest in Montego Bay – inject some summertime zip.

## Climate

These figures are for Kingston, but are virtually identical island-wide with the exception of Port Antonio and the Blue Mountains, where rainfall is considerably higher.

|  | Average daily temp (F max/min) | Rainfall (inches) |
|---|---|---|
| Jan | 86/67 | 0.9 |
| Feb | 86/67 | 0.6 |
| March | 86/68 | 0.9 |
| April | 87/70 | 1.2 |
| May | 87/72 | 4 |
| June | 89/74 | 3.4 |
| July | 90/73 | 3.4 |
| Aug | 90/73 | 3.5 |
| Sept | 89/73 | 3.8 |
| Oct | 88/73 | 7 |
| Nov | 87/71 | 3 |
| Dec | 87/69 | 1.4 |

# Basics

# Getting there from North America

There's no doubt that the Caribbean, in general, is an extremely popular destination from North America. And airlines and travel agents would be loath to admit that Jamaica is any exception. However, the relatively low profile it has on cruise itineraries, the scarcity of cheap flights, the fact that some airlines and tour operators have discontinued servicing the island, and the negative image Jamaica still has in America, have had an adverse effect on its popularity with North American travellers. However, just one hour and twenty minutes from Miami, and easily accessible by sea, Jamaica is nothing if not convenient.

## By air

There are few **cheap flights** to Jamaica. The airlines don't offer special student rates or air passes and the Caribbean doesn't fit too well into a round-the-world (RTW) itinerary. Apart from special promotions advertised from time to time (when the major carriers are engaged in a price war, for instance), the cheapest of the airlines' published fares is usually an **APEX** ticket, although this will carry certain restrictions: you have to book – and pay – seven, fourteen or 21 days before departure, spend at least seven days abroad (maximum stay 3 months), and you tend to get penalized if you change your schedule.

You can normally cut costs further by going through a **specialist flight agent** – either a **consolidator**, who buys up blocks of tickets from the airlines and sells them at a discount, or a **discount agent**, who in addition to dealing with cut-price flights may also offer complementary services such as travel insurance, car rental, tours and the like. Some agents specialize in **charter flights**, which may be cheaper than anything available on a scheduled flight, but again departure dates are fixed. With all reduced-rate operations, withdrawal penalties are high (check the refund policy).

Regardless of where you buy your ticket, fares will depend on the **season**. Seasonal definitions

---

### Airlines

**Air Canada** in BC ☎1-800/663-3721; in Alberta, Saskatchewan and Manitoba ☎1-800/542-8940; in eastern Canada ☎1-800/268-7240; in US ☎1-800/776-3000.

**Air Jamaica** ☎1-800/523-5585.

**American Airlines** ☎1-800/624-6262.

**Northwest Airlines** ☎1-800/447-4747.

**TWA** ☎1-800/892-4141.

**US Air** ☎1-800/622-1015.

### Discount travel agents and consolidators

**Airtech** ☎1-800/575-TECH or 212/219-7000.

**LTC Travel** ☎1-800/216-9776.

**STA Travel** ☎1-800/777-0112 or 212/627-3111.

**TFI Tours International** ☎212/736-1140.

**Travel CUTS** Canada: ☎1-800/667-2887 or 416/979-2406.

---

vary from airline to airline – and some consider the island a domestic destination not subject to such distinctions – but the period from around mid-December to mid-April is generally classified as **high season**, with the rest of the year considered **low season** (although various one-off events, like Spring Break and the reggae festivals, see fares unseasonably high and seats at a premium).

The following are typical high/low season APEX **fares** from US/Canadian cities to Montego Bay's Sangster Airport: Atlanta (US$335/315); Chicago (US$410/380); Charlotte, NC (US$408/361); Detroit (US$420/400); Orlando (US$300/270); LA (US$580/540); Miami (US$270/240); New York (US$390/350); St Louis (US$473/426); Toronto (CAN$490/$405); Vancouver (CAN$785/710). A few flights continue on, or fly direct to, Norman Manley Airport in Kingston – the extra leg will cost you anything between US$10 and US$65 on top of these prices.

Not surprisingly, **Air Jamaica** leads the field in flights to the island, with once-daily services to Montego Bay and Kingston from Atlanta, Baltimore, Chicago, Fort Lauderdale, New York (Newark and JFK) and Philadelphia, twice-daily flights to Kingston from Miami, a weekly connection from Los Angeles to Montego Bay, and twice-weekly flights from Orlando to Montego Bay. The other chief contender is **American Airlines**, with one daily direct flight from New York (JFK) to Montego Bay, three flights a day from Miami to Montego Bay and two from Miami to Kingston.

Plenty of other carriers are in the market, though, and it's worth calling around to see which are the most convenient for you – US Air, for example, offers the only direct flights to Jamaica from Charlotte, NC, while TWA flies from St Louis.

Finally, the Trinidadian airline BWIA International offers a thirty-day **air pass**, valid for travel around the Caribbean, which is available in the US. See p.21 for details.

## By sea

The archetypal luxury vacation – a **Caribbean cruise** – is a relatively accessible reality in North America. Scores of shipping companies peddle all-inclusive cruises of the Caribbean, and although prices on a luxury liner can scale the heights of silliness, a seven-day spin on a not-so-swanky ship should only set you back about US$500. The downside of choosing a cruise is that as you only get to see the tourist ports – and only for a few hours at that – the glimpse you get of each island is both hurried and unrepresentative. Mind you, the chance to live out your Jackie O fantasies might be ample compensation.

### Yachting

**Yachting** between the USA and the Caribbean is big business, and a very pleasurable way of getting to the island. There's a race from Miami to Montego Bay, The Pineapple Cup, in February, and a lot of yachters go over for the Montego Bay

---

### Cruise operators

The fares quoted below are for seven-day cruises, in single person/double occupancy "inside" (no ocean views) cabins, and are exclusive of port charges, which add an extra US$110 to US$130. All leave from Florida, and in each case, there is only one stop in Jamaica.

DOCKING IN MONTEGO BAY

**Commodore Cruise Line** ☎1-800/832-1122 or 954/967-2100; from US$498.

**Dolphin Cruise Line** ☎1-800/222-1003 or 305/358-2111; from US$485.

DOCKING IN OCHO RIOS

**Carnival Cruise Line** ☎1-800/327-9501 or 305/599-2600; from US$600.

**Holland America Line – Westours** ☎1-800/426-0327 or 206/281-3535; from US$699.

**Celebrity Cruises** ☎1-800/437-3111 or 305/262-8322; from US$699.

**Norwegian Cruise Line** ☎1-800/327-7030 or 305/445-0866; from US$649.

**Costa Cruise Lines** ☎1-800/462-6782 or 305/358-7325; from US$599.

**Royal Caribbean Cruises** ☎1-800/327-6700 or 305/539-6000; from US$749.

## Tour operators

**Air Canada Vacations** ☎ 1-800/74 8893 or 514/876-4141. *Montego Bay beach packages.*

**Air Jamaica Vacations** ☎ 1-800 622 3009. *All-inclusive trips to the island's premier tourist spots.*

**American Airlines Flyaway Vacations** ☎ 1-800/321-2121. *Standard all-inclusive vacations.*

**Elderhostel** ☎ 617/426-7788 or 426-8056. *Educational programmes for seniors, such as a twelve-day course in marine biology for US$1088 and an eight-day Coral Reef programme for US$763. Meals and lodging are included, but you have make your own way to the island.*

**Friendly Holidays** ☎ 1-800/221-9748. *Independent, customized tours of Jamaica.*

**STA Travel** ☎ 1-800/777-0112 or 212/627-3111. *Seven-night hotel/air packages from New York to Jamaica.*

**Sunburst Holidays** ☎ 1-800/MONTEGO or 212/567-2900. *All-inclusive customized packages to Jamaica.*

**Tour Host International** ☎ 1-800/THE HOST or ☎ 212/953-7910. *Specialist tour operator with an astonishing range of travel options, including Cockpit Country adventure tours, natural history tours, Kingston visits (including a car and a driver/escort at night), upscale "eco" tours, and trips to the big reggae festivals.*

**TourScan Inc** ☎ 1-800/962-2080 or ☎ 203/655-8091. *This Caribbean specialist scans some 18,000 tours from 200 brochures for the best value deals (including hotels, flights & tours) on a variety of general and specialist packages, and publishes its findings in a catalogue. This is available for US$4, refundable if you use TourScan to make your booking.*

**Travel Impressions** ☎ 1-800/284-0044. *Puts together the land portion of an island-hopping Caribbean tour.*

**Travel Jam** ☎ 1-800/554-7352. *No specific tours, but tailor-made packages.*

---

Easter Regatta. Marinas pepper the coast, and on arrival you have to go through customs and immigration, and pay a hefty tax. The US Coast Guard in Miami will steer you in the right direction (☎ 305/535-4470), or you can call US Sailing (☎ 1-800/-US SAIL 1 or 401/683-0800) or, in Jamaica, the Montego Bay Yacht Club (☎ 979-8038).

## Packages and tours

Although flights from North America are frequent and quite reasonably priced, and the island so small it's easy to explore independently, you might well be tempted by the comfort and convenience of a vacation **package**. If so, there are no end of all-inclusive deals available, most geared around lying on a north-coast beach for a week or two, and comprising flights, transfers, accommodation and airport taxes. Prices start from around US$620 for seven nights in low season, but generally hover around US$880 for a fortnight, occasionally going as high as US$2800. A few specialist operators offer more thematically designed **tours**, with itineraries geared around special interests or occasions – the big reggae festivals, for instance.

## Entry requirements

US and Canadian citizens don't need a passport to enter Jamaica but do need **proof of citizenship**.

---

### Jamaican embassies, consulates and high commissions

**The Embassy Of Jamaica**, 1520 New Hampshire Ave NW, Washington, DC 20036 (☎ 202/452-0660).

**The Jamaican Consulate General**, 767 Third Ave, 2nd & 3rd Floors, New York, NY 10017 (☎ 212/935-9000); 842 Ingraham Building, 25 SE Second Ave, Miami, FL 33131 (☎ 305/374-8431); 214 King St West, Suite 402, Toronto, Ontario, M5H 1K4 (☎ 416/598-3008).

**The Jamaican High Commission**, Standard Life Building, 275 Slater St, Suite 402, Ottawa, Ontario KIP 5H9 (☎ 613/233-9311).

This can take the form of a valid passport, a birth certificate supported by a driver's licence with photo ID, or a voter registration card supported by a driver's licence with photo ID. You'll also need a ticket valid for return or ongoing travel, sufficient funds to support yourself, and details of the place you'll be staying for the first couple of nights.

## Insurance

Before buying an **insurance policy**, check that you're not already covered. Some homeowners' or renters' policies are valid on vacation, and credit cards such as *American Express* often include some medical insurance, while most Canadians' provincial health plans typically provide limited overseas medical coverage. If you're

not covered – or for additional precautions – you might want to contact a specialist travel insurance company; see the box or ask your travel agent for a recommendation.

The cheapest coverage is currently with *STA Travel*, whose comprehensive policies for fifteen days in Jamaica start at US$48. Rates for a month start at US$80.

Note that most North American travel policies apply only to items lost, stolen or damaged while in the custody of an identifiable, responsible third party – hotel porter, airline, luggage consignment, etc. Even in these cases, you will have to contact the local police within a certain time limit to have a complete report made out so that your insurer can process the claim.

---

### Travel insurance suppliers

**Access America** ☎ 1-800/284-8300

**Carefree Travel Insurance** ☎ 1-800/645-2424

**Desjardins Travel Insurance** (Canada only) ☎ 1-800/463-7830

**STA Travel** ☎ 1-800/777-0112

**Travel Assistance International** ☎ 1-800/821-2828

**Travel Guard** ☎ 1-800/826-1300

**Travel Insurance Services** ☎ 1-800/937-1387

---

# Getting there from Britain and Ireland

The vast majority of British and Irish visitors to Jamaica are on some form of package tour which includes a charter flight direct to the island. This is certainly the simplest way of going about things, and even if you plan to travel independently, a seat on a charter is normally the cheapest way to get out there. But charters do have their drawbacks, especially if your plans don't fit exactly into their usual two-week straitjacket. As an alternative, a couple of airlines offer direct scheduled flights from London to both Kingston and Montego Bay, and you can find similar fares with other carriers that require a stopover in the USA. There are no direct flights from Ireland to Jamaica, but there are good connections via London and Manchester or, on *Aer Lingus* or *Delta*, via New York and Miami.

## Fares and flights

Start by calling the discount and specialist travel agents listed below; most of these can quote fares on scheduled and charter flights, although some, including *Campus*, *STA* and *USIT* (which all specialize in youth and student fares), can only quote for scheduled flights. Other good sources of information are the ads in London's *Time Out* magazine, and the travel pages in the *Observer* and other

Sunday newspapers. *Teletext* and *Ceefax* are also worth a look, as is your local travel agent.

Regardless of where you buy your ticket, fares will depend on the **season**. Seasonal definitions vary from airline to airline, but the period from around mid-December to mid-April is generally classified as **high season**, with the rest of the year considered **low season**. In July and August, however, when many British-based Jamaican families take advantage of the long school holidays to visit relatives, mid-priced "shoulder season" fares come into play.

---

### Airlines

**Aer Lingus**, 40–41 O'Connell St, Dublin 1 (☎01/844 4777) and offices nationwide; ☎0645 737 747 in Northern Ireland.

**Air Jamaica**, Central House, 3 Lampton Rd, London TW3 1HY; ☎0181/570 7999.

**Air UK Leisure**, Stansted Airport, Essex CM24 1AE; ☎0345/666777.

**American Airlines**, 15 Berkeley St, London W1X 5AE; ☎0345/789789.

**Britannia**, Luton Airport, Luton, Beds LU2 9ND; ☎01582/424155.

**British Airways**, 156 Regent St, London W1R 5TA; ☎0345/222111.

**Delta Airlines**, Oakfield Court, Consort Way, Horley RH6 7AF (☎0800/414767); 989 Upper Newtonards Rd, Dundonald, Belfast 4 (☎01232/480526 or 01/676 8080 in Northern Ireland).

**Virgin Atlantic**, Ashdown House, High Street, Crawley, West Sussex RH10 1DQ; ☎01293/747747.

### Discount agents

**Budget Travel**, 134 Lower Baggot St, Dublin 2; ☎01/661 1403.

**Campus Travel**, 52 Grosvenor Gardens, London SW1W 0AG (☎0171/730 8111) and offices nationwide.

**Caribbean Travel**, 367 Portobello Rd, London W10 5SG; ☎0181/969 6230.

**Council Travel**, 28a Poland St, London W1V 3DB; ☎0171/437 7767.

**Flightbookers**, 177–178 Tottenham Court Rd, London W1P 0LX ; ☎0171/757 2080.

**Joe Walsh Tours**, 34 Grafton St, Dublin 2 (☎01/671 8751); 117 St Patrick St, Cork (☎021/277959).

**The London Flight Centre**, 131 Earls Court Rd, London SW5 9RH (☎0171/244 6411) and other branches across London.

**New Look Travel**, 111 High St, London NW10 4TR; ☎0181/965 8212.

**Newmont Travel**, 85 Balls Pond Rd, London N1; ☎0171/254 6546.

**North South Travel**, Moulsham Mill Centre, Parkway, Chelmsford, Essex CM2 7PX; ☎01245/492882.

**Redfern Travel**, 1/3 Piece Hall Yard, Bradford BD1 1PL; ☎01274/733551.

**STA Travel**, 86 Old Brompton Rd, London SW7 3LH (☎0171/361 6262) and offices nationwide.

**Stratford Travel**, 41 Broadway, London E15 (☎0181/519 4921).

**Thomas Cook Flights Direct** ☎0990/101520.

**Trailfinders**, 42–50 Earl's Court Rd, London W8 6FT (☎0171/938 3366); 4–5 Dawson St, Dublin 2 (☎01/677 7888), and offices nationwide.

**The Travel Bug**, 125A Gloucester Rd, London, SW7 4SF (☎0171/835 2000); 597 Cheetham Hill Rd, Manchester M8 5EJ (☎0161/721 4000).

**USIT**, Fountain Centre, College Street, Belfast BT1 6ET (☎01232/324073); Aston Quay, Dublin 2 (☎01/602 1600) and offices across the Republic.

*Air Jamaica* offers **scheduled flights** from London Heathrow four times a week, on Wednesday, Thursday, Saturday and Sunday. The Thursday flight is direct to Kingston; the others stop at Montego Bay before continuing to the capital. *British Airways* flies from London Gatwick three times a week, on Wednesday, Friday and Sunday, stopping at Montego Bay and continuing to Kingston. Return **fares** with both airlines start at between £410 and £495 in low season, reaching £680–850 in high season.

A less convenient but often cheaper option is to change planes in the United States, normally in Miami. *Delta, Virgin, American Airlines* and *British Airways* all fly from London to Miami, with fares as low as £200 to £250 during the low season. From Miami, *American Airlines* and *Air Jamaica* both offer direct flights into Montego Bay and Kingston, with fares from around £140 to £170, according to season.

A number of **charter operators**, including *Britannia* and *Air UK Leisure*, fly from London Gatwick and Manchester into Montego Bay and Kingston. They are normally significantly cheaper than the scheduled flights but tend to arrive and depart at anti-social hours, and there is little or

no flexibility once the ticket is booked. Fares start at as little as £249–299 in low season, rising to £550–600 in high season. Most charter flights are for two weeks, although you can also find one-week and three-week options available.

Finally, if you fancy flying around more than one Caribbean island, *BWIA International* offers 30-day **air passes**, available in Britain, which let you do just that; see p.21 for details.

## Packages and tours

If you plan to do little more than stay in one place and soak up the sun, a **package holiday** can offer excellent value, often considerably cheaper (and more convenient) than arranging separate flights, transfers and accommodation yourself. There are all kinds of deals available, depending on whether you opt for an all-inclusive (hotel room plus all meals) room only, or self-catering option (usually a hotel room with simple cooking facilities). Most packages are for two weeks, and you may have to shop around to find a one-week or three-week deal.

All-inclusive packages at a three-star hotel start at around £775 per person for a week, £950 for a fortnight, based on double occupancy, while

---

### Specialist package and tour operators

**Airtours**, Wavell House, Holcombe Road, Helmshore, Rossendale, Lancashire BB4 4NB; ☎01706/260000. *One of the largest package operators into Jamaica, with a range of holidays in all the tourist hotspots.*

**Calypso Gold**, 1 Kingston Lane, Teddington, Middlesex TW11 9HL; ☎0181/977 9655. *Island-wide self-catering and all-inclusive packages, particularly good if you're after a niche tour like a Test match.*

**Caribtours**, 161 Fulham Rd, London SW3 6SN; ☎0171/581 3517. *Solid, upmarket group with expensive all-inclusive packages.*

**Hayes & Jarvis**, Hayes House, 152 Kings St, London W6 0QU; ☎0181/748 5050. *Exotic wedding packages to a range of hotels.*

**Kuoni Worldwide**, Kuoni House, Dorking, Surrey RH5 4AZ; ☎01306/742222. *Flexible package holidays and good family deals.*

**Thomas Cook**, 45 Berkeley St, London W1X 5AE and high streets across the UK (nationwide

☎0990/666222); 11 Donegall Place, Belfast (☎01232/242341); 118 Grafton St, Dublin 2 (☎01/677 1721). *Package holidays, charter and scheduled flights.*

**Thomson Holidays**, Greater London House, Hampstead Road, London NW1 7SD; ☎0171/707 9000. *Biggest operator into Jamaica, offering package holidays across the north coast.*

**Time Out Travel**, 54A Ilford Rd, London SE5 9HX; ☎0171/738 7077. *A range of accommodation packages, and tours tailored around specific local itineraries.*

**Tropical Places**, Freshfield House, Lewes Road, Forest Row, East Sussex RH18 5ES; ☎01342/825123. *All-inclusive hotel packages only but a wide choice of places to stay.*

**Virgin Holidays**, Ashdown House, High Street, Crawley, West Sussex RH10 1DQ; ☎01293/617181. *General room-only and all-inclusive package deals.*

---

room-only deals start at £450 per person for a week, £500 for a fortnight. Self-catering rooms start at around £550 per person for a week, £600 for a fortnight, again based on two people sharing. All deals include the flight and transfers from airport to hotel.

A handful of tour operators **offer specialized tours**, based, for example, around getting married or catching the West Indian cricket season. And if you just want to see Jamaica for a day, you could do worse than a **Caribbean cruise** (covered in more detail in "Getting There from North America"; see p.4); these start at around £1000 for a seven-day cruise, including a return flight to the embarkation point at Miami.

## Entry requirements

Citizens of Britain and Ireland can enter Jamaica without a visa and stay for up to six months. You will, however, need a **passport** and a return ticket or proof of onward travel. You might also be asked to show that you have sufficient funds to cover your stay, and to confirm that you have accommodation arranged for the first couple of nights. If you can't satisfy the immigration authorities on all counts, they have the right to deny you entry.

The **Jamaican High Commission** in Britain is at 1–2 Prince Consort Rd, London SW7 2BZ (☎0171/823 9911, fax 408 2545). There is no embasssy or consulate in Ireland.

## Insurance

Most travel agents and tour operators will offer you **insurance** when you book your flight or holiday, and some will insist you take it. These policies are usually reasonable value, though as ever, you should check the small print. If you feel the cover is inadequate, or you want to compare prices, travel insurance is sold by almost every travel agent, specialist insurance company or bank, with two weeks' cover for Jamaica averaging around £35, and a month's around £44. Policies issued by *Campus Travel, STA, Endsleigh, Frizzell* or *Columbus* (see box) are all good value. *Columbus* and some banks and building societies also do multi-trip policies which offer twelve months' cover for around £90.

---

**Travel insurance suppliers**

**Campus Travel** ☎0171/730 8111

**Columbus Travel Insurance** ☎0171/375 0011

**Endsleigh Insurance** ☎0171/436 4451

**Frizzell Insurance** ☎01202/292333

**STA** ☎0171/361 6262

**USIT** Belfast ☎01232/324073; Dublin ☎01/679 8833

---

# Getting there from Australia and New Zealand

Jamaica is no bargain destination from Australasia. There are no direct flights from Australia or New Zealand, so you'll have to take a flight to one of the main US gateway airports (Los Angeles, Miami or New York), and pick up onward connections from there.

The least expensive and most straightforward route is via Los Angeles or Miami, from where there are frequent flights to Kingston and Montego Bay. If you're planning to see Jamaica as part of a longer trip, **round-the-world** (RTW) tickets are worth considering, and are generally better value than a simple return flight. Whatever kind of ticket you're after, your first call should be one of the **specialist travel agents** listed in the box opposite. If you're a **student** or **under 26**, you may be able to undercut some of the prices given here; *STA* is a good place to start.

## Fares and air passes

All the **fares** quoted below are for travel during **low season**, and exclude airport taxes; flying at peak times (primarily Dec to mid-Jan) can add substantially to these prices.

Los Angeles is the main US gateway airport for flights **from Australia**; when they have surplus capacity, airlines frequently offer special fares to Los Angeles, which can be as low as A$1599; from LA,

*American Airlines* flies on to Kingston and Montego Bay for around A$350, giving a total fare of A$1949. Otherwise, the best you're likely to find are the *Air New Zealand*, *United* and *Qantas* regulars to Los Angeles, with connecting flights to Miami flying *American Airlines*, *Delta* or *United*: return fares to Miami cost around A$2259 from the eastern states, rising to A$2699 from Western Australia. From Miami to Kingston, return flights with *American Airlines* cost A$331, giving a total return fare in the region of A$2590–3030. **From New Zealand**, *Air New Zealand*, *Qantas* and *United* fly to Los Angeles, with connections on to Miami. Through fares to Miami start at NZ$2475; and the return to Kingston will add another NZ$365.

If you plan to indulge in some island-hopping around the Caribbean, *BWIA* **air passes** can be worthwhile; available for purchase in conjunction with any international carrier, these allow unlimited stopovers within the Caribbean within a thirty-day period. See p.21 for more details.

## RTW tickets

Given these fares and routings, **round-the-world tickets** that take in **Los Angeles**, **New York** or **Miami** are worth considering, especially if you have the time to make the most of a few stopovers; see "Getting there from North America", p.4, for more on reaching Jamaica from Los Angeles, New York and Miami.

Ultimately, your choice of route will depend on where else you want to go besides Jamaica, but here are a few sample itineraries to whet your appetite: starting from either **Melbourne**, **Sydney** or **Brisbane**, flying to Auckland to Papeete to Los Angeles to London (surface) to Paris to Buenos Aires to Melbourne, Sydney or Brisbane (from A$2299); or, starting from **Perth**, flying to Johannesburg to Amsterdam to New York to Los Angeles to Honolulu to Auckland to Perth (from A$2349). **From New Zealand**, you could fly from Auckland to Los Angeles to Rome to London to Bangkok to Melbourne and back to Auckland; fares for this route start at NZ$2499.

## Airlines

**Air New Zealand**, 5 Elizabeth St, Sydney (☎ 02/9223 4666); Level 18, 1 Queen St, Auckland (☎ 09/366 2400).

**American Airlines**, Level 8, 80 Clarence St, Sydney; ☎ 02/9299 3600 or toll-free 1800/227 101. No NZ office.

**Delta Air Lines**, Level 1, 36 Clarence St, Sydney (☎ 02/9262 1777); Dingwall Building

Level 2, 87 Queen St, Auckland (☎ 09/379 3370).

**Qantas**, Chifley Square, cnr Hunter and Phillip sts, Sydney (☎ 02/9957 0111); Qantas House, 154 Queen St, Auckland (☎ 09/357 8900).

**United Airlines**, 10 Barrack St, Sydney (☎ 02/9237 8888); 7 City Rd, Auckland (☎ 09/307 9500).

## Discount agents

**Anywhere Travel**, 345 Anzac Parade, Kingsford, Sydney; ☎ 02/9663 0411.

**Brisbane Discount Travel**, 260 Queen St, Brisbane; ☎ 07/3229 9211.

**Budget Travel**, 16 Fort St, Auckland (☎ 09/366 0061); other branches around the city (toll-free ☎ 0800/808040).

**Destinations Unlimited**, 3 Milford Rd, Milford, Auckland; ☎ 09/373 4033.

**Flight Centres**, Level 11, 33 Berry St, North Sydney, plus other branches nationwide (☎ 13/1600); National Bank Towers, 205–225 Queen St, Auckland (☎ 09/309 6171), and other branches countrywide.

**Northern Gateway**, 22 Cavenagh St, Darwin; ☎ 08/8941 1394.

**STA Travel**, 702–730 Harris St, Ultimo, Sydney; 256 Flinders St, Melbourne; other offices in state capitals and major universities (☎ 13/1776; fastfare telesales ☎ 1300/360960); Travellers' Centre, 10 High St, Auckland (☎ 09/309 0458; fastfare telesales ☎ 09/366 6673) and other offices countrywide.

**Thomas Cook**, 321 Kent St, Sydney; 257 Collins St, Melbourne; branches in other state capitals (☎ 13/1771 or toll-free 1800/064824); 96–98 Anzac Ave, Auckland (☎ 09/379 3920).

**Topdeck Travel**, 65 Glenfell St, Adelaide; ☎ 08/8232 7222.

**Tymtro Travel**, 314 Victoria Ave, Chatswood, NSW; ☎ 1300/652969.

## Packages and tours

**Package holidays** from Australia and New Zealand to Jamaica are few and far between, and many specialists simply act as **agents** for US-based operators, tagging a return flight from Australasia onto the total cost. **Cruises** account for the largest sector of the market: most depart from Miami, and because prices are based on US dollar amounts, they fluctuate with the exchange rate, but to give some idea, all-inclusive three-day cruises start from A$549/NZ$605, while seven-day cruises cost upwards of A$1000/NZ$1100. The luxury end of the market is also catered for by *Caribbean*

### Specialist agents and tour operators

**Caribbean Destinations**, Level 4, 115 Pitt St, Sydney; Level 38, Rialto South Tower, 525 Collins St, Melbourne (☎ 1800/816717). *Comprehensive range of tailor-made Caribbean holidays, including a wide range of accommodation packages and self-drive car rental in Jamaica.*

**Contours**, 466 Victoria St, North Melbourne; ☎ 03/9329 5211. *Choice of accommodation-*

*and-airfare package deals to Jamaica and other Caribbean destinations.*

**Creative Tours**, Level 3, 55 Grafton St, Woollahra, Sydney; ☎ 02/9836 2111. *Caribbean cruise agents.*

**Wiltrans**, Level 10, 189 Kent St, Sydney; ☎ 02/9255 0899. *Agents for a range of Caribbean cruise operators.*

*Destinations* and *Contours*, both of which offer **resort- and villa-based holidays** as well as cruises, with a choice of accommodation. Prices for all of these are suitably rarefied, starting around A$3500/NZ$5000 for two-centre two-week resort holidays (based on twin-share 3-star accommodation and low-season airfares from Australia), and rising inexorably.

None of the adventure-tour operators ventures to Jamaica; for independent travellers, the cheapest way to visit Jamaica is as part of a round-the-world or American holiday, making creative use of airpasses.

## Entry requirements

Australian and New Zealand citizens do not need a visa to enter Jamaica for stays of less than two months, but do need a **passport** and an ongoing or return ticket, and you may be asked to prove that you have sufficient funds, and somewhere to stay for the first couple of nights.

There are **no Jamaican embassies or consulates** in Australia or New Zealand.

## Insurance

**Travel insurance** is put together by the airlines and specialist groups such as those listed below, in conjunction with insurance companies. Policies are broadly comparable in premium and coverage, though *Ready Plan* usually gives the best value for money. A typical policy for Jamaica costs A$190/NZ$220 for one month.

---

**Travel insurance companies**

**AFTA** ☎ 02/9956 4800

**Cover More** ☎ 02/9968 1333 in Sydney; elsewhere ☎ 1800/251881.

**Ready Plan Australia** ☎ 1800/337462; New Zealand ☎ 09/379 3399

**UTAG** ☎ 02/9819 6855 in Sydney; elsewhere ☎ 1900/809462

---

# Information and maps

Before you leave home, it's worth contacting the nearest branch of the efficient Jamaica Tourist Board (JTB), which has plenty of information on the country, including brochures on the main tourist attractions and forthcoming events, lists of recommended accommodation island-wide, and a good road map.

Once in Jamaica, you can get the same information from JTB desks at the Kingston and Montego Bay airports, and JTB offices in the main towns. The offices in Kingston and Montego Bay also have small informative libraries, with clued-up staff who can usually help with local queries. None of the JTB offices provides an accommodation-booking service.

Jamaica has no entertainments **listing magazine**, so to find out what's going on, you have to rely on the newspapers, particularly the *Daily Gleaner*, and – the usual way of announcing forthcoming events – flyers posted up around the towns. We've given more specific advice on finding out what's on in the individual chapters.

## Jamaica on the Net

There's a growing amount of information about Jamaica available on the Internet, and you might

### JTB offices abroad

NORTH AMERICA

**Chicago:** 500 N Michigan Ave, Suite 1030, Chicago IL 60611; ☎312/527-1296, fax 527-1472.

**Los Angeles:** 3440 Wilshire Blvd, Suite 1207, Los Angeles, CA 90010; ☎213/384-1123, fax 384-1780.

**Miami:** 1320 S Dixie Hwy, Suite 1101, Coral Gables, FL 33146; ☎305/665-0557, fax 666-7239.

**New York:** 801 Second Ave, New York, NY 10017; ☎212/856-9727, fax 856-9730.

**Toronto:** 1 Eglington Ave East, Suite 616, Toronto, Ontario M4P 3A1; ☎1-800/233-4582 or 416/482-7850, fax 482-1730.

BRITAIN
1–2 Prince Consort Rd, London SW7 2BZ; ☎0171/224 0505, fax 224 0551.

Note: There are no JTB offices in Australia, New Zealand or Ireland.

### JTB offices in Jamaica

**Black River,** Hendriks Building, 2 High St, Black River; ☎965 2074, fax 965 2076.

**Kingston:** 2 St Lucia Ave, PO Box 360, Kingston 5; ☎929 9200, fax 929 9375.

**Montego Bay:** Cornwall Beach, PO Box 67, Montego Bay; ☎952 4425, fax 952 3587.

**Negril:** 20 Adrija Plaza, Negril PO; ☎957 4243, fax 957 4489.

**Ocho Rios:**Ocean Village Shopping Centre, PO Box 240, Ocho Rios; ☎974 2582, fax 974 2559.

**Port Antonio:** City Centre Plaza, PO Box 151, Port Antonio; ☎993 3051, fax 993 2117.

consider having a browse before you leave. Most of the sites so far are of limited use, but the best of what there is is listed below:

• **www.city.net/countries/jamaica** One of the most authoritative websites on the island, packed with advice on hotels, restaurants and forthcoming events, as well as a huge amount of more general information on the country.

• **www.jamaica–tours.com** Lists of all the main attractions, island-wide, and help on booking your vacation, wiuth hotel reviews and flight details.

• **www.uwimona.edu.jm** Website of the University of the West Indies, with all the college news and activities and dedicated sections on natural history and island tours.

• **www.webcity.co.jp/info/maeda/index. html** Big reggae site, with all the latest news, tributes, discographies, recommended buys and reggae charts.

• **www.jamaicans.com** Entertaining look at Jamaican idiosyncracies, with items on language, culture, music and cookery.

## Maps

For most places, the **maps** in this book should be all that you need. If you are touring or driving around the island the best map to get hold of is the free **JTB road map**, *Discover Jamaica*, which has a 1:350,000 scale map of the entire island, a 1:34,000 scale map of Kingston, and small sketch maps of the other main towns. The map is available from JTB offices abroad and, in Jamaica, from the offices in Kingston and Montego Bay – the smaller Jamaican offices are often out of stock.

Of the other island maps, the two best are *Hildebrandt* (1:300,000) and *ITNB* (1:250,000). If you're after something more detailed, 1:50,000 Ordnance Survey maps are published by the Survey Department, 23 1/2 Charles St, Kingston 10 (Mon–Thurs 9am–1pm & 2–3.30pm; ☎922 6630). Twenty of them cover the island – with nos. 13, 14, 18 & 19 dealing with the Blue Mountains – and cost US$10 each. If you can, get them before you arrive in Jamaica, as obtaining them from the Survey Department can be a laborious process.

# MAP AND TRAVEL BOOK SUPPLIERS

## UNITED STATES

**The Complete Traveler Bookstore**, 199 Madison Ave, New York, NY 10016 (☎212/685-9007); 3207 Filmore St, San Francisco, CA 92123 (☎415/923-1511).

**Rand McNally**, 444 N Michigan Ave, Chicago IL 60611 (☎312/321-1751); 150 E 52nd St, New York, NY 10022 (☎212/758-7488); 595 Market St, San Francisco, CA 94105 (☎415/777-3131).

**Traveler's Bookstore**, 22 W 52nd St, New York, NY 10019; ☎212/664-0995.

## CANADA

**Open Air Books and Maps**, 25 Toronto St, Toronto M5R 2C1; ☎416/363-0719.

**Ulysses Travel Bookshop**, 4176 St-Denis, Montréal; ☎514/289-0993.

**World Wide Books and Maps**, 1247 Granville St, Vancouver, BC V6Z 1E4; ☎604/687-3320.

Maps by **mail or phone order** are available from *Rand McNally*; ☎1-800/333-0136 ext 2111.

## BRITAIN

**Daunt Books**, 83 Marylebone High St, London W1M 3DE; ☎0171/224 2295.

**John Smith and Sons**, 57–61 St Vincent St, Glasgow G2 5TB; ☎0141/221 7472.

**National Map Centre**, 22–24 Caxton St, London SW1 0QU; ☎0171/222 4945.

**Stanfords**, 12–14 Long Acre, London WC2E 9LP (☎0171/836 1321); 52 Grosvenor Gardens, London SW1W 0AG (☎0171/730 1314); 156 Regent St, London W1R 5TA (☎0171/434 4744).

**Thomas Nelson and Sons Ltd**, 51 York Place, Edinburgh EH1 3JD; ☎0131/557 3011.

Maps by **mail or phone order** are available from *Stanfords'* Long Acre branch.

## IRELAND

**Easons Bookshop**, 40 O'Connell St, Dubin 1; ☎01/873381).

**Figgis Bookshop**, 56–58 Dawson St, Dublin 2; ☎01/677 4754.

**Fred Hanna's Bookshop**, 27–29 Nassau St, Dublin 2; ☎01/677 1255.

**Waterstones**, Queens Building, 8 Royal Ave, Belfast BT1 1DA; ☎01232/247355.

## AUSTRALIA AND NEW ZEALAND

**Bowyangs**, 372 Little Bourke St, Melbourne, VIC 3000; ☎03/670 4383.

**The Map Shop**, 16a Peel St, Adelaide, SA 5000; ☎08/231 2033.

**Perth Map Centre**, 891 Hay St, Perth, WA 6000; ☎09/322 5733.

**Specialty Maps**, 58 Albert St, Auckland; ☎09/307 2217.

**Travel Bookshop**, 20 Bridge St, Sydney, NSW 2000; ☎02/241 3554.

# Costs, money and banks

Though a little less costly than most other Caribbean islands, Jamaica is not a particularly cheap country to visit. Some things, like car rental and international telephone calls, cost more than in Europe and a lot more than in the US; for the staples, like accommodation and food, there's usually something to suit every budget, though the pickings are slim at the bottom end of the lodging market. Don't be scared to negotiate on prices – particularly in taxis and at markets and roadside stalls, the first price quoted is often an opening gambit, and even hotels and guesthouses are generally fair game for a bit of bargaining, especially during low season.

## Currency

Jamaica's unit of currency is the **Jamaican dollar** (J$), divided into 100 cents. It comes in bills of J$500, J$100, J$50, J$20 and J$10 and coins of J$5, J$1 J$0.50 and J$0.25. You may also see the smaller ten cent, five cent and one cent coins, although these are pretty much worthless and are gradually being phased out.

At the time of writing the **rate of exchange** is roughly J$35 to US$1 and J$56 to £1, although it is prone to fluctuation, with the local currency inexorably falling in recent years. As a result, the **US dollar** has emerged as an unofficial parallel currency, particularly at the north-coast resorts, and you'll often find prices for tourist services – hotels, restaurants, car rental and sightseeing tours – quoted in US$. When paying a bill, though, check in advance that your change will be given in the same currency or, if in Jamaican dollars, at a decent exchange rate.

## Costs

**Accommodation** is likely to be the major expense of your trip, although if you're prepared to put up with extremely basic options, you can find rooms in most of the main resort areas for around US$15–20. For something more salubrious, and certainly in Kingston and the south coast, expect to pay at least US$25–35, and closer to US$50–70 for a reasonable degree of comfort. Rooms apart, if you travel around by bus or shared taxi and get your food from markets and the cheaper cafés and roadside stalls, you can just about survive on a daily budget of around US$15–20 per day. Upgrading to one decent meal out, the occasional taxi and a bit of evening entertainment, expect to spend a more realistic US$25–30; after that, the sky's the limit.

## Travellers' cheques and plastic

Easily the safest and most convenient method of carrying money in Jamaica is in **travellers' cheques**, preferably in US dollars. These are available for a small commission from most banks, and from branches of *American Express* and *Thomas Cook*; make sure you keep the purchase agreement and a record of cheque serial numbers safe and separate from the cheques themselves. Once in Jamaica, they can be cashed at banks

---

### Pricing policy

Because of the volatility of the Jamaican dollar and the widespread quotation of US dollars for major expenses such as hotels and car rental, we've largely given prices in US dollars throughout the *Guide*. Restaurants and bars vary, with some quoting US, others Jamaican; where we give prices, we do as they do. For minor items like bus fares, short taxi rides or roadside snacks, drivers and vendors will always quote Jamaican dollars, and we have followed their example.

---

and cambios (you'll need your passport or other photo ID to validate them) for a small charge.

Major **credit cards** – *American Express, Visa, Mastercard* – are widely accepted in the larger tourist hotels, but don't necessarily expect the smaller hotels and restaurants to take them. You can also use your credit card to get **cash advances** at most banks, though you'll pay both commission to the bank and hefty interest to your credit card company. **ATM cards** can also be used to withdraw local cash at some banks, but don't rely on it – ask your home bank for a list of reciprocating Jamaican banks before you leave.

**American Express** is represented in Jamaica by *Stuarts Travel Service,* with offices at 12 Main St, Ocho Rios (☎974 2288); 40 Market St, Montego Bay (☎952 4350); Shop 10, Adrija Plaza, Negril (☎957 4887); and 23 Harbour St, Port Antonio (☎993 2609).

## Banks and exchange

**Banking hours** in Jamaica are generally Monday to Thursday 9am to 2pm and Friday 9am to 3pm or 4pm, though many branches of *Workers Bank* also open on Saturdays between 9.30am and 1pm. Other places to exchange money include: **cambios**, found at some supermarkets across the country, which usually offer a slightly better exchange rate, particularly when the currency is fluctuating wildly; at **exchange bureaux** at the main airports, where the rate is slightly lower than the banks; and at **hotels**, where, invariably, the rate is significantly lower.

Keep the official receipts when you change money, as you'll need them to convert any Jamaican dollars back to dollars/sterling when you leave – you are not allowed to take Jamaican dollars out of the country. Finally, whenever you get change, ask the cashier to give you some small bills – many shops, taxi/bus drivers and small restaurants won't be able to change a J$500.

The illegal **black market** is active in Jamaica, particularly when the currency is volatile, and you can expect to be approached to change money on the streets. The exchange rate offered is usually a little better than the banks, but bear in mind that counterfeit notes are common and scams rife on the black market, and that peeling off wads of cash in a public place makes you an obvious target for muggers. If you are going to risk it, never, ever hand over your cash until you've counted the Jamaican dollars you're given.

## Emergency cash

If you run out of money, you can arrange a **wire transfer** to most of the banks in Jamaica from your home bank account or that of a friend or family member. Bear in mind, though, that this is never cheap or convenient, and should be considered a last resort. *Western Union* (☎0800/833833 in the UK; ☎1-800/543-4080 in the US or Canada; ☎3229 8610 in Australia; ☎09/302 0143 in New Zealand; has branches across the island, including Kingston (☎926 2454).

# Getting around

A lot of people come to Jamaica, make straight for their hotel and spend the next fortnight lying on the beach. For those who want to see more of the island, though, there are a variety of ways to get around. Buses and minibuses run around the coasts, and to all towns and most rural communities in the interior; renting a car offers maximum independence, but will eat heavily into your budget, and if you just want to make the odd excursion or short trip, it can work out cheaper to take a taxi, or even hire a private driver. For longer trips, internal flights are reasonably priced, and a good idea if you're short of time or considering a two-centre holiday - say, Negril and Port Antonio.

## Buses and minibuses

According to the national *Daily Gleaner* newspaper, Jamaica's public transport system is "a dreadful source of punishment and wasted time for those who are forced to use it". And there's no doubt that Jamaica's **buses** – aside from the swanky air-conditioned "coaster" buses that ply certain north-coast routes – can be something of a nightmare. Timetables, if they exist, are rarely adhered to, drivers show little interest in the rules of the road, and passengers are squeezed in with scant regard for their comfort.

On the other hand, bus travel is absurdly cheap – roughly J$50 for 70 miles – and, if, like most Jamaicans, you can't afford to fly, take taxis or rent a car, you'll be doing a lot of it. Throughout the book we've explained where to catch buses and, at the end of each chapter, detailed the main routes and journey times.

Each town has a bus terminal of sorts, often near the market. The bus's destination is usually written somewhere on its front, and the conductor shouts it out again just before departure, scouting the area for potential passengers and cramming in as many as the vehicle will take, before the bus screeches off, jampacked with humanity and pounding with music. Buses will stop anywhere en route to pick up or drop off passengers (except in major towns, where they are restricted to bus stops and terminals). If you want to get off somewhere before the terminus, tell the conductor and fellow passengers where you're going and yell "one stop" at the driver once you're there. To get *on* a bus, just stand by the side of the road and wave.

Always keep as close as possible to your luggage – stories abound of travellers, unable to move for the crowd, watching as their bags leave the bus – and look out for the fare that locals are paying (it's not unusual for tourists to get charged extra). Having the right change will make your life easier too. Try also to travel during daylight – arriving in an unfamiliar place at night will make life more difficult, especially if you have to find accommodation. In fact, the earlier in the day you travel the better – being stuck in a bursting Jamaican bus on a boiling afternoon is no picnic.

### Minibuses

**Minibuses** ply many of the same routes as the buses – often gaily painted and captioned with the driver's "name" ("Mr Lover Man", "Country Boy" and the like) – but are often quicker, though they cost about the same and are just as crowded. They, too, depart from a town's central terminus, and though even less bound by timetables than their larger counterparts, asking around at the terminus should elicit approximate departure times. Minibuses, too, pick up and drop off freely en route.

### Cars

If you can afford it, **renting a car** is the best way of getting around and seeing Jamaica. Though some of the roads beggar belief – and knacker

---

### Car rental agencies overseas

**NORTH AMERICA**
**Avis** ☎ 1-800/331-1084
**Budget** ☎ 1-800/527-0700
**Dollar** ☎ 1-800/421-6868
**Hertz** ☎ 1-800/654-3001
**Thrifty** ☎ 1-800/367-2277

**BRITAIN**
**Avis** ☎ 0990/900500
**Budget** ☎ 0800/181181
**Hertz** ☎ 0990/996699
**Holiday Autos** ☎ 0990/300400
**Thrifty** ☎ 01494/442110

**IRELAND**
**Avis** ☎ 0990/900500; ☎ 01/874 5844
**Budget** ☎ 0800/181181; ☎ 0800/973159
**Hertz** ☎ 0990/996699; ☎ 01/676747
**Holiday Autos** ☎ 0990/300400; ☎ 01/454 9090

**AUSTRALASIA**
**Avis** ☎ 1800/225533
**Budget** ☎ 13 2727
**Hertz** ☎ 13 3039
**Avis** (New Zealand) ☎ 09/526 2847
**Budget** (New Zealand) ☎ 09/375 2222
**Hertz** (New Zealand) ☎ 09/309 0989

---

your suspension – it's a relatively easy country to drive in; distances are small, and a car can take you on some delightful back routes that you won't see if you're flying or travelling by bus. However, rental **prices** are high, starting (in high season) at around US$60 per day, including government tax. Third party insurance is normally included in the price; if you don't have a credit card that offers free collision damage insurance, you'll have to pay another US$12–15 per day to cover potential damage to the car.

There are rental companies all over the island, with the best selection in Kingston and Montego Bay, and we've listed them in the individual chapters. Renters range from reputable international chains to dodgy one-man-and-a-dog outfits; though the latter may appear less expensive, you're often better off going with the known names, which will normally offer guaranteed roadside assistance and are less likely to rip you off. To rent a car you'll need a current licence from your home country or an international driver's licence and, in theory, you'll need to have held the licence for at least a year. Most companies stipulate that drivers must be at least 21 (though some will rent only to drivers over 25). Before you set off, check the car fully to ensure that every dent, scratch or missing part is inventoried. When returning the car undamaged, ensure that you collect any credit card deposit slip.

### Rules of the road

Driving in Jamaica is on the **left**. The main A roads across the country are normally in excellent con-

dition, though once you come off them, you'll find the minor roads are often badly pot-holed. In parts of the country, including the Blue Mountains and Cockpit Country, roads are often little more than bare rock, and if you're planning to explore much in these areas, you should consider getting a **four-wheel-drive** (4WD) vehicle, though you'll pay a premium of around US$20 a day.

Jamaicans are notoriously bad drivers, with male drivers often dangerously macho and impatient. Watch out for overtaking traffic coming towards you – many drivers think nothing of overtaking a line of ten or more cars even if they can't see what's coming - and be prepared to spend a lot of time stuck behind large lorries on the main roads. Use the horn freely and, above all, drive defensively.

If you do have an accident, wait for the police before moving your car, and avoid making any admission of responsibility, or, for that matter,

---

### Hitching

Although many Jamaicans **hitch** rides – and will expect you to offer if you're driving by with a half-empty car – very few tourists do, and it's not something we recommend. There's a common assumption that tourists have plenty of money so, at the least, you'll be looked at as a curiosity; at the worst, you're exposing yourself to danger. If you're really short of cash, you're better off sticking to the buses.

---

accusations of blame – you don't want to get embroiled in a heated roadside argument.

Finally, the police often set up **speed traps** and **roadblocks**. If you're stopped, be friendly and polite and you'll normally be sent on your way, but drug searches are not uncommon.

### Local drivers

If you don't drive – or don't want to – but still want to travel independently around the island, it might be worth hiring a **local driver** to ferry you about; generally for between US$60 and US$100 a day. They often make excellent tour guides, but, especially if you're a woman alone, you might find the prospect of setting off in a car with a stranger a bit daunting. Obviously, we only recommend reliable drivers, whose names and numbers appear at relevant points throughout the *Guide*.

## Taxis

Although a rental car is useful for touring, if you're staying in one place for any length of time, you'll find that it often works out cheaper to get around by **taxi**.

What passes for a taxi in Jamaica varies from the gleaming white vans of the **Jamaican Union of Travelers Association** (JUTA; ☎926 1537), the official – and very expensive – carriers, to beaten-up old **Ladas** that crawl along the island's roads. Officially licensed taxis carry red numberplates with "PP" or "PPV" on them, but there are a number of rogue taxis, most of whom claim that their application for taxi status is being processed. The authorities advise against using the rogues but, obviously, it's up to you whether you trust the guy or not. Most towns have a reliable local taxi service that you can call (numbers are given throughout the *Guide*); during the day, it's usually just as easy to head to the local taxi rank or flag them down in the street.

On the whole, taxi **fares** are pretty reasonable in Kingston and the less touristed areas, even for long journeys; on the north coast, prices are rather more hefty – around US$5 for ten miles. Bear in mind, though, that few of the cars have meters, so always establish a price before you get in (or over the phone if you're calling for one). The first quoted price is normally just an opener; don't be afraid of negotiating. Once you've agreed on a price, a tip is unnecessary.

**Shared taxis** or "route taxis" - private Lada cars crammed with as many passengers as the driver/owner can fit in – operate on short, busy routes around the main towns, picking up and dropping off anywhere along the way in the same manner as the buses and minibuses. Some shared taxis are marked by the PPV numberplate, though many more are not, making them difficult to identify, except by the squash of passengers. Though they're normally perfectly safe, they don't often get tourists aboard, and it's not uncommon for a driver to assume that you wish to charter the taxi, in which case he will throw the other passengers out - make it clear that this is not what you want. Prices are much closer to bus fares than to taxi rates.

## Motorbikes and cycling

Jamaica should be much better for **cycling** than it is. Places like the Blue Mountains, perfect for biking, are not well geared towards independent cyclists, though several tours offer an easy, if expensive, way of seeing them on a bike (see p.109). Throughout the island, rental outlets are thin on the ground – we've listed them where they're available.

Renting a **scooter** or **motorbike** is easier, and can be an exhilarating way of touring the island. Outlets abound in the main resorts, and at US$30 per day, prices are very reasonable, and though in theory you'll need to show a driving licence, these are rarely asked for. Helmets are usually available and should be worn.

Zooming about on two wheels, though hugely enjoyable, is fraught with **danger** in Jamaica. Cyclists should stick to minor roads, and everyone should be watch out for potholes, madcap drivers and daft goats and dogs.

## Planes

If you're heading across country – say from Kingston to Montego Bay or Port Antonio – it's well worth considering one of the **internal flights** provided by *Air Jamaica Express* (☎923 6664), which are quick, efficient and sensibly priced. There are domestic airports at Tinson Pen in Kingston (☎924 8850), Montego Bay (☎952 4300), Port Antonio (☎923 6664) and Negril (☎957 4251), and another undergoing renovation in Ocho Rios. Private **charters** are available from *Wings Jamaica* at Tinson Pen (☎923 6573) and from *Timair* at Montego Bay (☎952 2516) and Negril (☎957 3394). For **sightseeing tours**

## Domestic flights

**Montego Bay to**: Tinson Pen, Kingston (Mon–Fri 8 daily, Sat–Sun 5 daily; 35 min; US$98); Negril (1 daily; 10 min; US$74); Port Antonio (1 daily; 40 min; US$104).

**Negril to**: Tinson Pen, Kingston (1 daily; 1hr; US$104); Montego Bay (1 daily; 10 min; US$74); Port Antonio (1 daily; 50 min; US$104).

Prices quoted are for a return trip.

**Port Antonio to**: Tinson Pen, Kingston (1 daily; 40 min; US$74); Montego Bay (1 daily; 40 min; US$104); Negril (1 daily; 50 min; US$104).

**Tinson Pen, Kingston** to: Montego Bay (Mon–Fri 8 daily, Sat–Sun 5 daily; 35 min; US$98); Negril (1 daily; 1hr; US$104); Port Antonio (1 daily; 40 min; US$74).

you're better off with *Helitours*, based in Ocho Rios (☎974 2265 or 1108) –a 15min helicopter ride around Ochi costs US$55 per person, while an hour-long island tour starts at US$200 a head.

## Organized tours

There's plenty on offer if you're after an **organized tour**; hundreds of operators crowd the resorts, most schlepping off to well-known attractions like

### Tour operators in Jamaica

**Caribic Vacations** ☎979 0114 or 1084, 952 4469 or 5013, fax 952 0891. *An excellent roster of reggae tours (see p.184), inexpensive Cuba excursions and Land Rover trips to interior waterfalls. Guides speak English, German and Dutch, and prices are reasonable, starting at US$20 for a half-day sightseeing tour to US$80 for a full day's jeep safari.*

**Eco Jamaica** ☎952 4488, fax 979 6363. *All-inclusive packages touring Jamaica's lesser-known attractions for three, four and seven nights from US$599 per person.*

**JUTA** ☎952 0813, fax 952 5355. *The largest tour operator in Jamaica, offering every con-*

*ceivable excursion within the limits of the well-beaten track, but prices tend to be a little high, at US$45 for a Blue Mountains trip.*

**PRO Tours** ☎978 6113 or 8129, fax 978 6139. *All the standard attractions plus specialist packages on art, architecture, natural history and birding.*

**Tourwise** ☎974 2323 or 952 6098, fax 952 0096. *Good for conventional tours island-wide.*

**Tropical Tours** ☎952 0400 or 2929, fax 952 6799. *A reliable company offering standard tours throughout Jamaica.*

### ALTERNATIVE TOUR OPERATORS

**Destinations** (formerly Sense Adventures), PO Box 216, Kingston 7; ☎927 2097, 960 5705 or toll-free 1-800/532 2271. *The original alternative operator – tales of its naked canoe trips are legendary – but, since the 1996 departure of its founder, no longer the best. Now concentrates solely on mountain hiking trips.*

**Explorers JA**, PO Box 188, Reading PO, St James; ☎0997 5798. *Montego Bay-based Ian Robinson offers extremely informed personalized tours – botany, birds, buildings, music, history – aboard a rattling but roomy Land Rover. Pricey at $200 per day including lunch, but the vehicle seats six. Call a week or so in advance.*

**Sun Venture**, 30 Balmoral Ave, Kingston 10; ☎960 6685, fax 929 7512. *Budget-friendly scheduled and custom-designed tours, starting at US$50 for groups of four or more. Mainstays include Cockpit Country caving, south coast safaris, and a serpent trail in quest of the Jamaican boa.*

**The Touring Society of Jamaica**, PO Box 118, Ocho Rios; ☎974 5831 or 944 8400, fax 974 5830 or 944 8408. *Based in Ocho Rios and Irish Town above Kingston, this slick outfit runs deservedly costly themed tours on anything from coffee to art, crafts to reggae, from US$250 for a group of four, and half-day, scheduled trips from US$75 per person.*

Rose Hall or Dunn's River Falls, or offering "high-light" tours of a specific area. At best, they are a hassle-free and comfortable means of getting around; at worst, they barely skim the surface of the country and its culture from the shelter of an air-conditioned bus. There also tends to be little variation in content from one company to another. Prices are generally comparable, too, starting from around US$25 for a simple half-day excursion to US$100 for full day-trips, including meals. Tours of specific sights are listed in the relevant chapters; listed in the box below are the largest operators, running trips throughout Jamaica, and several more **alternative-style** companies, which tend to be more rewarding and, consequently, more expensive – booking in a group spreads the cost and may get you a discount.

## Community tourism

**Community tourism** is a relatively new concept in organized tours in Jamaica, the idea being to encourage closer connections between the tourist and the community, through visits to private houses, farms, schools and craft centres. *Countrystyle* (☎962 3725, fax 962 1461), based in Mandeville, is one of the main organisers, arranging accommodation and customized itineraries island-wide; others include the *Bluefields People's Community Association* (☎955 8792, fax 955 8791) in the south-west, and the *Oracabessa Foundation* (☎975 3393), in St Mary on the north coast.

## Caribbean island-hopping

People often like to do a bit of **island-hopping** while they're in the Caribbean. Many, certainly, can't resist the lure of **Cuba**, just seventy miles north. *Cubana* (☎978 3410) flies to Havana from Kingston twice a week, with return trips costing US$187; *Caribic* (☎979 0322) flies from Montego Bay to Havana and Santiago de Cuba for a similar fare. Both companies can arrange accommodation. North Americans should note that Washington presently allows US citizens to visit Cuba but not to spend dollars.

*Air Jamaica* has just begun using Montego Bay as a hub airport, with connections to Cuba, Antigua, the Bahamas, St Lucia, Barbados, the Cayman Islands and the Turks and Caicos Islands. At present, round-trip flights to these islands are pretty expensive – starting at around US$207 for a round-trip to Cuba, US$282 to Barbados – though the airline already offers discounts for travellers visiting Jamaica on certain package holidays and expects to introduce reduced-price air passes for all travellers within a year or so.

More economical if you want to see a few islands is to buy a Caribbean **air pass** before you leave home. The Trinidadian **BWIA International Airways** (in the US ☎1-800/327-7401; in the UK ☎0181/577 1100; in Australia ☎02/9223 7004) sells thirty-day air passes, valid within the Caribbean region (including Venezuela and Guyana), which allow unlimited stops, though you can't zig-zag between islands. You must specify your routing, but not the dates, in advance; and each change incurs a fee of US$20 or the equivalent. Passes are available for purchase in conjunction with any international carrier if you're coming from Australia or North America, but only in conjunction with a flight into Jamaica with *BWIA* if you're coming from the UK. Passes start at US$399/£245/A$460/NZ$500.

# Accommodation

meet the JTB's sometimes rather pedantic requirements.

If you're in the mood, it is always worth **haggling** over the price of a room. Even in high season a lot of hotels have surplus capacity – the boom in all-inclusives has hurt the independent sector badly – and are sometimes desperate for custom. In low season, you have even more bargaining power, and it's not unknown for US$100 rooms to go for US$40. If you are going to negotiate, doing so over the phone will save you having to traipse around; if you do strike a deal, get the name of the person you're talking to in case the agreement has been "forgotten" when you arrive at the hotel.

## Hotels and guesthouses

Jamaica has no youth hostels and the **cheapest** places to stay are usually small, family-run **guesthouses** with pretty basic facilities. At rock-bottom prices (US$20 and under), rooms make for little concession to comfort; the ones that we recommend are normally clean and have some measure of security, though you can expect them to be cramped and box-like, with spartan furniture, shared bathrooms and a fan if you're lucky. Moving up in price, and into **hotel** territory, US$30–50 will normally secure a more tolerable place with a comfortable bed, hot water and, usually, a bar and maybe a place to eat; for a little more money you'll get a television and a phone and possibly air-conditioning. Once you're paying US$75, you can expect your hotel to have a swimming pool, a restaurant and air-conditioning; over US$100 you'll get a considerable degree of luxury. The top-price hotels are beyond most budgets but often worth a visit – expect top-quality architectural design, lavish artwork in the rooms and lobby, impeccably dressed staff, and swimming pools carved in exotic shapes or with their own tumbling waterfalls.

## All-inclusives

Jamaica was the birthplace of the "all-inclusive" hotel, where a single price covers your room and all meals, and often all drinks and water-

Accommodation is likely to be your biggest single expense while travelling in Jamaica. Although the country has far more choice than you'll find on other Caribbean islands, it's rare to find anywhere to stay for less than US$15-20 per night, and you usually need to pay at least twice that for a place with reasonable security and comfort. At the other end of the scale, Jamaica has some of the world's finest luxury hotels, and there are plenty of options in the middle. As you'd expect, you get what you pay for, although throughout the book we have emphasized places that we consider particularly good value.

The majority of visitors to Jamaica have their accommodation pre-arranged as part of a package deal, although this is by no means necessary. If you're not pre-booked, it's normally worth calling ahead to reserve a room for your first night or two to save hassle on arrival. After that, it's easy enough to call the next place you're heading to arrange a room, although if you've got your heart set on staying in a specific hotel or guesthouse, you should try to sort it out earlier.

Twice a year, the Jamaica Tourist Board publishes a list of approved accommodation island-wide, with details of their latest rates. It's a reasonable guide to what's available, but there are plenty of perfectly acceptable hotels and guesthouses which aren't included because they don't

sports too. *Sandals* and *Superclubs* are the best known of the all-inclusive chains, with around twenty hotels between them, but many other hotels are jumping on the bandwagon, offering all-inclusive deals side by side with room-only packages. Prices vary enormously, but bargain deals are rare.

The product offered by the all-inclusives is often excellent – sometimes verging on the madly luxurious – and, despite a blanket no-tips policy, staff are invariably as pleasant and accommodating as in other hotels. And there is something undeniably seductive about the idea of unlimited access to a hotel's facilities without having to reach for your wallet every time. There is a downside, though. Jamaicans call these places "tourist prisons", and indeed many guests do feel rather trapped after a couple of days – the fact that everything is already prepaid discourages them from getting outside the hotel compound to sample the island's many great restaurants and bars – and the giddy thrill of trying twenty different types of cocktail in an evening quickly evaporates. Besides, most all-inclusives offer **day or evening passes** for lunch, dinner or drinks and entertainment, so you might find it better to stay elsewhere and only visit once for a blow-out.

## Private homes

Hundreds of **private homes** throughout Jamaica are rented out to visitors, normally by the week. Ranging from small beachside chalets to grand villas, these are typically self-catering places, often with maid-service (occasionally with a cook and a security guard), and can make a reasonably priced alternative to hotels if you are travelling as a family or in a group. *JAVA*, the Jamaica Association of Villas and Apartments, has comprehensive details of 300 or so places to suit most budgets; contact PO Box 298, Ocho Rios (☎974 2508, fax 974 2967).

## Camping

There are surprisingly few **camping** options around Jamaica, although you'll normally find one or two in each of the main tourist areas, and some of the cheaper hotels will let you set up a tent on their grounds for a small charge. Expect to pay US$5–10 per person per night. **Camping rough** on the beaches is not recommended, as the risk of serious hassle and robbery is high. If you're considering a camping trip, it's worth contacting *JATCHA* – the Jamaica Alternative Tourism, Camping and Hiking Association – at PO Box 216, Kingston 7 (☎927 0357).

---

### Accommodation price codes

All accommodation listed in this guide has been graded according to the following **price categories**:

| ① under US$20 | ② US$20-35 | ③ US$35-50 | ④ US$50-70 |
|---|---|---|---|
| ⑤ US$70-100 | ⑥ US$100-150 | ⑦ US$150-200 | ⑧ US$200 and above |

Rates are for the cheapest available double or twin room during the off-season – normally mid-April to mid-December. During the high season, rates are liable to rise by up to 25 percent (though this is rare at the cheaper hotels), and proprietors may be less amenable to bargaining. Many of the all-inclusive hotels have a minimum-stay requirement – where this is the case, we have mentioned it in the text – and rates are quoted per person per night based on double occupancy. Although the law requires prices to be quoted in Jamaican dollars, most hotels give their rates in US dollars; payment can be made in either currency.

---

# Health

Travelling in Jamaica is generally very safe, health-wise. Food tends to be well and hygienically prepared – though you should be wary of some of the dirtier-looking roadside stalls – and the filtered and heavily chlorinated tap water is safe to drink, so bugs and upsets are normally limited to the usual "traveller's tummy". In rural homes you may be offered rainwater – while this is generally safe it is up to you to decide whether to risk it.

## Vaccinations and other precautions

Unless you have travelled to Asia, Africa, Central or South America, the Dominican Republic, Haiti or Trinidad and Tobago within six weeks of landing in Jamaica, **no vaccinations** are required to enter the island, though you might want to have hepatitis A, typhoid and polio shots if you're planning to hike or swim in rivers.

Jamaica is not malarial, but there are occasional outbreaks of **dengue fever**, carried by the *Aedes aegypti* mosquito, found throughout the island but particularly prevalent in Kingston. It's technically only fatal if you get it twice, but at the first sign of symptoms – extreme aches and pains in the bones and joints, dizziness, headaches, fever and vomiting – you should take to your bed for a few days. There's no effective vaccination, so your best prevention is to avoid mosquitoes (see "Creepy Crawlies", below).

Have a **dental check-up** before you travel and bring **prescription medicines** with you. A pre-prepared **medical kit** (see box) is also useful.

## Heat problems

Jamaica's **humid climate** can bring on a host of minor medical complaints in those unused to it. Open wounds take longer to heal and easily become septic, so make sure you wash and dress cuts thoroughly as soon as they occur; if you've no antiseptic to hand, white rum or even honey are effective substitutes. **Conjunctivitis** thrives in heat and bright sunlight – bring your usual treatment if prone. **Pityriasis**, a fungal infection that appears as circular crispy patches on white skin and as lighter patches of discoloration on black skin, is common but easily treated with anti-fungal creams, sulphur-based lotions or anti-dandruff shampoos containing selenium; the same goes for **athlete's foot** – wear open sandals as much as possible and flip-flops around the pool.

You'll need to be extra-scrupulous about personal hygiene, too, as blocked sweat ducts can cause **prickly heat**. To treat or avoid it, wear loose cotton clothes, take frequent cold showers without soap, dust with medicated talcum powder, and don't use sunscreen or moisturiser on affected areas.

**Dehydration** and **heat exhaustion** are other potential problems – at the first sign of light-headedness, headache, or nausea, lie down in a

---

### Aloe vera

Jamaicans are so convinced of the curative power of fast-growing **aloe vera** or "sinkle bible" (a corruption of the botanical name *Sempervivum*) that many dispense with titles altogether and simply call it the "healing plant". Noticeable for its thick, spiny-edged clusters of leaves growing close to the ground, aloe is the workhorse of Jamaican medicine – used to treat sunburn, heat rash, cuts, bruises, burns and all insect bites; mixed with water to make an eye wash to soothe conjunctivitis; used to condition sun-damaged afro hair; a treatment for skin conditions like eczema and psoriasis; and drunk with garlic to cleanse the blood – a daring feat, as it's very bitter.

Rastafarians use aloe in place of the Biblical hyssop, but you're most likely to encounter it in the hands of hustlers who peddle bottles of aloe massage on north-coast beaches. As it flourishes throughout the island, you can usually find it for free, but anyone will collect a stem for a few Jamaican dollars. To extract the gel, slice the stem in two, cut off the serrated edges, lightly scrape the mauve jelly and wipe it on. Be careful not to get it on clothing – it leaves a stubborn purple stain.

cool place and drink as much as possible; if you become seriously dehydrated, a salt/sugar solution in water helps replenish lost minerals. In case of serious **sunstroke** – signalled by vomiting and blurred vision – get to a doctor.

## Stomach problems

While serious stomach disorders are rare among travellers in Jamaica, the climate and unfamiliar food might well result in a bout of **diarrhoea** – or "running belly", as the locals call it. Washing and peeling fruit and vegetables, being choosy about where you eat and always washing your hands before you do so lessen the risk, but if you do come a cropper, rest and drink plenty of water, herb tea, fruit juice or clear soup; coconut water has excellent calmative properties and is packed with vitamins. Make up for lost minerals by drinking a glass of water mixed with a teaspoon of sugar and half a teaspoon of salt after every motion and once an hour. Eat plain foods like rice or bread and avoid fruit, fatty foods and dairy products. Conventional diarrhoea remedies alleviate symptoms but reduce the body's natural response to flush out the infection and should only be used if you cannot get to a toilet; i.e. before a long journey.

## HIV, AIDS and STDs

Government figures put the number of people with **AIDS** in Jamaica at 1605, with roughly ten percent more **HIV-positive**. However, HIV support workers estimate the true figure is up to ten times that. Given the high level of holiday liaisons and the local propensity for casual sex, figures seem set to rise and, even officially, have so far doubled every two years since the late 1980s. HIV is primarily a heterosexual problem in Jamaica, with tourist areas the worst affected; one in ten citizens in the Montego Bay area are HIV positive; one in five female prostitutes carries the virus. With an estimated 80,000 cases of other **STDs** (including syphilis) each year, Jamaica has a long way to go in sexual health education; only recently a radio advertising campaign saw fit to dispel the (widely believed) myth that STDs can be cured by having sex with a virgin.

---

**Advice** and **information** on AIDS, HIV and STDs is available on ☎ 0888 991 4444 (toll free) or ☎ 929 9408 or 9409.

---

Always use **condoms**. Bring them with you even if you don't plan on having sex; the main Jamaican brand "Rough Riders" and some US imports are available from pharmacies and street vendors – check the expiration date. If you notice unusual symptoms get treatment right away.

## Creepy crawlies: bites and stings

Prevention really is better than cure when it comes to encounters with insects. Avoid being bitten by **mosquitoes** by wearing long sleeves and trousers and using lots of *DEET*-rich repellent – especially in the early evening or after rain. Mosquito coils are sold everywhere and can be effective, and the widely available *Skin So Soft* has miraculous anti-mosquito properties. If you do get attacked, anoint the bites with aloe or calamine – and **leave them alone**; though hellishly tempting, scratching will lead to more irritation, scarring and infected sores.

Almost-invisible **sand flies** amass on beaches at dusk, inflicting a small, shiny bite with a lingering itch; Jamaicans use "rubbing alcohol" to soothe. Present wherever there is livestock, **ticks** and **grass lice** wait on grass stems for passing feet to feast on; defy them by wearing trousers tucked into socks, as repellent is ineffective. Though present year-round, tick populations peak between October and January, but even then they're only a problem in rural areas. They can be safely plucked from the skin, though you should apply antiseptic and ensure that you have removed the head as well as the body – leave infested clothes out to air. A lighted cigarette efficiently despatches the larger grass lice; locals dab with kerosene.

There are no **poisonous snakes** in Jamaica – rumours of the reappearance of the venomous black racer are as yet unsubstantiated – and **black widow spiders** are shy enough to make an encounter unlikely, though you should see a doctor if you think you've been bitten by either. Watch out for the red and black **"forty legs" centipede**, which measures up to five inches and imparts a nasty scarring bite if touched, even when dead.

### Beasts of the sea

Though they look vicious, **moray eels** and **barracudas** only attack if threatened, so keep away from them when snorkelling or diving. Other than

## A traveller's first-aid kit

Among items you might want to carry with you – especially if you're planning to go hiking (see "Sports and Outdoor Activities", p.42) are:

Antiseptic cream

Insect repellent

Plasters/band aids

Lint and sealed bandages

Imodium (Lomotil) for emergency diarrhoea treatment

Paracetamol/aspirin

Multi-vitamin and mineral tablets

Rehydration sachets

Calamine lotion

Hypodermic needles and sterilized skin wipes (more for the security of knowing you have them, than any fear that a local hospital would fail to observe basic sanitary precautions).

Thrush and cystitis remedies.

the harmless **nurse shark** occasionally seen around less explored reefs, sharks are rare along the heavily populated coast. **Spiny black urchins** are easily missed in a bed of sea grass – if you tread on one, remove the spines immediately, soak the skin in vinegar and see a doctor. **Jellyfish** are quite common, particularly in har-bours – the sting is painful but not serious and is easily treated by a doctor; supreme care should be taken to avoid the trailing purple **Portuguese man o' war**, rare but toxic. **Coral** can cut or cause a nasty reaction; don't touch the rash directly, but wash it with a diluted vinegar or ammonia solu-tion.

## Bush medicine

Jamaicans still make frequent use of "**bush medicine**" or "**balm**", a system of African herbal medicine introduced to Jamaica by slaves, fundamental to Maroon civilization for 300-odd years and still an important part of Myalist practice (see "Religion" in Contexts, p.337). Most Jamaicans have a rudi-mentary knowledge of plant medicine, but balmists or herbalists have a lifetime's experience, if no for-mal qualifications. One or two of these respected elders still prescribe from the traditional setting of a **balmyard**, distinguishable from other rural dwellings by coloured flags and hanging talismans. Consultations can be enlightening, but balmists tend to be secretive souls and you'll find a good one only through word of mouth.

Herbs can be taken as an infusion or decoction (usually as a tea), as a poultice, or in a hot "bush bath". Many households have a pot of cure-all **bush tea** permanently on the hob, made up of diverse ingredients like lemon, fevergrass, soursop, breadfruit leaves and pepper elder. Perhaps the most widely used single herb is **cerassee**, a climbing vine made into a very bitter tea – you can buy ready-made tea-bags if you develop a taste. It's said to cure practically everything, but is particularly good as a blood purifier and allegedly discourages mosquitoes. Inevitably, there are loads of plants geared around male virility – **chainy root**, **jack-in-the-bush**, **janta** (or cow-hoof leaf), **quassia** – the list of "front end lifters" goes on and on. **ganja** is boiled into a tea for asthma and eye problems; **leaf of life** conquers colds, hypertension and bronchial problems; **tuna cactus** treats dandruff, nerves and chronic pain such as arthritis. Among the best names are **search mi heart** and **shame o' lady**, both used for colds and stomach problems, but the prize goes to **ram goat dash along**, good for arthritis and debility. Simple **fruits and vegetables** are also attributed with specific healing properties – soursop is said to calm the nerves, and papaya (paw-paw) reputed to relieve indigestion, guava leaves are good for diarrhoea, tamarind soothes itchy skin and chicken pox, and coconut water cleanses the bladder.

Though most balmists stick to medicine, some are associated with **obeah**, or witchcraft, prescrib-ing grave dirt mixed with substances such as "**Oil of Keep the Dead**" or "**Oil of Deliver Me**" to ban-ish duppies, "**Oil of Come Back**" to win back a straying lover, or even "**Oil of Fall Back**" which dooms the imbiber to fail in everything they attempt.

## Hospitals, doctors and pharmacies

There are tiny regional **hospitals** throughout Jamaica, but most are overcrowded, underfunded and poorly equipped. The general rule is the larger the town, the better the hospital. There are two good, big public hospitals in Kingston, while Cornwall Regional in Montego Bay (see p.223) is the best equipped on the north coast. The easiest way to find a **doctor** in a hurry is to ask at your hotel. Most have a resident nurse or will be able to recommend someone locally – every town has a doctor or medical clinic. Most are reliable, but you'll have to fork out for the treatment and claim on your insurance once back home.

Every town has at least one **pharmacy**, with those in resort towns well stocked with expensive brand-name products; they will only issue antibiotics with a doctor's prescription.

Hospitals, private doctors, clinics and pharmacies are found throughout the island and listed in each chapter.

Finally, you'll often find various medicaments being peddled at **markets**. While some, like aloe vera and other natural remedies, are safe enough purchases, *do not* buy the red and black antibiotic capsules sold loose on market stalls – you have no way of knowing what you're taking.

# Food and drink

Jamaica's food reflects its motto – "Out of many, one people" – with distinctive contributions from each of the groups to have peopled the island, and though it's never made great strides overseas, the local cuisine is undeniably good. From fiery jerk meat, probably the island's best-known culinary creation, to its inventive seafood and ubiquitous rice and peas, the national diet is surprisingly varied. Snacking is good, too, with patties the staple fare, and there is a vast selection of fresh fruit and vegetables. Outside Kingston and the north-coast resorts, international eating options are limited, although you will find pizza and Chinese restaurants in most towns.

## Eating out

Cosmopolitan Kingston has the variety of eating options you'd expect in a capital city; elsewhere on the island, Jamaica's **restaurants** tend to be of two types: either the no-frills filling-stations patronized mostly by locals and with a standard menu of West Indian staples, or tourist restaurants with more in the way of decor and a menu geared towards American and European palates. We've listed a cross-section of options throughout the *Guide*, and it's always worth looking out for the local favourites if you're after some authentic "island colour" (as well as cheaper prices). Bear in mind, though, that such places often close early in the evenings – usually before 9pm.

In the cheapest, Jamaican places, expect to pay the equivalent of US$3–5 for a substantial plateful for lunch or dinner, and around half that for breakfast. Up a notch, moderately priced restaurants will charge more like US$8–12 for a main course, while at the upper end of the scale you'll be looking at US$15-plus for a similar dish.

### Breakfast

The classic – and totally addictive – Jamaican breakfast is **ackee and saltfish**. The flesh of the

Despite forming one half of Jamaica's national dish, **ackee** is a rather hazardous foodstuff. The fruits of the ackee tree must be picked only when their red pods have burst open to reveal the pale yellow arils inside; if forced open when unripe, ackees emit a toxic gas (hypoglycin), so poisonous that up to ten people a year still die from what's known as "**Jamaica poisoning**".

otherwise bland ackee fruit is fried with onions and peppers, then mixed with salted cod, producing a dish similar to scrambled eggs in looks and consistency. You'll usually find it served with the leafy, spinach-like **callaloo**, green bananas, fried or boiled dumplings, or **Johnny cake** – a sweet bread that varies widely in appearance from region to region. Other popular morning options include cornmeal porridge, steamed fish, or coconut "**rundown**" – coconut milk boiled with onions and flaked fish. Inevitably, tourist demands have resulted in a wider availability of the "continental" breakfast – rolls, jam, juice and coffee – and most moderate and expensive hotels will also have a good selection of local fruits.

### Lunch and dinner

Most of Jamaica's cheaper restaurants and hotels offer **chicken** and **fish** as the mainstays of lunch and dinner. Chicken is typically fried, grilled or curried, while fish – normally snapper, but occasionally grouper, kingfish or dolphin – can be grilled, steamed or "**escovitched**" – served in a spicy sauce of onions, hot peppers and vinegar (tastier than it sounds). Other staples include stewed beef, curried goat, oxtail and **pepperpot soup**, made from callaloo, okra and beef or pork, while more adventurous palates might fancy "**mannish water**" – goat soup, traditionally an aphrodisiac, served to a groom on his wedding night – and **cowfoot** or **cow cod soup** (made from a bull's genitals and, supposedly, an aid to virility).

The tradition of "**jerking**" meat is thought to date back to the seventeenth century, an invention of Maroon warriors keen to preserve the meat of wild pigs, and it's since become the island's most idiosyncratic – and flavoursome – cooking style. Seasoned in a mixture of island-grown spices, including pimento, hot peppers, cinnamon and nutmeg, the meat – usually chick-

en or pork, but occasionally sausage – is grilled slowly, often for hours, over a fire of pimento wood and under a cover of wooden slats or corrugated zinc sheets.

You'll find jerk on the menu at most tourist restaurants, though not so often in local places, and on the street in every town, where it's sold from small, home-made barbecues. With hard-dough bread and some roast breadfruit (often sold by the same vendors), it's the perfect picnic. If you're after the real McCoy, head for Boston Bay in Portland (see p.137), where you can get great meat from one of the original jerk centres, and a bottle of fiery marinade to take home.

Seafood is another Jamaican joy, with fresh **lobster** – occasionally curried but usually simply grilled with lemon or butter sauce, freshwater **crayfish** (known locally as janga) and **shrimp** on every upmarket restaurant menu. Freshwater shrimps are pulled from rivers across Jamaica, and you'll occasionally see groups of vendors offering bags of them, hotly peppered and ready to eat. **Seapuss**, also occasionally on menus, is octopus.

Once known as the Jamaican coat of arms, **rice and peas** (rice cooked with coconut, spices and red kidney beans) is the accompaniment to most meals, though you'll sometimes get **bammy** – a heavy, doughy, fried or (better) steamed bread made from cassava flour, **festival** – a delicious sweet fried biscuit, sweet or regular **potatoes** (the latter known as Irish potatoes), Johnny cakes or fried or boiled **dumplings**.

Though the island produces a fabulous array of fresh produce, **vegetarians** are only really catered for at Rastafarian **Ital** restaurants, where meals are exclusively meat-free, and in theory, cooked without salt. Mainstays include ackee and vegetable stews served with rice and peas.

In a bid to boost decimated fish stocks, the Jamaican government has enforced **closed seasons** on lobster and conch during their reproductive cycles – April 1 to June 30 and July 1 to Oct 31 respectively. It is **illegal** for restaurants to serve lobster or conch caught during these times, and while many will tell you that the stock is frozen and predates the deadline, this is obviously not always true, and you should avoid restaurants that don't comply with the law.

## Snacks

Along with jerk meat (see above), **patties** are Jamaica's best-known snack, a pastry case usually filled with minced beef, though occasionally with chicken, shrimp, ackee and saltfish or vegetables, and widely available in bakeries, cafés and snack bars. Many Jamaicans prefer **"bun and cheese"** – a sweet bun sold with a hunk of processed cheese that often passes for lunch – or **meatloaf** and **callaloo loaf**, both made with bread rather than pastry. Bakeries also offer buttery folds of **coco bread**, **bullas** – flat, heavy ginger cakes – rock cakes, fruit cakes and **gizzadas**, small tarts filled with shredded coconut and spiced with nutmeg and ginger. If you're lucky, you'll find **duckanoo** (also known as "blue drawers"), an African dessert made from cornflour, sugar and nutmeg, wrapped in a banana leaf and steamed.

## Fruits and vegetables

One of the delights of touring around Jamaica is stopping off at markets and roadside stalls to try the dozens of different **fruits** on sale. Bananas, oranges, pineapples and paw-paws (papaya) are the most common but, in season, there are plenty of others to choose from. **Mangos** come in all shapes and sizes, the suitably named **ugli fruit** looks like a disfigured grapefruit but is more tasty, while the origins and flavour of the Jamaican-bred **ortanique** are described by its hybrid name – orange, tangerine, unique. Small grape-like **guineps** (only available from July to October) are sold on the roadside all across the island; the brown, egg-shaped **naseberries** (sapodilla) are sweeter but need peeling; **sweetsops** look like pine cones and, as they ripen, the sections separate for eating. Other options include **guavas**, **soursops**, **star apples**, **June plums** and **otaheite apples**.

Ubiquitous **vegetables** include pumpkin and **dasheen**, like a yam but chewier. Of a variety of squashes, the fleshy **cho-cho** (also known as christophine) is the most common, and you'll also find **callaloo**, **okra**, **yams**, **breadfruit** and **plantains**.

## Drinking

Jamaica's water is perfectly safe to drink (see p.24), but for a tastier non-alcoholic **drink** during the day, look no further than the roadside piles of coconuts in every town and village (often with

a sign saying "ice-cold jelly"). The vendor will slice the top off one with his machete and you drink straight from the nut (with a straw if you're lucky), after which vendor will split the shell so you can eat the soft flesh, using the top of the nut as your scoop. **Sky juice** – cones of shaved ice flavoured with sticky fruit syrup or fresh cane juice – is also popular, usually served in a plastic bag with a straw, though the hygiene element is sometimes questionable.

Elsewhere, you'll find the usual imported sodas, plus Jamaica's own *Ting*, – a sweet and sparkling grapefruit drink– *Malta* (not surprisingly a malt drink), ginger beer and fresh limeade. Most places also sell **"box drinks"** – additive-filled, over-sweetened peanut punch (curiously popular), egg nog or orange juice. **Fresh juices** – tamarind, plum, guava, soursop, strawberry and cucumber – are always delicious if a bit over-sweet.

Jamaican **coffee** (see p.117) is usually excellent. The *Blue Mountain* brand, grown only on Jamaica's far eastern mountain slopes, is among the best and most expensive in the world, though the other local brews, such as *High Mountain*, *Low Mountain* or *Mountain Blend*, are also good. **Chocolate** is a popular breakfast drink, while **tea**, in Jamaica, means any hot drink – regular tea, fish tea (nicer than it sounds), herbal tea or even ganja tea; make sure you specify which one you want.

## Alcohol and bars

Jamaica's national **beer** is the excellent *Red Stripe*, available in distinctive bottles island-wide. If you need an alternative, *Heineken* is widely available, as is the Guinness-like *Dragon Stout*, and the major hotels and restaurants sometimes stock a couple of other brands. Decent **wine** is rarely an option; the local *Red Label* plonk is pretty grim, and you'll pay through the nose for America or European imports.

**Rum** is the liquor of choice, with a good variety at a range of prices. White overproof rum (and the even more lethal home-made stuff, John Crow Batty – often over 80 percent proof) is the poor man's friend – cheap, potent and available everywhere – best knocked back with a mixer of cola or *Ting*, though there are plenty of better sorts if you're after taste rather than effect, including simple gold rums and the older, aged varieties, left to mature in (and taking their colour from) charred oak barrels. *Appletons* and

*Sangster's* are two of the best producers on the island. Rum-based **liqueurs** are the other local speciailty; *Sangster's*, the best of the lot, has a liqueur factory at World's End near Kingston in the Blue Mountains (see p.115) and makes award-winning rum creams and liqueurs flavoured with orange, coffee, pimento and more. Finally, the coffee-flavoured *Tia Maria* is made on the island and widely available.

Jamaica's **bars** are generally rather macho enclaves, with groups of men sitting around, drinking rum and playing dominoes. They can present a good opportunity to meet local people, though single women won't always feel at home. Otherwise, other than the odd tourist spot, there aren't a lot of places geared up for drinking only, and you'll probably find that a restaurant with attached bar is your best bet.

---

### Stamina potions

Ever careful to safeguard their powerful libidos, Jamaican men consume gallons of potions to ensure sexual stamina. Drinks like **Billy Clarke** (a crimson decoction of a herb of the same name) or **tan-pon-it-long** are taken to enrich the semen and supplement the diet, and deemed necessary to see the Jamaican male through extended sessions of sexual olympics.

The most popular ingredient is **Irish moss**, a seaweed boiled and strained into a glutinous milky-white potion. Now available in tins, Irish moss is the main component in many stamina drinks including **magnum** (Irish moss and linseed), **strong back** (Irish moss, oats, peanuts, paw-paw, *Dragon* stout and a decoction of the strong back herb) and **pep-up** (Irish moss, *Dragon* stout, *Red Label* wine and liquified green corn).

Another popular tonic is **roots wine**, usually made by Rastafarian herbalists who mix various quantities of roots and herbs such as arrowroot, chainy root, bridal wisp, strong back and occasionally ganja, boiling them with molasses or honey to make an evil-smelling brew. Most people have their own recipes, but as preparation is time-consuming, many prefer to visit their favourite "juice man" who sells old rum bottles full of the stuff in most markets. If you're female, don't be surprised if a potential purchase is refused on the grounds that such drinks are a "man's ting".

---

# Communications

Though fairly efficient, Jamaica's telephone system is expensive for overseas calls; local calls are far cheaper, but you'll need to watch out for the shocking surcharges imposed by most hotels. The mail service is less dependable and, particularly within the island, can be extremely slow.

## Mail

Considering how small Jamaica is, it's amazing how long it can take for inland mail to get across the country. Don't expect a letter from Kingston to the north coast (or vice versa) to arrive in less than a week. International mail is also slow − reckon on around ten days to a fortnight for airmail to reach Europe or North America. Always use airmail, as surface mail takes forever.

Most towns and villages have a **post office**, normally open Monday to Friday 9am to 5pm. Those in larger towns have **poste restante** facilities − mail is held for about a month, and you'll need your passport or other identification to collect it − and a few have **fax machines**.

**Stamps** are sold at post offices and in many hotels. Rates are reasonable at J$8 for postcards anywhere in the world, J$11 for airmail letters to Canada and the USA and J$12 for airmail letters to Europe and Australasia. Finally, think carefully before sending anything valuable through the post; postal theft is increasingly common.

## Phones

Finding a **phone** is never a problem in Jamaica − most hotel rooms have one and distinctive blue phonebooths litter the island. **Rates** for local and long-distance calls within Jamaica are low, but if you're calling from your hotel, check the service charge first − most hotels impose a hefty mark-up on calls, sometimes over 1000 percent.

For calls within Jamaica, it's always much cheaper to use the public booths, operated by *Telecommunications of Jamaica* (*TOJ*). Almost all of these take **phonecards** only, available (in denominations of J$50, J$100 and J$200) from hotels, post offices, some shops and *TOJ* offices. For the few that take coins, you'll need J$5 bits.

All Jamaican telephone numbers (except some freephone ones) have **seven digits**. To dial locally, simply key in the number, to get anywhere further afield, prefix it with "1". Finding numbers is rarely a problem − if there is no phone book in your hotel room, reception will have one, or you can call **directory enquiries** from any phonebooth on ☎114.

**International calls** are more problematic, despite the recent introduction of international calling cards. Few of the phonebooths permit them, so you'll have to rely on your hotel (and cough up the exorbitant service charge) or, in larger towns, find a branch of *TOJ* or **Jamintel** (its international communications division), where you can place regular or collect calls, send and receive faxes, or send and receive telegrams (which are priced in Jamaican cents per word). Most offices are open Monday to Friday 9am to 4.30pm and Saturday 9am to 1pm. You'll also occasionally find **call-direct centres**, where a call is placed on your behalf and you're directed to a phone. Details of all of these places are given throughout the *Guide*. If you do find a phonebooth that permits international calls, dial ☎113, wait for the tone, press the # sign, and wait for the tone again before dialling your number.

---

**Useful numbers**

**Operator** ☎112

**International operator** ☎113

**Directory enquries** (domestic and international) ☎114

---

# The media

As in most countries, the best way to tap into the mood of Jamaica is to read its papers, tune in to its radio stations, or take a look at its television.

## Newspapers

Of Jamaica's three daily **newspapers**, the broadsheet *Daily Gleaner*, founded in 1834, is the market leader, both in terms of circulation and quality journalism. Rarely afraid to voice an opinion, particularly during the 1970s when it regularly condemned the Manley administration, it has recently eschewed political partisanship, and regularly harangues all parties. The paper's coverage of local news and sport is excellent, it enjoys the pick of the feature writers and has the best listings; overseas news is perfunctory but adequate.

The *Observer* is a recent arrival, founded by Gordon "Butch" Stewart (owner of *Sandals* and *Air Jamaica*) in the early 1990s. Tabloid in form but broadsheet in content, much of its news and feature journalism rivals the *Gleaner*, though it seems confused about its target readership. The *Star* is the island's tabloid, an afternoon publication from the *Gleaner* stable, full of salacious tittle-tattle. The independent *X News* plumbs even lower depths, but is excellent for entertainment listings.

Sunday brings weekend issues of the *Gleaner* and *Observer*, similar to the dailies with a few advertisers' supplements, and the rather dull *Sunday Herald*.

**International newspapers** – the main US dailies and the UK's Sunday broadsheets – are sold in major pharmacies and the gift shops of the bigger hotels, usually a couple of days out of date.

A couple of glossy, full-colour **magazines**, published every other month, will appeal to those interested in Jamaican music: *Jammyng* and *Reggae Times* print interviews with artists, features on the music scene and entertainment news; both cost J$100 and are usually available from bookshops and some gift shops.

## Radio

Jamaica's **radio stations** are predictably awash with island sounds – including stageshow broadcasts, talent showcases and festival coverage – though music faces tough competition from the daytime talk shows and sports coverage. Radio is much more popular than television in Jamaica, and an excellent way to appreciate the culture.

The upstart **Irie FM** is probably the most listened-to music station, easy skanking oldies in the morning giving way to harder core reggae and dancehall as the day wears on. *Irie* has edged ahead of the more long-standing **RJR** (Radio Jamaica Rediffusion), where talk and sport dilute the music. For many Jamaicans, talk shows are essential listening, as evidenced by the animated groups you'll see gathered round

### Radio stations and frequencies

**Fame** 91.5/98.1FM
**Irie** 105.5/107.7 FM
**JBC** 91.1 FM
**KLAS** 89.7 FM
**Love** 101.1 FM
**Power** 106.5 FM
**Radio Waves** 102.9 FM
**RJR** 90.5/92.9/94.5/103.3 FM

radios during their broadcasts. The anarchic Wilmott Perkins is the most entertaining presenter (*Klas FM*, Mon–Fri 10.30am–2.30pm), his ferocious attacks on authority figures attracting regular death threats and healthy ratings for his show "Straight Talk". Lawyer Ronnie Thwaites hosts "Independent Talk" (*Power FM*, Mon–Fri 5.30–9am), a more measured breakfast-time analysis of topical issues, while Beverley Manley's "Breakfast Club" (*Klas FM* Mon–Fri 6–9am) is another good morning news brief. For something altogether different, radical dub poet Mutabaruka's "Cutting Edge", (*Irie FM*, Tues 10pm–2.30am) lays down a Rastafarian viewpoint. Obviously,

schedules change; if you can't find what you're after, ask around.

Reception of the **BBC World Service** is patchy; early morning and late evening are the best times to find it.

## Television

You'll find a **television** set in most hotel rooms. The majority only pick up a handful of channels – usually the two domestic stations and maybe HBO, CNN and one of the North American network channels – though plusher hotels can access thirty to forty of the US channels.

The island's channels, **JBC** and **CVM**, are competent if rarely thrilling. Most Jamaicans don't have television sets, and output is limited to evenings and weekends, and dominated by news, local sport and interviews, though if you're a soap fan you'll want to catch the island's very own *Royal Palm Estates*. If you're desperate for international sports coverage, most towns have one or two bars with big-screen TV for major US sporting events – NFL and NBA games and occasionally baseball – though you won't find much from Europe. Try *Walter's* in Montego Bay, the *Wyndham Hotel* in Kingston, *Bill's Place* in Ocho Rios or *Risky Business* in Negril.

# Opening hours, festivals and entertainment

Jamaican offices are normally open for business between 8.30am and 4.30pm Monday to Friday, often closing for an hour at lunch, while shops are typically open from 8am to 5pm Monday to Saturday, although some close at noon on Saturdays. Sunday trading is rare, although you will find one or two pharmacies open in Kingston and at the major resorts, and we have listed these in the *Guide*. Museums normally close for one day a week, either Sunday or Monday, while most other places you'll want to visit – private beaches, waterfalls, gardens, churches and so on – are generally open daily.

The main **national holidays**, when virtually all shops and offices close, are:

New Year's Day (January 1)

Ash Wednesday

Good Friday

Easter Monday

Labour Day (May 23)

Independence Day (first Mon in Aug)

National Heroes Day (third Mon in Oct)

Christmas Day (Dec 25)

Boxing Day (Dec 26).

# Festivals and special events

Some of Jamaica's special events run throughout the year, such as the **Mutual Life Jazz Concerts** held at various locations on the last Wednesday of each month (details on ☎ 926 9024), but most are timed to coincide with the winter tourist season; main exceptions are **Reggae Sumfest** in August and **Spring Break**, when young Americans invade the big resorts. April is **carnival** time – though not on the same scale as in Trinidad, Jamaica's Carnival is a growing event, with more and more parades each year. Other mini-carnivals to look out for are Mandeville's Mangerine effort and the smaller Negril Carnival.

## CALENDAR OF EVENTS

### JANUARY

**Accompong Maroon Festival**, Accompong, St Elizabeth. All-day celebration of the 1739 Maroon peace treaty, held on January 6. Food and craft stalls, drumming, traditional dancing, speeches and a sound-system dance till dawn.

**Annual National Exhibition**, National Gallery, Kingston; ☎ 922 1563. Annual showpiece exhibition of new artists and established names.

**Heineken Startime**, various locations; ☎ 929 9200. Veteran artists perform at an enjoyable reggae festival that also takes place at other times throughout the year.

**Rebel Salute**, Brooks Park, Mandeville. Annual concert with cultural artists and DJs that attracts a large roots crowd. Sometimes held in February.

**Reggae Sunsplash** (see box).

**Reggae Superjam**, various locations; ☎ 929 9200. A mix of top-rated singers and DJs in a friendly, laid-back atmosphere. Also takes place at other times of the year.

**White River Reggae Bash**, White River Reggae Park, Ocho Rios; ☎ 974 2619 or 2489. Annual culmination of *Irie FM*'s year-round series of open-air concerts which attract the best veteran and DJ artists.

### FEBRUARY

**Bob Marley Birthday Bash**, Bob Marley Museum, Kingston (☎ 927 9152 or 926 6071), or at the Bob Marley Centre, Nine Miles, St Ann (☎ 0999 7003). Celebrations for the king of reggae are held at both sites on and around the anniversary of Marley's birthday on February 6. Ziggy Marley and the Melody Makers usually per-

form at one of them. Impromptu parties, dances and stageshows are also held throughout the island, particularly in Negril.

**UWI Carnival**, Mona, Kingston; ☎ 927 1660. The University of the West Indies' annual carnival celebrations with mas players, steel bands, reggae bands, soca jump-up and the crowning of a Carnival King and Queen.

### MARCH

**Spring Break**. In early March, American college students descend on the main resorts for a two-week JTB-approved orgy of beer drinking and slapstick antics. Student ID obtains discounts on hotels and events.

**Kite Festival**, Ocho Rios; ☎ 974 2582. An increasingly popular event attracting ever-bigger and more flamboyant home-made kites.

### APRIL

**Carnival**. The main festivities begin in Kingston in early April with costumed parades, concerts featuring Trinidadian soca artists and all-night parties. The show then moves around the island and peaks at Chukka Cove, St Ann, in late April.

### JUNE

**Ocho Rios Jazz Festival**, Ocho Rios; ☎ 927 3544. Largest jazz festival in Jamaica attracting performers from all over the world.

### JULY

**National Dance Theatre Company's Season of Dance**, Little Theatre, Kingston; ☎ 925 6129. Modern dance from this fabulous company throughout July and August.

Specific **dates** for most events are not listed, as these change from year to year; they appear in the JTB's **"calendar of events"** booklet, available from offices worldwide. Most of the bigger events are advertised nationally; local events are heralded on billboards

## Entertainment

If you don't mind a musical policy of reggae, reggae and more reggae, then you'll find plenty on offer in the way of **live music**. Though touring American soul artists and the occasional jazz festival provide occasional alternatives, it's the home-grown scene that dominates. Jamaican **theatre** – particularly roots plays and the annual pantomime – is also hugely enjoyable, an idiosyncratic insight into the Jamaican way of life.

### Stageshows

Most concerts – or **stageshows** as they're locally known – are well worth attending, as you'll see artists who seldom perform off the island sharing the bill with more familiar reggae luminaries like Buju Banton, Third World, Freddie McGregor, Dennis Brown and Gregory Isaacs. Most take place in open-air venues and are generally peaceful, with a friendly atmosphere and

---

**Negril Carnival**, Negril; ☎ 957 3110. Costume parade, mento bands, traditional dance and sound-system jams in the streets.

AUGUST
**Denbigh Agricultural Show**, Denbigh Showground, May Pen; ☎ 922 0610. The best in everything from beasts to beets in a carnival atmosphere.
**Independence Day Street Parade**, Kingston; ☎ 926 5726. Giant street parade through central Kingston to Liguanea Park to celebrate independence from the British. Colourful costumes and cultural performances, from traditional costumed Jonkonnu dancers to more contemporary gyrators.
**Miss Jamaica World Coronation**, National Arena, Kingston; ☎ 927 7575. Beauty pageants are still big business in Jamaica, and this is the crowning glory.
**Portland Jamboree**, Port Antonio; ☎ 933 3051. Sleepy Port Antonio comes alive with a series of concerts, parades and parties. Includes a float parade, church service, street dancing, and lots of local food and drink.
**Reggae Sumfest** (see box).

SEPTEMBER
**James Bond Festival**, Ocho Rios; ☎ 974 5831 or ☎ 975 3665. Annual celebration of all things 007 with guided tours of Goldeneye, Ian Fleming's erstwhile home, exhibitions of memorabilia and screenings of the classics.

OCTOBER
**All That Heritage and Jazz Festival**, Montego Bay; ☎ 979 2567 or 2584. A series of concerts

and cultural seminars, performances and displays that gets the town going in the slow (and rainy) season.
**National Mento Yard and Heritage Fest**, Jamworld Entertainment Centre, Kingston; ☎ 926 5726. Cultural groups show off their party pieces in this growing celebration of Jamaican culture.
**Oktoberfest**, Jamaica German Society Headquarters, Kingston; ☎ 927 6408. Annual celebration of all things Teutonic, with stalls, German food, dancing, games, top Jamaican bands and the obligatory beer drinking contest.
**Peter Tosh Memorial Bash**, *KD's Keg*, Belmont, Westmoreland. Annual roots and culture concert in memory of the reggae great; small, but one of the highlights of the stageshow year.

DECEMBER
**LTM National Pantomime**, Ward Theatre, Kingston; ☎ 926 6603 or 6129. Unmissable annual theatrical institution, with ribald jokes, great costumes, political commentary and traditional Jamaican song and dance. The whole shebang moves to Kingston's Little Theatre in February, and occasionally tours around the island.
**Reggae Kwanzaa**, various venues island-wide. Kwanzaa, the African Christmas (Dec 26–Jan 1), is celebrated in a large annual concert, held at venues across the island, featuring the best in cultural reggae.
**Sting**, Jamworld Entertainment Centre, Portmore and other venues across the island. Annual New Year celebrations featuring current top DJs and singers. The atmosphere can get a bit hairy.

---

plenty of stalls selling beers, rum and food, though some of the DJ-based shows attract a younger, predominantly male crowd and can get a bit fractious. Many are one-off affairs, but others – **Reggae Superjam**, **Heineken Startime** or the **White River Reggae Bash** among others – are established events that hire a fixed roster of artists and tour the island's venues; see the "Calendar of events" for further details

## Clubs

The party spirit is deeply imbedded in most Jamaicans, who like to dress up and let rip at the weekend. There's a lively **club scene** in Jamaica, at its most authentic in Kingston but also reasonably good along the north coast. Held indoors, most nights are sweaty and smoky in

the extreme, the music is super-loud, dancers vie with each other as to who can wear the least and move the most, couples wind their waists and gigolos prey on foreign women. Away from some of the more sterile in-hotel establishments, clubbing is lots of fun and generally inexpensive; you'll rarely encounter a cover charge of more than US$5, and the frequent "ladies nights" and weekday drinks promotions are well worth taking advantage of. Most towns also have a **go-go club** – generally full of men gawping at topless and naked female dancers.

## Sound-system parties

Altogether less formal, **sound-system parties** (known as "dances" or "jump-ups") take place all over the island at weekends, detailed more fully

---

### Sunsplash and Sumfest – Jamaica's reggae festivals

Every year, Jamaica's best-loved art form overwhelms the nation as the massive reggae **Sunsplash** and **Sumfest festivals** take to the stage. For months in advance, the festival build-up infects the whole country, flights from the US and Europe become desperately over-booked, beaches throng with fans from all over the globe and the line-up – which usually reads like a reggae hall of fame – is worried over in rum bars and on radio talk shows. By the time the sound equipment and lights arrive from Miami, hotel rooms have become a priceless commodity, the cost of living increases overnight and every available scrap of cardboard is appropriated by small-time entrepreneurs to be sold in the show-grounds as a "reggae bed" – an essential piece of equipment for tired legs, though only the foolhardy actually sleep on them.

A heady combination of ganja, rum, sea breezes and simply brilliant music, Jamaica's festival tradition began in 1978 when a small crowd of revellers enjoyed five trouble-free nights of roots reggae at Montego Bay's Jarrett Park. Jamaica's first Reggae Sunsplash set a positive tone; international attention was captured and two years on a capacity crowd of Jamaicans and tourists alike rocked to a killer line-up featuring Bob Marley and a host of other headline acts. Promotion in the US and Europe drew huge crowds to the quintessential shows of the 1980s, which coincided with reggae's strongest phase and were characterized by the legendary, laid-back "good musical vibes" that still differentiate them from the cool reserve and farcical posturing of regular stageshows.

By the beginning of the 1990s, however, legal wrangles and a series of venue changes – including a couple of dismal years in Kingston that scared off tourists and journalists alike – left Sunsplash struggling to recapture its early success. Sunsplash's future seems even more uncertain; recent developments include another (unconfirmed) venue change and a shift from a summer to a winter festival – leaving the traditional August dates free for its mightier rival. In 1993, newcomer Reggae Sumfest muscled in, snapping up the coveted Montego Bay location (by then shifted to Catherine Hall Entertainment Centre) and outshining its rival in terms of line-up and fun factor.

Yet even with the success of this Johnny-come-lately, the festival scene is not what it used to be; where crowds once reached 30,000 nightly, even Sumfest is lucky to draw 20,000 today. As artist fees have risen – peaking at J$1 million for DJ Beenie Man in 1996 – so ticket prices have become prohibitive for many Jamaicans, who increasingly prefer to attend sound-system jams rather than live shows. Some even argue that the changing focus of reggae – from the Bob Marley-style roots to today's immensely popular DJ-based dancehall – is just not appropriate to live performance any more. Despite all this, even today, with each festival boasting an average of around 100 acts spread over five themed nights, you'll get no better overview of the Jamaican music scene.

---

in Contexts (p.345). Loyal followers travel for miles to hear their favourite "selectors" (usually well-known figures) spinning exclusive tracks and, on a good night, see an established DJ take to the mike to improvise lyrics over a popular pre-recorded rhythm track. Most jump-ups are held in the open air at hurriedly fenced-in "lawns", and carry on until the early hours with the beer, rum and ganja consumption intensifying as the night rolls on. Most Jamaicans agree that the best dances are those held in remote country areas; noise restrictions are seldom enforced and the atmosphere is usually a lot more friendly than at city jump-ups or at "clashes" between two well-known sound systems, where aggressive under-currents often mar the fun. Tourists are infrequent but welcome visitors at dances; it's rare to be harassed – most Jamaicans are pleasantly sur-prised to see visitors taking an interest in this side of their culture – but as you're well off the beaten track and possibly in the company of drunken undesirables, you may want to tag along with a Jamaican escort.

## Theatre

Less energetic entertainment – though no less raucous – is available via a trip to the **theatre**, Jamaican-style. **Roots plays** are an institution, usually bestowed with titles – Boops, Baby Faada and so on – that reflect their bawdy ver-nacular content. With rich patois dialogue, plenty of easy-to-miss colloquial references and oceans of interaction from the audience, most perfor-mances are a riot and you're sure to get the over-

---

Sumfest **dates** are pre-fixed, starting on the first Tuesday following Independence Day on August 5, while Sunsplash is scheduled to take place each January – both plan to cut the usual five nights to four. Specialist Caribbean travel agents in the US, Canada and UK sometimes offer packages that include accommodation and entrance fees; you are issued with a voucher to be redeemed for a ticket in Jamaica, but though buying from home is fractionally cheaper, problems with counterfeit vouchers mean that it's usually simpler to pick up a ticket once on the island – nights are rarely sold out. Designated outlets (including JTB offices) are found in all the resorts. Nightly tickets (from US$30) or a season ticket armband (from US$120) are available for both festivals; for further information contact JTB offices worldwide (see p.13) or call ☎ 1-800/JAMAICA in the US. You can also contact Reggae Sunsplash International (☎ 960 1904 or 1905) or Summerfest Productions (☎ 979 1720 or 952 8592).

### HELPFUL HINTS FOR JAMAICAN STAGESHOWS

• Sumfest and Sunsplash generally adhere to published timetables, but otherwise, stageshows invariably start late. The gates may open at 10pm. but the first act often won't come on until 1am, so never leave your hotel too early; arriving at midnight will ensure an adequate view and enough stamina to last until the end.

• If it rains on the day of the show, it's likely to be a washout – most Jamaicans won't leave home if it means getting wet.

• Wear clothing suitable for the night-time chill and the early morning sun – it's a tradition for shows to continue well past daybreak. Despite having to stand in a field for ten hours, there are few pleasures more satisfying than watch-ing the sun come up as the cream of the per-formers take to the stage.

• Jamaican entertainers are uncompromis-ingly unreliable, and it's well worth checking that the artists you've come to see have actually turned up – even if the doorman confirms their presence, big names are unlikely to perform for a tiny crowd. Similarly, it's common for shows with mixed billings of veteran singers and trendy DJs to rapidly empty once the latter have left the stage, leaving the vocal acts with no audience and an excuse to slope off early.

• Don't worry about eating before a show. Vast quantities of curry goat, mannish water and fried fish are available at almost every stageshow – mobile vendors sell cigarettes and confectionery as well.

• Don't be alarmed by the practice of throw-ing firecrackers to demonstrate appreciation of an act; the more worried you look, the clos-er they'll be thrown. Move away if you don't like it.

---

all gist of a play even if you don't catch on to the more complex themes. Roots plays are staged at impromptu venues all around the island (listed in the relevant chapters), but particularly in larger towns, and details of performances are advertised in local papers – don't miss the chance to get a uniquely unfettered view of the Jamaican psyche.

If you're after more conventional drama, you're restricted to Kingston's Ward or Little theatres and the Fairfield Theatre in Montego Bay. Unmissable if you're on the island between December and February is the annual Little Theatre Movement **pantomime** (see "Calendar of events", p.34), a blend of folklore, song, dance and jokes that gets better every year. The Little Theatre is also the venue for performances by Jamaica's superb national **dance** company, NDTC, who combine African steps with European themes to great success, and often perform with the venerated NDTC singers.

### Cinema

If you tire of culture or partying, consider a trip to the **cinema**; most large towns have at least one, and away from the unbelievably violent martial arts epics or cheesy b-movies that dominate matinee schedules, you'll usually find programming on a par with release times in America. Be prepared for a lot more audience participation than you're used to, particularly in the less salubrious establishments.

# Sports and outdoor activities

As you'll quickly discover, sport is a Jamaican obsession – hardly surprising in a country that has produced so many world-class athletes. In bars, buses and taxis, if the music isn't blaring then the chances are that they're tuned into the cricket, football or horseracing, while the newspapers are awash with sports reports and statistics from Jamaica and overseas. The island is also a great place to indulge your own sporting passion, with excellent watersports and top-class golfing in particular.

## Spectator sports

Virtually every Jamaican has an opinion on **cricket**, the national game, and bringing it up in conversation is a surefire way to break the ice. If you get the chance to catch a match, you'll find the atmosphere very Jamaican – thumping reggae between overs and vendors hawking jerk chicken and *Red Stripe*. The Jamaican team is normally in action twice a year. In January, several matches of the *Red Stripe Cup* - four-day games against the likes of Barbados, Guyana and Trinidad and Tobago – are held at Sabina Park in Kingston. The more exciting one-day *Shell/Sandals* limited overs competition – against the same teams – is occasionally hosted in Jamaica in September/October, at Sabina Park, Jarrett Park in Montego Bay and Chedwin Park, near Spanish Town. On a grander scale, in March/April the West Indies team plays a series of international Test matches; one of the Tests is always held at Sabina Park and is definitely worth catching if you can.

**Football** (soccer) is also popular, with school-boy games attracting large and passionate crowds at grounds across the island. Although there is no professional league (many of the best players play in the United States), Jamaica's national side made a strong bid to qualify for the 1998 World Cup in France, in the process proving themselves the best team in the Caribbean. Although international matches, held at the National Stadium in Kingston, are relatively rare, the team's success has inevitably boosted local interest in the game.

**Athletics** is Jamaica's most internationally illustrious sporting field, winning Olympic sprint medals consistently from Arthur Wint in 1948 (when the island first entered the competition) through to the success of Deon Hemmings and Merlene Ottey in 1996. Most of the country's top athletes study and train abroad, and major track meets on the island are unusual.

Finally, the influence of satellite television and the enormous salaries on offer have led to a growing interest in American sports, particularly **basketball**. You don't see that much of it being played around the country, but there is concern (as throughout the Caribbean) that this new enthusiasm is deterring youngsters from traditional sports,

especially cricket, whose star players earn relatively little. Michael Jordan is an idol for most young Jamaican males and, though few Jamaicans have yet made a big name for themselves in US sports, once they do, the rush to follow suit and abandon the cricket field is inevitable.

## Participatory sports

Fabulous weather, excellent watersports, the widest variety of golf courses in the Caribbean, and a host of hiking oportunities make Jamaica a dream destination for **active sports** enthusiasts.

### Watersports

A permanently azure Caribbean sea studded with sumptuous coral reefs make **watersports** Jamaica's most obvious attraction.

**Scuba-diving and snorkelling** is concentrated on the north coast, between Negril and Ocho Rios. The state of the reefs is variable – much has been destroyed by tourism and aggressive fish-

---

### The rules of cricket

The laws of cricket are so complex that the official rule book runs to some twenty pages. The basics, however, are by no means as Byzantine as the game's detractors make out.

There are two teams of eleven players. A team wins by scoring more runs than the other team and dismissing all the opposition – in other words, a team could score many runs more than the opposition, but still not win if the last enemy batsman doggedly stays "in" (hence ensuring a draw). The match is divided into innings, when one team bats and the other fields. The number of innings varies depending on the type of competition: one-day matches have one per team, Test matches have two.

The aim of the fielding side is to limit the runs scored and get the batsmen "out". Two players from the batting side are on the pitch at any one time. The bowling side has a bowler, a wicket keeper and nine fielders. Two umpires, one standing behind the stumps at the bowler's end and one square on to the play, are responsible for adjudicating if a batsman is out. Each innings is divided into overs, consisting of six deliveries, after which the wicket keeper changes ends, the bowler is changed and the fielders move positions.

The batsmen score runs either by running up and down from wicket to wicket (one length = one run), or by hitting the ball over the boundary rope, scoring four runs if it crosses the boundary having touched the ground, and six runs if it flies over. The main ways a batsman can be dismissed are: by being "clean bowled", where the bowler dislodges the bails of the wicket (the horizontal pieces of wood resting on top of the stumps); by being "run out", which is when one of the fielding side dislodges the bails with the ball while the batsman is running between the wickets; by being caught, which is when any of the fielding side catches the ball after the batsman has hit it and before it touches the ground; or "LBW" (leg before wicket), where the batsman blocks with his leg a delivery that would otherwise have hit his stumps.

These are the bare rudiments of a game whose beauty lies in the subtlety of its skills and tactics. The captain, for example, chooses which bowler to play and where to position his fielders to counter the strengths of the batsman, the condition of the pitch and a dozen other variables. Cricket also has a beauty in its esoteric language, used to describe such things as fielding positions ("silly mid-off", "cover point", etc) and the various types of bowling delivery ("googly", "yorker", etc).

---

See p.332 of Contexts for more on the ecological aspects of Jamaica's marine environment.

ing techniques, and the whole stretch around Montego Bay is under enforced protection as a national marine park – but there are still some gorgeous sites very close to the shore. The fish are just as impressive, with multitudes of parrot fish, angel fish and trigger fish, as well as moray eels, turtles and the evil-looking barracuda. There are a handful of wreck dives – including several plane wrecks off the coast of Negril – and good trenches, overhangs and wall-dives. There are fewer decent sites on the south coast, and visibility is usually worse.

The main resorts are packed with operators offering dive trips and snorkelling excursions; the most reputable are listed throughout the *Guide*. For beginners, the most popular options are the one-day introductory **resort courses**, for around US$50, which offer basic instruction and a twenty-minute supervised shallow dive close to shore. The longer **PADI** (Professional Association of Diving Instructors) or **NAUI** (National Association of Underwater Instructors) **open-water certification course** costs US$300 to US$350 and takes a few days, with practical and theoretical tests, safety training and several dives. Once you're certified, you can dive without an instructor, though

you'll stil need to go with a licensed operator – expect to pay around US$55 for a two-tank dive.

**Parasailing**, **jet-skiing**, **water-skiing**, **kayaking**, **glass-bottomed boats** and **sailing** are also available at all of the major resorts and you can **surf** at Long Bay in Portland (p.138). **Deep-sea fishing** is best around Portland, particularly during October's Blue Marlin tournament. Fully equipped boats are available for rent in all the major resorts; at about US$350 per day the pursuit of big fish doesn't come cheap.

Away from the coast, **river rafting** is the big aquatic attraction, first popularized in the 1950s by movie idol **Errol Flynn** who saw that the bamboo rafts used to transport bananas along Portland's Rio Grande could be used for pleasure punting. The Rio Grande remains the most spectacular spot for an idle glide, but operators have also set up in Ocho Rios, Falmouth and Montego Bay (see pp.159. 190 and 229). Costs start at around $30 for a two-person raft.

**Swimming** is idyllic throughout Jamaica, particularly in the Rio Grande and White River in Ocho Rios. Dunn's River in Ocho Rios (p.158) offers the island's ultimate **waterfall climb**, but there are plenty more cascades, many completely untouristed. More relaxingly, **mineral springs** and **natural spas** are Jamaica's hidden gems – locals flock to Bath in St Thomas (p.123), Rockfort in Kingston (p.87) and Milk River in Manchester (p.293) for the restorative powers of the radioactive water, and

---

## Jamaica's golf courses

**Kingston**
**Caymanas Golf Club** ☎924 8144. 18 holes, 6844 yards, par 72.
**Constant Spring Golf Club** ☎924 1610. 18 holes, 6560 yards, par 72.

**Mandeville**
**Manchester Club** ☎962 2403. 9 holes (18 tees), 2863 yards, par 35.

**Montego Bay**
**Half Moon Golf Club** ☎953 2560. 18 holes, 6196 yards, par 70.
**Ironshore Golf and Country Club** ☎953 2800. 18 holes, 7119 yards, par 72.
**Tryall Golf and Beach Club** ☎952 5110. 18 holes, 6920 yards, par 71.

**Wyndham Rose Hall Country Club** ☎953 2650. 18 holes, 6800 yards, par 72.

**Negril**
**Negril Hills Golf Resort** ☎957 4638. 18 holes, 6333 yards, par 72.

**Ocho Rios**
**Sandals Golf and Country Club** 974 2529. 18 holes, 6600 yards, par 71.

**Port Antonio**
**San San Golf and Country Club** ☎993 9345. 9 holes. Closed at present.

**Runaway Bay**
**Runaway Bay Country Club** ☎973 2436. 18 holes, 6884 yards, par 72.

river **rising pools**, such as Roaring River in Westmoreland (p.275), are a sheer delight.

### Golf

Jamaica boasts no fewer than eleven **golf courses**, from the magnificent championship Tryall course near Montego Bay – home to the annual Johnnie Walker international – to less testing nine-hole links in Mandeville and Port Antonio. All are open to the public, except during tournaments (Tryall sometimes closes to non-members in winter); **green fees** vary from US$10 to US$100 in

---

### Jamaica's sporting calendar

#### JANUARY
**High Mountain 10km Road Race**, Williamsfield, Manchester; ☎963 4211. Strenuous mountain run.

**Negril Sprint Triathlon**; ☎957 4243. The 500-odd competitors undertake a half-mile swim, a three-mile run plus a fifteen-mile cycle ride along the coast at Negril.

**Red Stripe Cup Cricket Competition**, Sabina Park, Kingston; ☎967 0332. Annual inter-island clash.

#### FEBRUARY
**Carib Cement International Marathon**, ☎929 920. A 26-mile race from Kingston to Port Royal and back again.

**Chukka Cove International Polo Tournament**, Chukka Cove, St Ann; ☎972 2506. Internationally renowned players and lots of silly hats.

**Pineapple Cup Yacht Race**, Montego Bay Yacht Club; ☎979 8038. Yacht race from Fort Lauderdale, USA, to Montego Bay, where the winner is crowned.

#### APRIL
**Cable and Wireless Test Cricket**, Sabina Park, Kingston; ☎967 0332.

**Montego Bay Yacht Club Easter Regatta**, Montego Bay Yacht Club; ☎952 8262 or 979 8038). Annual boating fest that draws a lot of competitors from the USA.

**Motor Sports Championship Series**, Dover Raceway, St Ann; ☎978 2430. Championship motorcycle and car races in the hilly setting of Dover Raceway overlooking Runaway Bay. Local, amateur and international competitions. Other meets in the series take place in June, August, October and December

**Off-Road Triathlon**, Treasure Beach; ☎965 0552. An arduous swim, bike ride and run.

#### MAY
**Black River Fishing Tournament**, Manchester; ☎965 2074. Annual event hunting down the biggest tuna, marlin and wahoo the south coast can offer.

#### JULY
**Northern Telecom Youth Cricket Competition**, Sabina Park, Kingston; ☎967 0322. Annual youth cricket tournament.

#### AUGUST
**Hi-Pro Family Polo Tournament and International Horse Show**, Chukka Cove, St Ann; ☎972 2506. Local and international equestrian fanatics get serious in the competitions, as do the players on the polo field.

#### SEPTEMBER
**Fossil Open Polo Tournament**, Chukka Cove, St Ann; ☎972 2506.

**Montego Bay Blue Marlin Tournament**, Montego Bay; ☎9524425. Attracts top fishermen from the Caribbean and America.

**Shell/Sandals Cricket Competition**, Sabina Park, Kingston; ☎967 0322.

#### OCTOBER
**Port Antonio Blue Marlin Tournament**, Port Antonio; ☎923 8724. One of the older and more prestigious fishing competitions in the Caribbean, this one attracts big boys in big boats in pursuit of very big fish.

#### NOVEMBER
**International Karting Road Race**, New Kingston; contact Abe Zaidie ☎926 9342. Popularized in the movie *Cool Runnings*, this is Jamaica's Grand Prix of pushcart races, and attracts a big crowd.

#### DECEMBER
**Jam-Am Yacht race**, Montego Bay Yacht Club; ☎952 8262 or 979 8030. International boat race from Miami to Montego Bay.

winter, less in summer, and there are additional charges for caddies and club and cart rental.

## Hiking

Though the heat doesn't encourage strenuous exercise, **hiking** is by far the best way to get a flavour of the Jamaican countryside. The best opportunities are in the dense wildernesses of the **Blue and John Crow mountains** and **Cockpit Country**, where trails originally blazed by Maroon warriors lead deep into the Jamaican interior, though there are enjoyable minor walks elsewhere; all are fully covered in the text.

It is strongly recommended that you use a **guide** for all but the shortest of hikes, as it's perilously easy to get lost (see p.112 and 143 for major operators). Always stick to paths and trails; veering off into uncharted foliage not only encourages disorientation, but can destroy plants and lead to soil erosion. Never throw rubbish when hiking; even cigarette butts should be pocketed – a carelessly discarded cigarette can easily start a massive bush fire.

## Other activities

A labyrinth of **caves** networks Jamaica's limestone interior, and as many have been opened up as attractions with lights and stairs, you don't have to be an experienced spelunker to enjoy them. Best of the bunch are Nonsuch Cave in Portland (p.141) and Roaring River and Runaway caves in St Ann (p.179). Serious cavers should head for Cockpit Country, where the limestone is at its thickest and many of the caves are unexplored; Windsor (p.234) is the only easily accessible cavern.

**Horseback trail riding** is a lovely way of exploring the island, though some stables and their mounts are rather run-down; stick to those listed in the chapters or check with the JTB. The best stables are *Hooves* or *Chukka Cove* in St Ann and *Rocky Point* in Ironshore, just outside Montego Bay (see p.157, 175 and 225); the latter two also offer **polo**, **dressage** and **show-jumping** lessons.

**Cycling** is surprisingly under-promoted in Jamaica (see "Getting Around" p.19). An alternative to demure processions aboard colour-coordinated resort cycles is a guided **mountain-bike tour**, available in Negril (see p.253), St Ann's Bay (p.175) and the Blue Mountains (see p.109).

Finally, many upmarket hotels offer **tennis courts**, and for those who can't survive without their workout, the top-notch resorts normally provide **gyms** and **areobics classes**.

### Things to bring on a hike

**Clothes** – warm, waterproof layers are best, especially in the wet and chilly Blue Mountains. Always wear long trousers or leggings to protect against scratchy ferns, brambles and grass ticks.

**Shoes** – unless you're planning to do a lot of walking, hiking boots aren't essential, and a pair of stout shoes with good grip should suffice. Sneakers aren't advisable; they have less hold and don't allow feet to breathe. Clipping your toenails short will help avoid blistered toes.

**Food and drink** – concentrated high-energy foods such as chocolate, dried fruit or nuts keep you going, while a bag of cut sugarcane will maintain energy levels and quench thirst. Always bring water; isotonic sports drinks are available from the larger Kingston supermarkets.

**First-aid kit** – see p.26 for a list of recommended medicaments.

**Sundries** – insect repellent, high-factor sunscreen, good sunglasses, a good flashlight with spare batteries, and toilet paper.

# Shopping

The Jamaican souvenir industry is precisely that, with many of the carvings and knick-knacks mass-produced on a small scale with little variation from maker to maker. However, the most common products tend to be the best, and though your lignum vitae Lion of Judah may be a pitch pine copy of a thousand others, quality is generally good. Haggling is a natural part of the trade at crafts markets and stalls, but not in hotel boutiques and the more expensive air-conditioned shops.

## Where to shop

Virtually every town in Jamaica has at least one **market**, most selling fruit, vegetables and other produce, and often a limited selection of crafts. The main tourist centres have dedicated crafts markets, and these, along with the **craft stalls** (same products, higher prices) you'll see by the roadside everywhere, are the most enjoyable places to browse and buy. The range of t-shirts, wooden carvings, jewellery, straw goods, hats and assorted knick-knacks varies little from place to place, but the main **Crafts Market** in Kingston (see p.66) is by far the cheapest – expect to pay substantially more if you shop in Montego Bay or Ocho Rios.

Specialist **souvenir stores**, such as the government-run *Things Jamaican*, which has branches island-wide, also have a good stock of crafts and indigenous art, while local galleries often have paintings, scultures and woodcarvings for sale. They tend to be pricier than the markets and stalls, but the standard of merchandise is higher.

**In-bond** – or duty-free – shops are usually clustered together in glitzy plazas and malls, and their stock of perfume, spirits, designer clothes, brand-name watches, crystal, porcelain, diamonds and gold varies little. Savings range from 20 to 40 percent; all goods must be paid for in foreign (ie US) currency, and major credit cards are usually accepted. You'll need your passport and proof of onward travel.

## What to buy

There are many alternatives to Bart Marley (yes, Bart Simpson with dreadlocks and a spliff) t-shirts and bamboo shakers; a custom-designed pair of leather sandals, the ubiquitous string vests, bandannas and red-gold-and-green tassels for car mirrors are all available in market areas of most towns.

Not surprisingly, **reggae music** is big business in Jamaica, and fans will have a field day rooting through the record racks. The best music stores are in downtown Kingston (see p.84), but there are more than adequate outlets in most towns. As well as buying CDs, tapes and vinyl, you can also get compilation tapes made up for you, and pick up pirate recordings of recent stageshows and sound-system jams. Recordings cost about US$6.

Other good Jamaican gifts include the prettily packaged range of essential oils, soaps, candles and bodycare accessories from *Blue Mountain Aromatics*, made from natural local ingredients, and *Starfish Aromatherapy* oils also make classy gifts; both ranges are available from more upmarket gift shops. You can even take some Jamaican **flowers** home with you: *Exotic Flowers To Go* (☎953 5726 or toll-free ☎888 991 4234) offers a choice of thirty tropical blooms and foliage packed in a checkable travel-ready box for $30.

### Food and drink

For a taste of Jamaica back home, you can pick up fiery **jerk sauce** or viscous **guava jelly** at any supermarket – the main locally made brands, such as *Walkers Wood* or *Busha Brown*, are substantially cheaper when purchased in non-tourist shops. Jamaican **vanilla essence**, used in blended drinks, cakes and puddings, "**cocoa tea**", used to make the Jamaican version of hot chocolate, fresh **nutmeg** or the delectable **logwood honey**, sold in old rum bottles at any market, will all bring your memories flooding back.

**Rum** is an obligatory memento – gift shops sell

---

Especially on the north coast, you'll see **coral** and "**tortoiseshell**", products made from the endangered hawksbill turtle, on sale, but the trade in these protected species is **illegal** – don't buy. Though not illegal, conch shells, too, should be avoided.

cardboard "Jamaica Farewell" packages holding two or three bottles for easy transit, though these are usually cheaper in the airport departure lounge; savings can also be made if you buy from a wholesale liquor shop or supermarket. The *Sangster's* company produces excellent **liqueurs**, on sale everwhere, from its nerve centre in the Blue Mountains (see p.115), and the ubiquitous *Tia Maria* coffee liqueur is another must-have. Finally, a packet of **Blue Mountain coffee**, sold everywhere but most reasonably in situ (see p.117) is essential.

## Groceries and provisions

Most sizeable towns have fairly large **supermarkets** selling most items you'll find in shops at home, but **food**, particularly imported goods, is not cheap. Fresh **fruit and vegetables** are best bought at the markets, though expect to bargain over price, and ask for your "brawta" (a little extra) when finalizing a purchase. Women market traders will give tips on preparation and will not usually rip you off, though prices are inevitably a little higher for foreigners, black or white. **Smokers** will find that the cheapest way to buy Jamaican brands (*Craven A*, *Matterhorn*, *Rothmans* and *Benson and Hedges*) is by the carton at any wholesaler – you pay more at street stalls and small shops. Foreign brands are available at larger supermarkets, hotels and tourist gift shops.

# Drugs, trouble and harassment

Jamaica has a terrible reputation for violent crime; foreign documentaries flash images of poverty and gangsterism around the world, and the image that lingers is of drug-crazed, uzi-toting political rivals battling it out in the bloodbath of Kingston. Such adverse publicity encourages international perceptions of a "dark" land in political and social turmoil. However, while the island's murder rate is undeniably high – 900 violent deaths in 1996 alone – its nightmare image is vastly exaggerated, a hangover from the late 1970s, when the election violence that erupted during Michael Manley's turbulent administration (see Contexts, p.323) made headlines around the world.

The negative publicity has been difficult to shake off and, for a while, in the early 1980s, potential visitors stayed away in droves. In response, the government initiated a massive clean-up of the island's north-coast resorts, and today brigades of blue-uniformed tourist police patrol the boulevards, and the tourist board stresses that you are more likely to be mugged in New York than Montego Bay. Most tourists still steer clear of the capital – even rural Jamaicans are wary of going into "Town", and you'll be warned against going in all of the resorts – but such trepidation is largely misplaced, and you'll be surprised at how safe and friendly it feels. Drug-related organized crime *is* a frightening reality, but it's a reality that affects poor Jamaicans rather than tourists, and is restricted to isolated ghetto areas – pockets of west Kingston that you're never going to go to – and anywhere else, the vast majority of visitors experience no crime or violence during their stay.

At the same time, robberies, assaults and other crimes against tourists *do* occur, and you must take the **precautions** you'd take in any foreign city. Don't flaunt your wealth with fat rolls of bank notes, avoid walking alone late at night, don't go mad smoking ganja in the street – in short, use your common sense and you'll prevent potential problems before they happen.

### Hustling

**Hustling** – the hard-nosed, hard-sell pitches you'll be endlessly subjected to on the north coast – can be the chief irritation of time in Jamaica. Especially in Montego Bay, the tourist trade has long been adversely affected by the stream of young hopefuls (usually male) aggressively accosting foreigners in the street, plaguing them with offers of transport, ganja, aloe massage, hair-braiding and crafts. It's wearisome, to be sure, but much of what is perceived as harassment is really nothing more than an attempt to make a living in an economically deprived country, and while an inevitable few see tourists as easy prey for exploitation, most hustlers are genuine. Hustling is a game played in the true entrepreneurial Jamaican spirit; the sales pitch is finely honed and modified to match the perceived nature of the potential client, and the national aptitude for "lyrics" (artful banter designed to break down even the most hardened sensibility) can make encounters with street vendors an entertaining and educative experience rather than a trial.

Tourists are not the only victims of the entrepreneurial urge; city lights are haunted by regulars selling everything from a window wash to brooms, flowers, chamois leathers or newspapers, and the travelling peanut or cigarette vendors that pop up in the most unlikely places are often very convenient.

For a humorous insider's view of the hustler's art consult *Hustling Jamaican Style–A Guide to Tourist Service* (see Contexts, p.363) which lists the most popular products and provides suggested responses. p.207 of this book also has some suggestions.

### Homophobia

Anyone familiar with the theme of Buju Banton's *Boom Bye Bye* ("burn him up bad like an old tyre wheel") will know that Jamaica is overwhelmingly **homophobic**. Homosexuality is illegal in Jamaica, condemned as a sin by the church and the moral majority, and fuel for much hysterical press coverage. Attempting to argue with freely expressed prejudices is almost always a lesson in futility. This doesn't mean that you should avoid Jamaica if lesbian or gay – many hotels are managed by gay men and a lot of the smarter ones won't turn a hair if you ask for a double room – but don't expect to be able to display affection in public without attracting catcalls, sniggers, downright aggression, and possibly physical violence.

## Drugs

Though tourism officials are loath to acknowledge it, many people come to Jamaica in search of some of the finest marijuana in the world. Be warned, though, that Jamaican **ganja**, or "herb", packs a mightier punch than anything you've probably experienced before, and don't plan on doing much if you decide to partake; yellow-eyed Jamaicans who've been smoking since they were six can cope with a spliff before breakfast – you probably can't.

Most Jamaicans smoke their ganja **pure** in carrot-sized spliffs or a water pipe (chillum or cutchie), though some make a "blend" with ordinary cigarettes or whole tobacco leaf; this last, known as "fronta", is also used alongside dried sweetcorn husks or even paper bags as an alternative to rolling papers.

However, although you'd never guess it, those Jamaicans who smoke are in a minority; most islanders are Christians and neither take drugs nor approve of those who do. And despite its links with the Rastafari religion (see p.338) and frequent use as a medicinal draught, possession, use and export of any quantity of ganja is **illegal** and carries stiff penalties. Tourists are just as eligible for prosecution as Jamaicans; at any one time there are around a dozen foreigners awaiting trial in Jamaican jails.

If you are going to smoke, trust your instincts. You will be approached with offers; buy only from someone you feel you can trust, and *never* accept a spliff from someone you don't know – it may be laced with cocaine or crack, what Jamaicans call a "seasoned spliff". You should be equally wary of carrying ganja around the island; if you pass a car at the roadside flanked by a worried-looking white person and a swarm of cops, you can bet that the police are conducting one of their routine searches; wise Jamaicans conceal ganja carefully if they travel with it at all, preferring to pick up a little piece when they "reach".

Finally, tempting as it may seem, do not attempt to smuggle ganja out of the country; however devious you think your method, customs officials have seen hollowed-out sculptures, training shoes or roasted breadfruits before. Even carrying rolling papers can prompt protracted questioning.

## Other drugs

Though better known as a weed-smokers' paradise, Jamaica is also rife with **cocaine** and **crack**, with addiction to both a contributing factor in violent crime. Powder cocaine has long been the sweet-meat of choice for rich young Kingstonians, but the introduction of crack in the late 1980s ensnared a far wider following. Use is not restricted to the Kingston ghettos; Negril's reputation for drugs has attracted a significant number of crack-users, and cocaine has been a part of the scenery since wealthy tourists brought it with them in the 1970s. If you're fairly young, expect to be offered cocaine – and, less frequently, crack – in the tourist areas; if you're not interested, just say no calmly and firmly.

# Women travellers

Though violent sexual attacks against female tourists are rare, women travelling in Jamaica should prepare themslves for a quite unusual degree of scrutiny. Unaccompanied women receive a barrage of attention from Jamaican men, from hopeful innuendo – "gal, me a cry for you"– to frankly pornographic propositions, and a walk down the street will have you sized up by a thousand eyes – all of which is somewhat wearing after the first couple of days, particularly if your idea of a good holiday doesn't include "climbing aboard the big bamboo".

As casual sex is part and parcel of Jamaican culture, and lots of women *do* come to the island in search of romance, it will inevitably be assumed that you are in Jamaica to find a man – or several (see p.250). The news that you're not will often be greeted with incredulity, and the semi-professional gigolos who work the resorts will do their best to get you to change your mind. Foreign black women are just as much of a target as white, though generally get the "roots sister" approach and a tad more respect. If you're not interested, saying "no" and meaning it, and not wearing skimpy clothing off the beach, and avoiding eye contact with men you don't know, are your best defence; as a last resort you may want to assert that you already have a Jamaican boyfriend, though this can be seen to signify that you are playing the game and are a feasible challenge. Incidentally, the boyfriend-back-home excuse will only elicit, "but you're here for how long? Too long to go without".

In a social situation, Jamaican men are refreshingly direct, and while an open invitation to bed within the first five minutes of meeting can be disconcerting, you at least know where you stand; once the possibility of sex is out of the way you can move on to other agendas. Learn to listen to your instincts; the slightest hint of flirting means that you are probably about to be seriously propositioned, so assume that even the most innocent reaction may be interpreted as a sign of acquiescence – agreeing to play a game of pool can be read as a come-on.

If passion *is* on your agenda, don't have more than one partner in the same area; gossip spreads extremely quickly and Jamaican men do not take kindly to being "insulted" in this way (though of course it's OK for them). Though most men will help if they see a sister being seriously bothered, don't expect men (even friends) to extricate you from sticky situations of your own making, as this would encroach on another's machismo. Cope with your new status as a sex goddess with humility and humour; most of it probably has more to do with your foreign allure – or economic clout – than your personal charms, and a lot of the come-ons can be amusing.

## Jamaican women

As tourist centres are generally the preserve of male hustlers, it can be difficult to meet **Jamaican women**, and while most are friendly and older ladies inclined to shower you with maternal protection, some women display an understandable resentment towards the carefree, wealthy female visitors pursued by their men. Besides, most women are far too busy juggling childcare, cooking, cleaning and breadwinning to have time for idle chat.

From the dancehall queen to the market higgler, strong women rule Jamaica. They make up 46 percent of the labour force, the highest per capita ratio in the world, many employed at garment assembly factories or as domestic helpers, and earn an average weekly wage of J$800 (US$22). On top of this, they bear almost sole brunt of childcare responsibilities. Single parentage is an institution in Jamaica – eight out of ten children are born out of marriage, with women usually having several children by several partners. The common terms **"baby mother"** or **"baby father"** refer to parents who live apart. The

impetus for women to have more than one baby father is more often economic than libidinous – if one man doesn't recognize his responsibilities, perhaps another will – and the family court in Kingston has dealt exclusively with paternity disputes for the past twenty years.

Despite the respect they earn as matriarchs and wage-earners, Jamaican women have it tough in this sexist, macho and economically challenged country. They face an increasing threat of violence; the 1000 or so rapes reported annually are estimated to be only a fraction of those that take place, and marital rape is not legally recognized. Incest and domestic violence are also on the increase, there are virtually no sexual harassment laws and legal abortions are so difficult to get that they might as well be barred; thousands of botched back-street attempts kill and maim every year.

---

### Women's organizations

Most women's organizations are based in Kingston, and are presided over by the **Association of Women's Organizations in Jamaica** (2 Waterloo Rd, Kingston 10; ☎ 968 8260, fax 968 0862), an umbrella group which aims to direct, unite and empower women as well as lobbying for change in the law and female opportunities. It can act as a conduit if you want to make contacts or want information on specific groups.

**Woman Inc** (18 Ripon Rd, Kingston 5; ☎ 929 2997) runs a counselling service and crisis centre for victims of incest, rape and domestic abuse; the number above is a national helpline. **Sistren Theatre Collective** (20 Kensington Crescent, Kingston 5; ☎ 929 2457) is an internationally recognized feminist theatre company, with a sideline in publishing. It regularly tours the island with consciousness-raising plays and produces a monthly magazine.

# Directory

**Airport Departure Tax** For international flights, the departure tax is presently J$500, payable in local currency only at the airport when you leave. There is no tax on domestic flights.

**Children** Calm clear seas, shelving beaches, no serious health risks, welcoming attitude, make Jamaica an ideal destination for babies, toddlers and children. Though many of the larger hotels (the *Sandals* chain in particular) operate a couples-only policy, most welcome families. The Montego Bay *Holiday Inn* (☎953 2485), *Franklin D Resort* in Runaway Bay (☎973 4591), *Braco Pebbles* in Trelawny (☎954 0000), *Boscobel Beach* in Oracabessa (☎975 7331) and *Beaches* in Negril (☎957 9270) are all self-styled family resorts with extensive facilities, daily events and personal nannies, but there are plenty of others with kids' clubs for an afternoon off.

**Customs and immigration** Entering Jamaica, customs allow a duty-free quota of 200 cigarettes, 25 cigars, a pound of tobacco, a quart (two pints) of any liquor except rum and a quart of wine. The import of weapons and farm products (including plants, fruit and meat) is heavily restricted and if you're crazy enough to try to smuggle drugs into the country you'll risk severe penalties. When leaving, craft made in Jamaica attracts no duty. Note that visitors are given an immigration card on arrival, which must be returned to the Jamaican customs on departure.

**Disabled travellers** Only the largest hotel chains, such as *Holiday Inn, Superclubs* and *Sandals,* have ramps or lifts on their properties; the JTB can provide a full list of hotels with suitable facilities. The *Combined Disabilities Association* (53 Lyndhurst Rd, Kingston 5 or PO Box 220, Liguanea, Kingston 6; ☎929 1177, fax 920 9389) acts as an umbrella for other groups on the island and lobbies on behalf of Jamaicans with disabilities. It's a useful source of further contacts and information.

**Electric current** The island standard is 110 volts, with two-pin sockets, though a few of the older hotels still use 220 volts. Take adaptors for essential items – some of the upmarket hotels and guesthouses have them, but you shouldn't rely on it.

**GCT (General Consumption Tax)** A government tax of 15 percent is levied on goods and services in most hotels, restaurants and stores, and is usually added to the bill (rather than included in the advertised price).

**Getting married** Jamaica is a popular wedding destination. Only 24 hours' residence in Jamaica is required before you can apply for a marriage licence. You'll need a valid passport or a certified copy of your birth certificate; if you're under 21 you'll also need written parental consent; if divorced, a certified copy of the decree absolute, and if widowed, a copy of your previous partner's death certificate. Most people arrange the wedding through their hotel or tour operator – expect to have to provide the documents at least one month in advance. Alternatively, you can apply in person at the Ministry of National Security and Justice, Kingston Mall, 12 Ocean Blvd, Kingston (Mon–Thurs 8.30am–5pm & Fri 8.30am–4pm; ☎922 0080) – the paperwork costs US$150.

**Laundry** Most hotels have a laundry service, but check prices before handing over a huge load as some charge as much as US$2 for a single shirt. Most large towns have at least one public laundry (listed in the relevant chapters) but your best option is to follow Jamaicans and have clothes washed by hand – ask around for a trustworthy lady and bear in mind that your best garments may receive over-enthusiastic bleaching and scrubbing. A bag of clothes should cost US$8–12.

**Measurements** The country is slowly converting from the Imperial to the metric system – road-signs, for instance, now give distances in kilometres – but the former still dominates and is used throughout this book. The archaic measurement of a chain – 22 yards – is still used, though, if you're asking directions, "a few chains" can mean anything from 100 yards to a mile or more. Treat the direction "it's not far" or "just over there" with the same scepticism.

**Photography** Jamaica is made for pretty pictures. Take plenty of film and all the equipment you'll need – local costs for both are extortionate, and you'll have difficulty finding good filters and lenses, even at the in-bond stores. Humidity is the the photographer's main enemy – carry packets of silica gel in your camera bag, keep film cool and develop it quickly. Over-exposure can also be a problem: watch out for the glare from sea and sand, and try to take pictures early or late in the day when the sun is less bright. When photographing people, ask permission – some like it, others don't – and anticipate a request for a donation.

**Time** Jamaica is on Eastern Standard Time and does not adjust for Daylight Saving Time. Accordingly, it is on the same time as New York (one hour behind from spring to autumn) and five hours behind London (six hours from spring to autumn).

**Tipping** No tip is necessary at any restaurant that imposes an automatic service charge; 10–15 percent is the norm anywhere else. Taxi drivers do not expect a tip.

**Visa extensions** If you want to extend your stay, you can either leave and re-enter the island or apply to the Ministry of National Security and Justice, 12 Ocean Blvd, Kingston (Mon–Thurs 8.30am–5pm & Fri 8.30am–4pm; ☎922 0080), or the Immigration Office, Overton Plaza, Union Street, Montego Bay (Mon–Fri 8am–1pm & 2–4pm; ☎952 5381).

# The Guide

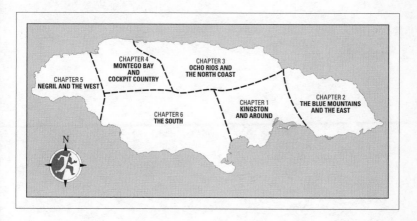

# Chapter 1

# Kingston and around

Intimidating and fascinating in equal measure, **Kingston** is unlike anywhere else in the Caribbean. Few tourists go near Jamaica's troubled capital, and, given its reputation as a city where gangs run riot and police cower in their stations, this is hardly surprising. And while the reputation is absurdly exaggerated, Kingston is certainly not a place for the faint-hearted. With a population fast approaching the million mark, it seethes with life, noise and activity, and if you're there for any time at all, you'll see the rough edges, some of them very rough indeed. In spots all over the city – particularly downtown, west of the Parade – thousands of people scrape a bare living, and the crowded tin shacks, the graffiti, the blaring radios and the stray goats and dogs create a sense of barely controlled chaos.

But it's easy to steer clear of the troubled areas, and it's worth making the effort to visit. Most people find that the city feels daunting at first – true of many unfamiliar cities – but that there is little of the persistent harassment which bedevils parts of the north coast. The pulsating, live-for-today vitality of the place injects a shot of adrenaline that can prove addictive. For many, the sights and sounds of the capital's non-stop street life are entertainment in themselves, and indeed you won't get a sharper insight into Jamaican life anywhere else, but the city is packed with more substantial draws besides. Kingston is the seat of government, the heart of Jamaica's commerce and the home of its high culture, and its exuberant atmosphere is tempered by a cool elegance and a strong sense of national history. A handful of interesting museums, galleries and churches can easily fill a couple of days of sightseeing; the island's best clubs, theatre and some great restaurants will take care of the evenings. If you follow the herd and avoid the capital, you'll have missed one of Jamaica's undoubted highlights.

Nearby, quite apart from the lovely Blue Mountains which overlook Kingston (and are covered in Chapter Two), plenty of other attractions surround the city. The area is littered with historic sites – Georgian monuments in **Spanish Town**, the forts of the English buc-

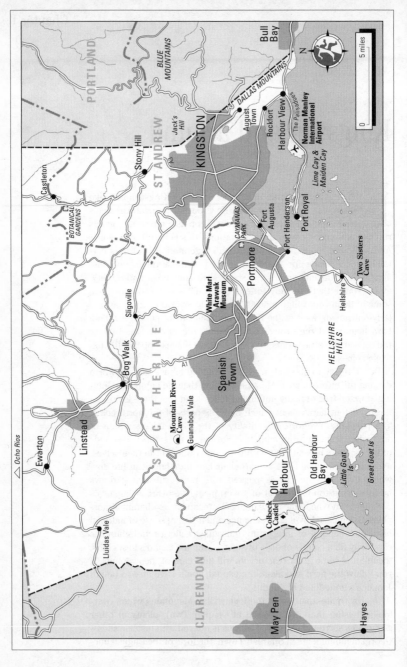

caneers in atmospheric **Port Royal** and **Taino caves** from pre-Columbian times at **Mountain River Cave** and **Two Sisters Cave** – and, for those who just can't cope without a beach, the white-sand **Hellshire beaches** and **Lime Cay** are the perfect places to get away from it all.

# Kingston

Founded at the tail-end of the seventeenth century, **KINGSTON** fast became the greatest city in the West Indies. The main impetus to growth was its fabulous location, built on an expansive natural harbour – the seventh largest in the world – which was to prove the cornerstone of Kingston's future trading success. Since those early days, the city streets have gradually found their way north and now reach as far as the foothills of the **Blue Mountains**, a truly glorious backdrop.

Kingston's main sights are divided between the area known as "downtown", which stretches north from the waterfront to the busy traffic junction of Cross Roads, and "uptown", spreading up into the ritzy suburbs at the base of the mountains. **Downtown** is the city's industrial centre, its factories and all-important port providing most of the city's blue-collar employment; the law firms, stock exchange and the Bank of Jamaica are also prominent features. The peaceful, grassy waterfront is a marked contrast to the busy streets of most of downtown, particularly the manic Parade square – a maelstrom of traffic and animals where hustlers flog cassettes, yams, sky juice and sundry worthless trinkets, yelling over a backdrop of booming reggae.

**Uptown** is different, and you may be surprised at how attractive and easygoing it feels, as suited businessmen and office workers go about their daily routine. Most of Kingston's hotels, restaurants, clubs and shopping centres are here, and it's where you'll spend most of your time. Some of the residential districts – places like Mona and Beverly Hills – are simply beautiful, while the central high-rises suggest a modern city anywhere in North America (although the coconut vendors and stray goats tend to give the game away).

In terms of **highlights**, many visitors make straight for the **Bob Marley Museum**, former home of the island's greatest reggae star and musical ambassador. There are also some grand old **colonial houses**, recently restored as museums, and an excellent **national art gallery**. There are plenty of good hotels and restaurants, and the city is the heartbeat of the country's music industry, with top-quality clubs and a busy live music scene, including an extravagant annual **Carnival** – well worth catching if you're on the island in April.

SOME HISTORY
Though the Spanish first settled in Jamaica in 1510, replaced by British colonists in 1655, there was little development in present-day

# Kingston

Kingston until 1692. The area held just a small pig-rearing village, glamorously known as Colonel Barry's Hog Crawle, and a handful of fishing shacks. All of the action was across the harbour on the island of Port Royal, then Jamaica's second city (after Spanish Town) and home to most of the country's leading lights. In 1692, however, a violent **earthquake** devastated Port Royal; several thousand people died instantly and the rest went scurrying for a more hospitable place to live. The Hog Crawle was the obvious choice – on the mainland but beside the harbour – and the former citizens of Port Royal promptly snapped up two hundred acres of land there.

Within a few months, the plans for the new town had been drawn up. New-born Kingston took its name in honour of William of Orange, king of England since 1688, and the town was laid out beside the water to take advantage of the existing **sea trade**. The road plan mostly followed a grid system (which remains largely intact today) with the big central square of **Parade** left open in the heart of town.

By the early eighteenth century, Kingston had become a **major port** for the transhipment of English goods and African slaves to the Spanish colonies of South America. Merchants, traders and brokers made rapid fortunes and began to build themselves ostentatious homes, while fresh waves of **immigrants** piled in to the booming city – some from Europe, some from other Caribbean islands, some from other parts of Jamaica, all in search of opportunity.

With its swelling population and rising wealth, the city soon began to challenge for the role of the **nation's capital**, though the authorities in Spanish Town – comfortably ensconced in their grand Georgian buildings – proved stubborn in handing over that role to their upstart neighbour. By 1872, when Kingston finally became Jamaica's capital city, many wealthy families were already moving beyond the original town boundaries to the more genteel areas that today comprise **uptown** Kingston. Meanwhile, the less affluent huddled downtown and in the **shanty towns** that began to spring up on the outskirts of old Kingston, particularly west of the city, their ranks swollen by a tide of former slaves hoping to find prosperity beyond the sugar estates

*Patrick Leigh Fermor's The Traveller's Tree paints a vivid picture of the Rastafari movement in Kingston's wastelands; see Contexts, p.359.*

Jamaica's turn-of-the-century boom, engineered by tourism and agriculture, largely bypassed Kingston's poor and helped to reinforce the divide between uptown and downtown. While the rich got richer and sequestered themselves in the new suburbs uptown, the **downtown** area continued to deteriorate, neglected by government and hit by a catastrophic earthquake in 1907 that destroyed almost all buildings south of Parade. Those who could afford to do so continued to move out, leaving behind an increasingly destitute population that proved fertile recruitment ground for the **Rastafari** movement during the 1920s and 1930s.

There were major **riots** during the 1930s, with the city feeling the knock-on effects of an island-wide economic crisis sparked by the plunging price of key crops like bananas amd sugar on world markets. The riots led to the development of local trade unions and political parties during the 1940s to speak for the workers and the dispossessed, but improvements in working conditions and the physical infrastructure were slow in coming. Finally, in the 1960s, the city authorities began to show some interest in reversing the decay. Efforts were made to give the old downtown area a face-lift; redevelopment of the waterfront resulted in a much-needed expansion of the city's **port facility** (still a vital part of the city's commerce today) and a smartening up of the harbour area with the introduction of shops, offices and even the island's major art gallery.

A mini-**tourist boom** was sparked by the new-look Kingston (and by the growing popularity of Jamaican music abroad), with cruiseships arriving to inject a fresh air of hope into the city. Sadly, the optimism proved short-lived. For the people of West Kingston, the redevelopment of downtown was only cosmetic. Crime – an inevitable feature in the crowded ghettos – was getting out of control, sponsored by irresponsible politicians who distributed weapons and patronage to their supporters. At election time (particularly in 1976 and 1980) hundreds of people were killed in bloody campaigns, many of them innocent bystanders. Tourists ran for cover, heading for the new beach resorts on the island's north coast, and the city sank into a quagmire of unemployment, poverty and crime.

For more on west Kingston's history, see p.68.

Today, Kingston remains a divided city. The wealthy have moved further and further into the suburbs, coming in to work in the smart uptown area of New Kingston but rarely venturing near downtown, while the ghettos remain firmly under the control of the political mafia. You have to look hard to find rays of hope, but there are hints that the city's fortunes may be turning. For the first time, senior politicians are starting to address the problem of the city's gangs and party factions and – a crucial development – admitting their own role in creating them. At the same time, there are proposals – from government and the private sector – to pour tourist development funds into the city, with the return of the cruise-ships the main priority. With tourism-generated money and a serious approach to tackling crime, Kingston may have a chance of regaining some of its former glory.

## Arrival and information

All international and most domestic **flights** land at **Norman Manley International Airport** on the Palisadoes – a strip of land that juts out into the Caribbean Sea south of the city. A number of **car-rental** firms have desks right alongside the arrivals area (see p.85); others will normally meet you there on request. A city **bus** runs from just outside the arrivals area to downtown roughly every half-hour (J$10); for a **cab**, the official fare for the thirty-minute journey to New Kingston is around US$18, although with all but the smartest cars this can normally be negotiated down.

The domestic airport of **Tinson Pen** (☎978 8068) is just to the west of downtown. From here, the city bus into downtown costs J$10 and takes ten minutes, while a cab to New Kingston costs around US$6.

If you're arriving by **car**, there are four main **entry points** to the city. Most visitors come in from the north coast on the busy A3 road, which runs straight through the northern suburbs of Stony Hill and Constant Spring and into the heart of uptown Kingston. Also from the north coast, the more tortuous B3 from Buff Bay will eventually bring you out at Papine, northeast of town; following the main Old Hope Road due west brings you into uptown. Coming from the west, Spanish Town Road divides at Six Miles on Kingston's western edge and signs point you downtown towards the airport or uptown towards New Kingston. From the east, Windward Road swings in past the turn-off to Port Royal and the airport – to get uptown, turn right on South Camp Road.

Most of the **buses** into Kingston pull in at the swarming **terminal** at the junction of Beckford and Pechon streets, just west of the crowded Parade. Local services run from there into New Kingston, although as Kingston's bus system is in such a state of disrepair (see below), you're best off getting a **taxi** from the busy rank here. Many buses from the north and west also stop at **Half Way Tree** in the uptown area, closer to most of the hotels.

### Information

The main office of the **Jamaica Tourist Board** (Mon–Fri 9am–4.30pm; ☎929 9200) is at 2 St Lucia Ave in New Kingston. It has maps, booklets, lists of places to stay and a useful little library. There's a smaller branch at Norman Manley airport (normally open to meet flights; ☎924 8024). The most useful **map** of the Kingston area is on the back of the JTB's free island map *Discover Jamaica*, with a handy separate plan of the city's downtown area.

There is no good listings section in any of the newspapers, but most of the theatres, cinemas and clubs advertise their activities in the national *Daily Gleaner*. Look out, also, for flyers slapped up around town heralding forthcoming stageshows and parties.

## Getting around

Finding your way around Kingston is pretty straightforward. Downtown uses a grid system while uptown is defined by a handful of major roads. You will quickly get used to the main landmarks and, as a reliable fallback, the mountains to the northeast serve as a good compass reference. The heat and the distances between places mean you're not going to want to do a lot of **walking**, though the downtown sights, in particular, are easily navigable on foot. Few people walk the streets at night in any part of the city.

**Taxis** are the quickest way of getting around the city and reasonably cheap; a ride from New Kingston to downtown costs around

*A list of Kingston's reliable taxi firms appears on p.86.*

The **pestering** of visitors, irritatingly widespread on the north coast, is relatively and refreshingly uncommon in Kingston. Nevertheless, as with any big city, there are plenty of scare stories and some places that you should steer clear of. There is serious poverty and political tribalism in large parts of west Kingston (see p.68) and you shouldn't even think of straying in there without an experienced guide. Downtown, too, has its dodgy areas and, once the business crowd has gone, it can feel distinctly hostile; unless you're arriving by bus or seeing a show at the brightly lit Ward Theatre, there is little reason to be there after dark.

With 500 murders in 1996 alone, the crime statistics for the city are ugly, although you should bear in mind that the majority of violent crime is domestic or the result of gang wars in the ghetto areas of west Kingston. Of course, criminals do venture out of these areas for the richer pickings of uptown Kingston, and the well-to-do are increasingly protected behind high fences, barbed wire, security guards and dogs. During the day, though, most of the uptown area feels fine, particularly once you're familiar with the main roads; at night, you're best off getting a taxi if you're travelling any distance.

US$5. Bear in mind that few cabs carry meters and you'll need to fix a price before you get in. Although it is standard practice to call for a taxi, particularly at night, they can almost always be flagged down on the main streets, and there's a bustling rank downtown at Parade.

Unfortunately, public transport isn't really a viable option, as the city's **bus system** is a chaotic nightmare. The government handed control to private operators in the 1980s and the resulting free-for-all has seen any notions of timetables and passenger comfort fly out of the window. Fares are absurdly cheap – J$5 to J$10 per journey around the city – but the overcrowding, aggressive sexual harassment and madcap driving deter all who can afford to do without. If you are determined to use them, Parade and Half Way Tree are the main terminals.

There are good reasons not to **drive** in Kingston. Car rental is expensive; it can work out cheaper to take taxis even if you're going as far afield as Spanish Town or Port Royal. City traffic can be hellish, and the quality of driving dangerously macho. And navigation is hindered, especially at night, by a paucity of street lights and road signs and an excess of potholes and jaywalking animals. Only if you're staying outside the city or planning to tour extensively should you need a car; rental firms are listed on p.85.

## Accommodation

Most of Kingston's **hotels** are scattered around the small uptown district of **New Kingston**, a convenient base for sightseeing and close to many of the restaurants, theatres, cinemas and clubs. Some of the cheaper places are in slightly insalubrious locales and, if you're stay-

# Kingston

*There are some dirt-cheap hotels **downtown**, but as these are only for the desperate and fearless, we don't recommend them.*

ing there, you'll need to watch yourself at night. Few of the city's hotels cater specifically for the tourist trade, relying instead on a steady stream of Jamaican and international business visitors; as a result, prices are not as seasonal as in the resort areas and there are few discounts available during the summer. Although it is normally wise to reserve in advance, finding a room is rarely a problem, except during the April Carnival and around Christmas and New Year.

If you don't fancy the hustle of the big city (and some of the hotels can get noisy at night), there are a handful of small hotels and guesthouses in the foothills of the Blue Mountains just north of Kingston. (Others, deeper in the mountains, are covered in Chapter Two.) As well as offering peace and spectacular views, these make good bases for hiking. If you want to explore the city, though, it can be expensive and time-consuming getting back and forth and, unless you have a car, you're probably better off staying in town.

## Kingston

**Altamont Court**, 1 Altamont Terrace; ☎929 5931, fax 929 2118. Pretty good location in the shadow of the gleaming *Jamaica Pegasus* hotel, with comfortable rooms and a small swimming pool. ⑤.

*The hotels and guesthouses listed here are marked on the map on p.73.*

**Artland Guest House**, 111 Waltham Park Rd; ☎923 4647. Basic spot a 15min walk west of Half Way Tree; all rooms come with fans. ①.

**Chelsea**, 5 Chelsea Ave; ☎926 5803. Basic and rather seedy accommodation, but cheap and in the heart of New Kingston. ②.

**Christar Villas**, 99 Hope Rd; ☎978 3933, fax 978 8068. Pleasant self-catering rooms and suites and a small pool near the Bob Marley Museum. ⑤.

**Crieffe Court**, 10 Crieffe Court; ☎927 7908. No frills but reasonable value at this functional hotel near the National Stadium. ②.

**Edge Hill**, 198 Mountain View Ave; ☎927 9854, fax 978 0779. Decent hotel-cum-motel on the eastern side of town near the National Stadium. The rooms, mostly self-catering, are sizeable but can be noisy at night – ask for one away from the main road. ④.

---

### Accommodation price codes

All the hotels detailed in this guide have been graded according to the following price categories. Note that the prices have been calculated as those for the cheapest **double** or **twin room** during low season, normally mid-April to mid-December. During high season, rates are liable to rise by up to 25 percent (though this is rare at the cheap hotels), and proprietors may be less amenable to bargaining. Although the law requires prices to be quoted in Jamaican dollars, most hotels give rates in US dollars; payment can be made in either currency. For more details see p.22.

| | |
|---|---|
| ① under US$20 | ⑤ US$70–100 |
| ② US$20–35 | ⑥ US$100–150 |
| ③ US$35–50 | ⑦ US$150–200 |
| ④ US$50–70 | ⑧ US$200 and above |

**Four Seasons**, 18 Ruthven Rd; ☎926 8805, fax 929 5964. Attractive, converted Edwardian home in New Kingston. Rooms in the original house are more atmospheric than those in the modern wing. ⑤.

**The Gardens**, 23 Liguanea Ave; ☎927 5957, fax 978 6942. Delightful complex of expansive two-bedroom townhouses set in gorgeous, flowered gardens with a pool and mountain views. Rooms and apartments (sleeping four) are available. ④.

**Holborn Manor Guest House**, 3 Holborn Rd; ☎926 0296. Friendly but rather basic family property in New Kingston. Rates include breakfast. ③.

**Indies**, 5 Holborn Rd; ☎926 0989, fax 926 2879. Compact, clean, slightly overpriced little hotel next to *Holborn Manor*, set on two levels around a garden courtyard and small restaurant. ④.

**International Inn**, 14 Derrymore Rd; ☎929 4437. Box-like rooms and rather unwelcoming staff, but cheap and close to New Kingston. ②.

**Island Club**, 1 Hopedale Ave; ☎978 3915, fax 978 3914. A bit run-down, but with great views over the city from its desirable perch in Beverly Hills. ⑤.

**Jamaica Pegasus**, 81 Knutsford Blvd; ☎926 3690, fax 929 5855. Liveliest of the two high-rise New Kingston hotels, attracting mostly business travellers, with a gym, tennis courts and outdoor pool. ⑦.

**Lynn's Guest House**, 36 Half Way Tree Rd; ☎929 7047. Very simple place, popular as a "short time" hotel, but in a decent location. ②.

**Mayfair**, 4 W King's House Close; ☎926 1610, fax 926 7741. A sound choice in a quiet area, with a pool and a lively bar. No unmarried couples. ⑤.

**Sandhurst**, 70 Sandhurst Crescent; ☎927 8244. Excellent value in a peaceful spot near King's House and the Bob Marley Museum, with a nice pool and a terrace restaurant overlooking the Blue Mountains. ③.

**Stony Hill**, Hermitage Dam Rd; ☎942 2357. Decent option if you're driving in from the north coast, signposted on the left near the gas station before you reach the Constant Spring shopping plazas. The rooms are perfectly acceptable and the staff friendly. ③.

**Sunset Inn**, 1A Altamont Crescent; ☎926 2017. Rather cramped and functional but central, and with small kitchens in some of the rooms. ③.

**Sutton Place**, 11 Ruthven Rd; ☎926 4580, fax 926 8443. Large, comfortable if impersonal hotel/motel with a pool, popular with local business travellers. A reliable fallback at busy times. ④.

**Terra Nova**, 17 Waterloo Rd; ☎926 2211, fax 926 9334. Very smart little hideaway set in landscaped gardens, with a small pool and elegant rooms. ⑦.

**Wyndham**, 77 Knutsford Blvd; ☎926 5430, fax 929 7439. Plush high-rise with a fabulous swimming pool, small casino, nightclub and top-class facilities. ⑦.

*Another alternative, handy for the airport, is the charming* Morgan's Harbour Hotel *in nearby Port Royal; see p.92.*

## Around Kingston

**Ivor**, Skyline Drive, Jack's Hill; ☎927 1460. Only three rooms in this one-time pastor's home, located high above the city and stuffed with old Jamaican books and prints. Memorable views and matchless tranquillity. ⑥.

**Jonraine Country Inn**, 7 West Kirkland Heights, Forest Hills; ☎944 3515. Friendly and cosy small hotel in the Red Hills area west of Kingston. Rather cut off from the city, but great views, especially at night, and good value. ⑤.

*For rooms in the Blue Mountains, see p.111–119.*

**Kingston**

**Maya Mountain Lodge**, Skyline Drive, Jack's Hill; ☎927 2097. Budget place and a local hangout, geared as a base for hikers but feasible for seeing Kingston if you've got a car or patience to wait for the bus. Rustic cabin rooms, and a campsite (with questionable security) from US$7 or US$14 if you rent a tent. ④.

## The City

Most people divide Kingston into two sectors – **downtown** and **uptown** – and we've adopted the same convenient distinction below. It'll take you half a day or so to check out the sights downtown, a little more to catch those uptown. The **National Gallery**, by the waterfront, is probably the highlight of the downtown area, while the nearby **Crafts Market** and Orange Street **record stores** are good places to go souvenir-shopping. This is also where you pick up the **ferry** to Port Royal (see p.87). Ten minutes' walk away, the busy **Parade** – one-time marching ground of the British army – is flanked by a couple of interesting churches, while, just to the north, **Headquarters House** is a grand old colonial home stuffed with historical relics.

Uptown has the more popular attractions, including the must-see **Bob Marley Museum** and the striking **Devon House** – home to the island's first black millionaire – with its clutch of gift shops, landscaped gardens and superb home-made ice cream. Also uptown, at Half Way Tree, the seventeenth-century **St Andrews' Parish Church**

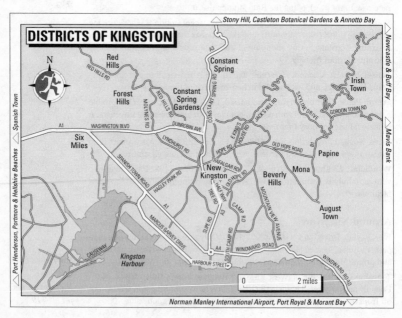

remains one of the key churches in Jamaica, second in historical importance only to the cathedral in Spanish Town (see p.98), while the **Hope Botanical Gardens** offer a quiet refuge from the noise of the city.

## Downtown

Flattened by an earthquake in 1907, **downtown** has lost most of its grand eighteenth-century architecture, though a handful of historic buildings can still be found among the old pavements of Rum Street, Water Street and King Street, and if you peer into the most unlikely yards you can occasionally find evidence of the intricate buildings that used to proliferate here.

Much of Kingston's economic strength still derives from its gorgeous, huge natural harbour. The **waterfront**, which once buzzed with ships carrying sugar and slaves, is a good spot to begin your tour of downtown, close to the **National Gallery** and the **Crafts Market** and a short walk from the main **Parade**, above which you'll find **Headquarters House**, and, just outside the old city boundaries to the north, **National Heroes Park**. Nearby, though very much off the beaten track, **west Kingston** has the country's most depressed ghettos – explosive and creative, the birthplace of many of Jamaica's musical success stories.

### THE WATERFRONT

Despite the large and rather ugly ships moored just offshore, Kingston's **waterfront** is a pleasant place to start your exploration of downtown; people and pelicans fish off the piers and planes land at the airport just across the water. The chief beneficiary of the city council's 1960s' bid to beautify elements of downtown, the waterfront saw its historic buildings swept away and replaced by spanking new high-rises – the icons of the era. Today, these modern monuments define the eastern end of the waterfront's main strip, Ocean Boulevard. They include the headquarters of the Bank of Jamaica on Nethersole Place, whose **Coin and Note Museum** (Mon–Fri 9am–4pm; free) has a collection of the country's currency that should fascinate the numismatic. Nearby at 14 Duke St, you can get a free tour of the **Jamaica Conference Centre** (Mon–Fri 9am–4pm; free), built in 1981 to host meetings of the United Nations' International Seabed Authority. This in itself probably won't have you queuing at dawn, but the building's lofty design and abundant use of glass and local crafts make it feel unlike anywhere else in the city.

West of here, the large, pink, forlorn-looking building on Ocean Boulevard was, until the late 1980s, the **Oceana Hotel**, built as the government's flagship for Kingston in a blatant attempt to entice business travellers – and their expense accounts – downtown. The target guests ignored it entirely and continued to enjoy the smarter hotels and

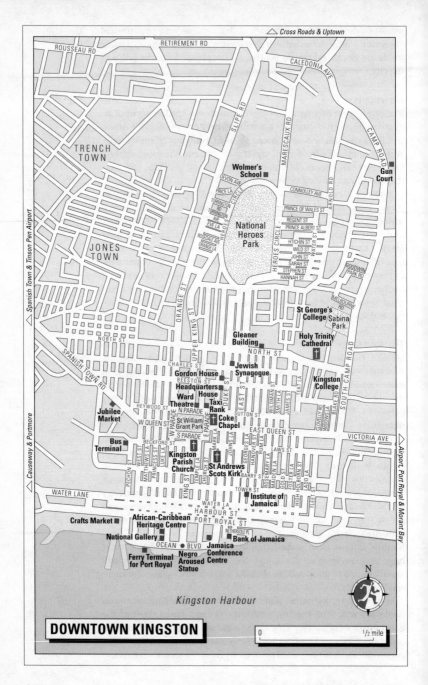

ROUSSEAU RD
RETIREMENT RD
CALEDONIA AVE

TRENCH TOWN

Wolmer's School ■

DEVON AVE
PRICE LA
CARRINGTON RD
TORRINGTON AVE
EVE LA

SLIPE RD

MARESCAUX RD

CONNOLLEY AVE

CAMP ROAD

Gun Court ■

National Heroes Park

PRINCE OF WALES ST
REGENT ST
PRINCE ALBERT ST
HTICHIN ST
WILD ST
JOHN ST
SARAH ST
STEPHEN ST
HANNAH ST

ARNOLD RD

GOODWIN PARK RD

JONES TOWN

ROSDALE AVE
ORANGELA

HEROES CIRCLE

MELBOURNE RD

St George's College ■

Sabina Park

Gleaner Building ■

Holy Trinity Cathedral ✝

NORTH ST

Kingston College ■

NORTH ST

SOUTH CAMP ROAD

ORANGE ST

UPPER KING ST

CHARLES ST
BEESTON ST

Jewish Synagogue ■

Gordon House ■
Headquarters House ■
Ward Theatre
N PARADE
W PARADE
W QUEEN ST
S PARADE
St William Grant Park

Taxi Rank ■

DUKE ST
MARK LA
EAST ST
SUTTON ST

WILMAN ST
SMITH ST

TEXT LA

COVELTY RD
WOOWNS LA

Coke Chapel ✝

EAST QUEEN ST

VICTORIA AVE

Jubilee Market ■

HEYWOOD ST

Bus Terminal ■

PECHON ST
WEST ST
MATTHEWS LA
PRINCESS ST
BECKFORD ST
UKE LA

Kingston Parish Church ✝
St Andrews Scots Kirk

JOHNS ST
GEORGE ST
HANOVER ST

LAWS ST
MARY LA
OXFORD LA
BARRY ST

HIGH ST
HOLBORN LA
LADD LA
FLEET ST

WATER LANE

KING ST
TEMPLE LA

WATER LA
TOWER ST

Institute of Jamaica ■

Crafts Market ■

African-Caribbean Heritage Centre ■

HARBOUR ST
PORT ROYAL ST

NETHERSOLE PL

National Gallery ■

OCEAN BLVD ●

Ferry Terminal for Port Royal

Negro Aroused Statue

Jamaica Conference Centre ■

Bank of Jamaica ■

Kingston Harbour

N

## DOWNTOWN KINGSTON

0 ............................ ½ mile

better nightlife of New Kingston and the hotel flopped; the official claim that private investors are on the verge of reopening it seems more than a little optimistic. Further along the boulevard, at the bottom of King Street, is a reproduction of the sculpture **Negro Aroused** by the late Edna Manley, wife and mother, respectively, of former prime ministers Norman Manley and Michael Manley, and one of Jamaica's leading artists. The bronze sculpture – a bent worker uncoils from bondage – represents the incipient labour movement and the spirit of unrest of the 1930s and is one of the icons of twentieth-century Jamaican art. The original is in the National Gallery (see below).

## THE NATIONAL GALLERY AND THE AFRICAN-CARIBBEAN HERITAGE CENTRE

For many people, the **National Gallery**, at 12 Ocean Blvd on the corner of Orange Street (Mon–Fri 9.30am–4pm; J$20), is one of the unexpected highlights of a visit to Kingston. The permanent collection here is superb, ranging from delicate woodcarvings to flamboyant religious paintings, and, of the several temporary exhibitions held each year, the Annual National Exhibition (normally Dec–Feb) showcases the best of contemporary Jamaican art.

Just inside the door, Christopher Gonzales' statue of Bob Marley was commissioned for Kingston's proposed Celebrity Park (see p.75); the statue (which bears little resemblance to the great man) was too eccentric for Marley fans and was consigned to relative obscurity here.

*See p.353 of Contexts for more on Jamaican art.*

At the core of the permanent collection are ten chronological galleries, housed on the first floor, representing the **Jamaican School**, 1922 to the present. Their era is generally deemed to begin with Edna Manley's 1922 *Bead Seller*, a dainty little statue which married a contemporary artistic trend (cubism) to a typical local image (the Kingston "higgler", or female street vendor) to create something distinctly Jamaican. Manley's sculpture and the "naive" paintings of John Dunkley (1891–1947) dominate the first galleries. Dunkley was a Kingston barber, and the first and most important of Jamaica's self-taught artists; his dark brooding local scenes are a far cry from the jaunty colours of modern landscape painters. He and Manley paved the way for others to paint what they saw around them and, in the work of artists like Albert Huie and David Pottinger – see his *Nine Night*, with its mourners turned trance-like during the ritual nine nights of grieving after a death – you can detect the early stages of a movement giving value and artistic identity to its own people and places.

The paintings of the prolific Carl Abrahams in the later galleries show a move towards abstraction that is capped by the idiosyncratically Jamaican surrealism of Colin Garland and the unsettling ghostly images of David Boxer, long-time curator of the gallery and a key figure in Jamaican modern art. Realism returns with the spooky recreation of a Trench Town ghetto in Dawn Scott's *A Cultural*

*The ferry to Port Royal departs from the pier at the bottom of Princess Street, near the National Gallery; see p.89 for details.*

*Object*, which has you walking in ever-decreasing circles through corrugated tin alleys to a disturbing climax. Look out, also, for the funky colours of Rastafarian Everald Brown whose vivid *Drum* sculpture recurs in his spiritual painting *Ethiopian Apple*. There is also a whole room devoted to the African-style sculpture and paintings of Revivalist Mallica Reynolds (aka Shepherd Kapo), which you'll either love or hate.

Downstairs, the **A.D. Scott Collection** displays a selection of Edna Manley's sculptures alongside some of the finest works of the island's biggest names, including Gloria Escoffery and Barrington Watson. Highlights include Watson's *Banana Loaders*, beautifully capturing the toiling banana workers in Post-Impressionist style, and Escofferey's *The Old Woman*, which suggests the esteem in which the seated grandmother, surrounded by her family, is held in Jamaica.

The rest of the permanent collection is rotated from time to time and includes a modern photographic display, a pre-twentieth-century exhibit, with its series of landscapes by itinerant European painters, and an international collection featuring such diverse sections as modern Cuban painters and the English Bloomsbury Group.

*Orange Street has the island's best record stores – see p.84.*

Just north of the gallery on Orange Street, the tiny, uninspired **African-Caribbean Heritage Centre** (Mon–Fri 9am–3.30pm; free) is a library and small art gallery with a few African drums and musical instruments and a long-standing exhibition on Marcus Garvey.

### THE CRAFTS MARKET

The **Crafts Market** (daily except Sun), housed in an unprepossessing iron building at the western end of Ocean Boulevard, is all that's left of the formidable market that for centuries was held at the bottom of nearby King Street. Originally a Sunday market drawing thousands of slaves on their day off, it got shunted a few hundred yards west during the 1960s' redevelopment of the waterfront, and never quite recaptured its heyday. Shopping here is generally a hassle-free experience, and you'll find loads of little stores selling t-shirts, carvings, jewellery and other souvenirs as cheaply as anywhere on the island. Unlike most places, though, don't expect to be able to bargain much on price.

### THE PARADE AND AROUND

Opposite Edna Manley's *Negro Aroused* statue, King Street runs north to the **Parade**, a large square left open by the original city planners and used as a parade ground by British troops during the eighteenth century, as well as for public floggings and hangings – most famously the hanging of the slave hired to assassinate Cuban independence leader Simon Bolivar during his visit to the island in 1818 (he failed, but perished for trying). Today, it's one of the busiest spots in town, with traffic racing around the central park, music blaring from radios and ghetto-blasters, crowds milling around the taxi rank and the bus terminus, and vendors hawking sky juice and cheap baubles. In the middle of the Parade, **St William Grant Park** (originally Victoria Park but renamed in 1977 for a 1930s' leader of the infant Jamaican trade union movement) offers a shady spot to catch your breath. Rather fierce statues of political rivals Norman Manley and Alexander Bustamante guard its north and south entrances, while Queen Victoria – the one-time "Supreme Lady of Jamaica" – stands to the east, looking a little lost among all the mayhem. There's an elaborate fountain in the centre of the park, prettily illuminated at night, and a small play area for kids.

Just north of the park on North Parade, looking like an elaborately iced birthday cake, the elegant **Ward Theatre** occupies a site with a long theatrical tradition – it is reckoned that public performances have been staged here since at least the mid-eighteenth century and probably earlier – although the present building dates only from 1911. It now hosts an annual pantomime every December and regular music and dance shows throughout the year. If you want to poke around, the building is normally open, and you're free to explore the gallery, stalls and – thrillingly, for those with thespian proclivities – even the stage.

*See p.83 for further details of performances at the Ward Theatre.*

On South Parade, just below the park, the **Kingston Parish Church** was first built in 1699, although little of the present structure pre-dates the 1907 earthquake. Airy and spacious, the church is used for important state funerals and such, although the regular congregation has dwindled almost to nothing due to migration out of the downtown area. The south wall has a marvellously wordy elegy to midshipman Edward Baker, who died in 1796 in a sea battle off Santo Domingo, and there are plenty of marble monuments to such notables as John Wolmer, founder of Wolmer's School (see p.72), and British Admiral John Benbow. An eloquent testament to colonialism hangs on the west wall, where plaques honour soldiers of the West Indian regiment who died (mostly of fever) on unheard-of campaigns in West Africa in the 1890s.

Queen Street runs west and east of the park. To the west, the enormous **Jubilee Market** (Mon–Fri) spills over onto the Parade, a colourful place to wander and pick up fresh fruit and vegetables, though the crowds can make it rather daunting. East of the park, the large red-brick **Coke Chapel** is a Methodist church dating from 1840 and erected over the remains of a smaller eighteenth-century chapel built by Thomas Coke, an early missionary. Methodism, along with other nonconformist religions, played an important role in Jamaica, its missionaries actively fighting for improvements in the conditions of slaves and, eventually, against slavery itself. Because of this, the Methodist church found itself in conflict with the Jamaican authorities and, like others, the Coke Chapel was ordered to close for several years in the early nineteenth century. There's little to see in the rather spartan interior, but it's a quiet retreat from the sun and the

# Kingston

**West Kingston**

**West Kingston** is Kingston's urban nightmare. Bob Marley sang fondly of growing up in the "government yards in Trench Town" but the reality of "the West" is of a huge underclass confined to crowded tenements, cardboard shacks and appalling poverty. The area – basically west of Parade, both north (Trench Town, Jones Town) and south (Tivoli Gardens) of the main Spanish Town Road – has seen some sporadic clean-up campaigns but it's a seemingly hopeless task.

In the city's early years, west Kingston was a popular residential zone – well laid out and central. Over the last century, though, an exodus of the wealthy to more chi-chi districts uptown led to west Kingston's decline, and a subsequent influx of the less well-off – men and women from rural Jamaica who headed for Kingston's bright lights but were unable to find either work or welfare. Crowded together, the very worst-off built their makeshift homes on the "**Dungle**" (dunghill) by Kingston harbour, where all the city's excrement was dumped before the introduction of a sewage system. There, they fought with each other, as well as with the dogs and John Crow vultures, for scraps of garbage from the dust-carts.

Criminal "**yardies**" were quick to take advantage of the conditions, recruiting gang members from the ranks of the poor, especially young men looking for the identity and protection offered by a gang or "posse". Robbery, muggings and drug sales brought in money and, with it, a measure of street credibility. The crime problem was exacerbated in the **1970s** as feuding political factions blatantly armed their supporters, asking them to intimidate opponents or drive them out of their "garrisons" or constituencies. In turn, the weapons helped the criminals to establish ever stronger and more extensive empires of drugs and prostitution.

Today, large areas of the West are little more than **armed camps**, daubed with murals and graffiti warning political opponents to keep out. There is nothing that the ordinary people can do to protect themselves; the murder rate is higher than anywhere else on the island, and the papers regularly carry stories of schoolchildren and other bystanders dying in the crossfire between the gangs. At election time – every four or five years – the place becomes a war zone. Despite the tales of tourists blithely wandering into Trench Town to film Bob Marley's childhood haunts (there's little else to see), this is not a place to venture without an experienced guide and a very deep breath.

*Perry Henzell's movie* The Harder They Come *(see p.92) is the classic account of a country boy falling in with the gangsters of west Kingston.*

crowds; the caretaker can usually be found nearby with a key – ask at the little shop in the compound.

Just south of Coke Chapel on Mark Lane, the bizarre octagonal **St Andrews Scots Kirk** (key from the resident caretaker; free) was founded in the early nineteenth century by local merchants of Scottish ancestry; the St Andrews Cross can still be detected in the church's stained glass window.

## THE INSTITUTE OF JAMAICA

Four blocks east of Coke Chapel, East Street runs south to the **Institute of Jamaica** (Mon–Thurs 9am–5pm, Fri 9am–4pm; free). Here you'll find the **National Library**, home to the best collection of books and old newspapers in the country, and the eminently missable **National Museum** (entrance round the corner on Tower Street) of Jamaica's natural history. Alongside the ranks of musty cabinets filled with dust-gathering stuffed birds, one of the more interesting displays explains the origins of the country's most important "economic plants" – sugarcane, bananas, coconuts and pineapples – almost all imported from areas of Asia during the early years of Spanish and British colonialism, and now widely grown for export. The museum has plenty of other interesting odds and ends – Taino *zemis*, African jewellery, old musical instruments – but, infuriatingly, these are only occasionally on display, spending most of their lives mouldering away in the basement.

## HEADQUARTERS HOUSE AND GORDON HOUSE

Two blocks west of East Street, **Headquarters House** on Duke Street (Mon–Fri 8.30am–4.30pm; free) affords a brief glimpse of Jamaican history. Built in 1755 by Thomas Hibbert, a wealthy local merchant, the house was part of a wager between four friends as to who could construct the most elegant building to impress a local woman (Hibbert lost the bet, but the winning house is no longer in existence – a shame as, given the cool elegance of Hibbert's design, it must have been a knockout). Jamaica's legislative assembly met here briefly in 1755 and moved in full-time between 1872 and 1960. During the intervening years the house was commandeered by the armed forces to serve both as its military headquarters and as the residence of the local general in charge.

Today Headquarters House is the home of the National Heritage Trust, whose offices are installed in the former bedrooms and on the recently walled-in veranda, but you're free to look around the rest of the house. The debating chamber, where the legislative assembly used to meet, is on the ground floor, filled with original furniture and a fine mahogany public gallery for visitors, and the walls hold large portraits of Jamaica's first political leaders and some of its National Heroes, including Sam Sharpe, Nanny and Paul Bogle. In the basement, the cool storage rooms contain more offbeat relics, including a bronze statue of Marcus Garvey and a painting by Noel Coward of his adopted home at Port Maria on the north coast (see p.170). Upstairs, you can climb to the look-out tower for great views over downtown Kingston, Port Royal and the Blue Mountains. From here Hibbert would watch his ships coming into the harbour and, later, the generals could keep an eye on any enemy boat movements.

*For more on Jamaica's National Heroes see p.71.*

Next to Headquarters House is the rather less imposing **Gordon House**, home to the parliament since 1960 and named for National Hero George William Gordon. Gordon, a lay preacher who consistently advocated the rights of the poor, proved a constant thorn in the side of the establishment. In 1865, the authorities found a flimsy pretext to accuse him of involvement in the Morant Bay Rebellion

*See p.122 for more on the Morant Bay Rebellion.*

and he was summarily executed, despite widespread protest from black Jamaicans. Today, the House of Representatives meets here most Tuesdays at 2pm (and at the same time on Wednesdays and Thursdays if there is sufficient business) while the Senate sits in the chamber on Fridays at 11am. Entrance to the public gallery is free, and when the chamber is empty you can ask the marshall to show you around. To be honest, the debates are normally pretty soporific for spectators, although it can be fun to catch political veterans like the Jamaican Labour Party's Edward Seaga in action.

## THE JEWISH SYNAGOGUE

The striking white building on Duke Street above Gordon House is the **Jewish Synagogue**. It's kept locked but you can normally find the caretaker on the premises during the week; you'll need to pay a small donation for him to open the place up. Jews were among the first Europeans to settle in Jamaica during the sixteenth century, fleeing the inquisition in Spain. Even here, though, they were still obliged to practise their religion in secret, a fact remembered today by the sand scattered on the floor of the modern building, which symbolically muffles your footsteps as you wander around.

In 1882, the synagogues of the two Jewish congregations, the Ashkenhazi and the Sephardic, were both destroyed by fire and an amalgamated synagogue was built on this site (although a handful of rebel members of each congregation refused to mix and went off to found their own synagogues). The present building dates from after the 1907 earthquake, with substantial repairs effected after Hurricane Gilbert. The exodus of Jamaica's Jews, both from downtown Kingston and from the island (part of the general flight of whites during the 1970s), means that the present congregation is tiny, but the building, with its mahogany staircase and gallery, is still worth a visit if you're passing.

## EAST OF DUKE STREET

A couple of blocks east of the synagogue, the **Gleaner Building** (closed to visitors) on the corner of North and East Streets holds the offices of the *Gleaner* and *Star* newspapers. The *Gleaner* has reported on events in Jamaica since it was founded as *de Cordova's Advertiser* in 1834; never afraid to voice its strident opinions, and particularly scathing during the first administration of Michael Manley, the paper remains the most influential and widely read of the country's three dailies. Five minutes' walk further east along North Street and you come to the Catholic Church's large-domed **Holy Trinity Cathedral**. A caretaker is supposed to guard the premises but don't hold out too much hope of finding him there, or the cathedral open, except during services. During termtime, hundreds of schoolchildren mill around the area, spilling out of nearby high schools **Kingston College** and **St George's College**, the latter founded by the Jesuits in 1850. Just around the corner from the cathedral is **Sabina Park**, home of the Kingston Cricket Club – the oldest sports club in the Commonwealth Caribbean – and venue for international test matches and many of the inter-island games.

*See p.38 of Basics for more on Jamaica's cricket fixation.*

NATIONAL HEROES PARK AND AROUND

Ten minutes' walk north from the Gleaner Building, **National Heroes Park** (better known locally as the Racecourse) is a large but rather desolate stretch of grass enclosed by iron railings and popular with local goats. If you're on foot it offers a chance to escape the traffic that hammers around it, but it can feel threatening, even during the day, and you'll want to stick to the outer edges. The park held the city's racecourse for more than a century before it got shifted to the more salubrious New Kingston and from there to its present location west of the city at Caymanas Park. After independence, the government decided to convert part of the area into a monument to Jamaica's National Heroes (see box); Norman Manley, Alexander Bustamante and Marcus Garvey are buried beneath the futuristic Shrine of Monuments – a series of stone, marble and bronze memorial busts and figures dedicted to each of the Heroes – at the south end of the park. Nearby is a bust of Antonio Maceo and a statue of Simon

---

**Jamaica's National Heroes**

Since independence the Jamaican parliament has elevated seven of the island's greatest people to the status of **National Hero**, all of whom carry the title "The Right Excellent". As yet, none of the Heroes comes from the worlds of sport or music, but it is widely anticipated that Bob Marley will be next to join the pantheon. Former prime minister Michael Manley, who died in 1997, is another popular candidate, as is sprinter Merlene Ottey, who would become the second female and the first living National Hero. The present National Heroes are:

**Paul Bogle** (unknown–1865). Baptist preacher involved in the 1865 Morant Bay Rebellion and executed for his participation.

**Alexander Bustamante** (1884–1977). Labour leader, founder of the Jamaica Labour Party and first prime minister of the independent country from 1962 to 1967.

**Marcus Garvey** (1887–1940). Founder of the Universal Negro Improvement Association and widely viewed as the father of the black power movement.

**George William Gordon** (1820–65). "Free coloured" leader of Jamaica's nationalist movement after slavery, accused of involvement in the Morant Bay Rebellion and executed.

**Nanny** (birth and death unknown). Legendary eighteenth-century female leader of the Windward Maroons in their battles with the English.

**Norman Manley** (1893–1969). Lawyer, founder of the People's National Party and leader of Jamaica's movement for independence.

**Sam Sharpe** (1801–32). Baptist preacher executed after leading the 1831 slave rebellion in Jamaica's western parishes.

Bolivar, independence leaders in Cuba and South America respectively and inspirational to Jamaica's early nationalists.

At the north end of the park, on Marescaux Road, are the colourful, wooden buildings of **Wolmers High School** and **Mico College**. Wolmers, founded in 1729, has proved a formidable centre of academic achievement, counting prime ministers and governor-generals among its alumni. Nearby Mico, the largest teacher-training school in the West Indies, owes its foundation in 1834 to the eleventh-hour refusal of an Englishman to marry Lady Mico's niece back in 1670. The intended dowry was invested for a number of charitable purposes, and eventually used to found teacher-training colleges in various parts of the Caribbean.

East of here on Camp Road are the headquarters of the Jamaican Defence Force (the island's equivalent of an army) and the notorious **Gun Court**. Established in 1972 during the early years of Michael Manley's first administration to deal with the proliferating number of firearms offences, the place is still a harsh prison, protected by high-security fences and reams of barbed wire. **Cross Roads**, quarter of a mile above Mico and the dividing line between uptown and downtown, marks the intersection where Kingston's principal roads meet. There's little to it other than a busy market and the **Carib Theatre**, the city's oldest cinema, presently being rebuilt after a catastrophic fire in 1996.

## Uptown

The phrase "uptown Kingston" is used as a catch-all for areas of the city north of Cross Roads, including the business and commercial centres of **Half Way Tree** and **New Kingston** as well as residential areas like **Hope**, **Mona** and **Beverly Hills**. Up until the late eighteenth century uptown was mostly rural, sprinkled with livestock farms (known as pens) and sugar estates. Gradually, as Kingston's wealthy merchants acquired this land in a bid to escape from the noise and crowds downtown, the city began to spill out of its original waterfront site. The process has accelerated during the past half-century and newer and more fashionable districts have been created further and further north of the old city, extending right across the old Liguanea Plain and into the foothills of the Blue Mountains.

Most visitors make a beeline for the **Bob Marley Museum** and the colonial-era **Devon House**, both just above New Kingston on the traffic-crazed Hope Road, uptown's central thoroughfare. Further east are the pleasant **Hope Botanical Gardens**, and Mona, home to the country's university, while, to the north, the main arteries fan out into the Blue Mountains and the ritzy suburbs of Red Hills, Stony Hill and Jack's Hill.

### New Kingston

The heart of uptown is the high-rise financial district of **New Kingston**, found in an eccentric triangle bounded by Trafalgar Road, Old Hope Road and Half Way Tree Road. In the early twentieth cen-

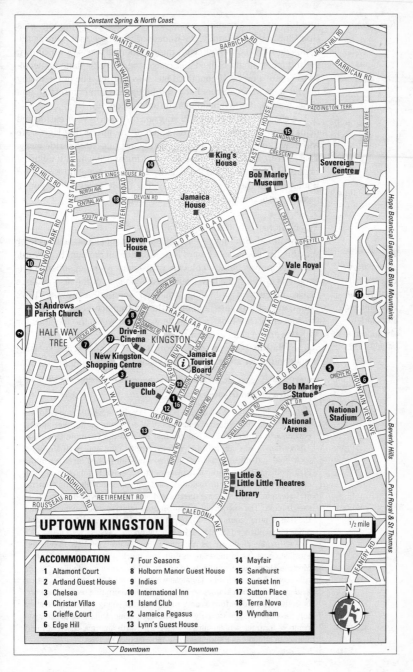

Constant Spring & North Coast

GRANTS PEN RD

BARBICAN RD

JACK'S HILL RD

BARBICAN RD

UPPER WATERLOO RD

PADDINGTON TERR

LIGUANEA AVE

EAST KINGS HOUSE RD

15 SANDHURST

RED HILLS RD

CONSTANT SPRING ROAD

WEST KINGS HOUSE RD

CRESCENT

14

King's House

Bob Marley Museum

Sovereign Centre

Hope Botanical Gardens & Blue Mountains

NORTH AVE

DEVON RD

CENTRAL AVE

18

Jamaica House

4

HILL CREST AVE

HOPEFIELD AVE

EASTWOOD PARK RD

WATERLOO ROAD

SOUTH AVE

HOPE ROAD

Devon House

Vale Royal

10

HAUGHTON AVE

TRAFALGAR RD

MUSGRAVE RD

11

St Andrews Parish Church

1

BELMONT RD

MELROSE RD

HUMPHRIES RD

NEW KINGSTON

LADY MUSGRAVE RD

2

HALF WAY TREE

CECELIO AVE

8

9

Drive-in Cinema

5 CRIEFFE RD

17

7

New Kingston Shopping Centre

KNUTSFORD BLVD

LANE

Jamaica Tourist Board

i

6

MOUNTAIN VIEW

3

Liguanea Club

19

CRES

WORTHINGTON AVE

OLD HOPE ROAD

Bob Marley Statue

National Stadium

HALF WAY TREE RD

12 16

1

ALTAMONT

HANING RD

National Arena

ARTHUR WINT DR

OXFORD RD

13

SWALLOWFIELD RD

BEVERLY HILLS

RIPON RD

BELMONT RD

Beverly Hills

LYNHURST RD

TOM REDCAM AVE

Little & Little Little Theatres

Library

Port Royal & St Thomas

ROUSSEAU RD

RETIREMENT RD

CALEDONIA AVE

0          ½ mile

DEANERY RD

**UPTOWN KINGSTON**

N

Downtown      Downtown

**ACCOMMODATION**

| | | | | | |
|---|---|---|---|---|---|
| **1** | Altamont Court | **7** | Four Seasons | **14** | Mayfair |
| **2** | Artland Guest House | **8** | Holborn Manor Guest House | **15** | Sandhurst |
| **3** | Chelsea | **9** | Indies | **16** | Sunset Inn |
| **4** | Christar Villas | **10** | International Inn | **17** | Sutton Place |
| **5** | Crieffe Court | **11** | Island Club | **18** | Terra Nova |
| **6** | Edge Hill | **12** | Jamaica Pegasus | **19** | Wyndham |
| | | **13** | Lynn's Guest House | | |

tury this was an attractive grassy area, the location of the Liguanea Golf Club and later, briefly, the Knutsford Park racetrack. During the 1950s and 1960s, though, with the commercial areas of downtown getting increasingly choked and congested, the city planners decided to create a new self-contained business district. The horse-racing moved west to Caymanas Park, the Liguanea Club contracted, and bank, hotel and office buildings started to shoot up.

The chances are that you will **stay** and do much of your **eating** and **drinking** in or around this area; some of the interesting sights are within walking distance, the rest are a short bus- or taxi-ride away. There are few places of note in New Kingston itself, although the **Liguanea Club**, opposite the *Jamaica Pegasus* hotel on Knutsford Boulevard (in theory members only, but easily accessible if you're passing), still retains its old colonial buildings.

## THE NATIONAL STADIUM AND AROUND

The **National Stadium**, which hosts most of Jamaica's premier sporting fixtures, is just east of New Kingston on Stadium Boulevard. The stadium was built to coincide with Jamaica's independence celebrations in 1962; the first event was the raising of the new nation's black, green and gold flag, followed soon after by the 1962 Commonwealth Games. Although the centrepiece of the stadium – the soccer pitch – looks a little the worse for wear, the facilities for athletics and cycling are first-rate.

The **National Arena** next door houses smaller-scale sporting events and other shows. There are plans to convert the grassy area

*For information on events at the National Stadium and National Arena, call ☎929 4970.*

---

### Jamaica at the Olympics

Although, like other West Indian islands, Jamaica is world-famous for its cricket, it also has a tremendous record of achievement in other sports, particularly **athletics**. The country first entered the **Olympic Games** in 1948 when it was still a British colony. Arthur Wint and Herb McKinley took gold and silver in the 400 metres, and Wint picked up silver in the 800 metres. That record of achievement, remarkable for such a small country, has been kept up over the years, with sprinters like **Don Quarrie** and **Merlene Ottey** winning medals and acquiring a devoted following in the process. The success of Jamaican-born athletes who have run under the flag of other countries – Britain's Linford Christie is just one example – has only enhanced the country's reputation.

Two explanations are usually given for Jamaica's athletic excellence. First, success (as in most sports) offers a quick way out of the ghetto – Merlene Ottey, for example, born and raised in a poor rural village, is *the* role model for many young Jamaican women. Second, the vision of political leaders like **Norman Manley** – who himself held a sprinting record in schoolboy athletics for over forty years – made sure that young athletes were given top-class facilities, particularly the National Stadium, and the opportunity to compete for track scholarships to colleges in North America – used by many Jamaican athletes as a springboard to international success.

opposite into a **Celebrity Park**, with statues of the island's leading names, but at present only a slightly mournful figure of Bob Marley stands by the road. The hills to the east house Jamaica's **Beverly Hills**, almost as affluent as the Los Angeles suburb it was named after. No longer the first-choice neighbourhood for wealthy Kingstonians (locals reckon that many of the smart houses were built by drug money), it still provides stunning views across the city and out to sea.

Further south on Tom Redcam Drive, the squat, wooden **Little Theatre** was built in 1961 to house the Little Theatre Movement, which from its inception in 1942 pioneered organized theatre in Kingston. The theatre hosts the LTM's annual pantomime and seasons by the globally recognized National Dance Theatre Company and the Jamaican Folk Singers. The wooden memorial outside is to Greta Fowler, energetic founder of the LTM, while the small building next door is the site of the innovative **Little Little Theatre**, where modern Jamaican playwrights are given an airing. The unimposing **Parish Library** (Mon–Fri 9am–6pm, Sat 9am–5pm; free), half a block further down Tom Redcam Drive, has an expansive if somewhat disorganized West Indian collection, and visitors can borrow books on payment of a small deposit.

*The LTM's pantomime is premiered at the Ward Theatre; see p.67.*

*See p.83 for further details of performances at the Little and Little Little theatres.*

## HALF WAY TREE

On the other side of New Kingston, a mile or so away, is the congested area known as **Half Way Tree**. Before it got swallowed up by the expanding city, Half Way Tree was a tiny village and the capital of the parish of St Andrew. Its central plaza – today a busy shopping area and one of Kingston's key road intersections – once provided a resting-place for farmers travelling into the city's markets. The eponymous cotton tree under which they sheltered is long gone and a clock tower now stands in its place, a 1913 memorial to British King Edward VII.

A handful of restored colonial buildings stand near the square, the most notable of which is the red-brick **St Andrews Parish Church** (always open; free). Though largely submerged by the modern buildings that have arisen around it, this is still a tranquil and gently alluring edifice. Built in 1666, it's one of the oldest religious sites on the island, though the present model is the fourth incarnation, renovated (with typical Victorian vigour) in 1879 after earlier ones were wrecked by hurricane and earthquake. Grand Latin memorials in the floor date back to 1692, the marble tablets on the walls commemorate English soldiers and Jamaican civil servants, and there are some delicate stained-glass windows. Outside, the massive **graveyard**, with its crumbling tombs, ancient and modern, is a fascinating spot to kill some time if you don't mind the company of large numbers of goats.

## DEVON HOUSE

Fifteen minutes' walk east from Half Way Tree, the immaculate **Devon House** at 26 Hope Rd (Tues–Sat 9.30am–5pm; J$110 including guided tour) was built by Jamaica's first black millionaire in 1881, and is still the grandest house in the city.

Born in Kingston in 1820, building contractor George Stiebel made his fortune gold mining in Venezuela, returning home in 1873 to snap up 99 properties throughout Jamaica (ownership of 100 was prohibited by law). Among these was Devon Pen, where he built the house that was his Kingston home until he died in 1896.

Bought by the Jamaican government in 1967, the house has gradually been furnished with West Indian and European antiques as well as more modern Jamaican reproductions. It makes for a diverting hour's exploration, despite the enforced tour, which can be rushed and monosyllabic – don't be afraid to take your time. Some eccentric pieces – a folding bagatelle table, unique porcelain chandeliers and an 1821 Broadwood piano – offset the obligatory portraits and rather predictable furniture. There are a couple of obituaries of Stiebel on display in the games rooms; look out also for the print of French Admiral de Grasse surrendering to Admiral Rodney after the crucial naval battle of les Saintes in 1782, which confirmed British naval superiority in the Caribbean.

*Devon House is replete with places to eat; see p.79.*

The landscaped grounds of Devon House make a fine place for a leisurely stroll, and you've a good chance of running into one of the numerous wedding parties who come here for their photos. The former stables now house a handful of reasonably priced gift shops – chief attraction at which is the heavenly home-made "I Scream" – and you can get a decent Jamaican lunch at the *Grog Shoppe*, which is not as painfully quaint as its name would suggest.

Rumour has it that nearby Lady Musgrave Road, which circuitously bypasses Devon House, was built at the request of the wife of Anthony Musgrave, Jamaica's governor from 1874 to 1883, so that she could get to King's House (see below) without having to pass such a fine house owned by a black Jamaican.

*The governor-general, the Queen of England's representative in Jamaica, has the notional powers of a head of state although, like the Queen, he retains only vestigial political authority.*

## JAMAICA HOUSE AND KING'S HOUSE

Guardhouses further up Hope Road mark the entrances to **Jamaica House** (closed to visitors), used as the prime minister's office, and **King's House** (Mon–Fri by appointment; free; ☎927 6424), official residence of the governor-general. You can get a tour of a few of the latter's rooms, including the ballroom, with its portraits of Jamaica's governors through the centuries, and the banqueting room, which has full-length portraits of Britain's George III and Queen Charlotte. A little south of here on Montrose Road, **Vale Royal** is the official residence of the prime minister but closed to visitors.

## THE BOB MARLEY MUSEUM

For reggae fans, the **Bob Marley Museum** at 56 Hope Rd (Mon–Tues & Thurs–Fri 9.30am–5pm, Wed & Sat 12.30–5pm; J$180) is the whole point of a visit to Kingston, and even if you're not a disciple, it's well worth an hour of your time. Marley's Kingston home from 1975 until his death from cancer in 1981, and still much as it looked when he lived here, the building is a gentle monument to Jamaica's greatest musical legend (see p.184). A guide meets you by the ticket office at the front gate, pointing out the mural *The Journey of Bob Marley Superstar* that decorates the outside wall and Rasta artist Jah Bobby's colourful statue of Marley with his preferred guitar and football. The hour-long tour takes in the room where Marley was almost assassinated during the 1976 election campaign – the bullet holes still much in evidence – after which he left Jamaica for a two-year exile in Britain. The stage dresses of the I-Threes, Marley's backing singers, and his own favoured denim stage shirt are on display below the stairs, alongside the rod of correction and the Order of Merit presented to him by the Ethiopian Orthodox Church and the Jamaican government respectively.

Upstairs, there is a recreation of *Wail 'n' Soul* – the tiny, shack-like Trench Town record shop where Marley used to hang out with band members Peter Tosh and Bunny Wailer – and a room wallpapered with thousands of newspaper articles on Marley and a chart of all the cities he played worldwide, with prominence given to gigs in Africa, particularly the independence celebrations in Zimbabwe in 1980. Gold and platinum discs rewarding sales of the albums *Exodus* (1977), *Uprising* (1980) and *Legend* (1984) hang above the stairs, and familiar tracks are played as you explore the house.

The tour ends behind the house in the theatre that once housed Marley's Tuff Gong recording studio. There's moving footage of the "One Love" concert held during the bloody election year of 1980, at which Marley brought together rival party leaders Michael Manley and Edward Seaga, and a film of interviews with the great man cut together with appropriate music videos – the return to Africa and *Exodus*, celebration of "herb" and *Easy Skanking*. Afterwards, you can escape from the clutches of the guide to look at the excellent photo gallery, with pictures of Marley in New York during his final tour, with the police after the assassination attempt, and playing a lot of football. You'll also get a chance to buy CDs and t-shirts at the gift shop, and the on-site *Queen of Sheba* restaurant offers a small menu of vegetarian Ethiopian food and fruit juices. Don't be surprised if you see Ziggy or other Marley family members hanging around the house or playing soccer on the tiny pitch out front.

*The Tuff Gong studio, run by Ziggy Marley, is now south-west of town at 220 Marcus Garvey Drive (☎927 7103), and free tours are available.*

*See p.184 for more on Bob Marley.*

### HOPE BOTANICAL GARDENS AND COCONUT PARK

Hope Road forks a quarter of a mile east of the Marley museum, just past the Sovereign shopping centre. Its eastern continuation, Old Hope Road, heads towards Papine and the Blue Mountains. In the early days of English settlement in Jamaica. Major Richard Hope, an officer with the invading forces of Penn and Venables (see p.314), set up a thriving sugar estate here in the late seventeenth century, with a stone aqueduct (parts of which can still be seen today) bringing water down from the Hope River. In 1881 the government acquired 200 acres of land from the Hope Estate and laid out the **Hope Botanical Gardens** (daily 9am–5pm; free) in much the same form as you see them today.

*A good walk south of the gardens, in Mona, is the campus of the University of the West Indies, where you'll find Kingston's best **bookshop** (see p.84).*

Entered on your left as you head up Old Hope Road, the gardens have been rather neglected in recent years, particularly since Hurricane Gilbert struck in 1988, and labelling is virtually non-existent, but the expansive lawns are good for escaping the din of the city and popular with weekend strollers. **Coconut Park** (Sat & Sun 10am–6pm; J$30), just north of the gardens, is a children's fairground with some excellent rides, and there's a small **zoo** (daily 10am–5pm; J$40) nearby, with lions, monkeys, mongooses and tropical birds. If you're driving from the city, turn off the Old Hope Road about 400 yards past the main entrance to the gardens (following the signs for Coconut Park); take the road under the aqueduct and around to the left to a small parking area.

SKYLINE DRIVE AND INTO THE BLUE MOUNTAINS
It is only a short drive from Kingston into the Blue Mountains. Even if you don't have time to make the trip, if you have a car it is worth going up onto **Skyline Drive** for spectacular views across the city. To get there follow either East King's House Road or Barbican Road to their northern end where they join Jack's Hill Road for the climb onto Skyline Drive itself. The drive presents you with a series of great panoramas of Kingston and across the harbour to Port Royal – imagine watching the catastrophic earthquakes of 1692 or 1907 from up here – before bringing you out on the Gordon Town Road. From there you can turn right, to return to Kingston through Papine, or left to travel up into the mountains (see Chapter Two).

*If your budget will stretch to it, Ivor (see p.80) is a fabulous place to stop for lunch on Jack's Hill.*

## Eating

After the sun goes down and the heat lifts, the Kingston area is hard to beat for open-air eating. Particularly uptown – which is where you'll want to be in the evenings – you'll find a wider choice of **restaurants** than anywhere else in Jamaica and an excellent standard of food. Most places offer variations on traditional Jamaican fare, from tiny jerk bars to exquisite local seafood establishments, but if you snoop around, you'll also find good Chinese, Indian, Italian and even Middle Eastern cuisine. Places downtown are less refined, usually doling out lunch to local workers or snacks to those on the move. **Fast-food** chains have boomed around the city recently, concentrated downtown around the Parade, uptown in New Kingston behind the high-rise hotels, and in all the shopping malls. Though short of atmosphere, some of these – *Mothers, Juici Beef* and *Tastee* – are good for snacks while you're sightseeing during the day.

## Downtown

**Bench and Bar Restaurant**, 5A Port Royal St. Opposite the *ScotiaBank* tower, this inexpensive place is one of the best options downtown, with great breakfasts, curried chicken and steamed fish lunches, and an after-work crowd in the evenings.

**Dukes**, corner of Duke and Queen streets. Crowded spot near the Coke Chapel serving local lunches – chicken, fish or stewed beef with rice and peas.

**King's Ital**, 16–18 Slipe Rd. Vegetarian café popular with Rastas, and adorned with signed photos of the reggae musicians who seem to be regular visitors. Great, inexpensive tofu and ackee stew, pastries, patties and natural juices.

**Luv 'n Oven**, 22 King St. A good patty stop if you're making your way between the waterfront and the Parade, with filling meat and vegetarian options.

**Metropolitan**, 53 Church St. Another inexpensive lunchtime place popular with local businesses, serving decent Jamaican and Chinese dishes.

**Ocean Restaurant**, Ocean Towers, 8 Ocean Blvd. Unpromising-looking café facing the sea, just around the corner from the National Gallery, but with reasonable, very affordable chicken, goat and fish lunches.

**Patty King**, corner of East and Water streets. Good place for patties and cakes near the Institute of Jamaica, with a daily special for J$120.

## Uptown

**Café Central**, 21 Central Ave; ☎968 4811. Cosy little outdoor bar near the *Terra Nova* hotel, with an excellent and reasonably priced selection of wines and cheeses as well as pasta, fish and meat dishes.

**Calcutta**, 11 Holborn Rd; ☎960 0211. Authentic, inexpensive Indian food with excellent callaloo, chicken and beef rotis.

**Chelsea Jerk Centre**, 7 Chelsea Ave (closed Sun). Popular shack open till midnight with reasonable jerk pork and chicken.

**Countryside Club**, 19 Eastwood Park Rd; ☎929 9403. Attractive and romantic outdoor venue with good seafood and interesting theme nights. Music most Thursday evenings. Open all day but occasionally booked for private functions, so it's worth calling ahead.

**Crossings New World Café**, 94 Old Hope Rd; ☎978 3547. Trendy bar downstairs and an intimate restaurant upstairs serving good Jamaican food at moderate prices and a wicked Sunday brunch. Just above the junction of Old Hope Road and Mountain View Avenue.

**Devonshire Restaurant**, Devon House; ☎929 7029 (closed Sun). Classy, costly Jamaican dishes in a cool and elegant setting.

**Eden**, Central Plaza, Constant Spring Rd (closed Sat). Good Ital food and juices served in this shopping centre until 8pm.

**The Emperial Kish-Inn**, 2 Hillview Ave, off Eastwood Park Rd. Rasta Ital eatery for bargain-priced breakfast and lunch, such as stew with soya mince, fried fish and vegetables. Natural juices and home-made cakes are available, as are lengthy discussions on Rastafari.

**Fish Place**, 136 Constant Spring Rd. Quite a ride out of the centre of town but worth it for the spicy conch soup alone, quite apart from excellent fish, scallops, crab and lobster. Expect to pay around J$500 per person.

*In restaurant listings, we have given a phone number only for those places where you might need to reserve a table.*

# Kingston

**The Grog Shoppe**, Devon House; ☎929 7029 (closed Sun). Standard Jamaican meals at lunchtime and a more European flavour (and prices) in the evening. Quite a popular spot for drinking at weekends, too.

**Guilt Trip**, 20 Barbican Rd; ☎977 5130 (closed Mon). Interesting variation on traditional Jamaican dishes – try the red snapper with ginger and paw-paw – with a regularly changing menu but consistently good seafood. Prices start at J$500.

**Heather's Garden Restaurant**, 9 Haining Rd; ☎960 7739. Reasonable Jamaican food in a quiet location with an extensive, moderately priced menu and a seafood speciality.

**Hot Pot**, 2 Altamont Terrace. Popular spot for typical Jamaican, with fish and bammy, curried goat and stewed beef at the lowest prices around.

**Indies Pub and Grill**, 8 Holborn Rd, opposite *Indies Hotel*. Easy-going out-door café with an eclectic, inexpensive menu featuring steaks, fish and chips, pizza and Lebanese dishes.

**Jade Garden**, Sovereign Centre; ☎978 3476. Smart business-set restaurant with some of the best Chinese dishes in town, most of them J$500–800.

**Lychee Garden**, New Kingston Shopping Centre; ☎929 8619. Reasonably priced but rather formal Chinese restaurant.

**Lyn's Vegetarian Restaurant**, 7 Tangerine Place. Friendly and super-cheap café near Half Way Tree serving vegetarian stews, tofu and great fresh juices. Closes at 7pm Mon–Thurs & 4pm Fri.

**Orchid House**, Devon House; ☎927 7029. Pretty authentic Thai food, with good fish and prawn dishes, in swanky Devon House surroundings.

**The Pantry**, 2 Dumfries Rd. Lunch-only restaurant with solid Jamaican dish-es popular with the New Kingston business crowd.

**Pegasus Café**, *Pegasus Hotel*, Knutsford Blvd; ☎926 3690. The best place in town for afternoon tea – sandwiches and fabulous cakes from J$100.

**Raphael's**, 7 Hillcrest Ave; ☎978 1279. Excellent, moderately expensive Italian food served outdoors, near the Bob Marley Museum, under a spreading lignum vitae tree. Pasta, beef and fish dishes and a separate ice cream bar.

## Outside Kingston

**Blue Mountain Inn**, Gordon Town Rd; ☎927 1700. Gourmet food – seared breadfruit chips, exquisite steaks, lobster and fantasy desserts – in a fabulous setting, a 20min drive into the mountains. Expect to pay upwards of J$1250 for dinner.

**Forbidden Heights**, *Jonraine Country Inn*, 7 West Kirkland Heights, Forest Hills; ☎944 3515. Friendly service, delicious Chinese food and great views.

**Ivor**, Jack's Hill; ☎927 1460. The four-course dinner (J$1250) and three-course lunch (J$900) menus changes daily, but expect to find superbly cooked lobster or other local seafood. The views over Kingston are spectacular.

**Rock Pub**, Gordon Town Rd. Small shack on the far side of Hope River just opposite the turn-off to Skyline Drive, with decent seafood from around J$250. Park by the sign, walk across the bridge and it's on your left.

# Drinking and nightlife

Kingston has few good places that cater specifically to **drinkers**, but there are plenty of excellent cafés, restaurants and hotel bars uptown that make decent venues for a swift beer or a more protracted soak. In many parts of the city, the typical **bar** is a tiny room where a handful of men sit around drinking rum and playing dominoes. If you are walking around downtown during the day you'll probably pop into one or two of these places; remember that foreigners are rarely seen here and, although it can be a good opportunity to meet local people (and drink pretty cheaply), you may encounter some initial suspicion or aloofness. When choosing a bar, bear in mind that you'll rarely want to walk between places at night, and taxis are the best way of getting around.

Kingston's active **club** scene ranges from smart laser shows with big-name DJs, state-of-the-art equipment and the latest dancehall to small dark oldies clubs for the retro-crowd. Anticipate a cover of around J$100–200 – more if there's a band on; the *Gleaner* advertises regular "ladies' nights" when women get in free. As you'll find island-wide, nothing much happens before midnight except on Friday, when "after-work jams" at places like *Mirage* and *Cactus* pull an early-evening crowd of bright young things. **Security** at most of the clubs is tight and you'll be checked for weapons on your way in. You'll occasionally find impromptu **street parties** happening around town, with a sound system stacked up and beer and jerk vendors ready at hand. Feel free to join in – everybody's welcome.

*There are street parties in Port Royal's main square on Friday and Saturday nights; see p.92.*

**Live music** in the capital is less predictable, but often more interesting, than the anaesthetised reggae dished up for tourists on the north coast. The big event is **Carnival**, a riotous five-day street party in April, adopted from the islands of the Eastern Caribbean in 1991 as competition for established north-coast Sunsplash and Sumfest festivals. Jamaica's top DJs, singers and bands – Bounty Killer, Beenie Man, Lady Saw et al – are usually in action around the city, as are reggae legends like Gregory Isaacs and Dennis Brown, playing anywhere from the regular clubs to open-air gigs at the Hellshire beaches (see p.94) and in the grounds of various hotels. Unusually for Jamaica, you'll find plenty of Trinidadian and Bajan calypsonians and steel bands playing too, reflecting the influence of the Eastern Caribbean, and, undoubtedly, the island's own soca stars Byron Lee and the Dragonaires. The concluding weekend, an intoxicating cacophony of sound and colour, sees marching bands, brightly-painted floats and extravagant costume parades through the city streets.

*See p.349 of Contexts for more on Jamaica's current music scene.*

Even if you can't make Carnival, the build-up can be almost as lively, with full dress rehearsals noisily spilling out onto the streets for several weeks before the main event and a party atmosphere taking hold of the city. Otherwise, the busiest times, musically speaking, are during the summer, particularly in the build-up to Sumfest, when the whole island hots up, and around Christmas. Many of the big events –

*Details of the Reggae Sunsplash and Reggae Sumfest music festivals appear on p.36.*

Kingston

whether bands or DJs – are put on at private homes or at one of the city's numerous "lawns" or open spaces; the promoters arrange private security and charge a "gate"or entrance fee. Keep an eye out for posters and billboards all around town advertising these.

## Bars

**Café Central**, 21 Central Ave. Small, civilized outdoor bar, the best place in town for a glass of good wine and a lump of cheese. See "Eating", p.79.

**Chaser's Café**, 29 Barbican Rd. Popular hangout with a decent beer selection and music that gets cranked up to conversation-killing levels.

**Chicago Inn**, 53 Slipe Rd. Easy-going local bar for a quick one if you're heading up from downtown, though not an area to hang around in after dark.

**Crossings New World Café**, 94 Old Hope Rd. Small, fashionable bar with occasional live jazz on Tuesday, a regular late-night crowd and good food upstairs. See "Eating", p.79.

**Grog Shoppe**, Devon House. In the grounds of Devon House, this is a good place to finish your day's sightseeing with a drink outside under the giant cotton tree, especially on Friday when a band plays. See "Eating", p.80.

**HQ**, Mark Lane. Local bar just off Parade above the Scots Kirk, and useful if you need a beer to wash away the dust of downtown.

**Indies**, 8 Holborn Rd, opposite the *Indies* hotel. Central location and a mellow atmosphere that's popular with late-night revellers at weekends.

**The Magnum Specialist**, Grove Rd, off Half Way Tree. Natural juice outlet of choice for everyone from Mona dreads to reggae stars, with a superb array of juices from gingery june plum to okra. Worth a visit for the experience alone.

**Mango Tree Café**, 11 Holborn Rd. Rather scruffy outdoor bar next to the *Calcutta* restaurant (and with the same menu), but often open after most other places have closed.

**Mayfair Hotel**, 4 W King's House Close. One of the liveliest bars in town, particularly in the early evening when the after-work hordes pour in. A couple of bottled English beers as well as the usual Jamaican brews.

**Peppers**, 31 Upper Waterloo Rd. Popular outdoor bar that pulls a post-work clientele and serves moderately priced jerk chicken and pork.

**Priscilla's**, upstairs at 109 Constant Spring Rd. Pleasant and easy-going roof bar with views over the city; Sixties and Seventies Jamaican music on Friday and Saturday nights attracts the older media and professional set.

**Raphael's**, 7 Hillcrest Ave. Trendy spot tucked away from the city streets near the Bob Marley Musuem. Busy on Friday evenings but normally a mellow place to sit at the outdoor tables with a drink. See "Eating", p.80.

**Sandhurst Hotel**, 70 Sandhurst Crescent. Spreading terrace with views up to the mountains and a very relaxed atmosphere. Not as popular as it used to be, but a reasonable option if you just want a quiet night out.

## Clubs and live music

**Cactus**, 13 Portmore Plaza, Portmore; ☎988 2319 (Wed–Sun). Competes with *Mirage* for number one spot in the Kingston area, but its location – a 20min drive west of the city – is an impediment. Still, it's usually packed at weekends and on Wednesday (dancehall night) and worth the trip for the live shows.

IAN CUMMING

Kingston lights from Jack's Hill

IAN CUMMING

Carnival queen

Bob Marley statue, Kingston

Papa San at Sabina Park, Kingston

Blue Mountain peaks

Devon House, Kingston

Getting down

Fort Charles' cannons, Port Royal    Coffee estate, Blue Mountains

Kingston – downtown looking up

**Chances**, 5 Dumfries Rd; ☎968 3682 (Wed–Sun). Small and rather pokey club hidden away beside a gaming joint in central New Kingston; Stone Love or other big-name sound systems sometimes set up here during the week.

**Countryside Club**, 19–21 Eastwood Park Rd; ☎926 3010. Well-designed outdoor venue that hosts some of Kingston's main gigs, hidden behind security gates close to Half Way Tree.

**Extremes**, Portmore Mall, Portmore; ☎939 2950 (Wed–Sun). Popular with the Portmore crowd and a big dancehall night on Sunday, but not really worth the trip west unless you're club-hopping.

**Godfathers**, 69 Knutsford Blvd; ☎929 5459 (Wed–Sun). No longer the first choice of fashionable Kingstonians, but it's in a central location and there's still plenty of posing from the teenybopper brigade.

**Jonkanoo Lounge**, *Wyndham Hotel*, Knutsford Blvd; ☎926 5430. Relatively sedate, as you'd expect from a hotel-based venue, but a good and very upmarket (if rarely crowded) disco and occasional live bands.

**Mirage**, Sovereign Centre, 106 Hope Rd; ☎978 8557 (Tues–Sat). One of the best clubs in Jamaica – upscale but with a mixed uptown/downtown crowd, particularly for dancehall night on Tuesday. Pool tables, a separate bar and crash-out sofas in the (extra cost) VIP lounge.

**Mutual Life Building**, 2 Oxford Rd; ☎926 9024. Live jazz – a rarity in Kingston – on the last Wednesday of each month and always popular. The resident band often supports well-known overseas artists; definitely worth looking out for.

**Peppers**, 31 Upper Waterloo Rd; ☎925 2219. Top outdoor venue with big name stageshows every month.

**Rodney's Arms**, Port Henderson; ☎988 1063. "Thursday night to Rahtid" is the ad you'll see around town for this place, and that's when the sound system gets cranked up and a small crowd descends from the city.

**Turntable Club**, 118 Red Hills Rd; ☎969 2966. Oldies, ska and rocksteady club a couple of miles west of central Kingston. Keep an eye out for one of the excellent festivals occasionally held here.

*Although Kingston has no listings magazine or newspaper, the Daily Gleaner advertises most of what's going on in the city.*

# Theatre and cinema

Next to popular music, **theatre** is Kingston's strongest cultural suit. The performance scene is limited but buoyant, with a small core of first-rate writers, directors and actors – including Trevor Rhone, Oliver Samuels, Aston Cooke and David Heron – producing work of a generally high standard. Most of the plays are sprinkled with Jamaican patois, but you'll still get the gist. Comedies (particularly sexual romps and political satire) are popular, and the normally excellent annual **pantomime** – a musical with a message, totally different from the English variety – is a major event, running from December to April at both the **Ward Theatre** (☎922 0453) and, later, the **Little Theatre** (☎925 6129).

Kingston's **cinemas** invariably screen recent mainstream offerings from the States. They're popular with Jamaicans, with tickets at around J$150 – anticipate standing for the national anthem beforehand and a lengthy snack break in the middle. Most of the cinemas

*Dance comes to the fore during the National Dance Theatre Company's annual summer residency at the Little Theatre.*

are uptown and include the **Palace Cineplex** (☎978 8286) at the Sovereign Centre, the **Island Cinemax** (☎920 7964) at the Island Life Centre on St Lucia Avenue and the **Odeon** (☎926 7671) at 11 Constant Spring Rd. There are even a couple of drive-ins – the best being the **New Kingston Drive-In** (☎929 5670) on Dominica Drive – perfect for the Jamaican climate.

## Shopping and galleries

A multitude of American-style malls means that **shopping** in Kingston is nothing if not convenient. The major players – the *New Kingston Shopping Centre* on Dominica Drive, the *Sovereign Centre* on Hope Road and the two *Manor Park Centres* on Constant Spring Road – house everything you can imagine buying, although the heaving Jubilee Market downtown (see p.67) and the smaller market at Cross Roads are more exciting places to look for fresh **food**.

For **books**, the *University Bookshop* at the University of the West Indies in Mona is far and away the superior choice for both novels and books on Jamaica, though *Sangsters* (branches at Ward Plaza, 106 Old Hope Rd and 33 King St) and *Bookland*, 53 Knutsford Blvd, are reasonable and more central, while *Reader's*, at Liguanea Plaza, 134 Old Hope Rd, has a decent second-hand collection. *Headstart Books*, 54–56 Church St, is a downtown bookstore-cum-craftshop concentrating on all things African and roots Jamaican, with an excellent collection of hard-to-find titles as well as Rasta-made crafts, greeting cards and posters.

As you'd expect, reggae fans are in shopping heaven in Kingston, and downtown's Orange Street is the place to go – you'll find loads of **record stores**, many of them attached to studios and pressing plants and attracting crowds of young hopefuls and red-eyed dreads. There have even been proposals for developing the lower end of the street into a living music museum, with a section tracing the history of Jamaican music. *GG's Records*, on the corner of Orange Street and Parade, is particularly well stocked, and as vibrant and loud as its location, while *Prince Busta's* further down Orange Street is known for its collection of rare oldies. *Rockers International*, 135 Orange St, carries an extensive stock of old rocksteady and reggae classics; *Techniques*, at no. 99, has a good selection of old and new stock alongside (unaccountably) in-car accessories. *High Times*, in the Kingston Mall at 12 Ocean Blvd, is owned by Earl "Chinna" Smith, who plays with Ziggy Marley and the Melody Makers, and is a shrine to reggae and Rasta. Staff will make up compilation tapes to your requirements and can usually track down even the most elusive and obscure Jamaican release.

For Jamaican **souvenirs** of the t-shirt, woodcarving and jewellery variety, try the Crafts Market downtown (see p.66); more expensively, check out the gift shops at Devon House or *Patoo*, in the Upper

Manor Park Centre, which has prints, books, spices, coffee and a host of other items. *Sangster's* devilish **rum** factory at World's End (see p.115) has an outlet at 17 Holborn Rd (closed Sat).

Kingston also has a vibrant art scene and there are excellent **galleries** across the city. The *Frame Centre Gallery* at 10 Tangerine Place (Mon–Fri 9am–5pm) is a fine place to start, with a good variety of local work on display. The *Grosvenor Galleries* at 1 Grosvenor Terrace and the *Mutual Life Centre* at 2 Oxford Rd (Mon–Fri 10am–6pm) both host exhibitions by contemporary Jamaican artists, while if you want to splash out, try the art shops at Devon House (Tues–Sat 9.30am–5pm) and the *Pegasus* and *Wyndham* hotels (the last has a great collection of paintings by Portland artist Ken Abendana Spencer in its lobby). Finally, the *Art Centre* (Mon–Fri 9am–5pm & Sat 10am–4pm), near Papine at 202 Old Hope Rd, sells local art, and there is a chaotic jumble of paintings and sculptures in the gallery opposite.

# Listings

**Airlines** *Air Jamaica*, 72 Harbour St (☎922 3460); *American Airlines*, 26 Trafalgar Rd (☎924 8305); *British Airways*, 25 Dominica Drive (☎929 9020); *BWIA*, 19 Dominica Drive (☎929 3771); *Cayman Airways*, 23 Dominica Drive (☎926 1762); *Cubana*, 22 Trafalgar Rd (☎978 3406).

**Airport** The information number for Norman Manley International Airport is ☎928 6077; the number for Tinson Pen domestic airport is ☎978 8068.

**Ambulances** Call ☎110 for a public ambulance, ☎926 8624 for a private one.

**Banks** The main banks have branches city-wide including: *Bank of Nova Scotia* at 2 Knutsford Blvd, 6 Oxford St and 125 Old Hope Rd; *Mutual Security Bank* at 18 Trafalgar Rd, 134 Old Hope Rd and 37 Duke St; *Citizen's Bank* at the Sovereign Centre, 17 Dominica Drive and 15A Old Hope Rd. Most of those uptown have ATMs.

**Car Rental** Reliable firms include *Avis*, Norman Manley Airport (☎924 8013); *Bargain*, Norman Manley Airport (☎924 8293); *Caribbean*, 31 Old Hope Rd (☎926 6339); *Don's*, 1 Worthington Ave (☎926 2181); *Island*, 17 Antigua Ave (☎926 8012); *Value*, 8 Worthington Ave (☎926 0921).

**Doctors and dentists** Ask your hotel to recommend a doctor or dentist, or contact the University Hospital (see below).

**Embassies** Almost all of the embassies and consulates are based in New Kingston. They include the British High Commission, 26 Trafalgar Rd (☎926 9050); the American Embassy, 2 Oxford Rd (☎929 4850); and the Canadian High Commission, 30 Knutsford Blvd (☎926 1500).

**Golf** Kingston has two excellent golf courses open to the public, west of the city at Caymanas Park (☎922 3388) and north at Constant Spring (☎924 1610).

**Hospitals** Kingston's public hospitals are the University Hospital at Mona (☎927 1620) and the Kingston Public Hospital downtown on North Street (☎922 0227). There are a number of private hospitals in New Kingston, including *Medical Associates* at 18 Tangerine Place (☎926 1400) and *Andrews Memorial* at 27 Hope Rd (☎926 7401).

**Laundry** All of the hotels will wash laundry and there is a drop-off/pick-up service at *Supersuds*, 13–15 National Heroes Circle (☎967 3791), and *Speedy's*, 108 Red Hills Rd (☎924 5846). *Supercleaners* at the Sovereign Centre (☎978 5116) offers a pricey drycleaning and laundry service.

**Newspapers** Sunday newspapers from England and many US publications can be found in the big pharmacies and at the gift shops at the *Wyndham* and *Pegasus* hotels in New Kingston.

**Pharmacies** There are pharmacies at most of the shopping malls. *Monarch*, at the Sovereign Centre, is open Mon–Sat 9am–10pm, Sun 9am–3pm.

**Police** The main station is at 79 Duke St (☎922 9321). In emergency, call ☎119.

**Post Offices** The GPO is at 13 King St downtown (☎922 2120) and there are a number of branches around town. Stamps can also be bought at most hotels.

**Sports** International and major domestic soccer and cricket matches are played at the National Stadium (☎929 4970) and Sabina Park (☎967 0322) respectively. Horse-racing and (occasionally) polo can be seen at Caymanas Park (☎922 3338).

**Taxis** Reputable operators include *Blue Diamond* (☎937 1604); *Blue Ribbon* (☎928 7739); *Candy* (☎925 0649); *Checker* (☎922 1777); *Eagle Force* (☎923 4236).

**Telephone** *Telecommunications of Jamaica*, downtown at 15 North St and uptown at 52 Grenada Crescent (both Mon–Fri 8am–4pm), has cardphone booths that allow international calls cheaper than anywhere else in town.

**Travel Agents** *Grace Kennedy Travel*, 19 Knutsford Blvd (☎929 6290); *ITS*, 75 Old Hope Rd (☎978 7038); *Stuart's Travel Service*, 9 Cecilio Ave (☎929 2345).

# Around Kingston

There are some excellent options around Kingston if you want to escape from the city for a day or two. The one-time fortress city of **Port Royal** in particular is worth a half-day visit, with nearby **Lime Cay** providing a good spot for a swim afterwards. **Spanish Town**, the nation's capital from 1534 to 1872, offers the third limb of Jamaica's "Historic

---

### Tours from Kingston

All of the places around Kingston can be explored on an **organized tour** from the city. You shouldn't need a tour to see Port Royal, easy to reach on the ferry and small, safe and relaxed enough to wander around alone, but it's not a bad option for Spanish Town, which is a bit awkward to get to and – as a major industrial city – can feel rather unwelcoming. *Heritage Tours* (☎938 2578) – run by the head of Jamaica's National Trust – has excellent guides, well-versed in the area's history, and offer half-day tours to both places for around US$25 per person – less if there are four of you taking the tour – including transport from your hotel. It can also arrange trips to less-visited places like Mountain River Cave and the Two Sisters Cave. Other reputable operators in Kingston include *Destinations* (☎929 6368), *ITS Tours* (☎978 8703) and *Pro-Tours* (☎978 6139).

Triangle" (with Kingston and Port Royal); again, half a day is more than ample to see the remains of the city's superb Georgian architecture and to tour the oldest Anglican cathedral in the "New World". Fragments of a more ancient culture remain in the old Taino haunts of **Mountain River Cave** and **Two Sisters Cave**, although both are tricky to reach without a car, while the **Blue Mountains** (see Chapter Two) and **Castleton Botanical Gardens** offer hiking and undisturbed nature. For something even more relaxing, **Rockfort Mineral Baths** have reasonably priced spas while **Hellshire's** lovely white-sand bays, just south of the city, are immensely popular at the weekend.

# East of Kingston

Windward Road, the main route east out of the city, follows the coastline out of Kingston, scything through an ugly industrial zone of oil tanks and a cement works that towers over the ruined defensive bastion of Fort Rock, now the **Rockfort Mineral Baths**. A mile or so further on, a right turn takes you on to the **Palisadoes**, a narrow ten-mile spit of land that leads out past the international airport to the ancient city of **Port Royal**, from where it's a short hop to the tiny island of **Lime Cay**.

### Rockfort Mineral Baths

**Rockfort Mineral Baths** (daily 8am–6pm; J$60 to use the pool, J$380 for a spa) offer one of the few public swimming pools in the Kingston area as well as some rather luxurious private spas. This was the site of the British Fort Rock, first strengthened against a threatened French invasion in 1694 and remanned in 1865 amid fears that the Morant Bay Rebellion further east might spread to Kingston. Today, the baths sit in a neat modern facility – an oasis in the surrounding dusty terrain – and offer a laid-back chance to enjoy some pampering. The small mineral spas, which seat two people comfortably, are all fitted with Jacuzzis and you're allowed to wallow in them for up to 45 minutes. The mineral water, which is piped from a local spring, is moderately radioactive; it is claimed that the radioactivity helps to infuse the therapeutic minerals into the body, though obviously it puts some people off.

*If you need rehydrating after your spa bath, there's a small café and juice bar on site.*

The hills above Rockfort rise up to the **Dallas Mountains**, named after Robert Dallas, a local eighteenth-century plantation-owner whose grandson, George Miflin Dallas, became Vice President of the United States in 1845 and founded the eponymous city in Texas.

### Port Royal

**PORT ROYAL**, a short drive or ferry ride from downtown Kingston, captures the spirit of early colonial adventure better than any other place in Jamaica. A tiny island for centuries, this little fishing village is now joined to the mainland by the **Palisadoes**, a series of small cays that silted together over hundreds of years and, with a bit of

# Around Kingston

human assistance, now form a roadway and a natural breakwater for Kingston's harbour. For several decades in the late seventeenth century, Port Royal was a riotous town – the notorious haunt of cutthroats and buccaneers, condemned by the church as "the wickedest city on earth". Only a few traces of those days remain – much of the old town is now a sunken city, submerged under fifty feet of water – but the Jamaican government and the private sector are slowly beginning to appreciate the potential allure of its romantic past. A major archeological museum is in the pipeline and there is even talk of a cruise-ship port. For now, though, Port Royal is still a good place to catch a whiff of the history of pirates and pieces of eight and of an egregiously proud city brought to its knees by natural disaster.

## SOME HISTORY

When Britain captured Jamaica from Spain in 1655, most of the country's population of two or three thousand lived in the capital city of Spanish Town, a few miles from what is now Kingston harbour. Two things were immediately obvious to British tacticians. First, to prevent any other power from repeating the simple strategy with which they had conquered the island, strong **defences** were required all around the harbour. Second, with their navy tied up with wars in Europe, they needed to recruit local support to help defend the new colony.

Port Royal at this time was uninhabited but, surrounded by deep water, it had been a perfect place for the Spanish to moor up their

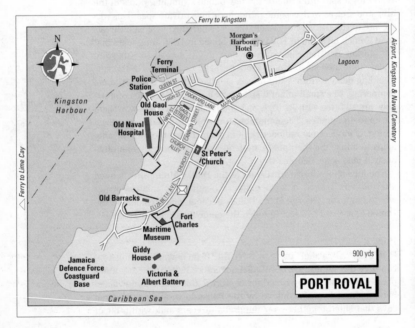

sailing ships for cleaning and caulking. Now the British turned it into a **battle station**, with five separate forts covering all of the angles from which enemy ships could approach, and a palisade at the north to defend against attackers coming over the cays. As added protection they encouraged the buccaneers who had for decades been pillaging the area to sign up as "**privateers**" in the service of the king.

Port Royal boomed. Merchants took advantage of the city's great location to export sugar, logwood and pimento and import slaves, bricks and supplies for the growing population. The privateers wreaked havoc on the ships of Spain. The fabulous profits of trade and plunder brought others to service the town's needs; brothels, taverns and gambling houses proliferated, and by 1692 the population had swollen to six thousand. Rents were as high as in the most fashionable parts of London and the world's finest wines and silks were readily available.

The huge **earthquake** that struck the city on June 7, 1692, dumped half of Port Royal into the sea, killing two thousand people in seconds; within a week a thousand more had died. Of the remaining population, most fled for Kingston at the first opportunity (see p.56), while the rest died or deserted when a massive fire swept the island in 1702.

Despite the destruction, Port Royal continued to serve as the country's **naval headquarters**. All the great British admirals of the eighteenth and early nineteenth centuries were stationed here at some point in their careers, plotting the downfall of the French, whose presence in the area grew increasingly threatening up until the time of the Napoleonic Wars. However, with the rapid expansion of Kingston during the last century, Port Royal has been increasingly marginalized. Today it is a small and tidy fishing village, proud of its very low crime rate, and it retains its naval traditions as home to the Jamaican coastguard.

## GETTING THERE

Unless you are **driving** – in which case follow signs southeast from Kingston to the airport and keep going past the turn-off – the most pleasant and convenient way to get to Port Royal is on the little blue-and-white **ferry** (J\$6 each way; 30min) that leaves regularly from the pier at the bottom of Princess Street in downtown Kingston, near the National Gallery.

A **bus** (J\$10; 25min) runs several times a day from the Parade via Harbour View, while a **taxi** will set you back around US\$25 in each direction.

## THE TOWN

Port Royal makes an impression before you even reach dry land; look back to sea as the ferry docks on the northwest shore and you'll get not only a great view of the harbour, but a clear idea of the area's strategic military importance and a glimpse of its former limits. The

**Around Kingston**

*See the box on p.91 for more on Port Royal's pirates.*

*At the time of writing the ferry leaves Kingston Mon to Sat at 6am, 7am, 10am, 12.30pm, 3pm, 5pm & 7pm, and on Sun at 11.30am, 2.30pm, 4.30pm & 6.30pm, returning from Port Royal 30min later. To confirm the times, call Morgan's Harbour Hotel or the JTB in Kingston.*

old city once extended way out across the harbour, but since the 1692 earthquake, ninety percent of it has been submerged under fifty feet of water, its key sites marked by several buoys.

Once on land, what remains of Port Royal is easily navigable on foot. Five minutes' walk from the harbour, behind the old garrison wall, is the decaying two-storey **Old Naval Hospital**. The prefab iron structure was shipped over from England and put up here in 1819; it now serves as offices for the National Heritage Trust. Although numerous arte-facts have been recovered from the sea and stored in the building, plans to reopen to the public remain on hold at the time of writing. Take a wander around if there's no one to show you the place.

*In the likely event that St Peter's is closed when you visit, ask the local ven-dors or the staff at Fort Charles for the caretaker.*

Ten minutes' walk away on the main Church Street, **St Peter's Church** (irregular opening hours) was built in 1726 and, apart from the roof, has survived largely intact since. It is unremarkable apart from an intricately carved mahogany and cedar organ loft; marble tablets on the walls emphasize the role of the navy in this area. More interesting are the ancient tombs in the small and rambling grave-yard, particularly that of the Frenchman Lewis Galdy. Swallowed by the earthquake in 1692, an eruption seconds later spat him out into the sea from where, amazingly, he scrambled to safety. No doubt a pillar of the church thereafter, Galdy lived until 1739. Next to Galdy's grave is a tomb for three small children who died in the earthquake and whose remains were found in the rubble of their col-lapsed house during underwater excavations in 1992.

A left turn out of the church leads down the main road to fascinat-ing **Fort Charles** (daily 9am–5pm; US$4). Originally known as Fort Cromwell (but renamed after King Charles II was restored to the British throne in 1660), this was the first of the five forts to be built here, though it never saw any action. The first structure was wooden but, following the Great Fire of London in 1666, British laws required that all such buildings in the colonies be made of brick. The present fort looks much as it did in 1692, except that then it was immediately bordered by the sea on three sides. The red-brick build-ing to your left as you enter is the storage room, where the all-impor-tant gunpowder was kept dry. In the courtyard, the **Maritime Museum** (same opening hours) gives a lucid history of Port Royal and displays items – bottles, coins, slave shackles and so on – dredged up from the underwater city. Look out, in particular, for the National Geographic recreation of the city at the time of the 1692 earthquake.

The raised platform on the other side of the small parade ground is known as **Nelson's Quarterdeck**; the great commander (incredi-bly still under 21) used to pace up and down here spoiling for a fight with the French. From the quarterdeck you can see how the land has built up around the fort – over a foot per year – as the sea has con-tinued to deposit silt against the former island. The two structures that now stand between the fort and the water both date from the

1880s (opening hours as for fort). The squat, rectangular **Giddy House** was an ammunition store, while the circular bunker beside it was the **Victoria and Albert Battery** – an emplacement for a nineteenth-century supergun. The 1907 earthquake dropped the gun turret several yards into the earth, while the store room somehow remained intact but tilted at a seventeen-degree angle. Try walking across it without slipping over.

There are two other points of minor interest in Port Royal. Heading back towards the main square, turn left after St Peter's Church, then right and third left onto Gaol Alley. The distinctive block building on your right is the **Old Gaol House** (closed to visi-

---

### Pirates and buccaneers

The early history of Port Royal is inextricably linked with adventurers. The first **buccaneers** were a ragged crew of outlaws and fugitives, European outcasts who banded together on the island of Tortuga, north of present day Haiti. They lived by hunting wild pigs and cattle (first brought to the island by the early European explorers) which they smoked on a wooden frame known as a *boucan* (hence the name). As they grew more organized and more daring, they began to raid the treasure ships sailing between Spain and its New World colonies.

After Britain conquered Jamaica in 1655, the newly installed authorities embarked on an open-door policy, issuing a general invitation to these buccaneers to set themselves up in Port Royal and use it as their base for attacks on the Spanish enemy. In return for official status as **"privateers"**, they were obliged to deliver ten percent of their haul to the Crown. Privateering flourished and Port Royal turned into a city marked by extreme wealth and a constant threat of violence.

The privateers' reversal of fortune came in 1671 when a peace treaty was signed between Britain and Spain. Despite the treaty, **Henry Morgan** – the most famous of the buccaneers – sailed from Bluefields Bay in Jamaica to plunder the wealthy Spanish colony of Panama. Although there is some evidence that the British authorities connived at this attack, Morgan and the Jamaican governor, Thomas Modyford, were recalled to the mother country to face official sanction. Modyford was sacked to appease the Spanish while Morgan, having insinuated his way into royal favour, was made lieutenant-governor in his stead, returning to Jamaica with a new brief – to stamp out piracy by persuading his former colleagues to adopt a life of peace.

Many of the buccaneers, now officially termed **"pirates"** to mark their loss of favour, refused to give up their exciting and profitable lifestyles and continued to plague ships throughout the Caribbean. In turn, they were ruthlessly hunted down by Morgan and his successors, and hangings at a spot called Gallows Point on Port Royal were frequent until as late as 1831. The most famous success for the authorities came in 1720 when "Calico Jack" Rackham and his sidekicks, female pirates Anne Bonney and Mary Read, were captured during a party near Negril. Rackham's body was squeezed into a tiny cage and left on Rackham's Cay, just east of Port Royal, as a warning to others; the women both got conveniently pregnant and were spared the gallows, although Read later died in prison.

*See p.251 for more on Calico Jack.*

tors), built before the 1692 earthquake and once used as a women's prison. Slightly out of town on the road back to Kingston, the **Naval Cemetery** marks the final resting place of many of Port Royal's long-forgotten sailors. Buccaneer-turned-politician Henry Morgan (see box) was buried here too, but the earthquake tipped his body into the sea along with a large part of the old graveyard.

Finally, there are a couple of **beaches** around Port Royal but both sea and sand are pretty dirty and, if you want to **swim**, you're better off taking a boat out to the cays (see below). Otherwise, the dive shop at *Morgan's Harbour Hotel* runs **diving** and **snorkelling** trips to some of the best sites on the south coast and offers diving certification courses. You can also arrange deep-sea **fishing** or a gentler boat ride into the mangrove swamps to look at the local birdlife, particularly impressive during the pelican breeding season from February to April.

LIME CAY AND OTHER ISLANDS

Just fifteen minutes from Port Royal, **Lime Cay** is a tiny uninhabited island with white sand, blue water and easy snorkelling. It was here that Ivanhoe ("Rhygin") Martin – the cop-killing gangster and folk-hero immortalized in the classic Jamaican movie *The Harder They Come* – met his demise in 1948. Boats run regularly from *Morgan's Harbour Hotel* (see below) or you can ask the fishermen at the pier to take you – the going rate is J$250 per person round-trip. On Sundays, when the hip Kingstonians descend, food and drink stalls are set up on the beach; at other times, take your own picnic.

If you desperately want your own private island, ask to be dropped at **Maiden Cay**, a tiny, shadeless sandspit popular with privacy-seeking nudists, or **Twin Cays**, shadier but with poorer swimming than at Lime Cay. En route to any of these, you'll pass the once heavily-armed **Gun Cay**, still bearing evidence of its eighteenth-century fortification by the British, and the fast-disappearing **Rackham's Cay**, a palpable victim of beach erosion.

PRACTICALITIES

The only place to **stay** in Port Royal (convenient also for the airport, five minutes' drive away) is the elegant *Morgan's Harbour Hotel* (☎967 8030, fax 967 8073; ⑤); it also has a dive shop and a good and reasonably priced restaurant, *Sir Henry's*. Several cheaper **eating** options near the ferry pier serve excellent seafood; the most popular is *Gloria's Rendezvous* at 5 Queen St, where you can enjoy a tasty plate of fish and bammy and watch the pelicans and frigate birds fishing just offshore. Otherwise, there's *Buccaneer's Roost* around the corner with a similar menu, a patty store on the same block, and local women selling fried fish in the main square. At weekends, speakers are stacked up in the square for an outdoor **party**, playing dancehall on a Friday and oldies on Saturday. A big crowd piles down from Kingston, and it's a great opportunity to enjoy a very easy-going Jamaican street party.

# West of Kingston

Southwest of Kingston, a **causeway** (closed to outgoing traffic Mon–Fri 6.30–9am and to incoming traffic Mon–Fri 4.30–7pm) connects the city to the bland but booming dormitory town of **PORT-MORE** in the neighbouring parish of St Catherine. Portmore itself has nothing of interest – although you might find yourself clubbing there (see p.82) – but **Port Henderson**, a brief detour away, has a handful of colonial-era relics and fine views across Kingston harbour. Below Portmore, the road cuts across the eastern fringe of the **Hellshire Hills** – a vast and scrubby limestone expanse – and down to Hellshire's white-sand beaches and the ancient Taino base of **Two Sisters Cave**. Further west, the former capital city of **Spanish Town**, a run-down shadow of its former self, still retains some graceful architecture, while the less accessible **Mountain River Cave**, **Colbeck Castle** and **Old Harbour** each offer a distinct glimpse into Jamaica's varied history.

## Port Henderson

Established as a port in the 1770s, when it was the embarkation point for residents of Spanish Town (then the capital city), **PORT HENDERSON** became a popular spa town and fashionable resort area during the Victorian era. It's now a small village with a few restored eighteenth- and nineteenth-century buildings, including the bar and restaurant at **Rodney's Arms**, named for the British admiral in charge of the local naval station during the late 1900s. Past here, towards the Jamaican Defence Force base, a trail leads up to **Rodney's Look-Out**, from where the admiral kept an eye peeled for French warships. The JDF keep-out signs aren't exactly welcoming, however, and you may prefer to take in the panorama by simply walking or driving up the hill past the restaurant.

To get to Port Henderson, take the left-hand exit as you cross the causeway from Kingston, then turn right onto Augusta Drive and left at the roundabout. En route, it's worth stopping off to look at the substantial old English fort at **Fort Augusta**, back at the far end of Augusta Drive. The British indulged in a frenzy of fortification around Kingston harbour during their tenure here, and this was their main sea defence on the western side. First built in 1740, it's now used as a women's prison and is closed to visitors.

### PRACTICALITIES
**Buses** and **minibuses** run to Port Henderson from Parade and to Portmore from Parade and Halfway Tree. There is nowhere to **stay** in Port Henderson itself, but Augusta Drive is lined with accommodation options, most of them short-time "love hotels" for couples escap-

ing Kingston for a discreet rendezvous. Of the more traditional places, *La Roose* (☎998 4654; ③) has very reasonable air-conditioned rooms, while *Jewels* (☎988 6785; ③), a little further on, has a nice pool beside its oceanfront restaurant. *Rodney's Arms*, justifiably the most popular local eatery, serves excellent seafood; the restaurant at *La Roose* is also good, dishing up fried chicken, fish and lobster, and there are plenty of fried fish shacks along the causeway. There's a great weekly club night at *Rodney's Arms*, which draws Kingston's good-timers, but otherwise there's only the decidedly average disco at *Jewels*; *Cactus* and *Extremes* in nearby Portmore are livelier.

*Details of the clubs recommended here appear on p.83.*

### HELLSHIRE AND THE TWO SISTERS CAVE

Possibly the least touristed part of Jamaica, the arid **Hellshire Hills**, covered in low, dense scrub and bushy cacti, extend for around a hundred square miles west of Kingston. Around 500 to 1000 years ago, this forbidding landscape was home to Taino Indians and, later, to runaway slaves. For now, though, virtually the only inhabitants are the migrant birds, a few conies and a handful of Jamaican iguanas, thought extinct for half a century until their rediscovery here in 1990. Low rainfall and the unwelcoming limestone terrain have deterred people from settling out here, although the expansion of the suburb of Portmore threatens to encroach on the area's eastern half. It's not a bad place to **hike** if you're interested in seeing one of the island's genuine wilderness zones. Don't try it on your own – it's easy to get lost and there are some nasty sinkholes; the *Iguana Conservation Group* at the university in Mona has some excellent guides and offers trips for US$60 per person (details on ☎927 1660).

*Buses from Parade and Half Way Tree in Kingston run roughly every hour to the Hellshire beaches, but stop short of the Two Sisters Cave. There's nowhere to stay in Hellshire.*

The eastern edge of Hellshire is marked by a series of lovely coves and beaches; the road south through Portmore hits the coast beside the **Great Salt Pond**, an old Taino fishing spot, and continues to **Fort Clarence beach** (Wed–Fri 9am–6pm, Sat & Sun 8am–6pm; J$60), which has showers and a café, and **Hellshire beach** (no entry charge). Both places buzz with Kingstonians at the weekend – Hellshire, in particular, becomes chaotic with reggae booming and stalls competing to sell the freshest fish, lobster and festival; many people reckon that the food here beats anywhere in town.

*Minor Taino finds from all over the island are on display at the White Marl Arawak Museum near Spanish Town (see p.100).*

Beyond the beaches, the road leads south to the intriguing **Two Sisters Cave** (9am–5pm daily; donation), signposted on the left. Ancient earthquakes in the area created subterranean chambers here, with streams trickling through them and a series of brackish pools – a perfect shelter (later a hideaway) for the island's first inhabitants, the Tainos (see p.100). It's an eerily quiet place, but there's usually a guide sitting at the entrance who will take you around and explain how the caverns came into being. Taino tools, pottery and hunting weapons have been found in those chambers which have been explored – more lie deeper under the surface, only accessible to divers – and you can just about make out a painted face, drawn beside the old entrance to the cave to ward off evil spirits.

## Spanish Town

Capital of Jamaica from 1534 to 1872, and still the island's second city, industrial **SPANISH TOWN**, twelve miles west of Kingston, today shows only vestigial traces of its former glory. Few tourists visit and, to be honest, it's not a place that you'll want to linger in for long, but the Georgian **square** – with possibly the finest collection of Georgian architecture in the Americas – and the great old **cathedral** – Jamaica's premier church and the oldest surviving Anglican cathedral outside England – repay the small effort involved in getting here from Kingston.

SOME HISTORY

Spain's first attempt to create a city in Jamaica foundered when its chosen site at **New Seville** on the north coast proved well-suited only to the spread of disease. Its second choice at St Jago de la Vega (as Spanish Town was then known) proved more durable; there was fertile ground, no mosquito-ridden swamps and it was only a short

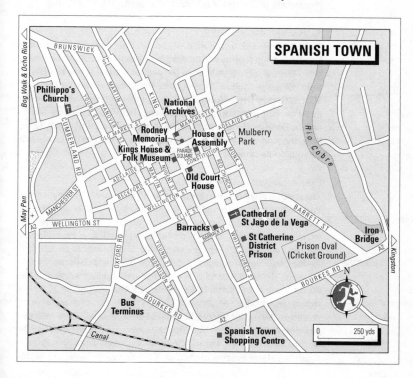

march from two good south-coast harbours (present-day Old Harbour and Kingston). The site also had great look-out points over the surrounding plains, although this proved of little help during English invasions in 1596 and 1643, when the city was comprehensively sacked. Sadly, there are almost no relics of the Spanish-era wooden and adobe buildings left today, although an extensive tunnel system is believed still to run under the centre of town – a hiding place for the Spaniards and their booty during English raids.

Soon after the English captured Jamaica, the country experienced a boom in trade and, gradually, the newly created port city of Kingston began to flourish as the centre of population and commerce. Although huge sums were spent on Spanish Town's major public buildings in the late eighteenth century to boost the city's prestige, the authorities cut their losses and eventually moved the capital to Kingston in 1872, leaving Spanish Town to decay. Today, parts of the city are desolate, rumoured to be entirely controlled by political gangs. More optimistically, though, there *is* some economic revitalization, with local industries – particularly in the busy free-trade zone – producing garments for export and cigarettes for the local market, and locals pushing hard for development funds and recognition of the area's potential as a "heritage tourism" site.

### ARRIVAL AND ORIENTATION

Spanish Town lies to the west of the Rio Cobre river with Bourkes Road, the main highway from Kingston, running across its southern end, fifteen minutes' walk from the central square. If you're **driving** from Kingston, follow Washington Boulevard (from uptown) or Marcus Garvey Drive (from downtown) out of the city. Regular **buses** make the half-hour trip from Parade and Half Way Tree to the terminus on Bourkes Road (J\$15), while a **taxi** costs about US\$15. Once here, the main sights can easily be explored on foot, as the city is still laid out on its original neat grid system.

### PARADE SQUARE

The starting point for any visit to Spanish Town should be the graceful **Parade Square**, centrepiece of the whole city. There is a charming little park at its middle, with a shabby fountain and a few royal palms, while the buildings around are splendid showcase examples of Georgian architecture. On the north side, the **memorial to Admiral Rodney** by English sculptor John Bacon was commissioned by the Jamaican House of Assembly to commemorate Rodney's defeat of the French navy at the battle of les Saintes, off Guadeloupe, in 1782 – a victory which ensured Jamaica's safety from invasion for several centuries. Bacon put Rodney in classical dress, in accordance with the artistic convention of the time, and the seaman is flanked by a couple of rare and intricate Louis XIV cannons, taken from the French flagship and still bearing the herald of the Sun King. In the 1870s the memorial was briefly moved to Kingston, but the aggrieved citizens of Spanish Town banded together and intimidated the authorities into returning it. Check out the mural above Rodney, depicting his arms and motto and a picture of the French ship sinking.

A number of Spanish buildings, including a sixteenth-century tavern, were demolished to make way for the memorial and the adjoining buildings, which today include the **National Archives** (Mon–Fri 9.30am–4pm), with records dating back to the early days of English settlement, and, opposite, the ruined **courthouse**, built early in the nineteenth century in symmetry with the memorial but badly damaged by fire in 1986.

On the west side of the square is the porticoed, red-brick facade of the **King's House**, built in 1762 and the official residence of the Governor of Jamaica until the capital was moved to Kingston. The facade is all that remains of the building, following a catastrophic fire in 1925, but there's a great little **folk museum** in the former stables at the back (Mon–Fri 9am–5pm; J$5). Among the many noteworthy pieces on display are an ancient wooden pump-action fire engine, made by Merryweathers of London, several old carriages, and early sugar-making equipment, including an animal-operated press for extracting juice from sugar cane and copperpot boilers for separating the sugar crystals from the juice. The main body of the museum has displays on Jamaican architecture and crafts, with the emphasis firmly on upholding African traditions.

The former **House of Assembly**, opposite the King's House, was built in the same year and to the same dimensions. The Assembly – representatives of the plantation owners and other bigwigs – met here until 1865 when, following the Morant Bay Rebellion (see

*Life at King's House is painstakingly described in* Lady Nugent's Journal, *the chatty, often patronizing, but totally engaging diary of the governor's wife. See* Contexts, *p.359.*

---

**Jamaica's death row**

The jail at Spanish Town, built right behind the cathedral, is home to Jamaica's notorious **death row**, the only place in the country that carries out capital punishment. In the recent past hundreds of men have awaited their execution here in appalling conditions, some of them for as long as fourteen years. In 1993 the cases of Earl Pratt and Ivan Morgan were brought before the Privy Council in London, which still sits as Jamaica's final court of appeal. Convicted of murder in 1979 and sentenced to hang, Pratt and Morgan had on three separate occasions heard the death warrant and been taken to the cells adjoining the gallows. Each time they received a last-minute reprieve. The Privy Council overturned the death sentence on the two men, finding that the length of time they had spent on death row was "cruel, inhumane and degrading". The verdict, which makes future executions increasingly unlikely, has not gone down well with the vast majority of Jamaicans, who, in the face of soaring crime figures, express widespread support for the penalty. It has also increased pressure on the government to abandon the archaic reliance on the English House of Lords as the ultimate arbiter in Jamaica's legal matters, a hangover from colonial days.

p.122), Jamaica abandoned its constitution and became a Crown Colony with direct rule from Britain. Today, the building is the seat of local government, reflecting Spanish Town's fall in the rankings. It is not officially open to the public but you can normally sneak in to look at the grand mahogany staircase and the chamber upstairs.

### THE CATHEDRAL

From Parade Square, a five-minute walk south down White Church Street leads to the **Cathedral of St Jago de la Vega** (daily 9am–5pm; free), Jamaica's most important church and the oldest Anglican cathedral outside England. It stands on the foundations of the six-teenth-century Church of the Red Cross, and the black-and-white tiles in the aisle are thought to date from that Spanish building. Important monuments crowd the cathedral, many of them carved in England by leading sculptors of the time like John Bacon and John Wilton, reflecting the status and wealth of the colony during the eigh-teenth century.

The **Blessed Sacrament Chapel**, to the left of the altar, holds a memorial to Basil Keith, governor of Jamaica during the 1770s; the sculpture by Wilton was the first monument in the country to be built with public funds. The **Lady Chapel**, on the other side, has a cheru-bic monument to another governor, Thomas Effingham, sculpted by Bacon. Slightly differing versions of the Jamaican coat of arms, with its Taino figures, crocodile and pineapples (once a sign of great wealth), can be seen on the Effingham monument and on the stained-glass window behind the altar. Also in the Lady Chapel, the memori-al to one Hugh Lewis on the south wall features the only **death mask** to be found anywhere in the Caribbean.

Throughout the cathedral are eloquent memorials to former gov-ernors, bishops and other leading figures of Jamaican society. William Chadwick was the only principal of Jamaica's first universi-ty – the Queen's College – which opened in 1873 for seven students but survived for just one year. Matthew Gregory established a benev-olent fund for poor whites in 1765, aimed at getting a trade for the boys and a husband for the girls. John Colbeck, whose tomb is by the south door, was a soldier with the original English invading force in 1655 and is believed to have been the designer of Colbeck Castle, a few miles west from Spanish Town. Other tombs were mass burial sites for victims of cholera epidemics or those who died on ships en route to the colony.

Outside, you can spend an hour exploring and deciphering the ancient gravestones under the mango trees. Note the **gargoyles** with Negroid features – considered to be unique anywhere – standing guard over a south window. Below them, a number of early gover-nors found their final resting place, including Modyford and Lynch, as well as Martha Ducke, an early settler "most barbarously mur-dered by one of her own Negro slaves" in 1678.

OTHER SIGHTS

The old **iron bridge** spanning the Rio Cobre near where you drive into town was erected here in 1801 after being cast in England, and was the first of its kind in the Americas. In town, the attractive old English **barracks** building, west of the cathedral along Barracks Street, dates from the late eighteenth century. Before this the soldiers had been based in private houses dotted around town, which was seen as a threat to discipline. Cannons stand at the entrance to the barracks, as they once did at each of the public buildings, as a place to hitch up your horse.

A short walk from Parade Square down Constitution Street brings you to **Mulberry Park**, formerly the site of a monastery where mulberry trees were grown to produce silk and today an infirmary for the indigent. It has also been a Jewish cemetery and, though now overrun with banana trees, the old headstones – some in English, others in Hebrew – have been propped up around the park's perimeter.

North of the square, on the corner of French and William Streets, is an unremarkable Baptist church, first built in 1827 but badly damaged by the 1951 and 1988 hurricanes. It is popularly known as **Philippo's Church** for its associations with James Philippo, a missionary who campaigned for the abolition of slavery and the establishment of "free villages" for emancipated slaves. These free villages were an important part of the development of Jamaican society after emancipation. The plantation owners were strongly opposed to allowing the erstwhile slaves to set up their own communities, hoping that they would be forced to return to semi-serfdom on the plantations. They reckoned without the missionaries, however, mostly Baptists like Philippo, who bought up old estates, sub-divided them and sold them off to the former slaves on generous terms. A church and a school were usually the first buildings erected in these new villages, with the houses going up around them, and this pattern of development can still be seen in parts of the country.

PRACTICALITIES

There are no good hotels or guesthouses in Spanish Town,which is most often visted as a day-trip from Kingston. A smattering of **restaurants** around the town centre serve typical if unexciting chicken and fish meals; try *Cecil's* on Martin Street, five minutes from Parade Square, or there are a couple of snack-bars on Bourkes Road near the bus stop.

## Around Spanish Town

A handful of places near Spanish Town merit a quick stop, particularly if you're driving. The small but worthy **Arawak museum** is beside the main road just east of the city while, eight miles to the northwest, **Mountain River Cave** – home to some rare

Taino cave paintings – takes considerably more effort to reach, but rewards the trouble. If you're heading west, you'll pass through the bustling little town of **Old Harbour** – if you're in a car, the ruins of nearby **Colbeck Castle** invite a quick detour – while the route north from Spanish Town passes through the dramatically scenic **Bog Walk Gorge**.

## WHITE MARL ARAWAK MUSEUM

Two miles east of Spanish Town on the main A1 highway, the **White Marl Arawak Museum** (Mon–Fri 10am–4pm; J$20) is a brave but slightly forlorn attempt at a monument to these ancient Jamaicans. Though the major Taino – or Arawak – relics found in Jamaica were taken out of the country long ago – many of the best ending up in the British Museum in London – the museum makes a valiant, largely successful effort to portray the Taino people and their way of life. There's also a recreation of a large *zemi* and a display of tools, pottery and other artefacts recovered from the archeological site surrounding the museum.

---

### The Taino

Jamaica's Tainos (known locally as Arawaks) were part of an Amerindian tribe that came in several waves to the Caribbean, starting around 400 to 500AD, sailing in long dug-out canoes from the Orinoco delta of South America. Originally settling in eastern islands like Trinidad and Barbados, conflict with the Caribs – a more aggressive Amerindian tribe who followed them – pushed the Tainos further and further west, and they probably reached Jamaica around 900AD, six hundred years before Columbus.

Although they lived simply, Taino civilization was peaceful and reasonably sophisticated for the time. They cultivated corn, cassava and cotton, brewed beer and grew and smoked tobacco. Early travellers wrote of their exceptional skill and patience in hunting and fishing, using canoes made from hollowed-out cotton trees, and they did business with nearby islands, trading pottery and woven cotton items, such as hammocks, for ornaments made of gold and copper. Their religious rituals centred around the *zemi*, a ceremonial idol carved from wood or stone that was both worshipped and, often, entombed with the body at burials.

Between half a million and a million Tainos lived in Jamaica when the first Spanish settlers arrived in 1510 although, apart from their presence on the national coat of arms, barely a trace now remains. Indeed, when the English conquered the island in 1655 they claimed that the Tainos were extinct, slavery, indiscriminate slaughter and Old World diseases like smallpox having taken their toll. There are a handful of contemporary accounts of the Tainos but most of what we now know of their way of life comes from lucky finds of carvings and tools and archeological excavations of their *middens*, or rubbish tips, scattered across the island. Parts of their language have also endured, with words like barbecue, canoe, tobacco and hammock finding their way into European vocabularies.

---

## MOUNTAIN RIVER CAVE AND GUANABOA VALE

Although Taino petroglyphs or stone-carvings have been found throughout the Caribbean, there are very few instances of their **painting** that survive. Accordingly, the fifty or so black drawings on the ceiling of **Mountain River Cave** – human figures, a turtle, frogs, other animals and abstract sketches – are an extremely important historic relic. Don't expect anything spectacular; the figures are small, amateurish in the extreme and it's not always easy to make out what they are supposed to be. The real pleasure of this isolated spot is the tiny glimpse offered by the paintings – among the few visible markers left by the island's first inhabitants – into Jamaica's pre-Columbian history.

First uncovered in 1897, the small cave has been thoroughly documented by the Smithsonian Institute in Washington DC and is now a National Trust site. To reach it, drive northwest from Spanish Town towards Lluidas Vale through the pretty and ancient village of **Guanaboa Vale**, childhood home of Jamaican National Hero and former political leader Norman Manley. A **church** has stood here since 1675 – very early in the period of English rule – although the present structure mostly dates from 1845, after repeated hurricane damage to the original. A couple of miles uphill beyond Guanaboa, a small signpost on your right marks the entrance to the site. Ask at the adjoining house for a guide to take you to the cave. It's a gruelling half-mile walk, involving a couple of steep slopes through banana, coffee and jackfruit trees. You'll also cross a narrow river which, a hundred yards downstream, has a small waterfall and a refreshing swimming spot.

## BOG WALK GORGE AND THE ROAD TO OCHO RIOS

The excellent main road from Spanish Town to Ocho Rios, a little over an hour's drive, runs north past Bog Walk and Ewarton. The first part of the drive is very scenic, the road cutting through the deep **Bog Walk Gorge**, a towering limestone canyon carved out of the rock by the Rio Cobre over the centuries. Cars cross the river at **Flat Bridge**, an eighteenth-century stone bridge that has no sides and occasionally loses reckless drivers into the slow-moving river. All along the route you'll see farmers selling their colourful crops – bananas, oranges, sweet potatoes and, in season, fabulous mangoes and luscious naseberries. If you're passing on a Saturday, **Linstead**, eight miles north of Flat Bridge still has a traditional weekend market. **Sligoville**, six miles east of Bog Walk, was the first free village in Jamaica, named after the pro-emancipation Marquis of Sligo, former governor of the island, though there's precious little to see today.

## OLD HARBOUR, OLD HARBOUR BAY AND COLBECK CASTLE

Driving between Kingston and the south or west coasts, the route takes you through the busy little town of **OLD HARBOUR**, nine miles west of Spanish Town. Crowded, noisy food markets spill over onto the road near the town centre and traffic always seems to get

**Indians in Jamaica**

**Indians in Jamaica**

In 1845, just over a decade after slavery was ended in Jamaica, *The Blundell* landed at Old Harbour Bay. The event marked the start of a new bout of colonial social-engineering in Jamaica, for the ship carried the first load of indentured Indian labourers. The abolition of slavery and the subsequent refusal of many ex-slaves to work for their former masters provoked a drastic need for cheap labour on the sugar estates. The estate-owners, having failed to import the required workers from Europe, China and Africa, turned instead to the poverty-stricken states of northern India.

Thirty-five thousand Indians came to Jamaica before the Indian government put a stop to it in 1917. In theory, the labourers were to work on the estates to pay the cost of their passage from India and would have the chance to earn money to send home before returning themselves at the end of their contracts (generally 5–7 years). In fact, almost all were forced to work under appalling conditions of semi-slavery for miserly pay (if any) and the majority remained and died in Jamaica, establishing close communities and continuing to celebrate traditional Hindu festivals like Diwali, Holi and Hosay. They still constitute probably the largest ethnic minority in the country (although on nothing like the scale of Trinidad and Guyana), but in recent decades their separate identity has begun to disappear as they have been assimilated into the wider community. Today their most potent legacy is a taste for curry and for ganja, introduced to Jamaica by the first wave of labourers.

clogged up around the central square, giving you time to admire the **clock** in the Victorian tower, which has kept pretty much perfect time since it was first installed here in the seventeenth century. Three miles south, the fishing village of **OLD HARBOUR BAY** was, four hundred years ago, an important harbour for the Spanish as they settled in and around Spanish Town. Columbus stopped here to meet with Taino leaders in 1494, and in 1845 the first wave of Jamaica's Indian indentured labourers docked here (see box). Columbus named the area Cow Bay, after the **manatees** or sea-cows that once proliferated offshore. Few of the gentle creatures have survived centuries of slaughter at the hands of local fishermen, and the only things you'll find here now are fishing boats, shacks and a few stalls selling fresh fish and lobster – as you'd expect, it's a good place to stop for a tasty fried-fish lunch. Just offshore, the virtually uninhabited **Great Goat Island** was used as a US Navy base during World War II, and is now home to a few fishermen who shelter in the crumbling barracks.

Two and a half miles from Old Harbour lie the ruins of **Colbeck Castle** (always open; free). These are among the oldest ruins in the country and, like Fort Charles at Port Royal, speak of the constant fear of invasion held by the early English settlers. The castle was built on land granted to John Colbeck, an officer with the English invasion force that captured Jamaica from the Spanish in 1655, strategically placed within ten miles of both the coast and the capital

Spanish Town. It is probable (though the date of construction is uncertain) that it was Colbeck who had it fortified with the massive walls of imported brick and local cut stone. A perimeter wall had a smaller guardhouse – probably a combination of a living quarters and a defensive position – at each corner.

No records have been found detailing the identities of the workmen, but it seems likely that the work was done by slaves under the guidance of skilled artisans from England. The circular brick windows on the ground floor are unusual and the brick arches that front the main building are equally striking, suggesting that decoration, as well as defence, was important to the architect. The rest of the castle is rather dilapidated, with collapsed staircases and exposed timbers hinting at a grand design.

It's a bit of a palaver to get to Colbeck. Turn inland at the clocktower in Old Harbour and continue until the road splits in three; take the centre route and follow the winding road (the ruins loom up on your left after a while) until you cross a bridge. After about four hundred yards take the first left down a gravel road/dirt track. Follow this for just over a half a mile to the castle – if it has been raining you may want to walk rather than risk getting your vehicle stuck.

## North of Kingston

The main A3 artery shoots north from Kingston, shearing through affluent suburbs and the western foothills of the Blue Mountains. First stop, fourteen miles along, is **Castleton Botanical Gardens** (daily 9am–5pm; free), which occupy fifteen acres adjacent to the Wag Water River. Established in 1862, with support from London's Kew Gardens, Castleton quickly became the best-stocked garden in the Caribbean, and many of the plants that now dominate the island – the ubiquitous **poinciana** for example – were first introduced here. Despite the damage caused by recent hurricanes (and by official neglect) the gardens are still an important research station and well worth a stop if you're passing. The guides, who are no longer paid and survive only on tips from visitors, are quite excellent; chief guide Roy Bennett has been here for over sixty years.

*The gardens can be reached by bus from Kingston's Parade.*

The gardens are well set out and easy to explore. There is a bewildering variety of palm trees, as well as coffee, cocoa and ebony, all of the island's perfume and spice plants, and a diverse collection of foreign plants and trees. The peace and quiet attracts a lot of birdlife, and you may well spot Jamaica's national bird – the streamer tail hummingbird also known as the "**doctor bird**", supposedly for its resemblance to a doctor in Victorian costume – and the tiny bee hummingbird, one of the smallest birds in the world. When you've finished your tour, there is a small **bar** on the other side of the road, and, further down, a larger **café** and more open space with access to the river if you want to swim or take a picnic.

# Travel details

It is impossible to predict accurately the frequency of buses and minibuses in the Kingston region – service is often chaotic and delays and cancellations are frequent – so the figures below are only general guidelines. However, on the most popular routes you should be able to count on getting a ride within an hour if you travel in the morning; things normally quieten down later in the day. On less popular routes, you're best off asking for probable departure times the day before you travel.

### Buses and minibuses

**Kingston** to: Black River (4 daily; 4hr); Mandeville (6 daily; 3hr); Montego Bay (3 daily; 5hr 30min); Negril (2 daily; 6hr); Ocho Rios (4 daily; 3hr 30min); Port Antonio (via Annotto Bay, 4 daily, 4hr; via Morant Bay, 3 daily, 4hr 30min); Port Royal (7 daily; 25min); Spanish Town (12 daily; 30min).

**Spanish Town** to: Black River (2 daily; 4hr); Mandeville (6 daily; 2hr 30min); Montego Bay (3 daily; 5 hr); Negril (2 daily; 5hr 30min); Ocho Rios (3 daily; 2hr 30min).

### Ferries

**Kingston** to: Port Royal (Mon–Sat 7 daily, Sun 4 daily; 30min).

### Flights

**Kingston** to: Montego Bay (Mon–Fri 8 daily, Sat & Sun 5 daily; 35min); Negril (1 daily; 1hr); Port Antonio (1 daily; 40min).

# Chapter 2

# The Blue Mountains and the east

Towering behind Kingston and enticingly visible from anywhere in the island's eastern third, the **Blue Mountains** conform with few people's mental image of Jamaica, land of sand, sea and reggae. At 28 miles, the mountains form one of the longest continuous ranges in the Caribbean, and their cool woodlands, dotted with coffee plantations and often shrouded in mist, offer some of the best hiking on the island and a welcome break from the heat of the coast. The most popular hike is to **Blue Mountain Peak** – at 7402ft, the highest point in Jamaica – but there are dozens of other trekking possibilities, and more relaxed options for non-hikers, including the **botanical gardens** at Cinchona, the **World's End liqueur factory** and a chance to visit the estates producing some of the most expensive **coffee** on earth.

Bisected by the mountains, the island's two easternmost parishes are relatively unknown outside Jamaica. To the south, **St Thomas** is historically one of the country's poorest and least developed regions; tourist development remains negligible here, although there are a couple of redeeming features if you want to get off the beaten track. The mineral springs and botanical gardens at **Bath**, an attraction for several centuries, have been neglected since Hurricane Gilbert ravaged the area in 1988, but remain delightful. For the intrepid few, a handful of hotels are slowly springing up on the south coast's best beaches, particularly at **Lyssons** and **Retreat**, where you'll find small swathes of deserted golden sand.

By contrast, the northeastern parish of **Portland** is one of the most beautiful regions of Jamaica, though high rainfall and a longish drive from the island's main airports mean that tourists are relatively few. All the more reason to come – the wetter climate supports the most outstanding natural scenery in the country and, if you stay in the parish capital, **Port Antonio**, you'll be close to great waterfalls at **Reach Falls** and **Somerset Falls**, you can hike in the tropical **rainforest** or take a more gentle rafting trip on the **Rio Grande**. The

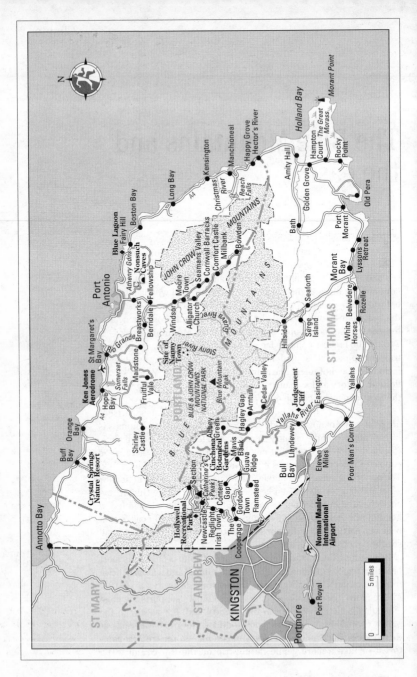

**beaches** are less spectacular than those further west, but they're far less crowded and boast some lovely places to stay.

The main **A4 highway** runs all the way around the coastline of Portland and St Thomas, and most points along it are reachable by bus, but you'll need a car to explore much of the interior.

# The Blue Mountains

The **Blue Mountains** begin where Kingston ends, and a starker contrast would be hard to imagine, with the chaos of the city replaced by a tranquillity and a gentle beauty that, at its best, is truly staggering. The mountains are named for the mists that colour them from a distance, and their craggy slopes form an unbroken, undulating spine across Jamaica's easternmost parishes, a tropical wilderness with a cool, wet climate that you won't find anywhere else in Jamaica.

*Rainfall averages 75 inches a year in some parts of the Blue Mountains.*

The northern slopes of the mountains are covered by a huge quilt of dense, primary forest – easily the largest on the island – but deforestation has badly affected the southern side, where great chunks have been cleared by coffee planters, farmers, squatters and (catastrophically) Hurricane Gilbert in 1988. To try to protect the wilderness from further devastation, 200,000 acres of the Blue and neighbouring John Crow Mountains were designated as a **national park** in 1993, with the stated aims of managing natural resources for long-term sustainable use and generating income opportunities through eco-tourism. To help in the latter, great **hiking trails** have been carved into the interior of the forest, often following ancient mule trails over the mountains.

*Hiking and rafting in the gorgeous Rio Grande valley, on the north side of the mountains, is described on p.142.*

Most visitors to the park come here to hike up **Blue Mountain Peak** (see p.119) or follow the well-maintained trails around **Hollywell** (see p.114); though exceptionally beautiful, the northern reaches are too remote and tough-going to be attempted by anyone except the most determined hikers. Elsewhere in the mountains, the

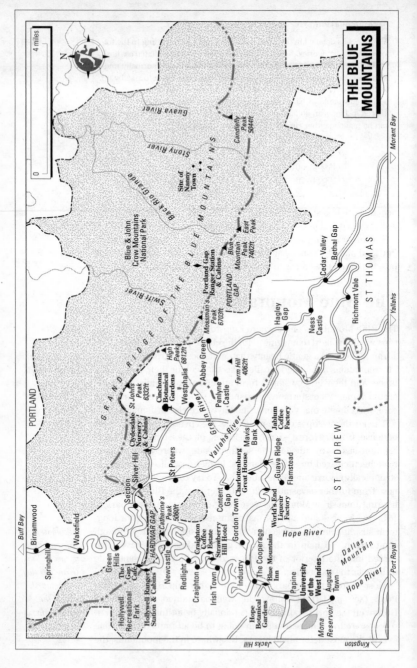

THE BLUE MOUNTAINS

botanical gardens at **Cinchona** (see p.116) are another delightful spot, a magical splash of colour 5000ft up, while the liqueur factory at **World's End** (see p.115) is a definite oddity in these parts but just-ly popular.

**The Blue Mountains**

*See p.144 for more on the Windward Maroons.*

In population terms, though the dense forest provided perfect cover for the Windward Maroons during the seventeenth and eighteenth centuries, the mountains have historically proved largely inhospitable. Even today, the population remains low, concentrated in small settlements like **Gordon Town** and **Newcastle**, or scattered around the edges of the national park, where people farm and raise cattle on the denuded slopes. Many visitors find the mountain people more gentle and welcoming than Jamaicans elsewhere – particularly compared to the heavily touristed north-coast strip – despite the evident poverty and grinding workload many of them face. If you're driving around, you'll pass some of the women who walk miles to pick coffee beans on the main estates, and a lift will be much appreciated.

**Tourism** in the mountains remains small-scale. There are a few hotels, some of them quite spectacular, and a couple of backpackers' hostels (detailed throughout the text), but **coffee** is the mainstay of the local economy. Dark and earthy, Blue Mountain coffee is consid-ered one of the world's best by experts, and prices reflect that assessment, though you can usually find it cheaper here – at the hotels or coffee factories or direct from the farmers – than anywhere else on the island. There are also several moderately diverting **coffee estate tours** for those keen to see how the stuff is produced.

## Getting around

You'll need a **car** to get the most out of the mountains. The principal access road, the B1, cuts straight through the slopes, connecting Kingston with Buff Bay on the north coast; a right fork at the small village of **The Cooperage** leads to Mavis Bank, the main access point for Blue Mountain Peak. The route is atrocious in parts – sometimes down to the bare rock – so expect some bone-rattling. If you plan to head off these main routes, particularly to Cinchona or Abbey Green, you'll need a four-wheel-drive.

Public transport will only take you as far as the main settlements – from Papine, just northeast of Kingston, **buses** go to Newcastle via Irish Town, and to Mavis via Gordon Town. **Cycling** is an attractive option if you've got your own mountain bike (finding one to rent is almost impossible). Several hotels run day-long biking expeditions, among them the *Mount Edge Guesthouse* (US$60; ☎944 8392; see p.113), calling in at small coffee farms and private homes. *Blue Mountain Tours* (US$80; ☎974 7075) picks you up from Port Antonio or Ocho Rios, drives you up into the mountains and lets you freewheel sixteen miles or so down to a waterfall near Buff Bay (see p.115).

### The mountain environment

The Blue Mountain range is Jamaica's oldest geographical feature, formed in the Cretaceous age (between 144 and 65 million years ago). Though the peaks are named for their cerulean tint when seen from afar, some of the rock actually is coloured blue by crossite minerals.

Categorized as montane (the technical term for high-altitude woodland), the **forests** are mostly native soapwood and dogwood evergreens with a few blue mahoe, mahogany and teak, but the eucalyptus and Caribbean pines introduced in the 1950s are starting to dominate even in the primary forest above Hollywell. The primeval-looking cyathea (tree fern) with its patterned trunk and top heavy fronds is particularly distinctive; the tallest are over 150 years old. Below the dense canopy is a layer of **shrubs**, of which the red tubular flowers of the cigar bush are the most identifiable. Every tree trunk or exposed rock is festooned with brightly coloured epiphytic ferns, mosses and lichen; most common are the inexhaustible swathes of dirty lime-coloured old man's beard. Wild strawberries, raspberries, blackberries and rose apples provide a free feast at middle altitudes, and you'll doubtless encounter the prickly vines of climbing bamboo, the only variety native to Jamaica. The tiny white flowers appear only once every 33 years, when each and every one blossoms simultaneously – but as they last bloomed in 1984 your next chance to see them is 2017. The mountains support over five hundred species of **flowering plant**, including around 65 varieties of orchid. Begonias, blue iris, lobelias, busy lizzies and fuschias proliferate, while wild ginger lilies perfume the air.

Other than mongooses, coneys and the wild pigs which roam the northern slopes, there are few **mammals** in the mountains. You may hear the scuffles of feral cats, mice and rats in the undergrowth, and Jamaican yellow boas inhabit the lower slopes in small numbers. The presence of bats is poorly documented; you're most likely to see them around the limestone slopes of the John Crow Mountains. By contrast, **birdlife** flourishes; the forests ring out with the evocative whistle of the rufous-throated solitaire, and mockingbirds, crested quail doves (known as mountain witches), white-eyed thrushes, blackbirds and Jamaican todys add to the cacophony, backed by the squeaking mating calls of tree frogs.

The mountains are the sole habitat of one of the rarest and largest **butterflies** in the world, the six-inch **Giant Swallowtail**, but its distinctly patterned dark brown and gold wings rarely flutter into view – again, the warmer John Crow range yields the most sightings. Insects, on the other hand, are multitudinous, particularly during the summer months when it's common to see thousands of **fireflies** clustering on a single bush and lighting it up like a Christmas tree.

See p.325 of
Contexts for
more on
Jamaica's
environment.

### Hiking

See p.42 of
Basics for
advice on
hiking.

Extreme weather conditions, ecological protection projects and lack of funding mean that of the thirty recognized **trails** in the park, only twenty or so are open at any given time; ask at any ranger station. For a comprehensive description of available walks refer to *The Hiker's Guide to the Blue Mountains* by Bill Willcox (available from *Maya Mountain Lodge*).

**Park practicalities**

At present, there is no charge to enter the park or to use its hiking trails,
though an access system and fees will be in place by the millennium, when
you'll have to purchase a **permit** (around US$5) from the Jamaica
Conservation and Development Trust, 95 Dumbarton Ave, Kingston 10
(☎960 2848, fax 960 2850) or at one of the park's three **ranger stations**,
located at **Hollywell**, **Portland Gap** and **Millbank**. Theoretically always
open, these can provide advice on weather conditions and trail access, and
ordnance survey maps are on display for reference. None has a phone, but
you can make prior contact through the administrative **park office** at
Guava Ridge (Mon–Fri 10am–4pm; ☎0997 8044 or 8069).

As Kingston-based hiking groups take to the trails in the summer
months, the **best time to hike** is during the winter; it's cooler and the
trails are at their quietest. If possible, avoid the rainy season
(May–June & Sept–Oct), when you're almost guaranteed to get
drenched.

All the usual common-sense guidlelines apply to hiking in the
mountains. Bring the standard equipment (see p.42), including
**drinking water** – wild pine bromeliads hold over a pint of water
between their leaves, but as they're home to insect nymphs and tree
frogs, you'll only be tempted to sup in an emergency. Bins are rare,
so carry a plastic bag to take rubbish home.

## North to Newcastle

Heading up the B1 from northeast Kingston, the first place you reach
is the tiny village of **THE COOPERAGE**, sitting on a junction in the
road and named for the Irish coopers who worked here in the early
nineteenth century, making the wooden barrels in which Blue
Mountain coffee was shipped abroad. A left fork leads up a winding
road for three miles to **IRISH TOWN**, where the coopers lived.
Today, it's a small farming town, dominated by the magnificent
*Strawberry Hill* hotel (☎944 8400, fax 975 7158; ⑦). The brain-
child of Island Records magnate Chris Blackwell, this former working plantation opened as a hotel in 1994 to a blaze of architectural
awards, and is one of the most attractive places to stay in all Jamaica.
It has a strong rock and roll pedigree – the Rolling Stones and U2 are
regular visitors, and Bob Marley was brought here to convalesce
after being shot in 1976. Its twelve luxury cottages, all made from
local materials and imaginatively designed with Jamaican heritage in
mind, show off hand-carved fretwork, louvered windows, mahogany
four-poster beds and antique furniture. Sunday **brunch**, at around
US$15 per person, is an institution, and well worth the journey if
(like most people) the hotel is outside your budget.

Beyond Irish Town is **Craighton Estate** (☎944 8224; Mon–Fri
9am–3pm; US$20), a Japanese-owned coffee plantation. Caffeine
addicts will enjoy the enthusiastically presented (though heftily

# The Blue
# Mountains

*The* Maya
Mountain
Lodge, *on the
outskirts of
Kingston, is
reviewed on
p.62.*

## Hiking guides and organized groups

No matter where you're walking in the Blue Mountains, it's almost always advisable to use a **guide**; given the changeable weather conditions and poor hiking maps (in a terrain with few obvious landmarks), it's very easy to get lost. Security can also be a problem for unaccompanied hikers, particularly on the Kingston side of the mountains. A guide will ensure your safety, clear overgrown paths and provide an informed commentary. Alternatively, you might consider hooking up with an **organized group**, most of which have their own vehicles, especially as getting to walks off the beaten track can be problematic on your own. The following outfits are all recommended.

**Blue Mountain Adventure Tours**, Section (via the park office ☎0997 8044). Walks with local guides from US$20 to US$50 per day depending on the experience of the guide (some have specialities like birds or botany) and the size of the group, but you'll have to make your own way to Section.

**Destinations**, *Maya Mountain Lodge* (☎960 5705 or 927 2097). Based at the lodge (see p.62), this outfit offers a variety of hikes, some starting right at its door, others on the Hollywell trails or to Cinchona or Blue Mountain Peak. Groups of five or more pay US$55 per person per day for guide, transport and lunch, or US$27.50 for guide alone.

**Sun Venture**, 30 Balmoral Ave, Kingston 10 (☎960 6685, fax 929 7512). Blue Mountain Peak by day or night; the former involves camping at the peak, waking for the dawn and tackling East Peak before you descend. Other options include wilderness trails through the northern slopes and an ambitious three-day crossing of the entire Grand Ridge, a mighty range of peaks that forms a boundary between Portland and St Thomas, not strictly within park boundaries. Costs start at US$50 per day for single hikers, US$35 per person for groups of three or more and US$70 per person for groups of three or more on overnight hikes. Transport is included in all prices.

**Touring Society of Jamaica**, Strawberry Hill (☎944 8400, fax 944 8408). Upmarket outfit specializing in all-inclusive custom-designed tours for bird watchers, coffee fanatics and botanists from US$250 per day for a group of one to four. Escorted mountain walks to Cinchona and local waterfalls cost US$55 per person (minimum 6 persons).

**Veterans Hiking Group**, c/o Ian Wallace at the Forestry Department (☎924 2667). A Jamaican club happy to include non-members in its weekend hikes throughout the Blue and John Crow mountains; you'll be expected to contribute to transport costs. Most excursions take place in the summer.

priced) hour-long tour, which shows you how the seedlings are nurtured into mature plants, and lets you taste the finished product in the small but charming eighteenth-century great house. Call ahead to ensure that a guide will be there to meet you. From Craighton, the road continues through the tiny village of **REDLIGHT**, named for the former brothels that kept the Irish coopers entertained.

Four thousand feet up from here is **NEWCASTLE**, an old British military base established by Major William Gomm in 1841 to escape the yellow fever raging on the hot, swampy plains below. The main road cuts across the **parade ground**, now a training ground for the Jamaica Defence Force, which still features old cannons and the insignia of the various regiments stationed here during the past century or so, while the nearby military graveyard remembers the dead of that period with its neat, white crosses. From the parade ground the views across the mountains and down to Kingston are dazzling and almost vertiginous, while behind you, immediately above Newcastle, **Catherine's Peak** (5060ft) – named after Lady Catherine Long, the first woman to climb it, in 1760 – marks the highest point in the parish of St Andrew.

For **accommodation**, *Tree Tops* (☎974 5831, fax 974 5830; ⑤), just below Newcastle, makes a marvellous hiking base if you have your own transport. The stylish two-bedroom house has a delightful garden full of busy lizzies and begonias and a practically unbroken view of Kingston from its verandah; it also has mountain bikes for guests to use. A little further down the hill, *Mount Edge* (☎944 8392, toll free 888 991 4292; ②) is a rest-stop/guesthouse/restaurant, which also runs a variety of local activities, from biking tours to excellent monthly full- moon parties, with occasional mento bands and plenty of Kingston trendies.

## Hollywell Recreational Park and Section

A couple of miles past Newcastle, the mountain pass 4000ft up at **Hardwar Gap** is named for a British army captain who supervised the construction of the road from here to Buff Bay (and who must be turning in his grave at its present condition). On your left you'll pass the atmospheric **Gap Café** (closed Mon), where you can get good, cheap Jamaican meals for around J$500 or just have a drink on the charming garden terrace. The building was constructed in the 1930s, originally designed as a way-station for those travelling into the mountains by horse and carriage, and Ian Fleming wrote *Dr No*, the first James Bond novel, while staying here in the 1940s.

Just beyond the café is the entrance to the **Hollywell Recreational Park**, over 4000ft above sea level, always cool and often bathed in mist; when it clears, you get a spectacular unbroken view over the shimmering Kingston streets, Port Royal and Portmore below. This 300-acre "park within a park" is the gateway to the mountains proper and had protected status before the rest of the area. Easily accessible from the city, it's long been the green space of choice for Kingstonians, and is consequently one of the busier parts of the mountains, latticed with enjoyable hiking trails. Call at the ranger station (100yd beyond the café) if you plan to hike; otherwise carry on along the road to the opposite ridge, where you'll find a picnic spot with tables, covered gazebos, water faucets and a malodorous toilet. The forest rising up sharply behind the ranger station is **Oatley Mountain**, site of several trails (see below) and a river, although you'll rarely get hot enough here to want to swim. To the east is Mount Horeb and the Fairy Glades trail, where pines are out-

*The word "Gap", which features in placenames all over the mountains, refers to the valleys between the peaks.*

*See p.167 for more on James Bond in Jamaica.*

numbered by the twisted trunks of soapwood and dogwood trees and clusters of orchids and wild pines. The park was extensively replanted with Caribbean pines after Hurricane Gilbert and remains a sanctuary for a wide variety of birds.

## Trails around Hollywell

The popularity of **trails** around Hollywell means that most are well maintained, but as rain can wreck these dirt tracks overnight, it's worth checking at the ranger station before you set off. As always, a **guide** is recommended – he or she should be aware of many more trails in addition to those listed here, which are the most popular and easily accessible. As most of these trails are not circular, you'll have to arrange for a pick-up at the end – discuss this with your guide.

**Catherine's Peak** (1.5 miles; 2hr). Steep, misty hike along a concrete road that branches off the B1 just north of Newcastle and winds its way up to Catherine's Peak (5060ft), with roadside tree ferns, rose apple trees and excellent views of Kingston if the mist clears.

**Cold Spring** (4.5 miles; 6hr). This trail starts half a mile north of St Peters (on the road that runs from Silver Hill to Content Gap), winds north and joins the **Clifton Mountain trail** (2 miles; 2hr 30min), also from St Peters, half a mile before Newcastle. They run parallel before terminating at Newcastle and offer some nice Kingston views when the canopy subsides.

**Fairy Glade and Mount Horeb** (2.5 miles; 4hr). A trail so beautiful that it's over-used and often closed – check at the ranger station. You strike into forest from the B1 near the *Gap Café* and curve steadily uphill through intricate forest, with some strenuous half-climbing stretches up 4849ft Mount Horeb. A thick field of wild ginger lilies often blocks the final stretch; make sure your guide has a machete. You emerge onto the concrete road above Newcastle and can combine this trail with Catherine's Peak by turning left once you reach the road.

**Middleton Mountain** (3 miles; 4.5hr). Fairly difficult, mostly uphill trek starting at Cascade Waterfall and ending at Wakefield district on the B1; the trail parallels this road along a considerably more serpentine route through the bush. You ford a shallow river in two places and get some good views of the unravelling mountainscape.

**Oatley Mountain** (5 miles; 40min). Easy, pretty varied circular hike through the tunnel-like jungle of diminutive Oatley Mountain. There are a couple of lookout towers and viewing platforms from which to enjoy the views. You can continue on the **Waterfall trail** (1.5miles; 1hr 30min) – a mildly testing scramble along a river bed to the Cascade Waterfall just off the road by *Green Hills Guesthouse*. Landslides have reduced the waterfall and swimming hole to a trickle.

**Wallenford** (1.5 miles; 3hr). A fairly strenuous hike starting just west of Section. There are a couple of confusing turn-offs before the finish at Cedar Valley, and it's easy to lose your way; a knowledgeable guide is essential.

**Woodcutters' Gap** (1.5 miles; 3hr). A signposted track that forks off the Catherine's Peak road, plummets down into a valley (Woodcutters' Gap itself) then heads steeply up it to meet the B1 just east of Hollywell. Lots of climbing and fairly difficult.

If you want to **stay**, there are three cabins (①), which you'll need to book in advance through the park office (see p.111). The basic facilities – foam-mattressed beds without bedding, indoor cooking range and cold shower – take second place to the marvellous setting, a Kingston view from your doorway, complete seclusion and plenty of pure mountain air. You can also camp for US$5 per person. For a little more comfort, *Green Hills Guest House*, (☎0997 4087 or 952 6590, fax 952 6591; ③), a mile past Hollywell, is an ancient wood-panelled home with basic rooms, a grubby shared bathroom and erratic water supply. It's a bit musty, but as the mists clear, early morning views across Hardwar Gap are awe-inspiring and the house is surrounded by wildflowers. At both places, you'll have to bring your own food; at weekends a fresh produce and soft drinks stall sets up near the ranger station.

Beyond Hollywell, gravel replaces tarmac. Three miles past the ranger station is **SECTION**, a friendly little town that, as home to the *Blue Mountain Adventure Tours* hiking group (see p.112) and sever-al small-scale coffee farmers, is a great place to both hire a hiking guide and buy some coffee (a pound of beans should cost about US$15). The few houses aren't much to look at, but the laid-back attitude of the locals gives an insight into mountain living. There's a small shop for beers and snacks, and coffee farmer James Dennis offers cheap and basic **accommodation** (①); any local will be able to direct you.

At Section, the road begins its attractive seventeen-mile descent to Buff Bay on the north coast (see p.146); there's little of specific interest to see, but you can stop for a dip at the small **Fishdone waterfall**, about nine miles before Buff Bay – turn left just before the white bridge. A second road forks east from Section to Silver Hill, winding its way between lushly vegetated peaks to Clydesdale and Cinchona (see p.116).

## The World's End liqueur factory

The right fork from The Cooperage heads past the tiny riverside vil-lage of **Industry** to undistinguished **GORDON TOWN**, the only size-able settlement in the Blue Mountains, built around a neat central square, with a couple of small snack bars and the usual giggling gag-gles of smartly turned-out schoolchildren. Crossing the bridge here and heading three miles east brings you to the colourful **Sangster's World's End liqueur factory** (☎926 8888; Mon–Fri 10am–4pm; free) – an improbable but very welcome sight two and a half thou-sand feet up the Blue Mountains. This brightly muralled building is the production centre for one of Jamaica's smallest but most suc-cessful rum-makers. Dr Ian Sangster came to the island from Scotland in the 1960s, founding the factory in 1974 with a couple of barrels of rum, a handful of spices and a big mixing pot. Sangster's success since then has been impressive, with international prizes for his gold rum, overproof rum, rum cream and coffee liqueur.

Your 45-minute tour starts in the tasting lounge – the best part of the visit – where your guide explains the production process and you can sample a dozen or so of the rums and liqueurs on a small outdoor patio. It's an atmospheric place, with views up the mountains towards Newcastle, doctor birds swooping in to feed beside you and ancient cannons from Port Royal (see p.87) scattered around. Inside, the factory is surprisingly simple – basically a large mixing drum and a bottling plant – with a planning room that looks like a chemistry lab. You take in a tiny museum, with old flagons and decanters from around the world, before winding up in the well-stocked shop.

Call ahead if you can to arrange your tour; although drop-in visitors are welcomed, you'll appreciate the tranquil atmosphere more if you arrange not to arrive at the same time as a big party.

### Flamstead and Cinchona Botanical Gardens

Heading east from *World's End*, the road forks at the hilltop junction of Guava Ridge, from where two consecutive right turns will take you past **Nyumbani** – Michael Manley's private mountain home and coffee estate – to the **Flamstead plantation** (call ahead to arrange a tour on ☎960 0204; US$50), once the site of a magnificent great house that was home to Governor Edward Eyre (see p.122), British Admiral Horatio Nelson and subsequent naval captains, but has since been turned to rubble by a series of hurricanes. Today, the tourable plantation grows Blue Mountain coffee, and in an area where every turn you make offers jaw-dropping vistas, the panoramic view over Port Royal and the Caribbean Sea is unsurpassable.

The northern fork of Guava Ridge takes you into the heart of coffee country. At the tiny hamlet of **CONTENT GAP**, you can **stay** in the small but prettily designed rooms at *Pine Grove* (☎977 8001; ⑤), set in peaceful gardens that look down over the mountains.

Two miles further north of here, tucked into a remote pocket of the mountains and accessible only by foot or four-wheel-drive, is **Clydesdale**, an old coffee plantation converted into a nursery in 1937 by the Forestry Department. It's the only commercial tree plantation remaining in the mountains, with row upon row of Caribbean pines neatly arranged up the hillsides, networked by several paths that make for a pleasantly shady walk. It's usually completely deserted so you'll need to bring a guide. Just before the road swings to the right toward Cinchona, you'll see a charming white-painted house by the riverbank, originally built to process coffee beans. It's an idyllic spot to stop and swim, and the house is sporadically available to rent (☎924 2667 or 2668; ②). There's floor space for up to five, but you'll have to bring everything with you, including bedding, and be prepared to bathe in the river and cook on a fire.

From here, you can drive within a mile of **Cinchona Botanical Gardens** (no set hours; free), bearing left up the steep path that snakes through the precipitous vegetable patches and coffee groves that cover Top Mountain – the gardens are at the summit, and their orderliness is a surprise after the rugged and wild hillsides below. Clinging to the ridge opposite Blue Mountain Peak and overlooking the Yallahs River valley, the ten-acre maintained gardens were initially a commercial venture, planted with Assam tea and cinchona trees – which produce quinine, used as an anti-malarial before the advent of modern drugs – in 1886. However, the inaccessibility of the site and competition from Indian plantations led to the project's decline, and it became a government-run public garden in 1968, still an important centre for botanical research.

The cinchona trees have all died out now, battered by the hurricanes, but the gardens are magical nonetheless. Several varieties of eucalyptus whistle in the breeze, and Norfolk Island pine, Japanese cedar, weeping cyprus, rubber and camphor trees flourish in the mist. The vivid walled flower beds are bursting with blooms, and wild coffee smothers the slopes. You can see it all on the **Panorama Walk**, preferably accompanied by one of the gardeners (leave a tip), which takes you through a tunnel-like thicket of Holland bamboo, past a broken-down old caretaker's house and back to the main house, an ancient oblong of stone that still contains most of its original fittings.

---

### Blue Mountain coffee

The story of **Blue Mountain coffee**, rated as one of the world's finest, is a long and turbulent one. Coffee trees were introduced to Jamaica from Ethiopia in 1728 by Governor Sir Nicholas Lawes, and found to flourish on the cool slopes of the Blue Mountains. Cultivation of the crop reached new heights of excellence in 1801 when expert coffee growers flooded into Jamaica from revolution-torn Haiti. At the same time, the craze for coffee houses in Europe fuelled a massive demand for the beans and, during the first half of the nineteenth century, Jamaica was among the world's main exporters, producing up to fifteen thousand tons of beans per year.

The industry suffered its first crushing blow with emancipation in 1838, as streams of former slaves left the plantations to set up their own small farms. Soon afterwards, Britain abolished preferential trade terms for its colonies; under free trade, direct competition from the excellent coffees of South America crippled the small Jamaican farmers. The industry's decline continued into this century, with periodic hurricanes wiping out entire plantations.

After World War II, the government took belated steps to save the Blue Mountains plantations. It established quality guidelines for both cultivation and processing, stipulating that only coffee grown at a certain altitude could claim the *Blue Mountain* name (you'll see other Jamaican coffee around the island called *High Mountain* or *Low Land*). This exclusivity heightened the coffee's cachet, and helped to underpin its reputation worldwide. The biggest boost for the industry came during the 1980s as Japanese companies, with a big domestic market for Blue Mountain coffee, invested huge amounts in the best of the plantations. More than ninety percent of the stuff is now sold to Japan, reducing the amount available for export elsewhere and contributing to the extremely high price that you'll pay for it in Europe and North America.

There are several other trails to enjoy around Cinchona; the garden supervisor will rustle up a guide for a nominal fee. One of the most rewarding paths is the sticky six-mile hike down to Mavis Bank (see below), and the historic, ten-mile **Vinegar Hill** trail to Buff Bay, an old trading route that the British used to transport supplies from Kingston to the north coast.

If you want to **stay** in Cinchona, US$3 will buy you floor space in the house, but you'll need to bring food and bedding with you; you can also camp in the grounds for the price of the water you use.

## Mavis Bank and Abbey Green

Heading east from Guava Ridge, the next settlement along is **MAVIS BANK**, nestled in the Yallahs River valley. Accessible by bus from Papine on Kingston's northeastern fringe, neat arranged Mavis Bank is the last full-scale village on the route to Blue Mountain Peak; if you're driving, this is the place to park – in the lay-by opposite the police station – as only the sturdiest Land Rover can tackle the terrain beyond. The focal point is the *Hikers Guide Rest Stop* in the centre of town near the white-painted church, where you can get an inexpensive Jamaican meal or pick up a guide. There's also a post office, bakery and a few hole-in-the-wall shops, all located along the town's single street, and a government-owned **coffee factory** (tourable by appointment ☎924 9503) on the west side of the village. You can **stay** at *Forres Park* (☎927 5957, fax 978 6942; ①–③), a new rest-stop in a private coffee plantation ten minutes from the centre; guides are available for local walks (US$15 per day).

*Both hostels provide guides for around US$25; they'll also supply mules for US$40 if you can't manage the walk up Blue Mountain Peak.*

You *can* start the hike up to the peak from Mavis Bank, along the steep and strenuous Farm Hill Trail from the church, but most people prefer to begin from **ABBEY GREEN**, just over five miles northeast, whose two hostels (call ahead; see below) offer Land Rover pick-up from Mavis Bank for US$30 per carload; on the way up, you'll pass through **HAGLEY GAP** – a steeply inclining one-street village where you can buy last-ditch provisions and get a hot meal from a small-scale cookshop – after which you'll traverse the least road-like road in Jamaica, with huge gullies carved through the clay by coursing water.

Of Abbey Green's rustic but perfectly comfortable **hostels**, *Whitfield Hall* (☎926 6612 or 0927 0986; ①/④) is the most atmospheric, set in an old stone planters' house, with a huge grand piano, a log fire, and geese in the yard. The low ceilings and pre-war kitchen add to the old-world effect, but there's an air of a regimented school dorm about the place, with lists of rules tacked prominently on the walls. You sleep in bunks or in a self-contained cottage, and there's camping for US$7. A few hundred yards down the road is the more liberated *Wildflower Lodge* (☎929 5394; ①–④), a two-storey house popular with younger hikers. Bedding choices are similar, though there are also private double rooms and the camping is marginally cheaper; there's also a gift shop, cavernous kitchen and dining room.

Whichever lodge you choose, it's a good idea to arrange to have a **hot meal** (US$5–7) prepared ready for your return; you'll need it.

## Blue Mountain Peak

Jamaica's climbing rite of passage, **Blue Mountain Peak** (7402ft), the highest point on the island, seems daunting but is actually relatively easy. It is magnificent by day – when you can marvel at the opulence of the canopy, the thousands of orchids, mosses, bromeliads and lichens, the mighty shadows cast by the Peak, and the coils of smoke from invisible dwellings below – and thrilling by night, when after a magical moonlit ascent, Kingston's lights occasionally twinkling in the distance, you find yourself at Jamaica's zenith as a new day dawns, arguably the most heartstopping experience the island can offer.

From Abbey Green, the climb to the peak is just under seven miles, and should take three to five hours depending on your fitness level. If you're staying at one of the hostels, you can start at around 2am and catch sunrise at the Peak; if you can synchronize your walk with a full moon, you'll get beautiful natural floodlighting. Regular signposts make the route easy to follow without the aid of a guide, but in this remote area it's sensible to go with someone who knows their way. Don't stray onto any of the tempting "short cuts" – it's illegal, you'll damage the sensitive environment, and you'll almost certainly get hopelessly lost. Rescue patrols can take days to find you, by which time you'll be in serious trouble.

The first stretch of the trail, aptly named **Jacob's Ladder**, is the most arduous – a series of scree-covered, corrugated switchback turns through open pastures and thick forest. The halfway point – around 4.5 miles or two hours' walking – is **Portland Gap Ranger Station**, where you can rest at the gazebo, fill up water bottles and leave a note for the sleeping rangers estimating your return time. A coffee shop is planned, but for now there's just a sporadically open tuck shop, some smelly pit toilets, a water pipe, a barbecue and two very basic cabins (①) – bring your own bedding and cooking utensils. Two subsidiary treks branch off from Portland Gap, though the more beautiful, the **Mossmans Peak trail** along Grand Ridge (4 miles; 6hr), is littered with fallen trees and not always open. Just before the ranger station, a sign points to the dangerous **Breezy Gully trail**; though mostly off-limits, you can still go as far as the small gap where the sheer drop creates a wind vortex that sucks up anything you throw in.

Once past Portland Gap, it's another three and a half miles to the peak through twisted montane and eventually low-lying elfin forest, in which the gnarled soapwood and dogwood evergreens are so stunted by low temperatures, exposure and lack of nutrients that they grow no higher than eight feet. You're still only about 6000ft up, but you might already be feeling dizzy or faint from the rising alti-

*If you're here
before sunrise,
there is a
derelict cabin
(full of
charred
timbers,
rubbish and
the occasional
rat) for shelter
while you
wait.*

tude; if so, take it slowly and eat a high energy snack. At around 7000ft, the plateau at **Lazy Man's Peak** is where many hikers call it a day, but it's worth struggling on for another twenty minutes, as a far more spectacular panorama awaits you at the peak.

If you've arrived before dawn, you'll be completely bowled over. The inky black slowly melts into ever-intensifying pinks, oranges and purples until finally a hint of wispy blue heralds the sun and reveals ranges unravelling like a sea of crumpled corrugated cardboard. It's quite possible you'll be here alone, the highest person in Jamaica and feeling –literally – on top of the world. As the sun burns off the mist, the panorama becomes recognizable; you can make out Cinchona and, on a good day, Buff Bay and Navy Island to the north and Kingston, Portmore and coastal St Thomas to the south – and if visibility is especially good, you may even catch a glimpse of Cuba, seventy miles away to the north. You get a heady perspective of the ranges you've crossed to get here, and a rather depressing view of the deforestation towards Kingston.

Before you begin the descent, if you're not too exhausted, the hour-long hike to sister summit **East Peak** is an alluring, occasionally precarious diversion, though only the most experienced guides know the way – convince yourself you've hired the best.

This is the furthest you can go into the Blue Mountains, as thick forest and treacherous, unexplored terrain means that even the burly pig hunters seldom venture further east, preferring to enter the John Crows from Millbank in Portland (see p.144).

# St Thomas

**St Thomas**, nestling below the mountains, is probably the most neglected of Jamaica's parishes. Historically troublesome, it has traditionally suffered from lack of government support; as a result, most of the villages you'll pass through feel desperately poor and tourist facilities remain meagre. The coastline between Kingston and **Morant Bay**, the parish capital, is mostly scrubby and unattractive, despite the backdrop of the Blue Mountains, and there is little to the town itself. East of here, though, the scenery improves, becoming quite spectacular in places. There are a couple of good, off-the-beaten-track beaches at **Lyssons** and **Retreat**; the rambling old spa town of **Bath**, up in the foothills of the mountains, merits a visit in its own right; and the romantically inclined can make for the deserted **Morant Point**.

## From Kingston to Morant Bay

Heading east from Kingston, past the tiny settlements of **Bull Bay** and **Cow Bay** – named for the manatees that were caught and slaughtered here in the seventeenth and eighteenth centuries – and a couple of rather dirty beaches, you'll come to the village of **ELEVEN**

**MILES**, where a roadside marker recalls **Jack Mansong**, an eighteenth-century Jamaican Robin Hood figure. "Three Finger Jack" – so named due to a hand injury sustained in a fight with a Maroon leader named Quashie – was a runaway slave turned bandit, the scourge of British soldiers and travellers but, in the best tradition of the romantic highwayman, unfailingly courteous to women and children. He hid out near here for several years in the late eighteenth century, terrorizing the island with his daring crimes, before being cornered and killed by a group of Maroons acting in league with the British. Back in England, contemporaneous fascination with this romantic hero inspired several plays and even a West End musical.

North off the main highway here, a road leads up into the hills towards the tiny village of **Llandewey,** from where there's a fabulous view over the thousand-foot wall of **Judgement Cliff**. The cliff was created by a massive landslide in 1692, caused by the same earthquake that flattened Port Royal a few miles west (see p.56); local legend claims that its fall buried a particularly cruel and rapacious local landowner – hence the name.

Back on the highway, the arid, scrubby landscape is refreshingly broken at **Poor Man's Corner**, the mouth of the Yallahs River, one of Jamaica's longest waterways – a trickle for most of the year but a raging torrent during rainy season. Just east of here is **YALLAHS**, a village best known for its **giant salt ponds**, divided from the sea by a narrow spit of land. Bacteria occasionally go on the rampage, turning the water a reddish colour, and scientists reckon that some of the micro-organisms are actually archeo-bacteria, among the earliest of the earth's life forms. Past Yallahs, the village of **WHITE HORSES** is named for its white limestone cliffs – with a couple of small brown-sand beaches nearby if you feel like a splash – and, just beyond, you'll pass the fertile **Rozelle** and **Belvedere**. The family of Captain Dow Baker (see p.127) once owned much of this land; today, it's still made up of large sugar cane and papaya plantations, and is the last home of the Jamaican yellow snake, though you've little chance of spotting one.

### Practicalities

You're unlikely to want to stay around here, and **accommodation** options are negligible, except for a great old plantation guesthouse at the foot of the mountains, a few miles north of Llandewey. *Arntully Guesthouse* (☎982 2939; ①) is incredibly peaceful, reachable only by four-wheel drive and visited by very few people, with comfortable rooms and an attractive verandah; bring your own food. Don't expect gourmet **cuisine** anywhere en route, but you can normally get decent Jamaican meals at the *Ackee Tree* restaurant in White Horses or the *A & I* restaurant in Yallahs, where you'll also find several good jerk stalls.

# Morant Bay, Lyssons and Retreat

The dusty town of **MORANT BAY**, parish capital of St Thomas, is perhaps best known for having witnessed some of the ugliest moments in Jamaica's post-emancipation history. Edna Manley's life-size, grim-faced **statue** of national hero Paul Bogle stands in the town square where he was hanged after leading the 1865 **Morant Bay Rebellion** (see box), and a plaque on the nearby courthouse honours the "patriots" who died alongside him. Bogle and the others are buried behind the courthouse, built on the site of the old courthouse razed in the rebellion. There is a monument to them and,

---

### The Morant Bay Rebellion

A generation after emancipation, living conditions for Jamaica's black population were still extremely difficult. High unemployment and heavy taxation hit the poor hard, and the transition to a free society was hindered by the bias of the authorities. Courts invariably supported white landholders in cases for trespass or squatting against the small farmers, who struggled to find decent land to cultivate, and there were frequent outbreaks of rioting across the island. Some of these were over rumours of re-enslavement, others were protests at taxes, food shortages or lack of access to property, and it was only a matter of time before they would spiral out of control.

*Paul Bogle Day is celebrated every year in Morant Bay on October 11.*

In St Thomas, local Baptist preacher **Paul Bogle** – supported **by George William Gordon**, a wealthy mulatto member of the National Assembly – began to organize demonstrations against the inequity of the legal system. In August 1865, he led a group that marched 45 miles to Spanish Town to protest to the island's governor, Edward Eyre – Eyre refused to meet them. On October 7, Bogle and his supporters went en masse to the Morant Bay courthouse, trying to disrupt the proceedings against local men. The authorities saw their chance to arrest a troublemaker and issued warrants for Bogle's arrest, but the police who tried to capture him were attacked by a mob and forced to swear oaths of loyalty to Bogle before they could escape.

On October 11, Bogle and his men marched into Morant Bay from nearby Stony Gut, raiding the police station before attacking the courthouse where the local council was meeting. Eighteen soldiers and council members were killed as the crowd's frustration erupted, with the courthouse burned and looting widespread through the town, and the rioting quickly spread throughout St Thomas. The government, fearing that the whole country would soon be engulfed, gave free rein to the army to stop the riots, and the protesters were crushed with brute ferocity. A staggering 430 people were executed, including Bogle and Gordon; another six hundred men and women were flogged and over a thousand homes razed to the ground.

The rebellion marked a key political and social watershed for Jamaica. Governor Eyre, the man behind the repression, was immediately recalled to England and fired. Jamaica's constitution was suspended and replaced with direct rule from the home country, allowing British governors to impose reforms, for example in education and the legal system, that would never have got past the local elite under previous governments. Although progress for the poor was still painfully slow, Jamaica remained relatively peaceful until well into the next century.

---

nearby, a number of old cannons from the **British fort** that once stood on this spot. There's not much else to the town, though walk west past the attractive **Anglican church** – across the square from the courthouse – and you'll reach the crowded daily **market**, bursting out of its long-standing home and a good place to pick up fresh fish and vegetables.

The coastal road runs below the main part of the town; to get to the square, turn uphill at the smart *Morant Villas Hotel* (☎982 2418; ②) and the road leads up to South Street, where you can park by the court-thouse. The **hotel** itself is fine, though there's not much reason to stay in town when you can stay on two lovely beaches just to the east. **Lyssons** and **Retreat** are golden stretches of palm-fringed sand that easily outshine the rest of this coastline. In Lyssons, the *Golden Shore Beach Hotel* (☎982 9657; ②), at the end of the track opposite the *Forever* supermarket, offers the best value, with a pretty private beach and a small gazebo bar. Retreat has the more elegant, though rather soulless, *Whispering Bamboo Cove* (☎982 1788; ③), again with its own beach, and the prominent but slightly chaotic *Goldfinger Guest House* (☎982 2644; ②). Meals are available at each of these places, with self-catering also an option at *Goldfinger*. All these hotels are popular with European backpackers.

For **food**, the restaurant at the *Morant Villas Hotel* is among the best in the area, with inexpensive local dishes of fried fish and chicken. The *Chef's Sea View* on the Lyssons road is also good, and both venues offer occasional **live reggae shows** in the evenings. Should you be in Morant Bay on October 11, **Paul Bogle Day** is celebrated with a road race starting from his home village of Stony Gut, six miles away, and there is a big party in the town square.

# Bath

Heading east from Morant Bay, a road cuts inland at Port Morant. Six miles from the coast, and right on the edge of a jungle, the little-visited village of **BATH** was born when a runaway Spanish slave stumbled across some hot mineral springs here in 1609. He found that the springs cured wounds he had incurred during his escape and, slowly, the word spread. After the British took Jamaica, they carved a road through the hills from the coast to get here (still an exceptionally pretty drive today) and erected a spa building in 1747.

Colonists came from all over the island to treat their various ailments, the wealthy built their fashionable summer homes nearby, and for a while in the early 1700s Bath glittered in the spotlight. However, the atmosphere was soon soured by disputes between political factions (specifically, supporters of the Jacobite and Hanoverian dynasties competing for the throne back in England), hurricane damage also took its toll, and Bath fell from favour. By the late eighteenth century, it had become a ghost town, with only ten residents. Today, it's a quiet and rather backward country village,

**St Thomas**

surrounded by jungle (see below), with a straggle of visitors coming to take the waters. You may run into the odd tourist or someone up from Kingston taking treatment for rheumatism or arthritis, but it's just as likely that you'll have the place to yourself.

Reached along a one-mile road from the town centre, the **spa** (daily dawn to dusk; J$40) now adjoins the rambling old *Bath Fountain Hotel* (☎982 8410; ②), with a dozen small cubicles each housing a sunken tiled bath. There are natural hot and cold springs a little way up the Sulphur River, which flows past the hotel, and the two are diverted to the spa and mixed to provide you with water at a tolerable temperature. The water is high in sulphur and lime and, like most mineral baths, slightly (though not, they insist, dangerously) radioactive. The charge covers use of a towel and a twenty-minute bath (any longer is not recommended in case you dehydrate).

To explore some of the nearby **jungle** – a thick forest of trees, vines and lianas spreading for miles on either side of the river – head up into the hills along the path running parallel to the river. Just beyond the spot where the hot water is piped as it comes out of the rock, you can scramble down the bank to swim in the river. Waterfalls tumble prettily through the trees, and hiking trails (see p.142) lead from here for miles across the Blue Mountains and into Portland; knowledgeable guides are scarce, but the hotel may be able to help.

At the bottom of road to the hotel and spa are the **Bath Botanical Gardens** (daily dawn to dusk; free). The gardens were established in 1779, a small patch of land where many plants – including cinnamon, jacaranda, bougainvillea and mango – were first introduced to the island. For a century or more, this was a thriving little spot, but the ravages of time and Hurricane Gilbert have ensured that little remains of the original, carefully ordered scheme. None of the trees is labelled anymore, but you'll see descendants of the **breadfruit trees** first brought from Tahiti by Captain Bligh of HMS Bounty in 1793. The gardens also house guava trees, royal palms, bamboo and crotons, and it is a pleasant and shady spot to stroll for fifteen minutes or so and test your botanical knowledge.

*See p.132 for more on Captain Bligh and the breadfruit.*

### Practicalities

A daily **bus** (2hr 30min) runs to Bath from the Parade in Kingston; buses from Port Antonio will only get you as far as Port Morant, where you can connect with the Kingston bus or take a taxi, for a truly beautiful drive through the jungle.

If you want to **stay**, the coral-pink *Bath Fountain Hotel* (☎982 8410; ②) is supremely quiet and old-fashioned, and includes free access to the baths, though the damage to roof and rooms inflicted by Hurricane Gilbert (see box) is only slowly being repaired. The hotel's dining room offers tasty Jamaican **meals** and some excellent fruit juices, and the town also holds a couple of tiny rum shops and snack bars.

**Hurricane Gilbert**

In September 1988 **Hurricane Gilbert** pulverized Jamaica. By the time the carnage had stopped, 45 people had died, 500,000 were left homeless – their tin shacks went down like ninepins – and agriculture was laid waste, with US$50 million worth of damage to banana, coffee, sugarcane and other crops. Sections of the Blue Mountains were denuded as the winds uprooted trees and hurled them down the slopes and, with electricity out for days, looting was widespread, particularly in Kingston. Aid poured into the island – US$125 million from the USA alone – and, in many parts of the island, particularly the main tourist areas, life returned to normal with remarkable speed. However, in the hardest-hit eastern parishes of Portland and St Thomas, it has taken a lot longer to repair the damage, and even today you can still find traces of Gilbert, as at the *Bath Fountain Hotel* (see opposite), still under renovation a decade on.

## The southeastern corner

Back on the coast, the tiny fishing village of **PORT MORANT** was a key harbour and shipping point during the eighteenth century, protected in its heyday by several bristling forts that dotted the coastline. The forts are now long gone and, except when the fishing boats are unloading their shiny catch, the place has a sleepy and rather melancholy feel.

East of here, the main highway skirts the far southeastern corner of the island, and it's a gorgeous six-mile drive – a seamless feast of banana, sugar and coconut plantations – to the next village, the shabby, run-down settlement of **GOLDEN GROVE**. You won't want to stop here, but a quick detour south will bring you to **Rocky Point Bay**, one of the best and most secluded beaches in this part of the country. A sizeable fleet of small fishing boats is based here, normally out from dawn until the early afternoon when some of their catch starts frying at the bar. Tourists are extremely rare – expect your presence to provoke considerable curiosity – and you can stroll for miles down the beach without bumping into a soul.

Also starting at Golden Grove, a track leads out to the hundred-foot **Morant Point lighthouse** (open daily; free), cast in London, England in 1841. The lighthouse marks the easternmost point of Jamaica and was put up here by Kru men from Sierra Leone, among the first free Africans to be brought to the island after the abolition of slavery. It's a deserted and windswept spot, but you won't find anywhere else on the island so serenely isolated, and you can climb the lighthouse and look out over the bay and back to the Blue Mountains.

Continuing north from Golden Grove, the road leads uphill, with a magnificent panorama behind you over pretty **Holland Bay** and the mangrove swamps of the **Great Morass**. A little further on, **Hector's River**, halfway up Jamaica's east coast, marks the boundary between Portland and St Thomas.

# Portland

**Portland**, north of the Blue Mountains, is generally considered the most beautiful of Jamaica's parishes – a rain-drenched land of lush foliage, sparkling rivers and waterfalls. **Port Antonio** is the main resort and your most likely destination; it's a small and not particularly attractive town but it makes a good base for sightseeing and there are a couple of fine **beaches** a short ride away. The waterfalls at **Somerset Falls** and (a bit further afield) the gorgeous **Reach Falls** are within striking distance while, if you head into the interior, you can be poled down the **Rio Grande** on a bamboo raft or hike through the rainforest along the centuries-old trails of the Windward Maroons. An increasing number of visitors are venturing east of Port Antonio for the more laid-back pleasures of **Long Bay** – with a growing young travellers' scene and the best surf in Jamaica – while the roadside vendors in **Boston Bay** continue to offer some of the most authentic jerk pork in the country in a dazzling oceanside setting.

SOME HISTORY

Even after the conquest of Jamaica by Britain in 1655, Portland was one of the last of Jamaica's parishes to be settled. Although its obvious capital-to-be, Port Antonio, blessed with two natural harbours, was superbly located for trade and defence, reports of the difficult terrain and the constant threat of Maroon warfare deterred would-be settlers. Eventually, the Crown was obliged to offer major incentives, including grants of land, tax exemptions and free food supplies, before the parish was officially formed in 1723.

Like the rest of the country, Portland's early economy was dependent on sugar, with large estates scattered around the parish. However, as the industry declined in the nineteenth century, Portland's fertile soil proved ideally suited for the surprise replacement crop – **bananas** (see box). As the country's major banana port, Port Antonio boomed, ushering in a golden era of prosperity for the town and the region. Steamer lines and businessmen poured in from Europe and North America and, in 1905, the town's first **hotel** was built on the Titchfield peninsula. Cabin space on the banana boats was sold to curious tourists, who found themselves rubbing shoulders with the rich and famous – publishing magnate William Randolph Hurst, banker J.P. Morgan, actress Bette Davis et al – swanning in on their private yachts.

The reign of the banana was to prove relatively short-lived – blighted by hurricane damage and Panama disease from South America – but the high-end tourism it had helped to engender soon became a key revenue-earner. With the enthusiastic patronage of movie stars like Errol Flynn (see p.139), Port Antonio's place in the glitterati's global playground was assured. The first luxury hotel in

Jamaica, *Frenchman's Cove*, was built here, and remains a testament to faded glamour to this day.

Celebrities still sequester themselves in Portland and there's a burgeoning backpacker scene at Long Bay, but the area can't yet compete for the mainstream vacationer, losing out to the more accessible and better-marketed resorts of Montego Bay, Negril and Ocho Rios. Agriculture is still important, though, and the region's lush vegetation provides vast amounts of fruit and vegetables for domestic and export markets. The movie business, too, periodically injects much-needed cash into the economy – recent films shot here include *Cocktail, The Mighty Quinn, Clara's Heart* and *Lord of the Flies* – but the area is a long way from the prosperity of its heyday.

---

### Bananas

First brought to Jamaica from the Canary Islands as early as 1520, the **banana** was long considered an unpalatable vegetable, fit only for animals and slaves. The turning-point in its popularity came in 1871, when sea-captain **Lorenzo Dow Baker** took a shipload of bananas from Port Antonio to Boston to see whether he could drum up any interest for the fruit in the United States. His gamble paid off handsomely – he had barely unloaded the crates before the entire stock was sold for a healthy profit, setting off a mass demand for the "new" fruit that would bring him (and others like him) colossal fortunes over the next couple of decades.

With sugar already in decline by the second half of the nineteenth century, Jamaica's farmers rushed to plant the new crop of "green gold", and Portland's high rainfall and fertile soil secured its position as the island's leading production centre. Banana production went ballistic, with output hitting highs of around thirty million stems per year. With little employment available elsewhere, armies of workers arrived from all over the country to earn the pitiful sustenance wages available to planters and pickers, who lived in wretched conditions on the edge of the plantations.

The arrival of banana ships at the wharves was signalled by blasts on a conch shell throughout the interior, followed by frenetic activity as the labourers cut the stems and carried the fresh fruit off the estates and onto the waiting trucks. At the dock the bananas were unloaded from the trucks and taken to the checkers, who ensured that the stem had the nine hands of bananas required for it to count as a bunch – hence, in the banana boat song, *Day O*, "six hands, seven hands, eight hands, bunch!". Once the stem was carried aboard the ship, the tallyman gave the carrier a tally to redeem for pay later, and the workers made their weary way back to the plantation or to the nearest bar.

Sadly for Portland, the boom didn't last for long. By the 1920s, a combination of disease and hurricane damage had decimated Jamaica's banana crops, and the decline was compounded by the disruption of shipping during World War II. Nevertheless, the precious banana remains the country's second most important official agricultural commodity (behind sugar) and still accounts for around four percent of Jamaica's total exports.

# Port Antonio

**PORT ANTONIO**, a magnet for foreign visitors during the 1950s and 1960s, today feels like an isolated backwater and a bit bad-tempered with it. A quiet and rather shabby settlement, there's not a huge amount to see, nightlife is fairly quiet and there is little in the way of watersports or shopping. But, to be frank, you're not here for the town. The highlight of this area is the great **outdoors** – waterfalls, river trips, hiking, splendid tropical scenery and some lovely beaches – and Port Antonio is the perfect base for exploring it all.

### Arrival and information

Flights arrive at **Ken Jones Aerodrome**, six miles west of town in St Margaret's Bay, from where a taxi into the centre costs around J$300. **Buses** and **minibuses** from Kingston (3hr 30min) and Montego Bay (5hr) pull in at the main terminus by the seafront on Gideon Avenue or by the town's central square on West Street (which also serves as the main taxi rank). If you're **driving**, the A4 highway runs straight into and through the town, whether you're coming from the east or the west.

The **Jamaica Tourist Board** office (☎993 3051) is upstairs at the City Centre Plaza on Harbour Street, although it doesn't have much in the way of local information, just a few scant brochures on hotels and attractions.

### Getting around

Port Antonio is a small town and its position, sandwiched between the mountains and the sea, makes it easy to navigate. One good way to get your bearings is to head up to the *Bonnie View Hotel* (see p.131), high above the town and with great views of the area. You can comfortably **walk** between the handful of sights in a couple of hours, while most places of interest outside town (and all of the beaches) can be reached by **public transport**. Shared taxis run along the main road as far as Boston Bay, or occasionally to Long Bay, for a maximum of J$40; most drivers are amenable to a small detour for a little extra cash, say to the beaches at Dragon Bay or Fairy Hill, although your fellow passengers might not be too amused. Because you'll want to

---

**Safety and harassment**

Most visitors find Port Antonio something of a relief after the harassment of the north coast, and any hassle you do encounter tends to be fairly half-hearted. There is also a relatively low crime rate, despite the odd night-time robbery on the Titchfield peninsula. Even so, it is worth taking the normal precautions: don't flash wads of cash around or wander off the main streets after dark. For some reason, the police quite often set up roadblocks east of town and it's not unusual for tourists to have their cars searched for drugs. If this happens to you, be helpful and friendly and you shouldn't be detained long.

---

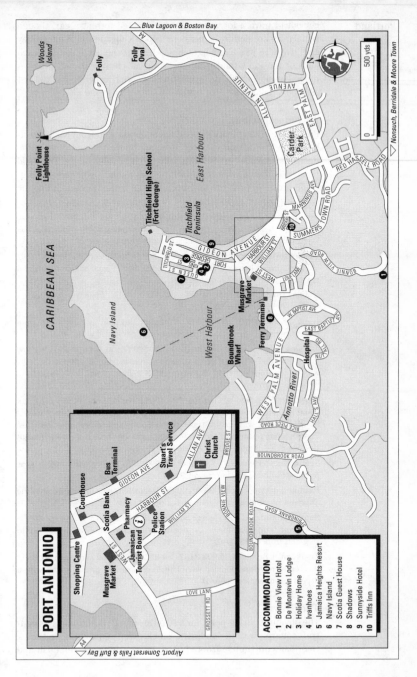

# PORT ANTONIO

**ACCOMMODATION**

1. Bonnie View Hotel
2. De Montevin Lodge
3. Holiday Home
4. Ivanhoes
5. Jamaica Heights Resort
6. Navy Island
7. Scotia Guest House
8. Shadows
9. Sunnyside Hotel
10. Triffs Inn

get out of town a lot, you might be tempted to rent a **car**, though rental rates are slightly higher here than in Kingston and Montego Bay and, if you're just planning a single trip for the day – say to Reach Falls or the Rio Grande – it can work out cheaper to use a taxi. A **moped** or **motorbike**, if you can find one, is a cheaper option and just as handy, though, as ever, watch out for potholes and mad drivers.

## Accommodation

Port Antonio has plenty of good **accommodation**, from basic guest-houses to Errol Flynn's former residence on Navy Island. Most of the inexpensive places are in town, with the best value on the Titchfield peninsula, though watch yourself here at night. If you can afford it, you'll probably prefer to stay in one of the better hotels that line the coast for around eight miles east of Port Antonio (see p.137).

**Bonnie View Hotel**, Bonnie View Rd; ☎993 2752, fax 993 2862. Fantastic views over the twin harbours from this long-standing hotel, which also has lovely gardens and a nice pool, but is overpriced and in need of renovation. ⑤.

**De Montevin Lodge**, 21 Fort George St; ☎993 2604. Good value in a lovely old gingerbread house, a relic from colonial days. Clean, simple rooms and great food from the restaurant downstairs. ③.

**Holiday Home**, 12 King St; ☎993 2882. Comfortable, friendly guesthouse on the Titchfield peninsula. ②.

**Ivanhoes**, 9 Queen St; ☎993 3043. Clean and tidy no-frills guesthouse opposite the ruins of the old *Titchfield Hotel*, and pretty good value. ②.

**Jamaica Heights Resort**, Spring Bank Rd; ☎993 2156, fax 993 3563. Mellow guesthouse that offers excellent value in a great location high up in the hills, with its own "private" river and waterfall, as well as a small pool. Taxis from town charge around J$200. ④.

**Navy Island**, reached by ferry from the West Street harbour; ☎993 2667, fax 993 2667. Ten smart but overpriced cottages on a private island, once owned by Errol Flynn, with nature trails, tennis courts and several quiet beaches. There's a fine restaurant, though most cottages also have self-catering facilities. Room No. 1 and the Top House have the best views. ⑥.

**Scotia Guest House**, 15 Queen St; ☎993 2681). Very basic option near *Ivanhoes* with rooms starting at US$8. ①.

**Shadows**, 40 West St; ☎993 3823. Fairly simple rooms in an annexe to the *Shadows* restaurant and nightclub, but decent value. ②.

**Sunnyside Hotel**, 5 Fort George St; ☎993 9788. Basic place opposite the *De Montevin Lodge*, just above the ocean. Rooms, several of which look out to sea, start from US$8. ①–②.

**Triffs Inn**, 1 Bridge St; ☎993 2162, fax 993 2062. Good mid-range option in the centre of town, popular with Jamaican business travellers, and with a decent restaurant attached. ③.

## The Town

The obvious starting-point for a stroll around Port Antonio is its **central square**, with a landmark **clocktower** opposite a red-brick Georgian **courthouse** fronted by an elegant fretwork verandah and always milling with people. Due north from here, the **Titchfield peninsula** juts out into the Caribbean Sea, bisecting Port Antonio's **twin harbours**. The tip of the peninsula once held the British **Fort George**, whose ancient cannons and crumbling walls today form part of Titchfield High School, alive with noisy open-air lessons and frenetic games of football and netball. The short wander up from town takes you past the **De Montevin Lodge** hotel – high-Victorian gingerbread architecture at its best – and the ruins of the **Titchfield Hotel**, Port Antonio's first and once owned by Errol Flynn.

Just below the clocktower, on West Street, compact **Musgrave Market** is the liveliest spot in town, friendly, easy-going and crammed with stalls. Fresh fruit and vegetables are the market's strong point, but there's also a busy trade in fish, meat and clothes, and a handful of crafts and souvenirs. The rest of West Street reeks of faded glory; particularly nostalgic are the once beautiful wooden house at no. 21 – now home to a small art gallery – and the office of the local MP opposite.

Further up West Street, past the **ferry terminal** for Navy Island (see below), **Boundbrook Wharf** is still the loading point for bananas being shipped to Europe and the United States. This is the place that inspired the banana boat song *Day O* – "Work all night for a drink of rum, daylight come and me wanna go home" – though the back-breaking work is now much simplified, with the bananas packaged centrally and mechanically loaded at the wharf.

Back in town, the red-brick Anglican **Christ Church** on Bridge Street, Romanesque in design, is the most prominent of Port Antonio's many churches. Built on the site of an earlier church in 1840, its numerous memorials date as far back as the late seventeenth century. The eagle lectern was donated in 1900 by the Boston Fruit Company, a firm owned by Captain Dow Baker (see p.127) which owed its foundation and much of its profits to the trade in bananas between Port Antonio and North America. You'll probably be grabbed by one of the ancient assistants who guard the church and dish out nuggets of local history to visitors – expect a request for a donation.

Across the road from the church, a stiff half-mile walk up Bonnie View Road takes you to the **Bonnie View Hotel**. A long-established, though rather run-down hotel (see p.130), this is a great place to head on arrival as the views are magnificent. From the front you look over the town and the twin harbours while, from the lovely back garden, you can see into the heart of the Blue Mountains. Hiking trails into the hills start from here and, with a bit of advance notice, the hotel can organize half-day horse-back tours of the area (from US$30 per person).

## NAVY ISLAND

The largest of the small islands that dot the Portland coast, **NAVY ISLAND** is a five-minute boat ride from the mainland. The British navy used it for storage and barracks in the early eighteenth century – hence the name – and Captain Bligh landed here in 1793, bringing

Portland

See p.139 for
the full
swashbuckling
Errol Flynn
story.

breadfruit plants from Tahiti. A later adventurer, Errol Flynn, came to Port Antonio in 1947 and, taken with the beauty of the island, immediately bought it as a private retreat for entertaining Hollywood starlets. Local legend – one of the myriad Flynn myths – says that he lost it in a poker game less than a decade later.

Today, the 64 acres are home to an upmarket **hotel** (see p.130), once Flynn's home, with a small **gallery** covered in posters and stills from his movies; outside, the wreck of his fishing boat sits mournfully by the water's edge. Elsewhere, some gentle nature trails carve through the island's lush vegetation, where you can spot ducks, cows and egrets among the coconut-palms (watch out for mosquitoes if it has been raining). There are a couple of good **beaches**, each with its own bar; the north beach (nudist only) is slightly the better of the two, though it gets very narrow at high tide.

---

### The breadfruit and the Bounty

Up until the late eighteenth century, Jamaica – like most of the West Indian islands – was not self-sufficient in food, relying on imports (particularly from North America) to feed the ever-increasing slave population. As a result, the American War of Independence (1775–81), which severely disrupted food supplies, brought tragedy to the islands, with thousands of slaves dying of malnutrition and related disease. To eliminate this catastrophic dependence, planters immediately lobbied the British government for a source of cheap food that could be grown in the islands, with the starchy, nourishing **breadfruit** – about which the great explorer Captain Cook had rhapsodized, "if a man plants ten of them . . . he will completely fulfil his duty to his own and future generations" – top of their wish list. In due course, the British designated *HMS Bounty* to bring breadfruit plants from their native Tahiti, and appointed one **Captain William Bligh** to command it.

Setting sail from England in 1787, the *Bounty* arrived in Tahiti the following year after a long and dangerous journey around Cape Horn, and captain and crew were treated as royalty by the islanders, garlanded with flowers and showered with gifts and hospitality. But Bligh had little time to waste, and insisted on loading up the breadfruit plants and moving on. Three weeks later, facing another arduous crossing under a captain who seemed to care more for his plants than for his men, the ship's crew, led by second-in-command Fletcher Christian, mutinied. Bligh was cast adrift in the middle of the Pacific Ocean with a handful of loyal followers, while Christian and his acolytes made for Ascension Island and their place in history.

Incredibly, Bligh survived. He eventually found his way back to England, where he was cleared of any blame for the loss of the *Bounty* and entrusted with command of another ship, *HMS Providence*, to complete his mission. The Jamaican House of Assembly voted him a substantial gift of 500 guineas to encourage his endeavours on their behalf, and the *Providence* left England in 1791, finally delivering the breadfruit to the island in February 1793. The plants were sent on to Bath Botanical Gardens (see p.123) for propagation, and eventually spread throughout the island, an important step towards Jamaican self-sufficiency.

Ferries make the trip roughly every hour from the West Street pier; the J$50 charge includes the return journey and use of the facilities.

## Eating

A number of inexpensive **restaurants** in town offer a standard Jamaican menu, and there are cheap Italian and Chinese options, too. If you're after something more international, you'll need to head east of town to the Blue Lagoon or one of the ritzier hotels (see p.138).

**Caribbean Hut**, Allan Ave. Great, spicy jerk chicken and other inexpensive fast food in this brightly painted hut just over the bridge going east out of town.

**Cartoons**, 15 West St. A good place to pick up snacks during the day, with filling patties, home-made cakes, ice creams and fruit juices.

**Daddy Dee's**, 17 West St. Popular, inexpensive local restaurant offering hearty breakfasts, brown fish stew, curried goat, fried chicken and fresh fruit juices.

**De Montevin Lodge**, 21 Fort George St; ☎993 2604. A great spot for good-value traditional Jamaican food – like pepperpot soup and escovitched fish – served in a charming old dining room.

**Golden Happiness**, corner of Harbour and West streets. The best Chinese food in town, with a huge menu of chop suey, sweet and sour and masses more, and very cheap to boot.

**Huntress Marina**, West St. Great place to hang out on the waterfront, with grilled lobster as good and as reasonably priced as you'll find anywhere.

**Jah Mek Yah**, Allen Ave. Small, functional takeaway café beyond *Caribbean Hut*, dishing up spicy fish, chicken and festival.

**Shadows**, 40 West St. Excellent omelettes and good Jamaican meals served at a pleasant bar with gazebo or in the smarter, less atmospheric restaurant.

**Survival Beach**, Allan Ave. Tiny hut on the beach, quarter of a mile past *Caribbean Hut*, selling inexpensive fish and vegetarian food.

**Trattoria Romagna**, above *Mutual Security Bank* on West St. Inexpensive, good-quality pizzas and pasta.

*In restaurant listings, we have given a phone number only for those places where you might need to **reserve** a table.*

## Drinking, nightlife and entertainment

Port Antonio suffers from a shortage of good places to **drink**, and the few places that exist are often very quiet. The oceanfront *Huntress Marina* on West Street normally has the most people and atmosphere, while the terrace at the *Bonnie View Hotel* offers spectacular views. The *Square View Pub* in the main square is a small local hangout with the cheapest drinks in town; *Tensi's*, above *Homelectrix* on West Street, is also popular with locals. *Shadows* (see above) is a little more salubrious, with bars upstairs and down and an odd, rather restrained disco for the older swinger.

On the **club** scene, the colourful *Roof Club* at 11 West St (daily; J$50) is the busiest spot most nights of the week (though rarely before midnight); DJs pump out the latest dancehall and reggae, with the occasional oldies night, and there's a staggering list of cocktails at the bar. *Lexus*, almost directly opposite (Wed–Sun; J$50), is a less spectacular alternative, with similar sounds and a big crowd on Friday and Saturday. *Blue Jays*, west of town at 24 Boundbrook Road, sometimes has live **bands** at the weekends. If you're around in August, you should catch the lively **Portland Jamboree** (details on ☎933 3051), which wakes the place up with concerts, parades and parties. In October, the **prestigious Port Antonio Blue Marlin Tournament** (☎933 3051) attracts serious anglers who carouse the streets in the evenings.

## Listings

**Airlines** *Air Jamaica Express*; ☎923 6664.

**Airport enquiries** The information number for Ken Jones Aerodrome is ☎993 2405.

**American Express** *Stuarts Travel*, Tunnel Plaza, Harbour Street (☎993 2609).

**Banks and money** There are plenty of banks along Harbour and West streets. Outside regular opening hours, *Citizens Bank* at 28 Harbour St (☎993 9755) is open on Saturday morning, while *ScotiaBank*, at Harbour St, is open until 4pm on Friday. Slightly better exchange rates are available at the town's cambios; one is upstairs at the *Ekklesia* supermarket on Harbour Street, another at *Kamals* on West Street.

**Car and bike rental** *Derron's* (☎993 7111), east of town at Drapers, will deliver to your hotel, as will the more reliable *Don's* at the *Trident Hotel* (☎993 2241); prices start at US$70 per day plus insurance. *Olimett*, 5 Market Square (☎993 9799), has scooters and motorbikes from US$30 per day, while *Sea Coast Bikes* on West Street (☎993 9330) sometimes has bicycles from US$9 per day.

**Doctors** There are several clinics on Harbour Street, including Dr Adams at no. 6 (☎993 3742) and Dr Parvataneni at no. 1 (☎993 3578).

**Hospital** The public hospital is on Nuttall Road; ☎993 2646.

**Laundry** The *Town Talk* store, next to the library on Harbour Street (☎993 9847), has the only drop-off/pick-up service in town.

**Library** The Portland Parish Library is at 1 Harbour St (Mon–Fri 9am–7pm; Sat 9am–1pm; J$100 deposit; ☎993 2793).

**Pharmacy** The *City Centre Plaza Pharmacy* (Mon–Sat 9am–7pm) is opposite *Scotiabank* on Harbour Street.

**Police** The main station is on Harbour Street (☎993 2546). Call ☎119 in an emergency.

**Post Office** The main branch is on Harbour Street opposite the clocktower.

**Shopping** Crafts and souvenirs are sold at the new Port Antonio mall near the clocktower, in Musgrave Market and in the small arcade near *ScotiaBank*. The best supermarket is the *Ekklesia* at 28 Harbour St.

**Taxis** The main rank is in the central square, or call the Port Antonio taxi co-operative (☎993 2684) or *JUTA* (☎993 2684).

**Telephone** The *Call Direct Centre* is opposite *Citizens Bank* at 29 Harbour St (Mon–Sat 8am–10pm, Sun 2–10pm).

**Travel agents** *Stuarts Travel*, Tunnel Plaza, Harbour Street; ☎993 2609.

# East of Port Antonio

The rugged stretch of coast east of Port Antonio is one of the most attractive parts of Jamaica, with some good beaches, a series of smart hotels and authentic jerk cooking at **Boston Bay**. A couple of the beaches, admittedly, are private, but several more – notably **Fairy Hill** and **Dragon Bay** – are free or carry only a nominal entry charge. The **Blue Lagoon** – made famous by the eponymous 1980 movie – is also nearby, and is another great place for a swim.

## The Folly

Perched on Folly Point peninsula, on the eastern coastal outskirts of Port Antonio, the **Folly** is the sorry ruin of what was, briefly, one of the grandest houses in Jamaica. Built in 1902 for American banker Alfred Mitchell and widely applauded as a model of mock-Grecian architecture, the concrete house was a model of ostentation – until the roof collapsed in 1935, a victim of shoddy construction and the shortsighted use of saltwater in the cement mix, and the place was left to decay. Only the pillars and half a staircase remained standing, and today, graffiti-daubed and strewn with litter, they form a grim testament to lost glamour. Quirky and evocative, the shell's dramatic presence is not lost on film-makers, and you'll see it in movies and in pop videos by the likes of Shabba Ranks and the Fugees.

Just across the water, tiny **Woods Island** was once joined to the mainland by a stone causeway, and Mitchell had a small zoo built on it for his pet monkeys. Nothing remains from that time, but swimmers can cover the short distance to create their own private retreat. Take care if you're swimming – undercurrents can be strong.

## Trident Castle, Frenchman's Cove and San San

Looming up suddenly as you make your way east, the fantasy **Trident Castle** is the most prominent landmark for miles around – a huge, white Disney-like edifice with each of its gleaming towers topped by a pointed roof. The castle began life in the 1970s as a rel-

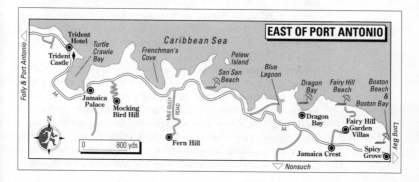

atively modest home for a European baroness with big land-holdings in the area. She was forced to sell after running into financial trouble, and the new owners got increasingly carried away with elaborate additions. Robust enough to have survived Hurricane Gilbert with barely a lost slate, the castle is occasionally rented out for private functions but is not otherwise open to the public.

Continuing east, **Frenchman's Cove** is the erstwhile site of one of the area's most famous hotels, home from home for royalty and A-list celebrities during the 1950s and 1960s. The once sumptuous hotel has deteriorated (though there is talk of reopening) but the **beach** (J$50) is still maintained and very popular, with food and drink vendors doing the rounds in the afternoon. The easily missed entrance is opposite the turn-off to the *Fern Hill Hotel*.

Two miles east, **San San** is a narrow but gorgeous strip of white sand beside a wide crescent bay. Access rules vary from year to year; it's presently open only to residents of certain exclusive hotels but, particularly when it's quiet, you may still be able to talk your way on. Just across from here is the tiny but beautiful **Pelew Island**, great for snorkelling or lazing if you're up to the swim out there.

## The Blue Lagoon, Dragon Bay and Fairy Hill

The **Blue Lagoon** is where 14-year-old nymphet Brooke Shields (and the now obscure cherub Christopher Atkins) – child castaways on a desert island – frolicked naked in the movie of the same name. There's no beach, but it's a peaceful place to swim, if a little cold (the lagoon is fed by underwater streams running down from the mountains). The whole effect is very picture postcard, the water a remarkable shade of blue and dropping to 180ft at its deepest spot, surrounded by rocks, trees and flowers. There is a US$3 entry fee for use of the simple facilities – namely shade and a seat – but the charge is knocked off your food bill if you eat at the restaurant (see p.138), which projects out into the sea at the edge of the lagoon.

It's hooray for Hollywood again a couple of miles east at **Dragon Bay**, where a protected sandy beach adjoins the *Dragon Bay Hotel*, half a mile from the main road and normally open to the public (entrance J$50). It offers a lovely cove to swim and snorkel in – the hotel's *Lady G'Divers* (☎993 3281) also offers scuba diving – and access to the self-same beach restaurant and bar where Tom Cruise juggled his bottles in *Cocktail*.

**Fairy Hill** (also known as Winifred's), a mile or so on, is one of the biggest and most appealing public beaches on this side of the island. The wide golden crescent of sand is justly popular with tourists and Jamaicans, and there's a small reef just offshore, perfect for snorkelling (you'll need to bring your own gear) or just lounging in the shallows. The beach has food and drink facilities, changing rooms and a notable absence of hassle, mainly owing to the self-appointed beach-keepers who'll normally ask for a small donation, and is just under a mile from the main road, down the rather bumpy track that starts almost opposite the *Jamaica Crest Resort*.

## Boston Bay

Though blessed with a perfectly good public beach twinkling with fishing boats, **BOSTON BAY** is better known for the **jerk stands** that line its main road every afternoon. Jerking of meat is thought to have originated in this part of the country – the Maroons hunted wild pigs here and smoked the meat to preserve it – and many of Jamaica's premier jerk cooks will tell you that they learned their trade in Boston. Obviously, the top talents have been poached by the tourist centres, but the pork and chicken you'll be offered here is still tasty, succulent and truly authentic. Reckon on around J$100 to J$150 for enough meat and roast breadfruit (an excellent accompaniment) for one person and take your picnic off to the beach. If you've room in your bags, buy a jar of the fiery home-made jerk sauce – you won't find better anywhere.

*See p.28 of Basics for more on jerk cooking.*

*Boston Bay's water can get choppy; if you want to swim you're better off at nearby Fairy Hill (see p.136).*

Buses, minibuses and shared taxis run to Boston Bay from Port Antonio. There are a couple of inexpensive **guesthouses** (see below), but this is a place to eat, not sleep.

## Accommodation

The coastline east of Port Antonio is packed with good **places to stay**, though none is as cheap as you'll find in town. Bear in mind, that transport links around here are poor, and if you don't have a car, you'll be reliant on taxis – expect to pay J$150–200 to Port Antonio from any of these places. All are marked on the map on p.135.

**Dragon Bay**; ☎993 8514, fax 993 3284. One of the best-value options in the area – a large, lively hotel with a small pool, 30 pretty villas and its own white-sand beach. ⑤.

**Fairy Hill Garden Villa**; ☎993 8205 or 3666. Attractive whitewashed villa near the best public beach in the area with four small rooms and a four-bedroom apartment. ③/ ⑥.

**Fern Hill**; ☎993 3222, fax 993 2257. Good-value, slightly ramshackle hillside hotel, with a large airy terrace overlooking San San, spacious grounds, several pools and friendly staff. Just under a mile uphill off the main road. ④.

**Jamaica Palace**; ☎993 2020, fax ☎993 3459. Bizarre fantasy hotel, with the pretensions of a European chateau, a huge black and white tiled patio and a swimming pool in the shape of Jamaica. ⑦.

*Most of the hotels along this stretch have snorkelling equipment for loan or hire.*

**Mocking Bird Hill**; ☎993 7267, fax 993 7133 Eco-friendly hotel, peacefully set in the hills above San San and filled with sculptures and paintings by artist and co-owner Barbara Walker. Great for watching the sun set over the Blue Mountains. ⑤.

**Spicy Grove**; ☎993 8515. Tatty Boston Bay guesthouse that nonetheless offers the cheapest kip on this strip. ②.

**Trident Hotel**; ☎993 2602, fax 993 2590. The epitome of tasteful luxury, with lawns, peacocks and delightful cottages by the sea. A serene and fabulous place to stay if you've got the money. ⑧.

## Portland

### Eating

There's a good selection of **places to eat** on this side of Port Antonio, with a clutch of hotel restaurants at the pricier end, and several good roadside joints if you're on a tight budget.

**Blue Lagoon;** ☎993 8491. Right beside the lagoon and one of the prettiest locations in the country, serving quality jerk meat, fresh fish and lobster. Live jazz on Saturday night. Daily until 10pm Thurs–Sun; lunch only Mon–Wed.

*In restaurant listings, we have given a phone number only for those places where you might need to reserve a table.*

**Fern Hill;** ☎993 3222. Marvellous views and reasonable, moderately priced Jamaican food make this a good lunch spot.

**Jamaica Palace;** ☎993 2020. Elegant, expensive European-style restaurant, big on steaks.

**Mocking Bird Hill;** ☎993 7267. Good, quiet restaurant with a daily vegetarian option and an emphasis on locally grown food.

**Nazarite**, between Folly Point and Trident Castle. Roadside shack, marked by a colourful fruit stall, with Ital food and superb fresh juices. Closed Thurs.

**Trident Hotel;** ☎993 2602. Haute cuisine Jamaica-style at the poshest and priciest option on this coast, with white-gloved waiters and a smart dress code.

**Woody's.** Inexpensive local café, a little way east of *Jamaica Palace*, with good Jamaican staples and an easy-going attitude.

### Drinking and nightlife

You can have a quiet **drink** on the waterfront at the *Blue Lagoon* restaurant (Thurs–Sun only) or in the *Drunken Dragon Pub* at the *Dragon Bay* hotel. Some of the major hotels lay on evening **entertainment**, although they often don't advertise outside the hotel itself, and you'll really need to head into Port Antonio if you're after even half-serious nightlife. *Dragon Bay* has mento and reggae bands several nights a week; bands also play at *Tiffany's* nightclub at the *Jamaica Crest*, an upscale place that pulls a crowd from town at the weekend.

## The Flynn estates, Long Bay and Reach Falls

The stretch below Boston Bay is **Errol Flynn country**. The erstwhile screen idol bought much of the land between Boston Bay and Fair Prospect in the 1950s, and his widow, Patrice Wymore, still manages the 2000-acre estates, growing coconuts and guavas, and raising beef cattle.

### Long Bay

South of here, the main road cleaves to the coastline, offering great views over the surf pounding in on this unprotected side of the island. The major attraction here is **LONG BAY**, where a mini-tourist industry – unusual on the barely developed east coast – is developing. A wide crescent of sand with a laid-back atmosphere and the best surf in Jamaica, the bay has been attracting a smattering of European backpackers for the last decade, some of whom have

### Errol Flynn

By the time he arrived in Jamaica in 1947, **Errol Flynn**'s movie career was already in decline. The era of the swashbuckler was drawing to a close, and the Australian actor – star of classic Hollywood action movies like *The Sea Hawk* and *Captain Blood* – had begun to fall from favour with the studios. Nonetheless, sailing ashore at Kingston in his yacht *Zaca*, Flynn quickly worked his way into local legend. Even today, you'll occasionally find people recounting (increasingly improbable) stories of his strength, powers of seduction, formidable drinking and addiction to gambling – he reputedly lost Navy Island, just off Port Antonio, in one particularly unfortunate bet.

Flynn loved Jamaica. Soon after his arrival, he bought the *Titchfield Hotel* in Port Antonio as well as Navy Island; later, with third wife Patrice Wymore, he set up a ranch near Boston Bay and planned a castle-like home up in the John Crow Mountains. For a while, he threw wild parties at his hotels – pulling a string of celebrities to the island – but unsuccessful efforts to resurrect his movie career and continuing bouts of heavy drinking and ill-health were already taking their toll.

During his final years Flynn spent much of his time in Jamaica, living at Titchfield with the teenage actress Beverley Aadland. At his death in 1959 Aadland asked that he should be buried in Jamaica, but Wymore insisted that his body go to Hollywood. Today, despite the tarnishing of Flynn's reputation over the years, the people of the area remember the one-time heart-throb with considerable affection.

---

settled here and opened guesthouses. The odd bar and disco cater to the demand for entertainment, but it's a far cry from the developed resorts on the north coast. Tourists are outnumbered on the beach by local fishermen and Rastas, and the whole place feels a bit like Negril must have in the 1960s – vaguely alternative, with a lot of dope-smoking and general hanging out.

There isn't much to the village, which seems to have grown up piecemeal on either side of the main road. The north end of the beach is where you'll find Jamaica's premier **surf** scene, though you'd never know it from the paucity of board-rental outlets. The locals propping up the beach bars should be able to help, and they'll also know of anyone who'll take you out **fishing**. **Swimming** is good here, too, but watch out for a dangerous undertow and rip tides. If you stay in Long Bay, try to get up early to catch the **sunrise** over the ocean – it's staggering.

*Negril is covered in Chapter Five; see p.239.*

**Buses** and **minibuses** run to Long Bay from Port Antonio and, less frequently, from Kingston. There's an increasing wealth of budget **accommodation**, though few places have phones so you'll have to turn up and take a chance. The best central options, simple but reliable, are *Seascape* (②) and *Long Bay Chalet* (②), while slightly north is the charmingly rustic *Blue Heaven* (②), and just south is the pretty two-bedroom cottage of *Rose Garden* (③). All will provide **meals** on request, or you can get Ital food at *Lion King* and local dishes at *Sweet Daddy*, both near the central gas station. Evenings in Long Bay are quiet, with just a few beach bars and rum shops to constitute a drinking scene, although the *Bamboo Lawn* bar has an occasional **disco** and, at weekends, the speakers get stacked up by the *Sunset Strip Pub*.

## Reach Falls

South of Long Bay, before crossing the Christmas River, you'll pass the tiny village of **Kensington**, birthplace of Father Hugh Sherlock, who composed Jamaica's national anthem in 1962. Just over the water, the *Ranch Bar* (☎993 6138; ②) is a peaceful place if you need to crash for the night, and offers the only camping in the area (US$6). Almost exactly halfway down Jamaica's east coast, **Reach Falls** (daily dawn to dusk; US$4) is one of the loveliest spots on the island, with the Drivers River running through some sumptuous rainforest before cascading over the falls into a wide, green pool. The thirty-foot waterfall itself is not particularly spectacular – though you might recognize it as the place where Tom Cruise cavorts with his lady love in *Cocktail* – but the hike up the river makes it one of Portland's definite highlights.

The side road to the falls winds for a little over three miles through some dazzling countryside to a small parking lot. The entrance fee includes the cost of a tour guide who will take you on a thirty-minute trek upriver through the rainforest – climbing up beside the waterfall, picking your way across slippery rocks, swimming through deep pools and wading along the riverbed. You can ask to be taken to the base of **Mandingo Cave**, where a trickle of water drops over one hundred feet, though it's quite a tricky climb. You follow the same route returning downriver, ending (if you can muster the courage) with an exhilarating jump into the deep pool at the base of the falls.

Just off the main A4, the falls are only practically accessible by car. A round-trip taxi from Port Antonio costs around US$50, although at quiet times you may be able to persuade a driver to do the job for half that.

## The Rio Grande valley

Portland's interior – the **Rio Grande valley** – is a fantastically lush and sometimes impenetrable hinterland of tropical rainforest, rivers and waterfalls. The **Rio Grande** – one of Jamaica's major rivers – pours down from the Blue Mountains through a deep and beautiful valley. This is real virgin forest, with none of the soil erosion and deforestation found on the south side of the Blue Mountains.

Despite its beauty, the valley is little explored and many people only get as far as the **Nonsuch Caves** on its outskirts. Those tourists who do venture in are here to **raft** the river, though a few are discovering the superb **hiking** options, which range from gentle riverside walks to strenuous overnight pilgrimages up into the mountains. This is Maroon country, and many of the rivers and springs are named after local leaders – Nanny, Quao, Quashie and Quako. The major

*For more on the Maroons, see p.314.*

remaining Maroon settlement is **Moore Town**, though its past is more of a draw than its present, and while some of the other **villages** have a lovely setting and fascinating names – Alligator Church, Comfort Castle – you'll only want to visit if you're craving rustic isolation.

## Nonsuch Caves and Athenry Gardens

Four miles south of Port Antonio, on the outer fringes of the Rio Grande valley, the **Nonsuch Caves and Athenry Gardens** (daily 10am–4pm; J$175) are an obvious and mildly entertaining first stop in the interior. The fourteen ancient subterranean chambers were used by Taino Indians in pre-Columbian times (although their relics were removed to the University of the West Indies long ago), and now house some impressive stalactites and plenty of bats. The guides who shepherd you through the well-lit passages deliver a well-oiled patter, and they'll point out fossils of fish, coral and sea sponges from the days – around one and a half million years ago – when the whole of Jamaica was still underwater. Once you've emerged back into the sunshine, take a stroll around the expansive **gardens** adjacent to the caves; they command a magnificent view over the coastline and are packed with ginger lilies, bougainvillea, royal poinciana trees and the like.

*For more on the Tainos, see p.100.*

The road up to the caves is in a dreadful condition, although your slow progress will allow you to appreciate some spectacular views of the John Crow Mountains.

## Rafting the Rio Grande

Once just an easy way to transport bananas to the loading wharf in Port Antonio, **rafting** down the majestic Rio Grande has been Portland's most popular attraction ever since Errol Flynn began organizing rafting races for his friends in the 1950s. Today, it's a delightfully lazy way to spend half a day – the sun can get fierce, so take a hat or umbrella.

From the put-in point at **Berridale**, six miles southwest of Port Antonio, thirty-foot rafts – made of lengths of bamboo lashed together, with a raised seat at the back that can hold two people and a small child – meander down the river on a three-hour journey through some outstanding scenery before terminating at the *Rafters' Rest* restaurant at St Margaret's Bay (see p.146). The raft captain stands at the front and poles the craft downstream, stopping periodically to let you swim or buy snacks from vendors positioned along the route.

**Tickets** (US$40 per raft) are sold at the put-in spot by *Rio Grande Attractions Ltd* (☎993 2778), or occasionally by hotels and tour groups in Port Antonio. Because it's a one-way trip, **transport** can be a problem. If you're driving, you can leave your car at Berridale and have an insured driver take it down to *Rafters' Rest* for around US$5. A taxi to Berridale and back to Port Antonio from *Rafters' Rest* costs around US$10 each way. If you're desperate to save cash, the

Berridale bus from Port Antonio runs close by the put-in point, and buses to Port Antonio from Kingston and Buff Bay pass the entrance to *Rafters' Rest* approximately once an hour for J$10 each way.

You'll occasionally find people touting **unofficial rafting trips** for a lower price; don't hand over the cash until you've finished the journey at *Rafters' Rest*, and don't go with anyone unless you feel completely comfortable with them.

## Hiking

Although some of the villages they once connected are long gone, the old parish council "roads" provide the basis for a number of **hiking trails** into the Rio Grande valley; others follow traditional pig hunters' routes. Many of them feature occasional reminders of

*Once a sizeable village, **Nanny Town** is today just a scattering of crumbling and overgrown ruins, but remains an important symbol of Maroon history, allegedly haunted with the ghosts of vanquished British soldiers.*

### Some hikes

The hikes listed are merely the most popular, pleasant or spectacular, but there are many more to explore.

**Bath** (8–10 miles; 4–5hr or 6–7hr). Two routes, both starting at Millbank and with swimming holes along the way. The Cuna Cuna Pass is easier, as it's mostly downhill through shady forests, while the longer route through Corn Puss Gap dips and climbs over hills and gullies and is altogether more strenuous with less shade.

**Nanny Town** (10–15 miles; 2 days). A strenuous two-day excursion from Millbank through untouched forest of unparalleled beauty to the site of the eighteenth-century Maroon hideaway, but you'll need determination, a love of nature and a tent to do it.

**Road End** (2 miles; 2hr). From Bowden, this easy hike follows what's left of a road cut by British settlers, now overhung by towering tree ferns and affording great views back into the valley. You pass Three Finger Jack spring and can turn off for a swim in Quako River, then walk back downstream past swimming holes and waterfalls to the meeting point with the Rio Grande. Return on the road or make your way back to Bowden through the bush.

**Scatter Water Falls** (0.75 miles; 20min). The shortest, easiest and most popular hike in the area, usually done from Berridale (see p.141). From Berridale's main "square" steps lead to the Rio Grande river, where a free government ferry drops you on the far bank. From there it's a twenty-minute walk to the falls, following the bank of the Saw River and crossing a small footbridge. There is a bridge (or if it's down, you can wade) to the base of the falls where a fallen tree has created a small pool, good for a dip. A further fifteen-minute hike up the falls leads to the Foxes Caves, which you'll need a flashlight to explore properly.

**White River Falls** (4 miles; 7hr). Starting from Millbank, this great hike traces the beautiful White River for quite a tough climb through virgin rainforest to a series of fabulous high waterfalls. The trail gets slippery and is fairly tough going with lots of uphill scrambling, but at the first fall you get your reward – a swim in the freezing froth. There are seven cascades in all, but most people go only as far as the first two or three.

Maroon occupation, from half-buried sugar pans to the remains of a deserted village above the Quako River.

Hiking in the valley is an entirely different experience to the Blue Mountains. The lower limestone John Crow Mountains are hotter and wetter – a waterproof is essential – and the humidity can make walking uncomfortable, though the proliferation of mineral springs and Rio Grande tributaries means that you're never far from somewhere to cool off.

One or two of the peripheral hikes, such as Road End, listed opposite, can be done on your own, but a **guide** is essential if you're heading deep into the valley. Far and away the best organization is Port Antonio-based *Valley Hikes* (Mon–Sat 9am–5pm; ☎993 3881), an excellent, eco-friendly, non-profit group which charges between US$10 and US$100 per person according to duration – it also rents out boots for US$5. All the guides are local and really know their stuff – they offer all the hikes covered in the box as well as horse-riding excursions (1hr 30min; US$30) and combined rafting and hiking tours (from US$60). The only other reputable organization is Kingston-based *Sun Venture Tours* (☎960 6685), which offers hikes on request along pig hunters' trails (from US$50 per day for lone hikers; US$35 per person for groups of 3–6 or US$70 per person for groups of three on overnight treks).

Valley Hikes *can also be contacted via the* Mocking Bird Hill *hotel; see p.137.*

## Moore Town

Eleven miles inland from Port Antonio, **MOORE TOWN** is Jamaica's principal Maroon settlement, founded, so the legend goes, by the semi-mythical **Nanny** (chieftainess of the Windward Maroons and now a National Hero) in the mid-eighteenth century. Today, it's a small, quiet place at the end of a winding rocky road, with few signs and little apparent sense of its historical importance. The road goes straight into the heart of the village, with houses and small shacks scattered beside it and across the adjacent fields. You should, as a matter of protocol, check in by saying hello to the Maroons' **Colonel** or chief. There are presently two of them: Colonel Harris, a knowledgeable elder whose house is the first on the right after the post office, and Colonel Stirling, to whom leadership was officially passed in 1995, who lives a little further up. There's no charge for looking around, but you may be asked for a donation to a planned (though probably far-off) Maroon museum.

**Bump Grave**, a monument to Nanny and supposedly the site of her grave, is in the town's small central square, and is pretty much the only thing to see. It's a stone tomb, with a plaque to the "indomitable and skilled chieftainess", and the Maroon and Jamaican flags fly side by side overhead. Otherwise, apart from the usual profusion of schoolchildren, Moore Town feels deserted. Many villagers live scattered around the nearby hills, and if you stand on the monument you'll see houses perched in the most unlikely places.

## The Windward Maroons

When the Spanish left Jamaica in 1660, they armed and freed most of their African slaves and encouraged them to fight a guerrilla war against the new British colonists. Over the years, the ranks of these guerrillas – known as "wild ones", or *cimarrones*, corrupted to **Maroons** by the British – were boosted by runaway slaves from the sugar plantations. They set up small communities in inaccessible parts of the island, with the **Windward Maroons** establishing themselves in the Blue Mountains and the Trelawny Maroons making a base in Cockpit Country (see p.236). As they grew in confidence, the Maroons raided British settlements for weapons and supplies and, by the 1720s, they had become such a serious menace that the British decided to send the troops in.

The Windward Maroons had their headquarters high up in the mountains at **Nanny Town**, virtually inaccessible to the British soldiers who were unfamiliar with the area and were periodically slaughtered on their forays into the rainforest. Eventually, in 1734, British army captain Stoddard dragged swivel guns up the south side of the Blue Mountains and bombarded the settlement, scattering the Maroons and forcing them to move south. Still the British couldn't flush them out, though, and five years later a peace treaty was signed, giving the undefeated Maroons a semi-independent status that they retain today, as well as five hundred acres of land in the Rio Grande valley, on which they established their new base at Moore Town (see p.143).

Today, the Windward Maroons have been virtually assimiliated into the wider Jamaican population. Though some of the elders remain fiercely proud of their heritage – and a handful still speak the traditional Coromantee language – most young Maroons see little opportunity in their mountain villages, and move to the cities for work, inter-marrying with other Jamaicans. Within a generation there are likely to be few pure-blood Maroons left.

*The former village of Nanny Town is visitable on an arduous two-day trek from Millbank; see p.142.*

If you're lucky you'll catch a **cricket game** in the grassy square across from the monument – given the precarious position of the pitch at the edge of the Wildcane River, several fielders normally stand up to their ankles in water to catch any well-struck balls before they disappear downstream. Alternatively, you can hike up to **Nanny Falls**, following the track north through town for around forty minutes. A guide will help you to find the best places to swim and can take you on a longer hike through the jungle if you wish; ask around for a suitable person and arrange a fee.

Moore Town is served by two daily **buses** from Port Antonio, one in the early morning, the other early afternoon (J$20 each way). Each bus takes about ninety minutes and comes straight back down, so your best plan is to go up on the first bus and come back on the second. Take a **picnic** as there are no restaurants, and don't miss the bus back as there's nowhere to **stay**; if you get stuck, the colonels might know someone with a room for the night.

### Millbank

Little-visited **MILLBANK** – the last sizeable town in the Rio Grande valley – nestles deep in the John Crow Mountains five miles south of

Moore Town. Sizeable here means a couple of basic shops, a playing field and a community centre, but the town also contains one of the three Blue and John Crow Mountains National Park ranger stations (see p.111). You're in prime Maroon country here, and many of the town's older inhabitants (a healthy diet and clean mountain air mean that many residents are pushing 100) will happily tell you tales of Maroon history, while the younger locals can escort you to derelict Maroon settlements that don't appear on the maps.

Millbank's setting is spectacular; rainforest rises up all around and the perfume of wild ginger lilies hangs heavy in the air. It's also the starting point for several good **hikes**, the most popular (detailed on p.142) heading to **White River Falls**, seven high cascades on the other side of the Rio Grande river.

As the road stops at Moore Town, getting to Millbank involves taking the right fork at Seaman's Valley via **Alligator Church**. You'll pass the diminutive communities of **Ginger House** and **COMFORT CASTLE**, where the *Gingerbread House* **bar** is the area's only source of entertainment, with loud rocksteady and reggae played well into the night. The only **place to stay** in the area is *Ambassabeth Cabins and Campsite* (☎938 5036; ①) at **BOWDEN**, an hour's walk southeast of Millbank – rangers are happy to give you a lift if they have time. The down-to-earth wooden cabins have no electricity or running water but bags of atmosphere and ingenuity, and traditional Maroon meals are prepared on an open fire. Call ahead to arrange transport from Kingston or Port Antonio, and bring your own groceries.

Between Millbank and Bowden, a rope and board **suspension bridge** provides the only dry means of crossing the Rio Grande for miles around and is an important link for locals. Once past *Ambassabeth*, the road widens into an improbably large thoroughfare, built in the late 1970s by British ex-servicemen granted large tracts of crown land. Harsh conditions and lack of modern conveniences prompted a swift exodus and the now grassy track melts abruptly into the bush at Road End, less than a third of the way to its intended destination at Bath.

## West of Port Antonio

The A4 winds prettily west from Port Antonio, criss-crossing an old railway track torn up by Hurricane Allen in 1980. It threads through a series of tiny fishing villages, peppered with stalls selling local fruit and vegetables, and has a couple of good lodging options along the way. You can stop for a splash at **Somerset Falls**, relax at the **Crystal Springs** resort or explore the towns of **Buff Bay** and **Annotto Bay**. Buses run between Port Antonio and Buff Bay every hour or so in both directions and will stop wherever you ask.

### St Margaret's Bay, Somerset Falls and Hope Bay

Heading out of Port Antonio the highway passes through **Norwich** – birthplace of heavyweight boxer Trevor Berbick and occasional home of singer Eartha Kitt – and the tiny village of **ST MARGARET'S BAY**, where the Rio Grande empties into the sea, before reaching **Somerset Falls** (daily 9am–5pm; J$100), part of the cascading Daniels River and often torrential. A concrete stairway provides access to the "cool pool" – a refreshing place to have a dip and slide over the rocks – and, further up, to the main falls where, at quiet times, your entrance fee gets you a boat ride to the spectacular "hidden falls" beyond, otherwise inaccessible but tantalizingly visible from a trail just before the cool pool. Below the falls, there's a **café** and a small farm with geese, ducks and the odd peacock.

The four-mile stretch between St Margaret's Bay and the busy little village of **HOPE BAY** holds a handful of quiet but interesting places to stay. *Rio Vista Villas* (☎993 2244; ③), just east of *Rafters' Rest*, has great views over the Rio Grande and a relaxed atmosphere, while the basic but beautiful *Content* (☎953 2387; ②), in the mountains about three miles south of Hope Bay, offers cottages on a forty-acre farm growing avocados, grapefruit and medicinal herbs. Finally, just west of Hope Bay, the gorgeously located *Swift River Cove Hotel* (no phone; ②) has comfortable rooms and a restaurant, and is the best place in the area for **swimming**, with both the river and black- and white-sand beaches on its doorstep.

St Margaret's Bay has a couple of roadside shacks selling cheap **meals**. Slightly classier, the *Rafters' Rest* restaurant has typical, Jamaican dishes as well as hamburgers and sandwiches. *Burkies* is the best spot for local dishes in Hope Bay.

## Crystal Springs, Buff Bay and Annotto Bay

Heading west from Hope Bay, the **Crystal Springs nature resort** (daily dawn to dusk; free) is a quasi-botanical gardens signposted off the main road just before Buff Bay, on the site of a seventeenth-century sugar plantation. A river runs through the large rambling gardens, where you'll find a fine collection of orchids and an old waterwheel. The **mongoose** was introduced to Jamaica here in 1872, in an attempt to wipe out the cane rats that were wrecking the local sugar harvest. The plan backfired badly as the mongooses, showing more catholic taste than had been anticipated, turned their attention to the island's harmless coneys and iguanas and devastated their respective populations. Mongooses are still all over the place and, if you're driving around the country, you'll often see them legging it across the road with gay abandon.

*Buff Bay is the starting point for a rocky but spectacular drive through the Blue Mountains to Kingston.*

Beyond Crystal Springs is the easy-going town of **BUFF BAY**. There's not a lot to see, but you might want to poke around **St George's** Anglican church, the oldest building in town. There's been a church on this site since 1681, although the present building mostly dates from 1814.

The road continues to **ANNOTTO BAY**, a busy little one-street town named after the annatto dye once produced locally from the pulp of indigenous trees. Pause – or at least slow down – to gasp at the staggering number of churches here, many of them, admittedly, little more than tin shacks daubed with the name of the religious affiliation. The best-looking example is the red and yellow **Baptist church**, built in 1892, its entrance guarded by old cannons, the meagre remains of British Fort George.

The only good **accommodation** along this stretch is at the *Crystal Springs* resort (☎996 1400; ③), with delightful old-fashioned wooden cabins, or camping for US$15. There's a good **restaurant** on the premises, but you're better off at Buff Bay's excellent *Pacesetter*, almost opposite the church, with great curried goat and rice and peas. Annotto Bay has the serviceable *Travel Halt*, with decent patties and juices, and the *Snack Shop*, housed in the old railway station. Nightlife is limited but possible; Annotto Bay's *Roots Club* (daily; no cover) is a colourful disco with occasional go-go dancers, and Buff Bay's *Sea Waves Club*, just east, has been known to rock at the weekend.

# Travel details

### Buses and minibuses

It is impossible to predict accurately the frequency of buses and minibuses in the Blue Mountains and the East – service is often chaotic and delays and cancellations are frequent – so the figures below are only general guidelines. However, on the most popular routes you should be able to count on getting a ride within an hour if you travel in the morning; things normally quieten down later in the day. On less popular routes, you're best off asking for probable departure times the day before you travel.

**Port Antonio to:** Boston Bay (4 daily; 20min); Buff Bay (4 daily; 1hr); Kingston (via Buff Bay, 4 daily; 3hr 30min; via Morant Bay, 2 daily; 4hr 30min); Long Bay (4 daily; 50min); Montego Bay (1 daily; 5hr); Moore Town (2 daily; 1hr 30min); Morant Bay (2 daily; 2hr 30min); Ocho Rios (1 daily; 3hr).

**Morant Bay to:** Kingston (3 daily; 2hr); Port Antonio (2 daily; 2hr 30min).

**Bath to:** Kingston (1 daily; 2hr 30min).

**Papine to:** Mavis Bank (2 daily; 1hr 20min); Newcastle (2 daily; 1hr 10min).

### Flights

**Port Antonio** to: Kingston (1 daily; 20 min); Montego Bay (1 daily; 45min); Negril (1 daily; 1hr 25min).

**Chapter 3**

# Ocho Rios and the north coast

P ot-holed as it is, the **north coast** road is the busiest tourist route on the island. Traffic belts between the most commercial resorts, and hundreds of hotels, bars, jerk stands and craft shacks line up to catch the passing trade. The attraction is obvious, as the road sweeps through the diverse parishes of **St Mary**, **St Ann** and **Trelawny**, past sparse mangrove coastline, luscious farmland

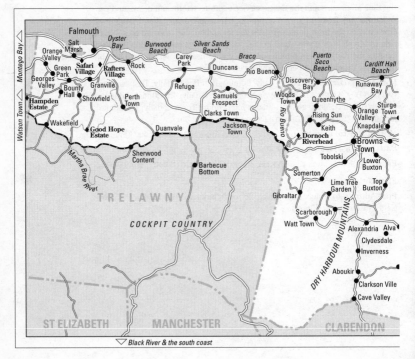

and sweeping cane or coconut plantations, and parallel to miles of white-sand beaches with reefs less than a hundred feet out to sea. Yet the north coast can seem like Jamaica at its most forlorn – many of the sights appear contrived, much of the accommodation is in fenced-in all-inclusives, and the ingrained practice of tourist **hustling** can make every interaction feel like a sales pitch. Nonetheless, the area does offer Jamaica's highest concentration of things to do and a certain energy noticeably absent in more tempered parts.

Much of the tourism development is centred on the "garden parish" of **St Ann**, so called because of the fertile soil and relative flatness that make the land easy to cultivate. The parish has also spawned luminaries such as **Marcus Garvey**, **Bob Marley** and **Winston "Burning Spear" Rodney**, and is widely considered the spiritual centre of the island. The nucleus of St Ann and the home of the famous **Dunn's River Falls**, **Ocho Rios** is fast becoming Jamaica's most popular holiday destination, with all the high-rise blocks, buzzing jet-skis and thumping nightlife you could ask for, while just a few miles to the east, the quiet coastal villages of **Oracabessa** and **Port Maria** are disturbed by little other than birdsong. West of Ocho Rios, **St Ann's Bay**, parish capital and site of ruined Spanish settlement **Sevilla Nueva**, makes a refreshing change to the glitz of its neighbour, while the developing resort towns of **Runaway**

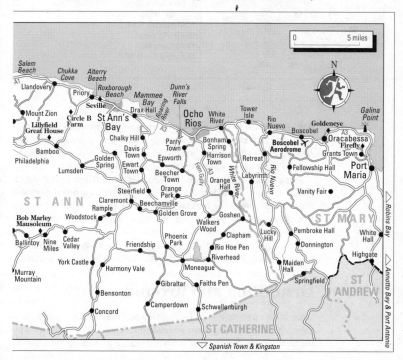

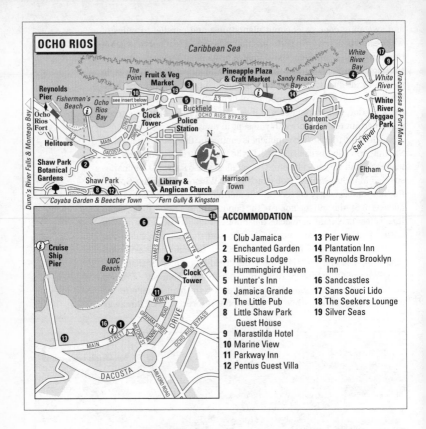

**OCHO RIOS**

Caribbean Sea

White River Bay · **17** · **9** White River

**Oracabessa & Port Maria** ▷

The Point · Fruit & Veg Market · **3** · Pineapple Plaza & Craft Market · Sandy Reach Bay · **4** White River Reggae Park

Reynolds Pier · Fisherman's Beach · **10** · **19** · A3 · White River Reggae Park

Ocho Rios Bay · see insert below · **5** Buckfield · OCHO RIOS BYPASS

Ocho Rios Fort · Clock Tower · Police Station · **15** · Content Garden

Helitours · MAIN · DACOSTA · DRIVE · N · Salt River

Shaw Park Botanical Gardens · **2** · Eltham

Shaw Park · **8** · **12** · Library & Anglican Church · Harrison Town

▽ Coyaba Garden & Beecher Town · ▽ Fern Gully & Kingston

◁ Dunn's River Falls & Montego Bay

**18**

**6**

Cruise Ship Pier

UDC Beach

JAMES AVENUE · EVELYN STREET

**7**

Clock Tower

NEWLIN ST

**11**

**16** · **1**

GRAHAM STREET · MOREST · ANNE · ROAD · OCHO RIOS BYPASS

**13**

MAIN · STREET · DRIVE

DACOSTA · MILFORD ROAD

### ACCOMMODATION

| | | | |
|---|---|---|---|
| **1** | Club Jamaica | **13** | Pier View |
| **2** | Enchanted Garden | **14** | Plantation Inn |
| **3** | Hibiscus Lodge | **15** | Reynolds Brooklyn |
| **4** | Hummingbird Haven | | Inn |
| **5** | Hunter's Inn | **16** | Sandcastles |
| **6** | Jamaica Grande | **17** | Sans Souci Lido |
| **7** | The Little Pub | **18** | The Seekers Lounge |
| **8** | Little Shaw Park | **19** | Silver Seas |
| | Guest House | | |
| **9** | Marastilda Hotel | | |
| **10** | Marine View | | |
| **11** | Parkway Inn | | |
| **12** | Pentus Guest Villa | | |

Bay and **Discovery Bay**, where tourism is largely restricted to all-inclusives, maintain communities relatively unaffected by the influx of foreigners. Small villages and brashly advertised rest-stops punctuate the scenery as far as the windswept market town of **Falmouth**.

Inland, smack in the middle of St Ann, is **Nine Miles**, Bob Marley's birthplace and mausoleum, where an obligatory cache of hard-sell Rasta guides welcome hordes of reggae disciples. Away from this star attraction, though, you can drive for hours through the mostly undeveloped **interior** with only cattle for company, but as huge tracts of this land are private (some of it owned by territorial ganja farmers), such forays are best attempted with a local companion.

# Ocho Rios and around

Once the archetypal sleepy fishing village, **OCHO RIOS** (usually just called "Ochi") has long been overtaken but not yet overwhelmed by the tourist industry. The first town in Jamaica to be developed specifically as a resort, Ochi's growth has been rapid, and the planners seem to have forgotten aesthetics in their quest to attract the foreign dollar. The town thrives on the spending power of thousands of cruise-ship passengers who disembark each week, and is fully geared up to cater to their needs; neon-fronted in-bond malls, fast-food chains, slickly packaged attractions and overpriced "Hi-Lite" tours abound, and local culture takes a definite back seat. This is not the best place to get an authentic flavour of Jamaica, and you'll probably be disappointed by the meagre scrap of hotel-lined beach, but it's difficult not to be swept along with the tide of infectious humour and very urban insouciance. Harassment, though still a problem, has declined since the introduction of resort police in the late 1980s, so away from the main craft market the stress factor is minimal and there's less of the "sitting duck" atmosphere of the Montego Bay strip.

## SOME HISTORY

"Ocho Rios" – literally "Eight Rivers" – is a corruption of the Spanish name *chorreros* or *chireiras*, referring to the "gushing water" of local waterfalls. Less poetically, it was the site of several bloody battles when local Spanish governor **Don Christobel Arnaldo de Yssasi** – whose family had been in Jamaica for over 100 years – refused to give in to the British after their capture of the island in 1655. Major skirmishes took place at Dunn's River in 1657, Rio Nuevo in 1658 and Shaw Park in 1659, when Yssasi's men were attacked by a group led by his erstwhile ally, **Juan De Bolas**, a former slave who had defected to the British. In April 1660, Yssasi fled the island in a dugout canoe from **Don Christopher's Point** in St Mary, and the local Spanish legacy rests in a smattering of place names and the fragrant **pimento** tree, first discovered by the Spanish in St Ann, and commercially planted in the parish ever since.

The **British** left a more pervasive mark, with their huge sugarcane, pimento, lumber and cattle farms, but most of the planters were absentees and Ocho Rios remained little more than a fishing harbour until the twentieth century, when the dual concerns of **tourism** and **bauxite** began to physically sculpt the land and secure local prosperity. In 1923, the great house of a struggling citrus plantation at Shaw Park became Jamaica's first exclusive **hotel**. By 1948, it had been joined by four others – *Sans Souci, Silver Seas, Dunn's River* (now *Sandals Dunn's River*) and *Eden Bower* (now *The Enchanted Garden*) – and Ocho Rios looked set for a glowing future. However, though there were a few glorious beaches nearby, most were overhung by steep cliffs or cut off from the mainland by mangrove swamps, a significant problem in a destination sold on the premise of sand and sea. Meanwhile, perpetual crop failures led local planter **Alfred DaCosta** to chemically analyze the local earth; he found that the soil contained high levels of **bauxite**, the chief raw material used to produce aluminium. Foreign-owned companies Reynolds and Kaiser bought up huge

**Ocho Rios and around**

tracts of land, and in 1968, the newly formed St Ann Development Company clubbed together with Reynolds Jamaica Mines and the Urban Development Corporation to reclaim forty acres of land behind what is now Ochi's Main Street. The harbour was dredged, and Reynolds built a deep-water pier to load purified bauxite for export, while the UDC imported sand for the beach and built another jetty to accommodate cruise ships. Thirty years later, their efforts have brought about the thriving resort town of today.

## Arrival and information

Though a central terminus is planned, **buses** from Montego Bay and Kingston currently pull in at the empty lot on the corner of Main and Milford streets, within walking distance of most hotels. Tour companies (see Basics, p.20) operate daily runs in smart air-conditioned buses from Sangster Airport in Montego Bay for about US$30 round-trip; you pay at booths at the airport; *Caribic Vacations* also offers a one-way taxi trip (seats up to four; US$90).

The main **JTB office** (Mon–Fri 9am–5pm, Sat 9am–1pm; ☎974 2582 or 2570) in *Ocean Village Plaza* on Main Street (go up the private-looking staircase at the side of the building, and it's the first door on the left) has flyers on activities and hotels and dispenses use-

---

**Organized tours from Ocho Rios**

The Ocho Rios roster of **organized tours** is second only to Montego Bay's, in terms of quality and choice. Scores of comparably priced operators (most with in-hotel desks) will whisk you off to Dunn's River Falls or Nine Miles, though it's often just as easy to go on your own. Pick of the bunch is **Caribic Vacations** (☎974 9106), which offers all the surrounding attractions (from US$25), the Blue Mountains (US$60) and easily the best tour of Nine Miles (US$34); all prices are per person. Of the more adventurous operators, try the island-wide but Ochi-based **Touring Society of Jamaica**, at the Island Outpost office on Eden Bower Road (PO Box 118; ☎974 5831, fax 974 5830), which organizes pricey but very enjoyable excursions to inaccessible beauty spots like Spanish Bridge, a "North Coast Beach Hop" to remote local swimming spots, and custom-designed tours to suit your interests, from US$250 per day for four people including lunch and activities. German-run **Safari Tours** (from US$50 per day per person; ☎972 1958 or 0919) uses zebra-painted Land Rover jeeps and a refurbished old-time country bus on its adventurous small-scale excursions, which include river-tubing, mountain-biking and some lesser-known swimming holes and plantations. Finally, **Helitours**, 120 Main St, (☎974 2265 or 1108, fax 974 2183), offers expensive but unforgettable helicopter jaunts. Its "Jamaican Showcase" takes in Linstead, Bog Walk Gorge, Spanish Town, Port Royal, Kingston, the Blue Mountains and Port Maria (1hr; US$200 per person). A half-hour tour to Port Antonio over Port Maria costs US$110 per person and the cheapest option is 15 minutes above Ochi for US$50 per person. The rather staid "no pedalling" downhill bike trip from *Blue Mountain Tours* (see p.109) will pick up from Ocho Rios hotels.

---

*For details of island-wide operators see p.20.*

*An alternative to taking an organized tour is to hire a local driver and do some independent sightseeing; try Alton Smith (☎974 6352 or 0997 7573)*

ful local maps. There are smaller **information booths** at Pineapple Place Craft Market, *Taj Mahal Plaza* on Main Street and at the cruise-ship pier. Look out also for *Focus on Jamaica–Ocho Rios*, an annual free guide to local attractions. *The North Coast Times* (weekly; J$7) is a valuable source for one-off entertainment events.

## Orientation and getting around

Ocho Rios is small enough to explore on **foot**, and as activity is centred along two parallel shopping streets, **Main Street** and **DaCosta Drive**, it's not hard to get your bearings. The **clocktower** at the junction of the two is the unofficial town square, where the taxi drivers and hustlers hang out. Forking off toward the sea opposite, **James Avenue** is about as close as Ochi gets to a "ghetto" and can feel a bit hairy at night. You can walk east from the clocktower to Pineapple Craft Market in about half an hour, and the town thins out past the Coconut Grove shopping centre and the *Irie FM* studios, becoming little more than a roadside strip at White River bridge. Westward, Ochi tapers off at Dunn's River Falls, around five minutes' drive out.

The clocktower and the car park next to Ocean Village Plaza are unofficial **taxi ranks**; reliable firms are listed on p.165. The abundance of tourist dollars can mean unreasonably inflated fares – haggle as there is always another waiting; a charter from Coconut Grove to the clock-tower should be no more than US$8. **Shared taxis** can be flagged down anywhere at the roadside for most city drives for around J$15. **Car rental** agencies abound, though it's easier to walk if you're spending most of your time in town. Expect to pay US$60–$90 per day, or about US$400 per week; rates are reduced in the summer. **Bicycles** are a good option for getting around town (US$10–15 per day), as are motor-bikes (from US$30 for a moped). For reputable agencies see listings.

---

**Accommodation price codes**

All the hotels detailed in this guide have been graded according to the fol-lowing price categories. Note that the prices have been calculated as those for the cheapest **double** or **twin room** during low season, normally mid-April to mid-December. During high season, rates are liable to rise by up to 25 percent (though this is rare at the cheap hotels), and proprietors may be less amenable to bargaining. Many of the all-inclusives have a minimum stay requirement; where this is the case it is mentioned in the text. Although the law requires prices to be quoted in Jamaican dollars, most hotels give rates in US dollars; payment can be made in either currency. For more details see p.22.

| | |
|---|---|
| ① under US$20 | ⑤ US$70–100 |
| ② US$20–35 | ⑥ US$100–150 |
| ③ US$35–50 | ⑦ US$150–200 |
| ④ US$50–70 | ⑧ US$200 and above |

---

# Accommodation

While the fashion for **all-inclusives** is embraced even by some of the small central hotels, there are alternatives. The sheer volume of accommodation means good deals, particularly during the low season, and a decent spread of budget options, but prices overall are higher than in less developed areas. **Private villas** are big business on the north coast, as testified by the vast number of properties in and around Ocho Rios. Some of the more luxurious units can rent for up to US$10,000 per week, others go for as little as US$600 – not bad considering some sleep up to eight. Most villas are represented by *JAVA* (see Basics, p.23), though local operators include *Mammee Bay Villa Complex* (74 Main St; ☎974 5762), *Prospect Plantation* (☎974 2058, fax 974 2468) – whose five lavish villas share a clifftop pool – and local resident Regina McClurkin (☎973 3544).

*Flashy condos are available to rent at flashy prices at the Columbus Heights complex overlooking the bay (☎974 2940)*

**Hibiscus Lodge**, 83–87 Main St; ☎974 2676, fax 974 1874. The most attractive independent hotel in the area, hidden from the bustle in beautiful landscaped gardens set back from the road. Perched on the cliffs, the clean, pleasant rooms each have balconies, and there's a pool, Jacuzzi, tennis court, sun deck, sea access, excellent restaurant and a bar with swinging seats. ④.

**Hummingbird Haven**, PO Box 95, White River; ☎974 5188.Youthful budget-style complex off Main Street just past White River. Hexagonal wooden cabins have single or double beds (can take 4 at a push) and hot and cold water, and though there's no security the large grassy campsite (US$10 per tent) is surrounded by trees and a high razor-wire fence. ①/②.

**Hunter's Inn**, 86 Main St; ☎974 5627. Unmemorable but inexpensive rooms in a great location, popular with young travellers. Eight rooms with ceiling fan, hot and cold water. Snooker and pool tables, bar and restaurant. ②.

**Island of Light**, PO Box 6, Retreat, St Mary; ☎ & fax 975 4268. Tucked away on the inland road at Content, this "holistic development" centre and vegetarian guesthouse is an easy distance from Ochi but far enough to escape the clamour. Alternative therapies and camping available. ① /③.

**La Mer Dive and Beach Resort**, PO Box 335, 154 Main St; ☎ 974 5187, fax 974 2359. Friendly, small-scale option – the clean, spacious studios and apartments have tv and kitchenette, and there's a pool, tennis court and dive centre. A good bargain but 20min from town. ④.

**The Little Pub**, PO Box 256, 59 Main St; ☎974 2324, fax 974 5825. One of the busier spots in town owing to the the complex of shops, restaurants and juice bars on site. Rooms are quirky – some split-level with platform beds, most with attic-style sloping roofs, but all are spotless and inviting. ④.

**Little Shaw Park Guest House**, 21 Shaw Park Rd; ☎974 2177. Easy-going family-owned place in a tranquil garden overlooking town. Clean, basic rooms with private bathroom, hot and cold water. Space for camping, communal area with cable tv. Some cooking facilities, meals can be provided. ① /③.

**Marastilda**, White River; ☎974 2223. Situated on the far reaches of Main Street, just past *Sans Souci* and interesting largely because of its charismatic owner. Sparse but spacious and clean rooms with fridge and ceiling fan. Cooking facilities available, or there's a supermarket nearby. ②.

**Marine View**, 9 James Ave; ☎974 5753, fax 974 6953. The brochure's promises of "an aura singular in its enchantment" are optimistic, but the rooms in this family-run hotel are comfortable and clean, and there's a pool, slot machines, restaurant, bar and disco. ②.

**Parkway Inn**, 60 Main St; ☎974 2667. Central with clean, comfortable rooms, some with tv. Jamaican roots plays, boxing tournaments, bingo and fashion shows are staged at weekends, so it's often full of activity and noise. ③.

**Pentus Guest Villa**, 3 Shaw Park Rd; ☎974 2313. Rooms with bathrooms in the small but spotless home of a very knowledgeable local woman, for 22 years head housekeeper of *Shaw Park*; the clean and tidy may use her kitchen. ③.

**Pier View**, PO Box 134, 19 Main St; ☎974 2607, fax 974 1384. Busy and friendly apartment development next to the UDC beach, with a great atmosphere. Rooms or self-catering units with kitchenette. All have fridge, fan or a/c, satellite tv and access to pool and sun roof. ③ /④.

**Reynolds Brooklyn Inn**, 188 Main St; ☎974 2480. Small guesthouse above a bar/restaurant, with simple but clean rooms with shared bathroom and a predominantly Jamaican clientele. ①.

**Sandcastles**, Main St; ☎974 5626, fax 974 2247. In front of the UDC beach (guests get a pass), light and airy studios and apartments with cooking facilities and private balconies. Popular with families; the pool has a slide and a children's area. ⑥.

**The Seekers Lounge**, 25 James Ave; ☎974 5763. Basic rooms at the better end of this road. You get what you pay for – rather depressing rooms with a/c or fans and private or shared bath, plus pool table, bar and restaurant. ① /②.

**Silver Seas**, 66 James Ave; ☎974 2755 or 5005, fax 974 5739. One of the oldest hotels in Ocho Rios, popular with repeat guests. Spacious rooms with balconies overlooking the private man-made beach, watersports, scuba, satellite tv in bar area, tennis court, pool and restaurant. ④.

## All-inclusives

**Club Jamaica**, Box 342, Ocho Rios; ☎974 6632, fax 974 6644. Very central all-inclusive overlooking the UDC beach, with functional but uninspired rooms, a nightclub, pool, watersports and PADI dive operator (additional charge). ⑥.

**The Enchanted Garden**, PO Box 284, Ocho Rios; ☎974 1400/5346, fax 974 5823 (US & Canada call ☎1-800/847-2535). The whimsical name has a ring of truth; built on the site of the Carinosa botanical gardens and now owned by former PM Edward Seaga, this capacious all-inclusive boasts 14 natural waterfalls named by the likes of Mick Jagger, five restaurants, two pools, private beach club, two night-lit tennis courts, spa treatments, sauna, Turkish bath, fitness programmes, yoga and T'ai-chi, the largest aviary in the Caribbean, fruit orchard and every other imaginable frippery. ⑧.

**Jamaica Grande**, PO Box 100, Ocho Rios; ☎974 2201, fax 974 2162 (in US ☎1-800/228-9898, fax 602/443-6543). Situated at the end of its very own road off Main Street, this is Jamaica's largest hotel with 720 amenity-packed rooms, a man-made waterfall in the lobby, five restaurants, nine bars, private beach, fitness centre, three pools, gym, tennis courts, disco, mini-casino, children's activity programme and very little character. ⑧.

**Jamaica Inn**, PO Box 1, Ocho Rios; ☎974 2514, fax 974 2449. A 10min drive west of town along Main Street. Quietly elegant all-inclusive completely in the colonial tradition, popular with a ritzy list of repeat guests. Beautifully decorated rooms with balconies and manicured croquet lawns. No children under 14; jacket and tie required for dinner. ⑧.

**Ocho Rios and around**

**Plantation Inn**, PO Box 2, Ocho Rios; ☎974 5601, fax 974 5912. Graceful colonial-style resort a 5min drive west along Main Street. Rooms, suites and villas, all amenities, watersports, great beach and tennis courts with professional tuition. Breakfast and afternoon tea included in the price. Not strictly an all-inclusive, but most guests treat it as such. ⑥.

**Sandals Dunn's River**, PO Box 51, Ocho Rios; ☎972 0653, fax 972 1611. A 10min drive out of town toward St Ann's Bay, this is the lap of luxury for couples only, with gaudily decorated rooms, three restaurants, seven bars and the largest freshwater pool in Jamaica, but a rather disappointing slip of a beach. Nightly entertainment and gazebos that see plenty of weddings. Three night minimum stay. ⑦–⑧.

**Sans Souci Lido**, PO Box 103, White River; ☎974 2353, fax 974 2544. Flagship adults-only all-inclusive in the *Superclubs* chain (a 10min drive west of town along Main Street), the best in the area. Full spa facilities and mineral springs, three excellent restaurants, two pools, a magnificent white-sand beach, Jacuzzis, fitness centre, tennis courts, golf and all watersports. The strolling saxophonist, gazebos and low-key landscaping ensure an emphasis on romance. Three night minimum stay. ⑧.

**Shaw Park Beach Hotel**, PO Box 17, Ocho Rios; ☎974 2552, fax 974 5042 (in US ☎804/460-2343, fax 460-9420). Ochi's oldest hotel, though moved from its original location to the eastern outskirts. The wooden fittings and plantation-style decor are pretty, the concrete accommodation blocks are not. But the atmosphere is friendly and there's a pool, superb beach, all watersports, tennis courts and a gym. Three night minimum stay. ⑦–⑧.

## The Town and around

Apart from shopping – and it could take days to work your way through all of the malls and markets (see p.163) – or hanging out in a bar, activities in Ocho Rios town are limited; there's nowhere to

---

### Watersports

Although there isn't that much to see underwater at the UDC beach – you'll find much richer pickings east of the harbour or at the reef at the bottom of Dunn's River (see p.158) – it's lined with **watersports concessions**. Prices are high – even snorkel equipment can cost as much as US$20 per day, though bargaining usually brings this down a bit. Reliable operators include *Garfield's Dive Station* (☎975 4420 or 0995 3700) and *Oras Divers*, which also operates from *Silver Seas Hotel* (☎974 5005), or the supremely professional *Sea Dive Jamaica*, back from the beach at 74 Main St (☎974 5762). Larger hotels have scuba concessions, but you may have to buy a day pass to the property to use them, then pay for your dive on top.

The coast reverberates to the sound systems of the many private boats offering **cruises**. Day-trips go to Dunn's River for snorkelling and climbing the falls, with an open bar and lunch or snacks; sunset cruises include drinks only, but most operators offer dinner cruises too. Agents roam the sand soliciting custom for the cruises, some of which are racier than others; among the better organized operators are *Jamaica Pirate Cruises* (☎974 5762; day cruise US$25), *Wild Oats* (☎974 7044; day cruise $38, sunset cruise US$25, dinner cruise US$35) and *Red Stripe* (☎974 2446; day cruise US$38, sunset cruise US$25). All prices are per person.

promenade and the permanently busy streets hold little interest for sightseeing. **Main Street** houses the majority of hotels, bars, banks, shopping plazas and restaurants, as well as the fruit and vegetable market, the craft markets and the post office, while **DaCosta Drive** is Ochi's quieter back entrance and a slip road for fast traffic. **James Avenue** has a markedly different feel, home to two raucous night-clubs and not a place to linger after dark.

During the day, most of the tourist activity in Ocho Rios centres around the **UDC Beach** – also known as Mallards, Turtle and Ocho Rios Bay (daily 6am–6pm; US$1). Tucked under the tower blocks and accessible from Main Street, the white-sand beach is wide, attractive and well-maintained – and *the* place to hang out – but rather claustrophobic when packed to bursting and overshadowed by the bulk of docked cruise ships across the bay, when pollution can be a problem. It's also a lot smaller than it used to be, as since the 1980s a prime section at the eastern end has been appropriated by the island's largest hotel, *Jamaica Grande*.

## The botanical gardens

From the main roundabout at the western junction of DaCosta Drive and Main Street, a twenty-minute walk along Milford Road takes you to two of Ochi's better known pastoral attractions, both on the ill-maintained Shaw Park Road. The **Shaw Park Botanical Gardens** (daily 8am–5pm; US$3.50), 550ft above sea level and boasting stunning aerial views of town, do a cracking trade with cruise-ship passengers. The former grounds of a long-gone hotel, the small but creatively planted gardens are resplendent with unusual flowers, plants, trees – including a huge banyan – and grassy lawns reminiscent of England's Kew Gardens, and a near-perpendicular waterfall. You can walk unaccompanied but a guide will initiate you into the wonders of tropical horticulture. There's an on-site bar open until 4pm, and crafts and jewellery on sale at the gift shop.

About five minutes further up Shaw Park Road, the more intimate **Coyaba River Garden and Museum** (daily 8am–5pm; US$4.50) is a meditative and restful miniature hothouse of lush, well-watered flower beds bisected by streams teeming with mullet, koi carp, crayfish and turtles. Wooden walkways allow easy viewing of the heliconias, anthuriums, hot-pink ginger lilies and rampant vines. The museum houses a limited but thoughtful collection of exhibits, spanning Jamaican history, with special weight given to St Ann's own Garvey and Marley, and the café and gift shop are both above average.

At the top of Shaw Park Road is **BEECHER TOWN**, a nondescript village blessed with great views of Ochi and the surrounding coastline. From Twickenham Farm on the outskirts of the village, *Hooves Ltd* offers splendid, scenic slow-paced **horseback trail rides** (☎974 6245; 9.30am & 2pm; 1hr US$35, 2hr US$50; prices include transport and snacks), with informative guides who'll point out the many medicinal "bush" plants that grow here, most, apparently, geared around the male genitalia.

*The UDC – or Urban Development Corporation – Beach wins the prize for Jamaica's most prosaically named strip of sand.*

*Coyaba hold occasional but unmissable full moon parties; call ☎974 4568 for details.*

*See p.26 of Basics for more on the redemptive powers of Jamaica's "bush" plants.*

# Ocho Rios and around

## Ocho Rios Fort and Dunn's River Falls

Heading west of town along Main Street, a specially constructed wooden boardwalk parallels the road and allows easy pedestrian access to Ochi's biggest attraction. It passes the town's only historical feature, **Ocho Rios Fort**, sandwiched between the cruise terminal and a former slaughterhouse. The fort was built by the British in the seventeenth century and restored in 1780 to defend against a feared French attack, but there's little to see other than two cannons from the now derelict Mammee Bay Fort added by the Reynolds bauxite company in the 1960s.

Ten more minutes along the boardwalk is **Dunn's River Falls** (daily 9am–5pm, beach closes 6pm; US$5, plus a tip for the guide), Jamaica's best-loved waterfall – overdeveloped but still breathtaking, and justifiably the area's major tourist trap. Masked from the road by a complex of restaurants, craft shops and car parks, the magnificent 600ft waterfall cascades down to a pretty tree-fringed white-sand beach far cleaner than the UDC, with a lively reef within swimming distance – snorkel gear is available to rent from several touts.

*Rather unnecessary "Sticky Feet" – shoe socks to aid your climb – are available to rent on site (US$5).*

Impressively proportioned, with water running so fast you can hear it from the road below, the falls are surrounded by dripping foliage and more than live up to their reputation; even the profusion of concrete and commerciality that surround them detract little from their beauty. The main activity is climbing up the falls, a wet but easily navigable one-hour ascent. The rocks are regularly scraped to remove slippery algae and you can hold hands with one of the very experienced guides to prevent a stumble, but the cowardly can take the wooden steps by the side. It's thoroughly exhilarating, as you're showered with cool, clear water all the way up – wear a bathing suit. There is a restaurant and bar, craft and hair-braiding shacks and full changing facilities at the beach and at the top of the falls.

An alternative to the crowds and the admission price are the unmaintained waterfalls outside the enclosure. The best spot is a twenty-foot lagoon known as **the whirlpool**, with a small waterfall to climb and a natural Jacuzzi. To get there, take the main route to the falls but carry on up past the car park to where the tarmac ends. Follow the first dirt path into the bush to your right for five minutes.

*The craft stalls that line Fern Gully are pretty good – look for the Rastaman who lives in a cave at the roadside and makes fantastically eerie intuitive masks.*

There are several more waterfalls further up the road which you can drive or walk to, but you may need a local companion to find them.

## Fern Gully and beyond

Heading south for five minutes from the central Ochi roundabout along Milford Road brings you to **Fern Gully**, a densely vegetated and steeply inclining three-mile stretch of the A3 Kingston road, made famous by the arboreal splendour of the 500 or so varieties of fern that smother the roadside banks. First planted in the 1880s, the ferns are overhung by tall trumpet and mahoe trees that meet overhead, filtering the sunlight to create a cool, green-tinged tunnel. Moist and sheltered, the gully environment is ideal for ferns, but exhaust fumes from the heavy traffic have damaged and even wiped out some of the species, and there are regular calls for Fern Gully to be closed to traffic and developed as a beauty spot. This proposition makes even more sense in bad weather, as after heavy rains the gully is reduced to an impassable series of potholes, causing traffic jams that stretch right back into town. You can walk up from Ochi in about twenty minutes, but the whizzing traffic, lack of pavements and persistent roadside vendors make pedestrians vulnerable.

Once at the top of the Fern Gully hill and out of the undergrowth, the landscape opens up with eye-popping views across the pastures and hillocks of the eastern interior, with the misted Blue Mountain peaks just visible in the distance. Continuing along the A3, through emerald-green pasture lands dotted with dilapidated gingerbread houses and restored plantation homes, you eventually reach **MONEAGUE**, a quiet but beguiling town with a "magic lake" on its outskirts. The usual thirty-foot pond occasionally expands to cover some 2000 acres – it's all down to rainfall and the flow of underground rivers, though the romantically inclined mutter of mermaids and golden tables.

*You can rent a pedal boat to traverse the water – more fun when the pond's expanded, obviously.*

## East of town

On the far eastern stretches of Main Street, a nondescript building set back from the road opposite the Coconut Grove shopping centre houses the studios of **Irie FM**, Jamaica's most popular radio station (not open to the public). The first on the island with a 100-percent-reggae music policy – the airwaves were previously dominated by American soul, gospel and country and western – Irie has, since its first transmission in June 1990, championed the artistic and cultural legitimacy of a musical genre branded subversive until the early 1970s. Today, it provides the soundtrack for the nation – wherever you go you'll hear the music, the massively popular talk shows, and the fabulous patois jingles: "Irie FM – a fi wi station" or "My radio dial stuck pon Irie FM, and guess what – me nah bodder fix it", though its tendency to broadcast explicit dancehall lyrics at peak listening times, and its alleged failure to make royalty payments, occasionally land it in hot water. Irie has breathed cultural life into Ocho Rios – Steel Pulse, Burning Spear, Aswad and Third World among others have recorded at the station's Grove Studios, and the associated Roof Extension band provide the backing at many large stageshows, including Irie's own White River Reggae Bash (see p.34).

Past here, before reaching the bridge over the wide but sluggish White River that marks the parish boundary of St Ann and St Mary, Bonham Spring Road winds inland, taking you through Ochi's poorer satellite communities and past the sumptuous eighteen-hole *Sandals* golf course at Upton (see p.40 for details) and a couple of well-signposted pastoral attractions competing for the tourist dollar.

**Irie Beach** at *Bonham Spring Farm* (daily 10am–5pm; US$5) – owned by a Chinese-Jamaican family who also run an organic farming collective and a prestigious recording studio on site (look out for reggae

*See p.342 of Contexts for a wider discussion of Jamaican music.*

*For more on Jamaican radio, and a complete list of frequencies, see p.32 of Basics.*

*You can raft White River with Calypso Rafting (☎974 2527; 45min US$35 per person).*

stars chilling out after a session in the studio – Garnet Silk wrote much of his material at the waterside while recording here) – is a landscaped section of the White River, a breathtaking series of deep-turquoise freshwater pools wreathed by chaotically abundant plant life and flowers. There's a rope-swing, too, and a café serving natural juices, snacks and barbecued chicken or fish. A fifteen-minute drive from here is **Wilderness Resort** (daily 10am–5pm; US$3), with landscaped gardens and fishing ponds, a petting zoo, paddle boat and kayak rides. The 38 well-tended ponds are stocked with tilapia, and you can fish on a catch-and-release basis, or have your haul cleaned, scaled and cooked at the clubhouse.

Back on the coast and directly below Irie Beach, former ice factory turned commercial farm **Prospect Plantation** operates the most popular plantation tour in the area (1hr 15min tours Mon–Sat 10.30am, 2pm & 3pm, Sun 11am, 1.30pm & 3pm; US$12). You sit with 38 others on an open jitney (trailer), listening to an inaudible commentary while trundling through pimento and lime groves, coconut palms, cane patches, and ackee, breadfruit, mahoe and soursop trees, stopping only to sample fruits, admire the views, and potter around a stone church. **Horseback trail rides** offer a less confined tour of the property and go right down into White River gorge (1hr US$20, 1hr 30min US$35 – book 1hr in advance on ☎974 2058).

Finally, **Rio Nuevo Park**, signposted off the main A3, commemorates the battle that made Jamaica a British territory. There is little to see other than a rather decrepit monument, but the park is a pretty spot for a quiet walk, with lovely views down to the sea.

# Eating

As many of Ochi's **restaurants** aim to please the foreign palate, Italian, Chinese and "American" cuisine vie for your custom alongside the curry goat, and much of what Jamaican cooking there is is blander than it should be. For a truly tasty – and inexpensive – Jamaican meal, try the outdoor cookshop at the fishermen's beach west of town, where you'll be served hearty fish tea and well-prepared lunches of fish, rice and peas and Jamaican-style veg. Most places here stay open late, so you'll rarely be stuck for a midnight feast.

### Snacks

The recent influx of international **fast-food chains** divides office workers between those who opt for *Burger King* or *Kentucky Fried Chicken* (both on Main Street) and those who stick with the traditional patties and coco bread. The best place for the latter is *Taste Pleasures* in Island Plaza, which bakes a delicious callaloo loaf alongside the usual patties, meat loaf and pastries. Also in Island Plaza, *TCBY Yoghurt* sells over-sweet and expensive frozen yoghurt, while *Tropical Flavour* at Carib Plaza stocks the delicious Devon House "I-Scream" (see p.75). The ubiquitous *Mother's* has a 24hr branch at 17 Main St, serving burgers, chicken and ice cream.

## Inexpensive

**Father Ancient Ital Food Shop**, in the vegetable market (take the west entrance, turn to the left of the covered portion and it's next to the coal shop). Healthy vegetarian breakfasts and lunches popular with a Rasta clientele.

**The Healthy Way**, Ocean Village Plaza. Busy and efficient vegetarian take-away with a couple of tables offering veggie/tofu burgers and patties, soups, Ital juices, fruit salad, cakes and a different main dish each day.

**Fish World**, 3 James Ave. Deservedly popular with locals and a good place for a late meal. Fish served any which way, with bammy, festival or rice and peas, cooked right before your eyes on an open grill. Natural juices are made fresh daily. Open Mon–Sat until 2am.

**Jack Ruby's**, 1 James Ave. Typical Jamaican eatery with down-to-earth prices serving ackee and saltfish or callaloo with all the trimmings, cowfoot, oxtail, chicken and fish – lobster on request.

**Jah Roy's**, in the vegetable market (turn right as you enter). Supposedly open 24hr, but in reality whenever Jah Roy makes it in to work. Ital Rasta cooking; ackee, tofu and greens and natural juices by the pint.

**The Lion's Den**, on the A3, opposite Dunn's River Falls. Unusual wickerwork and bamboo-columned decor and an attractive upstairs chill-out lounge in a Rasta haunt serving up good seafood and plenty of anecdotes about a bamboo bed once slept in by Bob Marley.

**Mr Humphrey's Pizza Café**, 10 Evelyn St, off Main St; ☎974 8319. Fast and tasty pizzas, sub sandwiches, jerk chicken and pitta pockets. Free delivery.

**Ocho Rios Jerk Centre**, just before the rounadbout on DaCosta Drive. Popular with locals who appreciate the consistently good jerk pork, chicken, fish and barbecued spare ribs. Daily 10am–midnight.

**Parkway Inn**, 60 Main St. Small upstairs restaurant serving excellent Jamaican breakfast and lunch – with particularly good ackee and saltfish – on a verandah overlooking Main Street.

## Moderate

**Bibibips**, 93 Main St. Set back from the road, with a sports bar style and varied menu that includes curry goat, chicken, fish, lobster, burgers and veggie or meat curry and stir-fry. A relaxed place to have a drink outdoors, too.

**Blue Cantina**, 81 Main St. Slightly more salubrious than its rival of the same name across the road, with a wider menu of burgers, veggie and meat tacos, curry goat, chicken and steak.

**Café Mango**, Main St, opposite the entrance to *Jamaica Grande*. Neon-lit diner in a central location serving snacks (focaccia, nachos, subs), salads, chicken and festival, some Mexican dishes, pasta and pizza. A nice spot for a long lunch. Deliveries available.

**Double V Jerk Centre**, 109 Main St; ☎974 5998. The jerk meat and Jamaican specials take second place to the pool-table, occasional live music and constant loud reggae or calypso. Busy, vibrant and open very late, this is a great place just to hang out.

**Glenn's Restaurant and Jazz Club**, Tower Isle, 10min west of town on Main St; ☎975 4360. Jamaican food accompanied by taped jazz on weekdays and occasional live bands on weekends.

*In restaurant listings, we have given a phone number only for those places where you might need to **reserve** a table.*

**The Little Pub**, 59 Main St; ☎974 2324. American and Jamaican breakfast and lunch in a roadside café with a juice bar on site. Dinner – from filet mignon or surf 'n' turf to lobster thermidore – is dished up in the "entertainment area".

**Mayflower**, Island Plaza, Main St. Good Cantonese food – seafood specialities, pleasant service and reasonable prices.

**Minnies**, off Main St, 200yd beyond *Hibiscus Lodge*. You have to trek down a rather dark road to get to it, but the Ital-style vegetarian cooking – vegetable run-down, bean stew and soup – is well worth the trouble and the garden setting is attractive and detached from the traffic.

### Expensive

**The Almond Tree**, *Hibiscus Lodge Hotel*; ☎974 2813. Romantic clifftop setting, friendly service and a great gourmet menu, featuring superb seafood.

**Evita's**, Eden Bower Rd; ☎974 2333. The best pasta on the north coast, served on a gingerbread verandah overlooking the bay. Huge choice of starters, salads and soups (snapper stuffed with crab, sautéed shrimp with garlic, tomatoes and fettucine), main courses including fettucine bolognaise, linguine with pesto, seafood, and "Lasagne Rastafari" with ackee, callaloo and tomatoes, and calorie-packed desserts.

**The Ruins**, DaCosta Drive; ☎974 2442 or 2789. An Ochi institution, serving well-prepared Oriental and international food, some of it vegetarian. The real draw is the waterfall tumbling down into a fish-filled pool. Lunch is buffet-style and a cheaper way to get the flavour of the place.

## Nightlife and entertainment

*Billboards advertising one-off stageshows and sound-system dances – a truly Jamaican experience – spring up overnight around town.*

A **nightlife** magnet for tourists and locals alike, Ocho Rios has **bars** and **clubs** open every night of the week. Main Street and James Avenue are teeming with Jamaican-style rum shops and beer joints which can be fun, though expect plenty of attention whether you want it or not. White River Reggae Park, to the east of town, is the venue for the unmissable **White River Reggae Bash** put on by Irie FM, which swings into action several times a year and attracts big names in the reggae scene (details on ☎974 7240 or 5051). The stellar **Ocho Rios Jazz Festival** is held every June, with concerts at venues around town – for more information call the tourist board or the Jazz Hotline (☎927 3544). **Theatre** is on offer at the *Parkway Inn* on Main Street (☎974 2667), which puts on regular roots plays as well as boxing matches and lunchtime bingo.

### Bars

**Bibibips**, 93 Main St. A clifftop bar that's a laid-back place for a drinking session, with less of the distinctions made between tourists and locals that sometimes mar the more central establishments.

**Bill's Place**, 47 Main St, behind *Gem Palace* in-bond shop. Popular and lively, with satellite tv, occasional karaoke, friendly atmosphere and excellent cocktails.

**Double V Jerk Centre**, 109 Main St. Piped music keeps the bar-proppers going, and there's occasional soca or reggae parties at this vibrant little spot.

**Jamaican Hard Rock Café**, Coconut Grove Shopping Centre. Not part of the international chain, but a Jamaican version of an American bar. Its location on the outskirts of town makes it a little quiet, but good for a drink before going on to *Silks* next door. "Ladies" get two drinks for the price of one Mon–Fri 5.30–7.30pm.

**The Little Pub**, 59 Main St. One of the most popular hangouts in town. The busy bar shows football games and boxing via satellite tv, and is great for people-watching; the stage area hosts "Afro-Caribbean musical extravaganzas" – spangly-costumed Jamaican-style cabaret with a band.

### Clubs

**The Acropolis Disco**, above the Mutual Security building, 70 Main St (Wed–Sun). Dancehall and reggae oldies make "Crub-Crub" (as it's known) the best indoor club in town, with ladies', reggae and disco nights and a Friday happy hour. Cover around US$5.

**Jamaika-Me-Krazy**, *Jamaica Grande* (nightly). The newest addition to Ochi's club scene, with neon and infra-red decor, a clientele of tourists and rich Jamaicans and just the occasional reggae or soca track to remind you of where you are. That said, it's usually a lot of fun – it's permanently packed, the sound system's excellent, and the cover lets you drink your fill. Cover US$15–20.

**The Marine Disco**, 9 James Ave (nightly, but best at weekends). Next door to *The Roof* and competing with it to see who can make the most racket. Fun, but best avoided if you're feeling fragile or want to be left alone. Moderate cover.

**Roof Night Club**, 7 James Ave (nightly). The source of the belly-vibrating dancehall audible even from the far reaches of Main Street. Go to watch impromptu demonstrations of the latest dancehall moves from Jamaican protagonists or simply soak up the atmosphere. Cover US$5.

**Silks Disco**, *Shaw Park Hotel* (Wed–Sun). Touristy in-hotel disco which can be entertaining at the weekend. Cover around US$8.

## Shopping

**Shopping** is big business in Ocho Rios. Its three **craft markets** (daily 7am–7pm) have enticed many a hapless soul to leave the island laden with "Yeh mon it irie" and "Same shit, different island" t-shirts or Rasta hats complete with fake dreadlocks. A frantic free-for-all on cruise-ship days, these are otherwise great places to shop – among the dross you'll find really nice t-shirts and sculptures, and vendors have a wicked line in sales banter. The main market is to the right of Ocean Village Plaza, while the smaller Pineapple Place and Coconut Grove markets are further east towards *Hibiscus Lodge* and the all-inclusive hotels. The **fruit and vegetable market** on Main Street is good for a browse, though prices often shoot up at the sight of a foreign face; go as early as 7am if you plan a big purchase.

*George at stall no. 124 at the back of the main market has some of the best woodcarvings in town.*

As well as the craft markets, Main Street is lined with shopping malls housing a rash of near-identical **in-bond shops**. Prices in these are fairly competitive – though you may pay more for simple items like t-shirts and craft goods than in quieter areas – and the quality of merchandise is reliable.

**Ocho Rios and around**

For **books**, try *Everybody's Bookshop* in Ocean Village Plaza which carries a good selection of titles, some published only in Jamaica, plus magazines and foreign newspapers. *Disc and Dat Music*, in PJ Plaza on DaCosta Drive, stocks the latest **reggae** and can make up customized compilation tapes for US$5–6, and *Reggae Master* at 71 Main St is a good old-fashioned Jamaican record shack with a blaring sound system, while *Vibes Music Shack* in Ocean Village and *De Muzic Shop* in Island Plaza sell soul, gospel and country and western too. Ceramics and various other creative **souvenirs** are sold at the *Wassi Art Factory Outlet* at Great Pond in the hills above town, though you can buy the products in most local craft stores and the markets. *Living Wood* in Ocean Village does a good line in wooden sculptures, wicker baskets and small furniture manageable even on a plane.

Finally, there's a gorgeous **art gallery** and shop at Harmony Hall, ten minutes' drive out of Ochi at Tower Isle; set in a beautifully restored great house, the gallery features small but comprehensive and ever-changing collections of work by renowned contemporary Jamaican artists, and a variety of crafts. The shop downstairs sells a quirky collection of Caribbean books, aromatherapy oils and women's clothing, and there's a relaxing garden café-bar. The site hosts excellent occasional art and craft fairs.

## Listings

**Airlines** *Air Jamaica* has a local office (☎974 2566); for flight confirmations and information on other airlines see Montego Bay listings p.222. *Air Jamaica Express* (☎975 3254) should soon be running internal flights from Boscobel Airstrip (☎975 3101); call for details.

**American Express** *Stuarts Travel*, 12 Main St; ☎974 2431 or 2288.

**Banks and money** Most of the banks are on Main Street opposite Ocean Village Plaza. *Citizens Bank* is on Newlin Street, and the *Worker's Bank* on Graham Street opens on Saturdays (9am–1pm). For currency exchange, try *Island Plaza Cambio* opposite *Burger King* on Main Street and *Kamal's Cambio* opposite the clocktower; though it's a bit out of the way, *Rainbow Car Rentals* in Pineapple Place has a licensed cambio that consistently offers the best rates in town. Wire transfers are available through the *Western Union* outlet at *Pier View Hotel*.

**Car and bike rental** Many of the internationals have in-hotel branches in Ochi, or there's *Bargain*, Pineapple Place Shopping Centre (☎974 5298) and *Hertz*, Shop 5, Coconut Grove Shopping Centre (☎974 2017), but you'll often get a better deal from independents such as *Caribbean Cars* on Main and Evelyn streets (☎974 2123 or 2513), *Prospective* at Columbus Heights (☎974 2940), *Sunshine* at 154 Main St (☎974 5025 or 2980) or *Rainbow Car Rentals* at 21 Pineapple Place (☎974 7114). For cycles and motorbikes, reliable companies include *Abe* in Ocho Rios Mall, 73 Main St (☎974 7787 or 1008), *G & B* at 6 James Ave (☎974 4618/8247), and *VLD's Cycle World* at 8 Main St (☎974 7529).

**Doctors** Most hotels have a resident doctor or nurse; if not, call Dr Horace Betton and Dr Michael James at their surgery at 14 Carib Arcade on Main

Street (☎974 2005 or 5413). The Holistic Medical Centre is at 40 Ocean Village Plaza (☎974 6403).

**Hospitals** The nearest is *St Ann's Bay* (☎972 0150), a 15min drive from Ocho Rios.

**Laundry** *Carib Launderette*, 6 Carib Plaza (Mon–Sat 10am–7pm, Sun 9am–5pm), offers service (US$5) and self-service (US$4) washes; bring powder.

**Pharmacies** Ochi pharmacies are plentiful, well-equipped and often open late; best are *The Great House Pharmacy* on Main Street next to the *Little Pub* (Mon–Thurs 9am–7.30pm, Fri–Sat 9am–9pm) or *Ocho Rios Pharmacy* in Ocean Village Plaza (daily 8.30am–8pm).

**Photography** *Frank Bailey Studio* at 2 Rennie Rd and *Pugh's Photo Lab* in the Mutual Security Building, 70 Main St, both offer Kodak film, photographic supplies and 1hr developing.

**Police** The police station (☎974 2533 or 4588) is on Evelyn Street behind the *Texaco* garage that faces the clocktower; in emergencies call ☎119.

**Post Office** The permanently busy post office is on Main Street opposite the main craft market (Mon–Fri 8am–5pm, Sat 8am–noon).

**Supermarkets** *General Foods* in Ocean Village Plaza is Ochi's largest and carries a wide range of imported food alongside Jamaican staples. *KC Supermarket* at 28 Main St is smaller but offers wholesale prices on beers and liquor. Fruit and vegetables are cheaper and better at the market just beyond the clocktower.

**Taxis** Reliable operators include *Al's Taxi Service*, also reasonable for day charters (☎974 6352 or 0997 7573), *Maxi Taxi* (☎974 2971), *Rising Bird* (☎974 7339 or 5929) and *United* (☎974 4755).

**Telephones** Pay phones are dotted around town; expect long queues. Phonecards are available from *Mother's* on Main Street, the post office and pharmacies. Overseas calls can be made at *Jamintel* in the Mutual Security Building (Mon–Fri 8am–7pm, Sat 8am–noon); they also offer fax service and telegrams. Otherwise try the *Call Direct Centre*, 74 Main St (Mon–Sat 8.30am–10pm, Sun 9am–noon & 5–8.30pm). You can send faxes from the *Xerox Centre* in Ocean Village Plaza.

# East of Ocho Rios

As the clamour of Ocho Rios recedes, the A3 coast road narrows, making way for some of the most beautiful scenery on the north coast. Lushly vegetated cliffsides almost overwhelm the roads and the region has a languid allure markedly different to the neon titillation of Ochi. The main settlements, **Oracabessa** and **Port Maria**, flaunt the full pastoral aspect of rural Jamaica, with some small guesthouses and excellent little restaurants peppering the roadside. Beyond Port Maria, the coastline extends in an unbroken series of forested outcrops interspersed by deserted, volcanic-sand miniature beaches. Yet the area has more to offer than just fabulous coastline and fashionable beach clubs – inland hikes or drives uncover breathtaking vistas as the peaks of the Blue Mountains shimmer into view (see p.105).

*For guided hikes in the area contact Sonrise Beach Retreat in Robins Bay (☎ & fax 999 7169).*

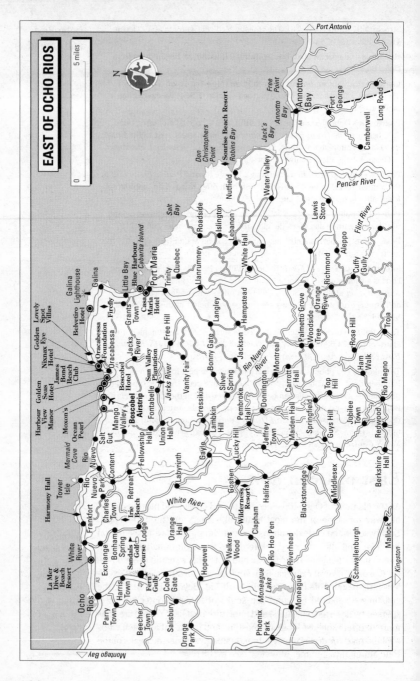

EAST OF OCHO RIOS

N

0          5 miles

△ Port Antonio

Annotto Bay
Fort George
Camberwell
Long Road
Free Point
Jack's Bay
Annotto Bay
Water Valley
Pencar River
Flint River
Lewis Store
Aleppo
Cuffy Gully
Richmond
Orange River
Woodside
Palmetto Grove
Tree
Rose Hill
Troja
Ham Walk
Rio Magno
Redwood
Berkshire Hall
Mallock
Schwallenburgh
Middlesex
Blackstonedge
Guys Hill
Top Hill
Jubilee Town
Maiden Hall
Springfield
Carrott Hall
Montreal
Donnington
Pembroke Hall
Jeffrey Town
Maiden Hall
Halifax
Clapham
Rio Hoe Pen
Riverhead
Wilderness Resort
Goshen
Lucky Hill
Gayle
Dressikie
Lambkin Hill
Silver Spring
Bonny Gate
Jackson
Hampstead
Langley
Vanity Fair
Free Hill
Jacks River
Sun Valley Plantation
Fontabelle
Union Hall
Fellowship Hall
Labyrinth
Orange Hall
Walkers Wood
Hopewell
Moneague Lake
Moneague
Phoenix Park
Orange Park
Salisbury
Cole Gate
Beecher Town
Fern Gully
Harris Town
Parry Town
Ocho Rios
La Mer Dive & Beach Resort
White River
Exchange
Bonham Spring
Sandals Golf Course Lodge
Harmony Hall
Tower Isle
Frankfort
Charles Town
Rio Nuevo
Irie Beach
Content
Nuevo Park
Mermaid Cove
Rio Nuevo
Ocean Pearl
Moxon's
Harbour View Manor
Golden Seas Hotel
James Bond Beach Club
Boscobel Hotel
Boscobel Airstrip
Mango Valley
Salt Gut
Oracabessa
Oracabessa Foundation
Nixmax Eye Hotel
Golden Seas Hotel
Golden Clouds
Goldeneye
Lovely Spot Villas
Belvedere Hotel
Galina Lighthouse
Galina
Firefly
Little Bay
Blue Harbour
Cabarita Island
Port Maria
Casa Maria Hotel
Grants Town
Trinity
Quebec
Llanrumney
White Hall
Lebanon
Islington
Roadside
Nutfield
Salt Bay
Don Christophers Point
Sonrise Beach Resort
Robins Bay
Water Valley

White River

Jacks River

Rio Nuevo River

White River

A3

A4

A3

A1

△ Montego Bay                    ▷ Kingston

Though ostensibly quiet, close proximity to Kingston and Ocho Rios has long made the region a favourite haunt of the rich and famous – Noel Coward and James Bond author Ian Fleming both lived here, and their old homes, **Firefly** and **Goldeneye**, are now prime tourist sights – and the surface tranquillity masks a steady hum of industry, with the dynamic Island Outpost company concentrating a sizeable part of its operation in Oracabessa and promising a full-scale tourist development that will change the region's face.

## Oracabessa

Lit by an intense apricot afternoon light that must have prompted its Spanish name *Orocabeza* or "Golden Head", **ORACABESSA**, some sixteen miles east of Ocho Rios, is a leisurely little town centred around a fruit and vegetable market (main days Thurs & Fri) and a few shops and bars. A centre for the export of **bananas** until the early 1900s, the wharves around the small natural harbour closed in 1969, and the town has snoozed quietly ever since.

Until now. Seventy acres of prime old port land – stretching all the way over to the Goldeneye estate – have been bought by Chris Blackwell's **Island Outpost** corporation, to be developed as a major open-plan community resort over a ten-year period. Island intends the Oracabessa project to be a sharp contrast to the usual fenced-off enclosures in which Jamaicans figure only as servants. Locals will set up their own businesses to provide the services, amusements and amenities – a move towards so-called "seamless tourism" and sustainable development. To kickstart the project, the **Oracabessa Foundation** (☎975 3393; Mon–Sat 9am–5pm) has opened in a green-painted shack just past the market, to prepare citizens for their role in the resort by fostering a sense of leadership, independence and community responsibility. It's also a useful local **information centre**, dishing out advice on hiking and accommodation, and the young members of its offshoot environmental/courtesy project, LYNX, patrol the streets in uniform t-shirts and caps.

*There's no public transport in Oracabessa, but Paramount Cars (☎994 2357) offers reasonable car-rental deals.*

The first phase of the resort development is already in evidence just off Main Street along Old Wharf Road at the **James Bond Beach Club** (daily 8am–6pm; US$5), already one of the trendiest private beaches on the island. It boasts translucent water, a small but near-perfect white-sand beach, a distinctively styled watersports centre and bar, and a huge bamboo stage which occasionally holds exclusive stageshows courtesy of the Island artist roster. Natural mixed drinks and meals are available, as are volleyball tournaments and jet-ski safaris to deserted bays.

*Already successful Island Outpost properties include* Jake's *and* Strawberry Hill *(see pp.291 & 111).*

If you're wondering why a Jamaican beach club should be named after a fictional secret agent, then head east along Main Street until Oracabessa merges into the residential community of **Race Course** where you'll find an unassuming white-walled bungalow with black-painted pineapples on the gateposts. **Goldeneye** was designed and purpose-built by British author Ian Fleming, who wrote ten of the *James Bond* novels within these walls, taking his hero's name from the author of the classic book *Birds of the West Indies* and many of his characters from various Jamaican friends. During the winters he spent here between 1946 and 1964, Fleming's house guests included Sir Anthony Eden and Princess Margaret. New owner Chris Blackwell has added Marianne Faithfull, U2 and Grace Jones to the guestbook and continued the tradition of having them plant a tree in the garden. You can see some of the trees and a distant glimpse of the house by peering in at the gate, which is only thrown open once a year for the **James Bond Festival**, an upmarket event featuring guided tours of Goldeneye, memorabilia auctions, displays of Bond artefacts and the chance to mingle with old Bond girls and baddies (see p.35 for details).

The right fork from the Oracabessa roundabout takes you to the most attractive plantation on the north coast, **Sun Valley** (daily, 1hr 30min tours at 9am, 1pm & 2pm; US$12). This working family-owned plantation concentrates on bananas and coconuts, and the tour explains their growth processes, takes in some interesting trees, flowers and bushes, and includes drinks, a light meal and some fruit-tasting. You can also see the lot on horseback (1hr; US$20).

## Accommodation

In addition to two large **all-inclusives** there are some really lovely small-scale **guesthouses** in the Oracabessa area, which range in price and facilities from the very cheap to the pretty plush.

**Boscobel Beach Hotel**, PO Box 63, Boscobel; ☎975 7331 or 7336, fax 975 7370. Sprawling family-oriented all-inclusive on the A3 just before the Oracabessa roundabout. Nice rooms, a large white-sand beach, petting zoo, playground, pools, tennis courts, watersports, gym, disco and numerous bars, plus constant childcare and an exhaustive kids' activity schedule. One child under 14 per adult stays free. Three night minimum stay. ⑦.

*Island Outpost plans a host of accommodations in Oracabessa to suit every budget, none of which has yet opened.*

**Golden Seas**, PO Box 1, Oracabessa PO; ☎975 3540 or 3094, fax 975 3243. An inexplicably fashionable but relaxed resort hidden behind trees next to the roundabout, with 1970s-style decor, a medium-sized yellow-sand beach with rather murky water, watersports, a pool with swim-up bar, watersports, tennis court and excellent piped reggae. Rooms have river or sea views. ⑤.

**Harbour View Manor**, Boscobel PO; ☎926 0029 or 2321, fax 978 6380. Private residence off the A3 just west of town, overlooking the bay and cooled by constant sea breezes. Rooms are decorated with delicate wall stencils and paintings, antique furniture and fresh flowers from the well-tended garden, and have access to the verandah and shared bathroom. Madame Curie the dancing turtle provides entertainment, and large German Shepherd dogs take care of security. There's a self-contained studio cottage at the bottom of the garden, and rates include a huge Jamaican/continental breakfast. ④.

**Lovely Spot Villas**, Race Course, Oracabessa PO; ☎975 3322 (in US ☎617/361-4416). Well signposted off the A3 just before Goldeneye, a small, friendly, family-run resort of self-contained villas at the sea's edge, with access to wonderful swimming and snorkelling. Discount for stays of a week or longer. Small bar area and meals available, though there are cooking facilities. ②.

**Moxons Villas**, Boscobel PO; ☎975 7219 or 7023. This hotel-cum-restaurant has seen better days, but its clifftop setting is starkly beautiful and rates for the eclectic range of villas are low. Rooms set back from the sea and ocean-facing apartments with cooking facilities. ②/③.

**Nix-Nax Rainbow Isle of Light**, off Main St, Oracabessa PO; ☎975 3364. Small American/Jamaican-run guesthouse with an unashamedly collective ambience – walls are adorned with consciousness-raising adages and alternative medical treatments are available. Rooms are basic with shared or private bathroom and communal kitchen. ①.

**Ocean Pearl Beach Resort**, Boscobel PO; ☎975 3164. Midway between Boscobel and Oracabessa, this small cliffside hotel has its own large and inviting beach, 1–4-bed apartments, a bar/restaurant and watersports. ③.

### Eating, drinking and entertainment

For a splurge, the *Golden Seas* hotel **restaurant** serves huge portions of expensive, well-executed Jamaican food. Directly opposite, *Big Mamma's Jerk Centre* offers good, cheap jerk chicken or pork and Jamaican staples. Perched atop a cliff on the other side of town, jovial and friendly *Dor's Sea Cliff Fish Pot* in Race Course has juicy fresh fish or lobster dinners and superlative conch soup and a nice circular bar for lounging and chatting (daily 24hr). A few hundred yards up the road, a nameless Ital food shack cooks up hearty portions of fish or vegetables. A little further afield, the thatched roadside bar and restaurant at *Ocean Pearl Resort* in Boscobel serves lobster and steak and puts on beach barbecues and Saturday night bonfires. Also in Boscobel, *Collette's Café-n-Lounge* offers Jamaican meals, reggae nights, seafood extravaganzas and a daily happy hour (6–7pm).

## Port Maria

**PORT MARIA** is oddly quiet for a parish capital, and though pleasantly lazy and picturesque, with lots of cut stone alluding to more auspicious times and far more in the way of shops and offices than Oracabessa, once you've admired the scenery and strolled the few shopping streets there's little to do.

The town's main attractions are all on its outskirts. As you round the twisting outcrops that protect the natural harbour, a stunning view of tiny and forested **Cabarita Island** is revealed right in the middle of the bay. You can arrange a combined fishing trip and island visit with one of the fishermen who moor their boats on the rather grubby grey-sanded central fishing beach. Around the next outcrop is the beautiful cut-stone **St Mary Parish Church**, dating back to 1861. Its cemetery extends down to the sea and the weathered gravestones stand testament to the abrasive properties of salty air; look out for the monument to black freedom fighter **Tacky** (see p.170). Opposite the church is the old police station, gutted by fire in 1988

*Port Maria's church and old police station are immortalized in scenes in the classic Jamaican movie Countryman.*

## The Tacky Rebellion

In the late eighteenth century, Port Maria saw one of Jamaica's bloodiest rebellions, an uprising that sowed the seeds for emancipation eighty years later. Led by a runaway slave known as **Tacky** (a European spelling of the Ghanaian name Tekyi or "the great") who was said to have been a chief of Coromantee descent, the rebellion sparked violent protests throughout the island and aimed at a complete cull of whites and the creation of an all-black colony. The revolt began on Easter Sunday 1760, when Tacky and a small group of slaves from local estates murdered their overseers and marched to Port Maria, killing the storekeeper at Fort Haldane and seizing arms and ammunition. Five months of fighting ensued, with £100,000 worth of damage done to nearby plantations. However, the thousand-strong slave army could not compete with the superior military force of the British, who utilized loyal slaves and Maroons (in accordance with the 1739 treaty) in the guerrilla warfare. The rebellion was savagely quashed and severe punishments meted out to the dissidents; Tacky was captured by Maroon marksmen and killed, his head cut off and displayed on a pole in Spanish Town. Others were chained to stakes and burned alive, gibbeted or hung by irons and left to die as an example to others contemplating sedition. After Tacky's death, many of his followers committed suicide rather than live enslaved. In all, 300 slaves died fighting, 50 were captured and executed and 300 transported abroad, but only 60 whites died.

but still displaying a plaque dedicating it to Alexander Bustamante (see p.246). A bridge crossing the polluted Ochom River brings you into the main town centre, a maze of intertwining streets and yellow stone buildings laid out in a rough grid formation.

## Firefly

The only public attraction around Port Maria, two miles away, reached by road from town or Oracabessa, is **Firefly** (daily 8.30am–5.30pm; US$10), Noel Coward's Jamaican home from its construction in 1955 to his death in 1973. Acquired by Island Outpost in 1992, the house remains much as Coward left it, his studio set up with a painting on the easel, the drawing room – where a string of illustrious guests were entertained – complete with two polished pianos, kitchen cupboards full of yellowing bottles and packets, and the table freshly laid as it was on the day the Queen Mother came to lunch in 1965. Coward died here in his bedroom and is buried on the property. The tour includes a complimentary drink (guides expect a tip) and there is a gift shop and café. The view to the east overlooking Port Maria bay and Cabarita island with the peaks of the Blue Mountains to the right is one of the best on the island. To the west lies **Galina Point** and **lighthouse**, the most northerly tip of Jamaica – you can see Cuba on a clear day. Pirate extraordinaire Sir Henry Morgan (see p.316) used the spot as a vantage point during his reign as governor three hundred years ago; gun slits in a ruined stone building here recall the buccaneer days.

**Practicalities**

Although there's precious little reason to **stay** in Port Maria, there are a few options should you choose to do so. *Blue Harbour*, a five-minute drive west (Port Maria PO; ☎994 2262; ③), built in the 1940s by Noel Coward who stayed here while waiting for Firefly to be completed, has attractive fan-cooled rooms, while *Casa Maria Hotel*, also just west (PO Box 10, ☎994 2323, fax 994 2324; ④), is a hotel of faded grandeur but appealing friendliness popular with long-stay Jamaicans. Slightly further out, in Galina, the secluded *Belvetiro Inn* (PO Box 151; ☎0919 7544; ①) has basic but clean rooms, a pool and good snorkelling. Finally, *Sonrise Beach Retreat* (Robins Bay PA; ☎ & fax 999 7169; ③) offers cottages, camping and dormitories in eighteen acres of gardens with a white-sand cove, undeveloped black-sand beaches and all sorts of sporting activities, and offers discounts for groups.

All the hotels can provide meals, but there are also plenty of small **restaurants**, such as the unceremonious *Almond Tree* at 56 Warner St, and **rum bars** aplenty; a few play rocksteady into the night on Saturdays and Sundays, and the weekend "ben-dung" (literally, "bend down", with items spread out on the ground) market adds a bit of bustle.

East of Ocho Rios

There are irregular buses to Port Maria from Ochi, Montego Bay, Kingston and Port Antonio.

# West of Ocho Rios

Though the coast between the top resort towns sees plenty of tourist traffic, the craft stalls, "Welcome to Jamaica" billboards and fruit vendors are generally restricted to the roadside, and even in the swiftly developing beach resorts of **Runaway and Discovery bays**, life continues relatively unfettered by the foreign dollar. With its thriving market and Georgian architecture interspersed with gently weather-beaten clapboard houses, **St Ann's Bay** is an attractive and unpretentious small town, with ruined Spanish capital **Sevilla Nueva** a few minutes' walk away. Historic but unkempt **Rio Bueno** marks the boundary of St Ann and Trelawny parishes and a distinct change in the landscape – from languid hills to rugged hillocks. Unexpectedly energetic interior villages such as **Browns Town** perch on the fringes of the Cockpits (see Chapter Four) and the panoramic views over deep valleys are constantly spectacular. The interior remains largely undeveloped save for the **Marley tomb** in central St Ann and some excellent tourist-oriented rum factories and river-rafting operations around **Falmouth**, capital of Trelawny and an architectural goldmine.

## St Ann's Bay and around

Eight miles west of Ocho Rios and stretching up the coastal hillside, **ST ANN'S BAY** is characterized by its porticoed shopfronts, sloping streets and old-fashioned but nonchalant atmosphere. Small enough

*Midway between Ochi and St Ann's Bay, behind the Roaring River generating station, is one of the prettiest secluded beaches in the area, known as "James Bond Beach" in reference to the Dr No scenes filmed here, and with its own waterfall.*

*Lillyfield Great
House, set in
the hills
behind St
Ann's Bay,
offers guided
tours and
lunch (call
☎972 6045).*

to cover on foot in an hour or two, it consists of two central thoroughfares, Bravo and Main streets, which meet in a crossroads. Main Street hogs all the action, lined with shops and a **market** which spills out onto the street on Fridays and Saturdays, selling everything from reggae tapes to string vests and skimpy dancehall duds.

The town's distinctive1860 **courthouse** dominates from its perch at the top of Main Street – you can enter as an observer during trials, though the bureaucratic rigmarole of the Jamaican court system is often more arresting than the cases themselves. Opposite the courthouse is the still operational **Eclypse Printery**, originally owned by an uncle of Marcus Garvey – you can still see the press where Garvey learned his first trade (see box).

Continuing down Main Street, a battered sign points to the ramshackle **Seville Pottery** warehouse, where you can buy excellent ceramics without the sales banter and mark-up of tourist shops – if you promise not to use them for liquor, the owner will sell you one of the beautiful blue-glazed bottles produced for Sangster's

---

### Marcus Garvey

Born in St Ann's Bay on August 17, 1887, the **Right Excellent Marcus Mosiah Garvey** was one of the most powerful black rights activists of the twentieth century. His outspoken denunciations of colonialism and racism and his concrete efforts to unite and empower the African diaspora influenced politicians, musicians and academics alike. His legacy remains one of the most significant in Jamaican history – Rastafarians call him a **black prophet** and his philosophies form the basis of their faith (see "Religion" in Contexts, p.334).

Reputedly of Maroon descent, Garvey's early years were dominated by the uncompromising attitude of his father, a master stone mason who earned enough to pursue multiple law-suits against those he felt had slighted him on racial grounds. Though lack of funds ended the young Garvey's formal education at fourteen, he continued to be tutored privately and spend long hours in his father's extensive library. Prodigious from an early age, Garvey was made foreman of his uncle's Eclypse Printery at eighteen, but small-town living offered scant opportunities, and in 1906 he moved to Kingston and found work as a printery foreman – a significant coup at a time when supervisors were usually white – and became an activist in the fledgling trade union movement. Disturbed at the institutionalized injustice meted out to black workers, Garvey left Jamaica in 1910 to search for better prospects in Costa Rica, where he worked as a time-keeper on a banana plantation and set up two workers' newspapers to highlight the deplorable conditions for West Indian migrants. During a stint in England in 1912, he took classes at Birkbeck College and read up on other black nationalists like Booker T. Washington, whose seminal text *Up From Slavery* was highly influential in fostering Garvey's ever-increasing militancy. In 1914, he returned to Jamaica and formed the **Universal Negro Improvement Association** (UNIA) "to champion Negro nationhood by redemption of Africa; to make the Negro race conscious, to advocate self determination, to inspire and instil racial love and self respect", but

---

liqueurs (see p.115). Further along the road, in the middle of a roundabout, sits an ornate **monument to Christopher Columbus** by Spanish artist Michele Geurisi – the adventurer strikes a noble pose above his sunken ships. Just before the road forks, the church of **Our Lady of Perpetual Help** is one of the few remaining Catholic houses of worship in Jamaica; the stone it's made of was resurrected from the original structure – Peter Martyr Church, the first stone church in Jamaica, built in 1524 by the Spanish as a part of Sevilla Nueva.

The quieter left fork of Main Street holds the **library** (Mon–Sat 9.30am–6pm), with its **Marcus Garvey memorial statue** on the front lawn. The outsize bronze stands before the words "We Declare to the World – Africa Must Be Free". Other than a parade in the town centre every August 17, the statue is the only distinctive evidence of Garvey's local connection (the house where he was born – 32 Market St – is a private residence); the library itself is a good source of information on his life and work.

# West of Ocho Rios

*Snorkelling and diving in quest of Columbus's sunken wrecks is a big draw. The best local operator is* Seascape Dive Village; ☎ *972 2573.*

Jamaica's middle classes weren't ready to embrace such a radical and he emigrated to the USA in 1916 to seek a more sympathetic audience. Black Americans identified so strongly that by 1920, the UNIA had become the largest black pressure group ever to exist in the US, with a membership estimated from two to six million. Despite being outlawed in most of the colonies, his self-published *Negro World* newspaper achieved the largest circulation of any black paper in the world, and with the financial backing of thousands who bought shares, Garvey formed the Black Star Line Shipping Company to foster trade links between black nations and enable repatriation to the African homeland.

Though known principally as a "Back-To-Africa" advocate, Garvey was equally concerned with improving the cultural and economic situation of blacks wherever they found themselves. His assault on post-colonial nihilism was his greatest achievement; eschewing the sense of inferiority and powerlessness fostered during enslavement, he advocated black pride and self-determination, using the historical achievements of Africans to animate blacks: "Up you mighty race, you can accomplish what you will."

Garvey was regarded a subversive in the US, and his supporters saw his 1922 imprisonment on a trumped-up mail fraud charge as an attempt to muzzle the message. After two years in Atlanta Federal Prison, pressure from UNIA members secured his release, and in 1927 he was deported back to Jamaica on a wave of publicity. However, his imprisonment had caused a loss of campaign momentum; the Black Star Line had foundered, and Garvey never recaptured his early success. Tiring of constant battles with authority, he moved the struggle to the UK, where he died in obscurity in 1940. His importance was only recognized posthumously – in 1964 his remains were returned to Jamaica by the state and interred in Kingston's National Heroes Park. In the 1970s, music inspired a resurgence of Garveyism in Jamaica, with Rastafarian musicians like Burning Spear immortalizing his life and work in song, and today his ideas remain central to the Jamaican national consciousness.

West of
Ocho Rios

*Hooves in Ocho
Rios (☎974
6245; 2 hr
30min; US$60)
organizes
excellent
horseback
heritage trails
of Seville.*

## Seville

St Ann's Bay is bordered to the west by the old Spanish village of **Seville**, Jamaica's first Spanish settlement (see box), but now an overgrown wasteland dotted with the crumbling remains of once-impressive buildings. On the other side of the road is **Seville Great House and Heritage Park** (daily except Mon 9am–4pm; US$3). Managed by the Jamaica National Heritage Trust, this is one of the few true heritage sites on the island, focusing on the lives, customs and culture of Tainos and Africans rather than celebrating plantation owners or "discoverers". A video presentation gives a detailed overview of Seville's history, and the museum displays intricately crafted Taino *zemis* (talismans used to ward off evil spirits) and other artefacts. Hidden in among unmaintained bush-land, the ruins of Seville itself are not visible from the main road, but you can ask at the great house for an accompanied walking tour of what remains –

---

### Christopher Columbus and the Tainos at Seville

The north coast is often referred to as "Columbus Country" – and though a little jaded the title is certainly apt, as the Italian-born conquistador got his first sight of Jamaica at St Ann's Bay. Sailing into the bay during his second voyage in 1494 to claim new territories on behalf of King Ferdinand and Queen Isabella of Spain, Christopher Columbus was so impressed by its beauty that he named it **Santa Gloria**. He was rather less enamoured during his fourth and final voyage in 1503, when the unseaworthy state of his worm-eaten, weather-beaten caravels forced him and his crew to spend an unhappy year marooned here in makeshift shacks, awaiting rescue from Spanish compatriots in Hispaniola. Plagued by illness and worried by the partial mutiny of his men, Columbus used a mixture of bribery and superstition (his prediction of a solar eclipse led them to believe he was a god), to coerce Taino Indians into providing food until their eventual rescue in 1504, after a year and a day on the beach.

Columbus died in Spain in 1506 but his son **Diego** was appointed Governor of the Indies and directed **Juan de Esquivel** to establish the first Spanish colony on the island – **Sevilla Nueva** – at what is today called Seville, in 1510. Situated on the site of the Taino (or Arawak) village **Maima**, the development of Sevilla Nueva eradicated Jamaica's Indian population in fifty years. The *encomienda* system of serf labour – the antithesis of the previously unfettered Taino lifestyle – was introduced and brutally enforced, and Caciques (Taino chiefs) selectively murdered; with their society in tatters and their forms of authority destroyed, the confused Indians were easily branded and enslaved, and along with Africans transported to the island by the Spanish, were conscripted to build the new city. Less robust than the Africans, the Amerindians were unable to bear a life of slavery; ill-treatment and European diseases soon eradicated those who didn't commit suicide, but while the Tainos expired, New Seville rapidly developed into a sizeable town, with churches, castles, irrigation and drainage sites and a wharf. However, its occupation lasted only until 1534, when the marshy, disease-inducing environment was abandoned in favour of Villa de la Vega or Spanish Town (p.95).

---

THE GUIDE: CHAPTER 3

a water wheel, parts of the Spanish Catholic church (the first on the island), sugar mill and the governor's castle poking through the foliage, as well as the sites of Taino villages and slave settlements.

## Around St Ann's Bay: Priory to Chukka Cove

The short coastal stretch west of St Ann's Bay is dotted with minor roadside communities. Past tiny **PRIORY**, a mile and a half along – where **Alterry** is a beautiful, usually deserted public beach with clear, deep water – is **LLANDOVERY**, home to a huge disused sugar factory, the Llandovery-Richmond estate, established in 1674 by the English. The shimmering factory chimneys are visible from the main road, and there is a beautiful waterfall on the property, but the land is private and access is at the discretion of the owners – ask at the farmhouse by the *Ocean Line Family Fun Park* (daily 9am till late; US$2 or US$5 to use the pool and water slide), a godsend for those with restless children, as there's a go-kart track, miniature golf course, pool with water slide, playground and muddy beach.

*The* Circle B Farm *(daily 10am–5pm; US$10/20), just inland of Priory, offers informal but informed plantation tours, with lunch optional.*

Just west is **Chukka Cove**, a colonial hangover of clipped polo fields, immaculate stables and luxury villas. Once part of the Llandovery-Richmond estate, Chukka is now the most prestigious equestrian facility and polo ground in Jamaica – matches are open to observers most weekends; call for schedules (☎972 2506). The beach ride (daily 9am; 3hr US$55) is fabulous; after a gentle hack through cattle pastures, you swim your snorting mount in the sea. Mountain rides (daily 9am & 2pm; 1hr US$30, 2hr US$40) are less energetic, and dressage and jumping are available. The barren volcanic cliffs to the left were used as a backdrop for scenes from the screen epic *Papillon*.

*Tomorrow's Times Today Bamboo Bicycle Tour (☎972 2144; US$50) offers great mountain bike tours through the hills and gullies.*

Chukka's exclusivity is forgotten once a year when the fields next door host Carnival in April, see p.34.

## Accommodation

Though **accommodation** choices are few around St Ann's Bay, you escape the dust and bustle of Ochi while staying close enough to enjoy its good points, and can relax in less restricted surroundings. *Starfish Beach Camping* (no phone), at the end of the road beyond *Seascape*, offers US$5 **camping** in an unfenced ground.

**Chukka Cove Villas**, PO Box 160, Ocho Rios; ☎974 5568, fax 974 5568. Luxury villas in lush gardens with fruit trees and a mineral pool, with access to deep-sea swimming and excellent snorkelling – paradise if you can afford it. ⑨.

**High Hope Estate**, PO Box 11, St Ann's Bay; ☎972 2277, fax 972 1607. A 10min drive inland from Priory, just west of town, an eclectically furnished 7-room hotel that's both intimate and luxurious, with fantastic views, a pool, extensive gardens, excellent food and free access to a private beach club. ⑥.

**Jamel Jamaica**, signposted off the A3 at Priory; ☎972 1031 or 1221, fax 972 0714. Extremely clean small hotel with a large courtyard, restaurant, slot machines, pool and access to the sea but no beach. ④.

**Seascape Dive Village;** ☎ & fax 972 2753. A bit hard to find – go down the slip road for the *Jamel Jamaica* and continue until the road turns. Friendly place with a fantastic setting and relaxed atmosphere, with rooms, comfortable villas and camping. Meals, pool and all sorts of watersports. ③/⑤.

### Eating and entertainment

Patty shops and small **restaurants** line Main Street in St Ann's Bay; *Square One* on Bravo Street is especially good for cheap Jamaican meals or snacks – chicken, patties, callaloo loaf and pastries. Fabulous sit-down meals are served at *The Mug* (☎972 1018), on the coast road behind *Artizans' Craft Village*, one of the north coast's best seafood restaurants; Jamaicans come from miles around for the excellent conch, fish, lobster and shrimp, served with sublime bammy, rice or chips. Wednesday is "Mug Night", when barbecued fish and chicken are added to the menu and opening hours are extended until 1am. Elsewhere, check out the *Seafood Specialist* at Priory – it specializes in seafood. For **entertainment**, sound-system dances and stageshows are occasionally held at Alterry beach and *Ocean Line* – look out for promotional posters.

## Runaway Bay and Discovery Bay

Sitting together halfway between Falmouth and Ocho Rios, two mini-resorts bask in isolated indolence, bayside oases where the "Jamaica no problem" maxim for once rings true. Dominated by sprawling all-inclusives, **RUNAWAY BAY** is the more developed of the two, though beyond the razor-wired fences and Italianate marble lobbies, life jogs along at a slow lick, with few organized attractions to draw in the crowds. Even more pacific than its neighbour, the crescent harbour of **DISCOVERY BAY** is dominated by the red-stained sphere of the Kaiser bauxite plant, with fewer hotels but a fantastic public beach and regular sound-system dances held right at the water's edge

*Contrary to popular belief, Discovery Bay is not so-named because of Columbus's first step onto Jamaican shores; that honour goes to Rio Bueno a few miles down the road.*

Theories abound as to the **naming** of the twin bays; while it's usually assumed that the "runaways" were Spanish troops fleeing the strong arm of the British in the late 1600s, it's more likely that the name refers to Africans who made the risky ninety-mile canoe trip to Cuba and freedom from slavery. Survivors were baptized into Catholicism, and calls for their return were denied on the grounds that Catholics couldn't be expected to live among sectarians.

### Arrival and getting around

Buses from Montego Bay and Ocho Rios arrive and depart from the small square outside *The Patty Place* in Runaway Bay, and from the A1/ B3 intersection in Discovery Bay.

As both communities spread out from the coast road, getting lost is practically impossible, though the barely paved tracks of the interior can seem a bit maze-like. Most things you'll want to do are within walking distance, but you may find it easier to jump in a shared taxi for the ride to Puerto Seco. *Sir Win's Love Line Taxi Service* (☎0999 7478 or 973 4954), private driver Daniel Melbourne (☎973 5294) and *Poochie's* minibuses (☎973 2509) are all dependable. Car rental is available from *Caribbean Car Rentals* in Runaway Bay (☎973 3539), while *Jake's* (☎973 4403), also in Runaway Bay, rents motorbikes and the odd bicycle – ideal for hopping between the bays.

West of Ocho Rios

## Accommodation

**All-inclusives** dominate the bays, but there are still some lovely small **hotels** and **guesthouses** towards Discovery Bay and around Hampton Road in Runaway Bay. There are also lots of luxury **villas** around the Discovery Bay headland, which can be cost-effective for large groups – a five-bedroom pad rents from around US$2000 per week. For further information, contact *JAVA* (☎974 2763 or 2508, fax 974 2967). *Sunflower Resort* (☎973 2171 or 2173, fax 973 2381) has some reasonably priced villas in the hills above Runaway Bay.

**Cliff's Apartments**, PO Box 33, Runaway Bay; ☎973 2061. Popular with Jamaicans and budget-conscious Europeans, this collection of apartments and rooms on Hampton Road enjoys the ambience of a Jamaican home – kids running around and lots of hanging out. ①/②.

**Hampton View**, Runaway Bay PO; ☎973 4337. Self-catering apartments in a characteristic Jamaican abode on Hampton Road – not flash but comfortable and homely, with kitchen and shared verandah. ②.

**The Pantharosa**, 100yd down the A3 Browns Town road; ☎973 5553. Self-contained, spacious and spotless apartments with cable tv and VCR. A lively bar in the huge backyard and home-cooked meals available. ②/③.

**Portside Villas and Apartments**, PO Box 42, Discovery Bay; ☎973 2007 or 3135, fax 973 2720. Split by the A3, a characterful complex of 32 pointy-roofed condos perched on the steeply inclining hillside with fantastic views over the bay. Two pools, watersports, tennis court, Jacuzzi, children's wading pool and tiny beach; one child under 12 stays free. ⑤.

**Runaway HEART Country Club**, PO Box 98, Runaway Bay; ☎973 2671–4, fax 973 2693. Outstanding service at reasonable rates in a government-sponsored hotel training school. Immaculate gardens, great patio restaurant, daily beach shuttle and good rooms; children under 12 stay free.③–④.

**Sharp's Flats**, opposite the *Patty Place* on Main St; no phone. Small rooms in beautiful clifftop gardens – functional, clean and excellent value. ②.

**Tamarind Tree**, PO Box 235, Runaway Bay; ☎973 4819 or 2678, fax 973 5013. One of the few remaining "old school" hotels, with a friendly atmosphere, restaurant, large pool, disco with black padded walls, and a choice between rooms and 3-bed cottages. Not far from some public beaches. ④/⑥.

**Tropical Inn**, PO Box 23, Runaway Bay; ☎ & fax 973 4681. Small, relaxed German-oriented hotel in the middle of town. Squeaky-clean rooms with the rare bonus of mosquito nets. Bar, restaurant, pool, small beach and lounge with satellite tv; tours and meal plans available. ④.

**Whilby Resort Cottages**; PO Box 111, Runaway Bay; ☎944 2701. Easy-going home-from-home right at the end of Hampton Road. Sweeping lawns, a

*For the best shopping in the bay area, head to the market inland at Browns Town; see p.182.*

# West of Ocho Rios

garden full of herbs and flowers, camping, laundry facilities, bicycles to borrow and a good spread of apartments. ②–③.

## ALL-INCLUSIVES

**Breezes Runaway Bay** (formerly *Jamaica Jamaica*), PO Box 58, Runaway Bay; ☎973 2436, fax 973 2352. The largest all-inclusive in the area, with a huge range of activities – gym, all watersports, scuba, pools, tennis courts, 18-hole golf course across the road, nightclub, a super-perfect beach (with a clothing optional area) and an emphasis on fun for over-16s. ⑧.

**Club Caribbean**, Salem, PO Box 65, Runaway Bay; ☎973 3507 or 4702, fax 973 3509. Appealing, unpretentious all-inclusive with a 1000ft imported-sand beach and an English-style pub, plus all the usual facilities. Rooms are basic garden cottages (no a/c) or suites in the main building. Children under 5 stay free, 6–12s at a reduced rate. ⑥.

**Eaton Hall**, PO Box 112, Runaway Bay; ☎973 2738 or 3403, fax 973 2432. Elegant rooms, individuality and no enforced merry-making. The dining area and pool perch on volcanic cliffs and most rooms face the ocean – swimming is marvellous. Pool, private beach, watersports, glass-bottom boat, scuba, tennis court and nightly entertainment. No children under 12. ⑤–⑥.

**Franklyn D. Resort**, PO Box 201, Runaway Bay; ☎973 4591 or 3067, fax 973 3071. Well-run family resort with cheerful atmosphere, attractive suites with terraces, numerous children's activities, all watersports, a pool, gym and disco, and loads of capable nannies. Excellent meals and a designated children's restaurant. Children under 16 stay free. ⑧.

## Runaway Bay

*The superb Superclubs golf course opposite the all-inclusive block is open to non-guests; there's a restaurant, bar and clubhouse on site (☎973 2561).*

Little more than a roadside strip, **RUNAWAY BAY** stretches lazily along the coast for three miles or so, a sun-bleached and lackadaisical melee of bars and hotels running to the satellite community of **SALEM** to the east, where you'll find the majority of shops and restaurants. The **all-inclusives** are clumped together in a single block in front of the best beaches – you know you're at the spot when you register the incongruous neatness. Runaway Bay is not a resort on the scale of Ocho Rios or Montego Bay, and as most holiday business takes place inside the all-inclusives, a non-Jamaican without a golf cart, resort bicycle or hotel entertainment co-ordinator is still a fairly rare sight; a shame, as the town is easily walkable and harassment and trouble are uncommon (though, as ever, be careful). However, as the new kid on the block of north-coast tourism and with several large hotels in the making, what little indigenous character there is may soon be eradicated.

*Independent operator Paul (☎0997 7141) offers great horse-riding in and around Runaway Bay.*

Other than the flurry of activity as buses come to a honking halt and vendors hawk their piles of cane and fruit around the miniature **town square** in front of the post office, there is little obvious activity in town, though there's plenty just up the B3 at **Dover Raceway**, a professional race track with regular advertised meets. For swimming, picturesque sugary-sanded **Cardiff Hall public beach**, opposite the *Texaco* petrol station, is popular with locals who congregate under the

Taking aim at Falmouth harbour

Lobster claw heliconia

Rafting on the Rio Grande

Banana man, St Mary

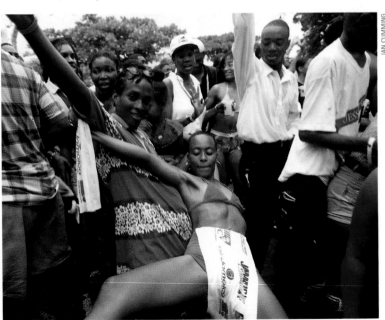

Carnival, Chukka Cove

Bamboo rafts on the Martha Brae

Long Bay, Portland

Falmouth police post, Trelawny

The doctor bird

Mobile record shack, Kingston

### Plantation culture and the story of sugar

When the British took control of Jamaica in 1655, they found three ramshackle **sugarcane plantations** recently deserted by the Spaniards, who had brought the plant to the island from southeast Asia but failed to develop it; a hundred years later, there were well over 400 plantations on the island. Having already established successful plantations in Barbados, the British were eager to transform Jamaica into a giant sugar-producing factory, offering thirty acres of land to any Englishman settling on the island. Hundreds took up the offer and the commercial cultivation of sugarcane began in earnest. Small concerns were quickly bought out and by the early 1700s, huge plantations covered practically all of Jamaica's most fertile land, with African slaves shipped in to do the dirty work and absentee owners reaping tremendous profits.

By the mid-eighteenth century, tax and trade incentives made Jamaica the largest sugar producer in the world and the richest of England's colonies. The planters celebrated their wealth by building the lavish **great houses** that still overlook cane flats from breezy hilltop perches. However, the abolition of the slave trade in 1834 and full emancipation in 1838 left a labour gap and marked the decline of the sugar trade. The Sugar Equalization Act of 1846 ended preferential treatment for sugar produced in the colonies and despite the influx of indentured workers from Africa, India and Europe (who were paid wages for the first time), the industry could no longer compete with cheaper sugar produced in Cuba and Brazil. In the twentieth century, the sugar industry is still Jamaica's single largest employer and accounts for nearly twelve percent of its overall exports, but poor rates of pay make industrial action a regular occurrence and inadequate technological advancement has seen a slide in productivity.

tree for dominoes and a beer. **Salem Paradise Beach**, at the Salem end of town, is not the promised elysium field – sound-system dances are occasionally held here and nobody clears up the debris. Midway between the two bays are the **Green Grotto and Runaway Caves** (daily 9am–5pm; US$3.50). Thought to have been used as a hideout by fleeing Spanish troops and possibly as a Taino place of worship, the caves are expansive and well lit with an underwater lake (short boat ride included), and would be tranquil were it not for the discordant musician with his ancient drum machine and electric guitar.

*You can buy freshly caught fish by the pound outside Salem Paradise beach – go early for the best bargains.*

### Discovery Bay

DISCOVERY BAY is more a coastal clutch of shops, snack bars and houses than a town. The **bauxite industry** is very visible here – the orange-stained wharf and dome-shaped storage chamber are even attractive in their immense ugliness. Jamaica exports over two million tons of "red gold" to US refineries annually, much of it from the plant at Discovery Bay; local big cheese Kaiser Bauxite pays its dues by financing all sorts of community projects, even sponsoring the push-cart derby held every August on the cricket pitch behind the plant (a good laugh if you're around).

*See p.307 for more on bauxite.*

# West of Ocho Rios

*Much of the go-karting footage in the movie* Cool Runnings *was shot in Discovery Bay.*

The broken-down structure as you round the bay is **Quadrant Wharf**, built in 1777 by British fearful of possibile French attack; its cannons have long disappeared, and only the basic stone structure and some rusting ironware remain. **Columbus Park** (daily 9am–5pm; free), on the western curve of the bay, is a well-signposted and glossy open-air museum exploiting the area's Columbus link. The artefacts are restricted to colonial times, but there are some interesting exhibits including a water wheel and cannon, and there's an (expensive) craft market on site.

**Puerto Seco beach** (daily 8am–5pm; J$20), bang opposite the shopping complex, is the best local swimming spot unattached to a hotel. The name is derived from the old Spanish title meaning "dry harbour" in reference to Columbus's reluctance to land in a bay with no fresh water (see p.186). Despite gleaming sand and crystal-clear water, it's relatively deserted on weekdays, and the gently shelving shoreline is good for families. There are full facilities and a good snack bar. **Discovery Bay beach**, just down a rutted dirt track, is free but can't compete. Past here, the eastern reaches of the bay are dominated by luxurious villas owned by the likes of white Jamaican entrepreneur Gordon "Butch" Stewart, while on the opposite outcrop, the University of the West Indies Marine Research Laboratory (☎973 2241) houses the island's only decompression chamber. The straight stretch of road beyond Columbus Park was used as an **illegal airstrip** by ganja exporters in the 1970s – in the still of the night they'd set up impromptu roadblocks, land their small planes and load bales of ganja aboard with the motor still running. The government finally wised up and installed concrete bollards at the roadside, smashing the planes' wings and putting a halt to proceedings on this part of the road at least.

## Eating

The bays' fancy **restaurants** are predominantly within hotels, and as most are all-inclusive you have to buy an expensive day or evening pass to eat there. The Jamaican **restaurants** serve hearty fare at attractive prices, and you can buy cheap and delicious fried fish and bammy or chicken and rice at any of the many roadside stalls.

**Afiya**, Cardiff Hall Blvd, Runaway Bay. Vegetarian restaurant and health food store serving excellent and imaginative wholefood cooking – brown rice is a priceless commodity after a few weeks of hardough bread and fried dumplings.

**Almond Grove**, Main Rd, Salem. Almost salubrious Jamaican eatery with a fairly extensive, moderately priced dinner menu.

**Auntie May's Bluebird Restaurant**, Runaway Bay. Good old-fashioned Jamaican restaurant. Huge breakfasts, soups (sublime conch, beef, or mannish water), and island standards, some Chinese food and lobster in curry butter. Take away available, full bar.

**Charlante Restaurant**, Salem. Small restaurant and bakery with the best ackee and saltfish and veggie patties around – go before 1pm or they'll have sold out.

**Con's Coffee Shop**, Discovery Bay. Thoroughly Jamaican – all the usual favourites accompanied by a steaming bowl of "hard food" – yam, boiled bananas and sweet potato.

**Island Queen**, Carib Plaza, Salem. Marvellous indoor café serving up chicken and chips, burgers, sandwiches, soup, ackee and saltfish, callaloo, patties and natural juices. Honey, home-made preserves, herb-infused vinegar and oils and pickled peppers are on sale at a fraction of gift-shop prices.

**Lagoon Park**. Peaceful setting next to Runaway Caves – you fish for your supper in a lake naturally stocked with red tail and perch, and have your catch cooked for you. Lobster and octopus are also available.

**Mackie's Bar and Jerk Centre**, off the A1 between the bays. Open-air circular bar and restaurant serving good, cheap jerk chicken and pork.

**Northern Jerk and Steak Pit**, Northern Plaza, Salem. Super-efficient shiny-countered indoor jerk house, with a selection of soups and a confectionery counter for late-night munchies. Open daily till midnight.

**The Rising Sun**, Runaway Bay; ☎973 2907. Swiss-run bistro opposite Cardiff Hall beach, serving salads, sandwiches, pizza, seafood, chicken and steaks. Deliveries available.

**Sea Shanty**, *Portside Villas*, Discovery Bay; ☎973 2007. Imaginative cooking in a seafront setting. The kingfish steak with cheese sauce is best, though the varied menu also features soups, meat dishes and fine desserts.

## Entertainment

There are innumerable **bars** at the Salem end of Runaway Bay; best is the *19th Hole Club*, complete with pool table, backgammon, dominoes, loud music and freshly cooked food. The *Marcus-y-Bob* complex on the road between the bays is a nice place for a cool coconut and a chat during the day, while Runaway Bay's *All Nations Bar* is a comfortable local watering hole. Don't bother with the seafood at **Seafood Giant** at the far western end of Runaway Bay – it's far better for a leisurely drink under the huge circular thatched roof.

Though the all-inclusives put on nightly **entertainment** (you can buy an evening pass to attend), there's plenty of alternative nightlife on offer. The *Tamarind Tree Hotel* disco is open to the public at weekends, though often very quiet (cover around US$5), and on Tuesday nights, an enthusiastic crowd heads to the *Quality Jerk Centre* opposite Green Grotto, for dancehall and oldies with the top

Bass Odyssey sound system. There's also an occasional Sunday-night oldies sessions at Puerto Seco Beach, and other nights at Cardiff Hall and Salem beaches. The *Reggae Palace Go-Go Club* in Salem is self-explanatory; it's open very late and packed at the weekends, with a moderate cover charge and a lot of underwear.

The proprietor of the *Almond Grove* puts on occasional **plays** which make for an insightful night of amateur dramatics – call ☎973 4652 to see if there's anything in production. Finally, if you're around in August, don't miss Discovery Bay's **Family Fun Day**, an uproarious blend of children's activities, push-kart racing, live music, sound systems and amateur comedy/cabaret.

## Browns Town

High in the hills above the twin bays, bustling **BROWNS TOWN** hums with the dynamism and industry absent along the coast below. Reached on the B3 from Runaway Bay, or the B5/B11 from Discovery Bay, Browns Town is a sizeable community with fantastic views and a booming central **market** (main days Wed, Fri & Sat); the stalls that line the main road overflow with fresh produce – six-foot pillars of sugarcane, yams and dasheens caked in red alluvial earth, and oranges tied into strings of ten – ferried in by small-scale farmers and sold by formidable higglers. Food is much better bought here than on the coast – quality improves once you near the source and people are too busy to bother about ripping you off. Bootleg name-brand clothing and tawdry knick-knacks also sell by the bucketload – this is *the* place for china figurines and fake flower displays. Even the proper shops are worthy of a root – *Charley & Son* on Main Street is a treasure-trove of ancient books with yellowing covers, tacky postcards and intriguing miscellany. The regional office of the Jamaica Cultural Development Commission (JCDC) on Main Street (☎975 0578; Mon–Sat 9am–5.30pm) will answer your queries. It also co-ordinates local dance and music groups entering the annual Mento Yard competition (see Basics, p.35), and can arrange for you to see local performances.

### PRACTICALITIES

**Restaurants** and **bars** line Main Street, among them *Win Mae's Highway Rest*, which serves huge portions of curried chicken and rice and peas for around J$100. If you want to **stay** and soak up the atmosphere, try the basic but comfortable rooms at *Meditation Heights*, just past the *Esso* petrol station on Huntley Avenue (☎973 4361; ①). Buses from Runaway Bay arrive two or three times a day; taxis are much more convenient.

## Marley's mausoleum and the St Ann interior

The B3 from Runaway Bay is the route to **Alexandria**, where you turn off for the only tourist attraction in the St Ann interior, Bob Marley's former home at **Nine Miles**. Though the scenery here is staggering – the distant Cockpits and sweeping hills and gullies of the Dry Harbour mountains are a photographer's dream – there are few specific points of interest, and the viciously potholed road will demand most of your attention. Small communities such as **Clarks Town** bear the names of European estate keepers and missionaries, and history is everywhere in a landscape strewn with the crumbling chimneys of unidentifiable sugar factories and stone churches built by Baptist missionaries. The main B3 from Browns Town runs to **Cave Valley** where Taino artefacts and petroglyphs adorn the walls of caves that mark the start of treacherous Cockpit Country (see Chapter Four, p.232).

From Alexandria, the narrow road off the B3 to the **Bob Marley Centre and Mausoleum** (daily 7.30am–7.30pm; US$5–10, depending on group size) winds through the hills past **Alva** and **Ballintoy** – you know you're in Nine Miles when you see the red-gold-and-green flags flying high above a fenced-off compound stretching up a hillock to the side of the main road. Just outside is the ticket office (where all visitors must sign in), a snack bar and a gift shop selling tapes and Marley memorabilia at high prices. Once you've paid your fee and the throng of Rasta guides have finished squabbling over who's giving the tour, you're taken up the hill and into the centre proper. On the brow is a prayer space to the left, usually filled with orthodox Rastafarians who come to worship and hold "reasoning" sessions. To the right is the wooden shack that Marley once slept in, complete with the "original" single bed he sang of in *Is This Love*, now decorated with photographs and scribbled notes from Marley disciples throughout the world. Opposite is an outdoor barbecue where Marley cooked up Ital feasts during rural retreats at the height of his career, and the Rasta-coloured "meditation stone" where he rested his head for contemplation with a marvellous view. You leave cameras and shoes outside before entering the **mausoleum** above, a brightly painted concrete building encasing the marble slab that holds Marley's remains. A stained-glass window filters red, gold and green sunlight over the stone, while candles, incense and fresh flowers make the mausoleum one of the more uplifting aspects of a place that in glorifying Marley's death seems only to succeed in highlighting the yawning gap left by his passing. Many Rastafarians – who eschew the concept of physical death – argue that Nine Miles is not his final resting place and that, like Haile Selassie, Bob Marley's bones will never be found.

In some ways, the centre is a bit of a disappointment; a permanent posse of hangers-on seem intent on the hard sell or swapping addresses with female foreigners while the desperate and under-funded commerciality sits ill in a country that puts so much emphasis on Marley's life and work, but nothing can detract from the beauty of the locale; the home of the original "Natural Mystic". This is one place it's better not to visit independently; Dutch reggae fanatic Franky Meeuws runs a well-designed and genuinely considered

**West of Ocho Rios**

excursion to Nine Miles with *Caribic Vacations* (☎979 1080 or 952 5013) that includes detailed commentary on Marley's life interspersed with rare cuts of his music played on the powerful in-bus sound system. Three-day reggae trips to Kingston with a studio visit are also available.

Otherwise, the place comes alive every **February 6**, when Marley's birthday is celebrated with a jump-up and sometimes a live show. For details contact Cedella Marley Booker, Ent (☎0999 7003) or simply turn up on the day (see also Basics, p.34).

---

### Bob Marley – King of Reggae

The legacy of the original ambassador of reggae is impossible to overemphasize. Jamaicans tend to regard their most famous compatriot with an emotional and religious reverence and his lyrics continue to strike a chord across every social strata. Born February 6, 1945, **Robert Nesta Marley** was the progeny of an affair between 17-year-old Cedella Malcolm and 51-year-old Anglo-Jamaican soldier Captain Norval Marley, stationed in the Dry Harbour mountains as overseer of crown lands. Marley's early years in the country surrounded by a doting extended family (particularly his grandfather and formidable "myalman" Omeriah Malcolm) and by the rituals and traditions of rural life had a profound effect on his development. Unlike most Jamaicans of mixed parentage, Marley clung to the African side of his heritage and revelled in the solidarity, freedom and rich cultural life of downtown Kingston, where he spent most of his later life. Marley was known as an intensely spiritual individual, emanating an almost-tangible energy and charisma. He was a lover as well as a thinker: his 1970s membership of the influential Twelve Tribes Of Israel – a Rastafarian sect that divides members by birth month into "houses" with a name and a colour – gave him the title of Joseph, "a fruitful bough" according to the Bible, and though his 1966 marriage to Rita Anderson lasted until he died, his appetite for women was great and he fathered eleven children by various women.

Fusing African drumming traditions with Jamaican rhythms and American rock guitar, Marley's music became a symbol of unity and social change worldwide. Between 1961 and 1981, his output was prolific. Following their first recording *Judge Not* on Leslie Kong's Beverley's label, his band, The Wailers (Marley, Bunny Livingstone and Peter Tosh), went on to record for the some of the best producers in the business – Joe Higgs, Clement "Coxsone" Dodd, Clancey Eccles and Bunny Lee – though most agree that the finest material was recorded in collaboration with innovative and volatile musical genius Lee "Scratch" Perry. In 1963, the huge hit *Simmer Down* (a warning to Kingstonians to cool down the increasing tension) meshed perfectly with the post-independence frustration felt by young Jamaicans and the momentum of success began in earnest, the Wailers' lyrics providing a script for the island's development from rude Boy to Rasta (see "Music" in Contexts, p.346). International recognition came when the Wailers signed to the Island label – owned by Anglo-Jamaican entrepreneur Chris Blackwell, who Marley saw as his "interpreter" rather than his producer. The first Island release was *Catch a Fire* in early 1973, and the eleven albums that followed all became

# Rio Bueno to Duncans

A Spanish-built stone bridge marks the St Ann–Trelawny border and
the entrance to **RIO BUENO**, a poverty-stricken village of crumbling
eighteenth-century buildings, too many skinny dogs and a peeling
police station, all cowering in the lee of a towering silver animal-feed
factory – fortuitously absent when the town was used as a set for *A
High Wind in Jamaica*. Yet despite its unprepossessing appearance, the town has a place in the history books. Having spent a night

---

instant classics. With the help of Blackwell's marketing skills, reggae
became an international genre. Differences with Blackwell – particularly
over his obvious concentration on Marley – led to the departure of Peter
and Bunny in 1974, but the group continued to tour the world with new
musicians and a new name – Bob Marley and the Wailers.

Inevitably, the socially aware Marley became embroiled in the factional-
ized and violent confusion of Jamaican politics, and in the run-up to a headline performance at the 1976 Smile Jamaica concert, staged by the government to quell rising tensions in an election campaign so dogged by violence
that Prime Minister Michael Manley declared a state of emergency, gunmen
burst into Marley's Kingston home and tried to assassinate him. The attempt
was bungled, and most of the shots hit manager Don Taylor (who made a full
recovery), though Bob and Rita incurred minor injuries. Undeterred, a ban-
daged Marley went on stage under heavy security. After the concert, Marley
left Jamaica to recover and record in Britain and the States, but as his international reputation grew, so did his popularity at home, and Jamaicans
began to embrace fully their home-grown megastar. Two years later, he
returned to the island for the first time since the shooting. Met by two thousand fans on the runway, Marley was back to perform for his people at the
historic **One Love Peace Concert**, the result of an unprecedented – and
short-lived – truce between the political garrisons of the PNP and JLP. The
headline act of a line-up that also included Peter Tosh singing solo and spit-
ting vitriol at the politicians, Marley ended his performance by enticing arch-
enemies Michael Manley and Edward Seaga on stage to join hands in a show
of unity – a huge coup. But Marley's call for unity and freedom was not
restricted to Jamaica; one of his greatest triumphs was performing the
protest anthem *Zimbabwe* at the independence celebrations of the former
Rhodesia, the last African country to free itself from colonial rule.

In the midst of a rigorous 1980 tour, Marley was diagnosed as suffering
from cancer, and despite treatments at an alternative clinic in Austria, he
died a year later in Miami, honoured by his country with the Order of
Merit. The Honourable Robert Nesta Marley OM died without making a
will, and years of costly legal wrangles over his US$46 million estate
ensued, with his widow eventually granted the lion's share. Rita Marley's
Bob Marley Foundation continues to sponsor the development of new
artists, and many of the Marley children have forged their own musical
careers – Ziggy, Cedella and Sharon have found success abroad as the
Melody Makers and Junior Gong, his son by 1976 Miss World Cindy
Breakespeare, is a respected DJ – but in the hearts of Jamaicans, the master's voice can never be equalled.

*See p.277 for
the Peter Tosh
story.*

*Bob Marley is
widely
predicted to
become
Jamaica's
next National
Hero; see p.71.*

anchored off St Ann's Bay during his "discovery" of the island in 1494, **Christopher Columbus** sailed west along the coast seeking a bay to land and find fresh water; with its rapidly running river and horseshoe dimensions, Rio Bueno is popularly agreed to be the "crescent harbour" he decided upon and recorded in his diary account.

The town today is nothing to write home about, though the British presence is evident in a ruined **fort**, named after Henry Dundas, British Secretary of War, and dating back to 1778, and **St Mark's Anglican church**, built at the sea's edge by the British in 1832. The original **Baptist church** was burnt to the ground in that same year by hostile Anglicans – the present incarnation was erected in 1901.

The town fell into decline following the abolition of slavery, though there are proposals for its development as a heritage site; until this comes to fruition, the only reason to visit is to swim in the rapidly running **Rio Bueno River** – best spot is the **Dornoch River Head pool**, a deep cliff-edged swimming hole surrounded by silk cotton trees and throngs of mosquitoes, reached on the B10 from Discovery Bay, though you'll probably need local help to pinpoint it. Baptist missionary and anti-slavery activist William Knibb used to baptize converts here, and a spiritual ambience lingers.

PRACTICALITIES

*Just out of town, the* Rio Bueno Travel Halt *(daily 8.30am– 5.30pm) has spotless bathrooms, a rarity in this neck of the woods.*

Although there is no earthly reason to **stay** in Rio Bueno, a vast all-inclusive has seen fit to open two miles down the road. *Braco Village* (Rio Bueno PO, Trelawny; ☎954 0019, fax 954 0020; ⑦–⑧) is a sprawling complex that strives to recreate a "real" Jamaican town – it even has its own town square (though obviously minus the traffic, goats and dirt). It's a mishmash of contrived architectural conceits – and it's fabulous; rooms are spanking new and amenities – gyms, pools, watersports, bars – are exhaustive. Also incongruous in Rio Bueno is *Gallery Joe James* on the western fringes of town (☎995 3044 or fax 953 5911; ③) – an **art gallery** that also offers good rooms and, in *The Lobster Pot*, expensive **seafood dinners**. Just out of town, *Richie Rich Yow Jerk Centre* sells great jerk, fish, chicken, fish tea, conch soup and very popular breakfasts.

*Signposted* Arawak Sunset Bar *is opposite a small undeveloped cave; the owner acts as unofficial guardian and guide (for a small fee of course).*

## Duncans and the beaches

A peaceful village huddled under Cockpit Country, **DUNCANS** has a supermarket, a few small-scale restaurants and bars, a pharmacy and a clocktower with a timepiece that hasn't worked for fifteen years. There's a huge **villa complex** here, *Silver Sands* (PO Box 1, Duncans; ☎954 2001, fax 954 2630; ②–⑦), and budget rooms at the *Sober Robin* directly opposite (☎954 2202; 1–②). Just out of town, the dirt-cheap and dependable *Montgomery's Holiday House* (Duncans PO; ☎954 0263; ①) stands alone in a field set back from the road.

The **coastline** parallel to Duncans is sublime – powdery white sand and big waves. The best beach is attached to the *Silver Sands* resort, though non-guests can normally use it for a fee; enquire at reception. Wide and windswept, the sand is famously white and the swimming superlative. Alternatively, there's Duncans **public beach**, basically a facility-free fisherman's beach that's so rocky it's hard to imagine how the boats ever manage to leave the shore. The turn-off for *Montgomery's Holiday House* marks a series of completely deserted bays – the water is quite shallow with some sea grass, but they're ideal spots for a secluded day by the sea. When you get **hungry**, try the *Prestige Fish Pot* at the roadside; for **drinks** head to the expansive *Rainbow Tavern*.

## Falmouth

Trelawny's capital reflects the history of the parish; at the height of the plantocracy there were 88 **sugar estates** in the region worked by thousands of slaves, and **FALMOUTH** – named for the English birthplace

*West of Ocho Rios*

*The B10 road that runs straight from the clocktower in Duncans is the easiest route into Cockpit Country from the north coast.*

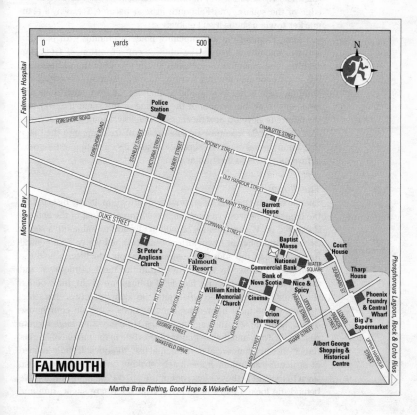

*Buses to
Montego Bay
and Ocho Rios
arrive and
depart outside
Courts in
Water Square.*

of parish Governor Sir William Trelawny – became the main port of call for sugar ships. Slaves were traded on the wharves and goods for the plantations unloaded while planters snapped up land and built elegant townhouses in Georgian style. In the late 1700s, Falmouth boasted more than 150 houses and a cage where the market now stands (akin to the one still standing in Montego Bay's Sam Sharpe Square – see p.211), used for locking up drunken sailors found on the streets later than the 6pm curfew. Though slavery was almost at an end when the town was dedicated as parish capital in 1790, Falmouth's central location and natural harbour ensured Trelawny's prosperity, and the town thrived where others declined, even after emancipation in 1838. However, the advent of the steamship – the first docked at Jamaican shores in 1837 – spelled the first step in the town's declivity. The harbour wasn't deep enough to accommodate these larger vessels, trade was diverted to bigger harbours and by the 1890s, Falmouth was something of a ghost town – the planters and traders had left for Montego Bay or Kingston, and their houses began to rot slowly in the sun and salty air. In 1896, the Albert George Market was built at the edge of the square, and Falmouth instead became Trelawny's main **market town**, a status it still enjoys.

Today, Falmouth is a compelling place brimming with paradox and incongruity. It boasts the highest concentration of **Georgian architecture** in Jamaica – possibly in the whole of the Caribbean – but many buildings are in a terrible state of disrepair; once majestic buildings now serve as dilapidated shelters for fowl, stray dogs and madmen – a visible symbol of the decline of the sugar industry and the failure to develop new business. Somehow, though, the ever-present trade winds inject a palpable breath of fresh air into the place that tempers the sense of stagnation, and its charming, easy-going nature only adds to its sunniness.

## The Town

The town centre retains its original grid formation, neatly bisected by the busy A1, the western continuation of the A3. Most of the activity is centred on **Water Square**, named in allusion to Falmouth's status as the first Jamaican town with access to piped water. The central fountain marks the spot of the stone reservoir which once held the fresh water pumped by water wheel from the Martha Brae river, and though marred by the lurid facade of a furniture chain, the wooden shop fronts and antiquated aspect lend the square plenty of character.

Some of the most impressive constructions – the old **courthouse** overlooking the sea, the sagging **Tharp House**, with a huge termite nest on the roof, and the porticoed **post office** in the middle of Market Street – are in commercial or municipal use, though still badly in need of structural attention. Immediately striking as you enter or leave town to the east is the conical roof of the 1810 **Phoenix Foundry**. It's behind the locked gates of **Central Wharf** – where sugar, rum and

slaves were shipped and traded during Falmouth's heyday – along
with several dilapidated stone warehouses and crumbling plaster-
board set dressings from the filming of *The Wide Sargasso Sea*.
There are plans afoot to develop an open-air museum of the history of
colonized Jamaica around the main historical structures, with a museum on slavery. Call Jamaica Heritage Trail (☎954 3033 or ☎0999
4674) for developments or to go on an excellent **walking tour** of
Central Wharf and all the town's other sites.

The stately **Baptist Manse** on Market Street is thought to have been
inhabited by Baptist minister and anti-slavery campaigner William
Knibb, whose efforts did much to facilitate emancipation. Once ruined,
the manse is now being carefully restored, though is not yet open to the
public. The **William Knibb Memorial Baptist Church** stands on the
corner of King and George streets, a commemoration of Emancipation
Day, July 3, 1838, when slave irons, collars and whips were
ceremonially buried in its grounds; Knibb himself is also buried here.

Falmouth was built on land originally owned by plantation magnate Edward Barrett, and was even known as Barrett Town for a
while. **Barrett House** on Market Street was once the family's appropriately fine domicile, but is now in a state of near-collapse, liable to
cascade into the street below at any minute; it's being repaired, but
for now you can't go inside. The house also has a tenuous literary
connection; having survived his three sons, Edward Barrett left his
Jamaican estates to his daughter on the condition that the man she
married took the Barrett name – the house was built by her husband,
Charles Moulton Barrett. The family moved to England and had two
sons, one of whom fathered the poet **Elizabeth Barrett Browning**.
Finally, the 1791 **St Peter's Anglican Church** on Duke Street is a
sepulchral structure, perfumed by wax polish and with a sun-
bleached cemetery that's usually spookily deserted.

## Out of town

Several more attractions lie immediately outside Falmouth. The most
visible is **Jamaica Safari Village** (daily 8.30am–5pm; US$6.50, boat
trip US$15), a haphazard menagerie on the A3 five minutes' drive
west of Falmouth. Like many small zoos, it's a bit depressing, but it's
the only place on the north coast where you can see Jamaican **crocodiles**. Ranging from tiny babies to alarming twelve-footers, the
crocodiles look fairly content; less fortunate is a lioness who per-
forms on command. There are mongooses, geese, peacocks and
pigeons and a cage filled with sluggish yellow boa constrictors. The
boat trip takes you through brackish mangrove swamps; repellent is
essential. Incidentally, this is the place James Bond used crocodile
heads as stepping stones in *Live and Let Die*.

Half a mile east of Falmouth at **Rock**, **Oyster Bay** is a phospho-
rous lagoon, so-called because of the incandescent illuminations of
micro-organisms. The water shines bright green when agitated and

you can see the trails of fish darting about. *Glistening Waters*, a restaurant and marina right on the lagoon (☎954 3229 or 3677), offers deep-sea fishing trips and night-time boat trips; bring your swimsuit and plunge into the eerie depths. Wide and wild **Burwood public beach** is 200 yards east down the road from *Time'n'place* (see opposite) – there are no facilities but it's clean,with good swimming and snorkelling.

Heading inland, the **Martha Brae River** is Trelawny's longest waterway and **raft trips** along it are a big attraction for Montego Bay tourists –follow the battered signs from Water Square for about three miles to the put-in point at Rafter's Village (daily 9am–4pm; 1hr 15min; US$35 per two-person raft). The leisurely trip takes you past banks overhung with silk cotton and mango trees and under towering banyans festooned with vines. There are a few craft stalls on the riverbank, floating bars and a constant mosquito offensive – bring repellent.

The Martha Brae road is also the route to **Good Hope Great House** (arrange a tour on ☎954 3289; free, but tips welcome), a Georgian dream house in a 2000-acre working plantation – follow the signed turn-off along a muddy and rutted road. Built in creamy English stone and set in gardens full of flowers and hummingbirds, this beautifully furnished Tharp family home is a serene nod to colonial splendour; you can have a look around, take tea on the terrace or follow a trail ride through the plantation, which contains the remains of the slave hospital and parts of an aqueduct.

Still further into the interior is **Hampden Estate** (Mon–Fri 9am–4pm; US$12) – a rum distillery and great house surrounded by vast sugarcane flats and a road littered with fallen cane from the trucks that shuttle between field and factory in cutting season. The polished mahogany and family portraits in the great house are dull in comparison to the **sugar factory tour** where the hot, dirty process of extracting sugar and rum from raw cane unfolds. The walkways are narrow and some steps a bit wobbly, so children under ten are not allowed. The cobweb-festooned distillery is thick with the sickly-sweet smell of fermenting cane, and you get to sample the abrasive "jancro batty" overproof white rum – at about 170 percent proof, the innocuous-looking liquid could strip paint.

### Accommodation

With Montego Bay so near, few people choose to **stay** in Falmouth, but there's a fair spread of accommodation and it's certainly a more relaxing place to rest your weary head.

**Bodmint Resort**, Rock; ☎954 3551. A range of villas next to the phosphorescent lagoon, with fully equipped kitchens and screened porches. Tasty Jamaican food, babysitting and various water-based trips. ③–⑧.

**Falmouth Resort**, Duke St; ☎954 3391. The only accommodation in the centre of Falmouth, with small, basic rooms, a bar and restaurant. ②.

**Good Hope Guest House**, PO Box 50, Falmouth; ☎ & fax 954 3289. Tastefully restored and classy; rooms in the main house, apartments in the Coach House or Counting House, pool and stables. All-inclusive plans available. ⑦–⑧.

**Greenside Guest House**, Salt Marsh, Falmouth; ☎954 3127. Elementary rooms with ceiling fan and cold water, mainly used by locals. ①.

**Roi's Villas**, Salt Marsh, Falmouth; ☎954 3852, fax 954 3324. Villas overlook a brackish lagoon good for fishing and bird watching, and are large and comfortably decorated, with kitchen and hot and cold water. ③.

**Time'n'Place**, PO Box 93, Falmouth; ☎954 4371. A wooden cabin on stilts right on the public beach with a bar and restaurant steps away and a great atmosphere. ③.

## Eating and entertainment

For **snacks**, *Nice and Spicy* on Water Square sells pastries and patties, and there are loads of **restaurants** around town – some, like the *Ackee Tree* at Salt Marsh, are your basic jerk stop, while the fabulous beachside café/bar *Time'n'Place* offers tasty burgers, fries, curried chicken, fish, pizza rolls, key lime pie and fruit smoothies laced with rum – as well as hammocks, a white-sand beach, great swimming and snorkelling, domino tournaments and occasional parties. *Glistening Waters* at the Rock marina (☎954 3229 or 3677) does a good line in seafood – but bring repellent as mosquitoes are rampant. Busy *Down South* between Falmouth and Greenwood cooks fish any way you like it and makes a mean carrot juice, and for a splurge sample the superlative but expensive nouvelle Jamaican cuisine at Good Hope Great House – reservations essential (☎954 3289).

For **entertainment**, look out for billboards advertising shows at the *Wet'n'Wild Entertainment Centre* at Rock, also a nice place for a **drink**. Otherwise, apart from at *Time'n'Place*, you'll be rubbing shoulders with Jamaicans in Falmouth's many rum bars – try the *One Love People Club* at 4 Lower Harbour St. The tiny **cinema** is at 33 Market St (☎954 4191).

# Travel details

Until *Air Jamaica Express* (☎923 6664) resumes flights to Boscobel airstrip, the only public transport along the coast is the haphazard **bus** system. Coasters, minibuses and the occasional old-style country bus ply the road between around 6am and 7pm, with a reduced service on Sundays, with little or nothing after 5pm. There are so many buses shooting along this stretch of the coast that we haven't put frequencies below – but you shouldn't have to wait any longer than thirty minutes for a bus; for pick-up points see relevant areas. The interior is a different matter entirely; areas that are covered have only one daily service, usually departing at the crack of dawn and returning to base in the early evening.

**Travel
Details**

**Buses**

**Falmouth to**: Discovery Bay/Runaway Bay (40min); Duncans (20min);
Montego Bay (30min); Ocho Rios (1hr 15min); St Ann's Bay (55min).

**Ocho Rios to**: Duncans (55min); Falmouth (1hr 15min); Kingston (2hr);
Montego Bay (1 hr 45min); Oracabessa (30min); Port Maria (45min);
Runaway Bay/Discovery Bay (40min); St Ann's Bay (20min).

**Runaway Bay/Discovery Bay**: to Browns Town (30min); Duncans (20min);
Falmouth (40min); Montego Bay (1hr 15min); Ocho Rios (30min); St Ann's
Bay (20min).

# Chapter 4

# Montego Bay and Cockpit Country

**M**ontego Bay is unashamedly Jamaica's tourist capital. Hundreds of foreigners flood in every day, seduced by a heavily marketed Caribbean dream of swaying palm trees, lilting reggae and cocktails at sunset. In many ways, Montego Bay delivers; sitting pretty in a sweeping natural harbour, hemmed in by a dazzling labyrinth of protected offshore reefs, and cradled by a majestic arc of hills, it's furnished with enough natural attributes to fill any brochure. The town itself, though marred by uninspired architecture, over-development and relentless hassle that can exhaust even the most laid-back visitor, is indisputably the reigning old madam of Jamaican resorts; gossipy, belligerent and overdressed but also absorbing, spirited and lively, particularly during its world-renowned summer reggae festival.

Concentration upon the traditional pleasures of the Caribbean fantasy has left the surrounding countryside largely undeveloped, save for the public plantations and converted great houses on the fringes of town, most famously **Rose Hall**, site of Jamaica's massively embellished legend of voodoo and sexual intrigue. Inland, the landscape rises sharply toward the hillside retreats of Montpelier and Kensington, all once part of the huge **sugar estates** that were the backbone of the area before tourism took off in the 1920s. Sugar is still big business here, and the downtown air is thick with the smell of burning cane during harvest season. Many of the estates have opened their doors to visitors, and the magnificent settings are worth the trip alone. Elsewhere, in the verdant **Great River valley**, you can raft through silky green water at **Lethe** or feed a hummingbird at the beautiful **Rocklands bird sanctuary**, high above the bay and an oasis of serenity.

Less than two hours' drive from the centre of town lies an area so untouched by any kind of development that it's something of a parallel universe. The uninhabited limestone hillocks of **Cockpit Country** are the antithesis of the palm trees and concrete of the

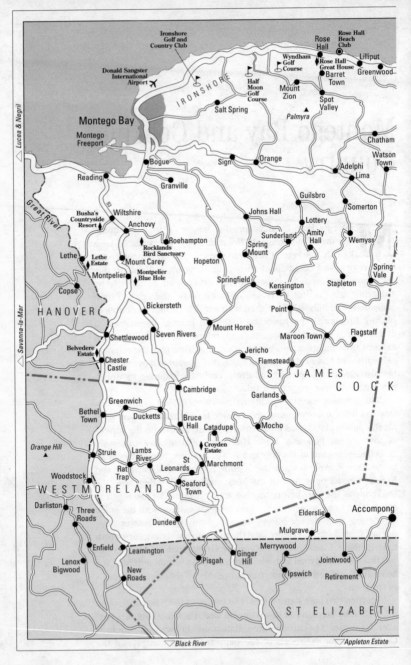

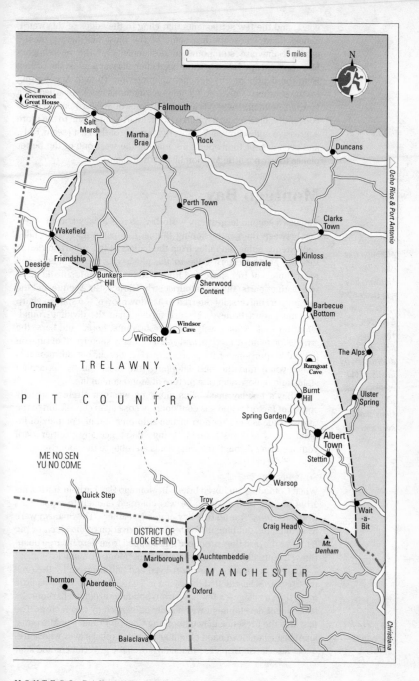

coast, and the few settlements that cling to the edges of this weird, almost lunar landscape are some of the most fascinating on the island. Some are still home to descendants of the once-mighty **Maroons**, escaped slaves who waged guerrilla war against the British from the depths of this impenetrable interior. Though **Accompong** on the southern side is still a semi-autonomous state governed by a Maroon council, these Trelawny Maroons of western Jamaica are conventionally seen as a watered-down lot in comparison to the more aggressive and secretive Windward Maroons of the east (see p.144), and even accept tour operators, making the west one of the better places to learn a little Maroon history first-hand.

# Montego Bay

Jamaica's second-largest city – **MoBay**, as it is locally known – nestles between the gently sloping Bogue, Kempshot and Salem hills, and extends some ten miles from the haunts of the suburban rich at Reading at its western edge to the plush villa developments and resort hotels of Ironshore and Rose Hall to the east. It's made up of two distinct parts: the main tourist strip **Gloucester Avenue** and the city proper, universally referred to as "**downtown**" – a split so sharp that most tourists never venture further than the dividing roundabout on foot. A long walkway of restaurants, hotels and bars, the strip is the main attraction, and you'll certainly spend a lot of time on the public portions of its postcard-perfect beach, but downtown is where you'll find the best shopping, the most quietly rewarding sights and a more accurate picture of Montegonian life.

MoBay's holiday mask slips along its **western** stretch, an ugly sprawl of factories and gas containers, whose main concession to the tourist trade is the **Freeport cruise-ship pier** and its complex of in-bond shops and restaurants. Things don't get any prettier until you're cutting through the cane fields en route to the suburbs.

*Although like any other city, Montego Bay has its danger spots, it's not Kingston. You'll be hounded to distraction by hustlers, but otherwise the usual precautions should keep you safe.*

SOME HISTORY

When Columbus anchored briefly in Montego Bay harbour during his 1494 voyage to the island, he was charmed enough to name it *El Golfo de Buen Tempo* (the bay of good weather). The Spanish were less romantic, dubbing it *Manterias*, a derivation of *manteca* or pig fat, after the lard they produced and shipped from here in large quantities. Eventually, the English corruption, "Montego", stuck.

Spanish occupation was short-lived and half-hearted; by the time the Spaniards hastily fled the island in 1655, Montego Bay was little more than a village – a few haphazard buildings around a harbour. Its subsequent development was heavily influenced by two factors. The first was the presence in neighbouring Cockpit Country of **Maroons**, an African-Jamaican band of militarily skilled rebel slaves whose frequent attacks on British settlements cowed the government and kept

*See p.314 for more on the Maroons.*

THE GUIDE: CHAPTER 4

the town from prospering until a peace treaty was signed in 1739. By this time, **sugar production** was booming throughout Jamaica and the turnover of the area's many plantations saw the harbour thronging with ships, and lavish cut-stone town houses and travellers' inns spreading back from the waterfront. Plantation culture built Montego Bay and nearly destroyed it; the 1831 **Christmas Rebellion** (see p.212), the first and most important of the violent slave revolts that prefaced emancipation, began in the foothills behind the town and burned almost all the estates to the ground.

After the collapse of the sugar trade, the city spent a hundred-odd years in limbo; many of the grander buildings were destroyed by fire or hurricanes and it was not until the early twentieth century that Montego Bay entered another period of growth, beginning when Sir Herbert Baker advocated the redemptive powers of the Doctor's Cave waters (see p.209) in the 1920s. Since then, Montego Bay has thrown full weight into its metamorphosis as the ultimate **tourist town**. Initially the trade was restricted to rich North Americans and Europeans who built holiday homes around Doctor's Cave or arrived on a banana boat to stay in the town's first hotel, the *Casa Blanca*. Sangster International Airport grew from the original single airstrip built in the late 1940s, and the town was poised for development as a major resort. Its population increased four-fold between 1940 and 1970, with Jamaicans from all over the island moving in to work at the hotels that sprang up alongside the best of the beaches. In the 1960s, the Freeport peninsula was manually constructed on land reclaimed from the sea, and Montego Bay's position as a premier port of call on any Caribbean cruise was assured.

More recently, Montego Bay achieved fame as the base for Jamaica's **reggae festivals** – the first ever Reggae Sunsplash took place here in 1978 and newcomer Sumfest is resident today – but over-development and a reputation for aggressive hustlers led to a decrease in tourist arrivals in the late 1980s and early 1990s, and as Montego Bay approaches its twentieth anniversary as Jamaica's second city, town planners and tourism officials are haggling over an uncertain future, though a state cash injection for beautification projects may just enable the city to live up to its self-appointed title of "The Complete Resort".

## Arrival, information and getting around

Over eighty percent of visitors to Jamaica arrive at **Sangster International Airport**, right by the sea three miles east of the town centre and a mile from the Gloucester Avenue tourist strip. As you'd imagine, it's fully geared up for the newly arrived tourist, with a 24-hour **cambio** and a branch of the *NCB* bank, a tourist-board desk and numerous hotel, ground transport and car-rental booths. **Luggage trolleys** aren't permitted past immigration, but the official red-capped porters will carry your bags for US$1 a piece.

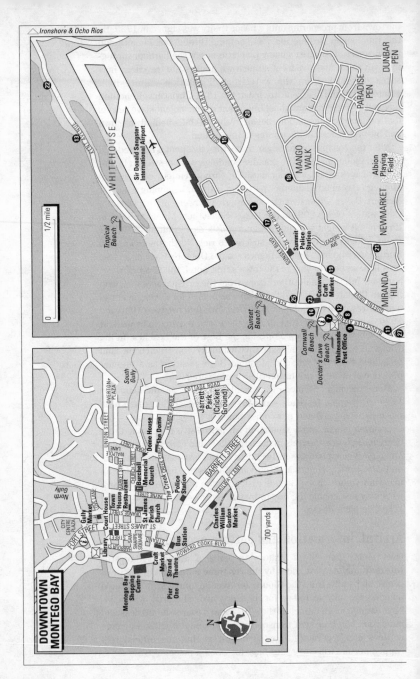

DOWNTOWN
MONTEGO BAY

City Centre Plaza

North Gully

Library
Court House
Town House
Restaurant
St James Parish Church
Gully Market Lane
Burchell Memorial Church
The Dome
Dome House

Montego Bay Shopping Centre

Craft Market
Strand Theatre
Pier One
Bus Station

Charles William Gordon Market

Police Station

FORT STREET
ST JAMES STREET
SAM SHARPE SQUARE
ORANGE STREET
CHURCH STREET
MARKET STREET
MARBLE LANE
WALPOLE LANE
UNION STREET
Overton Plaza
South Gully
COTTAGE ROAD
RAILWAY LANE
PARK LANE
STRAND STREET
HARBOUR STREET
BARNETT STREET
HOWARD COOKE BLVD

The Creek
Jarret Park (Cricket Ground)
FUSTIC AVENUE

N

0    700 yards

WHITEHOUSE

Tropical Beach

Sir Donald Sangster International Airport

Sunset Beach

Cornwall Beach

Doctor's Cave Beach

Whitesands Post Office

Cornwall Craft Market

Summit Police Station

MANGO WALK

NEWMARKET

MIRANDA HILL

DUNBAR PEN

PARADISE PEN

Albion Playing Field

GLOUCESTER AVENUE
KENT AVENUE
SUNSET BLVD
DE LISSER DRIVE
LEADERS AVE
ALICE ELDEMIRE DRIVE
OCEAN DRIVE

22
13
20
15
16
1
17
25
23
19
21
24
14
7
12
8
9
11
27

0    1/2 mile

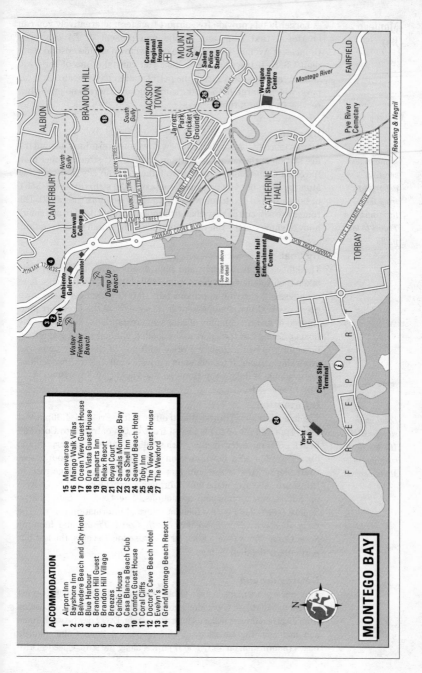

## ACCOMMODATION

1   Airport Inn
2   Bayshore Inn
3   Belvedere Beach and City Hotel
4   Blue Harbour
5   Brandon Hill Guest
6   Brandon Hill Village
7   Breezes
8   Caribic House
9   Casa Blanca Beach Club
10  Comfort Guest House
11  Coral Cliffs
12  Doctor's Cave Beach Hotel
13  Evelyn's
14  Grand Montego Beach Resort

15  Manevarose
16  Mango Walk Villas
17  Ocean View Guest House
18  Ora Vista Guest House
19  Ramparts Inn
20  Relax Resort
21  Royal Court
22  Sandals Montego Bay
23  Sea Shell Inn
24  Seawind Beach Hotel
25  Toby Inn
26  The View Guest House
27  The Wexford

**MONTEGO BAY**

Larger hotels provide free airport transfers; alternatively you can charter a **taxi** from any of the omnipresent *JUTA* drivers – Gloucester Avenue, Queens Drive or downtown should cost no more than US$8. If travelling *very* light you can take one of the local **shared taxis** that leave from the petrol station past the airport's car park, which charge J$15 for the same journey. There is no public bus service from the airport.

## By road

*For details of regional bus services departing from the terminus, see Travel Details, p.238.*

All **bus** journeys end at the busy new downtown **terminus**, behind the fire station at the corner of Harbour and Barnett streets. Other than the *Soon Come Shuttle* (see below), there are no city buses serving Montego Bay, but you can charter a taxi to the strip (around US$5), or take a shared taxi to anywhere in town for no more than J$20. The routes are set, and as they change frequently you'll need to ask somebody to show you the relevant departure point within the bus station.

## By boat

Though visitor harassment and high disembarkation charges have taken their toll in recent years, some 400 ships still drop anchor here each season, carrying approximately 10,000 passengers into town every week. Cruise-ship passengers disembark at the **Freeport pier**, centred in its own complex of shops and restaurants. Reps board the boats offering bus transport to designated in-bond shops and attractions, or you can negotiate a price with one of the many taxis that await ship arrivals. If travelling on a private craft, full marina facilities are available at the nearby Montego Bay Yacht Club (☎979 8038).

## Information

*Local radio station HOT 102 has good coverage of MoBay events.*

The main **Jamaica Tourist Board** office (Mon–Fri 9am–4.30pm, Sat 9am–1pm; ☎952 4425) is just in front of the entrance to Cornwall Beach off Gloucester Avenue, with smaller booths at the airport, the library garden area downtown on Fort Street, the Harbour Street Craft Market, the cruise-ship pier and the Holiday Village mall in Ironshore. All carry maps and informative freesheets and can advise on hotels, restaurants and attractions. The Cage in Sam Sharpe Square (see p.211) is an excellent informal information centre. The daily *Western Mirror*, weekly *North Coast Times* and monthly *Soon Come News* (see p.202) all advertise local events; the last has particularly detailed listings.

## Getting around

After many years of inadequate **public transport**, there is finally a decent way for tourists to get about Montego Bay – although vociferous opposition from local taxi drivers make its future uncertain. Every day between 10am and midnight, the conspicuous, cartoon-painted **Soon Come Shuttle** buses (information on ☎979 0057) travel along the strip, Queen's Drive

## Organized tours

Hundreds of **tour companies** operate out of Montego Bay; most have booths at the airport and offices along Gloucester Avenue and offer similarly priced trips to independent plantations and great houses. The **best operators** are slightly more adventurous: *Intrepid Explorers*, PO Box 188, Reading PO, St James (☎997 5798), for instance, arranges brilliant custom-designed tours for US$150 a day for a group of up to six, with a week's notice; *Caribic Vacations*, 69 Gloucester Ave (☎979 0114 or 953 9877), offers islandwide specialist and reggae tours and trips to Cuba; *Jamaica Sightseeing*, 1 Kent Ave (☎952 6590), boasts a semi-alternative roster including a "Rasta Beach Picnic"; and *Travel International*, at Cotton Tree Complex opposite the airport (☎952 9362), operates a *Hedonism II* special to Negril. Alternatively, hire a **local driver** and do some independent sightseeing; see p.224 for recomendations.

Listed below are the best **tour sites** and most popular **organized excursions**. All can be seen independently as well as on a package.

**Appleton Estate**, Siloah, St Elizabeth (☎963 9215; Mon–Sat; US$12). This classic half-day tour crosses the edge of Cockpit Country into St Elizabeth to the orderly Appleton rum distillery in Siloah. You see the progression of cane to molasses and finally rum, view the ageing stills, taste various varieties and come away with your own miniature bottle.

**Barnett Estate**, Fairfield, Montego Bay (☎952 2382; daily; US$20, US$8 for transfers). Jitney (trailer) trip around the 3000-acre cane plantation that covers the Montego Bay valley. Includes a tour of recently refurbished Bellfield Great House and a drink in the magnificent converted sugar mill bar. You can also explore the estate on a horse from Barnett Point stables (US$40; 1hr).

*See p.215 for
more on
Barnett Estate.*

**Croydon in the Mountains**, Catadupa, St James (☎979 8267; Tues, Wed & Fri; US$45). Half-day tour to Croydon Estate, a 132-acre working coffee and pineapple plantation in the foothills of the Catadupa mountains in the St James interior. Barbecue lunch and fruit tasting included in the price.

**Hilton High Day Tour**, St Leonards, St James (☎952 3343; Tues, Weds, Fri & Sun; US$50). So-called because it once included a balloon ride – now a little short on thrills but still enjoyable. You are bussed up Long Hill through Montpelier and Cambridge to the diminutive Hilton plantation house, whose small grounds contain a piggery and stables (30min US$15). You get breakfast, lunch, a stroll around the village and local school, a bus ride to the German settlement of Seaford Town and its museum, and a drive back through the western outskirts of Cockpit Country.

*One breath-
taking way to
see Montego
Bay and
Cockpit
Country is on
a helicopter
ride from
Helitours
(☎979 8290;
15min US$55).*

**Maroon Attraction Tours**, 32 Church St (☎979 0308; Tues, Thurs & Sat; US$55). The only tour company granted permission by Maroon officials to carry visitors to Accompong (see p.236). Includes a stop at Kensington to view the Sam Sharpe monument, tours of Accompong and Maroon Town, with introductions to "authentic" Maroons. Breakfast, lunch and live Maroon/mento band included. The views and countryside passed are spectacular and it's a hassle-free path to Accompong.

and out to Ironshore, belting out reggae and selling US$1 Red Stripe. There are two set routes, both departing from the lay-by opposite *Walter's* bar at the downtown end of the strip: "central" (every 15min) heads to the Montego Bay (LOJ) mall, then loops back to cover Queen's Drive and the strip as far as Sunset Beach; "eastern" (every 45min) goes all the way up the strip and out to Rose Hall. Both can be flagged down en route. **Fares** are fixed; central is US$1and eastern US$2, no matter how far you travel on either route. Payment is by **token** only, available from locations displaying the distinctive *Soon Come* parrot insignia.

*The people behind the Soon Come Shuttle also produce the Soon Come News, a useful monthly listings magazine replete with special offers, and run the Soon Come Fun programme of social events along the strip.*

Otherwise, as there are no public buses serving downtown or the strip, **walking** is your most convenient option. You shouldn't experience any problems along the strip even at night, but in the middle of town it's better to walk in company until you get your bearings. For trips further afield, don't be afraid to follow the local example and cram in to a **shared taxi**; most leave from the bus station or Gully Market (see p.211), but there are unofficial pick-up/drop-off points along the strip outside Walter Fletcher and Cornwall beaches. The cheapest place to pick up a **private taxi** is the downtown taxi park at the intersection of Market and Strand streets, but there are also stands opposite Doctor's Cave Beach and at the *Paradise Club* at Miranda Ridge, an elevated complex of shops and resturants on Gloucester Avenue, and any tourist walking the streets is assailed with offers. Be prepared to haggle and always settle the price before you get in; downtown to Sunset Beach should cost around US$5. **Horsedrawn carriages** depart from outside the *Grand Montego Beach Resort* and the Fort Street Craft Market to trot up and down Gloucester Avenue for US$25 per hour.

*See p.224 for a list of reliable taxi firms.*

Constant tailbacks during the daily rush hours (8–10am and 4.30–6.30pm) make **driving** a frustrating experience in town, although you might want a car for independent sightseeing elsewhere. International **car rental** companies have booths at the airport, while most local operators are located along the lower section of Queen's Drive/Sunset Boulevard (listed on p.222). Rates are high, but most operators offer reductions for weekly rentals; expect to pay around US$70 a day in high season and US$50 at other times. Motorbikes (from US$45 per day), scooters (from US$30 per day) and bicycles (from US$10 per day) are also available from most of the local companies.

## Accommodation

As you would expect, the range of **accommodation** in Jamaica's top tourist city is staggering. This is prime **all-inclusive** territory, with the swankiest enclaves out at suburban Ironshore just east of town. Most people, however, stay along the Gloucester Avenue **strip** – busy, buzzing and swarming with hustlers. Opting for a hotel on **Queen's Drive**, the road just above the strip, or **downtown** reduces the likelihood of being accosted as soon as you step outside; it's also cheaper, with proprietors more amenable to bargaining. Many hotels include free airport transfers in their rates, and more distant properties throw in a free beach shuttle. As this is tourist territory, places are up to international standards and, unless otherwise stated, rooms come with air conditioning, tv and phone.

**Accommodation price codes**

All the hotels detailed in this guide have been graded according to the following price categories. Note that the prices have been calculated as those for the cheapest **double** or **twin room** during low season, normally mid-April to mid-December. During high season, rates are liable to rise by up to 25 percent (though this is rare at the cheap hotels), and proprietors may be less amenable to bargaining. Many of the all-inclusives have a minimum stay requirement; where this is the case it is mentioned in the text. Although the law requires prices to be quoted in Jamaican dollars, most hotels give rates in US dollars; payment can be made in either currency. For more details see p.22.

| | |
|---|---|
| ① under US$20 | ⑤ US$70–100 |
| ② US$20–35 | ⑥ US$100–150 |
| ③ US$35–50 | ⑦ US$150–200 |
| ④ US$50–70 | ⑧ US$200 and above |

Most **budget** options are downtown, with a few more opposite the airport, but in such a tourist-oriented town, even the cheapest rates are pretty high. With so much to choose from, it's rarely difficult to find a vacancy, unless you hit town during Sumfest season – mid-July to mid-August – when it's practically impossible to find accommodation if you don't have a reservation.

## Gloucester Avenue and the beaches

**Bayshore Inn**, 27 Gloucester Ave; ☎979 5087. Cheerful gingham rooms above a great jerk restaurant (see p.216) at the less frantic end of the strip. Reduced-rate weekly rentals available. ③.

**Belvedere Beach and City Hotel**, 33 Gloucester Ave; ☎952 0593, fax 979 0498. Friendly small hotel with a restaurant, bar and pool, although as rooms overlook the road it can be noisy. Live jazz once a month. ③.

**Blue Harbour**, Sewell Ave; ☎952 5445, fax 952 8930. Quirkily decorated small hotel perched above the strip with good views, a nice pool and a restaurant serving breakfast and lunch. A range of rooms, all scrupulously clean; the cheapest are a bit gloomy. ③–⑤.

**Caribic House**, 69 Gloucester Ave; ☎979 0322, fax 979 3421. A busy German-run hotel opposite Doctor's Cave Beach with clean rooms and a few "penthouse suites". ②/③.

**Coral Cliffs**, 165 Gloucester Ave; ☎952 4130, fax 952 6532. Colonial-style hotel with a large verandah restaurant and lounge, and a pool. ④.

**Doctor's Cave Beach Hotel**, Gloucester Ave; ☎952 4355–9, fax 952 5204. One of the better strip hotels, with funky lobby decor, pool, Jacuzzi, restaurant, bar and small gym, across from Doctor's Cave Beach. Rooms are pretty uniform, but the friendly atmosphere wins lots of points. ⑤.

**Evelyn's Guest House**, Kent Ave, Whitehouse; ☎952 3280. So close to the airport it shudders with every take-off, this is otherwise a lovely new guesthouse right on the sea's edge, with capacious, clean rooms above a restaurant serving the only roti in town (see "Eating", p.218). ③.

# Montego Bay

*Montego Bay's wealthiest visitors head for Round Hill resort, eight miles out of Montego Bay near Hopewell (see Chapter Five, p.242). It's the island's classiest hotel and literally swarming with the rich and famous.*

**Manevarose Resort**, 17 Claude Clarke Ave, Whitesands PO; ☎952 1842, fax 940 3881. Small property overlooking the airport, so a bit loud. Airy rooms, a large pool, rooftop bar and restaurant and a canary cage out back. ②.

**Ocean View Guest House**, 26 Sunset Blvd; ☎952 2662. Modest guesthouse near Cornwall Beach, with basic rooms but a convivial atmosphere. ②.

**Reading Reef Club**, PO Box 225, Reading; ☎952 5909, fax 952 7217. Superbly appointed hotel, right by Bogue Lagoon. Large private beach, bright rooms, restaurant, bar, pool and a PADI dive centre. ⑤.

**Relax Resort**, 26 Hobbs Ave; ☎979 0656, fax 952 7218. Tranquil place on a side road above Sunset Boulevard with pretty landscaping, spanking new rooms and apartments, a pool, shop, restaurant and bar. ④/⑤.

**Royal Court**, Sewell Ave; ☎952 4351, fax 952 4532. Big on health and natural healing, this resort has fancy rooms, some with kitchenette, juice bar, pool, hot tub, steam room, gym and restaurant. All-inclusive plans available. ④/ ⑤.

**Sea Shell Inn**, Mabel Ewen Drive, Whitesands PO; ☎979 2983, fax 979 9836. Excellent location, back from the road opposite Cornwall Beach. Rooms are a little shabby but clean, functional and popular with Europeans on a budget. ③.

**Seawind Beach Hotel**, PO Box 1168, Montego Freeport; ☎979 8070, fax 979 8425. Infamy is courted by these multi-coloured towers of all-inclusive fun on the Freeport peninsula. Facilities include tennis, pool, watersports and private beach with nude section, but rooms are all similar and rather dark. ⑤.

**Toby Inn**, 1 Kent Ave; ☎952 4370, fax 952 6591. Friendly hotel in large gardens, popular with German tour parties. Rooms are attractive, with wooden furniture and balconies, and there's a pool, restaurant and bar. ④.

**The Wexford**, 39 Gloucester Ave; ☎952 2854, fax 952 3637. Very pink both inside and out, with serviceable rooms and apartments, a pool, bar, restaurant and slot machines. ④.

## Queen's Drive and downtown

**Airport Inn**, Queen's Drive; ☎952 0257, fax 952 5391. Two minutes from the airport, and clean and reliable. All rooms have kitchen facilities, and there is a pool and bar/restaurant. ③.

**Brandon Hill Guest House**, 25 Peter Pan Ave, Brandon Hill; ☎952 7074 or 979 5759. Rooms need refurbishing, but are airy and neat with ceiling fan. There a bar, restaurant, pool and large lounge adorned with Jamaican art. ③.

**Brandon Hill Village**, 11 Coke Ave, Brandon Hill; ☎952 2563, fax 952 9016. Funkily designed rooms and self-contained apartments; good value for those on a budget. All units have fan and kitchenette; apartments have tv. Most guests are Jamaican, and the atmosphere is friendly and quiet. ②/③.

**Comfort Guest House**, 55 Jarrett Terrace, Barnett View Gardens; ☎952 1238. Family-run place with a Christian slant – ideal for those seeking a reserved but friendly atmosphere. Comfortable rooms, tv lounge, sun deck and home-cooked meals. ③.

**Jenny's**, Rose Heights, c/o North Coast Cruises, Whitesands PO; ☎979 6963, fax 979 0843. Three rooms, one with its own bathroom, in a family home in Rose Heights, a hilly suburb with great views. Communal kitchen (though meals are available) and lounge with satellite tv. ①/②.

**Mango Walk Villas**, Mango Walk, c/o PO Box 179, Kingston 5; ☎952 1472
or 1473, fax 940 3093. Spacious, inviting villa complex in the hills above
Queen's Drive, with big, bright studios and apartments, a pool, restaurant
and small shop. ④–⑥.

**Ora Vista Guest House**, PO Box 351, Richmond Hill, Union St; ☎952
2576. A superb, friendly guesthouse with unrivalled atmosphere and great
views. Rooms are simple, with no a/c, but clean and homely, and there's a
pool, bar, kitchen, sun deck and communal lounge. Excellent Jamaican food
available. ②.

**Ramparts Inn**, 5 Ramparts Close; ☎979 5258. A quiet, friendly small hotel
just off Queen's Drive, with elegant rooms, a pool, bar and restaurant. ④.

**The View Guest House**, Jarrett Terrace, Barnett View Gardens; ☎952
3175. Commendable guesthouse with a real Jamaican flavour; good food,
fair-sized pool, nice views and big function lounge which hosts a popular
Friday night party. Rooms are comfortable and basic; a US$5 supplement
gets you a/c. ③.

## All-inclusives

**Breezes**, Gloucester Ave; ☎940 1150–7, fax 940 1160. The newest addition
to the strip, right on Doctor's Cave Beach with more opulence than character. Amenities are comprehensive – pool, Jacuzzi, gym, watersports, tennis
courts, games room, restaurants, bars, poolside grill and nightly entertainment – but the rooms, though plush and comfortable, are badly designed;
even suites lack natural light and use of space is impractical. Minimum stay
two nights. ⑧.

**Casa Blanca Beach Club**, Gloucester Ave; ☎952 0720, fax 952 1424. This
low-rise development was the first hotel in MoBay, and while it doesn't look
much from the outside and has comparatively few facilities – only a pool,
restaurant and bar – it has far more character than some of the rivals. ⑥.

**Coyaba Beach Resort**, Little River PO, Ironshore; ☎953 9150–3, fax 953
2244. The most intimate all-inclusive in the vicinity, with less of the snob-
bishness of some of the larger hotels. Rooms are tasteful, with lots of extras.
Pool, all watersports, restaurant and bar, tennis courts, beautiful beach and
good offshore reef. ⑦.

**Grand Montego Beach Resort** (formerly *Jack Tar Village*), Gloucester
Ave/Kent Ave; ☎952 4340–4, fax 952 6633. Friendly and comfortable, with
oceanfront rooms and a lovely private beach with "clothing optional" section,
watersports, pool, gym, sauna, Jacuzzi, tennis courts, restaurant, beach grill
and bars. Loud and lively entertainment and piped music all day long. ⑥.

**Half Moon Golf, Tennis and Beach Club**, PO Box 80, Ironshore; ☎953
2211, fax 953 2731 (in US ☎1-800/237-3237; in UK ☎0171/730 7144, fax
938 4793). Lauded as the most luxurious property on the island, short on
atmosphere but with brilliant amenities: a shopping village, equestrian centre, 18-hole golf course, half-mile beach, all watersports, two public and 49
private pools, tennis courts, croquet lawns, spa, sauna and Jacuzzi, disco, six
restaurants and various bars. You can choose to stay off the property at the
ten gorgeous affiliated *Russell Villas* (☎953 3009, fax ☎953 2732; ⑦–⑧),
which have access to the facilities, but cost slightly less. ⑧.

**Holiday Inn Sun-Spree Resort**, Ironshore; ☎953 2485, fax 953 9840.
MoBay's only family-oriented resort, with childcare facilities and daily activi-

ties. Recently refurbished but still disfigured by ugly 1970s-style room blocks. Facilities include restaurants, bars, disco, beach, watersports, pool, tennis and basketball courts, gym, slot machines and games. Children under 12 stay free; 13–19s pay US$50. ⑥.

**Sandals Montego Bay**, Whitehouse; ☎952 5510, fax 952 0816 (in US ☎305/284-1300, fax 667 8996; in UK ☎0171/581 9895, fax 823 8758). MoBay's largest *Sandals* property, with the emphasis on fun and frolics for a young and racy clientele. Tucked behind the airport in Whitehouse, it's all here for the taking: a huge private white-sand beach with watersports, tennis courts, gym, disco, lavish nightly entertainment, four restaurants and four bars that keep most guests permanently on the property. Three night minimum stay. ⑨.

## The strip: Gloucester Avenue and the beaches

Though it stretches for less than two miles, Montego Bay's glittering oceanfront tourist strip is the focal – sometimes only – point of many a Jamaican vacation. Occupying the whole of **Gloucester Avenue** and stretching north into **Kent Avenue**, this holiday highway builds to a bottleneck around throbbing Doctor's Cave Beach, and the short stretch between here and buzzing Cornwall Beach literally pulsates with commercialized gaiety; brightly clad women stroll along balancing baskets of fruit on their heads, taxi drivers shadow your every step and hustlers hunt in smiling packs. This is where you'll find the majority of MoBay's tourist hotels and restaurants as well as the best beaches, bars and clubs, so even if you don't check into a strip hotel, you'll find that you spend a lot of time here.

Starting at the roundabout that filters Howard Cooke Boulevard, Queens Drive and Fort Street traffic, the first stretch of Gloucester Avenue is a kind of no-man's land split in two by an elevated section of a one-way traffic system and bordered by the only sizeable undeveloped beach in town (see p.210). Easily missed on the upper section of Fort Street and overtaken by the adjacent craft market, **Fort Montego** is an uninspiring hulk of stone with an even less impressive past. Dating back to the eighteenth century, the fort was built by the British to guard against foreign attack, but its cannons were fired only twice, both times with disastrous results; in a salute to celebrate the capture of Havana in 1760, one of the corroded guns misfired and killed its operator, later in 1795 – in the fort's only recorded attempt at a defensive attack – it mistakenly opened fire on one of its own vessels, the schooner *Mercury* carrying a cargo of dogs imported to hunt down Maroons. Inevitably the shots missed. Infinitely more absorbing, **Fort Street Craft Market** is a favourite haunt of persistent hair braiders but a relatively relaxed spot for a bit of bartering. Loosely arranged around steep steps that make a useful short cut to Sewell Avenue and Queen's Drive, stalls sell the usual array of carvings and t-shirts.

Though Gloucester Avenue runs parallel to the sea, the water is mainly obscured by the hotels and bars that carve the beach into private sections. The only place to fully appreciate the sweep of the bay is from the strip's only **green space**, more of a thoroughfare than a public park, in the old hospital grounds opposite the restaurants and bars at Miranda Ridge, just above the strip. The bucolic illusion is rudely shattered just past the park at **Margueritaville** (daily 10am-3am; free), a mini-lido-cum-restaurant-cum-bar that proudly displays the tackiest facade along the strip, a mock-stone clad, neon-flashing shrine to the worst in US kitsch and glitz. The bar and outdoor eating deck are built right over the sea; below there's a watersports area with boat berths and swimming platforms, while on the roof there's a Jacuzzi, sun deck, and – best of all – a 110ft water slide (US$1) which sluices down into the sea and draws tourists and locals alike in their hordes.

The strip builds in intensity as it approaches the magnificent Doctor's Cave Beach, becoming a seamless parade of bars, cafés and identical in-bond shops that doesn't slacken up until past Cornwall Beach. Behind the last few stores here is diminutive **Cornwall Craft Market**, massively oversold by its vendors who spend more time outside trying to induce you in than tending their stalls. The hotels peter out as Gloucester becomes **Kent Avenue** at the junction with Sunset Boulevard and continues to hug the coast. Locally known as Dead End Road, Kent Avenue passes tiny Sunset Beach (see p.210) before ending abruptly at the wall marking the distant section of the airport runway. The last of the strip proper, **Sunset Boulevard** is home to a small complex of forlorn shops and bars, countless car rental outlets and the rather grand **Summit Police Station**, the only one in Jamaica with its own pool. At the airport roundabout, the boulevard becomes

*The best of the strip's countless bars and restaurants are reviewed on p.219 and p.216.*

---

### The MoBay hustle

The constant tourist presence in Montego Bay has spawned a multitude of young **hustlers** trying to earn a living selling crafts, ganja, hair braiding or their services as a guide (or gigolo – see p.250). Unless you're encased in an all-inclusive, your every move will be shadowed by someone trying to sell you something. It's tiring, it's irritating, and it's easy for visitors to lose perspective, bristling with tension and regarding every encounter as adversorial. You can't really blame the hustlers for trying, though, and whether or not the harassment becomes a problem depends largely upon your attitude. Resign yourself to being frequently approached, and learn how to deal with it. Hustlers play on guilt and use psychological trickery. Lines like "Don't you remember me from the hotel/car rental shop/airport/beach?" are designed to suck you into dialogue – of course you've never met them, but once you've stopped, the sales pitch begins. If you ignore the outstretched hand or catcall the response is often "Wh'appen, you too good to talk to a black man?". If you're white, don't fall into the liberal trap of buying things you don't want just to avoid looking racist. Don't try to avoid the issue by giggling or hinting that you may be interested another time; if you mean no, say no, in a friendly but straightforward manner. Keep your sense of humour and treat street sellers as people, and you'll minimize potential problems and maybe even make some friends.

---

part of **Queen's Drive**, an inland road that runs parallels to Gloucester Avenue – essentially a fast traffic route straight through MoBay (and popularly known simply as the top road, Gloucester Avenue being the bottom), pavements are sporadic and walking can be risky, though the views over the bay are fantastic. After a mile or so, the road forks left to the small fishing community of **WHITE-HOUSE**, a quiet residential zone seldom visited by tourists and refreshingly hassle-free. Roadside vendors sell excellent fried fish and festival, and the sand at **Tropical Beach** (see p.210) is as fine as you'll find anywhere.

## The beaches

*Walter Fletcher, Doctor's Cave and Cornwall beaches are open daily between 9am and 5pm; each charges J$30 to enter.*

The strip, of course, wouldn't exist were it not for Montego Bay's prize asset: a dazzling bay with miles of protected coral reef (see box below) and some beautiful beaches. Much of the coastline has been snapped up by the hotels and carved into private chunks, but there are three main managed **public beaches**, all with showers, changing rooms, snack outlets and watersports concessions and a minimal entrance fee.

Opposite Fort Street Craft Market, **Walter Fletcher Beach** is closest to downtown and the more family-oriented of the three, with a wide expanse of gently shelving sand and tennis and basketball courts. However, pollution from the nearby gully outlet makes it unwise to swim after heavy rain, when the water smells anything but briny. Walter Fletcher is popular with day-tripping Jamaicans; the parking lot fills up with buses from as far afield as Kingston most weekends, giving the beach a less commercial feel than its neigh-

---

### Montego Bay Marine Park

Though offshore MoBay became officially protected in 1974, regulations were seldom enforced, and the reefs remained open to attack from plunderers, spear fishers, snorkellers, divers, boat anchors and industrial pollution. In an attempt to stem the destruction, **Montego Bay Marine Park** was opened in 1992 – Jamaica's first national park, with environmental regulations strictly enforced within its boundaries. Running west from Sangster Airport to Great River, just past Reading, the park comprises over nine square miles of coral reef, sea grass beds and mangroves, zoned into watersports, fishing and fish nursery areas and patrolled by three rangers. Within the park it is illegal to mine sand, damage or move coral, shells and seaweed, fish without a permit or drop litter. Mooring buoys have been introduced along the major reefs, spear fishing has been banned, and a larger mesh is being used in wire traps. With two days' notice, rangers lead educational diving and snorkelling expeditions; there's no charge but donations in cash or kind (particularly depth gauges) are gratefully accepted; details are available from the office at Cornwall Beach (PO Box 67, ☎952 9709). For more on the conservation movement in Jamaica, see p.333 of Contexts.

---

## Watersports

Montego Bay is justifiably famed for its deep turquoise waters and abundant reef systems, some close enough to swim to from the main beaches. Discarded rum bottles and tyres can be disconcerting, but the deeper reefs are alive with fish, rays, urchins and the occasional turtle and nurse shark. There are hosts of similarly priced **watersports operators** on each beach and within the larger hotels; naturally, we list the most reputable below. Pamphlets and information are always available from the Montego Bay Marine Park office (see opposite).

### DIVING AND SNORKELLING
The following offer guided dives (around US$35), certification courses (from US$300) and equipment rental (from US$15). Like every other watersports operator in Montego Bay, they also rent **snorkel gear** for around US$10 a day – most also offer guided snorkelling tours of the best reefs.

*Jamaica Rose*, Tropical Beach and *Norma's*, Reading; ☎953 2417 or 952 6261.

*Poseidon*, Reading Reef Club and *Margueritaville*; ☎952 3624 or 6088.

*Reef Keeper*, Walter Fletcher Beach; ☎979 0104.

*Resort Divers*, Montego Bay (LOJ) shopping centre; ☎952 4285.

*Seaworld, Cariblue Hotel*, Ironshore; ☎953 2180.

### BOAT TRIPS
**Boat trips**, with an open bar and sometimes lunch, are always popular and usually fun, if bawdy on-deck humour is your bag. Most depart from the *Pier One* complex on the Freeport peninsula and sail around the bay to the airport reefs with a stop for snorkelling. Pick of the bunch are *Calico Cruises*, which operates the only wooden sailing ships in town (☎952 5860; 5hr day cruise US$50; 2hr evening cruise US$25), and *Freestyle* (☎0995 2912; 5hr day cruise US$50, 2hr day cruise US$35, 2hr 30min sunset cruise US$25), whose well-maintained catamarans stop at *Margueritaville* (see p.218) to ride the water slide.

    **Glass-bottom boats** operate from all the main beaches and sail out to the airport reefs for around US$20 for half an hour. *MoBay Undersea Tours* at *Margueritaville* (☎940 2493; 1hr 30min; US$34) has a semi-submersible vessel which takes you ten feet underwater. Go in the morning for the best light or try a night tour to catch the nocturnal marine life. If you'd rather go it alone, you can rent a fully equipped **sport fishing boat** from around US$600 per day; best of the lot is *Jupiter* (☎952 9391), though *Lucky Lady* (☎952 4285) and *Horizon* (☎953 3992) are also reliable.

*Thrill-seekers can **parasail** from Margueritaville (☎952 4285; 15min US$130), while **jet skis** are available all over the place for US$35 for half an hour.*

bours. Locals squeezing through the fence from the waste ground next door add to the informality.

    Half a mile further north lies the famous **Doctor's Cave Beach**, Montego Bay's premium portion of gleaming white sand and see-through water. The beach was put on the map in the late nineteenth century when local doctor and sea-bathing advocate Alexander McCatty founded the *Sanatorium Caribbee*, an exclusive private bathing club that's still in existence today (though a lot less choosy);

in the 1920s visiting English chiropractor Sir Herbert Baker was so impressed by the curative potential of the waters that he published an article in the English press extolling their efficacy. The beau monde flocked and MoBay's tourist industry was born. The rapidly deepening waters really are the best in town and facilities are excellent, though there is little shade and it gets very crowded at the weekend.

Separated from Doctor's Cave by unattractive breeze-block walls, **Cornwall Beach** is the most intimate and laid-back of MoBay's public beaches. It's a young person's beach, with music pumped out from giant speakers and topless bathing common (though theoretically prohibited); inevitably, it's popular with Jamaican gigolos, and female visitors should expect constant, usually good-natured approaches. There's a lively bar, built around a giant almond tree, favoured by local professionals and off-duty policemen who stop by to drink, play dominoes and catch the sunset.

If the big three are too crowded for your tastes, head past the strip to Whitehouse (see p.208) and **Tropical Beach** (daily 9am–5pm; US$1), a much quieter private white-sand stretch that nonetheless offers full facilities and watersports, and has a nice shady area with seating and occasional stageshows. Alternatively, right by the airport, and consequently dogged by the racket of landings and take-offs, **Sunset Beach** is a thin but attractive strip of public sand popular with Jamaicans. The water is shallow and there are no facilities, but snorkelling is good and the view over the bay is fabulous, providing the best free sunset seat in town.

## Downtown

After the flamboyance of the strip, **downtown** announces itself with its very own stretch of undeveloped shoreline right opposite the dividing roundabout. The contrast couldn't be more marked: **Dump-Up Beach** is a dilapidated place where pigs root through rubbish bags and the dispossessed camp out. The sand is white enough, but this is one of the dirtiest parts of the bay; overflow from the Catherine Hall sewage plant, alongside untreated human waste and garbage from downtown squatter settlements, drain directly into the sea via the many rainwater gullies. It's not a place to swim, but it is the popular venue of local soccer matches and a disappointing Saturday **flea market**.

*This is a prime area for pickpockets – don't take out wads of cash when paying for small items, use ATM machines in daylight, and keep cameras in a closed bag.*

Shooting off from the roundabout, the main route into the centre of town is **Fort Street**, a clamorous thoroughfare with dancehall flooding out from storefronts and all manner of pushcarts and vehicles jostling for space with the thick human traffic. A short way along, there's a little garden area housing a **JTB information booth** and the useful **parish library** (Mon–Sat 9.30am–6pm), which carries a fair stock of Caribbean books; it would be a tranquil spot were it not for the cigarette, newspaper and Rizla vendors who noisily tout their wares from the garden wall. Past here, over the bridge across North Gully, you enter town proper. The covered market to the left is popularly known as **The Gully** (the correct name, William Street Market, is seldom used), a lively fruit and vegetable market where hardough bread and callaloo are sold out of supermarket trolleys and bartering is common at the stalls; a Jamaican companion will ensure reasonable prices.

Running parallel to Fort Street, **Orange Street** is lined by shabby shops and dingy bars that back onto the Canterbury squatters' community. The zinc-roofed clapboard dwellings cover the entire valley behind Orange Street, petering out at the red-earthed playing fields of MoBay's main high school, Cornwall College.

*Star Wholesale in The Gully give big reductions on bulk buys of three or more of the same item – it sells everything from cigarettes to saltfish.*

## Sam Sharpe Square and the craft market

Fort Street comes to an abrupt end at **Sam Sharpe Square**, the heart of downtown. Characterized by its central fountain and seemingly permanent stream of screaming traffic, this cobbled pavement area was until recently dominated by illegal vending rackets, every pavement obscured with displays of leather sandals, cheap watches, toys and bootleg designer imports presided over by knife-wielding Kingstonian immigrants. Vociferous local complaint has succeeded in moving most of the vendors on, but it's still a good idea to watch where you tread.

The square is bordered by a jumble of old and new architecture, including **The Cage**, built in 1806 as a lock-up for disorderly seamen and runaway slaves whose custodial shenanigans so damaged the original wooden walls that they were replaced with the red-brick and stone that stands today. In 1811, the rooftop belfry was installed, used to ring out a 2pm curfew warning; after the second ring at 3pm, any slaves still on the streets were locked up. The building is now a cambio and lotto outlet (Mon–Sat 9am–6pm), run by Irish exile Michael Moore, and a good place to stop for directions and local information. Just outside, National Hero Sam Sharpe (see below) is commemorated in a **bronze statue** by Jamaican sculptor Kay Sullivan, which depicts him in full evangelical flow before a crowd of converts.

The expanse of ruined land just off the square, beyond the junction with Market Street, now serves at the central taxi park and is all that remains of the old **courthouse**, long destroyed by fire but almost imaginable in the two lone pillars that still mark the entrance. Market Street itself is unremarkable; even the **Burchell Memorial Church**, where Sam Sharpe lies buried, is hulking, unattractive and uninteresting. Market Street ends at the junction with Harbour Street where you'll find the town's main **craft market**, a surprisingly hassle-free place to shop if you don't treat the inventive sales pitches as bamboozling. The 200-odd stalls sell every type of Jamaican craft (see p.221), and there are a couple of good, cheap restaurants patronized mostly by the vendors.

## Sam Sharpe and the Christmas Rebellion

Over the course of just over a week, slavery in Jamaica received the blow that would kill it forever. The **Christmas** or **Baptist Rebellion** began on December 27, 1831; by its end on January 5, 1832, twenty thousand slaves had razed nearly 160 sugar estates, causing damage to the value of £1 million – a massive drain on the British exchequer. It was the largest slave uprising in Jamaican history, and set in motion the process that led to the abolition of the slave trade in 1834 and full emancipation in 1838.

The rebellion was led by **Sam Sharpe**, a house slave working for a MoBay solicitor. Though this nascent martyr took on the surname of his master in accordance with tradition, his sideline as deacon of the town's Burchell Baptist Church made him anything but servile – at the time, the Baptists were Jamaica's most radical and outspoken critics of slavery and were rightly seen as a threat by the British establishment, particularly as religious congregations were the only gatherings legally allowed to slaves. The church taught Sharpe to read, and through international newspapers he learned of English anti-slavery sentiments and became convinced that emancipation in Jamaica was imminent, a reality that planters were trying to suppress. A powerful orator, Sharpe formed a secret society dedicated to banishing slavery, and planned a non-violent withdrawal of labour over the Christmas period. Talk of the insurrection spread fast through St James estates and even the planters became uneasy as December 1831 drew to a close. By the night of the 27th, passions were running high. The peaceful protest soon degenerated into anarchy; tipped off by the estate owners, the militia were out in force, and the more miltant slaves responded by lighting bonfires at the highest point of the Kensington estate to signify the start of a full-scale rebellion. Others followed suit and within days western Jamaica was burning as the cane fields and great houses were destroyed one by one. The response of the British militia was brutal. Though damage was predominantly restricted to property and only fourteen whites died, soldiers gunned down 1000 slaves and Montego Bay magistrates handed down a further three hundred execution orders during the emotionally charged six-week trial that ensued. Sharpe himself was hanged in the MoBay square that today bears his name and buried in the harbour sand, though his remains were later exhumed and interred in the vault of Burchell Memorial Church.

## Church Street

The four streets that feed off Sam Sharpe Square are MoBay's busiest, packed with stores and offices. Of these, **Church Street**, branching off from the square's southern corner, is the most architecturally interesting. Dominating the street is **St James Parish Church** (if locked, ask at the office opposite or call ☎952 2775), built from creamy cut stone in the shape of a cross – it was considered the showpiece of the parish when the original structure was completed in 1782. In 1957, an earthquake destroyed the foundations and the building underwent major repairs. Inside the church, the virtues of Rosa, first wife of John Palmer of Rose Hall (see p.225), are commemorated in a John Bacon verse and sculpture, set to the left of the altar. Outside, the well-maintained graveyard contains the ornate but weathered graves of deceased planters, many standing at erratic angles since the earthquake.

Opposite the church is the **Gallery of West Indian Art** (Mon–Wed & Fri 9am–5pm, Thurs 9am–2pm, Sat 9am–3pm; free), more of an expensive craft shop than a gallery but still worth a look. The collection is eclectic, with lots of intensely coloured "primitive" Cuban and Haitian works alongside the near-identical Jamaican sunset scenes that turn up islandwide. Next to the gallery is the elegant facade of the **Town House**, its weathered stone walls and stately grace rendering the surrounding concrete even more ill-favoured. Constructed in 1765 by local merchant David Morgan, the building has served as a private home, church manse, Masonic lodge, warehouse, synagogue and hotel – Queen Victoria spent the night – before becoming the smart restaurant, favoured by lunching ladies and visiting dignitaries, it is today (see "Eating", p.216).

## Dome Street and Jarrett Park

At its very top Church Street becomes Dome Street, which loops down to Water Lane, Creek Street and the South Montego Gully. The principal feature of an otherwise quiet street is **Dome House**, built as a wealthy planter's residence in the late 1700s and now restored to its former glory after a long period of disuse. It's still a princely building, with the classic proportions of plantation architecture; large sash windows, cool cut stone and an interior rich with original mahogany floors and fittings – it's currently a rehearsal and performance space for dance and theatre groups. Aqueous street names hint at the centrality of water to the history of this part of town; the now disused well in front of Dome House was originally linked to the **Dome** on Creek Street below – a solid stone circle topped with a peeling wooden roof that looks rather incongruous these days in the midst of all the hardware stores and racing traffic. Originally built over the stream that provided Creek Street with a name (it's still flowing along concreted banks), the Dome's thick walls mask two floors; the upper portion was originally occupied by the "Keeper of the Creek", who supervised collection from what was Montego Bay's main and only source of fresh water until a piped supply was made available in 1894.

*For details of forthcoming events at Dome House, call ☎952 2571 or 1134.*

Moving west from the Dome along Creek Street, you reach the junction with **St James Street**, downtown's liveliest shopping strip. Tatty hole-in-the-wall emporia vie for space with neon storefronts and sidewalk vendors, all fighting to be noticed against a background symphony of non-stop reggae and shouts of "sky juice" and "peanuts and *Wrigley's*". East of here, Creek Street rises sharply uphill, changing names and eventually reaching **Jarrett Park**, MoBay's premier cricket ground and the original site of Reggae Sunsplash (Bob Marley and the Wailers made their only festival appearance here in

*Cricket
matches are
well advertised
in local papers
and on
MoBay's HOT
102 radio
station.*

1979). Even if you're not a cricket fan, attending a match is highly entertaining, as much for the crowd-pleasing dancehall that booms out during every break in play as for the aficionados' impassioned running commentaries. Tickets (US$3–8) are sold at the gate, but you should get to the larger games early to ensure a seat; alternatively, you could follow the local example and catch the match for free from one of the surrounding hills.

### Barnett Street and Charles William Gordon Market

The least tourist-friendly part of downtown, **Barnett Street** – reached by following St James Street south from Sam Sharpe Square – is a raucous belt of supermarkets and mini-malls choking in a constant fug of traffic fumes. After St James Street, this is where you'll find the best shopping in town, though not of the duty-free t-shirt and packaged rum variety. Look out for the artistic storefront of *Lyle's Intensified Inn*, featuring caricatured policemen and Rastas and a strongly worded admonition to any prostitutes or pimps foolish enough to linger outside. Barnett Street is also the site of the town's notorious main **police station** and lock-up, so run-down that the inmates sleep ten to a cell on concrete floors and the officers make regular appeals for donations. Turn down Railway Lane for the main fruit and vegetable outlet, **Charles William Gordon Market** (also known as Fustic Market). Straddling the disused railway tracks and the impoverished houses that make up MoBay's most notorious "ghetto" (though it's luxury by Kingston standards), the market is a visceral whirl of tarpaulin-covered stalls selling enormous mounds of earth-covered yams, sweet potatoes and cassava alongside deep orange pumpkins, bunches of scallion and thyme, fat fingers of green bananas or plantain and a kaleidoscope of fruits. Goat belly and cheap chicken back are bartered in the pungent indoor meat section, where higglers make up temporary beds beside their pitches at the end of a day's trade. Main days are Wednesday and Saturday, but goods are always on sale and you get better deals here than at Gully Market. You can refresh yourself with a jelly coconut or Day-Glo sky juice from one of the ever-present vendors – look for the lone guy selling fresh cane juice, a far more refreshing choice.

At the end of Barnett Street, the traffic opens up and passes over Montego River. Here, the roadside takes on an incongruously lush aspect; giant bulrushes and emerald reeds flourish in the greyish semi-sewage and egrets roost in the few remaining poinciana and palm. Beyond the river is Westgate shopping centre, where a fairly good road branches off towards Adelphi and ultimately Cockpit Country.

## West of town

Barnett Street shoots off from the dividing roundabout to become the the A1, and takes you through MoBay at its least inspiring, a grim industrial estate perfumed by the slaughterhouse. The flotsam-filled yards and warehouses don't let up until well past the painted zinc fence circumventing **Catherine Hall Entertainment Centre**, stageshow venue and home of Reggae Sumfest (see p.36). The road ends at a fork, the right prong leading to **Freeport Peninsula**, a depressingly empty thoroughfare suspended in a limbo of factory fronts and abandoned marshland backing onto the Bogue Lagoon. The shipping wharves seem to sum up the desolation; fuel silos block out the view of the bay and hundreds of cars sit marooned until their owners can afford to get them through customs. The sole sign of life is at the **cruise-ship piers**, an incongruously flashy mass of expensive shops and restaurants that springs into action on docking days. Otherwise, you might wander up here for the **nude beach** (US$5) on the *Seawind* hotel grounds, a shallow reef beach with some sea grass, or for a drink or a tasty lunch at the posh **Yacht Club**, ostensibly for members only but covertly accessible to tourists; if so, shared taxis ply the route.

The left fork takes you past the rambling wilderness of Pye River Cemetery, from which a turn left and another right leads through mile upon mile of undulating cane to **Barnett Estate** (daily; US$20), a 3000-acre plantation occupying most of the MoBay basin. The nerve centre of the estate is a huge palm-thatched barn specially refurbished to shelter visitors as they wait for their guide to arrive – he's the one in faintly ridiculous "period" costume. The forty-minute jitney tour is pleasant enough, but the highlight is a walk around **Bellfield Great House**. Less stately than Rose Hall or Greenwood great houses (see pp.225 and 227), Bellfield's sweeping verandah and gleaming cream paintwork make it look contemporary, though it dates from 1735. Inside, the refurbishment is slick, with fittings brought in from all over the island: "pineapple" beds laid with best linen, Dresden china in showcases, eighteenth-century kitchen implements and a spectacularly bad life-size model of former owner David Kerr, all crimson cheeks and outraged expression. You can also tour the estate on horseback astride a mount from the impeccably run **Barnett Point Stables**, but you'll need to call an hour or so ahead (☎952 2382; 1hr US$40).

Right of Pye River, the A1 takes you out of town through more cane fields, skirting the coast at Bogue and the lavish villas of the well-to-do at **READING**. More of an extended residential zone with a petrol station than a town, Reading is notable mostly as site of the **Desnoes and Geddes factory**, producer of national brew *Red Stripe*. The private life of founder Paul Geddes came under the public microscope in 1995 when his estranged common-law wife won a J$6m palimony lawsuit in recognition of the 32 years she had spent supporting him while he built up his empire – which would have been a significant victory for women had she not lost the lot on appeal. A few hundred yards further on, past *Norma's* restaurant (see p.217), clipped bougainvillea hedges and a tiny sign mark a roadside **mineral spring**, maintained by a talkative Rasta who has built his home adjacent to the brackish pool (and will expect a small contribution for a bathe). The cool, clear, pitch-black depths are slightly unnerving to enter but wonderfully refreshing once you're in, and the Montegonians who visit this low-profile little spot swear by its rejuvenative powers.

A mile or so further down the coast road is **Budhai's Gallery** (daily 9am–5pm; free), owned and run by Cuban-born artist Neville Budhai, charismatic leading light of the local arts scene and recipient of the prestigious Institute of Jamaica Centenary Award. His distinctive line-drawings, watercolours and lithographs are on sale, but the man alone makes the gallery a worthwhile stop.

## Eating

Montego Bay's resort status ensures a fair share of swanky **restaurants** alongside the more usual Jamaican eateries, though many offer bland "international" fare or watered-down Jamaican dishes at inflated prices. Pricier tourist restaurants almost always offer free pickups, and it's worth calling ahead or checking the *Soon Come News* guide for promotions and special offers. Aside from notable exceptions such as *The Native*, Jamaican food is at its best from small-scale cookshops and restaurants; for **fish**, head for Whitehouse. There are plenty of US-style **fast-food** outlets around town, including Jamaica's first *McDonald's* at Blue Diamond shopping centre in Ironshore and a *Burger King* in a bus on Gloucester Avenue. The concrete balustrades of Sunset Beach are a popular spot for takeaway consumption.

---

### Snacks

Patties, callaloo loaf, coco bread and pastries are generally found only at downtown pastry shops, though vendors wheel pushcarts of them into the strip's craft markets. The best **bakeries** are *Butterflake Pastry* on Harbour Street, *Viennese Pastry* on the corner of St James and Union streets, *Chin's* on Market Street and *Juci Beef* on St James Street. The **Montego Bay (LOJ) shopping centre** on Howard Cooke Boulevard has an excellent **food court** with a great view over the bay: decent purveyors include *Ron's*, *Select Pastries and Deli* and *Pizza Delite*, while **vegetarians** – ill catered for in Jamaica – will appreciate *Caffe Espresso*, serving a wide range of international coffees, falafel, burgers, soups, cakes and shakes, with no animal fat used in cooking. Elsewhere, cheap and tasty jerk is sold at the *Pork Pit* on Gloucester Avenue; sweet teeth can be satisfied at the **frozen yoghurt** outlet underneath, while *24-7* next to the Gully Market is the best **ice cream** outlet downtown. *Tony's Pizza* (☎952 6365), in a permanently parked red-and-white van opposite Cornwall Beach, sells pizza, sub sandwiches and wonderful pineapple and ginger juice until 2am, while for **all-night** macaroni cheese or callaloo and saltfish with dumplings try the cookshop to the right of *Star Wholesale* in the Gully Market, but be prepared to jostle with crowds of hungry Jamaicans fresh from the clubs.

## Queen's Drive and downtown

**Georgian House**, corner of Orange and Union streets. Attractive eighteenth-century building with a garden, serving well-made, inexpensive Jamaican food.

**I'N'I Paradise**, Queen's Drive. Rastafarian vegetarian restaurant just beyond the airport serving authentic Ital food in attractive red-gold-and-green bamboo shacks. Excellent natural juices including roots wine and cane juice.

**Lychee Garden**, 18 East St; ☎952 9428. Arguably the best and certainly the costliest Chinese food in town. The Peking duck is superb, as are shrimp in sweet and sour sauce and lobster stir-fried in ginger.

**Norma at the Wharfhouse**, Reading; ☎952 2745. Spectacular setting on a wooden boardwalk with a fantastic view of the bay and city lights. Changed daily, the sophisticated menu offers unusual combinations alongside more familiar dishes and is invariably delicious – devilled crab-back with red-leaf lettuce salad is excellent, as are any of the wicked desserts. Closed Monday.

*In restaurant
listings, we
have given a
phone number
only for those
places where
you might
need to
reserve a
table.*

**Ray's Vegetarian Top Tasting Restaurant**, Railway Lane. Popular Ital cookshop – go early as the food usually finishes by 3pm. Veggie burgers, ackee, cabbage and callaloo, tofu sandwiches, soups, stew peas, and proper Ital juices – peanut punch, roots wine, papaya and the like. Excellent stuff.

**Richmond Hill Inn**, Union Street; ☎952 3859. The overpriced seafood-based menu isn't that exciting, but the setting – on its very own hill at the top of Union Street – is intensely romantic; the view covers the whole bay.

**Rite Stuff**, Westgate Plaza. Bustling breakfast and lunch café popular with office workers. Soup and cheesecake are the highlights, but there are lots of salads and very good vegetarian options too.

**Smokey Joe's**, 19 St James St. Cheap and tasty local, serving no-nonsense Jamaican lunches and dinners in a comfortable atmosphere.

**Tigers**, 23 St James St. Buffet-style Jamaican café frequented almost exclusively by locals. All the usual dishes with some vegetarian food available.

**The Town House**, 16 Church St; ☎952 2660. Fashionable basement restaurant in a beautiful eighteenth-century building (see p.213), reeking of old-world gentility. The dinner menu (New York steak, red snapper papillot, shrimp and lobster creole) is expensive, but the daily lunch special, taken at one of the pews in the lounge area, is great value.

## Gloucester Avenue and the beaches

**Baba Joe's Hut**, Kent Ave, Whitehouse. Small-scale diner where a friendly crowd of locals enjoys huge portions of delicious steamed or brown stew fish, lobster and sea puss.

**The Brewery**, Miranda Ridge, Gloucester Ave. Late-opening spot above the strip. Extremely varied menu with daily specials (like oysters in lemon butter), a big burger selection, lots of salads and some Mexican (avoid the nachos). Good value and pretty views.

**Café Gran Caribe**, Gloucester Ave. Unimposing street café opposite Doctor's Cave Beach serving excellent Jamaican and American food, with particularly good breakfasts. The roadside setting is pleasant, but you sometimes feel like sitting bait for the hustlers.

**Da Grill**, *The Wexford*, 39 Gloucester Ave; ☎952 2854. Best for a leisurely breakfast on the lovely bayfront verandah: choose from an all-you-can-eat buffet in the week or brunch specials at the weekend.

**Evelyn's**, Kent Ave, Whitehouse; ☎952 3280. Famous for its unusual way of preparing roti, usually a spicy split-pea pancake but reinvented as a flat fried dumpling to back up fried fish or curry chicken. Call ahead for the conventional version served with dahl. Other dishes span the Jamaican spectrum, with lots of seafood.

**Guangzhou**, Miranda Ridge, Gloucester Ave. The only Chinese restaurant on the strip, and very good it is too. The indoor dining room is a bit gloomy in the daytime, but a 15 percent weekday lunch discount pulls in the punters.

**Margueritaville**, Gloucester Ave; ☎352 4777. The loudest place on the strip. International menu with a Mexican flavour, and American-style service with the emphasis on fun. Hidden behind an aquatic wall mural, *Marguerites* next door has elegant decor, upscale atmosphere and an innovative menu featuring reef snapper in a coconut run-down sauce and a divine hot banana and guava rum cheesecake; there's a flambé grill for table-side cooking as well.

**The Native**, 29 Gloucester Ave; ☎979 2769. The best place on the strip for a sit-down Jamaican meal – not cheap so take advantage of reduced-rate buffets and lunch specials. Try the "Boonoonoo's Platter" of ackee, curry goat, jerk chicken and escovitched fish, rice and peas and plantain. The regular Jamaican cookery classes are invariably entertaining.

**The Pelican**, Gloucester Ave; ☎952 3171. Long-established restaurant popular with locals and tourists. Highlights include cornmeal porridge or American/Jamaican breakfast, the daily lunch specials (fricassee chicken to cow foot) and desserts – rum pudding and coconut or banana cream pie.

**PJ's**, 17 Kent Ave. Excellent open-air jerk centre, serving platters of curried lobster, steamed fish and vegetables as well as jerk meats and all the trimmings.

**Quartz**, Cornwall Craft Market. Tiny soot-blackened open-air cookshop selling the tastiest and cheapest meals along the strip, served in a box with rice and peas, yam, sweet potato, roast breadfruit and avocado.

**Star of India**, Kent Ave; ☎952 9201. MoBay's only Indian restaurant, with consistently good kormas and tikkas, plenty of vegetarian options and superb stuffed naan. Popular with foreign residents bored with Jamaican cuisine.

**Sunset Restaurant and Bar**, Gloucester Ave. Tiny, easily missed place that's the only really authentic Jamaican bar and restaurant along the strip, as suggested by the clientele – taxi drivers and Jamaican couples.

**Tapas**, Corniche Rd; ☎952 2988. Innovative and delicious Mediterranean food in a place that's upscale but affordable, and blessedly detached from the strip; take the small road to the left of *Coral Cliff* hotel.

**Walter's Bar and Grill**, Miranda Ridge, Gloucester Ave; ☎952 9391. Menu highlights are the sizzling fajitas and copious nachos, though the salads and sandwiches are also good, and the setting is relaxing.

## Drinking, nightlife and entertainment

Surprisingly, Montego Bay is not particularly lively at **night**; the strip takes on a ghostly hush as the cruise ships glide out of the harbour and visitors hole up in their all-inclusives. Official attempts to get tourists out after dark with a Monday night mini-carnival along the strip have faltered – noise from the mobile discos and a host of security problems mean the event is often cancelled. You'll find **bar culture** forming an integral part of your MoBay weeknights: the strip's string of bars packed with gigolos hunting for fresh meat, North Americans and business-suited Jamaicans glued to big-screen NFL action and the unwary pickling themselves in rum punch. *Walter's, The Brewery* and *PJ's* are still enduring in the face of *Margueritaville's* imminent take-over as the place to be. If you're set on drinking yourself silly, do so in the sheltered surroundings of an all-inclusive – an **evening pass** (US$20–30) entitles you to unlimited drinks and sometimes food, with the occasional cheesy floorshow as part of the bargain; the most popular spot is *Breezes* overlooking Doctors Cave Beach. **Clubs** tend to get really busy only on weekends, though *Club Paradise* on Gloucester Avenue and certain enjoyably seedy downtown establishments attract a crowd of die-hards most nights; all get going by 11pm and keep the pace until the small hours. Cover charges vary, but you're unlikely to pay more than US$5. The weekend is ritually celebrated throughout downtown, with small-time **sound systems** setting up on street corners and the rum flowing free; these are local parties, not the preserve of tourists, but you should be fine with a Jamaican escort – recommended for all downtown bars and clubs.

*Exercise some caution if you venture away from the strip at night – take a taxi and leave your valuables at the hotel.*

## Bars

**The Brewery**, Miranda Ridge, Gloucester Ave. Friendly pub-style venue, permanently packed with young Jamaicans, who spill out onto the terrace bar on Tuesday and Friday's karaoke nights.

**Dead End Bar**, Kent Ave. Open 24hr, a laid-back spot perfect for sunset- and plane-watching. Thursday night is given over to oldies, with classic reggae and rocksteady churned out until the last punter leaves.

**Hi-Lites Café**, 19 Queen's Drive. Very quiet, but with a great view across the bay, simple food and a daily happy hour between 6 and 7pm.

**Margueritaville**, Gloucester Ave. Aquatic activity takes a backseat to American sports (admission charge for big games). Lively theme nights, special offers, drinks promotions and fabulous bay views but an irritating token payment system for drinks. The dancefloor opens nightly at 10pm, daily happy hour is 5.30–6.30pm and an all-inclusive cover charge of US$10–15 is sometimes imposed on weekends.

**Pirate's Perch**, above *Sunset Deli* on Gloucester Ave. Small bar with pool table, slot machines and a busy verandah.

**PJ's**, 17 Kent Ave. Hugely popular outdoor bar, attractively set under towering bamboo and silk cotton trees. There's nightly live reggae, and carnival nights (Mon & Wed) with craft stalls, traditional dancing and Rasta drummers. Persistent rent-a-dreads and ganja hustlers are the only drawback.

**Walter's Bar and Grill**, Miranda Ridge, Gloucester Ave. A MoBay institution, usually packed, with satellite sports coverage and live jazz or reggae every Friday. The small upstairs disco opens at the weekend or whenever enough customers demand.

**Zee Bar**, *The Wexford*, 39 Gloucester Ave. Popular with Montegonians, hence Thursday's Locals Night, when drinks, wings and pizza are all US$1 and classic reggae plays all night. Satellite sports and slot machines.

## Clubs

**Bottle Inn**, 11 Union St (nightly). Late-opening club with ultra-violet light and a certain louche charm. Wednesday is dancehall night, Thursday is old hits. Recommended for a taste of real Jamaican clubbing.

**Club Inferno**, Rose Hall (Thurs–Mon). Expansive outdoor setting that's quiet unless there's a concert on. Friday through Monday are the biggest club nights, with reggae dominant, but it's a bit of a trek from the strip just for a DJ. US$5 cover if there's a stageshow.

**Club Paradise**, Miranda Ridge, Gloucester Ave (nightly). The prostitutes and gigolos can be too attentive, but they can't spoil the fun. Mostly reggae with some R&B and dance, the best selection coming from female DJ Jackie. Cover US$3, women free on Thurs.

**Club XS**, Blue Diamond Shopping Centre, Ironshore (nightly). Popular with a fairly smart Jamaican crowd and improved by a breezy outdoor area. Various theme nights, with a usual cover of $3.

**Flamingo**, Sugarmill Rd, Ironshore (nightly). The usual X-rated go-go dancing and all-round lasciviousness occasionally make way for phenomenally popular jams by the best of the Kingston-based sound systems. Cover US$3–5.

**Goldfingers**, Market St (nightly). Dingy dancehall club downtown favoured by kissing couples and expert Jamaican dancers – make sure you know your butterfly from your body-basics.

**Hurricanes Disco**, *Breezes*, Gloucester Ave (nightly). Brand new, state-of-the-art hotel club, with dancehall, Euro-techno and R&B until dawn. Heaving on Saturdays, with the gigolos out in full force. Cover US$20, including all drinks.

**The Keg**, 2 Barnett St (nightly). Friendly local hangout on the corner of Harbour Street with a popular oldies session every Wednesday. Cover US$3.

**Lollypop on the Beach**, Sandy Bay; ☎953 5314. Though it's 10 miles out of town, many Montegonians trek west to this seaside venue for the occasional stageshow, while tourists are bussed in for all-inclusive reggae shows with dinner, drinks and a floodlit 15min glass-bottom boat ride (US$50 including transport).

**Pier 1**, Howard Cook Blvd (nightly). Oldies on the boardwalk during the week (free) and a pumping club at the weekends. Fridays are busiest, with upfront dancehall and R&B until dawn. A bit of a meat market, but as MoBay's premier nightspot it's essential nonetheless. Cover US$5.

**Royal Palm**, Orange St. Nightly go-go dancing and white rum drinking.

## Entertainment

Unless you're content with a diet of tired in-hotel floor shows, you'll often be climbing the walls for **live entertainment** in MoBay. **Music** is the town's strongest suit, with regular live reggae at various strip venues and at the beaches, where you'll occasionally find stageshows and open-air sound-system nights, generally more pleasant than the hot and smoky indoor venues. **Cornwall Beach** is the most regular spot, with raw dancehall every Tuesday night (8pm–1am; US$4) and a large stage for concerts. Usually ad-hoc affairs at Tropical Beach or

*Club Inferno*, the major events (including Reggae Sumfest; see p.36) are held at the **Catherine Hall Entertainment Centre** on Howard Cooke Boulevard. August and the whole winter tourist season are the best time to catch the larger **annual shows** such as Sumfest, Sting and Reggae Kwanzaa, which move from venue to venue across the island. Traditionally the suicide season for those in the tourism business, rainy October sees the **All That Heritage and Jazz** festivities, a week-long series of concerts on the strip with world music and jazz alongside the reggae. Finally, for a sedate evening, the *Belvedere Hotel* puts on live jazz on the last Saturday of each month, and *Doctor's Cave Beach Hotel* has a jazz trio in the lobby bar every Thursday and Sunday.

*For more
details on
MoBay's
annual events
see p.34.*

Otherwise, there are two **cinemas** in town: the characterful, rather shabby *Strand Theatre* downtown at 8 Strand St (☎952 5391) and the smarter *Diamond Cinema* at the Blue Diamond Shopping Centre in Ironshore (☎953 9540). **Roots plays** are staged at *Chatwick Gardens Hotel*, 10 Queen's Drive (☎952 2147), and occasionally at the Strand; for serious theatre catch one of the excellent Montego Bay Little Theatre Movement productions at *Fairfield Theatre* (☎952 0182).

# Shopping

As a major cruise-ship port, much of MoBay's consumer activity centres around **in-bond shopping**, with countless flashy malls given over to identical jewellery, perfume and leather goods outlets. They're all much of a muchness, but City Centre Mall on Fort Street is the least ostentatious. Better for general purchases, Montego Bay Shopping Centre – usually referred to as the LOJ (Life of Jamaica) Mall – on Howard Cooke Boulevard has a great selection of browsable stores, including the *Fontana Pharmacy* – great for gimmicky souvenir mugs, pens, stationery and knick-knacks – and the best **bookstore** in town, *The Book Shop*, with a range of Caribbean titles unmatched outside Kingston.

You can't move for **crafts** in MoBay. The best market is the huge Harbour Street complex (daily 7am–7pm; see p.211), packed with straw and wicker work, belts, clothes, jewellery, t-shirts and woodcarvings; some of the best woodwork is at *Kelly's Sculpture Creation*, shop 190. The Fort and Cornwall craft markets along the strip (daily 8am–7pm) are worth a look but tend to be a little more expensive with less variety. Elsewhere, check out *Things Jamaican* at 44 Fort St or the Rasta-inspired *Tafara*, 39 Union St.

Head downtown for the best **art** shopping – the *Gallery of West Indian Art* has a huge range of works; more affordable are *Irie Creations* in Sunshine Plaza opposite the main craft market. Try also *Budhai's* in Reading (see p.216) and *Ambiente Gallery* at 10 Fort St for Jamaican and Cuban prints and originals at upscale prices, and the *Cultural Arts Centre* at 31 Gloucester Ave for arty goods.

Downtown **record stores** offer the Jamaican speciality of custom-made reggae tapes (around US$2) as well as CDs and vinyl. Try *El Paso* at 3 South Lane overlooking Sam Sharpe Square, *Federal* at 18 Strand St, *Top Rank* in Westgate Plaza and *Bay City* in Sunshine Plaza overlooking Church Street. *Reggae Rhythms* in the Blue Diamond Centre also sells videos, books and photographs. For sound-system session tapes and bootleg recordings of recent stageshows (US$5–6), check the regular vendor in the Market Street car park; the quality is surprisingly good, but ask for a test play before you buy.

For miscellaneous odds and ends, browse around the untouristy stores downtown. **St James Street** holds a branch of the dependable *Sangster's* book chain and *Dominion Stationery*, with an excellent selection of 1970s postcards and a small but quality selection of yellowing books, while **Barnett Street** is best for useless souvenirs – right at the end by Post Office Number 2, the *Natural Apparel Shop/Ras Natango Designs*, 8 Filandy Plaza, specializes in clothing and accessories made from hemp, as well as wall hangings and cannabis-related books. If you want to take home some rum, the cheapest option is to club together and buy it wholesale from *C&J Liquors* on Harbour Street, though the *Jamaica Farewell* pre-packed boxes from in-bond shops are easier to carry and only a little more expensive.

# Listings

**Airlines** *Air Jamaica* (☎952 4300 or 4100); *American Airlines* (☎952 5950); *British Airways* (☎952 3771), and *Continental* (☎952 4495) are all based at Sangster International Airport.

**Airport enquiries** Sangster International Airport's ticket, flight and baggage information line is ☎952 5530 or 5531.

**American Express** *Stuarts Travel*, 40 Market St ; ☎952 4350.

**Banks and money** Several banks congregate around Sam Sharpe Square; most efficient are *Bank of Nova Scotia* (also at Westgate Shopping Centre) and *Mutual Security Bank* (also on Gloucester Ave opposite Cornwall Beach). *NCB* is just off the square at 41 St James St, with another branch at the airport; both have ATMs. There's a *Citizens Bank* at Montego Bay (LOJ) Shopping Centre, also with an ATM, and a *Mutual Security Bank* on Gloucester Avenue opposite Cornwall Beach. There are cambios at The Cage in Sam Sharpe Square, *Chin's Pastry*, 10 Church St, *King Midas*, 37 Gloucester Ave, and *Alvin Wallace*, Shop 144, Harbour Street Craft Market. Alternatively most of the in-bond shops on Gloucester Avenue operate unofficial cambios. Wire transfers can be collected from *Western Union* above *Hometown Supermarket* on Church Street, though *Moneygram* is a little cheaper – pick-up points are the *Lotto Shop*, 6 Market St or *Stuarts Travel*, 40 Market St.

**Car and bike rental** All the major companies have offices at the airport or Queens Drive/Sunset Boulevard: *Avis* (☎952 4543), *Budget* (952 3838), *Hertz* (☎979 0438) and *Thrifty* (☎952 5825). Local operators are usually cheaper; most reliable for regular cars are *Praise*, 18 Queen's Drive (☎952 0982), *Solid*, 32 Queen's Drive (☎952 7484), *Travel International*, Cotton Tree Complex, Queen's Drive (☎952 9362), *Utas*, MoBay Club, Gloucester Ave (☎979 3465) and *Westshore*, 32 Queen's Drive (☎979 3450 or 6849). *Hot Tops*, Miranda Ridge, Gloucester Ave (☎979 9187) rents only **jeeps** and is very efficient. For **motorbikes** try *Kryss*, also at Miranda Ridge (☎940 0476), *Montego Bikes*, 21 Gloucester Ave (☎952 4984) or *Tanka* in the forecourt of *Manevarose* hotel on Queen's Drive (☎979 3955).

**Consulates** Only the Canadian Consulate (☎952 6198) and US Consulate (☎952 0160) have offices in Montego Bay, both on Gloucester Avenue. Embassies and other consulates are all based in Kingston (see p.85).

**Dentists** Try Dr Marlene Foote, 14c Market St (☎952 3016), or the Montego Bay Dental Clinic, 19 Gloucester Ave (☎952 1080).

**Doctors** Most hotels have a doctor or nurse on duty or on call. Recommended practitioners are Dr Anthony Vendryes, whose surgery is at the *Royal Court* hotel on Sewell Ave (☎952 4351), or Dr Shirley Campbell at 15 Union St (☎952 0305).

**Hospitals** Cornwall Regional Hospital, Mount Salem (☎952 5100 or 5105) is the best public hospital outside Kingston. The best private institution is Doctor's Hospital in Fairfield (☎952 1616).

**Laundry** Most hotels have a laundry service but there are some fairly good laundries. *Bay Fabricare Centre* at 4 Corner Lane (☎952 6987) is chaotic but central, and its one-hour dry cleaning service is convenient. *Hot Line Laundry* below *Upper Deck Condos* on Sewell Ave (☎979 3204) is friendly, with a good pick-up and drop-off service. *Wonder Wash* in Westgate Plaza (☎940 1143) has MoBay's only coin-operated machines.

**Immigration** Immigration Office, Floor 3, Overton Plaza, Union Street (Mon–Fri 8am–1pm & 2–4pm; ☎952 5381). Visa extensions, lost passports – go early to avoid the queues.

**Pharmacies** There are plenty of pharmacies downtown: best equipped are *Clinicare* on Sam Sharpe Square (Mon–Sat 9am–8pm, Sun 10am–6pm), *Fontana*, Montego Bay (LOJ) Shopping Centre (Mon–Sat 8am–7pm) and *R Zacks*, 30 Union St (Mon–Sat 9am–8pm). The only one on the strip is St James Pharmacy at Shop 4 St James Plaza (Mon–Sat 9am–6pm).

**Photography** You can buy or develop film at *Photo Express*, City Centre Mall, Fort St (☎952 3120), at *Salmon's*, 32 St James St (☎952 4527), and at *Ventura* at 22 Market St (☎952 2937).

**Police** Montego Bay has three police stations; the largest is at 14 Barnett St (☎952 1557). If your car is impounded, go to the station at 29 Church St (☎952 4396); visitors are usually told to take complaints or crime reports directly to the Tourism Liaison Unit at Summit station on Sunset Boulevard (☎952 1540). In an emergency, dial ☎119; the Woman Inc rape crisis line is (☎952 9534).

**Post Offices** The two main post offices are named Number 1, on the corner of Fort Street opposite the library, and Number 2, at 120 Barnett St. There is a postal agency (Whitesands PO) on Gloucester Ave next to Doctor's Cave Beach; you can pick up post-restante mail at all three, but Whitesands is the least frenetic.

**Supermarkets** There are large supermarkets in Westgate Plaza on Barnett Street, Overton Plaza on Union Street and Blue Diamond Shopping Centre in

Ironshore. *Hometown* at 19 Church St is the best of the downtown bunch. Mini-marts on Gloucester Avenue are pricey but convenient; try *Sunset Supermarket and Deli* opposite *Casa Blanca* hotel or *Cleveland Supermarket* in the *MoBay Club* building, which opens until 10pm daily.

**Taxis** Reliable firms include *Doctor's Cave Stand* (☎952 0521), *In Your Hands*, (☎952 4863) and *Joseph* (☎979 9425 or 952 9694). The Market Street taxi stand is the choice of locals (6am–1am; ☎952 6329 or 979 9061); ask for Boxer, Neville or Jahson (sic), by far the most reasonable and reliable drivers. Ricardo Hutchinson (☎952 7032) is an excellent independent licensed driver especially good for long distances and tours. Patrick Clarke (☎0819 5832 or 0999 5816), a member of *JUTA*, is also dependable.

**Telephones** The strip is fairly well served by public phones and there's a large bank of them outside the TOJ office on Union St. Overseas calls are cheapest at *Jamintel*, 10 Fort St (Mon–Fri 8am–7pm, Sat 8am–noon), which also offers fax and telegram services, though you can also call home from The Cage in Sam Sharpe Square.

**Travel Agents** *Friendly Travel Service*, 18 Strand St (☎979 5797); *International Travel Service*, 14b Market St (☎952 2485); *Stuarts Travel*, 40 Market St (☎952 4350).

# Around Montego Bay

Away from the shops and the beaches, there's plenty to see around Montego Bay, and though many of the attractions – like **Rose Hall**, with its ghoulish reputation and theme-park ambience – are so hyped-up that you couldn't miss them if you tried, others, such as the **Rocklands bird sanctuary** or the **Belvedere Estate**, have a quiet charm and natural beauty that are effortlessly seductive.

Other than **rafting** down the Great River from Lethe, few people head into the **St James interior** – a shame, because the rolling hinterland pastures are spectacular in places. St James was prime plantation territory under the British and a few of the old estates have kept their land and opened it up to the public. Polished boiling pots and repointed stone mills illustrate the mechanics of the sugar industry, and lavishly restored great house interiors froth over the planters' lifestyles, but there's little to commemorate one of the most significant phases in Jamaican history: the **Christmas Rebellion** of 1831 that began in St James and set the wheels in motion for the abolition of slavery.

## East along the coast

*Ironshore's all-inclusives are covered along with Montego Bay accommodation on p.203.*

With its endless reefs and postcard beaches, the eastern stretch of coast beyond Montego Bay has long been the preserve of the more expensive all-inclusive hotels. As a consequence, the A1 coast road is a pleasure to drive; straight and smooth, it zips through the plush residential belt of **IRONSHORE**, home to two of the island's best **golf courses**, the independent *Ironshore Golf and Country Club*

(☎953 2800) and the *Half Moon Golf Club* (☎953 2211),host of the Red Stripe Pro-Am tournament. The area was once part of a vast sugar plantation; from Sugarmill Road you can see the remains of crumbling chimneys and an aqueduct.

There's some of the island's best **horse-riding** at the *Rocky Point Stables* at the *Half Moon* complex (☎953 2286). Trail rides take you into the mountains and back down to the sea, where saddles are removed and you and your mount cool off in the brine (1hr 30min US$50, 2hr 30min US$70). Dressage, show jumping and polo lessons are also on offer, and you can watch a polo match most Tuesdays.

## Rose Hall

Romanticized plantation history comes into its own at **ROSE HALL**, site of the infamous **Rose Hall Great House** (daily 9am–6pm; US$10), inspiration for Jamaica's best-loved piece of folklore, the tale of a voodoo practitioner who ruthlessly disposed of her husbands and is still said to haunt the corridors. Built between 1770 and 1780 by its first owner, planter and parish custos (the old English term for a mayor) John Palmer, the dazzling white stone structure, set back from the A1 and surrounded by gardens, woods and a swan-filled pond, is difficult to miss. Rose Hall makes much of the vastly embellished legend of Annie Palmer, the "White Witch of Rose Hall", and the rather mechanical guided tours that run every fifteen minutes milk it shamelessly. You gasp at blurred photos that supposedly show the face of an unknown woman in the mirror, and gawp at Annie's bedroom, symbolically redecorated in shades of red, and the terrace from which she allegedly pushed a maid to her death. As the house was unoccupied and widely looted during the nineteenth century, almost all of its current contents have been transported from other great houses or from overseas. The silk wallpaper, magnificent mahogany staircase and furnishings are attractive (if not from the right period), but the fake food and on-site Olde English pub – legacies of a gaudy refurbishment in the mid-1960s – rather spoil the romance.

Nevertheless, the grounds are lovely, although these too have a violent past, this one authentic. In 1963 the district was the site of the **"Coral Gardens Massacre"**, a bloody altercation between police and Rastafarians – then commonly viewed as vicious, anti-white, drug-crazed maniacs – whose right of way through the Rose Hall grounds to their vegetable plots was being threatened by property speculators developing the house into the tourist attraction it is today. After months of contention, a policeman sent to arrest the dissidents was attacked with a spear and a petrol station was set on fire. The army was called in, and during the ensuing bloodbath eight Rastas died and others throughout the island were thrown into jail. Obviously, nothing marks the spot, and it's ironic that Rose Hall glorifies a violent fairy story while ignoring the blood spilt to make it so glamorous.

*The* Stables *(formerly* The Oasis*) in Parkway Plaza is a restful place to stop for a no-nonsense Jamaican meal.*

*The* Soon Come Shuttle *will take you as far as Rose Hall.*

*For more on Rastafari, see p.338 of Contexts.*

*Herbert DeLisser's bodice-ripping* The White Witch of Rose Hall *is a thrilling narrative version of the story; see* Contexts, *p.359.*

## The White Witch of Rose Hall

Jamaica's most famous horror story centres on **Annie Palmer**, the "White Witch of Rose Hall". A beautiful young woman of Anglo-Irish descent, Annie Mary Patterson's early years are cloaked in mystery. Born in either England or Ireland, she was the only child of small-time property owners John and Juliana Patterson, who brought her to live in Haiti as a little girl, where she learned the voodoo art. The date of her arrival in Jamaica is unknown, but it's said that she came to Kingston as a fresh-faced seventeen-year-old in search of a husband. Being young and white, she was granted access to high society functions and her brooding good looks soon captured the attention of John Palmer, incumbent of Rose Hall and grand-nephew of its architect, John Palmer. They married in March 1820, but the union was not a happy one; seven years on and bored with her insipid husband, Annie took a young slave lover. Palmer found out and whipped her severely; Annie took her revenge by placing poison in his wine, smothering the dying man with a pillow. She went on to stab and strangle two more husbands, and seduce and murder a succession of white bookkeepers and black slaves. Even to those slaves she wasn't sleeping with, she was a cruel and sadistic mistress, meting out excessive punishments for minor misdemeanours.

However, Annie's cruelty proved to be her undoing, and she was murdered in her bed in 1831. No-one knows for sure whose hands encircled her neck, but some accounts point to an old and powerful balmist whose pretty granddaughter had been in competition with Annie for the attentions of a young English bookkeeper, until the older woman set an "ol' hige" vampire upon her rival, killing her within a week.

Gripping as it is, there's barely a shred of truth in the story. Annie Palmer did exist (she's buried in a concrete grave to the left of the house), but by all accounts she was a peaceful woman with no discernible tendencies to sadism or lechery. She may have become confused over the years with Rosa Palmer, the original mistress of Rose Hall who did have four husbands, but she was said to be unwaveringly virtuous. Nonetheless, most Jamaicans choose to believe in something more sinister, and visiting mediums swear to strange visions and the discovery of buried effigies in the grounds.

The Rose Hall empire extends a few miles up the coast to the non-descript roadside community of **LILLIPUT**. Just past the signs for the *Jamaican Bush Doctor and Palm Reader*, where roots wine and bush medicine are dispensed alongside negligible clairvoyant advice, lies **Rose Hall Beach Club** (daily 9am–5pm; US$8) a recently land-scaped beach with full tourist amenities that's advertised as the safest in Montego Bay – presumably because the locals can't afford to swim there any more. Every Monday and Thursday, the beach hosts the Miskito Cove Beach Picnic (☎952 5164; US$55), an all-inclusive fun day comprising an open bar, lunch, watersports and a cruise.

The towering *Wyndham Rose Hall* resort (see below) dominates the rest of the Rose Hall district. Its expansive (and expensive) **golf course** contains a beautiful waterfall seen in the Jamaican James Bond classic *Live and Let Die*, and is an excellent spot for a walk even if you don't play golf – though you should check at the hotel before entering.

PRACTICALITIES

The *Wyndham Rose Hall* **hotel** (PO Box 999, Montego Bay; ☎953 2560, fax 953 2617; ⑦) is an ugly high-rise with an incongruously plush lobby, a pristine private beach and five bars and restaurants. There's a simpler place to stay two miles inland at *Dunns Villa* (Little River PO, ☎997 5077; ③), a small family-run resort with a pool, Jacuzzi, restaurant and mountain bikes for rent. Rooms are pleasantly decorated but overpriced; haggle.

The best place to **eat** in the area is the *Ambrosia Restaurant* at *Wyndham Rose Hall* (☎ext 77), serving top-notch, top-whack Mediterranean dishes with an accent on seafood.

## Greenwood

Five miles west from Rose Hall, the A1 passes through scrubby mangrove swamps and opens up with a magnificent sea view at diminutive **GREENWOOD**. Perched on a hill overlooking the sea, the dull grey stone of **Greenwood Great House** (daily 9am–6pm; US$10) dominates the few houses and bars below. Surrounded by luscious flowering gardens, the house itself has none of the flashy allure of Rose Hall, and has managed to retain most of its original contents as well as a listless eighteenth-century ambience. Built in 1790 by relatives of the Barrett family of Wimpole Street film (see p.189), the house was used primarily for recreation and entertaining and contains their original library, an extensive collection of ancient musical instruments, a court jester's chair and custom-made Wedgwood china. The Barretts clearly had an eye for scenery – the forty-foot verandah commands a panoramic view of the sea unbroken by land, and, doubtful as it may seem, you really can see the curvature of the earth. The tour, which ends in the bar set up in the original kitchen area, is enjoyable enough, but is soured by a rather cavalier attitude to the property's slave history; there's just a cursory reference to a man trap used to catch runaways and a leg iron displayed on the wall like an ornament, while, with an apparent lack of irony, the young female guides are dolled up as eighteenth-century servants.

Nearby, **Cinnamon Hill Great House** was also built by the Barretts, but is now the private home of country and western star Johnny Cash, a local hero both as a singer (country music is incredibly popular in Jamaica) and for his regular contributions to children's charities and schools. Just outside Greenwood, the fluttering flags mark the first buildings of the **Bob Marley School for the Arts**, currently being built in two hundred acres as the island's premier musical training centre.

PRACTICALITIES

You can **stay** at the Bob Marley School for the Arts (☎954 5252, fax 953 3683; ③), in spacious roots-style rooms with beautiful wicker furnishings, clover-shaped skylights, fans, patio doors and a fantastic view of the coastline. Otherwise, there are all-inclusive, self-contained apartments at *Sea Castles* (☎953 3250, fax 974 5912; in US ☎1-800/752-6824, fax 212/924-8038; ⑦) in a huge property right on the coast between the *Wyndham* hotel and Greenwood, with a pool, private beach, watersports and two restaurants.

For **eating and drinking**, the *Far Out Fish Hut*, on the coastal side of the A1 just beyond Greenwood, serves the best fish and bammy on the island, and is always packed despite high prices. Cheaper Jamaican food is available at *Turtles Inn*, half a mile further down the road and worth a visit for the home-made conch soup alone.

# The St James interior

Shooting off from Reading on Montego Bay's western flank, the well signposted B8 inland road plunges straight into tropical St James. The initial steep incline, known as Long Hill, that parallels the Great River valley affords occasional glimpses of the lush palms and ferns of the chasm below. Most visitors venture here to raft the river and hike at **Lethe**, although there are more worthy attractions further on, including the superlative **Rocklands Bird Sanctuary**, the interesting **Belvedere Estate** plantation and the unique German settlement of **Seaford Town**. The B8 is the quickest route to Savanna-la-Mar and the south coast (see p.274), so traffic is pretty heavy. Striking west out of downtown Montego Bay, Fairfield Road takes you into a strikingly beautiful landscape. Country roads overhung with dripping foliage pass over swift streams and hug the edges of the Cockpit foothills, and the tarmac barely grips the edges of steep valleys lined by tiny hamlets such as **Kensington**, the key flashpoint of the Christmas Rebellion.

If you don't have a car, you'll often find **transport** a problem in the interior. Buses are practically non-existent towards Kensington, so your best bet, if you're heading somewhere fairly near the B8, is to hop on a Savanna-la-Mar bus, get off as near as possible and complete the journey on foot. It's usually much easier to join an organized tour or hire a private driver (see p.203).

## Lethe and around

The rafting and plantation tour that **LETHE** is locally famous for encourages plenty of tourists and a money-grabbing streak in some of its locals, though it's otherwise a very friendly community. Less than ten miles from MoBay and well signposted from the B8, it's a pretty village set amid cool and vividly green hills, with a graceful stone bridge, built by slaves in 1820, straddling the gushing Great River.

On your left as you enter, the village's focal point is **Lethe Estate** (☎952 0527; daily 9am–4pm; ⑦), a banana plantation chock-full of touristic opportunities. Most visitors opt for a jitney tour of the grounds (US$30–45, depending on duration and content), with lunch, fruits, liqueur-tasting and a stop-off at **Rheas World**, a rather contrived set-up of labelled flowers, morose-looking caged coneys and squawking geese. There are plenty of combinations available, but it's all a bit over-packaged, and your best option by far is to ignore the jitneys and naff "village tours" and opt instead for a **horse ride** (1hr 30 min; US$40) or **hike** (guides from the estate cost US$10–20 per hour and expect a tip) from Lethe to the nearby New Milns district, a better way to get a flavour of the countryside. **Rafting** is another huge pleasure – the 45min trip (US$35 for two people) takes you past banks dripping with vines and overhung by trees. It rains a lot up here so the usually clear water often takes on a muddy aspect, but it's still safe for swimming. There are a few rather turbulent spots where the shallows tumble and bubble over rocks; the bamboo rafts scrape the bottom a little, but the punt-handlers are far too experienced to sink.

You can **stay** on the property in expensive rooms with balconies overlooking the river, with a breezy verandah restaurant, a bar, tv lounge and a huge pool. There's a cheaper option a few miles down the main Lethe road at **Copse**, where Francisca and Neville Brown (ask anyone for the white lady and the Rastaman) own a small plot of **camping** land (US$10 a pitch).

On the road up to Lethe you'll notice the signs for **Busha's Countryside Resort** (☎952 0712, daily 9am–5pm; free), 300 acres of usually deserted private land that contain the remains of an old slave village. The Jamaica National Heritage Trust has removed most of the artefacts but a few scant vestiges remain – rusting sugar kettles lie half covered by earth and weather-beaten gravestones struggle to stay upright. You can **hike** (around US$10 per half day for a guide) or **horse ride** (1hr US$30, 2hr US$50) through exposed cattle pastures and into the nearby woods or attend one of the car-racing meets occasionally held at a small track on the property. There are pretty but overpriced **rooms** and **apartments** (④) with fan, kitchenette, balcony and free breakfast; check out the "Divorce Suite", complete with pull-out sofa for those awkward moments.

## Rocklands Bird Sanctuary and Feeding Station

Reached along a terrible road off the B8 just before the right turn for Anchovy, **Rocklands Bird Sanctuary and Feeding Station** (☎952 2009; daily 2.30–5.30pm; US$10) is unique in Jamaica. The flowered home and gardens of celebrated ornithologist Lisa Salmon, it's the only place on the island where hummingbirds are confident enough to drink sugar water while perched on your outstretched finger. Feeding peaks at around 4.30pm when the air thrums with tiny wings; over a hundred varieties of bird have been known to visit, including orange quits, vervain and national bird the streamer-tailed doctor. Ill health and age mean that Ms Salmon is seldom seen, but her assistant Fritz is extremely knowledgeable and can take you on bird-watching trails through the property and beyond (US$8) – a nature walk through the gardens is included in the entry fee; serious ornithologists should call ahead.

*Anchovy itself consists of little other than a school, post office and a couple of snack bars, with not a small, salty fish to be seen.*

## Montpelier and Belvedere Estate

About three miles further along the B8 is **MONTPELIER**, 2000ft above sea level and surrounded by citrus groves, arable land and cattle and ganja fields. The crumbling stone buildings in front the hilltop Anglican **church**, reached along a muddy track off the main road, are all that's left of one of the largest sugar estates in western Jamaica, burned to the ground during the Christmas Rebellion (see box, p.212). A rusting plaque marks the spot of the ensuing skirmish between British forces and the "black regiment".

A further fifteen minutes' drive along the track, the 800-acre **Montpelier Blue Hole Nature Park** (☎0909 9002; daily 9am–4pm; $2) claims to be a botanical garden but is more like a pastoral retreat. The views across the hills are awesome, and there is a huge swimming pool, an aqueduct dating back to 1747 and a series of breathtaking swimmable and climbable waterfalls along the Blue Hole river, a tributary of the Great River. You can **camp** in the park for a nominal fee; simple **food** is available from the thatched bar if you call ahead, or you can bring your own picnic. Guide Clifton Allen will hike around the property with you.

Just beyond Montpelier, the B8 forks; right takes you over the interior mountains to Shettlewood and on to Savanna-la-Mar in Jamaica's far west. The communities along the road are diminutive; only **Ramble** boasts a petrol station and a police station. A nice stop along the way is the *Capital* bar at **Haddo**, marked by a distinctive curved facade adorned with an unusually accurate painting of Bob Marley. The left fork takes you to the most attractive open plantation in the area, **Belvedere Estate** (☎952 6001 or 957 4170; daily 9am–4pm; US$10), a well-organized fruit and cattle farm that does good business with tour operators. More enjoyably explored independently, the coconut, citrus and banana fields are impressive, the waterfall and pool (managed by a 300-year-old dam) provide excellent swimming, and the many ruined buildings – most of the plantation was burned during the Christmas Rebellion – have been lovingly restored.

*Christmas Rebellion leader Sam Sharpe was once a slave at Belvedere.*

## Seaford Town

From Belvedere it's an hour's drive along an inconsistently tarmacked road to **SEAFORD TOWN**. At first glance, this is just another rural community, but a you'll soon notice that a lot of the older residents are white. In 1834, the British administration, fearing that forthcoming emancipation would result in widespread chaos and a mass exodus from the sugar plantations, began a pre-emptive programme of European settlement throughout the island's interior. To establish a "civilizing" white presence throughout Jamaica, and, more importantly, snap up the best land and labour before the slaves could, it drafted in over a thousand Germans over the next two years, promising them land and prosperity after a set period of indentured toil. Between 1834 and 1836, 251 Germans settled in Seaford Town, a 500-acre plot of land donated by Lord Seaford of nearby Montpelier. The rest of the immigrants scattered throughout Jamaica's interior and blended into existing communities; Seaford Town remains the only Jamaican town to be deliberately established by the government.

The new arrivals, many unused to farm labour, found life in rural Jamaica difficult, and when the rations they'd been allocated for the first year ran out, became as impoverished as their black neighbours. Intense hardship and tropical diseases depleted their numbers, and within just a couple of years many of the survivors emigrated to the US. Enough remained, however, for their legacy to be obvious today. Despite some racial intermixing over the years, a tradition of inbreeding has ensured that quite a few of the town's residents still have blonde hair, blue eyes and (almost) white skin.

*For an easier
route to
Seaford Town,
turn left at the
Montpelier
fork of the B8,
then head
right at
Marchmont.*

However, beyond the proudly displayed artefacts in the museum, little German culture has been retained around town. Traces are seen in the pointy roofs and gingerbread fretwork of some of the older houses, but German speakers are restricted to the very old, and people are more likely to have rice and peas than sauerkraut for their dinner. The diminutive **Seaford Town Historical Museum** (daily 9am–5pm; US$2), on a grassy knoll below the Catholic Church of the Sacred Heart, tells the story of Seaford's German heritage, with photographs of the original settlers and a plaque listing their names and occupations (one man was a comedian). As the museum is usually locked you'll need to ask at the church to enter.

## The Cockpit fringes and Kensington

From Seaford Town, you can drive east through the pretty hilltop village of **St Leonards**, site of the *Hilton High* tour (see p.201). Just north of here, the ragged road takes you through tiny **MARCHMONT** – look out for the red-gold-and-green-painted board home of the local bush doctor just off the road. A couple of miles further on is **CATADUPA**, once the main tourist stop of the now-derelict train line that ran from Montego Bay to Kingston. Today, cows and goats pick at the grassed-over sleepers, though the gingerbread-style station house, with its peeling paint and panelled walls, exudes a faded romance. Just before Catadupa, you pass signs for **Croydon Estate**, 132 acres of pineapple plantation occupying the last stretches of accessible land before the Cockpit hillocks make large-scale farming a commercial impossibility.

From Catadupa, the road lurches crazily along the western fringes of Cockpit Country, passing lazy-looking communities like **MOCHO** where untethered goats stare wild-eyed at the sun and housewives hang their washing out to dry on hedges. City folk disparage the residents of this backwoods village as unsophisticated country bumpkins. There are several villages called Mocho in Jamaica, all located in remote rural areas – a common colloquial insult is to tell someone they're from "up a Mocho sides", and the *Dictionary of Jamaican English* interprets the name as "a place of symbolic remoteness – a rough, uncivilized place".

Three miles on at diminutive **Flamstead**, the road splits; right heads for **Maroon Town**, which despite its name has no contemporary Maroon connections, while left takes you the four miles to **KENSINGTON**. Despite huge historical significance as the place where the first fires of the Christmas Rebellion were lit (see p.212), the only hint of the past is a roadside plaque. Past Kensington, the views over gaping valleys are marvellous; John Crow vultures whirl high on the thermals and you get the occasional glimpse of the sea behind the trees. You're only thirteen-odd miles from Montego Bay, but the contrast couldn't be more striking. If you want to **stay**, head for *Orange River Ranch* (☎979 3294, fax 953 9619; ④), set in 1000 acres of land complete with a swimmable river, hiking trails, a 110-year-old great house and countless groves of raggedy banana trees. Rooms are simple and functional with a balcony, and there's a restaurant, bar and pool as well as some of the nicest hotel staff you'll encounter.

# Cockpit Country

The most bizarre landscape in Jamaica, **COCKPIT COUNTRY** is an uncanny series of improbable lumps and bumps covering roughly 500 square miles of Trelawny Parish, just south of Montego Bay. Thousands of years' worth of rain and river water flowing over the porous limestone surface has created a rugged karst topography of impenetrable conical hillocks dissolved on each side by a drainage system of sinkholes and caves. The region is one of the most intriguing parts of the island, not least because of the place names peppered throughout it: Me No Sen You No Come, Wait-a-Bit, Quick Step and Rest and Be Thankful District, though the last appears on aged maps only. Cockpit Country is also known as The District of Look Behind in reference to the justifiable paranoia of English soldiers who made hot, comfortless and usually ill-fated missions through the area tracking Maroons, whose superior local knowledge and guerrilla strategies brought most of the sorties to a bloody end.

*The Cockpits are believed to be the stamping ground for all manner of spirits and duppies and are avoided by more superstitious Jamaicans.*

Save for a few pockets on the outskirts and along the central ten-mile trail from Windsor to Troy, Cockpit Country is uninhabited. Hunters make regular forays into the interior in search of feral pigs, but otherwise the few locals congregate at **Windsor**, **Albert Town** and **Accompong**, their economy based on small-scale farming, coffee-production and – cloaked by the region's thick foliage – ganja-growing.

Only a fraction of this land is accessible, and you can't get far independently, so what follows is not a geographical tour but a few of the highlights. Wherever you go, the scarcity of tourists and the lack of environmental damage make Cockpit Country unmissable: a sanctuary of incredible untouched beauty, particularly in the early mornings when low-lying mists and a silence broken only by bird calls give it an almost primeval feel.

### Hiking and caving in the Cockpits

Despite popular disbelief, **hiking trails** do exist in Cockpit Country, usually maintained by local residents, though the further you get into the interior the rougher they become. Windsor and Albert Town are the most accessible starting points for hiking, where you should pick up a local guide, essential not only to stop you getting lost but in case of any accident – if you fall down a hole here, there will be nobody around to get you out. The main ten-mile trail through Cockpit Country starts at Windsor and runs straight through the middle to Troy on the southern outskirts, though it gets very overgrown towards the middle. The first few miles are relatively easy and foliage-free, but in the heat of the day it's an arduous eight-to-ten hour trek that few would want to undertake; you're in the midst of foliage most of the time so there are few open vistas and little to interest you after the first couple of hours, but you'll certainly feel a sense of achievement if you complete it. Of course, you don't have to go the whole way; the first couple of hours from Windsor give you a pretty good idea of what's to come. If you set out from Troy, the trail is mostly downhill and a lot easier-going – the best plan is to base yourself at Windsor, hire a guide there and drive to Troy early enough to make the hike back to Windsor before nightfall.

*Never hike alone or unguided in Cockpit Country; maps are useless, sinkholes extremely dangerous and there's no-one to help if you run into problems.*

Informed and well-organized **guided tours** pointing out rare plants and birds seen along the pig-hunting trails that network the Cockpit interior are available from *Sun Venture* in Kingston (☎960 6685). For basic hikes around the more open land near Albert Town, try local community group *Trelawny Adventure Guides* (☎0919 6992). As the going is rugged, and accommodation usually primitive, you'll need a stout pair of shoes or boots with good grip, something waterproof, something warm (winter evenings are pretty cold), a torch, water bottle, and heavy-duty mosquito repellent to deter the mosquitoes: Cockpit Country's limestone pools are an ideal breeding ground. Allow double your usual walking time, as an ostensibly simple trek can take hours longer if you have to chop at foliage to clear your path.

**Cavers** would find Cockpit Country irresistible were it not for the lack of infrastructure. Though 250-odd caves network the area, only Windsor is easily accessible; the rest are little explored and there is no specialized group to guide you. If you have caving experience, contact the Jamaica Caving Club via the geology department at the University of the West Indies in Kingston (☎927 6661 or 927 2728); it runs occasional spelunking expeditions in the area. Another possibility is US Peace Corps volunteer Brian Zane (via ☎0990 6034) in Albert Town, who guides visitors into the caves around the village, and has plenty of caving and abseiling equipment. Alan Fincham's essential *Jamaica Underground* lists and measures all the island's caves, but is difficult to get hold of – the Caving Club might be able to help.

*Non-
ornithologists
can join the
Cockpit field
trips made by
the Gosse Bird
Club (☎ 927
8444).*

### Flora and fauna

Though soil forms only a thin cover over the Cockpit limestone, underground rivers ensure enough irrigation for flourishing **plant life**, in some cases so thick that a chainsaw would be more appropriate for chopping your way through than the conventional machete. Close inspection of tree trunks often reveals miniature orchids, and giant bromeliads hang from the boughs overhead. The Cockpits are also great for **ornithologists**; this is one of the few places where you'll see – and hear – profusions of shrieking green parakeets. The rare Jamaican blackbird is also seen here – and the forests support all 27 endemic Jamaican species of bird. The feral **pigs** that root through the undergrowth are descended from those reared by the Maroons, and with hundreds of caves, **bats** are common – all 22 Jamaican varieties are found in the region. The limestone also provides a perfect cover for the **Jamaican boa** or **yellow snake** as well as the **black racer**, a venomous variety that was thought extinct until pig hunters began to report bites on their hunting dogs.

### Getting there and around

If you're **driving** in from Montego Bay, you can take either of the roads that lead off the A1 near Westgate Plaza, though as these are narrow, potholed country lanes, a quicker route is to drive along the coast to Falmouth (see p.187) and head inland at Rock along the B11. As with most of the Jamaican interior, Cockpit Country is poorly served by **buses**. For Windsor, a limited daily service runs from Falmouth to Clarks Town and Sherwood Content, the best places from which to catch a lift to Windsor itself; buses for Albert Town also depart from here. If all that sounds like hassle, you might want to consider joining an **organized tour** from MoBay (see p.201); *Maroon Attraction Tours* are the only carriers authorized to visit Accompong, but big companies like *Caribic* offer trips to Windsor on demand. Alternatively, you could approach the Maroon owners of *Linkage Guest House* at 39 Church St (☎ 952 8753) who run more informal excursions – prices start at about US$50 a day per person.

Once you're there, by far the best mode of transport is a **car**. Most makes of regular car will suffice, but a four-wheel-drive is preferable. Otherwise local people are extremely amenable with **lifts**, usually for free but sometimes for a small charge; just flag down anything that passes.

## Windsor

Smack in the middle of Cockpit Country's accessible northern edge and reached via a dirt track from the tiny village of Sherwood Content, **WINDSOR** is the most heavily visited settlement in the region, as tour buses pull in to its star attraction, **Windsor Cave**. Documented to stretch as far as three miles underground, the cave itself is an eerie maze of dripping water and huge twisting columns of fused stalagmites and stalactites. Its innocuously small mouth exhales a constant, clammy wind, except at dusk, when hundreds of bats – the cave is home to seven species – sweep majestically out on feeding forays. Experienced cavers or the foolhardy can follow the slippery path for about two and a half hours, emerging deep into the mountains and walking back to Windsor overground. As it's completely undeveloped and pitch black inside, the best way to see it is with a guide; Franklyn Taylor, owner of the village's convivial red-gold-and-green painted bar, and his brother lead tours for US$5–10 dependent upon group size.

Franklyn's also your man for **hiking**, a big activity here as Windsor is the starting point for the only trail that crosses Cockpit Country. There's not much else to Windsor save for a couple of nice swimming spots along the Martha Brae River which rises by the cave, a few fields of coffee and the stately **Windsor Great House** (☎0997 3832; ①), recently renovated and privately owned, with a huge open verandah and a couple of facility-free **rooms** for budget travellers – meals are available at extra cost.

# Albert Town

The best way to see the southern Cockpits is from **ALBERT TOWN**, an isolated but friendly hillside community at the southeastern edge of the area. It's fairly small, with thirty-odd buildings dotted around a central square and residential areas extending down into the valley below. It's also the only place other than Windsor to offer any kind of organized **hiking tours** – and as you're not quite into deep forest the going is a lot easier. Though they're so new they haven't yet got a proper office, *Trelawny Adventure Guides* (☎919 6992 or 0990 6034) are surprisingly efficient. Lawrence is by far their most experienced guide, and can take you along trails known only to locals, and to **Quashie River Sink**, a 120ft sinkhole complete with swimmable river and waterfall and a 2.5-mile-long cave; prices start at US$15 per day.

The easiest route into Albert Town is via the B11 from the north coast at Rock. At Clarks Town, you join the B10, a poor excuse for a road that offers fantastic views and some of the best white-knuckle driving in Jamaica. The road takes you past the **Barbecue Bottom** district, notable for the scarily steep cliffs that sheer off from the roadside and provide superlative views of the Cockpits and cane fields below. Off the road just south of Barbecue Bottom is **Ramgoat Cave**, another pitch-black abyss that you'll need a knowledgeable guide to find, let alone enter.

There's no formal **accommodation** in Albert Town, but a number of local families offer bed-and-breakfast, most with private bathrooms and meals at extra cost (details on ☎0919 6992; ②–③). Basic but tasty Jamaican **food** is available from the three-storey *Ataurus Restaurant and Bar*, the best place in town to sink a few beers and admire the stunning views from the back verandah. There's a fried chicken vendor, small mini-mart and a petrol station in the town square. Weekend **jams** take place at the *Upstairs Club* in the centre of town.

## Accompong

Sitting on one of the precipitous hillocks that make up outer Cockpit Country, **ACCOMPONG** boasts breathtaking views and is the last remaining Maroon settlement in western Jamaica.

Named after the brother of Maroon hero Cudjoe, Accompong came into being in 1739, when as part of the peace treaty that ended the first Maroon War, the British granted the Maroon people 15,000 acres of land (see p.314) upon which to create a semi-sovereign community (however a missing zero meant that only 1,500 acres were made available, a matter of continuing contention). Several such communities, including Trelawny Town in St James, were also given land and the Maroons set about a peaceful life in the hills, raising animals and farming. In 1795, however, a Trelawny Town Maroon caught stealing a pig in downtown Montego Bay was publicly flogged, ironically by one of the runaway slaves the Maroons had captured and returned to the plantations in accordance with the peace treaty. His kinsmen rebelled once again and the second Maroon War flared up. Though the Trelawny Town Maroons could muster only 300 fighters, the British took no risks and sent in 1,500 soldiers and hunting dogs to track them down and wreck their villages. Accompong, the only Maroon village in western Jamaica that chose to remain neutral, was allowed to stand.

*Herbal medicine is still the tonic of choice in Accompong; a booklet,* Welcome to the World of Maroon Traditional Medicine *is locally available (US$3). Ask to see Carlton Smith if you want a consultation.*

Still ruled by a Colonel, the citizens of Accompong are beginning to doubt the benefits of their semi-autonomous status; though the Colonel still makes judgements and the residents pay no taxes or rates, this independence has meant years of state neglect; roads are fixed only when the Maroons can raise the money and the whole town is served by one public phone box. Modern Accompong clings to its heritage, but it's fighting a losing battle. A one-street village with a church, school and a bar, only the palm-thatched roof and woven bamboo walls of the local community centre belie an alternative history. Though older residents claim direct descendancy from fearsome Maroon leaders Nanny and Cudjoe, there are relatively few "real" Maroons left in the town – in the last thirty years over two thirds of the population have left to pursue jobs in urban areas or abroad and even current Colonel Meredie Rowe has a day job as a MoBay policeman. The secret "Coromantee" language has vanished from daily use, resurfacing only in traditional songs and ceremonies and the survival of Maroon culture has become less important to a younger generation more interested in dancehall than Goombay drums or Akan chants.

Today, Accompong feels more or less like any other rural Jamaican village, though a rush of would-be guides craftily try to impose an entrance fee (there isn't one, though a donation to the school is always appreciated). Its sights consist of a musty **church** on a hillock overlooking the main town, a **memorial to Cudjoe**, co-signatory of the 1739 treaty, set on a small concreted podium that serves as the town square, and a tiny **craft centre** opposite that's usually locked – vendors will open it up and show you the goods but other than the odd goatskin drum they differ little from what's on offer in resort markets. In a valley below the town is the **Peace Cave** where the treaty was signed. You should be able to arrange for somebody local to take you there, but it's so small and insignificant-looking that it's hard to imagine that history was made here; it's a couple of miles' walk through pretty, undulating hinterland that's more of an attraction than the destination. The best and most interesting time to visit is for the annual **Accompong Maroon Festival**, held on January 6 to celebrate the signing of the peace treaty (see box).

### Practicalities

There are several ways to get to Accompong, the easiest by heading north from Maggoty in St Elizabeth (see p.296) to Vauxhall, and asking from there. You can also drive up from Albert Town, skirting the southern edge of Cockpit Country along the B10/B6. Other than arranging to **stay** in a private home, you can rent one of the three basic rooms at *Peyton Place Pub* (①) just up from the town square; it also serves **food**.

---

**Accompong Maroon Festival**

Every **January 6**, Accompong Maroons from all over the island come home to celebrate the most important day in their calendar – the anniversary of the 1739 peace treaty. Like everything else in Jamaica, the Accompong festivities start late. Under a towering mango tree on the outskirts of the town, a suckling pig (always male according to Maroon tradition) is roasted on a spit, to be communally eaten just before the real highlight of the day, when Maroon leaders adorned by the vines used as camouflage by their ancestors make their way up from the Peace Cave, where they have drummed, danced and chanted since dawn. Goombay drums beat complicated rhythms in anticipation and the town's aged hornblower sends the haunting tones of an abeng horn (a cow horn once used as a musical instrument and means of communication) echoing across the hills, signalling the approach of the elders. The drumming reaches a climax as the parade arrives and the assembled mass joins in with call-and-response Akan war songs. The procession moves through the village, paying respects at the homes of former Colonels and those too old to participate, finishing at the town square for speeches and performances from traditional Maroon dance groups who whirl around and are sprinkled with a traditional dash of white rum. Eventually, the drums make way for towers of speaker boxes, and the party continues in an all-night sound-system jam.

---

# Travel details

### Buses

Buses from the main bus station in Montego Bay can take you throughout the island, but you'll have to change midway for longer journeys. The terminal is pretty well organized by Jamaican standards and even has signs directing you to each route, but as there are no timetables your best bet is to turn up the day before and ask, particularly if your destination is off the beaten track. Below are the main routes covering places listed in this chapter. Services run from around 6am until 6pm. There is a reduced service on Sundays, with little or nothing after 5pm.

**Montego Bay** to: Anchovy (daily; 40min); Catadupa (daily, 1.5hrs); Falmouth (every 20min, 30min); Reading (every 30min; 10min); Rose Hall (every 30min; 15min); Savanna-la-Mar (every 40min, 40min).

### Flights

**Montego Bay** to: Tinson Pen, Kingston (Mon–Fri 8 daily, Sat–Sun 5 daily; 35 min); Negril (1 daily; 10 min); Port Antonio (1 daily; 40 min).

# Chapter 5

# Negril and the west

T hough Jamaica's **western tip** is often associated only with the seven miles of sand at **Negril**, there's a lot more than beach life to the parishes of Hanover and Westmoreland. At only 174

square miles, **Hanover** is the island's smallest parish, and despite the deceptively steep-looking coastal rise to the 1789ft peak of the central Dolphin Head range, it's also the flattest, ensuring the **lowest rainfall** in Jamaica and invariably sultry weather in the extreme west. Sleepy capital **Lucea**, with its Georgian buildings and decaying grandeur, is slated for heritage development, but for now remains a languid and charming shrine to the past. Other than the ever-hopeful roadside refreshment stops and craft shacks, there's little tourism development long its stretch of coast. The smooth cattle pastures and deserted white-sand coves beg for exploration, while the odd abandoned windmill and crumbling walls of long-deserted estates remain untouched. Split in two by Hanover and Westmoreland, sybaritic **Negril** has a front-row sunset seat, the longest continuous stretch of white sand in Jamaica and a geographical remoteness that provides this ultimate chill-out town with a uniquely insouciant ambience. "Discovered" by wealthy hippies in the 1970s, Negril is still immensely popular with those who favour fast living and corporeal indulgence, and is easily the best place outside Kingston for **live reggae** and **nightclubs**, though its reputation as "sin city" means an over-quota of ganja and cocaine hustlers and an inevitable edginess. However, even though the main menu is sun, sea, smoke and sex, there are plenty of natural attractions around Negril, including the **Great Morass**, the **Royal Palm Preserve** and some marvellous **reefs**. Beyond Negril, the landscape stretches out into the flat south-coast plains and tourism gives way to agriculture. Irrigated by the meandering Cabarita River, **Westmoreland** was once Jamaica's foremost **sugar-growing** parish and though rice is now an equally popular crop, cane plantations still surround the main commercial town and parish capital **Savanna-la-Mar**. Exports have significantly declined in recent years, leaving districts without tourism receipts struggling to find new industries and lending an air of pastoral neglect to the

---

**Accommodation price codes**

All the hotels detailed in this guide have been graded according to the following price categories. Note that the prices have been calculated as those for the cheapest **double** or **twin room** during low season, normally mid-April to mid-December. During high season, rates are liable to rise by up to 25 percent (though this is rare at the cheap hotels), and proprietors may be less amenable to bargaining. Many of the all-inclusives have a minimum stay requirement; where this is the case it is mentioned in the text. Although the law requires prices to be quoted in Jamaican dollars, most hotels give rates in US dollars; payment can be made in either currency. For more details see p.22.

| | |
|---|---|
| ① under US$20 | ⑤ US$70–100 |
| ② US$20–35 | ⑥ US$100–150 |
| ③ US$35–50 | ⑦ US$150–200 |
| ④ US$50–70 | ⑧ US$200 and above |

quiescent coastal villages. Until long-standing plans for a huge all-inclusive near Whitehouse are realized, the **southwesterly point** remains deliciously quiet, with beaches dedicated to fishing rather than aloe massages and sun loungers. **Bluefields** and neighbouring **Belmont**, birthplace of the late **Peter Tosh**, are small but lively once you scratch beneath the surface, and have the best undeveloped beaches in Westmoreland. Fishing also dominates **Whitehouse**, a main port of call for north-coast hotel food buyers; both towns are ideal if you want peace, quiet and few other foreign faces.

# West towards Negril

The west tip begins where Montego Bay ends. Past the bridge over the mouth of Great River, the A1 coast road twists and turns past **Hopewell**, home of the finest hotel on the island, and villages that decrease in prosperity the further they are from the tourist towns. Though the haunting coastal scenery is a constant enticement into the interior, there's little to occupy you other than the swimming at **Mayfield Falls** or the mini-museum at Alexander Bustamante's **Blenheim** birthplace, and as most people choose to remain within sight of the Caribbean Sea much of the land remains uncompromisingly indifferent to tourism; even the many hiking possibilities of the central **Dolphin Head** range are unexploited. Market town **Lucea** breathes a little life into the area, and further west the build-up to Negril begins, with a closer concentration of roadside bars and rest-stops around **Green Island** and **Orange Bay**. Riding and diving at bounteously situated **Rhodes Hall Plantation** and swimming at the marvellously secluded **Half Moon Bay** beach are the last vestiges of calm before the onslaught of Negril.

## Hopewell

The first sizeable town west of Montego Bay, dormitory town **HOPEWELL** is quite content to let MoBay deal with the tourists, to the extent that some residents seem positively to resent a foreign face. Other than browsing through the general stores that surround the bedraggled and unjustifiably pricey **vegetable market** (main day Sat), there's little in this one-street town to keep you busy. The hills around are scattered with multiple zinc and plaster fundamentalist churches – *The Watchtower* is the unofficial village newspaper – and an evangelical mood dominates, broken only on Friday evenings, when a local sound system strings up on the main road and blocks traffic way into the night. The **coastline** around town is not ideal for swimming, but there are occasional sandy spots; most popular is **Steamer Beach** just past the murky fishermen's beach, marked by the rusting iron shell of a wrecked boat. The slim white stretch gets packed in the early evening and on weekends when kids descend for an after-school bathe and dominoes slap down on the verandah tables of the *Old Steamer Tavern*.

There is just one **hotel** in Hopewell – *Round Hill*, PO Box 64 (☎952 5150, fax 952 2505; in US ☎1-800/237-3237; in UK ☎0171/602-7181; ⑦–⑧) draped across an entire hillside just east of town – but it is indisputably the classiest in Jamaica. From the swimming pool that starts inside a villa and drips over a cliff into the sea to the Ralph Lauren-designed bar and the eclectically furnished villas, the 98-acre property exudes taste and opulence. JFK and Jackie O, Audrey Hepburn, Clarke Gable and Queen Elizabeth II gave the hotel a reputation for glamour which today attracts an autograph book of famous names. Ordinary Joes may use its facilities – the main pool, tennis courts, gym, art gallery, restaurant and all watersports – for a US$20 daily fee. Otherwise, there are plenty of possibilities for **private rentals** if you ask around, and as Hopewell is nicely detached from MoBay but close enough to to enjoy its benefits, it's worth having a go.

*Shared taxis
run between
Hopewell and
MoBay; fares
are around
J$20, cars
leave every
10min from
the main street
and terminate
in St James
Street.*

You won't go hungry in Hopewell. There's an excellent bakery renowned for its hardough bread, and a great **restaurant**, *Love Bird* on Bamboo Hill, which churns out ackee and saltfish, chicken and curry goat to its local regulars. Just west of town, seafood dominates at three restaurants directly in front of the fishing beach, all serving comforting conch and fish soup as well as steamed or fried fish: *Jamaika MiKrazy* is the most upmarket.

## Tryall and Mayfield Falls

Three miles west of Hopewell, a towering **water wheel** at the roadside marks the old **Tryall Estate**, a once huge sugar plantation detroyed in the Christmas Rebellion (see p.212) that's now Jamaica's most prestigious **golfing hotel**. Until 1996, the *Tryall Golf Tennis and Beach Resort* (PO Box 1206, Montego Bay, ☎956 5660, fax 956 5673; in US ☎305/670-4911, fax 670-4948; in UK ☎01753/684810, fax 681871; ⑦–⑧) hosted the annual Johnny Walker World Championship tournament; the smoothly undulating eighteen-hole green is the best-kept, and reputedly most challenging, on the island, though you'll need deep pockets to examine it; low-season fees start at US$75 plus mandatory caddie service. The hotel, in the plantation's refurbished great house, is unstintingly luxurious; rooms come with every conceivable trapping and most of the self-contained villas have private pools. The 800yd beach is fully equipped for watersports and there are tennis courts and a waterfall pool on site.

The road that turns inland here overlooks the foothills of the **Dolphin Head Mountains**, a languid series of low-lying hills said to resemble a dolphin (though no-one seems to know *where* you get this perspective). Most of the hillocks are partially cultivated by small-scale farmers, and there's none of the cool air or remoteness of full-scale ranges like the Blue Mountains (see Chapter Two). A right fork right at **Cold Spring** leads to the appealing surrounds of **Cascade** and **Pondside**, where there are plenty of undeveloped waterfalls – you'll need local help to find them, and to do any walking in the area, as this is prime ganja-growing territory. However, the best way to get a flavour of the Dolphin Head surrounds is to visit the 22 mini-cascades and numerous swimming spots at the private **Mayfield Falls** in the eastern reaches (daylight hours; US$12, US$20 inc lunch). The steep entrance fee shouldn't put you off – the tranquil walk through bamboo-shaded cool water with swimming holes every twenty yards is a fabulous, sensuous treat compared to the contrivances of the more famous Dunn's River Falls (see p.158) – but the difficulty of finding it might: signs dot the route from Tryall via Pondside, but you'll probably have to ask about a dozen times. A thatched restaurant, bar, restrooms and precarious bamboo and log bridge mark the start of a clamber along the greenery-laden river bed. A guide (leave a tip) helps to carry belongings, points out the easiest route and the best naturally formed swimming pools, and will tell you the local names of the trees, flowers and vines along the banks; wear a swimming costume and bring flip-flops as the stones are tough on bare, wet feet – mosquitoes can also be a problem. Once at the end, you walk back through richly fruited, hilly pastures dotted with yam banks and fluffy clusters of bamboo. Hiking guides are available for walks in the surrounding mountains.

*West*
*towards*
*Negril*

*From Cascade you can drive south straight to Savanna-la-Mar (see p.274), though the road is abominable in places.*

*Caribic Vacations (☎957 3309) offers full-day tours to Mayfield Falls from Negril; US$47 covers transport, snacks, lunch and entrance fee.*

## Sandy Bay and Mosquito Cove

Three miles west of Tryall, sleepy, suburban **SANDY BAY** was founded by Baptist missionaries as a free village for newly liberated slaves. Today it's just a strip of shops, cafés, bakeries and bars, with great views back along the coast to distant Montego Bay, and the incongruous *Lollypop on the Beach* (☎953 5314), a seaside entertainment venue packed to the rafters on Wednesday and Friday nights for its cheesy tourist-oriented reggae shows; it also hosts occasional sound-system nights and stageshows.

*See p.319 of Contexts for more on the free villages.*

Just west of town, pretty **Mosquito Cove** is named for the perfect breeding ground of the Maggoty River shallows; several tributaries meet here, spanned by a tiny stone bridge. The pesky mites didn't deter the Amerinidians – remains of **Taino settlements** have been found around here, though there's not a hint of them today. Instead there's a small **beach** of pebble-strewn yellow sand lined by wind-bent palms – assorted flotsam and jetsam hint at the strong undertow that makes swimming risky, so stick to paddling. There are a couple of bar-cum-jerk spots and craft stalls at the edges of the bay.

Inland of Mosquito Cove, horses graze in clipped pastures dotted with the odd run-down windmill, relics of the plantation days when the land was part of the Kenilworth estate. A superb example of old industrial architecture, Kenilworth's **great house** now serves as the

HEART Hotel Training School (daily 9am–5pm; free), signposted off an inland track just past the cove. There are no guided tours, but you can go in and have a look around the surrounding mills, boiling houses and distillery, all now listed buildings under the protection of the Jamaica National Heritage Trust.

## Lucea

Built around a crescent-shaped natural harbour where Henry Morgan (see p.316) moored ships during his respectable period as lieutenant-governor of Jamaica, **LUCEA** (pronounced Lucy) was a flourishing port town during the plantation era, its wharves thronged with ships exporting locally produced sugar. These days, only the occasional shipment of molasses leaves the docks, but the town has another card up its sleeve: the exceptionally tasty **Lucea yam**. A floury-textured tuber with excellent storing properties, it was exported in vast quantities to the thousands of Jamaicans who migrated in the late-nineteenth century to work on sugar plantations or as labourers on the Panama canal, and is still crucial to Lucea's economy.

Despite being the capital of Hanover, Lucea is no showpiece; peeling paint pervades, and even the best buildings display the odd broken window or sagging wall. The faded allure of the town's Georgian town hall and gingerbread fretwork of the older houses have long prompted calls for Lucea's development as a heritage resort, though in true "soon come" style, nothing's yet happened, and Lucea remains a sleepy sort of place. It's a beguiling town, a perversely aesthetic jumble of austere stone architecture and salt-and-sun-bleached clapboard houses, gaudy storefronts, and snack and rum bars, all clustered around a seething central bus park that hums with the raucous shouts of minibus touts and peanut vendors and the tinny strains of reggae tape stalls. The A1 twists straight through the centre of Lucea, past the bus park and the covered entrance of **Cleveland Stanhope Market**, which spills out onto the streets on Saturdays and draws villagers from miles around.

Just beyond the bus park is the imposing exterior of the once-majestic **town hall** and old **courthouse**, but inside the Georgian grandeur concedes to broken furniture, well-worn floor tiles and cluttered neglect. The roof of the courthouse is topped by an incongruously large **clocktower**. Still keeping perfect time after 170 years, the size of the clock betrays its misplacement – it was originally destined for St Lucia (Lucea's Spanish name was Santa Lucea) but was mistakenly sent to Lucea. Locals became so attached to it that they refused to exchange it for the more modest timepiece originally ordered, raising the difference through public collections. The tower was built with funds donated by a local planter of German origin on the condition that he had a hand in its design, hence the distinctive nippled dome of a German army helmet that forms its roof. The town hall overlooks the official town square, which serves as a traffic roundabout. Formally dedicated as **Alexander Bustamante Square** by England's Queen Elizabeth in 1966, the square was used as a period set for parts of the movie *Cool Runnings*.

West towards Negril

Lucea's western portion contains most of the older buildings; particularly noticeable from the road is the towering cut-stone steeple of **Hanover Parish Church**, which dates back to 1725. The church boasts some fine moments, one by the British sculptor John Flaxman. The cemetery's walled area is a **Jewish burial ground**, presented in 1833 to the large Jewish community who settled here during Lucea's commercial heyday. Toward the sea behind the church, **Rusea's School** (Mon–Sat 8am–4pm; free) was established in 1777 by a benefaction from French religious refugee Martin Rusea, who was so grateful for the help he received when washed ashore at Lucea that he bequeathed his accumulated estates to the parish upon his death in 1764; his disgruntled relatives were not quite so benevolent and contested the will for ten years. Originally located at the current Wesleyan mission house, the school was moved to the present site, an old army barracks, in 1900. Just past the school, through a small truck repair yard, is near-derelict **Fort Charlotte**, restored in 1761, though no one is sure when the foundations were first laid. Three of the original cannons remain, and the fort gives a fabulous sweeping view across the harbour.

*See p.335 of Contexts for more on Jews in Jamaica.*

As you leave town towards Negril, scrubby playing fields mark the way to Lucea's main bathing spot, windblown **Watson Taylor public beach**. This is not one of Jamaica's best and it's generally the preserve of locals who pick up the rubbish and maintain the rudimentary facilities. The miniature cove is sheltered by rocks, and there's a little sea grass, but the swimming is good and the water clean. Overlooking the beach is the excellent **Hanover Museum** (Mon–Sat 10am–4.30pm; J$50). A former British barracks, the red-brick building has also seen service as a prison, police station and firing range – you can see the original stocks and lock-up rooms complete with newly concreted stone "beds". Blackened timbers purport to the fire that almost destroyed the structure in 1985; it suffered a further battering from Hurricane Gilbert in 1988, the year it was awarded the prestigious Heritage Architecture Award. In honour of the settlements discovered at nearby Mosquito Cove (see p.243), recreations of Taino dwellings and canoes stand in the backyard, flanked by a traditional canoe hollowed from a silk cotton tree. Other artefacts have been donated by the still-flourishing Matapi Tainos in Guyana. The main museum offers a surprisingly comprehensive glimpse into local history, with old English weights and measures displayed alongside records of the west African ancestors of various Lucea citizens, maps, "jackass rope tobacco" (a long coil of dried tobacco leaves, resembling the rope used to tether a donkey and smoked by poor Jamaicans in the nineteenth century), a chunk of Lucea yam, and a copy of a harbour map hand-drawn by Captain Bligh. There's a good gift shop selling locally made crafts and a no-frills café on site.

*Lucea-based Hanover Historical Society (PO Box 35; ☎956 2584) is the best source of in-depth local information.*

## Around Lucea

From the town centre, a twenty-minute drive inland along the B9 will take you to **BLENHEIM**, birthplace of National Hero Alexander Bustamante. The shack in which Jamaica's first prime minister grew up has been converted into a tiny and frankly inadequate **museum** (daily 9am–5pm; free) displaying a scant pictorial life-story – future improvements are promised. Other than this, there is nothing to see in this tiny hamlet.

---

### Chief Busta

Wild-haired and brutishly handsome, **Sir William Alexander Bustamante**'s physical stature, charismatic appeal and legendary appetite for women earned him a fond notoriety in the ribald world of Jamaican politics. Born Alexander Clarke on February 24, 1884 into an impoverished family working on the Blenheim estate, Bustamante was architect of his own destiny, rising to political prominence through a mixture of insight, cunning and cynical manipulation of the illiterate populace who came to worship him as "Busta" or simply "Chief". He left Jamaica at nineteen in search of better prospects, and his years away are veiled in mystery. Though he's said to have begun cutting cane and labouring alongside other migrants, he returned nearly thirty years later with an assumed surname and enough wealth to become a small-time money-lender, a shrewd move that gave him clandestine influence before he entered the political arena.

Settling in Kingston, the Jamaica he returned to was still firmly under Britain's imperial grip and languishing with it; pay and working conditions for those lucky enough to have a job were abysmal, and the polarities between the ruling brown-and-whites and the black majority were as sharp as ever. Bustamante allied himself with the workers and became their unofficial spokesman, and his outspoken condemnation of these inequalities began to win support. By 1938 his "fire and brimstone" warnings of racial violence and black revolution (designed to scare the colonial authorities into action) were almost realized; fanned by Bustamante's inflammatory rhetoric, a violent confrontation between police and workers broke out at the West Indies Sugar Company in Frome, in Westmoreland, sparking a wave of rebellions and strikes that brought the whole island to a near-standstill for months. Eclipsing the tentative support for black nationalist labour leader William Grant, Bustamante formed the **Bustamante Industrial Trade Union** – still the island's main union – and became the leader of the labour movement among the rank and file.

See p.273 for
more on
Frome.

In 1940, distressed at the volatility of his speeches, the government seized on Bustamante's union involvement and imprisoned him as the ringleader of the 1938 unrest – he spent seventeen months in jail plotting his future. On his release in 1942 he formed the **Jamaica Labour Party** and swept to victory at the island's first election in 1944, trouncing his first cousin Norman Manley's People's National Party so decisively that Manley lost even in his own constituency. Though the PNP enjoyed a few years of power between 1955 and 1961, it was the JLP who ruled when Jamaica was granted independence in 1962, and Sir Bustamante – he had been knighted by Queen Elizabeth II in 1954 – who danced with Princess Margaret during the ensuing celebrations. He remained active in politics until 1967 and died a National Hero on August 6, 1977, aged 93.

---

The other inland road parallels the Lucea East River and circumvents the Dolphin Head Mountains, an undeveloped wilderness area known for its abundant bird life. At present there are no **organized tours** into the area; you may be able to arrange an ad-hoc guide at the tiny village of **Askenish**, the nearest settlement to the highest peak, or at Mayfield Falls (see p.242).

West of Lucea, the coastal scenery is immensely attractive; foliage drips down over the road from the inland side and deserted coves swing temptingly into sight around each precarious corner. **Gull Bay beach** (usually known as Bull Bay), five minutes west of Lucea, is a nice spot for a swim; the two pristine white-sand coves are usually deserted and *Sally Faithful's* across the road provides refreshments. At **Lance's Bay**, three miles west of Lucea, **Ron's Rat Bat Cave** (daily 8am–6pm; 2hr tour US$10) is signposted from the road. The bats provide a good harvest of guano, there's plenty of intricate stalactites and stalagmite formations, a swimmable mineral pool and faint wall murals said to be of Taino origin.

## Practicalities

You can see Lucea's sights on foot in a day, and as the only place to **stay** is the overpriced, anonymous *West Palm Hotel* (☎956 2321; ②), you'll probably leave town before dark. For **eating**, there's simple and delicious chicken or fish in a box with proper rice and peas at *Sam Wailers Café* behind the parade of shops opposite the bus park. Taking an ironic slant on the well-known chain of the same name, the *Hard Rock Café* by the town hall is another worthy Jamaican eatery. Practically all of the **buses** and **minibuses** that connect MoBay and Negril terminate at Lucea's central bus park; you simply change services to complete the journey. To avoid long waits, ignore the touts and choose a bus that's almost full. The fare from Lucea to Negril is around J$40.

# Green Island, Orange Bay and Rhodes Hall

A harbour town with a few shops and a post office, **GREEN ISLAND**, about six miles west of Lucea, attempts to attract tourists with its bars, jerk stops, occasional "authentic" sound-system dances and cut-price canoe trips (around US$20). The town houses the only secondary school for miles around and most of Negril's burgeoning youth population commutes to it daily. Just out of town, the *Crystal Bar* is a spanking new rest-stop facility for drinks or basic Jamaican meals, and small, clean, fan-cooled **rooms** are available at *JJ's Guesthouse* (☎956 9159; ②), on a breezy hill off the main road.

A mile down the coast, **ORANGE BAY** boasts the unspoilt **Half Moon Bay Beach** (daily 7am till late; free), full of the paradisical charm that originally brought tourists to Negril. The wide curve of white sand has no braiding booths, jet-skis or hassle, just a little sea grass and some small islets; nude bathing is perfectly acceptable and snorkel equipment cheap, and the **restaurant** (daily 7am–9pm) serves excellent chicken, fish and sandwiches. The overgrown flat track behind the restaurant was once an illegal airstrip used for ganja smuggling; today it hosts occasional dirt-bike races. Set back from the sand, the two extremely rudimentary wood cabins (③) contain only a bed (with linen) and a table; **camping** is also possible and security provided. The *Hurricane Bar*, in the small strip of bars past the beach, is the perfect place for a seafront beer.

Just past Orange Bay, **Rhodes Hall Plantation** (daily 7am–5pm; US$2) is a 550-acre coconut, banana, plantain, pear and coconut farm with two private **beaches** – one a shallow sea-grassy reef beach with a freshwater mineral spring bubbling under the brine, the other a more conventional sugar-sanded curve with watersports equipment and scuba via the reputable *Scuba World* (☎957 6290). Volleyball and football pitches and a restaurant/bar back onto the beaches, as do two luxurious two-bedroom **cottages** (⑤). **Horse-riding** is also an option; the well-kept mounts trot into the hills and along the beach (daily except Sat 7am, 10am, 1pm & 3pm; 2hr US$40). The property also covers an area of pristine **mangrove swamp**, home to a few wild Jamaican **crocodiles** – if you can't see any in the open section, you'll usually find some sunning themselves in a fenced-off enclosure.

# Negril

Jamaica's shrine to permissive indulgence, **NEGRIL** has metamorphosed from deserted fishing beach to full-blown resort town in less than two decades. Though it's hard to imagine once you've seen today's overdeveloped strip, in the late 1960s the population was well under a hundred and the only visitors were day-tripping Jamaicans. By the 1970s, hippies had discovered a virgin paradise of palms and pristine sand, and the picture of beach camping, ganja smoking and chemically enhanced sunsets set the tone for today's free-spirited attitude. Thanks to deliberately risqué resorts like the infamous **Hedonism II**, Negril is widely perceived as a place where inhibitions are lost and pleasures of the flesh rule. The traditional menu of ganja and reggae – Negril has a deserved reputation for its **live music** – draws a young crowd, but the north-coast resort ethic has muscled in too – all-inclusives pepper the coast and hustling has increased to an irritating degree. And though it guarantees the best sunsets in Jamaica, Negril's remoteness on the island's far western edge can be infuriating, with constant power failures, water lock-offs, telephone breakdowns and high prices.

Nonetheless, Negril shrugs off its minor irritations and remains supremely chilled-out – every conversation starts and ends with

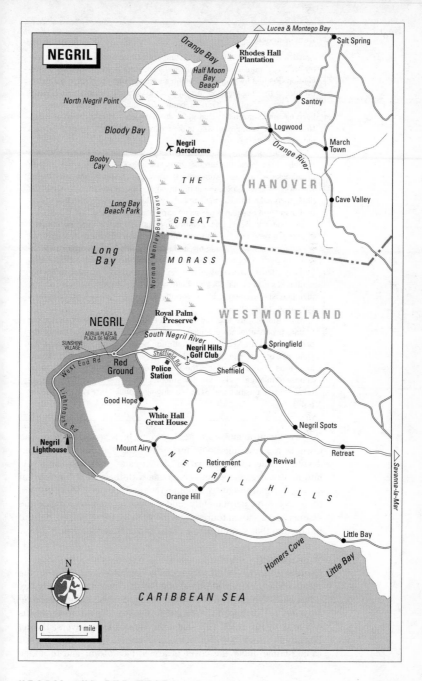

## Rent-a-dread

Jamaica is a carnal kind of country, and while there's no sex tourism industry as such, monetary-based holiday liaisons are a well-established convention. Fuelled by tropical abandon and the island's pervasive sexuality, the lure of the "big bamboo" prompts some unusual partnerships. Middle-aged women strolling hand in hand with handsome young studs has become such a normality that pejorative epithets – **rent-a-dread** or **rastitute** – for the young men who make a career out of these cynical liaisons have entered the lexicon.

The butt of many jokes, conventional specimens are muscle-bound models of the latest mini-trunks and expensive sneakers topped off with dreadlocks – or hair extensions if they can't manage the real thing. However, not all gigolos come in the same package; a rastitute is equally likely to appear in the form of an Ital-style Rasta who woos with talk of natural living and postulates sex as an expression of racial unity.

In a country of scant possibilities and high unemployment, becoming a gigolo is a practical career move for many young Jamaicans. Negril is a centre for this kind of trade-off, and many women regularly return specifically to partake of an injection of "Jamaican steel", some forming relationships that span several years of holiday time. This makes life rather difficult if sex is not a part of your holiday vision as single women are almost unanimously assumed to be out for one thing only – prepare yourself for a barrage of propositions.

Male tourists are less involved in the holiday romance scenario, but **female prostitutes** are common and men should expect to be frequently propositioned. In Negril, the prostitution scene is firmly ingrained – the main players are notorious, with the queen of the pack affectionately known as "Scotch Bonnet" (the fiery Jamaican hot pepper). If you do choose to indulge, make sure that you practise safe sex; one in five prostitutes are HIV-positive and STDs – including syphilis – are rife (see Basics, p.25).

---

"irie" or "no problem" – and addicts come back year after year. The town is a gathering point for string-vest-clad North American devotees collectively known as "Jamericans" who wax their hair into matted dreadlocks and commune with their local "bredrin" in a compound jargon of "yeh mon, iyree" and "respec". Many visitors have stayed on permanently, and the consequent blurring of the distinctions between tourists and locals make for a relaxed, natural interaction that's a refreshing change from other resorts.

### SOME HISTORY

Negril's isolation – until very recently completely cut off from the mainland by the Great Morass, Long Bay and the smaller Bloody Bay – has been central to its history; even its Spanish name *Punto de Negrilla* or "dark point" referred to the west tip's remoteness as much as to the black eels that once thrived in its rivers. During British rule, Negril's seclusion was used both to protect British ships sailing home under the cover of armed men-of-war and to attack

Spanish vessels straying off course to Cuba. It also provided an ideal hideout for **pirates** in the eighteenth century (see box below), and for the export of **ganja** in more recent years; in 1996, over-zealous coast guards opened fire on a seaplane owned by Island Outpost boss Chris Blackwell, assuming that the cargo was drugs rather than, as was the case, various members of the band U2 and country and western singer Jimmy Buffet; fortuitously the volleys missed and pop fans were spared a tragedy, though the shame-faced coast guards were cornered into a public apology. The town has also played a part in war: in 1814, fifty English warships and some 6000 men, including 1000 Jamaicans from the West Indian Regiment, sailed from Negril to Louisiana to fight the Battle of New Orleans.

In 1959, a coast road was laid from Green Island, and Negril was for the first time connected to the rest of Jamaica. Its beauty was soon discovered by foreign hippy travellers, who brought Negril's charms to wider attention and spawned a **tourist industry**. Developers were quick to step in, and by the early 1980s the once-empty curve of beach was smothered with all the trappings of a full-blown resort. International attention was captured by tales of debauchery at the notorious *Hedonism II* resort, and Negril's reputation as Jamaica's devil-may-care holiday hotspot was assured.

---

### Negril's women pirates

One of Negril's proudest moments came when the reign of **Calico Jack Rackham**, the most famous and notorious buccaneer to terrorize Jamaican waters, was brought to an end here in November 1720. Rackham – called "Calico" in reference to his preferred underwear – and his crew had moored their captured sloop in Bloody Bay to celebrate recent plunders along the north coast, unaware that their every move was bring shadowed by one Captain Barnet of the British navy. Made inattentive by rum punch, the pirates were quickly overwhelmed. Some surrendered instantly, but two, in particular, put up a mighty struggle – even turning their weapons on their more malleable crew members. Eventually, these last two were subdued – at which point naval officers were atonished to find that they were **women** in disguise. Famously ruthless and bloodthirsty in battle, **Anne Bonney**, Rackham's former mistress, and **Mary Read** formed a courageous double act and were instrumental in earning Rackham his infamy as a freebooter. At their trial, victim Dorothy Thomas noted that "they wore men's jackets and long trousers . . . each of them had a machete and a pistol in their hands, and cursed and swore".

Rackham was executed, his body displayed in an iron frame at the Kingston cay that now bears his name. Bonney and Read were also sentenced to death, but were spared when they declared themselves pregnant and eventually reprieved. Anne Bonney disappeared from recorded history, while Mary Read died of a fever and is buried in St Catherine.

# Negril

## Arrival and information

*Buses to Savanna-la-Mar and Lucea depart every half-hour; the fare is J$30–40.*

*Private taxis charge between US$50 US$150 for the MoBay to Negril trip; US$90 is fair.*

Arriving in Negril is straightforward; **buses** from Lucea drop off on the A1 just before the central roundabout – if you're staying on Norman Manley Boulevard, bus drivers will drop you off outside your hotel. Buses from Savanna-la-Mar terminate at the top end of Sheffield Road, from where you can charter a **taxi** to the West End or beach (see below) for about US$5. Domestic **flights** land at Negril Aerodrome at Bloody Bay; taxis are waiting but fares can be ridiculous – a reasonable price is between US$7 and US$10.

The **Jamaica Tourist Board office** is on the first floor of Adrija Plaza opposite the roundabout (Mon–Fri 9am–5pm, sat 9am–1pm; ☎957 4243); it stocks various local freesheets, all of which carry local maps, listings and news. Pretty-pink JTB **information booths** are located in the grassy park area of Long Bay beach, at the main craft market by the roundabout and on West End Road opposite *Tensing Pen* hotel.

## Orientation and getting around

*For bike and car rental outlets and taxis on the phone see p.271.*

Negril doesn't really have a "town centre", just a roundabout right on the coast that feeds its three streets: **Norman Manley Boulevard**, which runs parallel to the Long Bay and Bloody Bay beaches and the Great Morass wetlands; the quieter **West End/Lighthouse Road** which winds along the cliffs to Jamaica's west tip; and **Sheffield Road**, the route to Savanna-la-Mar.

You don't need a **car** if you're going to stay in town. **Shared taxis** run the length of the beach and West End Road all day every day, and charge between J$20 and J$50 from the roundabout to the lighthouse or Bloody Bay – you can flag them down anywhere en route. **Chartering a taxi** can be expensive, particularly at the far reaches of the cliffs, but competition is high, so you should be able to haggle – US$5 from the roundabout to Bloody Bay is reasonable. There is no local bus service to the roundabout from the beach or cliffs. Other than **walking**, by far the most popular and way of getting around is moped, motorbike or bicycle. **Dirt bikes** rent for around US$40 per day, mopeds from US$25 and bicycles from US$10.

### Organized tours

As Negril tends to attract those who want to stay put and relax, the roster of available **tours** in Negril is pretty paltry in comparison to Ocho Rios or Negril. Large operators (see below) offer the same roster listed in the Montego Bay chapter (p.201) and a few options in southern Jamaica. The smoothest operator is *Caribic Vacations* (☎957 3309), which from its office on Norman Manley Boulevard books a **Royal Palm Preserve tour** (full day; US$80) aboard a jeep, taking in Paradise Park in Westmoreland for lunch and river swimming then returning through the Savanna-la-Mar cane plantations and the West End, a **Black River Safari** (full day; US$68) stopping at the Appleton rum distillery in Siloah, continuing to the beautiful YS waterfall for a swim and lunch and finishing with a crocodile search by boat along the Black River, and a tour to Mayfield Falls (full day; US$47). Alternatively, local operators *Mr Tour Man* (☎0990 9608) and *Tutu Tours* (☎956 9223) offer all the nearby trips and are more amenable to bargaining. All quoted prices are per person.

**Bicycle tours** are an excellent way to explore the countryside; *Super Herb Bicycle Rentals*, opposite *Drumville Cove* on West End Road (☎957 0137), offers off-beat mountain-bike journeys around the surrounding hills and countryside and an insider's guide to Negril society. For the serious cyclist, *Rusty's X-cellent Adventures*, past the lighthouse on West End Road (☎957 0155 or 4944), has developed trails through the ganja landing strips and deserted beaches of greater Negril; the top-of-the-range mountain bikes and the pace demand good riding ability.

Alternatively, hire a **local driver** and set off on your own; Felix Wilmot (☎957 0139) and Romeo McKenzie (☎957 0094) are both recommended.

## Accommodation

Negril has over two thousand **beds**, split between the cliffs and beach. Easily the more popular location, the **beach** reeks of commercial vitality. Most hotels have commandeered semi-private areas of beach with sun loungers and security guards, while smaller hotels and those on the inland side of the road simply use whatever piece of sand is closest. Inland properties are often cheaper, but as they back straight onto the Great Morass, bugs can be a problem. The all-inclusives congregate towards **Bloody Bay**, well away from the polluted South Negril River. The quieter **West End** has a degree of privacy lacking at the beach, though steep open-access cliffs make it a bad choice if travelling with children. There are more budget options here and rates are often open to negotiation, especially if you're planning a long stay; *Dreamscape Villas* (☎957 4495) has serviceable, well-equipped "efficiency apartments" on the cliffs for extended rental.

As Negril's planning regulations prevent building anything higher than a palm tree, a lot of accommodation is in traditional circular palm-thatched **cottages**. Though much cooler than concrete, many of these are ludicrously easy to break into. A new innovation is the **pillar cabin**, a round cottage set on top of a stone column, with a shower below and the advantage of catching the best breezes. Locals cite the lonely reaches of West End Road as problematic in terms of **security**; wherever you stay, always make sure that doors and windows are secure and check ID before you let anyone in. Twenty-four-hour security is sensible if you plan to **camp**, though if you're willing to rough it and risk it, there are plenty of cabins and campsites with few facilities and negligible security on the morass side of Norman Manley Boulevard.

## The beach

**Arthur's Golden Sunset**, PO Box 21, Norman Manley Blvd; ☎957 4241, fax 957 4761. Long-established and reliable with inexpensive, plain but clean rooms or cabins with fan, kitchenette and private or shared bath. The restaurant serves tasty and inexpensive Jamaican fare. ②.

**Beachcomber Club**, PO Box 98, Norman Manley Blvd; ☎957 4170, fax 957 4097. Sparsely planted gardens with garishly painted accommodation blocks. Spacious rooms with four-poster beds, plus pool, games room and popular Italian restaurant. Under 12s stay free and baby-sitting is available. ⑤.

**Charela Inn**, PO Box 33, Norman Manley Blvd; ☎957 4277, fax 957 4414. French–Jamaican-owned place with gardens, pool, carpeted rooms with four-poster beds, and an air of cultured elegance. Rates include a cruise, watersports and folklore shows. ⑤.

**Firefly**, PO Box 54, Norman Manley Blvd; ☎957 4358, fax 957 3447. Rooms, studios and cottages, with an outdoor whirlpool, beach bar and free access to the *Swept Away* hotel's sports facilities. ③–④.

**Negril Cabins**, PO Box 118, Norman Manley Blvd; ☎957 4350, fax 957 4381 (in US ☎1-800/382-3444). Well-equipped cabins in a garden backing onto the morass. Excellent food and a full range of facilities, including a "private" section of Bloody Bay. Good for kids; up to three under-16s stay free in each room. ④.

**Negril Tree House**, PO Box 29, Norman Manley Blvd; ☎957 4287, fax 957 4368 (in US ☎412/231-4889, fax 231 5044). A clean, comfortable and appealing complex of rooms and villas. There's not a tree house in sight, but there is a pool, bar, restaurant and watersports. ⑤.

**Negril Yoga Centre**, PO Box 48, Norman Manley Blvd; ☎957 1397 (in US ☎813/ 263-7322). Yoga centre and guesthouse with attractive cottages of varying degrees of comfort surrounded by heaps of greenery. Wholefood cooking available. ③.

**Nirvana on the Beach**, Negril PO, Norman Manley Blvd; ☎957 4314, fax 957 9196 (in US ☎716/789-5955, fax 789-4753). Semi-luxurious wooden cottages in an unusually beautiful sand garden shaded by tall trees and dotted with sculptures and hammocks. Friendly atmosphere, kooky decorative touches and free pass to *Swept Away*'s sports facilities nearby. ⑤.

**Perseverance**, c/o Jules Jackson, Negril PO; ☎957 4333. Budget accommodation across the road from the beach; clean and comfortable with fan and shared or private bath. ②–③.

**Rondel Village**, PO Box 96, Norman Manley Blvd; ☎957 4413, fax 957 4915. Lots of greenery surrounding the fully equipped villas and comfortable rooms with tiny tv and occasional kitchenette. Two pools and a Jacuzzi. ⑤–⑥.

**Roots Bamboo**, Norman Manley Blvd; ☎957 4479. Friendly, efficient place that's one of Negril's most popular budget options. Cottages are small but cosy; some have private showers or there's a communal row. Cheap Jamaican restaurant and a campsite with 24hr security and showers. ②.

**Sea Gem**, Norman Manley Blvd; ☎ & fax 957 4318. Imaginative and stylish Mexican tiling, calico fabrics and mahoe four-poster beds in the main block. Alternatively, basic gingerbread cottages have optional kitchenette and a/c. Good restaurant on site. ④.

**Sea Splash**, PO Box 123, Norman Manley Blvd; ☎957 4041, fax 957 4049. Spacious, clean, upscale 1-bed units with screens, lounge and kitchenette. Attractive gardens with a pool, Jacuzzi, mini-gym, beach bar and gourmet restaurant; meal plans available. ⑤.

**T-Water Beach Hotel**, PO Box 11, Norman Manley Blvd; ☎957 4270, fax 957 4334 (in US ☎718/519-0634, fax 718/655-2335). Friendly, popular medium-sized hotel with a relaxed and happy atmosphere. All rooms have patios, some have kitchenette and tv. Pool and rooftop Jacuzzi, watersports, tv lounge and baby-sitting service. Rates include breakfast and lunch. ⑥.

**Westport Cottages**, c/o Joseph Matthews, Negril PO; ☎957 4736. Budget travellers' haven at the roundabout end of the beach. The basic cabins are starkly furnished but comfortable, with fan, mosquito nets, outdoor bathroom and communal cooking area. ①.

## West End

**Addis Kokeb**, PO Box 78, Summerset Rd; ☎ & fax 957 4485. Communal living in the main building or handsome hardwood cabins in fruited and flowered gardens. Cooking facilities are shared, and you can use the pool at *Summerset Village* next door. ③.

**Banana Shout**, PO Box 4, Lighthouse Rd; ☎957 0384. Simple but attractive cottages in lily-ponded gardens or right on the cliffs. Kitchenette, ceiling fan, hammocks on the verandah and Haitian art. The cliff portion has a diving platform, sun deck, its own cave and exceptional sunset views. ③–④.

**Blue Cave Castle**, PO Box 66, West End Rd; ☎957 4845. Pastel-painted castle on the rocks, a curious mix of high kitsch and careful luxury. Individually decorated rooms built over a cave that extends underneath the road (excellent swimming). Restaurant serves lunch and breakfast. ③.

**Catcha Falling Star**, PO Box 22, Lighthouse Rd; ☎957 0390, fax 957 0522. Attractive gardens criss-crossed by pathways, lots of grassy sunbathing spots and excellent sea access. Most of the split-level cottages have verandahs with hammocks, a few have waterbeds, and all have fridge and access to the communal kitchen. Rates include full breakfast. ⑤.

**Devine Destiny**, PO Box 117, Summerset Rd; ☎ & fax 957 9184. Fairly new resort set back from the main road, popular with tour groups and yet to develop an atmosphere but friendly. Centred around a large free-form pool and there's a daily beach shuttle. ④.

**Drumville Cove**, PO Box 72, West End Rd; ☎957 4369, fax 957 4971. Imaginative cliffside setting with a quiet serenity and eclectic accommodations. There's a bar, diving platforms, sun deck and restaurant. ③.

**Heart Beat**, PO Box 95, West End Rd; ☎957 4329, fax 957 0069. Family-run collection of cabins, cottages and rooms, all featuring lots of wood and Balinese fabrics. Two swimming/sunbathing decks and a cliffside gazebo. ③.

**Hog Heaven**, Negril PO, Lighthouse Rd; ☎957 4991. The secluded, peaceful rooms have kitchenette and patio with hammocks. There's a large freshwater pool and two saltwater whirlpools, plus a bar and restaurant. ④–⑤.

**Jackie's on the Reef**, Negril PO, Lighthouse Rd; ☎957 4997. Breezy alternative-style place with all sorts of holistic therapies on offer – massage, yoga, t'ai chi, you name it. Private cottages or expansive units in the main house, all simply but carefully decorated – there's a saltwater pool if the sea gets too rough. ⑤.

**Negril**

**Lighthouse Park**, PO Box 3, Lighthouse Rd; ☎957 4490. Sprawling, densely vegetated section of clifftop with basic but serviceable A-frame cabanas, villas and camping. There's a communal kitchen and a gazebo with hammocks. ②–③.

**Mariners Inn**, PO Box 16, West End Rd; ☎957 4348 or 4474, fax 957 4472. Medium-sized retreat with clean if unimaginative rooms, and facilities including a dive and kayak site, volleyball court and a games room patronized by local pool wizards. Great sea swimming and a boat-shaped bar. ④.

**Mirage**, PO Box 33, West End Rd; ☎957 4471, fax 957 4414. The round cottages (often privately rented) or tile-floored oceanfront rooms are much nicer than the hotel rooms, but all enjoy a large gazebo, sun deck, cliff access with diving board, and an excellent restaurant. ④.

**Native Shelter**, Negril PO, West End Rd; ☎957 0159. Self-contained apartments above and around a private home, with good security and a tranquil family atmosphere. ②–③.

**Ocean Edge**, PO Box 71, West End Rd; ☎957 4362, fax 957 4849. Atmospheric, budget-friendly property straddling the road. Accommodation is split between rooms, some with kitchenette, and two private cottages, and there's a cliff diving board, pool, Jacuzzi, restaurant and bar. ②–④.

**Primrose Inn**, c/o Gus/Martin Hylton, Negril PO; ☎957 4399. Basic "home from home" set back from the road in a yard dominated by a large ackee tree. Rooms are off an open corridor laced with hammocks; all have fan and double bed and most have a cold-water bathroom. Bad dogs take care of security. ②.

**Rising Sun**, c/o Kenneth Thorpe, Negril PO, Summerset Rd; ☎957 0260. Little beauty but lots of atmosphere, and popular with Jamaicans during the slow months. Rooms are clean but very basic, with a communal kitchen. ②.

**Rock Cliff**, PO Box 67, West End Rd; ☎957 4331, fax 957 4108. Attractive hotel with a large kidney-shaped pool. The cliffs are well landscaped with a restaurant, bar, PADI dive centre, tennis and volleyball courts. Rooms are adequate, some with kitchenette, and open to bargaining. ③–⑤.

**Rockhouse**, PO Box 24, West End Rd; ☎ & fax 957 4373. Enviable location, Mediterranean styling, magnificent thatched bar/restaurant and saltwater pool on a rock peninsula ensure unique and stylish comfort. Thatched studios or villas with glass-doored patio overlooking the ocean, outdoor shower, fan and bamboo four-poster beds draped with muslin nets. Innovative and deservedly expensive restaurant. Add 10 percent service charge. ⑤.

**Secret Paradise**, PO Box 56, Lighthouse Rd; ☎957 4882. Rambling resort that's quiet to the point of inertia but attractive and very private. Large clover-shaped pool, landscaped cove with nude bathing area, restaurant and bar. Rooms are pretty basic but very clean with fan; some have kitchen. The 5-bed units are good value. ③–④.

**Summerset Village**, PO Box 80, Summerset Rd; ☎957 4409, fax 957 4078. Set in seven fruited acres with a large pool, restaurant, bar and games room, the eclectic accommodation ranges from regular room blocks to a 5-bed wood-panelled thatch house. ③–④.

**Tensing Pen**, PO Box 13, Lighthouse Rd; ☎957 4417, fax 957 0161. Stylish and exclusive retreat in pretty clifftop gardens with imaginatively decorated bamboo and wood cottages graced with individual touches, and a well-equipped communal kitchen/lounge. Some of the cliffs are linked by a tiny suspension bridge. ⑤.

**Villas Sur Mer**, Negril PO, Lighthouse Rd; ☎957 0377, fax 957 0177. Thoughtfully designed and decorated luxury villas right on the cliffs, with marble bathrooms, breezy living rooms, full staff and a wooden boardwalk complete with pool and Jacuzzi. ⑥.

**Xtabi**, PO Box 19, West End Rd; ☎957 4336, fax 957 0121. Well-organized West End veteran with flowering gardens and a network of caves. Oceanside rooms are wooden cabins with private sun deck and sea access or two-storey concrete cottages with kitchen. Pool, open-air restaurant and bar and countless swimming platforms. ②–④.

## All-inclusives

**Beaches**, Negril PO, Norman Manley Blvd; ☎957 9270, fax 957 9269 (in US ☎305/ 284-1300, fax 667-8996; in UK ☎0171/581 9895, fax 823 8758). Spanking new and the only *Sandals* family-oriented resort in Jamaica, but as children over two can only stay in one of the more luxurious rooms (there are nine categories) and singles pay a US$100 surcharge, the excellent facilities don't come cheap. Three restaurants, pasta bar, beach grill, five bars, two pools, all watersports, tennis courts, a fitness centre, disco, nightly entertainment and supervised children's activities. Babies under two stay free, children up to 16 pay US$60 per night. Three night minimum stay. ⑨.

**Grand Lido**, PO Box 88, Norman Manley Blvd; ☎957 4010, fax 957 4317. One of the island's swankiest all-inclusives in a dream location on Bloody Bay, and altogether mellower than its nearby cousin *Hedonism II*. All watersports are included, as is a nightly cruise on the luxury *M/Y Zein*, former yacht of Aristotle Onassis, and there are four top-quality places to eat – book early for the fantastic *Piacere* restaurant. ⑨.

**Hedonism II**, PO Box 25, Norman Manley Blvd; ☎957 4200, fax 957 4289. Anything goes at *Hedonism II*, a fast-paced, singles-bar-on-sea, complete with nudist beach and popular late-night Jacuzzis. Though there are plenty of couples, the raunchy reputation attracts far more men (mostly North Americans) than women, and it can feel like one long stag night, but it's great fun if you're in the mood. ⑦–⑧.

**Negril Inn**, PO Box 59, Norman Manley Blvd; ☎957 4370, fax 957 4365 (in US fax 516/247 2839). Small-scale and relatively inexpensive. Rooms in B block are slightly larger than those in A; all have private balconies. Large outdoor restaurant, disco, games room, Jacuzzi, pool, watersports, tennis, basketball and badminton courts. No children under 12. ⑥.

**Poinciana Beach Resort**, PO Box 44, Norman Manley Blvd; ☎957 4100, fax 957 4229 (in US ☎305/749-3032, fax 749-6794). Middle-of-the-road luxury but friendly and good for children. Rooms are clean but bland, while facilities include sports bar, disco, two pools, Jacuzzi, watersports, tennis courts, gym, and a family fun park across the road. One child under 12 pays US$47 daily supplement, second child free. Three night minimum stay. ⑦.

**Swept Away**, PO Box 77, Norman Manley Blvd; ☎957 4061–6, fax 957 4040 (US ☎1-800/545-7937 or 305/666-2021, fax 666-8250; in UK ☎0181/367 5175, fax 367 9949). Extensive landscaped gardens and copious sports facilities make this one of Negril's finest; there's tennis, squash, basketball and racquetball courts, gym, regular and Olympic-sized pool with lap lanes, Jacuzzis, saunas, steam rooms, aerobics room, fitness circuit, spa facilities and watersports. Rooms are elegantly furnished, the beach grill and veggie bar serve up healthy snacks, and the main restaurant is award-winning. Three night minimum stay. ⑧.

# The Town

Negril doesn't really have a centre – just a roundabout feeding its three main roads – and most people leave the beach or cliffs only to change money, buy petrol or find a ride out of the area. However, **Sheffield Road** is the least tourist-oriented part of town and the closest approximation of a real heart. The police station, market stalls, petrol station, restaurants and constant crowds dodging beeping mopeds create an animation that's absent in the boulevard's beach-life or the West End's studied tranquillity. To the right of the roundabout are two **shopping plazas** – Adrija Plaza and Plaza de Negril; the parking lot in front is known as **Negril Square**, a base for taxi drivers, black-market currency touts and would-be guides. Nestled behind is **Red Ground**, a seldom-visited residential area that houses most of Negril's permanent population.

---

### Negril's drug culture

As any aficionado can tell you, Jamaica's best **ganja** (marijuana) grows in the fertile Westmoreland earth – well-flavoured and incredibly potent – and the trade to eager tourists plays a significant if covert part in the local economy. Many devotees make annual pilgrimages to find a place to chill out and partake of the local weed – international seed-swapping has produced interesting "name-brand" crossbreeds; alaska and skunk are only found locally. Herb is a part of daily life in Negril, so don't be surprised if your first potential supplier is your hotel porter and you lose count of the men who hiss "sensi" as you pass them in the street. Don't feel that you can light up wherever you choose, though – marijuana is as illegal here as it is anywhere else on the island, and there are plenty of undercover police around town who can and do arrest tourists and locals alike for possession.

Though Negril has been an unofficial ganja centre since its hippy heyday, there's also a great deal of **cocaine** and **crack** use around town. It's not especially noticeable and junkies won't accost you on the street, but a certain furtiveness around the late-night beach bars lets you know that it's there for the taking. Negril is also one of the few places on the island where you're likely to be offered locally abundant **magic mushrooms**, considerably larger and stronger than those in cooler countries. Some restaurants include them in cakes, omelettes or pizzas, and *Miss Browns* on Sheffield Road is the traditional spot for foul-tasting mushroom tea, though the proprietors report that hardly anyone asks for it these days.

---

# The beach

**Negril beach** is a near-perfect Caribbean seashore. The whiter-than-white sand is lined by palms and sea-grapes, the water is translucent and still, and the busy reefs ornately encrusted. It's also packed with tourists, locals and holidaying Kingstonians, and while it's great for lively socializing – the banter runs as freely as the rum cocktails, and everyone and everything is on show – the high concentration of human traffic inevitably draws a hard core of vendors and hustlers.

The hassle is constant and high-octane, and as well as the usual crafts, hair braiding and aloe massage – the last must have been invented in Negril – you'll be offered sex and drugs with alarming frequency.

Though hotels guard "their" portion of beach with security men and strings of floating buoys, the law keeps beaches public up to the shoreline and you can walk the entire seven miles in an hour or so, though it's a hot and thirsty business in the sun. The beach is roughly divided by the bank of all-inclusives at the outcrop splitting Long Bay and Bloody Bay. Beginning at the roundabout, **Long Bay** is the

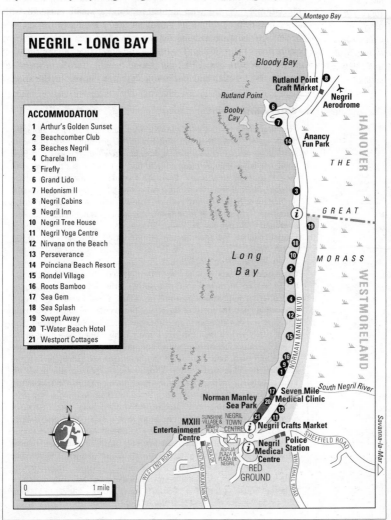

**NEGRIL - LONG BAY**

**ACCOMMODATION**

1 Arthur's Golden Sunset
2 Beachcomber Club
3 Beaches Negril
4 Charela Inn
5 Firefly
6 Grand Lido
7 Hedonism II
8 Negril Cabins
9 Negril Inn
10 Negril Tree House
11 Negril Yoga Centre
12 Nirvana on the Beach
13 Perseverance
14 Poinciana Beach Resort
15 Rondel Village
16 Roots Bamboo
17 Sea Gem
18 Sea Splash
19 Swept Away
20 T-Water Beach Hotel
21 Westport Cottages

*Cosmo's, towards Bloody Bay, is one of the best places to hang out if not staying at a beach hotel, with its own football field and plenty of action.*

most heavily developed, by day a rash of bronzing bodies and flashing jet skis; by night a chain of disco-bars dedicated to reggae, rum punch and skinny dipping. At the far end, the hotels give way to the grassy stretch of **Long Bay Beach Park**, with picnic tables, changing rooms, a snack bar and considerably fewer people. On Sundays, things liven up with the regular **Oldies Beach Party** (10am till early evening; free) – speaker columns blast and jerk stands sizzle. Towards the northern end of Long Bay on the Morass side of the boulevard is **Anancy Fun Park** (daily 9am–5pm; free), a themed entertainment centre with miniature golf, a small museum with rather humdrum exhibits on Jamaican life, a mini-steam train ride (US$2) and boating and fishing out into the Great Morass aboard paddle boats (1hr; US$8). The tilapia and perch that inhabit the dark and peaty waters cost US$2 per pound caught. Tackle is supplied, you pay US$1 to fish and can have your catch cooked on the spot.

---

**Watersports**

Two large reefs running parallel to the West End cliffs and four along the beach make **snorkelling** and **scuba** major Negril highlights. Reefs are sumptuous despite environmental damage, crowded with soft and hard coral, brilliantly coloured sponges and fish, octopuses, starfish and even the odd turtle or nurse shark. There are several **sunken wrecks** that have become artificial reefs, including a ganja smuggling plane that misjudged its landing at Negril airstrip and one that was sunk deliberately. Snorkel equipment is available at most hotels and from all watersports operators at around US$5 per day. For snorkels, scuba gear, guided dives and certification courses try *Blue Whale* (☎957 4438), *Marine Life* (☎957 4834), *Negril Scuba Centre* (☎957 4425), *Resort Divers* (☎957 4408), *Scuba World* (☎957 6290) and *Sundivers* (☎957 4336 or 4069). **Glass-bottom boats** are well represented along the beach and cost roughly US$16 for a 90min trip; touts also sail along the cliffs, as do **canoe owners**, offering impromptu pleasure or fishing trips. Rates vary greatly depending upon the mood of the owner but average at about US$40 per half day; you can also ask at the fishermen's beach behind the craft market. If really serious, you can hire a **sport fishing boat** from most of the cruise operators listed below and go after deep-water blue marlin, sailfish, wahoo and tuna. Bait, tackle, ice and beverages are usually included in half-day rates of around US$300. **Cruises** are an excellent way to see the local coastline, particularly at sunset; most operators throw in snorkelling and snacks and all have an open bar. Some sail down to Rhodes Hall plantation; try *Wild Thing* on a Tuesday (☎957 3392, 9am–3pm; US$60) or an early-evening champagne cruise to *Rick's Café* (Mon–Sat 4–7pm; US$35). Forty-foot catamaran *Indigo Cat* (☎957 0405; 10am–1.30pm; US$30) cruises along the cliffs with stops for snorkelling and slide rides at the *Pickled Parrot* and has a sunset party cruise (3–6pm; US$30). The *Red Stripe* (☎0990 9318; Tues, Fri & Sun 10.30am–1.30pm; US$35) sails to Booby Cay for a picnic and snorkelling and has daily sunset or morning cruises (3hr; from US$30). *Aqua Nova* (☎957 4323; 6hr; US$45) includes a picnic at Half Moon Bay.

If you prefer a quieter strip of sand, head for crescent-shaped **Bloody Bay** beyond Long Bay Beach Park. Named for the crimson innards of whales once butchered on the beach, this is the "private" domain of the luxury all-inclusives but still the least-developed stretch, much favoured for nude bathing and deserted enough to merit keeping a beady eye on your belongings – the sand backs straight onto scrawny bush, and robberies are not unknown. Stick close to the open-air barbecue towards the centre of the beach and you're sure to be looked after. The small forested islet in the centre of Bloody Bay, **Booby Cay**, appears in Jules Verne's epic movie *20,000 Leagues Under the Sea*. It's named after the **booby bird** or sooty tern, an ocean dweller that takes a brief respite to lay eggs on offshore cays, though centuries of egg collection and hunting mean you're unlikely to clap eyes on one these days. The all-inclusives hold barbecues here, though you can usually get a local fisherman to transport you for around US$10 – ask at the fishermen's beach behind the main craft market. On Bloody Bay's northern side is an attractive rocky inlet with rope swings slung over the trees and an excess of sea grass that negates swimming.

*Tiny Mary Gate of Heaven Catholic Church opposite the Beachcomber Club is worth a visit if only to see the jalousied windows and brightly painted heart-shaped fretwork.*

Beyond Bloody Bay, past the Orange River bridge, there are several deserted white-sand coves fringed by mangroves, creepers and trailing vines, favoured by Jamaicans for weekend beach parties. To get to them, take any of the dirt tracks that lead into the trees. Past reports of robberies and assaults make going in a group sensible.

## The Great Morass and Royal Palm Preserve

Jamaica's second largest **wetland**, the **Great Morass** comprises 6000 acres of rivers, peat bogs and grasses running directly parallel to the beach. Fed by rivers flowing down from the Orange and Fish River hills, the morass lies at the bottom of Negril's watershed recharge area and is crucial to the area's supply of fresh water. Acting as a giant natural filter, the wetlands also protect the reefs from being smothered by silt and earth run-offs and are a sanctuary for insects, shrimp, rare plants and birds – commonly seen species include Jamaican euphonias, parakeets and woodpeckers. Land crabs enjoy one of the few remaining perfect habitats in Jamaica, and are a common sight during the summer breeding months – often, unfortunately, squashed at the roadside.

*The island's largest wetland, also called the Great Morass, is covered on p.286.*

This rare habitat has long been threatened by pesticide and sewage pollution and proposals to remove peat fuel, but public outrage at the obvious destruction put a stop to the cut-and-drain activities of the government-owned Petroleum Company of Jamaica, and the 200-acre **Royal Palm Preserve** was created in the 1980s towards the south side of the morass as a means of protecting this crucial wetland and the plants and animals within. Tall and graceful but devoid of coconuts, the royal palm cluster is one of the largest single collections in the world, and it's magnificent; wreathed in creepers and vines springing up from the nutrient-rich bog below, in places the palms are thick enough to block out the hills behind and their stately presence lends a patently tropical air. Peat channels are now fishponds, there's a rickety bird-watching tower and a system of boardwalks which allows you to go deep into the morass without getting wet.

*Caribic Vacations (☎957 3309; US$80) runs jeep trips to the palm preserve, with a stop for swimming and lunch.*

The land is still owned by the PCJ, but apart from limited maintenance, little has been done to encourage or facilitate visitors, and despite being one of the most attractive sites in the Negril surrounds, the area remains difficult to get to. In 1996, local environmental groups put in a bid for the lease, documenting plans to create a wildlife centre and nature tourism destination, but as yet no one has won the lease and the preserve seems destined for continued stagnation. Although ostensibly private, it's usually possible to go in and have a walk by paying a small fee to the caretakers who inhabit the block of decaying rooms at the gates. Finding it can be tricky, but most locals know the way from the Negril Hills golf club. At present, other than the paddle boats at *Anancy Fun Park*, there are no organized boat trips into the morass, but you may be able to hire one of the fishing boats moored at the mouth of the South Negril River for a glimpse of its perimeter.

---

**Environment matters**

Rapid growth and unplanned development have had a devastating effect upon Negril's delicately balanced eco-systems. Norman Manley Boulevard cuts straight through what was originally swamp land, jet-skis and anchors have played havoc with the reefs, and on a bad day you can smell the sewage in Long Bay. Fed by nutrients from effluent and fertilizer run-off, algae flourish in the place of starfish and sea grass, and mangrove-felling has allowed the sea to slim down the precious beach and smother portions of reef with earth and sand that the trees once filtered. The population explosion means that houses built on captured land lack water supplies, garbage removal services and sanitation facilities. Children become ill from drinking and bathing in river water, rubbish is burnt or simply dumped into limestone sinkholes that provide a vital link in the natural water filtration systems and soak-away pit toilets drain straight into the sea. Though an improved sewage network is under construction, many hotels are not linked up to the system, and it's worth asking before checking in. However, the long-term picture is far from hopeless. With healthy support from Negril citizens, the **Negril Coral Reef Preservation Society** (NCRPS) has placed 35 mooring buoys at key points on the reefs and successfuly lobbied for official marine park status like that afforded the Montego Bay waters (see p.208). The **Negril Environmental Protection Trust** (NEPT) has a wider brief, declaring 80 square miles from Green Island to Salmon Point as the **Negril Watershed Environmental Protection Area**. To find out more about both groups, or to become a member of NCRPS (and receive the excellent monthly publication *Reef Rap*), visit their offices above the community centre in the main craft market (PO Box 27, Negril; ☎ & fax 957 4473).

---

# The West End

Beyond the overpriced cocktails and hallucinogenic sunset-watching at the infamous *Rick's Café*, the West End cliffs are the last vestige of truly laid-back Negril. Traffic is infrequent, as hairpin bends and pot-holed tarmac are traumatic enough for pedestrians, but the ostensible serenity masks the depression of an extended period of decline. Disruptive sewage works between 1995 and 1997, combined with the more obvious appeal of the beach, have almost eclipsed the West End's formerly massive popularity, though the remoteness, immaculate reefs and the thrill of diving from a cliff straight into fifteen feet of the crystal-clear Caribbean remain unbeatable, and the quietude often means that you've got some of the best places entirely to yourself.

The West End begins at the roundabout in the centre of town and meanders along the cliffs for some three miles, becoming Lighthouse Road at Negril lighthouse and winding inland to Orange Hill and ultimately Sheffield Road. The first stretch is the liveliest, with jerk shacks, bars, juice stalls and craft shops – including the official A Fi Wi Plaza **craft market** – lining the inland side and restaurants hanging over the sea's edge; there are a couple of ramshackle **beaches** where fishermen moor their canoes but the murky water makes swimming inadvisable. The road opens up a little once you get to the fancy Kings Plaza and Sunshine Village shopping malls, but the true West End begins over the next blind bend; the road narrows, the water clears and the hotels that carve up the rest of the cliffs begin in earnest.

As this is Jamaica's extreme westerly point, the **sunset view** from the West End is the best you'll see; most evenings the sky blazes with absurdly rich oranges, pinks and blues that intensify as the sun dips behind the horizon, eventually merging into the deepest of blues with a moon reflected way out to sea. Sunset-watching is an institution; most bars and restaurants offer sunset happy hours (see p.268) and the half-hour or so before dusk is the closest the West End gets to hectic. Coach parties descend in droves upon Negril's biggest tired cliché: undeservedly popular **Rick's Café** has the trade sewn up – you pay for your drinks with plastic tokens, cameras click and local lads play the jester by diving off the cliffs for dollars.

*Rick's* marks the last of the major development; from here on the road becomes a country lane and the hotels are interspersed with near-wild coastline. A main point of interest is **Negril Point Lighthouse**, standing 100 feet above sea level at Jamaica's western-most tip. Built in 1894, the 66-foot tower flashes a solar-powered beam ten miles out to sea and still contains the carefully preserved acetylene gas canisters that first provided the power, the original hand-wound pendulum that once regulated the beam and plenty of brass fittings. Port authority workers who live on site are usually willing to take you up all 103 leg-quivering steps to the top. Look out for the quaint crumbling outhouses preserved as listed buildings and the far-reaching roots of a huge silk cotton tree.

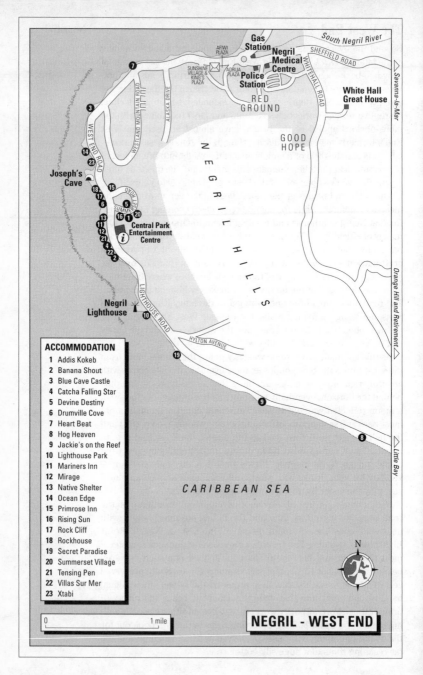

## ACCOMMODATION

1  Addis Kokeb
2  Banana Shout
3  Blue Cave Castle
4  Catcha Falling Star
5  Devine Destiny
6  Drumville Cove
7  Heart Beat
8  Hog Heaven
9  Jackie's on the Reef
10 Lighthouse Park
11 Mariners Inn
12 Mirage
13 Native Shelter
14 Ocean Edge
15 Primrose Inn
16 Rising Sun
17 Rock Cliff
18 Rockhouse
19 Secret Paradise
20 Summerset Village
21 Tensing Pen
22 Villas Sur Mer
23 Xtabi

0 ⸻⸻⸻ 1 mile

## NEGRIL - WEST END

## The West End's top spots

Many **hotels** will let you swim from their piece of cliff for the price of a drink, and though they all look pretty similar, some stand out. *Drumville Cove* has a friendly attitude to non-guests and a spectacular portion of cliff, while *Rockhouse* boasts a stylishly surreal salt-water swimming pool, a bar, excellent sea access and complete seclusion. The limestone cliffs are riddled with **caverns**, with a popular network below *Xtabi* hotel, though the ever-popular *Pickled Parrot* watering hole is in prime position for exploration of **Joseph's Cave**, one of the largest along the West End, made famous in the movies *Dr No, Papillon* and *20,000 Leagues Under the Sea*; the daredevil swings and waterslide above help to draw in the crowds as well. The cliffs are at their highest around *Rick's Café*, the venue of daily **cliff-diving** demonstrations; a less prominent place to have a go yourself is the *LTU Pub* next door. Below the lighthouse is a beautiful **cove** unconnected to any hotel, reached via a precarious wooden ladder, with rocks smooth enough to lie on and a small cave. Past the lighthouse, the cliffs peter out, coastal winds whip the sea into a frenzy and swimming becomes a little risky, but there is a sheltered spot just past the point where Lighthouse Road turns inland – turn straight onto the piece of undeveloped land and climb down the rocks.

## Negril Hills

Beyond the lighthouse the coast swings out of sight, but there's plenty of undeveloped land perfect for exploration by **bicycle** (see p.253 for outlets and cycling guides). As the cliffs and calm water diminish into a windblown ruggedness, there are fewer people, practically no hassle and a markedly rural atmosphere. Inland, the terrain rises into the dry limestone peaks of the **Negril Hills**, habitat of the non-venomous **yellow boa snakes** occasionally seen slithering across the road. The coast road becomes a dirt track here, and the tarmac swings into the interior through quiet **ORANGE HILL**, with flowered duck ponds on its outskirts and a host of quietly convivial **bars** along its single street. Orange Hill merges into residential **RETIREMENT**, home to the innocuous **Co-Metallic Restaurant and Lounge**. Marked by giant cast-iron painted flamingoes at the gates, this is the creative outlet of a local ironworker, whose enormous metal pterodactyls, hibiscus flowers and a five-foot-long centipede overlook the basketball court, bar, restaurant and a shady gazebo set up for domino tournaments.

*Stables offering 2hr trail rides to Whitehall include Country and Western (☎957 3250; US$30) and Mariner's Stables (☎957 0392; US$25).*

Past Retirement, the route loops back to Sheffield Road, giving wonderful views of the cane fields in the basin below and passing **Whitehall Great House**, a crumbling piece of colonial architecture that enjoyed a brief stint as a disco in the early 1980s, but has lain uninhabited since being gutted by fire in 1985. Only the stone shell and black-and-white floor tiles remain, but you can climb the foundations for a magnificent sweep over West End, the beach and the Great Morass. A peaceful spot for **horse rides**, the 187 acres of grounds contain an enormous silk cotton tree with grotesquely twisting limbs and quite possibly the widest girth of any on the island. There's a **bar** adjacent to the house staffed by men who try and charge US$5 for a rather superfluous tour.

### Homer's Cove and Little Bay

Continuing along the coast road around the western tip right until you touch the south side of the island, you reach the pleasant but rather dishevelled inlet of **Homer's Cove**. The once-pristine beach has been mostly eroded by sand-mining, but it's still a nice place for a swim and there are a few vendors selling drinks and snacks. Past Homer's Cove lies **LITTLE BAY**, the last piece of unspoilt coastline in the Negril hinterland, and an extremely attractive, uncommercial area despite the obvious lack of money. Seaside yards around here host one-off **sound-system dances**, where boulevard rent-a-dreads take a night off. The abysmally potted road is lined with ramshackle dwellings and down-at-heel guesthouses; look out for the sign to **Bob Marley's Place**, a spring the singer reputedly bathed in during regular visits in the 1970s. The **accommodation** here is rustic in the extreme and you'll need to have a good look at what's on offer before you decide to stay. Best option is *Tony's Ocean Rest* (☎0909 9976; ①–②), an extremely quiet place, with a bar, at the bay's far reaches.

## Eating

Negril's hippy associations are manifest in the high proportion of **Ital and health-food restaurants** alongside the usual chicken and fish, and you'll also find a lot of **pasta**, as many restaurants attempt to cater for the huge number of young Italians who visit en masse in the early summer. Vendors based at the first stretch of West End Road sell roast or fried fish, jerk chicken and soup; as many of these are no more than a shack, names come and go and phones are infrequent, but generally the less flashy the place, the cheaper the product. Many of the smarter restaurants offer free pick-up; call in advance. **Ganja cakes** turn up on some menus, particularly along

---

**Snacks**

For snacks and patties, try *Hammond's* towards the roundabout on West End Road – its vegetable or ackee and saltfish patties are by far the best in town, and it also sells good bagels, croissants and cakes. Opposite is *3 C's Pastry*, open 24hr for chicken, fish and curry goat alongside the pastries. *Fair Flakes* in the middle of the West End is a garish neon-clad outfit also open 24hr, and selling hot meals as well as pastries. Ice cream and fruit vendors make regular rounds of the beach if you can't be bothered to move; the *Yogurt Hut* at the *Bar-B-Barn* hotel sells frozen yoghurt flavoured with tropical fruits and Devon House "I-Scream" is available at *Cecile's Cafe* on Norman Manley Boulevard.

---

West End Road. For **fast food** try *King Burger* or *Shakey's Pizza* in Sunshine Village, which has a pleasantly breezy upstairs café area.

## Sheffield Road

**Rainbow Ital**, Sheffield Road. Excellent local Ital joint. Breakfast on proper ackee and saltfish with callaloo and cornmeal dumplings or try the beetroot-pink Ital stew with steamed fish. Full range of natural juices and ice cream.

**Sips and Bites,** Sheffield Road and West End. Popular with taxi drivers, the Sheffield Road branch is open 24hr, serving unadulterated Jamaican cuisine. The sister branch offers equally good cooking but closes at around 11pm.

**Sweet Spice**, Sheffield Road. The best place on Sheffield Road for cheap, delicious Jamaican food to take away or eat in.

**Three Sisters Restaurant**, Sheffield Road. Quite a way up, but worth the trip for Jamaican cooking in a friendly atmosphere. Pepper steak and oxtail curry goat as well as the usual chicken and rice. Carrot and beet or okra juice too.

*In restaurant listings, we have given a phone number only for those places where you might need to reserve a table.*

## The beach

**Alfred's Ocean Palace**, Norman Manley Blvd; ☎957 4469. Hearty American-style breakfasts accompanied by an early-morning pianist. Crepes and sandwiches at lunch and seafood, blackened chicken and pasta in the evenings.

**Cosmo's**, Norman Manley Blvd; ☎957 4330. One of the best, busiest spots on the beach, equally popular with Jamaicans and tourists. Excellent seafood – conch soup is a speciality – and the usual selection of chicken variations.

**Gambino's Italian Restaurant**, *Beachcomber Club*; ☎957 4170. Celebrated Italian eatery; dishes include fettucine with lobster, grilled fish, lasagne, carbonara and so on. Usually pretty busy.

**Kuyaba**, *Sea Gem* hotel; ☎957 4318. Thatch-roofed, open-sided restaurant with innovative decor, consistently good food and regular crowds. The frequently changed blackboard menu includes lobster in white wine and garlic, imported Italian pasta, steaks, snapper stuffed with crab in an orange sauce and vegetarian dishes. Puddings are not the best but still gooily satisfying.

**La Vendome**, *Charela Inn*; ☎957 4277. Celebrated, sophisticated French/Jamaican cuisine – duck à l'orange, veal with velouteé sauce, snapper in coconut, home-made ice cream and excellent bread – and a good wine list. Some vegetarian dishes.

**Marguerites** (formerly *Runaways*), Norman Manley Blvd; ☎957 9180. American breakfasts, sandwiches, salads, conch fritters, crab cakes, Oriental vegetable stir-fry, chicken kebab or chicken cordon bleu under a thatched roof.

**Tan-Ya's**, *Sea Splash* hotel; ☎957 4041. Gourmet indoor restaurant, with shrimp, snails, salmon, Cornish Hen (chicken with bammy), chicken with cashew nuts or julienne of chicken breast in a butter, sherry and cream sauce.

*Alfred's Ocean Palace holds a popular January volleyball tournament; teams are open to tourists.*

*There's an express branch of the Pickled Parrot on the beach; see opposite for review.*

## West End

**Archway Pizza**, West End Road; ☎957 4399. Pizza and pasta (including the mushroom variety) in 15min as well as sub sandwiches and fish or chicken with chips; free delivery anywhere in Negril.

**Café Au Lait**, *Mirage Hotel*; ☎957 4471. Fish in rundown sauce, Creole dishes and the deep-crust pizza with lobster, fish or vegetarian toppings.

Extensive wine list includes French imports – classy and highly recommended.

**Chicken Lavish**, West End Road; ☎957 4410. Choice spot for domino players, serving chicken and fish, Jamaican and Chinese style, steaks and pork chops.

**Countryside**, West End Road. Jamaican food with a touch of the Ital. Sweet potato and cornmeal pudding are delicious, as are the natural juices.

**Culture Yard**, Lighthouse Road; ☎957 0195. The menu is a bit limited – the main dish is hemp burger (soy burger with nuts and *real* ganja seeds), but they're delicious, high in fibre and quite unable to inebriate.

**Happy Bananas**, West End Road; ☎957 4071. Relaxed atmosphere, hospitable Dutch/German proprietors, attractive cliffside setting and an inventive menu that changes with the seasons; crepes, octopus salad or meat, fish and chicken in sauces from Red Stripe to satay. Strong vegetarian selection and live music every Saturday.

*There's a branch of Sips and Bites on West End Road; see opposite for review.*

**Hungry Lion**, West End Road; ☎957 4486. The best vegetarian food in town, with seafood as well. A walled courtyard affords privacy, and the food – meatless shepherd's pie with green lentils, lobster in lemon butter, black bean chilli, pasta primavera – is always good. The coconut cream pie is unmissable.

**Jamiana Inn**, West End Road; ☎957 4005. Pizza, pasta, eggplant parmesan, burritos, tofu dishes, veggie-burgers and lots of desserts; all very good and served indoors or in a sheltered courtyard.

**Just Natural**, West End Road. Inexpensive, fresh Jamaican food, callaloo omelettes, pasta, burritos and vegetarian options, in a beautiful shady garden.

**Pickled Parrot**, West End Road (☎957 4864) and the beach. Popular and efficient American-style bar and grill with two locations. The extravagant clifftop original serves large portions of tacos, fajitas and burritos alongside jerk chicken, seafood, formidable burgers and pizza. The beach version has a limited express menu of burgers, jerk and barbecued lobster.

**Planet Jamaica**, West End Road; ☎957 0298. Fashionable decor, upbeat Italian/Jamaican owners, and innovative Italian food. The seafood-based pasta sauces are invariably delicious but vegetarian options are unexciting.

**Rockhouse**, West End Rd; ☎957 4373. Romantically set on a boardwalk right over the sea, with excellent service and a menu that includes vegetable tempura, seafood linguine with garlic and conch fritters.

**Roy and Felix Serious Chicken**, West End Road. The fowl-heavy decor competes for your attention with wonderful chicken, fish and vegetarian options. Unintrusive musical accompaniment from a huge CD selection.

**Shark's Seafood Restaurant**, Summerset Rd. Delicious inexpensive fish and seafood – the tender, well-seasoned kingfish and dolphin steak are standouts.

## Drinking and entertainment

Most **bars** want you to spend the **sunset** with them and provide drinks promotions or happy hours as an incentive. As the cliffs give the best view, bars along the West End tend to be livelier at dusk, with the action moving to the beach after dark. The larger places are distinctly tourist-oriented, with neon, imported drinks, satellite tv and an air of enforced indulgence. If you want some local flavour try the darkened interiors of the **rum bars** and **beer shacks** along Sheffield Road or West End Road near the roundabout; the owner of the tiny nameless bar opposite *Heartbeat* hotel lets his penchant for earth-trembling reggae shatter the peace with a nightly session on the decks.

As there are only two proper **clubs** in town, most of the week-night dancing is offered by **beach bars** using their portion of sand as a dancefloor. These have agreed a nightly rotation system to share the business around a little; DJs play dancehall or Euro-disco and the **live music** usually consists of a no-name reggae band singing Bob Marley covers. Ask around to see which is on each night – Thursdays at *Risky Business* and *Alfred's* and Fridays at *De Buss* or *Alfred's* are particularly lively. Nights vary and new venues pop up with alarming regularity, but most locals keep abreast of the current hot spots, and as the beach venues are free you can walk from one to another in any case.

Large **stageshows** featuring well-known reggae artists are advertised on roadside billboards and through a car-with-megaphone system, and are supposed to start at 9.30pm and finish at 1.30am, but seldom do. Well-known artists and DJs perform regularly during the winter season; if a major artist is scheduled to play, it's always worth checking that they are actually there before you pay your money, as most have a reputation for unreliability (see p.37). Main **venues** for large shows are *Samsara*, *MXIII* and *Central Park* on the West End and *De Buss* on the beach, with occasional nights at *The Swamp* and *Cheap Bite* on Norman Manley Boulevard; cover charge is usually in the region of US$10.

Sound-system jams take place every weekend in Red Ground, Orange Hill and the surrounding communities. There's often a jam at the large lawn in front of the *One Love Rastawant*, off West End Road behind Adrija Plaza. Though the Negril Reggae Festival is a thing of the past, there's usually a huge **reggae extravaganza** around the Spring Break period in March. Two set fixtures in the local calendar are **Negril Carnival**, held annually in late April with costume parades and all-night dancing in the streets – contact the JTB for further information. The other main event is the annual **Bob Marley Birthday Bash** at *MXIII* each February 6, which usually attracts top reggae performers. See p.34 for details of both.

## Bars

**Alfred's Ocean Palace**, Norman Manley Blvd. Pretty busy with lots of table space, occasional live shows and a relative lack of pretension.

**De Buss**, Norman Manley Blvd. The trademark London bus used in *Live and Let Die* stands outside; inside there's piped or live music every night in a covered area and section of the beach. Occasional cabaret shows and drinks specials on Wednesdays.

**Irie Vibes Bar**, *Jamiana Inn*, West End Road. Indoor bar with tv and lots of chat. Two-for-one Red Stripe and rum punch every Thursday 4pm–midnight.

**Jahmerican**, West End Road. Breezy upstairs spot for drinking and dominoes.

**LTU Pub**, West End Road. Vastly superior to next-door *Rick's*; cliffside drinking, diving, snorkelling and food to boot.

**Mi Yard**, West End Road. High-rise bar that's tourist-friendly but positively Jamaican. Open 24hr for music, dominoes, drinking and jerk; always packed once the beach bars slow down after 2am.

**Peachy's**, West End Road. Dark but atmospheric 24hr bar and restaurant popular with hotel workers.

**Pickled Parrot**, West End Road and Norman Manley Blvd. The cliffside branch gets busy during the daily happy hour (3–5pm); beachside has an efficient ambience and good cocktails. Free rum punch at both locations at sunset.

**Planet Jamaica**, West End Road. Pretty cliffside bar area with daily two-for-one special offer between 5–7pm.

**Rick's Café**, West End Road. Overpriced tourist trap with crass limbo dancing and piped soca alongside the traditional spectacle of local boys diving from the high cliffs. The West End's main sunset event.

**Risky Business**, Norman Manley Blvd. One of the most popular beach bars complete with big-screen sports via satellite, nightly two-for-one specials and live reggae every Saturday.

**Yacht Club**, West End Road. Large thatched bar overlooking the sea. Less popular than in recent years but good for a heavy drinking session.

## Clubs

**Close Encounters**, Kings Plaza, West End Road (nightly). Every town has one, and this is Negril's go-go club, where scantily clad women gyrate for the drinkers. Cover US$1.50.

**Compulsion**, Plaza de Negril (nightly). Negril's largest indoor disco and pick-up joint, at its most entertaining and sweaty each Wednesday and Saturday. An experience not to be missed for the dodgy chat-up lines alone. Cover US$4, including a drink.

**Samsara Hotel Disco**, West End Road (Fri & Sat). Right on the cliffs and busy during the high season, with a simple music policy – reggae. Cover US$3–4.

# Shopping

**Crafts** are available practically everywhere you go in Negril. Dedicated craft shops pepper the West End and though the resort police and Chamber of Commerce have cracked down on **mobile vendors** by building dedicated plazas and patrolling the streets, plenty still roam the beach. The best place to buy is the **main craft market** at the roundabout end of Norman Manley Boulevard, with around a hundred stalls and a full spread of merchandise. Also good is A Fi Wi Plaza on West End Road between the roundabout and Sunshine Village. The Rutland Point market opposite Bloody Bay deals mostly with guests of the all-inclusives, so it can be more expensive but it's often quiet enough to make bartering worth the vendors' while.

*Bev's Boutique* at the far end of West End Road is good for African-print clothes and crochetwork. For unusual items try the shop at *Kuyaba* restaurant on the beach, which prides itself on stock that you can't find anywhere else in town, like painted tin "country buses" and primary-coloured enamelled tropical fish. Well-known Negril-based artist Geraldine Robins sells excellent **batik** and hand-painted t-shirts and fabrics from her shop on West End Road, and *Gallery Hoffstead* in Plaza de Negril has prints, originals and sculpture by owner Lloyd Hoffstead. You'll find **in-bond shops** in the plazas and hotels.

Basic **food** needs are met by the well-stocked *Hi-Lo* in Sunshine Village, or the older *Save-A-Dollar* in Plaza de Negril, which needs a good clean and a restock. The stalls at the top end of Sheffield Road have cheaper and fresher fruit and vegetables. If you don't want to stray too far from your hotel, *Deli Express* at the *Negril Beach Club* has a wide selection of cooked and raw meats, cheeses and breads; *Twin Stars*, near *Rick's Café*, is incredibly convenient if you're loathe to leave the West End. *Daley's* liquor store near the post office on West End Road offers discounts on bulk buys of **beer** or **spirits**; a good idea if you have a fridge in your room. Don't be surprised by Negril's high **prices**; the isolation means that all fresh food has to be transported in and you'll often be forced to pay over the odds for simple items.

## Listings

**Airlines** *Air Jamaica* (☎952 4300 or 4100); *Air Jamaica Express* (☎957 4251); *American Airlines* (☎952 5950); *British Airways* (☎952 3771); *Continental* (☎1-800/230-0856 or 952 4495); *Timair* (☎957 3374).

**Airport** The information line for Negril aerodrome is ☎957 3016.

**American Express** *Stuart's Travel*, 10 Adrija Plaza; ☎957 3410.

**Banks and money** The *Bank of Nova Scotia, Mutual Security Bank* and *Workers Bank*, are clustered around Negril Square – the latter opens on Saturdays between 9.30am–1pm. *National Commercial Bank* is in Sunshine Village. *Mutual Security* and *National Commercial* banks have 24hr ATM machines. All banks offer currency exchange and most do cash advances on credit cards; rates are substantially better than in hotels but around the same as the town's best official cambio, *Gold Nugget* at 5 Adrija Plaza (Mon–Sat 9am–5pm). Black market touts hang around Negril Square; if you choose to risk using them, try and get a Jamaican to accompany you. Wire transfers can be collected at *NCB* and *Mutual Security* banks, and at *Stuart's Travel*, 10 Adrija Plaza; *Western Union* has an outlet at *Hi-Lo* supermarket in Sunshine Village.

**Car and bike rental** *Don's*, Negril Aerodrome, Norman Manley Blvd (☎957 4366); *Elite*, Norman Manley Blvd (☎957 4657); *Jus Jeep*, West End Rd (☎957 0094 or 0095); *Prospective*, Norman Manley Blvd (☎957 4711); *Vernon's*, Adrija Plaza and Norman Manley Blvd (☎957 4522 or 957 4354). Bikes can be rented from *Boulevard Bike Rental*, Norman Manley Blvd (☎957 3326); *Dependable*, Norman Manley Blvd (☎957 4236); *Indian*

*Skonk*, West End Rd (☎957 3227); *Super Herb Bike Rentals and Tours*, (☎957 0137); *Negril Auto Sales and Rental*, Norman Manley Blvd (☎957 3198 or 0990 5082).

**Doctors and clinics** There are plenty of doctors and private clinics; try Seven Mile Medical Clinic on Norman Manley Blvd (☎957 4888), Negril Medical Centre on Sheffield Road (☎957 4926) or Dr Michael Clarke (☎957 3047). There is an optician in Kings Plaza, West End Road.

**Golf** *Negril Hills Golf Club* (☎957 4368), an extremely hilly and attractive 18 hole, 6,600 yard, par 72 course in the hills above town. The topography makes for a challenging game and there's a clubhouse and restaurant on site.

**Hospitals** The nearest hospitals are at Savanna-là-Mar (☎955 2533 or 2133) and Lucea (☎956 2233).

**Laundry** Most hotels will wash clothes but it's cheaper to hire a local lady; ask around – a load should cost US$5–7. *West End Cleaners* (☎957 0160) is rather inaccessible off Hylton Ave at the top of Lighthouse Road but will pick up and deliver between 8am–10pm daily. Washing costs J$30 per pound including soap. The *Village Laundry* (☎957 0165) on the back road behind Adrija Plaza is more expensive but convenient.

**Massage** Massage is a Negril institution; try Nadine Loeb at *Catcha Falling Star* hotel (☎957 0237), *Jackie's on the Reef* (☎957 4997), freelance practitioner Gloria (Joan) Spence (☎957 0137) or *Tropical Touch* (☎957 4287).

**Petrol** Negril's only petrol station is on Sheffield Road (daily 6.30am–11pm).

**Pharmacies** *Key West Pharmacy* is at 11 Sunshine Village (Mon-Sat 9.30am–8pm, Sun 10am–6pm); *Negril Pharmacy* is at 14 Adrija Plaza (Mon–Sat 9am–7pm, Sun 10am–2pm).

**Photography** *Colour Negril*, Plaza de Negril, and *Photo Prints*, West End Road; both offer free pick-up and delivery and one-hour processing.

**Post office** Negril post office is on West End Road next to A Fi Wi Plaza; open 9am–5pm Mon–Fri.

**Taxis** *Easy Going Cabs*, West End Road; ☎957 3227.

**Telephones and communications** There is a large bank of phone boxes opposite the main craft market; phone cards are available from pharmacies or the post office. Other than Sunshine Village, the West End is poorly served; there is a booth at *Bev's Boutique* and another towards the lighthouse. *Office Solutions*, Bouganvilla Complex, West End (daily 8am–11pm) offers relatively cheap local and overseas calls and a fax service; you can also send faxes from the Negril Chamber of Commerce office at A Fi Wi Plaza (Mon–Fri 9am–5pm).

# East of Negril

After Negril's glittering hedonism, the rest of the southwest can come as quite a surprise. Restaurants remain wholeheartedly Jamaican with mannish water and eye-rollingly insouciant service replacing waffles and exhortations to "have a nice day". Locals tend to be more genuinely friendly, if a little surprised that you've torn yourself away from a resort, and unfettered by high-rises and serviceable roads, the countryside is magnificent. Westmoreland's longest river, the multi-tributaried **Cabarita**, meanders down central hills through the vast cane fields around **Frome Sugar Factory** and the alluvial plains surrounding the concrete capital of **Savanna-la-Mar**, where brisk trade and honking horns fight against the soupy humidity. A few miles to the east, **Roaring River** marks its entrance above ground with a spectacular blue swimming hole, having carved out an inky cave on its way. Water is central to Westmoreland: irrigating the sugarcane and reducing turf to swamps or noticeable by its absence as you near the parched fields and dry riverbeds towards St Elizabeth. Since Indian workers first entered the scene in the mid-nineteenth century, the region's extensive wetlands have been mostly employed for the cultivation of rice – the potential for bird-watching and boat safaris has not been capitalized as it has further down the south coast, nor have the miles of beach at **Bluefields** or the unhurried charm of fishing village **Whitehouse**; though the peace of the last looks set to be shattered as long-standing plans to open a *Sandals* resort nearby are realized.

*See p.102 for
more on the
Indian
immigration.*

## Little London and Frome

Once out of Negril proper, Sheffield Road opens up into the pock-marked, fast-moving and truck-dominated route to Savanna-la-Mar, sweeping past cane fields neatly bordered by the stunning Fish River hills; stop to enjoy the view at the tiny roadside *Polly's* bar. After about nine miles, a cluster of buildings around a gas station signifies

---

### Sugar wars

The centre of some of Jamaica's most violent labour disputes, **Frome sugar factory** was built in 1938 by British company Tate and Lyle's subsidiary West Indies Sugar Company as the most modern facility in the West Indies, and is now government-run under the Sugar Company of Jamaica. The factory has long been beset by industrial disputes; constructed during a period of high unemployment, the promise of work drew job-seekers in their thousands. Most were unlucky, and even those who were given jobs received a pittance far lower than the salary they'd been promised. Under the fiery leadership of Alexander Bustamante, the workers banded together in protest and the dispute swiftly turned ugly; cane fields were set on fire and a full-scale riot broke out on May 3, 1938, which left four dead from police bullets and 100 demonstrators, including Bustamante, in jail. The reputation for volatility endures and Frome has been the centre of more recent difficulties triggered by the decline of the Jamaican sugar industry; machinery has never been updated, leaving the factory unable to compete with more efficient producers and operating at a loss. Re-mechanization is mooted as the only solution, but the inevitable loss of hundreds of manual jobs has understandably generated animosity – Frome remains the largest single employer in Westmoreland and its success is crucial to the overall prosperity of the area.

---

the start of **LITTLE LONDON**. Though the years have blurred racial origins, the local population was at one time dominated by Indians who came to Jamaica in the nineteenth century as indentured workers to labour in the cane fields and sugar factories. Most people pass through Little London with hardly a sideways glance, as there's little of obvious interest. However, it's a world away from the commerciality of Negril, and boasts some excellent places to **eat** and **drink**; try the gaily painted *Malcolm X Bar*, *First Choice* or *Rainbow Delight Pastry and Restaurant*. Best of the lot is the *Kingfish Kitchen* for traditional Jamaican cooking; the large lawn out back serves as an occasional venue for sound-system dances and the proprietors and regulars usually have a small party on a Sunday.

Flat savannah lands ideal for the cultivation of cane have long meant strong local ties to the **sugar industry**. The largest cane-processing factory in the area is **FROME**, about five miles northeast of Little London, which handles most of the cane from neighbouring plantations (see box). Though the factory is not officially open to the public, you should be able to arrange a tour by calling ahead (☎955 6080).

## Savanna-la-Mar

Capital of Westmoreland it may be, but there's little to keep you in the rather soulless confines of commercial **SAVANNA-LA-MAR**. It's the area's main shopping centre, but as the profusion of low-lying concrete keeps the air still and makes it a hot and uncomfortable place to wander about, most people depart as quickly as possible and there are no developed tourist attractions. The elements have given the town a battering – successive hurricanes flattened it in 1748, 1780, 1912 and 1948 and 1988; in 1748 the wind drove the sea far enough up central Great George Street that boats were left drydocked in the middle of the road.

Other than a couple of attractive gingerbread dwellings on the outskirts, you're stuck with the negligible appeal of **Great George Street**, the needle-straight main thoroughfare. The **courthouse** and parish administrative offices stand next to a cast-iron **fountain** with the warning "Keep the pavements dry" inexplicably inscribed on each side. The rest of the street is taken up with pharmacies and general stores, most selling the usual assortment of imported designer bootlegs, though if you want some true yard-style ragga string vests, Jamaican flag bandannas or barely-there dancehall attire, this is the place to go. Great George Street ends abruptly at the seashore; here you'll find the main fruit and vegetable **market** (main day Sat), and the ruins of **Savanna-la-Mar Fort**, declared the worst fort in Jamaica by a visiting admiral in 1755, who discovered that though vast sums had been devoted to defending the town, the fort was unfinished and one third of what there was had collapsed into the sea. Opposite is the West Indies Sugar Factory **pier**, from which sugar from the

Beach at Alligator Pond

Cliff jumping, Negril

Black River safari, St Elizabeth

Jake's, Treasure Beach

Orange seller, Mandeville

Long Bay beach, Negril

Different draughts

Treasure Beach, St Elizabeth

West End waters, Negril

The nanny state in Gut River

Bamboo Avenue, St Elizabeth

Cornwall Beach, Montego Bay

Frome factory is loaded for export. There's little to see other than crumbling walls and moored fishing boats.

## Practicalities

Savanna-la-Mar is a main junction of the Montego Bay/Negril route; all **buses** stop at the main bus station at the top of Great George Street and you can connect with services to the south coast and beyond. With so many pleasant options nearby, few choose to **stay** in Savanna-la-Mar, but you could join Jamaican regulars and rent a basic but air-conditioned room at *Orchard Great House* (☎955 2737; ①); there's a restaurant, bar and a pool on site. For **food**, try *Q's Restaurant and Bakery*, off the road just past the junction to Negril, for pastries and Jamaican/Chinese dishes.

*If driving to Montego Bay, take the A2 east to Ferris Cross and keep straight on at the petrol station – the signposts are very confusing.*

## Around town: Fish World and Roaring River

One good reason for hanging around town is **Fish World** (daily 8am–6pm; free), half a mile west off the A2, an expansive commercial fish farm on the outskirts of the Cabarita River wetlands that's making tentative steps towards developing itself as a tourist attraction. The precisely proportioned water nurseries are bursting with unhealthily pale freshwater tilapia – as they form the mainstay of many a hotel dinner menu, you'll probably have tried one already. The ponds are so jammed that a net is all that's needed to make a catch, but if you want to slow down the process you can fish for them (rod and tackle supplied). Tilapia cost US$2 per pound and you can have them fried on the spot. You can camp here for US$10, though the promised boating, birding and hiking advertised on the signs may not yet be available.

An easy escape about five miles north of Savanna-la-Mar is gorgeous **ROARING RIVER** near the small community of **Petersfield**, approached on a rutted road that you'll probably need directions to find, though there are plenty of signposts from town. Set in a former plantation and still surrounded by cane fields, a dazzling blue **mineral pool** and extensive **caves** have been developed with tourists in mind, though not on the scale of Dunn's River (see p.158) – don't let the partially deserved reputation for hassle put you off; the jaw-dropping beauty easily outweighs a bit of irritation from local kids. You enter past the brightly painted huts of **Freedom Craft Village**, where young men will attempt to stop your vehicle and charge you to go any further (a "village tour" costs US$20). Drive on, past the stone bridge that marks the first of a series of milky turquoise springs. Watercress grows wild along banks planted with palms and crotons and the forested hillside rises up unbroken – the village is further on past the main swimming spot at **Blue Hole Garden** (daily 8am–6pm; US$5). Overhung with trees and flowers, this thirty-foot wide natural spring of refreshing chilly azure water is said to be bottomless – the true depth has never been charted. The surrounding gardens are well kept but not over-landscaped, packed with unusual trees, anthuriums, narcotic white trumpet flowers, every variety of heliconia and several spots to immerse yourself amid gushing mini-waterfalls.

A huge silk cotton tree opposite Freedom Village marks the entrance to the **caves** (daily 8am–5pm; US$5). Ask for Shaper, a thoughtful Rastaman who can direct you to the best guides and dissuade some of the scramble for your custom. Steps up to the mouth, concrete walkways and lighting let you appreciate the full magnitude of the caverns, which range from broom cupboard to auditorium in size. Bats flit about, and there are two mineral pools for a disquieting swim in pitch-blackness – the water is said to be rejuvenative. The caves are marred only by graffiti carved into the rock and jagged edges where the quartz has been levered off and sold.

If you want to **stay** in Roaring River, there are two cool thatched cabins (②) in the Blue Hole Garden. Facilities (outdoor shower, mosquito screen and pit toilet) are simple but the setting is incredible. You can also **camp** at perfectly appointed tent sites (①). **Food** and **drink** are available from the **Lover's Café** in Blue Hole Garden; for a relatively remote spot, the menu is excellent: vegetable patties, garlic bread, spicy dumplings and fish.

## Bluefields and Belmont

East of Savanna-la-Mar, the coast road becomes the A2 and after the crossroads at Ferris Cross sticks close to the sea on its way to Bluefields and Whitehouse. Just before Ferris Cross, **Paradise Park** (no set hours; free, with tips for guides) marked by a drive of royal palms, is an extensive cane plantation offering swimming in the Sweet River, hiking in beautifully varied terrain (guides are available) and two-hour horse-rides (9am, 11.30am & 2pm; US$30) – a worthwhile diversion before you reach **Bluefields** and **Belmont**, contiguous, laid-back communities of picturesque fishing beaches and reef-fringed shallows.

Henry Morgan (see p.316) sailed from **BLUEFIELDS** in 1670 to attack Panama, and the calm seas and sheltered bay have attracted every generation of Jamaican settlers; it was one of the first Spanish settlements, and the dynamic local community association (see below), is attempting to reopen the old Spanish road to Martha Brae in Trelawny as a hiking route – though the distance and thick plant cover make this a rather distant possibility. The most interesting building in modern Bluefield is privately owned **Bluefields House** next to the police station, once a temporary home to "father of Jamaican ornithology" and inventor of the modern aquarium Philip Gosse, who researched *Illustrations of the Birds of Jamaica* and *A Naturalist's Sojourn in Jamaica* during an eighteen-month residence in 1844–45. In the gardens stand a **breadfruit tree** said to be the first in Jamaica, planted by Captain Bligh when he brought seedlings from Tahiti.

*See p.132 for
more on
Captain Bligh
and the
breadfruit.*

Bluefields merges imperceptibly into **BELMONT**, birthplace of the late **Peter Tosh** (see box, p.278). His body lies in a small red-gold-and-green **mausoleum** (daily 9am–5pm; donation) just off the road, decorated with cobwebs, stained glass and press cuttings. It's much less of an affair than the Marley mausoleum in St Ann (see p.184) and usually deserted.

---

### Peter Tosh

Consciously controversial, **Peter Tosh** (born McIntosh) was Jamaica's best-known lyrical agitator. Born an only child in Belmont on October 19, 1944, he was raised by an aunt in the west Kingston tenement yards then dominated by the explosion of hopeful harmony groups that transformed post-independence Kingston into a hotbed of aspirations. Every newly arrived country "bhuttu" (or bumpkin) wanted to be a singer and Tosh followed suit, embarking on a mission to reveal home truths from a ghetto perspective. He saved to buy his first guitar and in 1964 formed vocal trio The Wailers with teenage allies Bunny Livingstone and Bob Marley. In 1972 the Wailers signed to Chris Blackwell's Island label, a move that eventually terminated the original line-up permanently. They recorded *Catch a Fire* and *Burnin'* together while Tosh put out tracks on his own Intel Diplo HIM label (Intelligent Diplomat for His Imperial Majesty), all the time becoming increasingly bitter over pay and personal disputes with the man he referred to as "Whiteworst". By 1974, he and Bunny Livingstone went their separate ways.

Having already earned a reputation as the Wailers' social conscience and an uncompromising egotist, Tosh took on the mantle of chief critic of what he called Jamaica's "Babylon shitstem", publicly berating politicians for double standards and hypocrisy and lighting spliffs on stage with a cool disregard for the law. His bellicose militancy did him no favours with the island's police; in 1975 he was busted on a trumped-up ganja charge and beaten to within an inch of his life. As soon as his wounds had healed, he answered back with *Whatcha Gonna Do*, a cocky release chiding the futility of police brutality, smokers' anthem *Legalize It*, and the defensive *Can't Blame the Youth* – inevitable airplay bans ensured record sales and Tosh cemented his position as the roots reggae revolutionary.

Tosh stayed in Jamaica, but his ever-increasing status and fortune – collaboration with the Rolling Stones in 1978 and a deal with EMI attracted global recognition – drew awkward parallels with the sufferers' lot he expostulated and the international star he had become. In a country where money and fame draw a barrage of demands from old friends, needy causes and shady characters, the intensely spiritual and suspicious Tosh began to display signs of paranoia, believing himself both a victim of an establishment assassination conspiracy and haunted by duppies. His prophecies of destruction were fulfilled on September 11, 1987, when gunmen opened fire in Tosh's living room, killing him and two friends, and wounding five others. Rumours of the motive spread swiftly, some arguing that head assassin and renowned "bad man" Dennis "Leppo" Lubban was demanding financial retribution for a recent prison stint he saw as Tosh's rap, others muttering of a government-backed gagging.

Remembered by Jamaicans as a formidable ladies' man with a razor-sharp wit, Tosh himself provided his best biography; the "Red X" tapes shot on scratchy film in a darkened room show him philosophizing on his personal mantra, reggae and Rastafari and form part of the essential Tosh documentary *Stepping Razor Red X*.

**Practicalities**

The two villages are served by hourly **buses** from Savanna-la-Mar. If you want to **stay** in Bluefields, try *Casa Mariner* (Cave PO, ☎995 9897; ②) to the west of town, which has nine budget rooms with fan and air conditioning, a restaurant, popular bar, pool tables and slot machines, and an upstairs "conference room" that serves as a weekend disco. Another inexpensive and unusual option, *Shaftson Great House* (c/o Frank and Rosie Lohmann, Bluefields PO, ☎0997 5076; 1–②) sits above the bay (call ahead for free pick-up) with fabulous views, and offers dormitory-style bunk beds or private rooms with en-suite or shared bathroom. Meals are included in the rates but you can cook for yourself if you choose. There's a small pool, bar, pool table, lots of hammocks and extensive grounds; camping costs US$5. Just above the bay, five beautifully designed and furnished villas comprise the casually elegant *Bluefields Villas* complex (in US ☎202/232 4010, fax 703/549 6517; ⑧).

A few **bars** and **restaurants** group around the police station and post office in the "centre" of Bluefields. *KD's Keg Lawn and Restaurant* and the cavernous *Ocean Edge Pub and Restaurant* are both fine, but the hands-down best place to eat is *Jenny's Meals on Wheels*, a converted bus jammed between the road and the sea which never closes and is one of the most evocatively Jamaican eateries you'll find anywhere on the island. The food is the catch of the day, stuffed and fried on an open griddle; speciality is stuffed turbot and a huge pot of excellent vegetable-filled fish tea simmers around the clock. Next door is *Miss Jamaica Love Boat*, a revamped grounded and roofed ex-fishing vessel selling beers and natural juices. In Belmont, *KD's Keg Lawn and Restaurant* is the usual venue for the annual **Peter Tosh birthday celebration** in mid-October, a live concert featuring "roots and culture" performers.

For all local **information**, contact the excellent Bluefields People's Comunity Association (daily 9am–5pm ☎955 8792), whose ongoing programme of community tourism operates from headquarters next door to the *Ocean Edge Pub*.

# Whitehouse and Scott's Cove

As you continue along the A2 – through land known as **Surinam Quarters** in honour of the English who resettled here when the British colony was captured by the Dutch in 1667 – the scenery becomes drier but more agricultural, with swathes of pasture and plenty of cattle and goats. The road swings away from the coast but there are still some nice places to swim; ask locals to direct you to the best spots.

One of the main fishing ports on the south coast, **WHITE-HOUSE**, five miles down the road, offers little beach life but plenty of commercial bustle (though plans for a massive new *Sandals* resort will change all that). Turn off the main strip of shops at the fruit and vegetable **market** (Wed & Sat); passing some dusty cows and resigned-looking higglers, the track deposits you in the midst of the clapboard shacks and run-down bars at the **fishing beach**. If you get there early enough, you can watch the chicken wire traps being baited up with cow skin, balanced on canoes and sailed out to the shallows where the meat attracts lobster and fish. Huge hessian bags of flapping specimens are weighed and bartered over, while women scale furiously and cats prowl for scraps. Fish caught at Whitehouse is transported island-wide, and this tiny place hums with action (and odour) as the boats return from trips that can last as long as a week.

Just east of town, an attractive gingerbread house by the roadside boasts a sign for "**Lidia's Herbal Stuff Like Tonics**"; inside are imported Indian "remedies" such as "Keep Him" cream and lucky room-sprays.

Past Whitehouse, the coast road marks the Westmoreland/St Elizabeth border with a cache of purpose-built fish and bammy stalls at **SCOTT'S COVE**, manned by a friendly team of vendors who crowd around anything that stops. The fish is usually excellent, but ensure that your bammy has been soaked and fried – it's become commonplace to offer tourists the uncooked supermarket version.

### Practicalities

There are quite a few places to **stay** in Whitehouse, most of them – like the large, airy *South Sea View Guesthouse* (☎963 5172, fax 963 5000; ③) – deserted. By far the best option, and never empty, is *Natania's* (☎ and fax 963 5342; ④) in Little Culloden to the west of town. Rooms are beautifully simple with fan only – request an ocean-facing unit. There's a deck overlooking the sea, a pool, bar and a small beach, and its **restaurant** is the best in the area – go even if you're not staying, though there are also plenty of small-scale seafood places in central Whitehouse. In the evenings you can choose between hanging out in a rum bar or checking out *Club Klassique* (open nightly) on the main road, hottest and fullest for Wednesday's dancehall night, when salacious DJs often perform live.

# Travel details

### Buses

Tour company buses make daily runs from Sangster airport in Montego Bay to Negril (US$30), but public buses are as haphazard as everywhere else in Jamaica.

**Montego Bay** to: Lucea (16 daily; 1hr); Savanna-la-Mar (16 daily; 1hr).

**Lucea** to: Negril (20 daily; 40min); Montego Bay (20 daily; 1hr).

**Travel details**

**Negril** to: Lucea (20 daily; 40min); Savanna-la-Mar (20 daily; 40min).

**Savanna-la-Mar** to: Bluefields (9 daily; 40min); Montego Bay (20 daily; 1hr); Negril (20 daily; 45min); Whitehouse (16 daily; 50min).

**Flights**

**Negril** to: Kingston (1 daily; 45min); Montego Bay (1 daily; 20 min); Port Antonio (1 daily; 50min).

# Chapter 6

# The south

**M**ass tourism has yet to reach Jamaica's **southern** parishes. None of the all-conquering all-inclusives have opened here yet and the beaches aren't packed with sun-ripened bodies, but there are some fantastic places to stay and great off-the-beaten-track places to visit. It takes a bit of extra effort to get here – and you'll need a car or a tour to see one or two of the "hidden" highlights – but it's definitely worth it. If you're after watersports and heavy-duty nightlife, stick to the coastal resorts, but if you want to catch a glimpse of Jamaica as it was before the boom, head south.

The parishes that make up south-central Jamaica are immensely varied, with the landscape ranging from mountain to scrubby cactus-strewn desert, and from typically lush vegetation to rolling fields more redolent of the English countryside. To the west, in the beautiful parish of St Elizabeth, **Black River** is the main town – an important nineteenth-century port that today offers popular **river safaris** and a handful of attractive colonial-era buildings. If you're after somewhere to stay and swim, **Treasure Beach** is a better target – an extremely laid-back place with decent beaches and some lovely accommodation options – and if you want to tour around you can make for the **rum factory** at Appleton, the fabulous **YS waterfalls**, or drive around the tiny villages of the attractive and untouristed **Santa Cruz Mountains**.

Further east, the parishes of Manchester and Clarendon are less diverse and a little less appealing. Manchester has the major town of **Mandeville** – a possible inland touring base that makes a pleasant if unspectacular change from the coast – and the much smaller market town of **Christiana**, an unspoilt retreat with a single, delightful old hotel. The coast is less accessible, although a new road through the wild scenery between Alligator Pond and Milk River has opened up **Gut River**, one of the most picturesque spots on the entire island. The parish of Clarendon is total farming country, with large citrus groves in the north and sugarcane fields everywhere else, and offers a handful of unusual places to visit, from the mineral spa at **Milk River** to the seventeenth-century **Halse Hall**, just south of the market town of **May Pen**.

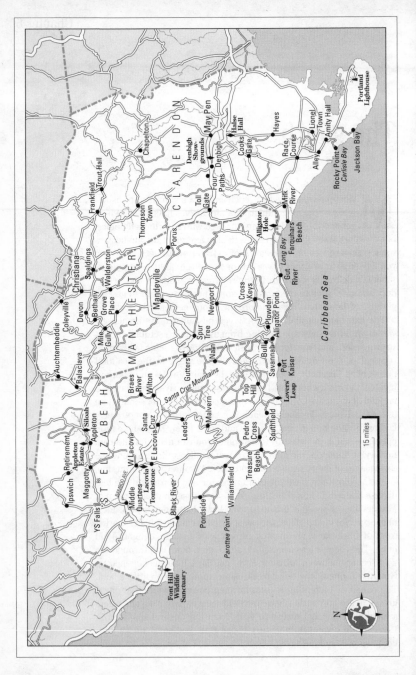

**Bauxite** is the crucial economic commodity in the area, mined at seams in the central highlands (particularly around Mandeville) and processed at refineries scattered over the parishes. **Agriculture** is also key: despite the dry climate (particularly west of the Santa Cruz Mountains), St Elizabeth produces much of the country's agricultural surplus and is known as Jamaica's breadbasket. Recently, **tourism** has begun to make a limited impact, though it is unlikely ever to approach north-coast levels – the emphasis is on small-scale "community tourism", avoiding the disruption to traditional lifestyles that the industry has caused elsewhere on the island.

### Getting around

Regular **buses** and **minibuses** run along the main routes between Kingston and Negril, giving easy access to the main towns of May Pen, Mandeville, Santa Cruz and Black River. From these centres, a network of buses fans out to smaller towns like Christiana, Treasure Beach and Malvern, though these services are much less frequent. Be warned, also, that many of the main attractions in the interior, like the YS Falls, Apple Valley and Appleton, are somewhat off the beaten track and can be hard to reach by public transport. **Driving** is the best way to see the hidden parts of the south; the roads are mostly good, but watch out for gullies on the smaller, coastal roads – they'll take the bottom out of your car if you hit them too fast.

# The south coast

New roads have opened up large parts of Jamaica's **south coast** in the last few years and it's now possible to drive along large stretches of it, particularly between Black River and Milk River, without losing sight of the sea. The scenery is often wild and unspoilt down here, though you'll need a car to see most of it as buses and minibuses tend to stick to the main, inland roads, making side-trips down to coastal villages as required.

Just east of Whitehouse (covered in Chapter Five), the gorgeous **Font Hill Wildlife Sanctuary** is a good place to start your south-coast tour, with some great beaches and a chance to go exploring for birds and crocodiles. Beyond Font Hill, **Black River** merits a visit for its crumbling architectural gems and **river safari** into the Great Morass, and, further round the coast, tiny **Treasure Beach** is probably the best place on the island to just stop, chill out and de-stress for a couple of days. Further east still, there's a great coastal drive from Alligator Pond to the tiny nature reserve at **Alligator Hole**, and you can stop off for a splash in the vividly blue **Gut River**. Finally, and usually the quietest place of the lot, the mineral spa at dry and dusty **Milk River Bath** is the perfect place to soothe away your mental and physical aches and pains.

If you spend any time in this part of Jamaica, you'll appreciate the importance of the local **fishing industry**. Tiny fishing villages are scattered along the coast with boats pulled up on stretches of the beach; even in tourist areas like Treasure Beach, fishing remains vital to the local economy. Many of the fishermen head for the **Pedro Banks**, about eighty miles south, for the best possibilities, with several thousand of them living on small islands there – known as the Pedro Cays – at any one time. If you're interested in going out on a fishing boat, ask around at any of the fishing villages; many fishermen will be grateful for the extra cash, but make sure you clarify whether you'll be expected to help out with the work.

## Font Hill Wildlife Sanctuary

Still little known by tourists, the **Font Hill Wildlife Sanctuary** (daily until sunset; free) – straddling the main road three miles east of Whitehouse – is one of the most delightful places on the south coast. Owned by the Petroleum Corporation of Jamaica, the three-thousand-acre sanctuary was established to provide some unspoiled land for swimming and nature walks. It also serves as a refuge for the endangered **American crocodile**, about two hundred of which live in the swamps at the eastern edge. The entrance to the sanctuary is at the western end of the main fence – distinguished by the blue and white topped posts – where you can drive down to a parking spot beside the beach. The beach is small but gorgeous, with clear turquoise water, and it's always quiet in the morning before filling up with parties of schoolchildren as the day wears on.

If you've got the energy, take a wander down the **hiking trail** that leads east into the woods. Many bird species have taken refuge in the sanctuary, and you stand a good chance of spotting doves, pelicans, egrets and herons. After four hundred yards, a path cuts down to the beach again and you can follow the shoreline as far as **Luana Point**, where a lone mangrove tree spreads its roots over the tidal flats just offshore. Pick your way across the flats and around the point and you'll find a large bay, picture-perfect and almost always deserted, although the swimming isn't great. If you're after the crocodiles, you'll have to find one of the sanctuary's wardens and ask him to take you. It's quite a scramble through the scrub to the ponds at the far end of the reserve and there's no guarantee of spotting the elusive creatures, but the African-style scenery – parched land scattered with cracked and broken acacia trees – makes the hike worthwhile.

**Buses** regularly pass the entrance on the main road and will drop you off outside if you ask. Take something to **drink** if you're planning to do much walking in the sanctuary; although there is talk of putting guest rooms and a café on the site, there are no such facilities as yet, and you'll have to head west to Scott's Cove and Whitehouse (see Chapter Five) or east to Black River.

# Black River

Although it's St Elizabeth's largest town, **BLACK RIVER** is a quiet spot, and most travellers only nip in briefly to take a boat trip on the river. It wasn't always this way: in the mid-nineteenth century the town derived substantial wealth from the trade in **logwood**, used to produce black and dark-blue dyes for the textiles industry and exported in great quantities from Black River's port. For a brief period the trade helped to make the town one of the most influential in Jamaica, with electricity, the telephone and the car all first introduced to the island here, and a big racecourse west of town. However, with the introduction of synthetic dyes, the trade in logwood began to dry up and, today, the only signs of those illustrious days are some wonderful but decrepit old gingerbread houses.

*For details of
the Black River
boat safari, see
p.286.*

**Buses** and **minibuses** stop behind the market, just off the High Street. Five minutes' walk away, the **Jamaica Tourist Board** (Mon–Fri 9.30am–4.30pm; ☎965 2075) has a small office on the upper floor of the Hendrick's building, 2 High St, but don't expect much in the way of useful information.

## Accommodation

Given that few tourists stop over in Black River, there's a surprisingly good selection of **places to stay**. Most of the cheaper options are just east of town on Crane Road, across the iron bridge, but there are several good choices in the town centre and the spectacular *Ashton Great House* a couple of miles to the north.

**Ashton Great House**, Luana, 2 miles north of town; ☎ & fax 965 2036. One of the nicer places to stay in this area of Jamaica, with a beautiful location high up over the surrounding plains and great views of the area and the Santa Cruz Mountains. It's a working farm, and you can arrange horseback rides. ④.

**Bridge House Inn**, 14 Crane Rd; ☎965 2361. The rooms are nothing special but this is pretty good value on the east side of town. ②.

The south coast

**Invercauld Hotel**, High Street; ☎965 2750, fax 965 2751. Attractive restored house on the seafront and a comfortable option close to the centre of town. ④.

**Port O'Call**, 136 Crane Rd; ☎965 2360, fax 965 2410. Probably the best of the options east of town, with a nice little pool and decent rooms. ③.

**South Shore Guesthouse**, 33 Crane Rd; ☎965 2172. Small, tidy guesthouse on the beach east of town. ②.

**Waterloo Guesthouse**, 44 High St; ☎965 2278. The first hotel in Black River, central but now rather run-down. ②.

## The Town

The nicest thing to do in Black River is to take a stroll along the **waterfront**, particularly attractive towards sunset, and check out the old wooden buildings, many with gorgeous colonnaded verandahs and gingerbread trim and most in a perilous state of collapse. The **Waterloo Guesthouse**, built in 1819, is reputed to have been the first place in Jamaica to get electricity – installed to provide air conditioning for racehorses kept in the old stables – and to have boasted the island's first telephone. Nearby, the gleaming white **Invercauld Hotel**, built in 1889, reflects the confidence of the town during its heyday. Heading back towards the town centre, goats roam in the grounds of **St John's**, the tidy parish church which dates from 1837 and has marble monuments to Robert Munro and Caleb Dickenson, benefactors of two of the schools at nearby Malvern.

There are a couple more attractive old buildings in the town centre, particularly the brightly coloured **Hendrick's building** beside the bridge, built in 1813 and now housing the Jamaican Tourist Board. From here you can wander down to the shore where you'll see men and boys fishing and maybe the odd crocodile feeding or hanging out by the ocean. Scant traces of the once fashionable town can be found a couple of miles west of here along the main road: **Abundant Spring** is an old spa, once attracting people from all around the area with its restorative waters but now a run-down and forlorn spot by the sea, while nothing at all remains of the nineteenth-century **race track** that stood across the road.

## The Great Morass and the Black River safari

The main reason most people come to the town is for a **boat safari** on the **Black River** which, at 44 miles, is Jamaica's longest. The river – so named because of the peat moss lining the river bottom that makes the crystal-clear water appear an inky black – is fed by various tributaries as it makes its way down from Balaclava, on the Manchester/St Elizabeth border, and is the main source for the **Great Morass** – a 125-square-mile area of wetland that spreads north and west of Black River and provides a swampy home for most of Jamaica's surviving crocodiles as well as some diverse and spectacular bird life. It's the best place to spot the crocodiles, a rapidly dwindling bunch, now protected by law, who once lived in great numbers around the coast of Jamaica until hunting and the deterioration of the swamplands began to take their toll.

The boat tour is a very pretty trip into the Great Morass, although the term "safari" promises rather more excitement than it delivers. You do have a virtually guaranteed sighting of crocodiles (albeit fairly tame ones), and there are some marvellous **mangrove swamps** where you can normally spot flocks of roosting egrets as well as whistling ducks, herons and jacanas, and you may run into the occasional shrimp- or crab-fisherman in his dug-out canoe. The boats run about eight miles upriver to a small settlement, where you can get some refreshment and take a swim – most people decline the opportunity, though crocodiles are rarely spotted this far north – before heading back down. To go on the ninety-minute tour, which costs US$15 per person, turn up at the dock or contact *St Elizabeth River Safari* (☎965 2229) or *Black River Safari Boat Tours* (☎965 2513). Both companies occasionally make trips further, along the narrower stretches of the Black River where the big tour boats can't go, and it's worth calling in advance to find out if there's any chance of getting taken along – reckon on another US$10 per person.

## Eating and nightlife

Black River is a quiet town and, though there are a couple of good **places to eat**, the evening **entertainment** options are strictly limited. If you're **snacking** during the day, there are a couple of good bakeries on the High Street and you'll find the odd jerk chicken vendor plying his trade nearby.

**Abundant Spring**, west of town. Small, reliable and inexpensive restaurant alongside the old mineral spa serving roast fish and Jamaican staples.

**Ashton Great House**, Luana ☎965 2036 (see p.285). Some of the best food in the area, particularly the seafood, though the price reflects the quality.

**Bayside**, 17 High St. Reasonable café serving the usual chicken and fish dishes for around J$150 and a good selection of cakes and ice cream.

**Bridge House Inn**, 14 Crane Rd. Often rather low on atmosphere, but the Jamaican food is consistently good and moderately priced.

**Jerk Pit**, at Ashton Great House. Excellent jerk chicken and pork served at outdoor tables around the eponymous pit.

**Panchos**, 9 High St, opposite *ScotiaBank*. No concessions to comfort but about the cheapest option for some local colour, with cowfoot or curry goat for around J$100.

### DRINKING AND ENTERTAINMENT

Most of your drinking and entertainment will be done at the places listed above. For an early evening drink, the bar of the *Waterloo Guesthouse* is often the busiest spot in town, popular with Black River's professionals. East of town along Crane Road, the *Sunset Beach Club* has a more earthy feel, with locals playing dice and drinking rum, while the nearby *Safari Club* has a more relaxed atmosphere. For music, *Abundant Spring* stacks up the speakers at the weekends, often pulling a crowd from town, with the latest sounds on Friday and Saturday and oldies on Sunday. The *Jerk Pit* also cranks up the music at the weekend, with occasional live bands.

## Treasure Beach and around

From Black River, a minor road cuts south to the coast beyond **Parottee Point**, passing some bizarre ironshore rock formations and a string of deserted bays en route to snoozy **TREASURE BEACH**. Though it's a tiny spot, with no watersports or nightlife worth mentioning, this easy-going community attracts those who simply want to unwind, and is slowly becoming the main tourist centre on the south coast. There is a good range of **accommodation** options, including some of the most delightfully rustic places in Jamaica, some great places to eat and a couple of diverting attractions, while the bays that make up the area boast some pretty beaches.

The **Santa Cruz Mountains** (see p.299) rise up from the sea just east of Treasure Beach and run northwest, providing a scenic backdrop for the village and protecting the area from rainclouds coming

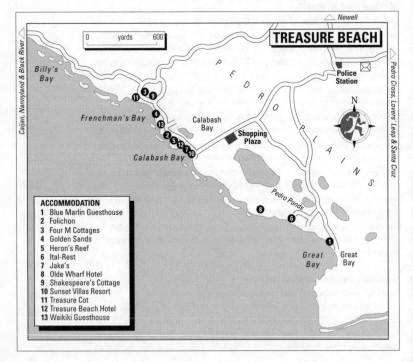

**ACCOMMODATION**
1 Blue Marlin Guesthouse
2 Folichon
3 Four M Cottages
4 Golden Sands
5 Heron's Reef
6 Ital-Rest
7 Jake's
8 Olde Wharf Hotel
9 Shakespeare's Cottage
10 Sunset Villas Resort
11 Treasure Cot
12 Treasure Beach Hotel
13 Waikiki Guesthouse

from the north. As a result, Treasure Beach has one of the **driest** climates in the country, and the scrubby desert-like landscape – strewn with cactus and acacia trees – often looks like the setting for a western. Despite the dry weather, though, this is very much farming country, and you'll see plantations of carrots, scallions, thyme, onions and watermelons scattered around the area.

## Arrival and getting around
Public transport links with Treasure Beach are not great, although several **minibuses** and **shared taxis** run daily from Black River; a regular taxi costs around US$20 each way. If you're **driving**, there are two approaches to the village. Most traffic arrives via the road from Pedro Cross, passing the police station and post office north of the village. A turn-off to the left leads to Great Bay while the main road continues towards Calabash Bay, where most of the recent tourist development has taken place. The newer, coastal road from Black River runs into the village from the west past a string of small bays and intermittent guesthouses.

*Treasure Tours* (☎965 0126) runs a good and reasonably priced **tour service** if you're interested in seeing the YS Falls, Gut River or other parts of the south from a base in Treasure Beach; if you want to tour on your own, the *Waikiki Guesthouse* (☎965 0448) rents **scooters** for around US$30 per day.

## The villages and beach
Treasure Beach itself is made up of a string of loosely connected fishing settlements. The chances are that you'll stay in **Calabash Bay**, where tourism is gradually displacing fishing as the main industry, though you'll still see brightly coloured fishing boats pulled up on the beach below the newly constructed hotels and guesthouses. To the east, **Great Bay** remains a basic fishing village with just a couple of guesthouses and some lovely beaches, while west of Calabash Bay the road runs out of town past **Billy's Bay**, a series of shacks and a lot of goats.

If you're in the mood for **sightseeing**, there are a couple of places worth checking out just outside Treasure Beach (see below). Otherwise, it's just you and the **beach**. The swimming is good, though you'll need to watch the undertow, which can get strong at times – ask at your hotel about present conditions. Although rocky headlands create occasional obstacles, you can stroll for miles on certain parts of the beach, particularly west of the *Treasure Beach Hotel*, and the bluff which protects the shore at Great Bay is a lovely place to walk and look out for the local seabirds.

**Fishing trips** with the local fishermen can normally be arranged without difficulty for around US$25 per person for a half day – ask the people at your hotel to put the word out that you're interested. There's no scuba diving to be had in the area, and snorkelling can be tricky because of the undertow and choppy waters, but *Jake's* offers canoe trips out to good, safe snorkelling spots for around US$10 per person. Finally, new **shopping plazas** are springing up around town with little consideration of aesthetics; if you're after souvenirs, the **candle factory** at *Jake's* offers something more interesting than the usual woodcrafts and t-shirts.

## Nannyland, Caijan and Lovers' Leap

*You can also camp or rent a room at Nannyland, Caijan and Lovers' Leap – see below.*

Right beside the road five miles west of Treasure Beach, **Nannyland** (daylight hours) is a sprawling seaside site dedicated to black heroes – particularly the Maroon leader, Nanny – with statues of and monuments to Martin Luther King, Paul Bogle and Sam Sharpe scattered around the grounds. It's usually deserted, with a bleak and slightly eerie feel, but the location, just above the ocean, is superb. A little further west, and less easy to reach, **Caijan** is a mountain retreat where Rastaman Brother John has built an extraordinary house into the mountainside, using the rocky outcrops as floor, ceiling or wall as required. The house is full of artefacts that John has collected on his world travels, including paintings, musical instruments, bits of pottery and other paraphernalia. Entrance is up a steep hill (you'll need a four-wheel-drive or the legs of a mountain goat), marked by an ancient pink Ford Prefect. If you can find anyone in, both places are normally welcoming to visitors, though you may be asked for a nominal donation.

On the other side of Treasure Beach, the Santa Cruz Mountains drop nearly two thousand feet to the sea at the sheer cliffs of **Lovers' Leap**, signposted off the main road at Southfield seven miles east. According to legend, two young lovers – slaves at a nearby plantation – came here while running away from their owners. They were followed to the edge of the cliffs and, preferring to die rather than be separated again, threw themselves into the sea. The views over the cliffs and out to sea are pretty spectacular (though not worth a major diversion), and if you're feeling reckless you can scramble part of the way down for an even better look at the drop. There's a new **café** and **viewing platform** on the site, too, though it rather spoils the feeling of isolation.

On the way to Lovers' Leap, you'll pass *Mayfield Ranch* (☎965 6234), which offers **horseback rides** from around US$15 per person on trails through the local farms and prairie-like landscape.

## Accommodation

There is a wide variety of **accommodation** in Treasure Beach, and more guesthouses are springing up all the time. **Camping** – available at *Caijan*, *Nannyland* and *Four M Cottages* for around US$10 per tent – is more feasible than in most parts of Jamaica, and there are plenty of villas, which can be usually rented by the night or by the week.

Of the **villas**, *Folichon* in Calabash Bay has four rooms (though only one double bed) and rents for US$100 per day; the adjacent *Herons Reef* has two rooms, sleeping four, and costs US$50 per day. Both places are on the beach beside *Jake's* and can be reserved on ☎963 8569. *Treasure Cot*, just east of *Jake's*, is an atmospheric two-bedroom guesthouse on the beach that rents for US$100 per day, bookable via *Jake's* (see below). Further west at Great Bay, *Blue Marlin Guesthouse* (☎965 0459) is on the site of a Taino (Arawak) settlement; the house is strewn with Taino artefacts, as well as colonial-era heirlooms collected by the owner, and the guesthouse – rented by the week only – costs US$1,000 for up to four people.

**Caijan**, west of Billy's Bay; ☎990 6641 or c/o *Jake's*. Fabulous mountainside setting with camping sites and a couple of cottages about seven miles west of town on the coastal road to Black River, the entrance marked by an old Ford Prefect. No electricity, but great views and atmosphere. You'll need a sturdy four-wheel-drive to get up there or ask to be collected. ②.

**Four M Cottages**, Calabash Bay; ☎965 0131. Six small, simply furnished rooms in a friendly house opposite the *Treasure Beach Hotel*. ②.

**Golden Sands**, Calabash Bay; ☎965 0167. Longstanding budget option on the beach, with rather basic rooms and self-catering facilities. ①.

**Ital-Rest**, Great Bay; ☎965 0248. Two cottages only at this gentle and beautifully landscaped place near the beach, each with separate rooms upstairs and down (ask for upstairs for the views and the breeze). No electricity but the owners will provide food. Turn right just before the *Seacrab* restaurant and take the first right. ②.

**Jake's**, Calabash Bay; ☎/fax 965 0552. Casual but delightful venue on its own tiny beach, with six brightly coloured cottages and an easy-going but cultured atmosphere. If you're not after luxury, this is one of the most charming options in Jamaica. ⑤.

**Lovers' Leap Guest House**, Lovers' Leap (no phone). Friendly place with fairly spartan rooms, and snacks and drinks at the bar downstairs. ①.

**Nannyland**, west of Billy's Bay (no phone). A couple of cabins and camping space in this sprawling shrine to Jamaica's black heroes, by the sea five miles from Treasure Beach. ①.

**Olde Wharf Hotel**, Calabash Bay; ☎965 0003, fax 962 5640. Large but quiet resort by the beach – a reasonable option if you're looking for a standard-type hotel. ③.

**Shakespeare's Cottage**, Calabash; ☎965 0120. Cheapest place in town, with four basic but clean rooms and a self-catering option. ①.

**Sunset Villas Resort**, Calabash Bay; ☎965 0143. Sizeable rooms with home-from-home creature comforts and a lovely seaside setting. ④.

**Treasure Beach Hotel**, Calabash Bay; ☎965 2305, fax 965 2544. Big, attractive resort with a pool and suites with oceanfront views on one of the best stretches of beach. ⑤.

**Waikiki Guesthouse**, Calabash Bay; ☎965 0448. Basic option by a small bay in the centre of Treasure Beach, opposite *Tiffany's* restaurant. ①.

## Eating and nightlife

Evenings are pretty low-key in Treasure Beach but there are a few
good options for **food** and a couple of new **bars** are being built to
cater for the slowly growing number of visitors. The roads aren't lit
at night, so you'll be wandering between places in the moonlight.

**Fishermen's Bar**, Calabash Bay. Thatched bar up the lane beside *Tiffany's*,
with a small disco and pool table out back. Easy-going local hangout that's
open after everywhere else has closed.

**Jake's**, Calabash Bay; ☎965 0552. Good option for dinner and usually one
of the busiest places in town, with a blackboard menu that changes daily but
normally includes fish and lobster.

**Moreen's**, Calabash Bay. Intermittently open restaurant next to *Trans-Love*
with cheap local meals.

**Seacrab**, Great Bay. Friendly local restaurant, near *Ital-Rest*, with good and
inexpensive Jamaican staples like escovitched fish and curried goat.

**Tiffany's**, Calabash Bay; ☎965 0300. Attractive restaurant serving excellent
lobster, octopus and fish dishes from around J$200.

**Trans-Love Bakery**, Calabash Bay. Laid-back thatched patio and the essential stop for breakfast or brunch, with fresh bread, cakes and fruit salads, as
well as regulars like ackee and saltfish. Also open for (equally good) dinner
during the high season.

**Yabba**, *Treasure Beach Hotel*; ☎965 2305. Good hotel food and enthusiastic service, though it's often quiet and consequently low on atmosphere.

# Alligator Pond to Alligator Hole

At first glance, the ramshackle fishing village of **ALLIGATOR POND**
– ten miles east of Treasure Beach – is not one of the most attractive
spots on the south coast. But if you're passing, it's worth stopping to
get the feel of a part of Jamaica completely unsullied by tourism, and
to eat some superb **seafood**. A number of small shacks sell lobster
and fish fresh from the boats; the most popular is *Little Ochi*, right
on the beach just to the west of the town square, which fills up at
weekends and holidays with hungry folk from Mandeville or even
Kingston. There's little reason to **stay** but, should you need to, the
uninspiring *Sea-Riv Hotel* (☎962 7265; ②) – west of town en route
to the Port Kaiser bauxite-loading pier – is right on the beach, while
*Breakers* (no phone; ①) is a small guesthouse one mile to the east.

From the square in Alligator Pond, a road leads east for eighteen
miles to Alligator Hole and Milk River. Recently laid, this gives a pretty drive through an isolated area known as **Canoe Valley** or the Long
Bay Morass, much of it along the coast, with goats and seabirds usually your only company. The area is barely touched by development
and remains a naturalist's paradise, with the dry, cactus-strewn
slopes in the west giving way to mangrove swamps – brilliant for
bird-watching – as you head further east. Halfway along the road
you'll cross **Gut River**, one of the most picturesque places on the
south coast. The river runs under the road towards the sea, emerging

**Manatees**

The **manatee** – an aquatic mammal that looks rather like a large, fat seal –
is found in the warm waters of the Atlantic Ocean and in the Caribbean
Sea. Also known as the sea cow, it's a very secretive creature; little is
known about its reproductive habits, for example, and studies have found
it tricky to monitor numbers. The nature park at Alligator Hole is the only
place in Jamaica – and one of few places in the world – where you can see
them in the wild.

Fully grown, manatees can reach up to fourteen feet in length, although
the great size is no cause for concern as they are strictly vegetarian – eating as much as four hundred kilos of sea grass per day – and doting on
each other and on their young. Columbus probably spotted them when he
first came to Jamaica in 1494 (although he claimed that he had seen mermaids), and there were certainly plenty around. Sadly, their slow and gentle lifestyle meant that they were (and are) easy prey for fishermen;
accordingly, even though they are now protected, fewer than 3,000 are
believed to survive in the Caribbean and only 100 in Jamaica.

in a clear blue stream edged by coconut palms, where you can swim,
snorkel and jump off the rocks. Frigate birds and egrets flap lazily
around, and even the best efforts of local developers, who are putting
up a café and bar (and may offer basic accommodation in the future),
can't spoil the beauty.

Continuing east towards Milk River, you'll pass the tiny nature
park of **Alligator Hole** (daily 9am–4pm; free), the part-time home of
a small number of **manatees**. It's a peaceful place to stop, with an
informative little visitor centre; if you're lucky, you'll see the gentle
creatures come in for their daily feed (usually in the late afternoon),
supplied by the caretaker-managers who hang out by the park, drinking and playing dominoes. Until recently, the managers organized
boat trips downriver to look for the manatees; these were officially
discontinued for insurance reasons but it's still worth asking if they'll
take you. **Crocodiles** (known locally as alligators) also inhabit the
area, although they are seen less often.

## Milk River Spa

The **hot mineral springs** near **MILK RIVER** – a couple of miles
inland from Alligator Hole – were first discovered in the early eighteenth century. Mineral spas were subsequently built in the area –
first opened to the public in 1794 – and are today housed in the basement of the *Milk River Hotel* (☎924 9544, fax 986 4962; ②). The
hotel is a lovely old wooden building, with comfortable rooms and
inexpensive meals on offer, and, though there's nothing spectacular
about the area, the dry climate and the laid-back atmosphere make it
a very pleasant place to spend a night.

Many of the guests at the hotel and spa are return visitors who
swear by the curative powers of the water for a range of ailments

from rheumatism to gout, nerve diseases and sciatica. Other visitors find their curiosity tinged with concern about the high radioactivity levels of the baths – more than fifty times that of the waters at Vichy in France – although the staff will assure you that this is quite harmless. The nine sunken tiled baths are big enough to have a good splash around in during the recommended fifteen minutes, although you'll probably just want to lie there and soak up the steam. You get free use of the spas if you're staying at the hotel; if you're visiting, they cost J$50 per time.

*Infrequent
buses run to
Milk River
from May Pen
(see p.309).*

Other than the spa, there's little to the village of Milk River other than the usual crowd of schoolchildren and smattering of churches. The river itself is named for its colour in the early morning, when it is shrouded in mist, but given that it is the home of a number of local crocodiles, swimming is not a great idea. A better option is the **Milk River Mineral Pool** (J$80) – an open-air swimming pool 150 yards from the hotel – though it's only open at weekends. Two miles beyond the spa, past rows of giant cacti, is the tiny fishing village of **FARQUHARS** which has, at its western end, a passable black-sand beach where you can swim in the ocean.

## East of Milk River

From Milk River, you can either head north to the main road for Mandeville and May Pen or continue east towards Lionel Town. After six miles, the latter B12 road passes through the quiet village of **ALLEY**, where **St Peter's Church** is one of the oldest and most attractive churches on the island. Founded in 1671 the present building mostly dates from the early eighteenth century. Inside the church, check out the tablets on the upper west wall, engraved with the Lord's Prayer and the Ten Commandments, and the 1847 organ. Outside there are a mass of crumbling tombs, many of the inscriptions ravaged by time. If the church is locked you can get the key from the rectory, next door beside the church hall.

Beyond Alley you'll pass a unique octagonal building at tiny **AMITY HALL**. Originally a sugar mill, probably built around 1800, the building now houses the **parish library** (Mon–Fri 9.30am–4pm), with the rooms above occupied by a local family (though you can ask to look around). Constructed from imported brick, rather than Jamaican limestone, this was an unusual building even in its own time. Ruins of the old sugar works, which closed in 1926, are dotted around nearby and there is a present-day refinery at **Monymusk**, a mile away. Unlikely as it now seems, Amity Hall was the site of an important battle during the French invasion of 1694. The French landed at Yallahs in the east of Jamaica (see p.121) and crossed the island, destroying sugar estates as they went. At Amity Hall, though, they lost over a hundred men in one short engagement with the British (probably on the site of the sugar mill) and fled, never to return, burning the coastal village of **Carlisle Bay** in spite as they left.

East of Amity Hall, the B12 road turns north for the bustling market town of **LIONEL TOWN**, crowded with traders, fruit and vegetable stalls and schoolchildren, or you can continue past the turnoff and head south for some of the most isolated places in Jamaica. **Jackson Bay**, roughly five miles from Lionel Town, is the only option if you want a swim although, frankly, it's not a particularly attractive beach. Very few tourists ever come here, and your presence will awaken considerable local interest. If you have a four-wheel-drive vehicle, you can head east before you reach the bay and a rough track carries you out along the deserted and scrubby **Portland Ridge** past mangrove swamps as far as the **Portland lighthouse**. There is talk of converting this area of wilderness into a national park but, for the present, it remains eerily quiet and unexplored.

# Inland to Mandeville

The A2 highway speeds inland from Black River, passing through some attractive countryside before making the long climb up Spur Tree Hill to **Mandeville**. The main road passes through **Bamboo Avenue**, with its walls of tall bamboo, and there are several interesting detours worth taking, particularly in the interior of St Elizabeth. There are gorgeous **waterfalls** at YS, **hiking** possibilities in the **Black River Gorge**, and the quiet and completely untouristed villages of the **Santa Cruz mountains**. You can also visit a **rum factory**, beautifully placed among fields of sugarcane at Appleton, on the southern edge of Cockpit Country (see Chapter Four). **Accommodation** options in the area are limited, though there are a couple of decent places at Santa Cruz and Maggotty, and you may want to consider visiting on day-trips from a base on the south coast or in Mandeville. **Getting around** is a breeze if you've got a car; public transport links into the interior are not brilliant though buses do run to most parts – for a couple of places, including YS, you'll need to take a taxi for a short part of the trip.

## Middle Quarters and YS Falls

As you drive northeast from Black River, you'll reach an intersection directing you north for Montego Bay or east towards Santa Cruz and Mandeville. Head east and you'll soon pass **Middle Quarters**, a small crossroads where groups of women sell spicy, salty **shrimp** from the Black River. Feel free to sample from the proffered bags before you buy; reckon on around J$50 for a small bag. The shrimp taste okay on their own, though better with hardough bread which the vendors occasionally have. Buy some to add to your picnic if you're heading to the YS waterfalls or take a few minutes out to crunch them on the roadside and have a chat with the women. Incidentally, don't be intimidated by the fiercely competitive approach of the sellers – they are often all members of the same family and if one is lagging in sales for the day, she will usually be thrust forward to clinch the deal.

Shortly after Middle Quarters, a left turn takes you two and a half miles north to **YS**, an area dominated by the **YS farm**, home of the magnificent YS Falls. The name is thought to derive from the farm's original owners in 1684, Richard Scott and John Yates, whose initials were stamped on their cattle and the hogsheads of sugar that they exported. Today the farm covers around 2,500 acres and raises pedigree **red poll cattle** – a Jamaican breed that you'll see all over the country – and grows papaya for export.

The **YS Falls** (daily during daylight; April–Dec closed Mon; US$9), a series of ten greater and lesser waterfalls, are great fun. A jitney pulls you through the farm's land and alongside the YS river to a grassy area at the base of the falls. You can climb up the lower falls or take the wooden stairway which leads to a platform beside the uppermost and most spectacular waterfall. There are lianas and ropes for aspiring Tarzans, pools for gentle bathing at the foot of each fall, and you can swim under the main falls and climb up into a cave behind them. Early morning is a good time to go, before the tour buses arrive; take a picnic and a book and, on a sunny day, you can comfortably spend a few hours loafing around on the grass and in the water. Cold beers and soft drinks are always available nearby.

A car is extremely handy if you're heading for the falls, as they're a little off the beaten track, but if you're relying on public transport, **buses** run along the main A2 highway south of YS between Black River and Santa Cruz. Ask the driver to drop you at the junction, and you can usually find taxis waiting to run passengers up to the YS farm – make sure you negotiate the price before you get in. There's nowhere to **stay** at YS – the nearest options are Maggotty (see below) or Black River (see p.285).

## Maggotty

East of YS and seven miles from the main highway, **MAGGOTTY** resembles a small Wild West frontier town. It's a dry, dusty place, most of whose inhabitants work at the **Appleton rum estate** nearby (see opposite), and, though there's little to see in town, there is some beautiful scenery nearby and a couple of good accommodation options.

Just south of town, the red-roofed *Apple Valley Guesthouse* (☎997 6000; ③) is a colonial-era great house with five comfortable rooms. It's a also a handy base for some good walking, and the owners can provide guides. The best **hike** is across the local farmland and down into the **Black River Gorge**, a deep and attractive ravine carved by the island's principal river. Around twenty minutes' walk from the guesthouse you reach the first of a series of 28 **waterfalls** and you can either wallow around there or trek for an hour or so down to the bottom. It's a straightforward walk to get down into the gorge although the climb back up can be a bit strenuous; the owners can arrange for you to travel down on a tractor if you're not up to the walk.

Inland to Mandeville

The guesthouse's industrious owners also run the *Sweet Bakery* just up the road, and the **Apple Valley Park** (daily 8am–5pm; free) opposite, a small nature park with ducks and geese, paddle-boats for kids, explanations of the medicinal value of Jamaica's herbs and a little farm. The park has a couple of very basic cabins (①), but the simple, clean rooms at *Poinciana Guesthouse* (①), up a slight hill opposite the police station, are better and cheaper. Each of the guesthouses will provide **meals** as required, or you can get typical Jamaican food in town at the *Happy Time* restaurant or good patties at the *Sweet Bakery*.

*See p.26 for more on the medicinal uses of Jamaican plants.*

Infrequent **minibuses** run to Maggotty from Black River and Santa Cruz. If you're **driving**, the road north from the A2 highway is in far better condition than the road running east/west between Maggotty and YS.

## The Appleton rum estate

Three miles east of Maggotty, the **Wray and Nephew rum estate** at **APPLETON** (☎963 9215; Mon–Sat 9am–3.30pm; US$12) has a great setting in the Black River valley among thousands of acres of

---

### Rum and raison d'être

**Rum** – once known as rumbullion or kill-devil – is the island's national drink, and you couldn't choose a better place to acquire a taste for the stuff. Jamaica was the first country to make rum commercially and it still produces some of the world's finest. **Overproof** is the drink of choice for the less well-off – it's cheap, lethally strong (64 percent alcohol) and, supposedly, cures all ills. If you can't handle the overproof, the standard **white rums** are the basis for most cocktails, while more refined palates go for the **darker rums**. During the ageing process these rums acquire colour from the oak barrels in which they are stored and, as they get older, you'll find they slip down increasingly smoothly with no need for a mixer.

Distilling of sugarcane juice started in Jamaica during the years of Spanish occupation, stepping up a few gears when the British took over in 1655, and rum became famous as the drink of the island's semi-legitimate **pirates** and **buccaneers**. The production process hasn't changed much over the centuries, although it has become fully mechanized, putting a number of donkeys out of work in the process. The sugarcane is squeezed to extract every drop of its juice, which is then boiled and put through a centrifuge, producing molasses. In turn, the molasses are diluted with water and yeast is added to get the stuff fermenting away. After fermentation, the liquid "dead wash" is sent to the distillery, where it is heated, and the evaporating alcohol caught in tanks. It sounds simple enough and it is, but when you discover that it takes ten to twelve tonnes of sugarcane to produce half a bottle of alcohol, you begin to appreciate all those fields of swaying cane a little more.

---

sugarcane fields. At 250 years old, this is the oldest rum producer in the English-speaking Caribbean and the best known of Jamaica's several brands. All of the rum produced here is sent for barrelling in Kingston (though some barrels are sent back here to age) and blending and bottling are also carried out in the capital.

You'll need a car to get here, or you can take a taxi from Maggotty. Though you're free to drop in, it's a good idea to call ahead to arrange a guided visit, if only to avoid your visit coinciding with a big tour party. The thirty-minute **tour** starts at an old press, where donkeys used to walk in circles to turn a grinder that crushed juice out of the sugarcane. Today it's all mechanized, though a donkey has been put back into service to demonstrate old techniques. From there you get to see the various pots, boilers and barrels used in the production process – interesting enough, though it's the fabulous smells that you'll really notice – and the tour concludes in a "saloon", where you get to sample the various products, before you adjourn to the bar for a couple more free drinks.

## Bamboo Avenue and Lacovia

Back on the main A2 highway, **Bamboo Avenue**, halfway between Middle Quarters and Lacovia, enlivens the drive to Mandeville. For several miles *bambusa vulgaris*, Jamaica's largest species of bamboo, has grown up on either side to create a pretty arch over the road. The place was once almost completely shaded by the bamboo but the sun now streams in through gaps created by Hurricane Gilbert and, some say, by official neglect. Just east of Bamboo Avenue, the village of **LACOVIA**, one-time capital of St Elizabeth, was once an important inland port for shipping sugar and logwood down to Black River for export. Today it is most notable for its **twin tombs**, just outside the *Texaco* petrol station, believed to contain the bodies of two young men killed in a local duel in 1723. One of the deceased is named as Thomas Jordan Spencer and the coat of arms on his tombstone suggests a connection with the family of Winston Churchill and Diana Spencer.

## Santa Cruz, Malvern and Spur Tree Hill

If you're in this part of the country, sooner or later you're likely to pass through **SANTA CRUZ**, the main settlement along the A2 and a pleasant, expanding market town, once famous as a livestock trading centre. There is no particular reason to stop off here, although you can fill up on fresh patties and delicious juices at *Paradise Patties* on Main Street. If you need to spend a night, the friendly *Danbar Guest House* (☎966 9382; ①), at Trevmar Park just south of the main road towards the west side of town, has seven very cheap rooms and the owners will cook to order, while the *Supreme Club*, at the junction of Main Street and Coke Drive, has raucous evening entertainment involving live bands and go-go dancers.

The road south from Santa Cruz to Treasure Beach and the coast (see p.288) is a beautiful (if slow) drive over the Santa Cruz Mountains. The drive takes you through a series of tiny villages and the quiet town of **MALVERN**. Like Christiana further north (see p.306), this is one of Jamaica's **coolest** towns, at around two and a half thousand feet above sea level, and, earlier this century, was an important summer retreat for foreigners and wealthy Jamaicans, though it's now almost bereft of tourists. Today, apart from a handful of top-notch schools and colleges established here in the 1850s, there's not much to the town, although the presence of returning residents who've made their money abroad is injecting an air of affluence – with grand houses springing up on the hilltops – and it's a pretty place to cruise around for a little while. There's nowhere to **stay**, although the nearby *Chariots Hotel* (☎966 3860; ②) in **LEEDS**, midway between Santa Cruz and Malvern, has a small pool and decent rooms. *Dolly's* restaurant and ice cream parlour, next to the petrol station in Malvern, has standard Jamaican **food** if you're after some lunch.

Heading east from Santa Cruz, the A2 continues to **Gutters**, on the Manchester/St Elizabeth border, where it begins the long and rather tortuous climb up **Spur Tree Hill** to Mandeville. Once known as "man bump", the switchbacking hill provides dramatic views over the southern plains, the Santa Cruz Mountains, and down to the sea, and there are a couple of good **bars** and **restaurants** to stop off at and enjoy the view: *Four Seasons* has a variety of local dishes and a verandah while, 400 yards further up, *Alex's Curry Goat Spot* is known island-wide for its curried goat and mannish water.

# Mandeville and around

You can almost feel the wealth in **MANDEVILLE**, Jamaica's fifth town. Big money started to arrive here in the 1950s as a result of the very visible **bauxite industry** that grew up around the town. More recently, returning expatriate Jamaicans, attracted by the cooler climate and the relatively low crime rate, have begun to invest their accumulated savings in large homes and small businesses around town. Tourism has been rather an unimportant sector in recent years, although from the early days of the *Mandeville Hotel* in the 1890s, the town was popular with British soldiers who came to escape the heat of the coastal areas and to recuperate from their fevers and diseases.

*For more on Jamaica's bauxite industry, see p.307.*

Nowadays, Mandeville is still a quiet town and by no means an essential stop on your tour of the island. However, it is a pleasant place to get away from the hustle and bustle of Jamaica's more touristed areas – you'll probably notice the lack of hassle – and makes a reasonable base for exploring the south and centre of the island. If you're here for any time, check out the old **great house** at Marshall's Pen and the more contemporary mansion at **Huntingdon Summit**, or while away an hour with a visit to a local factory.

# Arrival, information and getting around

**Buses** into Mandeville arrive at the south end of Mandeville Square, a small village green in the town centre surrounded by banks, super-markets and, usually, a crowd of people. Buses and minibuses for Kingston and Christiana (less often for the west and north coasts) leave from the same place at regular intervals, and the town's main **taxi rank** is alongside. If you're **driving** there are three separate entrances to town signposted from the highway – it's simplest to take the middle one, at the major roundabout, and follow New Green Road all the way into town. For sightseeing, a car is definitely a major asset; although you can see everything in the town centre on foot, getting out to, say, Marshall's Pen or Huntingdon Summit will require wheels.

There is no longer a tourist board office in Mandeville, so you'll have to rely on your hotel staff and the usual flyers around town for news of what's going on.

# Accommodation

Mandeville's **hotels** largely cater for business travellers – tourists are relatively few here – but there are a couple of decent budget places.

**Astra Country Inn**, 62 Ward Ave; ☎962 3265, fax 962 7979. A little out of the town centre, and a bit short on character – the place used to be a nursing home and still feels a little sterile – but there's a small pool, the food is good and the owners are a great source of information on the local area. It's also the base for the area's community tourism scheme (see box). ④.

**Fleur Flats Resorts**, 10 Coke Drive; ☎962 5109. Tidy self-catering apart-ments in a small hotel complex a 5min drive from town – follow the Manchester Road south from the central square, keeping right at the petrol station, and take the first left. ③.

---

### Community tourism

The creation of big tourist "ghettoes" on the north coast has completely disrupted traditional lifestyles there and means that, often, the only con-tact overseas visitors have with Jamaicans is when they are serving drinks or driving tour buses. In the face of its own, miniature tourist boom, Jamaica's south coast, where the absence of large-scale development offers visitors more of a feel of the "real" Jamaica, is keen to escape such insensitive development. Planners and hoteliers are showing increasing interest in the concept of "**community tourism**", which aims to contain and control tourism by fostering closer connections between the tourist and the community – through visits to schools, farms and craft centres – and persuading developers not to despoil the area. It's a positive, opti-mistic approach, but it remains to be seen whether the organizers' noble intentions will rein in some of the short-termist developers, beginning to sniff big possibilities on the south coast. For more information on the fledgling programme, contact Countrystyle Ltd (☎962 3725, fax 962 1461) at Mandeville's *Astra Country Inn*.

*See p.21 of Basics for more on community tourism in Jamaica.*

**Glenrock Guest House**, 3 Greenvale Rd; ☎961 3278. Not the most welcoming place in town but the rooms are OK and it's certainly the cheapest option. ②.

**Golf View Hotel**, 7B Caledonia Rd; ☎962 4471, fax 962 2858. Modern, well-equipped hotel designed around a central courtyard that holds a small pool. ③.

**Kariba Kariba Guest House**, 39 New Green Rd; ☎962 8006. Friendly little guesthouse whose rates include breakfast. ③.

**Mandeville Hotel**, 4 Hotel St; ☎962 2460, fax 962 0700. One of the oldest hotels in Jamaica and, though almost totally reconstructed and refurbished, still a pleasant and easy-going place to stay right in the heart of town. ④.

## The Town and around

Mandeville was founded in 1814 and still retains something of its early colonial air – most noticeably at the very English **Manchester Golf Club**, just west of the town centre. The first buildings were set out around **Mandeville Square**, a rather unkempt grassy space now also

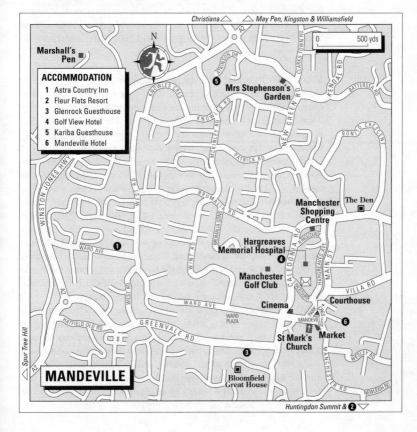

known as Cecil Charlton Park after a former mayor (see p.303, and this is the best starting point for a brief walking tour of the centre.

Built in 1819, **St Mark's Church** is on the south side of the park, behind the massed ranks of taxis, buses and vendors. The interior is pretty ordinary but, as usual, there are plenty of goats nosing around in the churchyard, and you could happily spend a few minutes wandering among them and checking out the nineteenth-century tombstones. On the other side of the park, the limestone **courthouse** is one of Mandeville's original buildings, completed in 1820 and still normally crowded, while the **rectory** (now a private home) alongside the courthouse dates from the same year. The nearby **police station** – once the town jail and workhouse – is the last of Mandeville's original structures.

North of here, at 25 New Green Rd, there is a **private garden** that will be of interest if you've a passion for anthuriums. Carmen Stephenson has the most impressive collections of plants in town, and she is a regular winner at the Mandeville Flower Show every May. Visitors are free to drop in for a tour of the garden (daily during daylight hours; US$2) with its well-ordered collection, which includes the rare white anthurium, orchids and **ortaniques** – a cross between the orange and the tangerine and Mandeville's contribution to the world of fruit.

## Marshall's Pen and Huntingdon Summit

Mandeville's more interesting sights are both a bit of a drive out of town. **Marshall's Pen** (daily by appointment ☎963 8569; US$10) is a lovely old great house, built around 1795 and originally used in the preparation of coffee beans for export. The driveway you enter through was the "barbecue", where the beans were laid out to dry in the sun, and the ground floor of the house, with its massive cedar floorboards, was where they were polished prior to their shipment to the US and UK for roasting and grinding. Nowadays this area has been converted to living quarters and also serves, together with a couple of rooms upstairs, as an interesting **museum**. The Suttons, owners of the house, have collected relentlessly over the generations; there are fabulous collections of shells and stamps, both from Jamaica and abroad, Japanese and Chinese artefacts, and a tiny array of Taino relics. If you're lucky, you'll be conducted around the house by the venerable Arthur Sutton – born in Mandeville in 1900 and with a keen interest in all aspects of local and family history.

The grounds are also great for **bird-watching** and serious ornithologists can arrange to stay at the house for around US$30 per person per night. Even if you are just passing through you are likely to see a doctor bird or two flitting around the gardens. Robert Sutton, Arthur's son, has co-written a leading book on Jamaica's birds; he and his wife Ann are loaded with information on the country's natural history and occasionally lead natural history tours of the south coast and Cockpit Country. If you have a particular interest, ask.

A more modern mansion is **Huntingdon Summit** (daily by appointment ☎962 0585; free), a Jamaican version of Elvis Presley's Graceland that's the home of the town's former mayor and self-made millionaire Cecil Charlton. The octagonal extravagance features a giant living room replete with antique furniture, seven bedrooms colour coded by their carpets and often esoteric furnishings, and a library stuffed with trophies and photographs of the great man meeting Jamaican and foreign dignitaries. The place is losing some of its lustre with age but still commands great views over the neighbouring countryside and an interesting perspective on Jamaica's nouveaux riches. You'll see Mr Charlton's **off-course betting shops**, from which he made his fortune, all over town.

To get there, follow the Manchester Road out of Mandeville, keeping right at the *Texaco* station. At the T-junction where the road ends, turn right onto Newport Road, then first left onto May Day Road for just under a mile, turning left down George's Valley Road until you reach the big green gates on your left.

### Coffee, chocolate and Pickapeppa sauce

It won't be the highlight of your time in Jamaica, but if you have some time to kill while you're in Mandeville you can visit a nearby factory. The **coffee factory** of Jamaican Standard Products (Mon–Fri by appointment ☎963 4211; free) is a couple of miles north of the town centre in Williamsfield. JSP makes a number of different foodstuffs – including tea, sauces and spices – but coffee, which they've been producing since the 1950s, is their mainstay; the factory roasts, grinds and packages beans for the superior Blue Mountain coffee as well as JSP's own "High Mountain" brand. The tour of the coffee plant is about as interesting as you'd expect (ie not very) but, afterwards, you have a chance to buy the products at pretty good prices.

On the same street, the **chocolate factory** of Pioneer Chocolate Company (Mon–Fri by appointment ☎963 4216; free) is a small family-run business that has been producing chocolate products since the 1920s. The cocoa beans are roasted here to give a chocolate flavour and the crushed beans are then put into a melter and separated into cocoa butter and cocoa powder. Much of the cocoa butter is exported for use in pharmaceuticals, like tanning lotion, while the powder is used for popular items like drinking chocolate. Pioneer also produces excellent chocolate bars, though it has only a tiny share of the domestic market. The owners have recently started to discourage visitors, mainly because of the risk of accidents, but if you have a keen interest it's worth calling to try to arrange a tour.

Finally, there's the **Pickapeppa factory** (Mon–Fri by appointment ☎962 2928; free), just beyond Williamsfield at the bottom of Shooter's Hill. In operation since 1921, the factory is active for nine months of the year (normally March–Nov) producing its unusual spicy sauce, made from home-grown tomatoes, onions, mangoes, spices and hot peppers. Though you'll see the distinctive bottles at restaurants across the island, 98 percent of the factory's production is for the export market.

## Eating, drinking and nightlife

As you'd expect from such a peaceful town the **nightlife** is pretty tame, but there are plenty of good **restaurants** and a lot of fast-food options and snack outlets at the ubiquitous malls (particularly at the Manchester Shopping Centre). You'll also find a handful of decent **bars** and **nightclubs**, including nearby *Jim's HQ*, one of the best clubs in Jamaica. There's a **cinema** (☎962 2177) on Caledonia Road, near the junction with Ward Avenue.

### Restaurants and snack bars

**Astra Inn**, 62 Ward Ave; ☎962 3265. Good and moderately priced hotel restaurant, though not worth the trip out if you're staying in town.

**Bamboo Village**, Ward Plaza, 35 Ward Ave; ☎962 4515. Pretty good Chinese restaurant, halfway between the town's main square and the *Astra Inn*.

**Bloomfield Great House**, Bloomfield; ☎962 3116. Italian/American place (formerly the renowned *Bill Laurie's Steakhouse*) under restoration at the time of writing, but in a fabulous spot south of Mandeville overlooking the town and likely to be top-notch. Head south on Caledonia Road, and take the first right after Greenvale Road.

**Bluebells**, Midway Mall, Caledonia Road. Reasonable spot for a cheap Jamaican breakfast or lunch, serving the usual staples.

*In restaurant listings, we have given a phone number only for those places where you might need to reserve a table.*

**Central Restaurant and Bar**, Caledonia Road; ☎962 1546. Just across from the more popular *Den* and serving similar meals, *Central* is less refined but the food is still good.

**Charcoals**, junction of Caledonia Road and South Racecourse; ☎962 9645. Good fish, lobster and natural juices at this easy-going and reasonably priced jerk bar. Closed Sun.

**The Den**, 35 Caledonia Rd; ☎962 3603. One of Mandeville's busier restaurants, with curried chicken and other typical Jamaican dishes served indoors or out.

**Gee's Café**, Manchester Shopping Centre. Best of a number of good eateries, juice bars and pastry shops at the back of this shopping plaza, with excellent Jamaican breakfasts and good cheap food throughout the day. Closed Sun.

**International Chinese Restaurant**, 117 Manchester Rd; ☎962 1252. Chinese food from an extensive menu, a short drive from town.

**Jerky's**, just off Caledonia Road between the *Golf View Hotel* and Caledonia Plaza. Good jerk chicken and pork from an intermittently open green bus; half a pound of meat with bread for J$100.

**Mandeville Hotel**, 4 Hotel St; ☎962 2460. Consistently good central hotel restaurant, though often low on atmosphere, with a varied menu of steaks, fish and curried goat.

## Bars and clubs

**Bally's**, above Manchester Road. Centrally located outdoor bar serving jerk chicken and pork and with an active sound system at the weekends. About 400 yards from Mandeville Square and a sharp left uphill.

**Charcoals**, junction of Caledonia Road and South Racecourse. Friendly bar/restaurant and occasional hangout for trendy young Mandevillians, particularly at the weekend.

**Fayors**, 33 Ward Ave, next to the Ward Plaza (Wed–Sun). Small dark venue that gets seriously crowded at weekends, belting out dancehall music and the best place for a dance in the town itself.

**Jim's HQ** (nightly except Mon). Excellent, popular club 11 miles west of Mandeville, with the country's big names deejaying Fri–Sun, and a good place for cheap food and drink during the week. Head west all the way down Spur Tree Hill, then left at Gutters for under a mile.

**Manchester Arms**, at the *Mandeville Hotel*. Pleasant quiet bar, fashioned after an English pub.

**Manchester Club**, corner of Caledonia Rd and Ward Ave. Definitely a colonial feel at this golf club, but a decent place for an early evening drink if you're cruising around.

**Merv's Cocktail Bar**, Caledonia Plaza, 11 Caledonia Ave. Simple, easy-going bar – good if you're looking for a bit of local colour.

**Sparkles**, Leaders Plaza, 41 Main St (nightly except Mon). Popular club playing a variety of dancehall, reggae and soca, though don't expect much action during the week.

**The Venue**, Manchester Shopping Centre (next to *Woolworth*). Mellow place for a drink, open to 11pm daily, and popular with an older crowd.

# Shopping

**Shopping malls** are everywhere in Mandeville. Probably the most extensive is the *Manchester Shopping Centre*, opposite the junction of Caledonia Road and New Green Road, where you'll find banks, an excellent *Hi-Lo* supermarket, craft stores, and a number of fast-food restaurants. *Bookland* at the centre has **books** on Jamaica and recent UK and US newspapers and magazines. There are two more **supermarkets** – *Moo-Penns* and *Super Plus* – beside Mandeville Square on East Park Crescent, and a good **record shop** at *Leroys*, Leaders Plaza, 41 Main St. The vibrant and colourful local **market** is at the southeast corner of Mandeville Square and a great place to shop for fruit and vegetables.

*The Magic Toy factory, in nearby Walderston, is a good place for souvenirs – see p.306.*

If you're nearby, drop in at the *SWA Craft Centre*, 7 North Racecourse behind the Manchester Shopping Centre, which evolved as a way of dealing with the problem of youth unemployment for girls. They are trained in various craft skills, such as embroidery, dress-making and cooking, and many of the products are sold in the centre. If you're not interested in the crafts there's normally some cooking going on and patties or plantain tarts worth trying.

# Listings

**Banks** Numerous banks around town include *NCB* at the Mandeville Centre
(☎962 2161), and *Scotia*, 17 West Park Crescent (☎962 2842) and at the
Manchester Shopping Centre (☎962 3139). If you're changing money, there
are cambios at the *Moo-Penns* and *Super Plus* supermarkets on East Park
Crescent.

**Car rental** *Candi*, Caledonia Road, opposite Manchester Shopping Centre
(☎962 3153); *Hemisphere*, 51 Manchester Rd (☎962 1921); *Maxdan*, 183
Ward Ave; *Moon Glow*, 3 Caledonia Rd (☎962 9097). From US$60 a day.

**Dentist** *Manchester Dental Associates*, 11 Manchester Rd; ☎962 1560.

**Golf** The nine-hole *Manchester Club* (☎962 2403), at the corner of
Caledonia Road and Ward Avenue, is the oldest club in the Caribbean and
costs around US$15 for a round and a caddy.

**Hospital** The public *Mandeville Hospital* is at 32 Hargreaves Ave (☎962
2067); the private *Hargreaves Memorial Hospital* shares the same address
(☎962 2040).

**Library** The Manchester Parish Library (Mon–Fri 9.30am–5.30pm; Sat
9am–1pm) is on Hargreaves Avenue, just above the hospital.

**Pharmacy** *Haughtons*, 18 West Park Crescent (Mon–Sat 8am–10pm, Sun
9am–8pm); *Fontanas*, Manchester Shopping Centre (Mon–Sat 8am–7pm).

**Police** The main station is on the north side of Mandeville Square; ☎962
2250. In an emergency call ☎119.

**Post Office** On South Racecourse (Mon–Fri 8.30am–4pm).

**Taxis** The main rank is on the south side of Mandeville Square, near the
parish church, or call *Manchester Taxis* (☎962 2021).

**Travel Agents** *Global Travel*, Manchester Shopping Centre; ☎962 2630.

# Christiana and May Pen

The south's two other main towns sit in splendid isolation, with the
emptiness of the interior between them. North of Mandeville, the
hills around the small market town of **Christiana** offer a view of a
very different, more rural, Jamaica, while unattractive **May Pen**, to
the east, is only worth a visit for its annual agricultural show, or for
the impressive great house at nearby **Halse Hall**.

## Christiana and around

The steep Shooter's Hill heads north from Mandeville, climbing up
above the ugly **Alcan bauxite plant**, with its lake of red mud. Just over
halfway up the hill you'll come to **WALDERSTON**, a small village at
the crossroads; turn left and left again up a dreadful track for the sweet
little **Magic Toy factory** (daily 9am–5pm). The small workshop makes
the very colourful wooden fish, jigsaws and similar playthings that
you'll see in hotel gift shops all over Jamaica – you can buy them here
at a considerable discount – and is housed in a lovely old house with
attractive gardens and fabulous views over the surrounding area.

### Jamaica's bauxite

**Bauxite**, the raw material from which aluminium is produced, is present in abundance in Jamaica's earth. Large-scale extraction began here during the 1950s, when three North American companies started local operations, and the mining and processing operations remain very visible as you travel around the country's interior. Much of the mining is open-cast, resulting in gruesome-looking red mud lakes like the one just outside Mandeville, while the ugly refineries spoil the landscape at various places around the country.

It may not be pretty, but the "**red gold**" is vital to Jamaica's economy. After tourism, it's the second most important contributor, employing around five thousand people and, more importantly, contributing about a quarter of the government's income and a half of the nation's export earnings. A third of the raw bauxite is shipped abroad for processing; the rest is processed at the island's four alumina refineries, and the resulting alumina is then sent abroad for conversion to aluminium. This last stage – the most profitable part of the process – cannot economically be carried out in Jamaica because of the lack of a cheap energy source.

The industry took a big hit during the 1970s, when Michael Manley's PNP administration imposed higher taxes on the multinational companies involved in extraction. The bauxite companies scaled down their operations dramatically and, in the face of increasing world competition and a declining price, it was a decade before the local industry recovered to a perceptible degree. Today, the industry remains under pressure, with world prices relatively low and new production centres in Australia and South America challenging Jamaica's market position. With little else to fall back on, the island has to hope that the industry it has relied on so heavily for nearly four decades can survive its modern challenges.

Continue north for **CHRISTIANA**, a small market town for the surrounding agricultural community, where potatoes, yams, ginger, coffee and cocoa are grown. Lofty and cool, three thousand feet up in the hills, the town was a popular resort for "old-style" tourism in the 1940s and 1950s when beaches and tanning were less fashionable than they are today. It's a simple one-street town with just a single hotel and not a huge amount to see – though you can organize a hike or two and a spot of caving – but if you're looking for a peaceful escape from the heat of the coast, it's an excellent choice. If you have a car, Christiana also makes a decent base for visiting Appleton and Maggotty to the west (see p.296) or Bob Marley's mausoleum to the northeast in Alexandria (see Chapter Three, p.184).

A hike to the lush gorge at **Christiana Bottom** is the big thing to do here. Head east beside the *NCB* bank in town, take the first left and then the second left downhill, where you can park beside a small house (it's not easy to find the way – if you get lost ask for the "blue hole"). From here, an often muddy track leads down through prolific ferns and bamboo to a **waterfall** and a cold but refreshing **pool**. North of town, beyond the village of **Coleyville**, the **Gourie State Park** (daily during daylight; free) has a number of hiking trails through its

pine woods; the nearby **Gourie Caves** and **Oxford Caves** offer some
challenging caving, and tours can be arranged through the hotel. With
a good flashlight you can explore on your own, though the underground routes are tricky and a guide is strongly recommended.

If you have a car, it's also worth taking a brief trip west of Christiana
to **BETHANY**. Head back downhill towards Walderston, take a right
turn beside the petrol station and bear left down a winding road that
leads through the cute village of **DEVON** and some very English
scenery. Nineteenth-century Moravian missionaries – the first
Christian missionaries to come to Jamaica – built a number of **churches** in the local area, and Bethany's, modelled on one in Hernhut,
Germany, and perched on the mountainside, is the most impressive.
The large, red-roofed church was founded in 1835 and the views over
the Dom Figuereroa Mountains and up to Cockpit Country are staggering. There isn't much to the church interior but, if it's locked, you
can get a key at the adjacent rectory, prettily gabled with gingerbread
trim. The countryside around here is green, rolling and quite un-
Jamaican with its hedgerows and dry-stone walls, but don't come out
this way if you're short of time – it's easy to get lost driving around as
there are no roadsigns and minor roads spin off all over the place.

## Practicalities

*Hotel Villa Bella* (☎964 2243, fax 964 2765; ④), 2km from the
town centre and the only **hotel** in Christiana, is one of the most
delightful small hotels in Jamaica. There's no pool or unnecessary
fripperies, but the place retains a colonial-era feel and is dotted with
interesting curiosities – plenty of art deco furniture, nineteenth-century china, old prints and the hotel's original guest book from 1941.
If *Villa Bella* is full or you prefer an even quieter location, *Glencoe
Bed and Breakfast* (☎964 2286; ④) in **Spaldings** – a tiny agricultural centre three miles east of Walderston – is a lovely old farmhouse dating from 1891, with spacious, well-kept rooms.

*Villa Bella* is the best place in town for **food**, many of the ingredients coming from its own garden, with delicious, experimental
Jamaican dishes from around US$10 for lunch and dinner. Options
in town include *Variations*, a cheap restaurant with local meals just
beyond the Syldian Court shopping centre, and the main road has a
smattering of inexpensive snack bars and patty shops. **Nightlife** is
quiet, but the *Lamplight Club* in town is open late every night and
has occasional live music or dancers.

Regular **minibuses** run up Shooters Hill from Mandeville and head
straight into town – ask them to drop you off if you're heading for the
hotel. If you're driving, the hotel is signposted on your right just
before you enter town; bear left and keep straight on for the town
itself. The *Villa Bella* organizes a variety of **tours** of the local area,
including mountain-biking, caving and hiking tours, for between
US$10 and US$30 per person.

# May Pen and around

Heading east from Mandeville, the A2 highway runs out of the parish of Manchester through **Porus** – a lengthy village easily identified by its displays of citrus fruit strung up by the roadside – and into **Clarendon**, one of Jamaica's least enthralling parishes. A right turn at Toll Gate takes you down to Milk River Bath on the south coast (see p.293), while continuing straight brings you to the capital of **MAY PEN**, a light industrial centre and an important market town with a population of over forty thousand. The highway actually bypasses the town, which is handy as there is no reason at all to stop there unless your bus is breaking its journey. However, if you're here during the **Denbigh Agricultural Show**, a three-day fair held in the Denbigh showgrounds just west of town – normally over the last weekend in July or the first weekend in August – then it's certainly worth stopping off. The event features displays of each of the country's parishes' agricultural produce, exhibits of prize livestock and a showjumping event. There's also plenty of live entertainment including singers, dancers and reggae bands and the usual array of food vendors and craft stalls. If you're planning to stay over, try to arrange a room well in advance.

*See p.35 of
Basics for
more on the
show.*

The best place to **stay** in town is the *Hotel Versailles*, just off the highway at 42 Longbridge Ave (☎986 2775; ④). If you're driving, take the right-hand exit towards May Pen at the main roundabout and there's a small signpost for the hotel about 400 yards down on your left. A cheaper alternative in town is the *Fairfield Guest House* on Fairfield Drive (☎986 4344; ②). The **restaurant** at *Versalles* serves reasonable food but, if you're just passing through town on the bus and have time to kill, you'll find a number of **patty shops** around the clocktower in the market square (where most of the buses originate and terminate). Alternatively, Chinese food at *Magic Wok* is probably the best option, near the clocktower and above *Maxie's* department store.

## Halse Hall

Rather more worthy of your time is the great house at **Halse Hall** (Mon–Fri 9am–5pm; free). The basic structure was built in the late seventeenth century by Thomas Halse, an English soldier who was active in the war against the Spanish, although the present building mostly dates from the 1740s. The wealth of the erstwhile owners is evident from the interior design; the sturdy mahogany doors and window frames in the airy living room are particularly impressive. The front of the house (you drive up at the back) has commanding views over miles of plantations and, to the south, over the less attractive alumina works of bauxite company Alcoa, present owners of the house. Don't miss the tiny **cemetery** behind the house, which holds the tombs of Halse and some of his descendants.

Halse Hall is due south of May Pen, just off the A2 highway. Take the exit south from the main roundabout towards the Jamalco alumina plant and the house is one mile down on your right. Several **buses** a day run past the house en route from May Pen to Lionel Town (see p.295).

## Travel details

### Buses and minibuses

It is impossible to predict accurately the frequency of buses and minibuses running the following routes – services are often chaotic and delays and cancellations are frequent – so the figures given below are only rough estimates. However, on the most popular routes you should be able to count on getting a ride within an hour if you travel in the morning; things normally quieten down later in the day. On less popular routes, you're best off asking for probable departure times the day before you travel.

**Black River** to: Kingston (3 daily; 5hr); Mandeville (5 daily; 2hr 15min); May Pen (3 daily; 3 hr 30min); Montego Bay (4 daily; 2hr 15min); Negril (2 daily; 2hr 20min); Santa Cruz (8 daily; 1hr); Treasure Beach (3 daily; 1 hr 15min).

**Christiana** to: Kingston (3 daily; 3hr); Mandeville (8 daily; 30min).

**Mandeville** to: Christiana (8 daily; 30min); Kingston (6 daily; 2hr 45min); May Pen (6 daily; 1 hr 15min).

**May Pen** to: Kingston (6 daily; 1hr 30min); Milk River (3 daily; 1hr); Spanish Town (8 daily; 1hr).

# Part 3

# Contexts

# The historical framework

The first human inhabitants of Jamaica were the **Tainos**, an Amerindian people speaking the Arawak language, who arrived in Jamaica around 900 AD. The Tainos originated from present-day Venezuela and Guyana in South America, making their way between the Caribbean islands by way of dug-out canoe. They were a peaceful people with a primitive stone age culture – fishing and foraging for subsistence – and they lived in scattered settlements all over the island, settling around sites with a good water source. Estimates of Taino numbers at the time of Columbus's arrival in Jamaica are hugely varied, but it is possible that there were as many as a million. Although Tainos living in the small islands of the eastern Caribbean were under attack by the more war-like Caribs by the fifteenth century, there is no evidence of any Carib attacks on Jamaica.

## The arrival of the Spanish

**Christopher Columbus** made his first expedition from Spain in search of a western sea-route to Asia in 1492. During his second "voyage of discovery", he landed at Rio Bueno on Jamaica's north coast, on May 6, 1494. The Tainos had learned of the violence of Columbus's men from their neighbours in Hispaniola (today's Dominican Republic) and there was a brief skirmish, easily won by the Spanish with their armour, dogs and superior weaponry. Columbus had little interest in the island (which he named

Santiago) but claimed it for Spain and moved on in search of China. During his fourth and last voyage in 1503, Columbus made an unfortunate return to Jamaica, his ships running aground on the coral reefs at St Ann's Bay. The explorers were marooned on the island for a year before a rescue ship could be summoned from Hispaniola, carrying them back to Spain where Columbus died two years later.

Spanish settlement of Jamaica began in 1510, when a group of settlers from Hispaniola, headed by Governor Juan de Esquivel, set up a base at Sevilla Nueva on the north coast. The initial plan was to look for gold but, other than the few trinkets the Tainos had collected in trade with other islands, there was none to be found. Nor was Sevilla Nueva a good site; surrounded by swampy land, the tiny Spanish population soon found its numbers threatened by fever. In 1534, King Charles I permitted a transfer of the capital, and the Spanish decamped to a better location near the south coast; Villa de la Vega, known today as **Spanish Town**, was to remain the island's capital until 1874.

Despite the successful settlement of Spanish Town, and the agricultural bounty that the country offered, Jamaica remained a backward colony until well into the seventeenth century. Early colonists established farms across the country – introducing cattle, horses and various food crops such as bananas and sugarcane – but mostly the island served as a stopping-off point between the mother country and the richer colonies of the Spanish Main. Ships stopped for cleaning and repairs and supplies of maize, cassava, pork and beef were taken on. Despite the low level of activity on the island, though, the Spanish soon managed to obliterate any traces of the native population. The Tainos fell victim to European diseases in their thousands, suffering severely, too, from the legendary cruelty of the Spanish. Incredible as it now seems, by the time of the British conquest of Jamaica in 1655, not a single Taino remained alive.

Because of the inability of the Tainos to provide the Spanish with the labour force they required, the importing of **slaves** from Africa began within a decade of the Spanish settlement of Jamaica. This was not a novel practice – slavery from Africa had been going on for centuries – but the new gold and silver mines of South America required a mass labour force, and the trickle of slaves slowly became a flood. Again, most of the traffic bypassed Jamaica but there was a steady growth, and there is evidence of the first runaway slaves, who gradually developed settlements of their own and were to prove a constant thorn in the side of the British after 1655 (see box below).

## The British conquest

Spanish Jamaica was not a well-protected colony. In 1596, Sir Anthony Shirley, an English adventurer, landed with five hundred men at Passage Fort near present-day Kingston and completely **sacked** Spanish Town. In 1643, the same thing was done by a small force led by a Captain William Jackson. Spain provided little or no assistance in defending the place, and gave scant impression of caring for its colonists.

In 1654, Britain's "Lord Protector" Oliver Cromwell, distrustful of sections of his armed forces whom he suspected of plotting the restoration of the monarchy, decided to send them against Spain's American possessions, far away from home. The British were well aware of the immense Spanish wealth in the area and, for over a century, British pirates and buccaneers like Francis Drake had been making a good living from looting their ships and cities. Cromwell sent fifteen ships under the command of General Robert **Venables** and Admiral William **Penn**, the father of the founder of Pennsylvania. The ships were fitted out in British Barbados before launching an assault on the city of Santo Domingo, capital of Hispaniola.

The assault on Hispaniola was a catastrophe for Penn and Venables. The Spanish resistance was well thought-out and the British troops were incompetently managed, retreating to their ships

---

### The Maroons

As we have seen, the Spanish armed and freed most of their slaves when they finally quit the island in 1660; these Africans joined comrades who had escaped from Spanish owners previously, and formed a band known as the *cimarrones*, a Spanish word meaning "wild" or "savage" that the British corrupted to **Maroons**. These Maroons lived in small communities in inaccessible parts of Jamaica's mountains and forests – particularly in the Blue Mountains in the east and Cockpit Country in the west – and, after the British arrival, found their numbers gradually swollen by new runaway slaves, particularly after slave rebellions such as the Clarendon revolt of 1690.

Most of the original Maroons were of **Coromantee** descent, from the region of modern-day Ghana, and, despite the upheaval of slavery, their shared language and traditions helped them to organize strong communities in their new environment. As their numbers grew, they periodically plundered British settlements for arms, animals and supplies, and they proved an effective deterrent to colonists who were considering settling in inhospitable areas like Portland.

Although British soldiers made regular forays against them, by the 1720s the Maroons had become such a serious menace that it was decided to take conclusive action against them once and for all. Forts and barracks were built at the edges of their territory and the British military might was turned towards wiping out this troublesome fifth column. Special troops were brought in, including a large party of Mosquito Indian trackers from Nicaragua, but, in extremely difficult and confusing terrain, they were often outmanoeuvred by the skilled **guerrilla tactics** of the Maroons. In places that now carry evocative names like "The District of Look Behind", whole parties of British soldiers were slaughtered, though one was normally left alive to carry the message of comprehensive defeat back to the authorities.

By 1739, though, the British had gained the upper hand, although it was apparent to them that winning a war against this "invisible enemy" would be costly and drawn-out. Accordingly, the First Maroon War was ended by a **peace treaty**, signed in the Maroon stronghold of Trelawny Town by British commanding officer Colonel Guthrie and old **Cudjoe**, the Maroon chief. The terms were that the Trelawny Maroons should stop attacking British settlements, return all future runaway slaves and provide assistance in the event of internal rebellion or foreign inva-

---

having lost around a thousand men yet without having properly engaged the enemy. There was little will for fighting on, but the leaders knew that to return to Britain without anything to show for their trip would be fatal. Jamaica was known to be a modestly prosperous and poorly defended place, so they set sail for the island, landing at **Passage Fort** in May 1655.

After the previous sackings, there were few Spanish left to fight for Jamaica: Spanish Town was quickly overrun, but the Spanish settlers were able to withdraw to the north coast, where they held the British at bay for another five years. The Spanish king hadn't given up entirely: in 1657, an invasion force from nearby Cuba engaged the British, but were defeated at the battle of Los Chorreros, present-day Ocho Rios. In 1660, British governor Edward D'Oyley led a force that defeated the Spanish at the battle of **Rio Nuevo**, near Ocho Rios, and the last of the Spanish finally left for Cuba. In the process of

leaving, the Spaniards freed and armed their slaves to continue the fight; these freed slaves proved an important boost for the growing band of Maroons.

Having anticipated further incursions, the Spanish had removed their valuable goods to the mountains before 1655, so there was little booty to show for the capture of the island. Penn and Venables returned to Britain and, despite the conquest, were promptly imprisoned in the Tower of London. Nevertheless, despite his disappointment over Santo Domingo, Cromwell soon came to appreciate the strategic importance of Jamaica and issued a proclamation encouraging emigrants, from Britain and from other colonies like Nevis, and offering land to settlers.

## Port Royal and the buccaneers

Immediately after the British conquest, large tracts of Jamaica were divided up between the

sion. In return, they were granted freedom, fifteen hundred acres of land around Cockpit Country, and a remarkable degree of autonomy, including the administration of justice in all cases except for those involving the death penalty. One year later, the Windward Maroons – those encamped in the Blue Mountains – signed a similar deal with the British.

For two generations the peace held, and Maroons lived as a semi-sovereign state within Jamaica. Both sides kept to the agreement, most notably in 1760 when a major **slave rebellion** broke out in St Mary, led by a runaway slave named **Tacky** (see p.170). Tacky and his followers took to the mountains, anticipating support from the Maroons, only to find that the poacher had turned gamekeeper, helping the British to suppress the uprising. However, in 1795, the public flogging of two Maroons in Montego Bay outraged the Maroon community in Trelawny and, with temperatures raised and neither side prepared to compromise, hostilities quickly flared again. Plantations were burned and planters killed, and the British army rushed to quell this internal conflict. For a while, the **Second Maroon War** followed the path of the First, with soldiers ambushed as they ventured into unfamiliar

territory, and the Maroons inflicting heavy losses.

However, the British were better organized this time and had at their disposal both dogs – imported from Cuba and quite terrifying to the Maroons – and warriors and trackers from Jamaica's other Maroon settlements. A generous peace offer was made by British General Walpole and the Maroons surrendered their arms, although not until several days after the terms of the peace offer had lapsed. Using this pretext, the British revoked the promise that the Maroons should be allowed to stay on their land, and five hundred of the Trelawny Maroons were **deported** to the freezing cold of Nova Scotia, although not before General Walpole had resigned in disgust at the authorities' duplicity. The deported Maroons stayed in Nova Scotia for just a year, setting sail for Sierra Leone from where, generations earlier, many of their ancestors had been brought to Jamaica as slaves.

Most of the Maroon communities in Portland and at Accompong in Cockpit Country remained relatively undisturbed by the ructions of the Second Maroon War and, protected by the 1739 peace treaty, continued to maintain a semi-independent status within the island.

officers who had served with Penn and Venables, their legacy still very apparent today. Officer Thomas **Hope** was given a huge estate near present-day Kingston, while Thomas **Halse** and John **Colbeck** established properties at or near modern-day Halse Hall and Colbeck Castle. The first priority of these new British settlers, though, was defence, to ensure that they could keep their newly won colony. Recognizing the strategic position of what is now Kingston harbour, they began immediately to build **fortifications** on either side of it, particularly on **Port Royal**. Five separate forts were built on the uninhabited island including the still-standing Fort Cromwell, renamed Fort Charles in 1660 when King Charles II was restored to the British throne.

In 1661, Edward D'Oyley became Jamaica's first non-military governor and, in 1664, the first **local assembly** was summoned. Sir Thomas Modyford became governor and encouraged local **"buccaneers"** to make Port Royal their base for attacks on Spanish dominions. These buccaneers had started out as a ragged collection of outlaws from their European homes, living on the island of Tortuga near present-day Haiti. By the mid-seventeenth century, they had evolved into a disparate but skilled collection of pirates, attacking ships around the region. The British saw a way of using these buccaneers to their advantage. By giving them official sanction as "privateers" and letting them use Port Royal as a base, they would provide some defence for the young colony; equally important, they would harass the Spanish enemy, attacking their treasure ships, and would be obliged to deliver ten percent of their haul to the British authorities in Jamaica.

Port Royal became a boom town. The security provided by the forts and the wealth provided by the privateers encouraged traders to set up, exporting sugar and spices and importing slaves and supplies for the growing population. Although Spanish Town remained the capital city, government figures set up home on the island alongside the merchants, and Port Royal became one of the wealthiest places in the world, with rents rivalling London's classiest districts. However, its ascendancy was to be short-lived; a devastating **earthquake** in 1692 plunged most of the island into the sea, and sent its residents fleeing for a new home across the harbour in modern-day Kingston.

By the 1670 **Treaty of Madrid**, the Spanish recognized British rule in Jamaica, and the brief era

of the privateers was over, though there was to be one last fling. Henry Morgan, most famous of the privateers, launched an attack on the Spanish colony of Panama, sailing from Bluefields Bay on Jamaica's southwesr coast. Though he claimed that he was unaware of the peace treaty, Morgan and Governor Modyford were recalled to Britain. Modyford was sacked to appease the Spanish while Morgan, having insinuated his way into royal favour, was made lieutenant-governor in his stead, returning to Jamaica with a new brief – to stamp out piracy by persuading his former colleagues to turn to a life of peace.

Naturally enough, many of the buccaneers, now officially termed **"pirates"** to mark their loss of favour, refused to give up their thrilling and financially rewarding lifestyles and continued to torment shipping throughout the Caribbean throughout the eighteenth century. But their heyday was past, and a succession of high-profile successes by the authorities – particularly the capture in 1720 of Calico Jack Rackham, with his female aides Anne Bonney and Mary Read – inexorably turned the screw on the remaining bandits.

## Sugar and development of the Jamaican economy

After the British had taken possession of Jamaica, and particularly after peace was made with the Spanish in 1670, settlers were encouraged to come out from the mother country with the offer of land grants and other financial incentives. Slowly, the island began to embark on the massive transformation from tiny colony towards its present shape and, without a doubt, the key factor in that change was **sugar**. Though first imported and grown by the Spanish, cultivation of sugarcane was to become a phenomenon under British rule, turning its West Indian colonies into much-prized possessions.

At first, there was little enthusiasm for sugar. **Tobacco** was the crop of choice, but Jamaican tobacco was unable to compete with the produce of Virginia. However, the settlers quickly realised the potential of sugar, which flourished in Jamaica's tropical conditions, and as the taste for the stuff boomed in Europe, the cultivation of sugarcane grew in leaps and bounds. The number of sugar estates in Jamaica expanded eightfold between 1673 and 1740 and, during the course of the eighteenth century, the island became the **biggest producer** of sugar in the world.

As Jamaica developed, more and more settlers were tempted out from the mother country, although most of the estate-owners, known as "**planters**", were absentee landowners, who spent most of their time in Britain and delegated control of their estates to local overseers. The planters amassed extraordinary fortunes from their Jamaican possessions and, as their wealth increased, it brought with it significant political power and influence in London. In turn, this new-found influence was used to nourish and protect the sugar trade, with huge duties levied on sugar imported from elsewhere and the price of Jamaican sugar kept artificially high. Given the lavish lifestyle led by the planters in Britain, few of the profits of sugar were ploughed back into the colony, although every plantation had its "great house" – the elegant mansions that often survive today (despite the fact that they were normally the first target during any slave revolt).

## Slavery

The success of the sugar industry, and the wealth of the planters, was, of course, predicated upon the appalling inhumanity of **slavery**. Like sugar, slaves had been in Jamaica during the Spanish rule, but on a tiny scale. Under the British, the development of the sugar estates called for a mammoth workforce and, with no indigenous labour available, the only option the planters could envisage was the importation of slaves from Africa, a business which had already been in existence for many years, providing labour throughout the Americas.

The **slave trade** was dominated by British merchants. Their ships sailed first to the west coast of Africa – from where most of the slaves were taken – carrying trinkets and other goods to barter for the human cargo. From Africa, many of the ships sailed direct to Kingston – the most important transhipment point in the region – where the slaves were unloaded into warehouses and sold at auction. From there, the ships would return to Britain, now laden with Jamaican products of sugar, rum and spices.

This triangular traffic brought great wealth to the traders, reflected among other things in the development of the major port cities of Bristol and Liverpool. Little attention was paid, though, to the plight of the west Africans, drawn principally from the tribes of the Coromantee, the Fula, the Ibo and the Mandingo. In the early days of slavery, many of these Africans were already prisoners before they were shipped, bought from local **chieftains** who had captured them in war.

As the needs of the colonies expanded, **raiding parties** were sent into the African interior to hunt for more victims, who were then marched across the continent to stockades on the coast. From there, the journey to Jamaica could take between six and twelve weeks, with the slaves kept in chains in the hold of the ship, crammed together with little room to stretch their limbs, let alone any sanitation facilities. Many died of disease or malnutrition; many others committed suicide if the chance arose, sometimes leaping from the ship rather than continue in captivity.

Despite the high rate of loss, it continued to be profitable for the slavers to ply their trade and, every year, several thousand slaves survived to become labourers on the estates or, on a smaller scale, domestic workers in the home. Inevitably, many of the transported slaves – uprooted from home and family and prohibited from using their own language – found the prospect of life on the plantations impossible, and there was continual **conflict** between slaves and slave-owners. Discipline, accordingly, was fierce, with severe punishment for any wrongdoer and the death penalty commonly imposed as a deterrent to others.

The **living conditions** of the slaves varied from estate to estate but, certainly in the early years, they were mostly squalid, with little living space or privacy. Slaves were often at the whim of cruel overseers, few of whom would ever be taken to task, however badly they treated them. As time went by, conditions slowly improved. Religious conversion played a part in this – once converted, slaves were usually given Sundays off to attend church – and encouraged slave-owners to treat slaves as humans for the first time. When food supplies to the island were disrupted, for example in the 1770s during the American War of Independence, slaves suffered badly; as a result, they were often given the opportunity to cultivate and market their own foodstuffs.

Yet, for every decent slave-owner who looked after his slaves properly, there would be another who cared little or nothing for their wellbeing. For most slaves, life on the plantations continued to be extremely hard.

## Rebellion

Given the harsh conditions of life, it is little surprise that **slave revolts** were a feature of Jamaican life from the time of the British conquest right up until emancipation in 1834, always dreaded by the authorities and invariably crushed with appalling brutality. In fact, slave rebellions in Jamaica – on average, every five years during the eighteenth century – were both more numerous and on a larger scale than in the United States or elsewhere in the British West Indies.

There were a number of reasons for this. First, there was an unusually **high ratio of slaves to whites** and, particularly during the seventeenth and eighteenth centuries, a relatively high ratio of African slaves to creole slaves (ie those born on the island and generally considered less rebellious). The island's mountainous geography encouraged rebels, by providing places to which they could escape and hide, and the high level of absentee slave-owners probably also encouraged revolts either through the cruelty of those left in charge or, conversely, because of a lack of attention to the risks of rebellion. In addition, though not exclusive to Jamaica, **social and religious ideas** fomented disorder, particularly at the turn of the nineteenth century, as abolitionists argued the case against slavery and missionaries challenged the religious orthodoxy about keeping blacks in their place. Finally, the revolution in **Haiti** in 1799, which threw out the French colonialists, provided slaves with a concrete example of a successful revolt.

The first major slave rebellion faced by the British came in 1673, when around three hundred Coromantee slaves from present-day Ghana, working at a large plantation in St Ann, murdered their owner and fled inland, massively swelling the ranks of the Maroons. Their success encouraged further revolts and, in 1690, five hundred slaves from the same part of Africa instigated a rebellion in Clarendon, though most were either killed or captured.

**Tacky's rebellion** in 1760, again with Coromantee slaves at its heart, was the major slave revolt of the eighteenth century, occurring during Britain's Seven Year War against France and Spain and lasting for five months. For the first time, a rebellion spread island-wide; sixty whites were killed, more than a thousand slaves were either killed or transported from the island, and there was colossal damage to property across Jamaica. After the rebellion, the British authorities continued to fortify the island, bolstering the armed forces and encouraging firmer dealings with the slaves.

For a while, the level of revolts died down but, in 1831, the **Christmas rebellion** was to prove the most serious slave uprising in the island's history. Though it lasted for just ten days, as many as 20,000 slaves were involved. By now, Jamaica's slaves were aware of moves towards abolition in Britain, and of the fierce hostility to such a move felt by the island's planters. There were strong rumours that slavery had actually been abolished, and that no one in Jamaica was going to tell the slaves.

**Sam Sharpe**, the rebel leader, was a slave in Montego Bay, reasonably educated and a leader in the Native Baptist church. Through the church, he organized a campaign of passive resistance, designed to coerce the slave-owners into declaring the end of slavery, but this had little chance of success and quickly erupted into a full-blown revolt throughout the island's western parishes. Though Sharpe and another five hundred slaves were either killed or executed, the seriousness of the rebellion and the brutality with which it was crushed intensified the abolition debate, both in Jamaica and in Britain, and accelerated the emancipation that Sharpe had been seeking.

## Foreign affairs 1670–1800

The threat of slave rebellions, and the two wars with the Maroons, were not the only problems faced by the Jamaican authorities during the eighteenth century. Although Spain had recognized British control of the island in 1670, the risk of **foreign invasion** was far from removed. In 1694, Ducasse, the French Governor of nearby San Domingo (present-day Haiti), launched an invasion of Jamaica; troops landed in St Thomas in the southeast and did tremendous damage to sugar estates across the country before they were repulsed at the battle of Amity Hall. Regular skirmishes with the French followed, with British Admiral Benbow killed during another defeat of Ducasse in 1702.

The frenzy of **fort-building** with which the British began their occupation of Jamaica was continued, with military establishments being put up around the coast, as well as in parts of the interior where regiments were being maintained to contain the threat of the Maroons. All of Britain's great naval commanders served time on the island, normally based at Port Royal, and the presence of such force undoubtedly contributed to the fact that there was not to be another foreign invasion.

In 1775, the **American War of Independence** had a profound effect on Jamaica. The Jamaican assembly sympathized with the thirteen colonies when they made their declaration of independence, but the British refused to concede and blockaded the eastern coast of North America, depriving the island of its ability to trade with the Americans. The resulting food shortage was dramatic – around fifteen thousand slaves are believed to have died of starvation – and prompted significant change on the island. Estate owners began to encourage slaves to grow food on small allotments, while the introduction of the **breadfruit** from Tahiti in 1793 helped the island take a big step towards self-sufficiency in food.

The French were not slow to take advantage of Britain's war with its former colony in North America, and a series of invasions of her West Indian possessions left Britain holding just Jamaica, Barbados and Antigua. In Jamaica itself, invasion seemed inevitable, but a crucial sea battle off the Windward Islands in 1782 – the Battle of **Les Saintes** – saw the destruction of the French navy by British forces under Admiral Rodney, and removed the threat of attack from the island for several generations.

## Jamaican politics 1700–1834

From the early days of British occupation of Jamaica, the chief authority on the island was the governor, appointed from Britain. An assembly of estate-owners was convened in 1661 to advise the governor on local matters, but control of key issues was kept in the hands of the British Crown. However, it wasn't long before conflicts arose between the interests of the early settlers and of the mother country, coming to a head towards the end of the century in discussions over the abolition of slavery. As creole society developed, and a new generation grew up who had actually been born in Jamaica, there were increasing demands for political power to be kept entirely on the island. Accordingly, in 1729 the British Crown recognized the local assembly as the source of all legislation on Jamaican matters.

Throughout the eighteenth century, power remained in the hands of the white planter class, with the right to vote given only to property owners. Gradually, given the sexual proclivity of the planters, a mulatto or **mixed race class** emerged who looked to their white fathers for an education and opportunities that were denied to the blacks. Although this mulatto class were not officially granted equal rights until 1832, many of its members exercised considerable political influence, and were to prove far more sympathetic to the black cause that anyone from the planter class had previously been.

By the end of the eighteenth century, the present-day **racial composition** of Jamaica was already pretty much in place, with the black population outnumbering the whites by over ten to one. Though political power rested with the whites, forces inside and outside Jamaica were soon to bring about a sea-change in the fortunes of the different racial groups.

## The abolition of slavery

In 1807 the British parliament prohibited its colonies from trading in slaves but the **abolition of slavery** itself – heavily opposed by the West Indian lobby, who feared the collapse of the local economy – was not finally passed until 1834. Despite the island-wide jubilation, though, the slaves were not yet given unconditional freedom; they were expected to continue working for their former masters, unpaid, for a six-year "apprenticeship". In 1838 the apprenticeship system was abandoned and the former slaves were, at last, free to demand wages or work elsewhere.

Many former slaves left the hated estates at the first opportunity, renting or squatting on a little landholding and establishing small farms. Across the country, missionaries set up "**free villages**", buying land, subdividing it and either selling or donating it to former slaves, who would also normally help with building the local church and school that the villages were based around.

The drain of workers from the estates, and the reluctance of many estate-owners to pay proper wages, forced them to turn to alternative sources of cheap labour. Already, during the 1830s, 1,200 Germans had been brought to Jamaica, with the promise of land grants once they had worked on the estates for five years. Other workers were brought from China, the Middle East and other parts of Europe, but it was India that was to provide the great majority of the new **indentured labour**.

Under a scheme approved by the Jamaican assembly in 1845, 35,000 Indians were brought to the island before the Indian government banned further traffic in 1917. The estate-owners promised that, once the workers had paid off the cost of their passage from India, they would be able to earn decent money to send home, before returning themselves at the end of their contracts. In practice, the Indians became the new slaves – working for scant pay under appalling conditions – and the majority never had the chance to return home.

Jamaica's sugar industry took another major blow in 1846, when a **free-trade** minded British government passed the Sugar Duties Act, forcing Jamaica's producers to compete on equal terms with sugar producers worldwide. At the same time, the development of **beet-sugar** in Europe also hurt the industry, contributing to the drop in the price of sugar and reducing demand for the West Indian product.

Although the sugar industry was far from dead, this series of setbacks forced the island to diversify out of its reliance on a single crop. A Royal Commission report recommended the encouragement of peasant proprietors and the substitution of other tropical products – such as coffee, coconuts and citrus fruits – for sugarcane. **Banana** cultivation was introduced in the 1860s and, for a while, became the boom crop as demand for the new fruit soared in Europe and America. By the end of the nineteenth century the older economic pattern of the Jamaican community had faded completely and a new organization was emerging. Only the scattered ruins of the plantation great houses and sugar mills – still found in even the remotest districts – now speak of the once great days of sugar.

## Post-emancipation problems

Jamaica's estate-owners were given a total of **£20 million compensation** for the loss of their slaves (most of which went to repay debts owed to merchants in Britain). There was no such compensation for the newly freed slaves. Life for them was far from easy and, in the mid-nineteenth century, there were two issues which caused them particular concern.

The first problem was **land**. Unless they could get somewhere to farm, the freed slaves had little choice but to return to the plantations and work as poorly paid wage labourers; getting their own plot of land guaranteed a degree of independence and gave them a bargaining tool for higher wages. Unfortunately for them, the planters were equally aware of this issue, and made it as hard as possible for the ex-slaves to get land, imposing high rents and taking action against squatters who tried to take possession of unused land. The second, related, issue was the one-sided **administration of justice**; the landowners generally dominated the magistrates' courts, and imposed heavy-handed penalties for squatting and other minor wrongs.

The downturn in the country's economy that followed the abolition of slavery and the introduction of free trade in sugar also took its toll on the freed slaves. Wages were kept pitifully low, taxes were imposed and unemployment rose as plantations were downsized or abandoned altogether. There were numerous **riots** and conspiracies, particularly in the early years of emancipation as rumours of re-enslavement were given strong currency, and there was even talk – fuelled by dissatisfied planters – of the island being annexed to the United States as a slave state. The last straw came during the American Civil War of 1861–65, when naval blockades cut off crucial supplies to Jamaica, causing food shortages and intensifying the economic problems of the poor.

The grievances of Jamaica's black population came to a head in 1865, when a major **rebellion** broke out in **Morant Bay** in St Thomas. Problems here were particularly acute, and compounded by the authorities, who removed a magistrate who was seen as too impartial and also removed from the parish council **George William Gordon**, a mulatto businessman openly sympathetic to the cause of the local people. On October 11, a band of rebels marched on the town, looting weapons from the police station, releasing prisoners from jail and attacking the courthouse, killing eighteen people.

The attack on the courthouse was swiftly followed up by raids on outlying plantations and estates and, fearing that the rebellion would spread throughout the island, Governor Eyre ordered a show of strength from the armed forces. Little mercy was shown as 430 people were killed and executed, including the rebellion leader, **Paul Bogle**, and the government also took advantage of the situation to execute leading political dissidents such as Gordon. Thousands more people were flogged and terrorized, and the brutal suppression caused horror throughout Jamaica and Britain.

## After Morant Bay

Although the Morant Bay rebellion did not spread outside St Thomas, and there was no evidence of an island-wide conspiracy, it provoked considerable change in the colony. After the rebellion, Governor Eyre had little difficulty persuading the assembly to abolish itself and, in 1866, Jamaica became a **Crown Colony**, with direct rule from Britain. This meant that, rather than having elected representatives, the governor appointed members of a legislative council who were responsible for policy on the island. Although this set back the cause of responsible government on the island for almost a century, it enabled certain reforms to be passed that would never have got past the planters and their representatives in the assembly.

Governor Grant, who replaced Eyre (fired by Britain for his role in the repression at Morant Bay), brought in important measures that helped to give Jamaican society a more modern shape. New courts were established, a new police force created and the Church of England was disestablished on the island. Roads and irrigation systems were improved, more money was spent on education and, in 1872, the capital city was transferred from Spanish Town to **Kingston**. This move was long overdue – most of Jamaica's trade – from slaves to rum – had been processed through Kingston's harbour for two centuries, bringing colossal wealth in its wake, and by any criteria the city was the right place for the seat of government.

There were downsides to the changes, of course. Taxes were raised to finance the reforms, and the unrepresentative political system frustrated the island's fledgling democratic movement for nearly eighty years. There was scathing criticism of the government by landowners for financial extravagance and inefficiency, while black leaders bemoaned the lack of any radical change and the continuities with the old system of government. On the whole, though, the new system kept the peace while preserving the status quo; the whites retained all political and social author-

ity, while the blacks were sufficiently mollified that there was little threat of upheaval for the rest of the century.

Away from politics, meanwhile, innovation in Britain's prized colony continued as the mother country continued to reap the rewards of its industrial revolution. In 1845 Spanish Town and Kingston had been joined by **railway** – the first outside Europe and North America – while, in 1891, the **Jamaica Exhibition** was held in Kingston and Spanish Town and drew a crowd of around 300,000 people. Also during the 1890s early **tourists** were brought to Jamaica, many sailing from North America on the banana boats that plied between the US east coast and Port Antonio in Portland. Trends were being started that would prove of crucial significance in the coming century.

## Jamaica in the twentieth century

The early twentieth century saw considerable **economic prosperity** in Jamaica, with particular booms in the banana and tourism industries. And the new wealth was no longer confined to the whites – **George Stiebel**, Jamaica's first black millionaire – had used his fortune to design some fine buildings, particularly Devon House in Kingston, and his example proved an inspiration to others. Inevitably, though, much of the new wealth bypassed the black masses, and serious **poverty** remained throughout the island. People were increasingly drawn to the new capital city to look for work, but many were left stranded in slums on the city's western edge with little prospect of income or employment. **Natural disasters** also took their toll. In 1907, Kingston was flattened by a devastating earthquake, and there were major hurricanes throughout the 1910s.

By the 1930s, as the **Great Depression** took hold worldwide, the positive effects of the economic boom had pretty much evaporated. The banana crop had been decimated by disease, never to regain the exporting heights of the early century, and sugar exports fell precipitately too as overseas demand dried up. In the face of the depression, US immigration laws tightened up, and the blocking of this perennial pressure valve resulted in further problems, sending unemployment figures spiralling. Riots in Kingston and around the island were commonplace, and **strikes** erupted too, with a major clash in 1938 between police and workers at the West Indies

Sugar Company factory in Frome leaving several people dead. Protests and looting followed island-wide.

1938, in fact, was to prove a key year in the development of modern Jamaica. Partly as a result of the battle in Frome, strike-leader **Alexander Bustamante** founded the first **trade union** in the Caribbean – the Bustamante Industrial Trade Union (BITU). An associated **political party** was born too, with the foundation of the People's National Party (PNP) by the lawyer **Norman Manley**. Both events gave a boost to Jamaican nationalism, already stirred by the campaigning of black consciousness leader **Marcus Garvey** during the 1920s and early 1930s, and increased the pressure for political reform and improvement in the condition of the workers.

## World War II and after

As it did worldwide, **World War II** fuelled the pressure for change in Jamaica, dramatically weakening European countries and loosening their grip on their colonies. Economically it was also a major catalyst for development – Jamaica was an important Allied base during the war and Britain was obliged to increase financial aid to the island. Jamaica was also called on to provide increased supplies of food to the mother country and, as sugar and other food industries expanded again, the disruption of shipping supplies led to the creation of local servicing industries and small manufacturing businesses. This all continued after the war and was boosted by major tourism and bauxite, whose commercial export began in 1952.

On the political front, a **new constitution** in 1944 introduced universal adult suffrage and the same year saw the first elections for a government to work in conjunction with the British-appointed governor. In 1943, Bustamante had split from Manley's PNP to form the Jamaica Labour Party (JLP) and it was the JLP that won the elections, succeeding on a populist appeal for "Bread and Butter", rather than the PNP's more intellectual call for independence. The two parties gradually drifted in different ideological directions, with the JLP adopting a basic liberal capitalist philosophy, and Manley's PNP leaning more towards democratic socialism. The JLP won again in 1949, not ceding power to the PNP until the election of 1955.

Taking office in 1955, one of Norman Manley's first priorities was the issue of independence. Both he and the British government considered that it was impractical for the Caribbean islands to "go it alone", and the idea of a West Indian federation was floated. However, right from the start such a federation faced awesome challenges. First, **economic development** in Jamaica and in Trinidad and Tobago during the 1950s – fuelled by the exploitation of bauxite and oil respectively – convinced many in both countries that they were strong enough economically to stand on their own feet. Second, **public opinion** in the large islands was largely anti-federation, with traditional rivalries between islands coming to the fore and many Jamaicans suspicious that they would have to subsidise the others. Third, the progress of self-rule, albeit somewhat limited, in Jamaica, created a class of local **politicians** who felt they could manage the island's affairs themselves, and were reluctant to share power with others in the Caribbean.

Accordingly, though the **West Indies Federation** was launched in January 1958, with its capital in Port of Spain, Trinidad, it never really stood a chance. Jamaica refused to accept the principle of federalism, arguing that it must be allowed to protect its own economic interests, even where these clashed with the other islands. Following the threat of sanctions from the federal government, Bustamante declared his opposition to the union in 1960 and, in a **referendum** called by Manley in September 1961, the Jamaicans voted categorically to leave, prompting the rapid disintegration of the federation. Disheartened though they were, the British had little choice but to accept the decision of the electorate. Within a year they had granted Jamaica its **independence**.

## Independence

On August 6, 1962, Jamaica became an independent state within the British Commonwealth, with Bustamante as its first prime minister. The early years of independence were marked by rising prosperity, as foreign investment increased, particularly in the bauxite industry. **Hugh Shearer** succeeded Bustamante after his retirement in 1967 and the JLP continued in power until the key elections of 1972. By then, the difference between the two main parties had become marked, with the JLP espousing a US-friendly liberal economic programme and the PNP – now led by Norman Manley's charismatic son **Michael** – an avowedly democratic socialist party.

**Michael Manley's victory in 1972** led to eight years of PNP rule, a period regarded by almost all Jamaicans as instrumental in fashioning the country of the late twentieth century. Until 1972, economic and political power had rested predominantly with the whites and the mixed race Jamaicans. Manley's slogans, such as "Power for the people", set out his desire to improve the conditions of the black majority and, to accomplish this, he would have to challenge the status quo.

The major reforms introduced by the PNP included a minimum wage, a literacy campaign, the distribution of land to small farmers, more public housing, and an improvement in funding for the island's education and health-care sectors. To finance these **"people's projects"**, Manley turned to businesses which had been largely protected from taxation, in particular the internationally owned bauxite industry. Increased levies on the industry proved counterproductive, though, as bauxite companies promptly scaled down their Jamaican operations, reducing the country's foreign exchange earnings. This blow was quickly followed by the effects of the 1973–74 oil crisis, which led to a tripling in the cost of the island's imported oil and further increased pressure on government spending. In the light of this, Manley sought to promote a greater degree of **self-sufficiency**, encouraging the use of Jamaican, rather than imported products.

In **foreign affairs**, too, Manley followed a different line to his predecessors. Rejecting close ties with the United States, the prime minister turned to the non-aligned movement, calling for increased aid and better terms of trade for third world countries, and forged particularly close ties with Fidel Castro's Cuba. Needless to say, the American reaction was furious; economic sanctions were applied and it became increasingly difficult for the island to attract foreign investment. Manley's problems were compounded by the **exodus** of wealthy white Jamaicans, withdrawing their capital and skills from the island at the time that they were most needed. Most left through fear of higher taxation and even the introduction of communism, but the rhetoric of Manley and his supporters didn't help as they gave broad hints to anyone dissatisfied with his

regime that there were plenty of flights leaving the island every day.

During the Manley years, politics in Jamaica became as polarized as they had been since self-rule was reintroduced in 1944. The opposition JLP, led now by **Edward Seaga**, launched blistering attacks on the "communist" administration, and the 1976 election – won by the PNP again – saw a disturbing increase in **political violence**. This was particularly true in the ghetto constituencies of Kingston which the political parties had turned into "garrisons" – distributing guns to their supporters and encouraging them to drive opponents away through intimidation. Despite criticism from human rights groups, Manley's response to the violence was to impose a **state of emergency**. The government established a non-jury "Gun Court" and passed severe anti-crime legislation providing, for example, a life sentence for anyone convicted of unlawful possession of a firearm.

During the PNP's **second term**, the lack of capital to finance his projects sounded the death knell for Manley's brand of democratic socialism. Foreign investment had fallen precipitately, local capital had been withdrawn from the island and, despite the empty shelves in the supermarkets, the cost of imports continued to outstrip exports. The government was forced to turn to the International Monetary Fund for assistance, and the resulting curtailment of public spending and the drastic cuts in social programmes alienated many erstwhile supporters. Violence flared again during the 1980 election campaign, with hundreds of people killed in shoot-outs and open gang warfare and, amid the carnage, the Jamaican people turned to the JLP for a new vision for their country.

## The JLP in power

Immediately after Ronald Reagan won the 1980 US presidential election, Jamaica's new prime minister Edward Seaga was the first foreign leader to visit him in Washington, and the **realignment** of the two neighbouring countries was perhaps the most important change in policy that Seaga brought about. The US took steps to open its markets to foreign imports and to encourage outward investment, most notably with the enactment of the Caribbean Basin Initiative (economic aid in return for free elections and co-operative governments), and foreign capital began to find its way back to Jamaica. However, Seaga was obliged to continue the cutback of government services, begun under the PNP, and his honeymoon with the Jamaican people proved short-lived.

In 1983 Jamaican troops assisted the US **invasion of Grenada**, launched to depose the Marxist leaders who had overthrown and executed prime minister Maurice Bishop. Taking advantage of a brief surge in popularity (and the absence of opponent Manley from the island), the JLP called a snap election. In protest at government tactics, the PNP boycotted the election, leaving the JLP in sole control of Jamaica's parliament, and re-elected prime minister Seaga gave himself various portfolios in the resulting government, including minister for finance, defence and culture. However, although his skills as minister of finance were widely praised, Seaga was unable to give the island's economy the boost it required and, in the face of rising poverty and unemployment, his lack of charisma and the concentration of power in his hands led to a fall in support. In 1989, Michael Manley and the PNP were returned to office.

Despite widespread fears of a return to the politics of the 1970s, the new-look Manley administration proved very different. The emphasis now was on continuity of policy and, although foreign relations with Cuba were restored, there was no more of the anti-American and anti-white rhetoric. The demands of the World Bank and the IMF continued to be met and a generally liberal economic policy followed. In 1992 Manley resigned the premiership on the grounds of ill-health, leaving his successor, **P.J. Patterson**, to continue the policy of continuity. In 1993 Patterson – the first black man to become Jamaica's prime minister – defeated Seaga and the JLP in the general election.

## Jamaica today

The backbone of the modern Jamaican economy is provided by tourism, bauxite and agriculture. A colossal amount of money is spent on encouraging **tourism** and counteracting the negative images of the island that have been seen abroad in recent years, although arrival figures have been pretty stable for several years at a little over a million people a year. **Bauxite** production has recovered from the blow the industry took in the 1970s although falls in prices worldwide have meant overall lower earnings.

**Agriculture** – particularly sugar and bananas – accounts for around twenty percent of export earnings. The potential of the sector remains vast, with great products and superb farming conditions, but the imagination required to expand and diversify output has been sorely lacking. A daunting problem that Jamaica faces with other West Indian islands is the anticipated removal of their privileged access to European markets, which will lead to fierce competition from the larger and cheaper agricultural sectors of South America. Also on the agriculture side, **ganja** farming and export – illegal but very widespread – also makes a major, if unofficial, contribution to the island's economy.

Unfortunately, Jamaica's export earnings from these industries are quite unable to keep pace with the nation's spending habits. Jamaica carries a substantial burden of **debt** to foreign banks, and much of the foreign currency earned is required to repay interest and capital on that debt. As a result there is little money available for urgently needed domestic programmes, such as education, roads or public transport. Retrenchment, built on interest rates of nearly 50 percent, has hit hard – officially, unemployment stands at around seventeen percent (though the real figure is probably significantly higher), and the glamour of the tourist resorts belies a lot of poverty in Kingston and rural areas.

The imbalance between earnings and spending has been compounded in the last decade by a staggering increase in foreign **imports**. The streets and shopping malls of Kingston are chock-full with flash cars and other foreign accessories, though there is no sign of any corresponding increase in export production to pay for it all. **Remittances** from Jamaicans working overseas help to reduce the earnings gap but even this is creating problems – it is widely felt that "easy money" from relatives abroad is creating a class of idle youngsters, who refuse to countenance the prospect of hard work.

On the **political** scene, major ideological differences remain a thing of the past. In 1995, JLP veteran Bruce Golding left the party to set up a third political force, the **National Democratic Movement**. As yet, there is little to indicate that the party has any new ideas on dealing with the country's problems at the turn of the twenty-first century. Many of the important political issues today are familiar ones throughout the Caribbean, although given the size of the island, relative to its smaller neighbours, they are often felt more extremely in Jamaica than elsewhere.

**Crime** is the key topic for most people. The "garrison communities", first established by politicians in Kingston and Spanish Town, have become safe havens for gangsters and drug barons, no longer in need of political support. Convicted Jamaican criminals have been deported to their home country from North America and Britain but, as they have committed no local crime, they are free as soon as they arrive home. With their overseas contacts, these deportees (numbering around 1,500 a year) have reinforced the garrison gangs and turned the drug business into a billion dollar industry. Gang warfare is a serious problem in the city ghettos, occasionally spilling out into "uptown" areas and thereby provoking more calls for action.

**Political corruption** is another much-lamented problem, with the party in power seen to dispense favours to its supporters and believed to use every available ploy to get itself re-elected. In the face of this cynicism, and a general feeling that successive governments have done little to alleviate poor economic conditions, disillusionment with politics is growing and a selfish material and a dangerous fatalism have both taken over large sectors of society.

Despite these problems, there remains much to be positive about in Jamaica. Democracy is still firmly rooted and there is a vigorous **culture of debate**, most noticeable in the numerous talk-shows that compete with reggae for radio airtime. There is growing enthusiasm for another attempt at serious regional co-operation, one example of which is the prime minister's support for a Caribbean Court of Appeal, to replace the British Privy Council as Jamaica's highest appellate court.

Leading entrepreneurs – most notably **Chris Blackwell**, former head of Island Records, and **Butch Stewart**, owner of Sandals – have elected to stay in Jamaica and invest their considerable fortunes in the island's development; Stewart's purchase and overhaul of the once-decrepit *Air Jamaica* has been particularly inspiring. Away from politics, Jamaican culture remains vibrant and the island continues to produce leading figures in **music** and **sport**, from Ziggy Marley and Buju Banton to Merlene Ottey and Courtenay Walsh. Whatever the challenges, it is hard to quench the island's spirit as Jamaica heads into the twenty-first century.

# The environment

Jamaica's four thousand-plus square miles make it the third largest island in the Caribbean archipelago. Unlike many of its neighbours, however, more than half of it stands over 1500ft above sea level, so Jamaica has mist-shrouded peaks as well as brilliant white-sand beaches. In fact, the island's landscape and topography vary immensely – from parched savannah plains and dry limestone forest to low-lying rainforest and wetland swamps, with richly vegetated undulating hills in between. Other than the metamorphic, sedimentary and igneous volcanic rocks of the Blue Mountains – Jamaica's oldest geological feature – most of the island's surface area is covered with soft, sedimentary limestone, at its thickest in central and western areas such as Cockpit Country

(see p.232), where rivers have carved out a labyrinthine network of conical hillocks surrounded by deep sinkholes and caves. Also abundantly present in Jamaica's earth is bauxite (see p.307), though the island's largest export mineral comes at a price – the caustic red mud deposits, still inadequately disposed of in unlined pits which seep into the watersheds and poison rivers and lakes.

There are about 120 **rivers** in Jamaica, the longest being the 44-mile Black River in St Elizabeth. **Mineral springs** bubble up from the earth throughout the island, many within caves and a few hot, such as at Bath in St Thomas (see p.123).

Over half of the land area is given over to **agriculture**, with vast plantations cultivating

## Natural disasters

Jamaica's geographical location and geological origins make the island highly susceptible to the elements, particularly during the rainy seasons, which run roughly from May to June and September to mid-October, when pre-hurricane tropical storms can cause flooding, landslides and road closures island-wide. After a few days of relentless sun and calm seas, these intense tropical storms can be exciting, but it's wise to avoid swimming or golfing during an electric storm.

Though the Caribbean is ranked third in the worldwide scale of annual **hurricane** occurrence, full-scale tempests are relatively rare in Jamaica. Twenty hurricanes hit between 1886 and 1991, the worst being Allen in 1980 and Gilbert in 1988 (see p.125), with the season

running from June through to November. News bulletins carry regular updates on the position and force of storms in the region, the Office of Disaster Preparedness (12 Camp Rd, Kingston 5, ☎972 9941 or 4101) issues guidelines for coping with a strike, and most hotels are well prepared during the season.

Jamaica is also prone to **earthquakes**; the most violent occurred in 1692, destroying Port Royal (see p.87), and in 1907, when much of Kingston was levelled. Most of the major faults are found in the east of the island – there have been over twenty earthquakes per century in Kingston and St Andrew, but only five in the western region. The last earthquake occurred in Kingston on January 13, 1993, a scale two quake that caused extensive damage.

coconuts, bananas, sugarcane, cocoa, coffee, citrus, rice and tobacco. However, farming has had a negative effect upon the island's environment; unstable mountain slopes are cleared for cultivation, resulting in landslides and soil erosion, while use – and misuse – of pesticides and fertilizers has led to loss of productivity. Slash-and-burn farming methods destroy acres of forest and animal habitats annually. The Jamaican gardener's adage "whatever you throw, it grow" is borne out in the island's abundance of trees and plants; of the **3,003** varieties of flowering plant, some 28 percent are endemic, though many have been introduced by successive colonists. Jamaica has always been an island, so all of its fauna and flora have evolved from ancestors that crossed a marine barrier. There may be relatively few indigenous species, but as Jamaica boasts many variations found only on the island it is an important centre of **endemism**.

Aside from its creepy crawlies and bats, Jamaica's animal life is pretty poor in comparison to its flora. There are few large mammals, though **camels** made a brief and embarrassing appearance in the eighteenth century, transported by planters to carry sugar and rum on the estates, but their preference for smooth ground and sand dunes made them unsuited to Jamaica's uneven and precipitous terrain. They spooked other livestock and had more or less died out by the late nineteenth century when historian Edward Long

described them as "the most useless animals on the island".

## Trees and shrubs

Jamaica has one of the highest rates of deforestation in the world (3.5 percent annually) and only five percent of its natural woodlands remain, but the island's tropical fertility ensures a richly variegated landscape. Trees are often planted for their shade-giving properties; the **guango**, with its symmetrical spreading branches, is popular, but the most arresting and majestic is the towering **silk cotton**, which often reaches more than 130ft in height, its buttressed roots spreading elegantly to meet the ground. Regarded as sacred in Ashante folklore, the silk cotton is surrounded by superstition; the silver roots are said to hide duppies, and the trees are associated with Myalist ceremonies. Naturally buoyant and easily carved, silk cotton trees were hollowed out into dug-out canoes by Tainos, and the fruits contain the cotton-like kapok. **Logwood** is extremely common and was once grown commercially for the dark-blue dye extracted from the trunk and roots – and in 1893 surpassed cane and coffee as the island's main export – until synthetic alternatives ended the trade. Bees flock to the perfumed yellow blossoms, and logwood **honey** is said to be the best available. The **annotto** was also exploited for the intense orange-red dye extracted from seed pods growing in clusters around its attractive pink flowers – Tainos used it as their principal body paint and it was a prime commodity during Spanish occupation – though it's extremely rare today.

You'll encounter the marbled blue-tinted wood of national tree the **mahoe** in countless craft items. Fast-growing and indigenous, the mahoe has a short straight trunk that grows up to 65ft, broad leaves and distinctive hibiscus-like flowers that change from yellow to orange and deep crimson as they mature. The rich red wood of Jamaican **mahogany** is regarded as the best in the world and has been so heavily exported that few trees are left – the custom of stripping the bark from young trees to extract a dye also helped to decimate populations. Those remaining grow in remote areas such as Cockpit Country and the John Crow Mountains, and can attain a height of 130ft. Another prized tropical hardwood, true **ebony** is found only in Jamaica and Cuba, though trees called "ebony" grow in other places. Now rare in primary forest, the orange and crimson flowers make it a popular garden shrub if trained.

Characteristically Caribbean, there are several varieties of ornamental **palm** in Jamaica. Often used to mark out driveways, the graceful **royal** at around 100ft is shaped like the perfect postcard palm, while close relative the **cabbage palm** manages a whopping 130ft, and has thicker and messier-looking fronds. There are several pseudo-palms in Jamaica – the unusual **screw pine** is easily distinguishable by its yucca-like leaves and spidery "silt-roots" that branch off from the bottom of the central trunk. Commonly planted in hotel gardens, the most attractive pretender is the **travellers' palm**, a member of the banana family – the name refers to mini-ponds at the base of the leaves that provide a convenient water source. Fronds fan out from the base in an enormous peacock's tail shape that can measure 30ft.

## Flowering trees and shrubs

If you fly over Jamaica's interior or look closely at any rural panorama, the greenery will doubtless be broken by occasional patches of deep red, courtesy of the **African tulip** or "flame of the forest". Flowering sporadically throughout the year, the clusters of blooms often cover entire outer branches; each bud contains a pouch of water – a natural water pistol very popular with children. Commonly planted in towns and hotel gardens for its distinctive and gorgeous crown of deep-

scarlet blossoms, the **poinciana** or "flamboyant tree" produces long brown seed pods, often polished and used as shaker instruments. Equally popular and familiar as a Christmas pot plant, the **poinsettia** displays a huge spread of bright green leaves that turn deep red in the cooler winter months; however the leaves are highly poisonous if imbibed. Twenty-nine varieties of **cassia** are found in Jamaica; most common are the pink and yellow flowering types, widely planted in urban parks. The showy blossoms cascade downward in tight clusters and develop into brown seed pods up to 2ft long. The smaller shrub *Cassia occidentalis* is equally pretty but known as "piss-a-bed" and "stinking weed" due to its nauseating odour.

The tree of life, **Lignum vitae** – so called because of its many medicinal uses – blooms with Jamaica's **national flower**, a subtle light blue shower that covers branch tips and makes a splendid show from afar. Trees are fairly small with twisting branches, heart-shaped fruits and a dense cover of dark and waxy leaves. Highly resinous, the wood is heavy enough to sink in water, and was extensively used in shipbuilding and as a suitably painful material for truncheons. The gum has long been used as a purgative and a treatment for syphilis and gout, while the detergent action of the leaves still usurps soap powder in remote areas. An urban staple known as "poor man's orchid", the **bauhinia** is a prolific purple-flowered shrub also known as bull hoof in reference to the cloven-shaped leaves.

## Fruit trees

Bearing Jamaica's national fruit, the 30ft **ackee** tree is one of the most common in Jamaica, with glossy ovoid leaves and crimson seed pods, the latter bursting open when ripe to reveal the yellow arils (see p.28 for more). Almost as prevalent are the spreading branches of the **breadfruit**, decorated by serrated, hand-like leaves and pockmarked, matt-green fruits; less widespread is its cousin the **breadnut** tree, similar in appearance but producing a two-inch nut.

**Cashew** trees are common and produce both fruits and nuts. Similar in appearance to red ackee pods, cashew apples produce the cashew nut but can also be cooked and eaten. The oily liquid in the shell is poisonous, while the sap produces an indelible ink. The **calabash** is a 30ft spreading tree bearing large globular fruits which are hollowed and dried for use as dishes and containers, or filled with pebbles to make musical instruments like the "shakka" or maraca. It's an odd-looking tree with leaves clustered in condensed spirals along long, thin branches. **Cocoa** trees are easily identifiable, with shiny dark-green leaves and ten-inch oval pods that grow in clusters from branches or sometimes the trunk, turning from light-green to brown when ripe; the beans inside are a popular delicacy when raw.

Versatile **coconut palms** are everywhere, with every part of their fruit used – be it for food or floor mats. The Jamaica tall coconut palm has been largely eradicated by lethal yellowing disease and is widely replaced by the hardier hybrid **mayapan**, a squat ten-footer with straggly yellowed leaves and orange-tinted nuts. Diminutive **guava** trees grow wild throughout the island and are also cultivated commercially for their green-skinned, pink-fleshed fruits. Fairly common in the interior, **jackfruit** trees grow up to 65ft and produce a globular, strong-smelling sweet fruit with pronounced pimples that can weigh as much as 40lb. With a satisfyingly rounded crown of leathery leaves over a short trunk, **mangoes** are one of the most beautiful trees in Jamaica, also boasting admirable shade cover and delectable fruits. Stumpy and rather nondescript, **naseberry** trees grow to around 50ft, with hairy brown fruits better known as sapodillas. Suited to wet areas, **nutmegs** attain a height of 60ft with plain but oily dark-green leaves and inconspicuous flowers which spawn a creamy yellow fruit that contains the nutmeg kernel. When ripe, the fruit splits to reveal the red aril (mace) and the nutmeg, soft enough to be chewed at this stage.

### Coastal trees

**Mangrove swamps** grow along the Jamaican coast and are central to the health of coastal ecosystems, affording protection from hurricane surges, filtering earth sediments and nutrients and providing a protected nursery for fish and crustaceans. Yet they often fall victim to short-sighted development, bulldozed to make way for housing and to facilitate sand-mining or used as fuel for charcoal kilns. Though not naturally a coast-dweller, the **Indian almond** can withstand drought and flourishes along the length of Jamaica's shores. Branches grow symmetrically, and though they don't taste much like conventional almonds, the nuts can be eaten once the

outer pods turn brown. A staple of all Jamaican beaches, the **sea grape** varies considerably in shape according to its environment; on exposed shores it lies low and twisted, but with less buffeting can attain a height of 50ft. The flat, round leaves are distinctively veined and turn a deep red as they mature. Once they've turned purple, the grapes are edible if a little sour. Fortunately very rare and definitely one to avoid is the **manchineel**, which grows to about 40ft with a wide-spreading canopy dotted with indistinct green fruits and flowers, all of which are extremely poisonous – even standing below a manchineel during rain incurs blistering.

## Plants

Borders and fences island-wide are enlivened by the multicoloured **croton** shrub; the yellow, red, orange and green leaves are extremely hardy and are also used in bush medicine. More than 550 species of **fern** thrive in Jamaica's hot, moist climate; silver and gold ferns are common, coated with a waxy substance on the underside which makes a natural tattoo. **Cacti** are best suited to the dry scrub of the Hellshire Hills and south coast plains, where some, such as the two **dildo** varieties, grow as tall as 20ft. The inner stems of **torchwood** are dried and lit as homemade torches in rural areas and bear a yellow fruit, while the **dildo pear** (*Stenocereus hystrix*) has a red fruit; both are edible. **Prickly pear** and the "smooth pear" or **cochineal cactus** are also common, the latter known as "roast pork" for its taste when cooked. Of climbing cacti, most spectacular is the **queen of the night**, which boasts a huge and powerfully scented flower that only blooms at night. The endemic **god okra**, with edible stems and crimson fruits, is often vested with supernatural powers as its aerial roots spread so far over rocks and trees from their triangular main stem that they appear to have no earth to support them. The epiphytic **spaghetti cactus** has 6ft skinny green stems that hang down from dead or living trees and bears miniature white flowers and berries. The flat-lobed prickly **tuna** cactus is widely used in bush medicine, said to cure dandruff, reduce swelling and relieve chronic pain.

Of Jamaica's **vines**, the rampant forest **cacoon** has a huge circular bean pod the colour of a burnished conker, while the triffid-type **duppy fly trap** bears the largest flower in Jamaica – an eight-inch purple heart-shaped centre from which 23-inch

## Ganja cultivation

Though there are two annual growing seasons, Jamaica's most infamous crop is mainly reaped between August and October, when the buds have received the full benefit of the summer sun and entire hillsides of 7ft bushes are harvested, the outer leaves discarded and the potent buds hung up and cured. Marijuana, or **ganja**, is not particularly easy to raise – many cultivators liken the task to bringing up a sickly child. Seeds must first be carefully germinated, then planted in open ground and stringently guarded against pests and birds. As buds attain maturity, the farmer must spend increasing amounts of time at the plot, feeding, watering and tending his crop as well as defending the valuable stems against thieves. Many use pesticides and expensive conventional fertilizers, though this is frowned upon and seen to produce a tainted version of the real thing; organic fertilizers such as bat guano are preferred to ensure top potency. Growers also face losing it all to the hands of the Jamaica Defence Force, who conduct regular eradication programmes as the fields reach maturity. Helicopters scour the hills for likely plantations while a ground crew sweeps through the countryside burning or spraying the plants with powerful insecticide. Unscrupulous soldiers are frequently known to accept a bribe in return for burning only a portion of the fields or not arresting the farmer, though as many policemen sell or smoke cannabis themselves, undocumented and highly profitable confiscations are reputedly common.

fly-catching spurs extend. A rotting-meat odour attracts flies to the inside of the flowers, where they are covered in pollen and released to pollinate other plants – contrary to popular belief, the insects are not consumed. Strings of shiny red and black seeds from the **John Crow bead vine** turns up on craft stalls island-wide; dangerously so, as this is one of Jamaica's most toxic plants. Growing prolifically throughout the island, the mimosa family's fascinating **shame'o'lady**, resembling a miniature bracken, closes its leaves to expose thorns on its stem at the slightest touch as protection against foraging animals. Equally intriguing is the epiphytic **wild pine bromeliad**, its 3ft pineapple-like leaves flourishing wherever there's a tree to host it. The rainwater collected between the leaves supports a variety of insects and even frogs, and the most protected specimens boast a pale crimson flower.

## Flowers

Jamaica's perennial summer keeps flowers constantly in bloom, and the rich soil supports a huge variety of **flowers**, from the lavish exotics of the lowlands, exported worldwide, to the delicate iris, begonia and azaleas of cool mountain climates. One of the most familiar sights is the brush-like deep pink **red gingers**. The bracts hide the small white true flower that grows from each tip once fully open, and the shiny, banana-like leaves are teamed with the blooms as a staple of flower arrangements. A close relative is the **torch ginger** which boasts one of the showiest heads in the world, a deep-crimson cluster of thick waxy petals nestled among leaf blades that grow to 15ft. Also ubiquitous are the forty vividly coloured varieties of the **heliconia** genus. Most popular are the various red shades of aptly named **lobster claw** and the red, gold and green cascade of the **hanging** heliconia, which looks like a series of fish hanging from a rod. Equally prevalent is the artificial-looking **anthurium**, a heart-shaped and shiny red, pink or white bract with a long penile stem protruding from the centre, and the spectacular **bird of paradise**, a mauve bent stem which resembles a bird's head graced by a deep orange crest.

Jamaica boasts 237 species of **orchid**, approximately 25 percent of which are endemic. Most are epiphytic and grow on living or dead plant or tree matter, and many are so small that you'll need a magnifying glass to appreciate them. There are far too many varieties to mention, but some of the most notable are pea-sized miniature orchids like **Lady Nugent's purse** or "**hot lips**", commonly seen in the pristine Blue Mountain and Cockpit Country forests.

Hedges and fences are beautified by several varieties of **flowering shrub**; the ubiquitous **bougainvillea** ranges from red to deep magenta, white, orange and pink, the colour provided not by the comparatively insignificant flowers but by the surrounding papery bracts. **Hibiscus** take on an abundance of hues and shapes but are distinguishable through the generic pollen-tipped stamen that grows from the centre. The lacy **coral hibiscus** has a cluster of tiny curling red petals and an unusually long stamen topped by another red frill, and there are hundreds of hybrid varieties. **Mexican creeper** is a clambering shower of delicate pink or white flowers used to beautify fences and walls. The unusual **angel's trumpet** boasts large white horn-shaped flowers that are mildly hallucinogenic, so don't get too close when inhaling the musky scent. **Bladderwort** is a carnivorous plant found mostly in the Black River morass, bearing trailing yellow flowers that float on water and feeding on insects lured by sweet nectar.

## Fauna

Jamaica's geological isolation precludes a rich variety of animals, and human habitation has decimated indigenous mammal species, with an estimated 37 species becoming extinct since the first settlements. Much damage was done by the introduction of the **mongoose** in 1872, which wiped out the Jamaican cane and rice rat population in little more than three years. Together with rats and mice first introduced via the galleys of Spanish ships, burgeoning populations of mongoose pose a significant threat to other Jamaican creatures, including traditional victim the Jamaican hutia or **coney**, a nocturnal rabbit-sized rodent that lives in hollowed trees or rock crevices. Other than **feral pigs** first introduced by the Spanish and still living wild in the interior 200 years later, Jamaica has no large land mammals, although semi-feral cats, dogs and, particularly, goats roam every corner of the island, especially prevalent in urban areas. The only other indigenous mammal is the **bat**, of which there are 21 varieties, referred to along with the country's huge moths as "rat-bats". Some are solitary tree-dwellers, but huge colonies inhabit Jamaica's caves, from which their droppings or guano have been harvested as a fertilizer, particularly prized for its effect on ganja plants.

### Birds

You can see approximately 250 species of birds, though many are migratory or come to the island only to breed. There are 25 indigenous species and 21 varieties found nowhere else in the world, which represents a greater level of endemism than in any other Caribbean island.

Quick-moving, brightly coloured **hummingbirds** epitomize Jamaican bird life at its most spectacular; the red- or black-billed streamertail or **doctor bird** is the national bird, though only males have the characteristic trailing double tail feathers and iridescent green breast. At under two inches, the **vervain** or bee hummingbird is the second smallest bird in the world. Its darting aerial techniques, surprisingly loud squeaky call and bee-like buzzing are far more notable then its grey-brown plumage. The endemic two-tone black and purple **mango hummingbird** is seldom seen in the urban flower gardens frequented by its braver cousins, preferring peace and quiet and defending its rural nesting sites with dive-bombing assaults and a sharp curved beak. Another nectar addict, the black and yellow **banana quit** punctures flowers with its curved bill and often hangs upside down from a twig to ensure a favourable feeding position. Equally eye-catching is the bright green back and red crest of the Jamaican **tody**, which digs a nest two feet underground during its breeding season. Squawking green **parakeets** and rare red- and black-billed parrots are found in quiet forested areas, like Cockpit Country. Glossy black, sharp-beaked **greater Antillean grackles** are to Jamaica what pigeons are to England. Their staring yellow eyes have resulted in the common name "shine eye" though they are also known as "cling clings" or "tinglings": Noisy and social, they live in groups and their harsh clacking call broken by a gentler whistle forms a constant background music wherever there are food scraps to be found. Commonly seen around cattle, the **white egret** often roosts on a ruminating rump in a mutually rewarding relationship that provides the egret with a constant supply of insects and the cow some relief from bloodsuckers.

Few sights are more evocatively Jamaican than the sight of a distant **John Crow vulture** swooping high over the hills. Though ugly and awkward on the ground, this scavenging carrion bird comes into its own in the air as it scans the land for the scent or sight of dead meat. Typically scrawny, its messy black plumage and bald red neck and head make it a convenient euphemism for people considered dirty, lazy or ugly. Easily recognizable by its harsh rasping cry is the 2ft **red-tailed chicken hawk**, dark-brown and black with a white breast and russet tail feathers, which feeds on rats, mice and occasionally chickens. Jamaica has two types of night-hunting **owls**, both surrounded by superstition. The unworldly call of the "**screech owl**" or white owl is said to bring bad luck despite its useful function as a vermin exterminator. Owls are generically referred to as patoos (their Ghanaian name), and the **Jamaican brown owl** is rarely known as anything else. Seldom seen away from country areas, the patoo feeds on moths and lizards and has a deep, hoarse cry that's said to be a harbinger of death and destruction – it's certainly disquieting on a dark night. The charismatic sea-dwelling **brown pelican** or "old Joe" frequents fishing harbours feeding on discarded scraps, though out at sea they dive for fish. Despite their dull brown coat, old Joes are facially expressive; the squat body, thin neck and long hooked bill with a food pouch on the underside give a faintly ridiculous aspect; survivors of Hurricane Gilbert will tell you that their flesh provides a bitter meal.

## Reptiles and amphibians

There are 24 species of **lizard** in Jamaica including the **iguana**; the Jamaican version *Cyclura collei*, native of the Hellshire Hills near Kingston, is found nowhere else in the world. A dinosaur-like beast, it attains a body length of 5ft. However, most of the lizards you'll see are one of the seven varieties of *Anolis* lizard – all are despised by many Jamaicans who refuse to enter the same room as a lizard and squash them like vermin. *Anolis lineatopus* has a mixed pattern of brown markings, while *Anolis grahami* and *garmani* are bright green and can darken their body skin if threatened. A variety of gecko, **croaking lizards** provide a throaty night-time call and are extremely common. The 2ft-long, dark-brown **galliwasp** has a particularly unfortunate reputation that has led to a massive decline in numbers; African superstition falsely argues that the bite is fatal and that if bitten, you must run to the nearest water source – if you get there before the galliwasp, you'll live. Though decimated by the mongoose, there are still six varieties of **snake**. Only the **black racer**, thought extinct but recently rumoured to have been spotted in Cockpit Country, is poisonous. Most snakes inhabit remote forests but are found in small numbers throughout the island. The largest is the Jamaican **yellow boa** or nanka, which grows to around 7ft and is bright yellow/orange when young, matur-

ing into a beautiful yellow and black, though during the day it rests in trees and sinkholes and is rarely seen. Popularly called the trophy dophy, the 1.6ft **thundersnake**, cream-coloured with rows of brown squares along a russet stripe, is said to be able to soothe sprains; chunks of its body are marinated in white rum which is rubbed into the skin – its willingness to be handled makes it easy to catch. Jamaica's two species of **grass snake** (*Arrhyton funereum* and *dromicus*) are also known as black snakes, both attaining a size of 1.6ft and uniformly brown with a white underside, found under logs or leaf litter. The **two-headed snake** or worm snake is so named because of its tiny head and larger tail, which comes equipped with a small "thorn" used to burrow into the earth. Fairly common throughout Cockpit Country, you'll usually find one through lifting stones or digging.

South-coast swamp inhabitant the American **crocodile** has been so extensively hunted that it is now classed as endangered and has been protected by law since 1971. The Black River Morass is one of the last places it lives wild, growing up to 12ft, though smaller specimens are more common. Generally non aggressive unless threatened, Jamaican crocodiles live mostly on small fish. The only native amphibians, there are 22 varieties of **frog** in Jamaica. Since their introduction in 1890 by the then-governor's wife Lady Blake, who apparently found their sound soothing, whistling frogs provide a regular night-time chorus throughout the island. There is one variety of **toad**, commonly called "bull frog", introduced from Barbados in 1844 as an insect killer, but most often seen squashed flat on country roads.

## Insects

By far the most noticeable Jamaican insects are the 120 varieties of **butterfly** and **moth**, which appear in all shapes, sizes and colours. Most striking but extremely rare is the six-inch **giant swallowtail** butterfly, seen only in the lower slopes of the eastern John Crow Mountains, matched in size by the multiple species of giant moths. One variety of solitary **wasp** (*Auplopus bellus*) prefers meat to pollen and stores its food in a self-built larder of loosely connected mud cells, incarcerating spiders by chewing their legs off, while cave-dwelling flies capture prey with silken home-spun fishing lines dangled from the ceiling. **Spider** species are comparatively few, and though there are none of the huge and hairy tarantula types, there are some pretty big ones; the orange, red and black **silk spider** measures around six inches. Its many-layered webs are an arachnaphobe's nightmare, at 3ft wide with attachment lines extending as far 6ft, they have been known to trap small birds. Less noticeable are **brown** and **black widows** that live under rocks and leaves, which though dangerous do not carry a fatal bite. Heavily armoured, dull brown and apparently without a sense of direction, **news bugs** are easily recognizable by their habit of bumping into walls and people; if one lands on you, it's said that important news is to come. Diamond-shaped and lime-green, "stinkies" are named after their offensive smell. Often referred to as white ants, Jamaica's seventeen species of **termites** construct huge nests along tree trunks and wooden buildings, which give off an excrement-like odour if ruptured.

### Marine life

Much diverse marine life is found around Jamaica's reefs. The sixty or so coral varieties include rotund **brain** coral, patterned with furrowed trenches, branching umber **elkhorn** and **staghorn**, stalagmite-like **pillar** coral and coolgreen **star** coral. Extremely striking are the **gorgonian** group of intricate soft coral **sea plumes**, **sea whips** and purple **sea fans**. Around the reefs, brilliant yellow **anemones** and red, brown, purple and green **sponges** provide a splash of colour, some growing up to three feet in diameter. **Crabs**, **Caribbean spiny lobsters** and spotted **moray eels** inhabit the crevices between corals. Harmless unless provoked, when they can inflict serious bites, morays open and close their mouths in a constant snarl as they draw oxygenated water over the gills. The patches of sandy seabed and sea grass fields between reefs provide a habitat for many animals; spiny black sea **urchins** are an obvious hazard – their needle-sharp barbed and venomous spines splinter off into the skin if stepped on (see Basics, p.26). Often picked up for a closer inspection by scuba guides, the spines of round white urchins are too short to puncture skin. **Sea cucumbers** are long, thin and off-white, sifting through the sea floor to feed on deposited nutrients, while five-armed orange and green **starfish** and queen **conch snails** move slowly along encircling grass blades

with their stomachs to ingest encrusted organisms. One of the most stunning inhabitants of the sea floor is the flat manta or **stingray**, often partially buried in sand. Though non-aggressive, the serrated tail spine is venomous but can only be used if the ray is partially immobilized by a bite or a badly placed foot. The camouflaged **scorpion fish** rests motionless on coral or sand looking exactly like a barnacle-encrusted rock – the spines of its dorsal fin carry a virulent poison.

Despite the effects of over-fishing (see "Threats to the environment", below), there are still over 700 varieties of **fish** in Jamaican waters. The commonest include multicoloured **parrot** fish, electric-blue creole **wrass**, red and yellow **snappers**, ornate **damselfish**, striped **grunts**, glassy sweepers, spiny puffers and rarer **tarpon** and **trigger fish**. The slender yellow and blue **trumpetfish** suspends itself vertically in the water awaiting smaller victims to drift by and into its mouth. Larger fish include **groupers**, **jackfish**, **dolphin**, **kingfish**, **tuna**, **marlin**, **bonita** and **wahoo**. The scourge of spear fishermen, silverysleek predatory **barracudas** impart a nasty bite if provoked, though the common **nurse shark** is benign unless attacked or cornered. In deeper water, **dolphins** are a common companion to boats, and pleasure cruisers often carry a conch shell to blow in answer to their squeaks.

Though increasingly rare, hawksbill and loggerhead **turtles** still lay their eggs on Jamaican shores, despite the continuing threat of capture. Though it is illegal to kill, capture or posses any part of a turtle living or dead, the trade in their meat and shells is lucrative. The Caribbean **monk seals** that once inhabited offshore cays are now believed to be extinct, and Jamaica's most engaging sea mammal, the **manatee** or sea cow, is extremely endangered; there are only about a hundred left in Jamaican waters, mostly along the less developed inlets of the south coast.

## Threats to the environment

As a developing country, the Jamaican environment has long suffered the effects of unplanned development and a lack of environmental awareness. While many of its **reefs** are still the beautiful underwater gardens of hotel brochures, they are under serious threat; a recent study reported that the island has lost 95 percent of its reefs in the last fifteen years as a result of over-fishing (and destructive fishing practice), sand-mining,

## Environmental and conservation associations

Environmental matters in Jamaica are the responsibility of the **Natural Resources Conservation Authority** (53 1/3 Molynes Rd, Kingston 10, ☎ 923 5155, fax 923 5070), which devises and enforces environmental legislation – you can report environmental outrages via the NRCA's toll-free hotline ☎ 0888 991 5005. More directly active are the voluntary conservation agencies, also useful for obtaining information on specific environmental concerns. The **National Environment Societies Trust** (46 Duke St, Kingston 8; ☎ 922 0667, fax 922 0665) and the **Jamaica Conservation and Development Trust** (95 Dumbarton Ave, Kingston 10; ☎ 960 2848, fax 960 2850) act as umbrella organizations for those listed below.

**Bluefields People's Community Association**, Bluefields PO, Westmoreland; ☎ 955 8792, fax 955 8791

**Friends of the Sea**, 6 James Ave, Ocho Rios; ☎ 974 9832, fax 974 6494

**Gosse Bird Club**, 2 Starlight Ave, Kingston 6; ☎ & fax 927 8444

**Jamaica Environment Trust**, 58 Half Way Tree Rd, Kingston 10; ☎ 929 2376, fax 929 1074

**Natural History Society of Jamaica**, Department of Zoology, UWI, Mona Campus, Kingston 7; ☎ 927 1202

**Negril Coral Reef Protection Society** and **Negril Environment Protection Trust**, PO Box 27, Negril; ☎ 957 3735, fax 957 4473

**Portland Environmental Protection Association**, 6 Allen St, Port Antonio; ☎ 993 9632, fax 993 3407

**South Coast Conservation Foundation**, 91a Old Hope Rd, Kingston 6; ☎ 978 4050, fax 927 3754

**Southern Trelawny Environmental Agency**, Albert Town PO, Trelawny; ☎ 0919 6992

**St Ann Environmental Protection Agency**, PO Box 21, Runaway Bay; ☎ & fax 973 4305

**St Elizabeth Environment Association**, 2 High St, Black River; ☎ 965 2074, fax 965 2076

**Trelawny Environment Protection Agency**, c/o Trelawny Chamber of Commerce, Shop 6, Albert George Shopping Centre, Falmouth; ☎ & fax 954 4087

**Wildlife and Environment Conservation Action Now**, Hope Zoo, Royal Botanical Gardens, Kingston 7; ☎ 927 1085

coral collection, industrial pollution and mass tourism. Dynamiting and chemical bleaching, which stun fish up to the surface for an easy catch, have also become common, with obviously disastrous effects upon reefs, which depend upon clean, clear water for their survival. A symptom of unusually high sea temperatures throughout 1995, coral bleaching has been reported on eighty percent of reefs around Jamaica's shores – killing the algae within the polyps and leaving the still-living coral to starve.

On land, **deforestation** and its associated problems are a major concern. Stripped slopes are overly susceptible to soil erosion and landslides, threatening hundreds of already rare animal and insect species and wreaking havoc with the island's ecosystems. Deforestation has been particularly severe in the Blue Mountains, which represent the watershed for the entirety of eastern Jamaica, causing water restrictions in the corporate area and an increasingly shallow Mona Dam.

For an island with such a high rainfall, Jamaica is in the perverse situation of facing a permanent drought entirely of human making. In the Yallahs Valley, a century of misuse – slopes cleared for coffee cultivation or slash-and-burn farming techniques – has left the valley vulnerable to the torrential rainy season deluges, which have flooded the valley and dumped huge amounts of earth onto former farmlands, leaving the slopes above bald and impossible to cultivate. The situation became so desperate that the government intervened as early as 1961, creating the Yallahs Valley Land Authority to rehabilitate the area through planting Caribbean pine, mahoe and eucalyptus to restabilize the slopes, although a lack of funding has resulted in poor maintenance.

Elsewhere, though eighty percent of household waste is collected by the government, the remaining twenty percent is simply dumped in open areas and gullies, resulting in poor hygiene, increasing levels of vermin and polluted water.

However, all is not lost. Thanks to the efforts of non-governmental conservation organizations there has been a marked increase in public awareness over the last few years, culminating in the first Green Expo held in Kingston in 1996, where exhibitors offered environmentally friendly goods, services and advice to over 1000 visitors. Through a US$200,000 donation from USAID,

Jamaica established two **national parks** (Montego Bay Marine Park and the Blue and John Crow Mountains National Park) as the first phase of the 1995 Protected Areas Resource Conservation (PARC) Project. The Negril Watershed has just become the third park, with a further six sites proposed for protected status, including Cockpit Country, Black River and the Hellshire Hills.

# Religion

With over 250 denominations and the highest number of churches per capita in the world, religion is a Jamaican vocation. Most Jamaicans are devoutly religious, and in this fundamentally non-secular society, faith features in every aspect of daily life. Over eighty percent of the population describe themselves as Christian, but there are also Jews, Quakers, Moslems and Hindus practising on the island alongside the American-influenced fundamentalist Church of God, Pentecostal, Seventh Day Adventist and Jehovah's Witness faiths. Popular ideology is governed by Biblical dogma, and most Jamaicans have an astonishing ability (and propensity) for quoting lengthy passages of scripture. Sunday piousness is fervently observed, reggae stars read from the Bible on stage and devote entire performances to unadorned preaching, graffiti artists decorate Kingston walls with apocalyptic Biblical verse rather than obscenities and the most popular newspaper agony columnist is addressed "Dear Pastor". Churches are at the heart of all Jamaican communities, providing subsidised housing, education, healthcare and a strong social focus – and this centrality is fundamental to Jamaican religion, in all its myriad forms.

## The development of Jamaican religion

The antecedent of most contemporary Jamaican cults and Christian sects is a wider

African religious tradition that arrived with the first wave of slaves. Considered as living machines with no Christian or human rights, slaves were denied formal religious instruction until the late-eighteenth century. This privation, together with the constant influx of new slaves, allowed for a continuing reinforcement of African tradition – although the planters attempted to quash it by banning drumming and persistently breaking up ceremonies.

**Missionaries** began arriving on the island in the late eighteenth century. Fighting against the indifference of the planters, they slowly began proselytizing increasing numbers of slaves. Owners were faced with a choice between having their slaves attend church on a Sunday or flaunt their heathen proclivities on a daily basis; they grudgingly bowed to the former, and a mass church culture was born.

Sunday mass became the only sanctioned gathering for slaves, and, ironically, contributed to emancipation, as firebrand black-activist preachers used their sermons to whip congregations into political action.

After emancipation, the British took a belated interest in the spiritual lives of black Jamaicans, and tried to "civilize" them into orthodox Christianity, but decades of religious neglect had permitted African belief systems to survive and flourish, and former slaves preferred to openly practise aspects of their folk culture. The time was ripe for a uniquely African-Jamaican phenomenon.

## Jamaican Jews

Though numbers have never risen much higher than 1000, **Judaism** has been practised in Jamaica since the sixteenth century, when small numbers of Sephardic Jews fled to Jamaica from Spain and Portugal during the Spanish Inquisition. Though they still had to worship in secret in a Spanish colony, the "Portugals" or "Marranos" could at least live without the threat of being tortured to death. Eager to avoid continued persecution, Jamaican Jews assisted the English in their capture of Jamaica by piloting ships and acting as negotiators in the Spanish surrender. Under English rule, Jews were not only able to worship openly, but were granted both English citizenship and the right to vote, going on to play a prominent role in contemporary civic and commercial life despite making up less than one percent of the population. Numbers were only minutely increased by the **"Syrian"** Jews that emigrated to Jamaica from the Middle East in the late nineteenth century. Though Jamaican Jews have only one recognized synagogue – the United Congregation of Israelites in Kingston, where the majority of believers are based – their commercial success has attracted anti-Semitic sniping, though the community's prime economic position in Jamaican society means that Jews suffer little direct persecution.

Some twenty years after the abolition of slavery, a new religious fervour swept Jamaica, initially carried along by the momentum of the newly popular Native Baptists and other Christian denominations but essentially resting upon the Revival, Pukkumina, Zion and Myal Afro-Jamaican cults that have remained active in Jamaica ever since. The **Great Revival** of 1860–61 was one of several religious revivals (also in 1831, 1840, 1865 and 1883) that signified a resurgence both of religious practices banned under slavery and a desire among blacks to rediscover and celebrate their African origins. It marked the beginning of a Jamaican religious tradition that threatened carefully constructed colonial hierarchies, and white Jamaicans were horrified at this "grossly perverted religious fervour" and "scenes of debauchery and hideous caterwauling".

By the end of the 1800s, the Jamaican elite was panic-stricken by the phenomenal popularity of the church led by self-declared messiah (and eventual lunatic) **Alexander Bedward**. His August Town branch of the Native Baptist Church adapted conventional theology, proffering a combination of black power and faith healing – he blessed the waters of Hope River and thousands flocked to Kingston for baptism or a miracle cure. He also prophesied that he would sprout wings and fly to Zion on December 31, 1921, and Bedwardites from all over Jamaica and the Caribbean descended upon Kingston to witness his departure;

Bedward stayed put, but used the mass gathering as an opportunity to spread the message. Inevitably, Bedward's black nationalist tendencies led to several clashes with the state; in 1895 he was tried for sedition but acquitted on the grounds of insanity, and eventually he was arrested as a vagrant and committed to Kingston's Bellevue asylum, where he died in 1930.

## Christianity

Christianity arrived in Jamaica with the Spanish, who built the island's first **Roman Catholic** church at Sevilla Nueva in St Ann (see p.174) in 1524. The British promptly outlawed Catholicism in 1655, and it was not freely practised until 1792; only between five and eight percent of Jamaicans are Catholic today.

The British replaced Catholicism with the Church of England, and divided the island into the ecclesiastical **parishes**, each of which had a church as its spiritual centre. The Church later became known as the **Anglican Church of Jamaica** and is far and away the island's dominant faith, though the Moravian, Baptist and Methodist missionaries who arrived on the island from 1754 established denominations that still thrive in force today.

The second-largest Christian denomination is **Baptism**, first brought to Jamaica by African-American ex-slaves **George Liele** and **Moses Baker** in 1783. The Native Baptist movement, as it was then known, incorporated numerous

African rituals into more orthodox forms of worship and was widely supported at its peak, with impressively large and still-functioning churches springing up all over the Jamaican interior throughout the 1800s. Following emancipation the Baptists were the first to set up **free villages** for liberated slaves, and became a main instigator and provider of free education for black Jamaicans.

Approximately ten percent of Jamaicans are **Methodists**, a faith strongly influenced by the African religious tradition and often connected to Revivalism (see below). Many black Jamaicans were converted to Methodism by missionaries from the Wesleyan Missionary Society who arrived in Jamaica in 1789 to set up the Coke Church in Kingston, assuring potential converts that their own religious traditions would survive within the blanket of the Methodist Church.

In recent years, the fundamentalist tenets of US Bible Belt churches have started proving immensely popular, with many Jamaicans becoming Seventh Day Adventists and Jehovah's Witnesses, while Pentecostals and the Church of God also have significant followings.

## Revivalism and Kumina

Essentially spiritualistic, the **Revival** movement, which came into being during the Great Revival, combines African and European religious traditions into a uniquely Jamaican form. It centres on the African acceptance of a synthesis between the spiritual and temporal worlds; an "animist" philosophy of a supernatural power that organizes and animates the material universe. Spirits have a distinct influence upon the living and must accordingly be respected, pacified, praised and worshipped through ritual dances, offerings and prayer. There are two branches within Revivalism; **Zionism** and **Pukkumina**. More overtly Christian, Zionism deals only with the heavenly spirits and angels of the Bible, while the more African Pukkumina worships earth-bound "ground spirits" such as deceased ancestors. Known as **bands** (the collective plural is always used), Revivalist congregations have a female (**mother**) or male (**shepherd** or **captain**) leader who acts as general advisor and governs meetings. Ceremonies are held in consecrated **mission/seal grounds** or **poco yards** which are specifically designated by spirits and marked by a tall central pole flying coloured flags to attract passing spirits and identify the site. The **tabernacle** is either in the open air, in a temporary bamboo structure or, increasingly, in a concrete building, decorated with symbolic candles, fruits, herbs, flowers and holy pictures, and containing an earthenware jug of water used in the rituals. Liturgies include the singing of "Sankeys" (hymns penned by the American evangelist Ira David Sankey), dancing, drumming, clapping and multiple-spirit possession (sometimes called **trumping**) induced by the hypnotic rhythms, controlled circular wheeling and dancing movements and the technique of **over-breathing**, a self-induced hyperventilation which results in a trance-like state of possession. Once inside a physical host, the spirit becomes an advisor to the whole flock and is controlled by the shepherd

### African death rituals

A prime time for the release of wicked duppies, **death** is surrounded by rituals designed to smooth the passage from one world to another, though these days many are remembered only by the elderly and restricted to rural areas. Within hours of expiration, the body is washed by two family members who begin at the head and feet and meet in the middle; the water is saved and poured into the grave. Mirrors are turned against walls to prevent reflections that may portend further deaths, and the house is ritually swept out with new palm brooms. If death occurred in bed, the body is placed so that the head rests at the foot of the bed to confuse any

lurking duppies, and the mattress may be turned over. Once the corpse leaves for the funeral home, the bed is left outdoors for three days to air out any negative spiritual residue. **Nine Night** ceremonies traditionally take place over the nine days and nights following a death, with friends and relatives "setting up" to remember, grieve and celebrate the deceased and ensure that their duppy doesn't return to haunt the living; food is cooked and consumed, stories told, rum imbibed and traditional dances performed. Today observance is usually restricted to the ninth night only, and sound-system speakers often take the place of drums and anecdotes.

who interprets messages received in "unknown tongues" or through the movements of the possessed. The drumming, chanting and dances are all of African origin, as are the traditional goatskin burru or kette drums (see "Music", p.342). Revivalism is concentrated in the eastern end of the island, and flocks are typically comprised of working-class higglers, domestic helpers or fishermen, with a higher proportion of women than men. Followers wear flowing white or coloured robes and cover their heads in a turban-style wrap.

Usually described as the most African of Jamaican cults, **Kumina** (also concentrated in the east) is less formally organized than Revival, and though still centred on connections between spiritual and temporal worlds and the evocation and worship of dead ancestors, **music** plays a far greater role. Indeed, Kumina is regarded as an art as much as a religion; the intricate and precise patterns of its **drumming** have had far-reaching influence upon latter-day forms such as reggae, and Jamaica's national dance company NDTC incorporates numerous Kumina **movements** into performances.

# Obeah

**Obeah** (from the Ashante term *obayi*, meaning a malicious spirit) is the belief in a form of spiritual power or witchcraft that can influence events – from curing disease to providing good fortune or wreaking revenge – and also manifests itself in individual ghosts or **duppies** (see box, below). Though dismissed by some as primitive nonsense – and theoretically outlawed, though prosecutions are rare – obeah, or "duppy business", is taken very seriously by large numbers of Jamaicans, with even the most God-fearing Christians resorting to an obeah practitioner in special circumstances. **Obeah-men** are paid to invoke or dispel a curse and usually dole out brown bags of special powders – the "powder of compliance", for instance, is comprised of roots and herbs, ashes, earth, blood, feathers – to sprinkle on the subject and bring on the desired effect – reversible only by a more powerful obeah-man. "Good" obeah-men are sometimes called **myalmen**; they use specific ceremonies to counteract evil or mischievous obeah and rid those possessed by duppies in a "shadow catch-

## Duppies

The Jamaican name for ghosts, **duppies** can be good but are generally malevolent and feared even by the most stringent non-believers. Duppies originate from the African belief that each person has two souls; after death, one goes up to heaven while the other may linger in the temporal world and can be easily persuaded by an obeah-man to do good or evil to the living. Believers consult obeah-men if they feel they've been "fixed" or cursed, and there are countless rituals, charms and substances used to ward off or invoke the spirits. A popular superstition warns that when walking on lonely roads at night you should carry handfuls of stones or matches and drop them as you go to ensnare any inquisitive ghoul – unable to count beyond three, the duppy is forced to remain on the spot in a perpetual inventory.

Alongside the ghosts of regular people, there are also specific fiends that haunt children's bedtime stories and have become intermeshed with Jamaica's folklore and culture. The **Ol' Hige** is a bloodsucking hag who leaves her skin at night to seek out succulent babies and feast on their blood. A crossed knife and fork and Bible are kept near a child's crib to ward off her attentions, but she can only be stopped by finding her skin and dousing it with salt and pepper. The **Rolling Calf** is a staple night phantom that appears as an enormous red-eyed bull draped with clanking chains and has a sickly rolling gait; to see it is dangerous, and to be attacked means certain death. Missing a foreleg, the **Three-Foot Horse** is sometimes ridden by the **Whistling Cowboy** and its breath is said to be deadly. The only duppy to appear during the day, the **River Mumma** combines the African belief in a river spirit with the Western mermaid legend. Appearing as a ravishing young woman, she sits near deep pools on river banks and exposed rocks, bewitching passing males with her beauty; once beguiled, the love-struck victims are pulled down to the river bed and drowned. The River Mumma is also one of the most commonly invoked spirits in Revivalism, particularly when ceremonies are held near running water.

ing" ceremony, commonly held around the roots of a silk cotton tree where duppies are said to hide. Myalmen are usually respected members of rural communities who prescribe herbal medicines for physical and spiritual complaints (see Basics, p.26) and minister at ceremonies to mark births, illness, and death – dangerous times when spirits are particularly active.

## Rastafari

From the reds, golds and greens that colour everything from shop hoardings to belts and buses, and the beaming dreads that adorn commercials and tourist brochures, the outer trappings of Jamaica's newest and most visible religious movement are inescapable. **Rastafari** has influenced all aspects of society from art and craft to politics, academia, language and particularly music (see p.346), but the movement was not always looked upon so favourably. The last 25 years have seen a complete societal volte-face from widespread revulsion and persecution (a favourite police pastime in the 1960s was to arrest Rastas on ganja charges and shear off their locks; as sacrilegious as the cutting of hair is to Sikhs) to the tentative acceptance of today. Nevertheless older Jamaicans still retain a deepseated prejudice against the "Blackheart Man", and despite a few notable exceptions, dreadlockwearing Rastafarians are poorly represented within the professions, their more prestigious supporters preferring to defend the faith without displaying the frowned-upon outer trappings.

### The development of the faith

Kickstarted in 1930s Kingston by Marcus Garvey, the **Rastafarian** movement centred on the capital and quickly attracted some vociferous advocates, and provoked widespread antagonism in the broader society. One of the most provocative early sympathizers was **Claudius Henry**, head of the self-made Kingston-based African Reform Church, and something of a charlatan. Aligning himself with Rastas through public speeches on white corruption and the necessity of repatriation, in 1959 he enraged the poorest sections of Jamaican society through the sale of thousands of cards purporting to be a ticket back to Africa. Hundreds of eager exiles sold all their furniture and descended upon Kingston on October 5 only to be disappointed as Henry reneged on his promises. The movement was further maligned

when Henry's church was raided and a quantity of detonators, guns, swords and conch shells packed with ganja were seized. Henry was imprisoned, but reports that his son was training a crack team of armed Rastas in preparation for an overthrow of the government led to a national manhunt and an island-wide state of emergency; a public relations disaster for a generally pacific movement.

Among early Rasta elders of a more sincere nature, **Leonard Howell** stands out as one of the most influential father figures. He established a Rasta commune at **Pinnacle**, an abandoned great house near Sligoville in St Catherine, where converts lived a self-sufficient lifestyle praising Jah, growing food crops and cultivating ganja. Despite countless police raids the community flourished for over thirteen years until Howell's 1953 arrest and permanent committal to an asylum. Those Pinnacle members who were not incarcerated drifted back to the slums of west Kingston, establishing the Back'o'Wall and the Dungle strongholds described in Orlando Patterson's seminal novel *The Children of Sisyphus* (see "Books", p.360) and setting up Jamaica's oldest Rastafarian camp at Bull Bay, east of Kingston. By the late 1950s, Rastafari was a serious faction in the volatile sphere of Jamaican religion, with at least fifteen different sects practising in Kingston alone. Yet the wider view, fuelled by hysterical press reports, was of a drug-crazed, violent underclass plotting the mass murder of white Jamaicans. Police harassment ensued throughout the 1960s, with Rastafarian communities bulldozed without notice and countless followers beaten and thrown into jail.

However, by the 1970s, things began to look more favourable. Poor Jamaicans in their thousands began to identify with the movement's militant analysis of a wicked state and its apparent disdain for the lot of the black sufferer. The socialist Michael Manley was the first politician to use the Rasta faith to his advantage –during a visit to Ethiopia in 1970 Manley was presented with an ornamental staff by Haile Selassie; a sacred relic that he dubbed the **"Rod of Correction"** and transported to every election meeting in every small village during the 1972 election campaign. Always favourable to a little showmanship, Jamaicans greeted the appearance of the sacred rod with evangelical fervour, and Manley reinvented himself as the Rastas' ally, employing their lexicon in

## Women in Rastafari

Inherently patriarchal, the traditional Rastafarian attitude towards **women** takes direction from Biblical concepts of an evil, impure and a potentially corrupting influence upon man. Initially, women ("daughters" or "sistren") could only be recognized within the movement and be shown their own innate sin through the guidance of a "king-man", the physical and spiritual ruler of the Rasta queen who takes responsibility for balancing her thoughts and for her spiritual development. Women are expected to be receptive to spiritual instruction at all times, and – unlike males – they are required to cover their hair when praying. They must never be seen in public without a hat or headscarf, and must dress modestly, avoiding revealing clothes (particularly trousers) and make-up. They are considered unclean during menstruation, when they are not permitted to prepare food for others or attend communal prayer sessions, and in camps are often completely isolated and excused from chores. Women are also greatly excluded from worship, prohibited from leading rituals and sharing the chalice and sometimes excluded from the most significant nyabinghis. However, since the 1970s and the rise of the more egalitarian Twelve Tribes group, women have begun to assert themselves within the movement, often with the active support of progressive, usually young, male Rastas, taking respected positions in the hierarchy and participating in all celebrations.

speeches and calling himself the "people's Joshua", able to lead Jamaicans into deliverance. He swept to victory on election day with the tacit support of the Rastafarian community and its many sympathizers. Governmental recognition of Rastafari was lent untold weight by the worldwide influence of **Bob Marley and the Wailers**, who brought international attention to Jamaica and forced an acknowledgement of the movement's legitimacy at home, and suddenly–almost overnight–the tide of public antipathy turned. Dreadlocks became chic and reggae Jamaica's number-one export, but these halcyon days were short-lived. With popularity came a certain commercialization of the faith, with many Rastas turning to the financial gains of the international ganja trade rather than to Jah. Conspiracy theories about infiltration by the CIA were supported to a degree even by Manley, who believed that his programme of "economic socialism" was deliberately destabilized by the US government. Twinned with the death of chief ambassador Marley in 1981, this general degeneration meant a loss of international prominence and local momentum, but Rastafari continues to develop its political and ideological strategies on home ground, remaining one of the most unique, challenging and fascinating of twentieth-century religions.

Though true figures are probably far greater, it is estimated that there are around 100,000 Rastafarians in modern Jamaica, many now describing themselves as "twenty-first century Rastas"; they allow women a more prominent and egalitarian role (see box) and even question the divinity of Selassie and criticize his questionable human rights record. Its worth bearing in mind that, though not all contemporary Rastafarians are orthodox followers. Known as **wolves** (criminals), **goats** (hypocrites), **foxes** (tricksters) and **jackasses** (novelty followers), many embrace the faith superficially, letting their locks tumble down for all to see, becoming "Rent-a-dreads" (see p.250), smoking the sacred herb and pontificating about Jah, Ethiopia and their personal friendship with brother Bob, but lacing their ganja with cocaine and washing down their jerk pork with a white rum.

### Beliefs and rituals

The Rastafari faith has its roots in the teachings of black activist and National Hero **Marcus Garvey** (see p.172). He advocated an anti-imperialistic, pro-black philosophy and prophetically urged Jamaican followers to "Look to Africa, where a Black King shall be crowned". When **Ras Tafari Makonnen** was crowned Negus of Ethiopia in 1930, taking the title Emperor Haile Selassie, King of Kings, Lord of Lords, Conquering Lion of the Tribe of Judah, Jamaicans looked to their bibles and interpreted his title as proof of divinity; Garvey was christened the **Black Moses** and Selassie became a messiah sent to redeem black people from their suffering at the hands of white oppressors.

Rastafari places Africans as the direct descendants of the original Hebrew Israelites and Africa as the promised land, offering a restructuring of black identity and an emphasis on black culture lost and maligned by centuries of "slave mentality". As a colonized country, Jamaica is part of the white, Western system of corruption and "downpression" – **Babylon** – which will ultimately destroy itself through its own innate wickedness in an appropriately apocalyptic manner.

The first tenet of Rastafari is the acceptance of Haile Selassie as God or **Jah**. *Kebre Negast*, the Ethiopian version of the Christian bible, places him in a legendary line of Ethiopian kings stretching directly back to King Solomon and Queen Sheba; it states that the Ark of the Covenant (and therefore the God of Israel) rests in Ethiopia rather than Jerusalem, and that Selassie is the 225th incarnation of the divinity – a latter-day Christ. Though the Rastafarian elders granted a private audience with Selassie during his 1966 visit to Jamaica report him saying "Holy priests, warriors and traitors, be still and know that I am He", Selassie never publicly acknowledged himself as a god and was said to be frightened rather than gratified by the adulation he received. Selassie died in 1975, but to Rastafarians, he became even more powerful – only the evil die, and as the Rastaman lives his life in the appropriate spiritual manner, his soul is immortal.

A second central doctrine is African **repatriation**, which became a real possibility through Haile Selassie's gift of land at Shashamene in Ethiopia for black people to return "home" to. Though the few who made the journey found life equally as harsh as in Jamaica, the belief in Africa – particularly Ethiopia or **Zion** – as a spiritual home persists amongst older Rastas. Younger followers, though, point to 1966, when Selassie publicly advised Rastafarians that they should "liberate themselves in Jamaica" before removing to Africa. The new cry of "liberation before repatriation" emerged, alongside a new politicization – traditionally, Rastas do not vote and refuse to enter the corrupt world of "politricks", but following Selassie's words, the movement became intensely political, with popular adherents such as Peter Tosh publicly decrying the manifestations of the bloodsucking Babylon "shitstem".

Most Rastafarians abide by basic principles taken from the bible. Proverb 15:17 "Better is a dinner of herbs where love is, than a stalled ox and hatred therewith" directs the strict **Ital** (nat-

ural and unprocessed) **diet**: no salt in cooking, no meat (pork, lobster and shellfish are particularly avoided, though many eat small fish – anything larger than 12in is probably predatory and representative of cannibalistic Babylon), and few dairy products. Some even abstain from rice and bread, eating only home-grown vegetables and pulses. Animal by-products such as leather and lard are also prohibited, as are alcohol, cigarettes and chemical stimulants. **Ganja**, however – or "herb", as Rastas prefer to call it – is seen as a religious sacrament, as referred to in Psalm 104:14 "He causeth the grass to grow for the cattle, and the herb for the service of man" and in many others. Though many followers smoke pretty much continually to aid their meditations or "reasonings", ganja is primarily used at prayer meetings when the communal pipe (chalice, cutchie or chillum) is stoked with the finest herb available, blessed with a prayer and passed round the group to the left. Alleged to have first grown around King Solomon's grave, the "holy herb" is said to enable deep penetration of thought as well as permitting a higher level of spirituality that transcends the petty distractions of the Babylonian world. **Reasoning** is central to the Rastafari faith, designed to reveal truth and elucidate the wickedness of the world and the Rasta position within it. Alongside these ad-hoc sessions, Rastafarians hold more organized gatherings, usually outdoors, known as **grounations** or **nyabinghis**, which go on for as long as three days.

**Dreadlocks** are also a biblical directive; Leviticus 21:5 commands that "They shall not make baldness upon their head, neither shall they shave off the corner of their beard, nor make cuttings in the flesh", and orthodox Rastafarians cover their hair in a knitted hat or wrap called a **tam**, believing it indiscreet and immodest to show it off. The reference to cutting the flesh informs Rasta opposition to surgery; most prefer to trust in herbal **bush medicine** and supplement their diet with a variety of stamina-building fruit drinks and herbal tonics such as the "roots wine" concoction consumed by Rastas and non-believers island-wide.

Finally, the Rastafarian **colours** of red, black, gold and green have a deep significance. Red symbolizes the blood spilled in Jamaican history, black is the African skin of 97 percent of the population, gold is the hope for the victory over oppression and green represents the fertile land of Jamaica – and Ethiopia.

## Sects

Though there have been many attempts to co-ordinate the Rastafarian movement, there are hundreds of divergent belief strands, sects and methods of worship. The **Rastafarian Centralization Organization** represents the newest attempt to unify the disparate chapters of Rastafari, holding yearly conferences and speaking for the wider movement on common issues. In recent years, the development of new sects with differing interpretations of the faith have caused some level of internal division. Some (including several of the Marley family) have moved towards the more Christian-oriented **Ethiopian Orthodox Church**, while others (like Marley himself) have opted to join the **Twelve Tribes of Israel** sect. Well-organized and well-connected, Twelve Tribes is now one of the more prosperous branches of Rastafari, with chapters in the UK and America, as well as one of the more progressive, with women taking a far more equal role. Members must read a chapter of the Bible every day, and are assigned a name and a colour based on twelve "houses" related to birth months (see box), and music plays a strong part in ceremony. Controversially, Twelve Tribes believe that redemption will be limited to only their 144,000 chosen few, and use the names Haile Selassie and Jesus Christ interchangeably when referring to God. At the other end of the spectrum, members of the reclusive and strictly orthodox **Bobo Shanti** sect are the high priests of Rasta, choosing to reject wider society and live self-sufficiently in semi-rural communes called **camps**, wearing their locks wrapped tightly in a cloth turban rather than the conventional knitted tam. Prayer meetings are continuous, and members leave only to sell the palm brooms and leather sandals made on site or to purchase foodstuffs that the commune is unable to produce.

---

### Houses and colours of the Twelve Tribes of Israel

The houses and colours of the Twelve Tribes of Israel begin in April according to the ancient Egyptian calendar used by the Hebrews or "Children of Israel". They are: April: Reuben, silver; May: Simeon, gold; June: Levi, purple; July: Judah, brown; August: Issachar, yellow; September: Zebulun, pink; October: Dan, blue; November: Gad, red; December: Asher, grey; January: Naphtali, green; February: Joseph, white; March: Benjamin, black.

---

# Music

Close your eyes practically anywhere in Jamaica and you'll hear music. Radios blare on the street, buses pump out non-stop dancehall and every Saturday night the vibrations of a thousand sound systems waft through the evening air. Music is a serious business here, generating an average of 100 record releases per week and influencing every aspect of Jamaican culture – from dress to speech to attitude. Reggae – and specifically the current strain of DJ-based dancehall – dominates, but Jamaicans are catholic in their musical tastes:

soul, hip-hop, rock, gospel and the ubiquitous country and western are popular, and international artists like Johnny Cash, Roberta Flack and Michael Bolton frequently play to sell-out Jamaican crowds.

## The evolution of Jamaican music

Jamaica has long been a musical island. The simple rhythms of the Amerindian Tainos were adopted by the Maroons; the drumming, Coromantee chants and songs of their **Myal** religious ceremonies and related **Kumina** dance movements (see "Religion", p.337) became the island's first established musical form. Principal instruments included the bamboo and Coromantee nose flutes, abengs (cow horns), conch shells and strum-strums – home-made banjos fashioned from a hollowed calabash strung with horsehair. These provided the melody, but by far the most important instruments were the gumbe and ebo **drums**, supplemented by **percussion** from shakers, scrapers and graters. But while the Maroons were sounding their drums and abeng horns through the hills, plantation slaves were expressing themselves in a considerably more restricted environment. Recognizing the drum as a principal instru-

---

### Traditional Jamaican dance forms

The syncretism of African and European culture in the plantations and beyond is particularly visible in traditional **dance**. Much of it emanates from the moves performed at Myal or Revival religious ceremonies, and most dances are purely African, often revolving around "dip and kotch" up-and-down movements or shuffling, hip-swinging styles that parallel the counter-clockwise movements of ritual dance. One of the most interesting dances is **etu**, danced at Nine Night Festivities (see "Religion", p.336), but otherwise performed only in Hanover by descendants of the original community of Nigerian slaves. It revolves around a process called "shawling", where the Revival Queen throws a scarf around the neck of

a fellow dancer who is ceremoniously dipped back, giving each individual a chance to demonstrate some solo footwork from the standard pose of a slight but flat-footed bent-kneed crouch. Still actively practised in Portland, **brukin' party** is danced to celebrate the emancipation of Africans from slavery; groups of red and blue sets perform in a mock contest before the king and queen of each colour.

Many of Jamaica's most well-known dance forms are incorporated into performances by the island's professional dance companies, and you can see practically every style ever danced at the annual Heritage Festival held each October in Kingston (see Basics, p.35).

---

ment of African warfare, the British tried to smother the provocative music of their minions, going so far as to prohibit "the beating of drums, barrels, gourds, boards or other such-like instruments of noise".

Yet African musical traditions survived on the plantations, most notably in the annual **Jonkonnu** masquerade parade, contemptuously dubbed "Pickaninny Christmas" by the whites. Jonkonnu was originally a religious ceremony using music and dance to evoke spirits – and named for its principal rhythmic component, the jawbone of a cow or horse played by scraping a stick across the teeth – and appropriated on the plantations to become a secular travelling pantomime. It incorporated British fife and drum marching rhythms and featured the fixed characters of a cow- or horse-headed leader followed by a king, queen and policeman, with companies of **Set Girls**, grouped by coloured sashes and skin tone. Jonkonnu is resurrected today as a tourist attraction. Other celebrations, such as those marking the end of the plantation year, were more European in flavour, with English maypole and morris dancing, and French quadrilles.

Another significant development was the rise of the **folk song**, created by workers in the cane and banana fields as a way to alleviate the arduous hard labour – an oral tradition that survives today. In the enormous canon of Jamaican folk music, there are traces of African, British, Irish and Spanish musical and vocal traditions, and heavy doses of Nonconformist hymns, arrangements and singing styles. Each of these influences is blended with characteristic Jamaican wit, irreverence and creativity. There are songs for courting, marrying, digging, drinking, playing ring games, burying – and just for singing, too. One of the all-time classics is "Hill and Gully Rider", a timeless ode to transport on an island strong on hills and weak on roads.

## The roots of reggae: burru to mento

After emancipation, the influx of free African workers rekindled support for the less European aspects of Jamaican music and society. The Great Revival of 1860–61 (see p.336) saw a massive resurrection of support for Myal, Kumina and Afro-Pentecostal Revival religious forms within which drumming, chanting and singing form an integral part of worship. The new prominence of the master **burru** drummer and his topical,

wickedly humorous social commentary signified the return of the **drum** to the heart of Jamaican music. A version of the African griot (a travelling one-man information agency who brought gossip and news to rural communities), the burru man originally accompanied fertility rites and played in plantation cane fields to keep machetes swinging to a steady pace, but later became a sort of smutty strolling minstrel. Burru songs were commonly associated with sinful and indecent practices, and dealt with situations seen as taboo in everyday speech. Musically influenced by Pukkumina and Revivalist drumming, the burru man would accompany himself on a three-part set of drums known today as **akete**, with complicated rhythms that would eventually work their way into Rastafarian music and develop into ska, rocksteady and finally reggae.

Over time, the burro man added a booming rhumba box (a wooden box with a hole on one side covered by metal strips which are plucked for an elementary bass sound) and home-made bamboo fifes, piccolos and fiddles to his repertoire. By the turn of the twentieth century, groups of burro men were banding together to perform at jump-ups and parties, singing souped-up and sophisticated versions of traditional folk songs – burru had become **mento** and Jamaican popular music was born. With a syncopated rhythm that got hips gyrating and bodies dipping forward or back in Kumina-esque abandon (a style of movement revived in the "bogle" dance of the early 1990s), pelvis-centred mento was closely related to calypso – the music of nearby Trinidad and Tobago – both through a predilection for rhythmic and lyrical sexual bawdiness and its humorous social commentary, and it dominated the Jamaican music scene for the first decades of this century. You'll still see mento trios–often referred to as calypso bands – performing welcome songs at north-coast hotels or forming the "authentic Jamaican culture" portion of an all-inclusive floor show.

## Big bands to ballads

By the early 1940s, mento was waning in popularity as thousands left the island to fight for Britain in World War II or find work in Cuba, Latin American and the US. They returned with a taste for new rhythms and musical styles – rhumba, salsa and merengue – as well as new musical technology; phonograph records and cheap radio sets, widely available and affordable for the first time. Taking their influence from Count Basie and Duke Ellington, **big bands** such as the Eric Deans Orchestra found moderate success playing international standards and cleaned-up versions of mento hits at hotel floor shows – the best were put on vinyl by West Indies Recording Limited (WIRL), a record label owned by then-entrepreneur Edward Seaga. However, despite the quality of these tightly orchestrated performances, the big bands were bypassed by the majority of Jamaicans in favour of the radio stations beaming black American R&B from transmitters in Florida.

By the early 1950s, Jamaica's music scene was concentrated largely in a few pockets of southwest Kingston that were later to spawn the island's best-known musical luminaries. The desperately poor communities of Trench Town, Jones Town, Denham Town and Greenwich Farm offered plenty of dancehalls and street corners where quick-thinking impresarios like **Duke Reid**, **Prince Buster** and **Clement "Coxsone" Dodd** played for the people on huge mobile disco sets, taking the latest R&B or blues to areas where few could afford to see a big band play live. Reid and Dodd were the first to exploit the full commercial potential of the **sound system** (see box, opposite), vying with each other to see who could spin the best selection, often acquired on record-buying sorties to the US, and employing the braggadocio that characterizes today's dancehall posturing. An ex-policeman who always carried a firearm, Reid was prone to arrive at a dance dressed to the nines in sequins and leather, his guns

## The producers

From the 1950s to the late 1960s, **Duke Reid** and **Coxsone Dodd** – along with King Edwards, although he never became a top producer –dominated Jamaica's music scene, commanding heavyweight respect among the music fraternity and churning out the majority of the island's hits. This pair of musical titans are widely credited with controlling Jamaican recording as the industry shifted focus from ska to rocksteady, and their "big fish in a small pond" infamy has shaped the way that the industry works at a basic level: a producer raises enough funds to build a studio; he then hires a team of session musicians to lay down rhythm tracks and scouts for a talented arranger to handle the daily running of recording sessions and Sunday auditions. The producer then chooses the right combination from his pool of vocalists, songs and rhythm tracks, puts it all together, presses vinyl copies and releases it.

Though the reign of Reid and Dodd remained watertight until the late 1960s, the prevailing mood had changed by the early 1970s. Artists got sick of being paid a single fee while the producers reaped the royalty benefits, and in-house arrangers balked at doing all the work while the producers sat back and enjoyed the rewards. As starting a label was merely a matter of raising the funds for studio time and vinyl pressing, a new breed of independent producer emerged. Some lasted no longer than a couple of releases, but others like Joseph Hookim, Jack Ruby, Harry "J" Johnson, Bunny "Striker" Lee, Joe Gibbs, Joe Higgs, Henry "Junjo" Lawes, Sonia Pottinger, Clancy Eccles and Augustus Pablo produced some of the finest reggae made in the 1970s. The most infamous and instrumental independent, however, was the eminent "Upsetter" **Lee "Scratch" Perry**, who started out as a bouncer for Prince Buster and graduated to running Coxsone's Studio One, where he worked with Marley and the Wailers on the definitive singles (*Small Axe*, *Duppy Conqueror*, *Sun Is Shining*, *Satisfy My Soul*) that were later reworked on the Island albums. In the late 1960s he built his **Black Ark** studio and set up the famous **Upsetter** label, releasing classic tracks such as Junior Murvin's *Police and Thieves*, Max Romeo's *Sipple Out Deh* (*War Inna Babylon*) and the definitive roots reggae LP *Heart Of The Congos*. Perry remained at reggae's cutting edge until the late 1970s, becoming one of the chief innovators of dub (see p.347) as a patron of the late King Tubby, before his legendary – and often consciously cultivated – mental instability (planting records in his garden, and burning down his own studio in a fit of pique) and refusal to compromise his musical vision to commercial demands led to a decline in sales.

## The cult of the sound system

Since the mid-1950s when Duke Reid and Coxsone Dodd discharged the first shots in a battle of heavy wattage, mobile discos known as **sound systems** have been intrinsic to the Jamaican music scene, laying the foundations of each genre's development, providing an opportunity to test crowd response or break new talent, and inspiring Jamaicans to follow their sound of choice with a loyalty that sometimes descends into antagonism. A simple arrangement of high-powered amplifiers and momentous speaker columns customized to give a heavy, belly-rolling bass, the sound system began as a way of bringing music to those who couldn't afford nightclub or stageshow cover charges, and is now the major form of entertainment for young Jamaicans. Some come to hear their favourite selector, the man who employs an almost clairvoyant intuition to play just what the people want, while others come for the prospect of hearing amateur and professional DJs chatting lyrics over a rhythm track – a tradition that began with a couple of introductory one-liners and expanded to full-blown commentaries – but it's the unique "dancehall vibe" that most people come to savour. Whether it's a country dance or a high-fashion Kingston session, the panorama is the same; packed with sweaty patrons bub-

bling alone or intertwining loins in a complicated exchange of body heat as rum and ganja fumes mingle with the steam from pots of mannish water soup, smoke from jerk chicken stands and the shouts of "Wheel and come again mi selectah!" as the music reaches a peak.

Since the early days when Dodd would set up on an opposite corner to Reid and try to poach his crowd with a mightier bass and a craftier play-list, **rivalry** has been central to sound culture – with the fiercest, most cacophanous battles known as "clashes". Buying a larger amp or a new set of speakers is one way of achieving dominance, but the most popular method is still to spin an exclusive record, a one-off "dub plate" acetate voiced over by the latest singer or DJ.

In the 1990s, the king of the sound-system scene is the mighty Stone Love Movement, whose raw reputation and ace selectors prompt followers to travel miles just to hear them play out, a following that has spread overseas. Even with this glory, though, the position of the sound system in its island of origin is becoming increasingly fragile, with recent noise pollution legislation and the closure of several major Kingston venues, and the days when a sound system could simply link up in the street and play into the early hours are drawing to a close.

cocked and ready to discipline any contenders to his throne.

By the mid-1950s, R&B's star had faded and the fickle Jamaican consumer was tiring with American imports. Quick to catch on to a new opportunity, men like Reid, Dodd and Leslie Kong began recording their own music – primarily soft and soulful ballads – using established vocalists and players who had cut their teeth on the big band circuit. The Gaylads, Jackie Edwards, Owen Grey, Jackie Opal, Laurel Aitken and Bunny and Skully were backed by some of the best session musicians Jamaica has ever produced – Roland Alphonso, Tommy McCook and "Deadly" Headley Bennett on saxophone, Don Drummond and Rico Rodriguez on trombone, Jerome "Jah Jerry" Haines and Ernest Ranglin on guitar, Lester Sterling on trumpet and keyboard virtuoso Jackie Mittoo. Initially, the producers used the WIRL (now

Dynamic) and Federal (now Tuff Gong) studios to record, but as soon as finances allowed, Reid and Dodd (among others) built their own rudimentary studios, giving them the names of their most popular labels, **Treasure Isle** and **Studio One** respectively. Around this time as well, in 1959, Chris Blackwell founded Island Records, which would go on to become arguably the most famous label in Jamaican music. It was a halcyon age for Jamaican music, a time of co-operation and innovation described by Ken Boothe, who began his career with Coxsone in the late 1950s: "Music was nice in them times; you could just go and sing on a corner, go look for some other singers and everybody used to talk and smoke and sing together."

## Ska licks

By the late 1950s, musicians and singers began flirting with the philosophies of **Rastafari**. Some went down to the Dungle in Kingston or Adastra Road in the Wareika foothills and jammed with master drummers like **Count Ossie** (Oswald Williams) and his **Mystic Revelation of Rastafari** band, collaborations that produced the first ever recording for the Jamaica Broadcasting Corporation (JBC). Reworked in 1993 to massive commercial success by Jamaican DJ Shaggy, their *Oh Carolina* was one of the most influential tracks recorded, a perfect example of the fusion of Kumina drumming, harmonic singing and unique rhythm that was later to develop in to ska, rocksteady and finally reggae. The Rasta drummers became well known on the Kingston entertainment scene via the popular Vere Johns Opportunity Knocks variety show (held every week at the Ambassador Theatre in Jones Town) when star Marguerita Mahfood refused to appear unless she was backed by Ossie and Mystic Revelation. Unwillingly Johns complied; to his surprise the drummers were a huge hit and went on to perform regularly at Kingston venues.

For Jamaican musicians, the late 1950s and early 1960s were a time of intense creativity, a period of exploring new rhythms and pushing the boundaries of jazz, R&B and Rasta drumming – an explosive combination that sometimes saw drummers and instrumentalists pitched against sound-system wattage. Meanwhile, session musicians were conducting their own experiments using the exaggerated shuffle rhythm of R&B and syncopated mento sounds, until somewhere along the way, the staccato, guitar-and-trumpet-led sound of **ska** emerged and captured the Jamaican musical imagination with effortless ease.

Following independence from British colonial rule in 1962, the future seemed full of possibilities. You can hear the euphoria in the music – joyous, up-tempo ska tunes that seem now not to express a care in the world – and it was the small independent record labels in west Kingston who were at the cutting edge. Ska lyrics provided a window into the evolution of Jamaica and its music, and with its home-grown roots and dancefloor beat, ska expressed the mood of the ghetto dweller. Tommy McCook grouped together the cream of the session musicians to form the now-legendary **Skatalites**, who released a host of massively popular instrumental tracks, like *Guns of Navarone*, and backed most of the era's popular singers – including Millie Small, who shot to international fame with *My Boy Lollipop*, pro-

duced by Chris Blackwell for Fontana. Other prominent ska tracks included Justin Hinds and the Dominoes' *Carry Go Bring Come*, the Ethiopians' *Train to Skaville* and a host of others on Beverley's, Federal, Treasure Isle and Coxsone's Studio One and Coxsone labels.

## Rude boys to rocksteady

As the post-independence glow began to fade, the ghetto youth became increasingly dissatisfied with their meagre slice of the pie and the **rude boy** era of violence, police brutality and ghetto dissent began, cinematically celebrated by Jimmy Cliff's portrayal of urban rebel Ivan in *The Harder They Come*, and musically documented in early Wailers cuts like *Rule Them Rudie* and *Let Him Go (Rudie Get Bail)*, a fractious stance that had generated 1964's *Simmer Down*, an appeal for calm among the youth.

While the musical critique of free Jamaica continued in releases like the Skatalites' 1966 *Independent Anniversary Ska*, subtle changes occurred in the music itself as Jamaicans began to demand something more leisurely. Producers accorded and began to slow down the tempo, guiding their artists toward a more benign lyrical output. Though the rude boy lament continued in cuts like *007 (Shanty Town)* from Desmond Dekker and the Aces, by 1966 Hopeton Lewis had produced *Take It Easy*, Stranger and Patsy were singing emollient **rocksteady** tracks about love and relationships in *When I Call Your Name*, while *Happy Go Lucky Girl* and *Only A Smile* by John Holt and the Paragons, *Queen Majesty* and *You Don't Care* by the Techniques with Slim Smith and Pat Kelly and *You Don't Need Me* and *I Caught You* by Brent Dowe's Melodians did something to temper the pressure in west Kingston. Characterized by the addition of the "one drop" drumming style and a more melodic tone, rocksteady carried the swing and swiftly eclipsed the ska sound. The king of the era was Alton Ellis, who put a name to the movement with his *Get Ready Rock Steady* track. It was a prolific time for Jamaican music, with labels like Studio One and, primarily, Treasure Isle literally pumping out the tunes, many set to rhythm tracks which still continue to be heard to this day (see box, opposite). However, rocksteady was a short-lived movement, and by 1968 it had been superseded by the tighter guitars, heavier bass and sinuous rhythm of reggae.

### The art of the rhythm track

Through what's known in Jamaica as the **rhythm track**, the basslines and chord sequences laid down during the rocksteady and reggae eras have become the foundation for practically all Jamaican music recorded thereafter. Realizing that there are only so many chords to play or pressed for time when studios charge by the hour, musicians and producers like Bunny Lee (one of the first to release multiple versions of the same rhythm) have capitalized on the best chord and bassline combinations, manipulating and reinterpreting them so often that most of the classic rhythm tracks have established names, usually gleaned from the song title with which they first appeared. Working as full-time studio session musicians throughout the rocksteady and early reggae eras, the likes of singer, bassist

and arranger **Leroy Sibbles** created many of the rhythms that backed hundreds of 1970s' reggae cuts and are still reworked into today's dancehall; hence the famous bassline which underpinned Eric Donaldson's *Cherry Oh Baby* was reworked by UB40 in the 1980s with their cover version and by Tony Rebel in the 1990s with *Sweet Jamaica*. Many of the older rhythm tracks (and some new ones) have been digitally reworked to become hugely popular backing tracks, and surface on as many as six hundred versions. The upshot is that listening to Jamaican music can feel like an exercise in déjà vu; you may or may not have heard a particular song before, but once you've listened to a fair portion of rocksteady and early reggae, you'll certainly be familiar with most of the classic rhythm tracks.

## Reggae to roots rock

So many artists contributed to the development of **reggae** that it's impossible to say who originated it – it's most likely that this ubiquitous Jamaican sound developed organically as a natural progression from rocksteady, but Toots and The Maytals' 1968 single *Do The Reggay* (sic) certainly cemented a name that Rastafarians will tell you derives from *rex*, meaning king. Hence reggae is the "king's music" – an apt allegory, as the appearance of reggae coincided with an explosion in the popularity of the Rastafarian movement.

From 1970 onwards, Jamaican music took an increasingly religious stance, with its main lyrical themes drawing reference from the tenets of Rastafari; repatriation, black history, black pride and self-determination. "Roots and culture" were the lick and reggae became a fully fledged protest music – anathema to the establishment, who saw a menacing, subversive message from a dirty and violent source, and banned it wherever possible; though the rum bar jukeboxes played whatever the radio stations wouldn't. Not until the international acclaim that greeted Bob Marley and the Wailers after they signed to Island Records in 1972 (see p.184), was reggae given island-wide approval for the first time.

A time of intense musical productivity, the 1970s stands out as the classic period of

Jamaica's best roots reggae. But while **Burning Spear** was singing *Marcus Garvey* and *Slavery Days* and Joseph Hill's **Culture** provided apocalyptic warnings of the time when *Two Sevens Clash*, the era also offered a sweeter side; the angelic crooning of more mainstream artists like **Dennis Brown** or **Gregory Isaccs** found an eager audience, their style becoming known as **lovers' rock**. Though lyrics rested mostly on love and affection, lovers' artists also had some bite; tracks like Junior Byles' *Curly Locks* (a song about the controversial move of falling in love with a Rastaman) highlight the uneasy relationship that Rasta and reggae still had with wider Jamaican society.

## Dub to DJ business

As the 1970s wore on, studio technology became increasingly sophisticated and producers began manipulating their equipment, using reverb or echo machines, over-dubbing techniques and snatches of dog barks or gun shots to produce some of the most arresting and penetrating music ever to emerge from Jamaica – **dub**. Using a remarkable level of inventiveness with often limited means, Jamaican engineers such as dub pioneers **King Tubby**, **Prince Jammy** and **Scientist** pre-dated the advent of the digital sampler by ten years and brought reggae back to basics, stripping down songs so that only bass, drums and inflec-

## Dancehall queens

Each Saturday night, hundreds of young women step into the dancehall wearing virtually nothing. Whether it's a latticework leatherette g-string and bra ensemble or a concoction of carefully arranged silver plastic straps, dancehall wear is usually topped-off with a white or violent-coloured wig, thigh boots and the essential "matey bag" (a mini-rucksack). These costumes are for one purpose – the sheer hype and self-promotion of "modelling" for the crowds who'll step aside to watch the wearers "skin out" and "shock out" – perform the suggestive gymnastics of the latest dances (see below) to the most overtly sexual tracks; the self-explanatory *Stab Up The Meat* by the queen of slackness DJ Lady Saw are guaranteed to have the "hottie-hottie gyals" filling the floor. Dancehall queens, as the wearers are called, are the icons of sound-system culture, a league of ghetto princesses ruled by a light-skinned uptown Kingstonian named Carlene, whose killer dress sense, athletic dancing style and pneumatic body have earned her the local status of a Hollywood film star. Other luminaries include pop crossover Patra, whose steamy videos have brought the phenomenon wider attention, and the Ouch posse of dancehall divas are celebrity guests at only the very best of sound-system nights.

Each new rhythm that appears on the dancehall scene spawns not only a hundred DJ or singer versions but – if it becomes really popular – maybe even a **dance** of its own. Most dances involve heavy gyration of the hips and lower body, the "winding", "skanking" or "water pumping" of the early1980s were a fairly innocuous way of slow-dancing, but in recent years, some of the dances have become ever more explicit. Some of the best to look out for – or have a Jamaican companion demonstrate, are the now old-hat bogle, butterfly, pepper seed and tattie or the more current sketel, body basics, mock the dread or go-go wind, and you'll occasionally see semi-professional ragga dance groups like the Chemical Boys performing the latest moves at stageshows and fun days all over the island.

---

tions of tone remained. Snippets of the original vocals were then mixed in alongside sound effects and two-line DJ sound-bites. Like ska, dub remained a primarily instrumental music for a short time; before long, scores of DJs clamoured to produce a dub voice-over, and producers plundered their archives and released dub versions of old cuts, while DJs provided the voice-over and even vocal tracks had a dub flip-side.

The cult of the DJ had begun in the sound systems, with resident DJs improvising a couple of lines of introductory patter at the beginning of a record. The ecstatic crowd responses encouraged them to spin it out, and soon they were delivering full-length monologues over the music, discussing topical events as well as the state of play on the dance floor. The craft was mastered by **U-Roy** – inspired by the earlier efforts of Count Machouki and Sir Lord Comic – who released talk-based singles to great success throughout the 1970s with roots sound systems like the venerable King Tubby's Hi-Fi, Tippertone, Sir George and Killermanjaro providing the backing for their live appearances. Meanwhile, the DJs' trade was expanded when Big Youth started talking over records in his cultural style, followed by the likes of King Stitt, Dennis Alcapone, I-Roy, Jah Stitch, Tappa Zukie, Prince Jazzbo and Dillinger, whose *Cocaine Running Around My Brain* scored a hit in the UK. As the violent elections 1976 and 1980 saw the pressure in Kingston building up, the sound systems multiplied and the DJs chatted about – or "**toasted**" – the times, analyzing the position of the ghetto youth in Jamaica from a dread perspective, and offered cultural distractions by setting the Psalms to song. Newcomers U-Brown, Ranking Joe, Josey Wales, Charlie Chaplin and Trinity continued in the same vein, touring Jamaica and the Caribbean with sound systems, and paving the way for the dancehall explosion of the 1980s.

In 1981, the Jamaican reggae industry was left in shock as Bob Marley succumbed to cancer and the music fraternity realized the enormity of their loss. Jamaica came to a standstill for two days as mourners viewed his coffin and lined the roads to watch the entourage on the final procession to Nine Miles. Though arguably not the greatest singer to emerge from Jamaica, Marley's influence and songwriting talent were immeasurable, and following his demise, reggae struggled to regain its direction and purpose. Groups like **Black Uhuru** recorded a succession of roots albums for Island, but the musical tide had already turned towards the DJ and Marley's legacy of cultural consciousness began to seem less appropriate to the world of cocaine-running and political warfare in the ghettos.

## Slackness in the dancehall

These days, you're far more likely to be assailed by a clamorous barrage of raw drum and bass and shouted patois lyrics than hear Bob Marley or Burning Spear booming out from Jamaican speaker boxes. The two-chord sound that earned DJ Shabba Ranks two Grammy awards in the early 1990s is the most popular musical form in contemporary Jamaica, named **ragga** (from "ragamuffin", meaning a rough-and-ready ghetto-dweller) or **dancehall** because that's where it originated and where it is best enjoyed. The genre first surfaced in around 1979, and was cemented in 1981 when a flamboyant albino DJ named **Yellowman** exploded on to the scene with his massive hits *Married in the Morning*, *Mr Chin* and *Nobody Move*. Yellowman's lyrical bawdiness and huge popularity signified the departure from roots reggae and cultural toasting to the sexually explicit and often violent DJ-ism that took hold in the 1980s. Though none were rawer than Yellow, who added energetic stage performances and self-deprecating humour to the expletives, other DJs – fuelled by a positive response from their Jamaican audience – emulated his lewd approach, and sexually explicit lyrics – or "**slackness**" – began to proliferate.

In 1985, Wayne Smith's hit *Under Me Sleng Teng* – voiced to the King Jammy-created rhythm of the same name – heralded the start of the computer age in the dancehall. Studios switched from analogue to digital recording formats and producers seized upon computerized rhythms as a quicker and cheaper way of putting out a record. The mixing board had become an instrument unto itself, with a new breed of producers like Bobby Digital, Donovan Germaine, Mikey Bennett, Dave Kelly and Patrick Roberts becoming the Reids and Dodds of the 1990s and DJs becoming the island's biggest stars. Vocalists also clamoured to ride the digital rhythms – singers like Frankie Paul, Michael Palmer, Little John, Beres Hammond, Barrington Levy, Pinchers, Wayne Wonder and Sanchez got the sweetness out of the rhythms and continue to record today.

Dancehall is massive today, though it's not to everyone's liking. Many Jamaicans charge the genre with wider moral decline as the DJs become the gangsta rappers of reggae with gold chains, flash cars, and in some cases, a seemingly limitless enthusiasm for automatic firearms. However, though some do songs seem intent on a glorification of violence, most simply reflect the lives of a thousand ghetto dwellers for whom violence and guns are a daily reality. Essentially, dancehall is a raw, rude, hard-core music designed to titillate and tease its Jamaican audience on home ground and beyond. Whether you like the lyrics or hate them, it's unlikely that you'll be able to resist dancehall's compelling rhythm and infectious hype, and while you're in Jamaica, it's futile to try.

## Reggae in the 1990s

Dancehall dominates Jamaican music in the late 1990s. Yet those worried about moral depravity can take heart: dancehall culture is going through another transitional phase, as the battle between cultural and slackness artists intensifies. In 1993, the conscious lyrics and staunch Rastafarian stance of singer **Garnet Silk** managed to conquer the dancehalls at the time when "gun bizness" and sexual slackness were the sole signifiers, and his immense popularity started the momentum for today's resurgence of cultural reggae. In 1994, Silk was killed in an explosion, but Everton Blender and Luciano have carried on where he left off, using musicians and actually writing their own material. It seems that the righteous are triumphing over the base; even the original "gold teeth, gold chain don gorgon" **Ninjaman**, a long-term crack addict and firearms advocate, has resurrected himself as Brother Desmond, a gospel singing born-again Christian, while rising megastar **Buju Banton** – who famously encouraged the murder of homosexuals, to mercifully widespread condemnation – has renounced his early lyrical vitriol, converted to Rastafari and now sings of Jah to the sufferers who've dubbed him the "Bob Marley of the Nineties". Ziggy Marley and the Melody Makers, Yvad and Ivanay are experimenting with acoustic reggae and conscious lyrics while "veteran" artists John Holt, Leroy Sibbles, Ken Boothe and the Mighty Diamonds do the stageshow rounds to satisfy the current demand for "**oldies**" hits. Capleton, Tony Rebel, Anthony B and Prezident Brown keep up the cultural pressure in the dancehall and

For the definitive history of Jamaican music, consult Steve Barrow and Peter Dalton's *Rough Guide to Reggae*, and for a musical trip through the years, try Island's unbeatable *Tougher Than Tough* four-CD collection.

singers Richie Stevens, Beres Hammond and Benjy Myers provide sweet love songs for the romantically inclined. Reggae has even made moves into the pop arena; Grammy winner Shaggy scored recent worldwide hits with *Boombastic* and the *Train Is Coming*, while Chaka Demus and Pliers' *Murder She Wrote* and *Tease Me* provided the now-staid Island Jamaica label with the biggest crossover hit in years. The on-going DJ feud between Beenie Man's Shocking Vibes stable and

**Bounty Killer**'s Scare Dem crew has now left the formerly formidable **Beenie Man** on the sidelines, and DJs have become such figureheads that the most popular have signature catchphrases; Bounty chants "Yeah yeah yeah yeah", Beenie warbles "Oh la di da" and new sensation Red Rat provides an ironic "On noooo". You'd be hard-pressed to find anywhere with a music scene as influential, vibrant and liberated as Jamaica's, and with the launch of the island's first all-reggae radio station **Irie FM** in 1990 (see p.159) and the thousands of young Jamaicans who dream of being the next Marley, Marcia Griffiths, Merciless or Lady Saw, it looks as though reggae's future prosperity is secure.

**with contributions by Steve Barrow and Greg Salter**

## DISCOGRAPHY

### Compilations

**Various** *Tougher than Tough: the Story of Jamaican Music* (Island, UK; 4-CD set). This is quite an investment but it would be hard to imagine a better compilation of Jamaican music. The discs cover just about every phase of the Jamaican musical story, from 1958 to 1993, beginning with a superb selection of pre-ska R&B, then moving through the ska and rock steady hits of the 1950s and 60s to an overview of reggae's manifold styles and sub-genres. The songs are gathered from a wide variety of labels – not just from the Island catalogue – and there are superb, virtually book-sized sleeve notes from Steve Barrow.

**Various** *This is Reggae Music Volumes 1–5* (Mango, UK). More crucial anthologies, if you prefer to pick your reggae years.

### Roots and Mento

**Count Ossie and his Mystic Revealers of Rastafari** *Grounation* (various labels). Traditional Rasta drumming accompanied by bebop and cool jazz horn lines, apocalyptic poems, and much chanting.

**The Jolly Boys** *Pop'n'Mento* (Cooking Vinyl, UK/First Warning, US) and *Sunshine'n'Water* (Rykodisc, US). Sunny and lewd, this is classic good-time mento from a band who have

been playing it for decades. Strongly recommended.

**Luciano** *Where There Is Life* (Island Jamaica, UK). An exceptionally well-crafted set that's a landmark in modern roots music.

**Various** *Drums of Defiance* (Smithsonian Folkways, US) and *The Roots of Reggae* (Lyrichord, US). Two excellent, well-annotated anthologies of the deepest roots music of Jamaica from the Maroon communities.

**Various** *From Kongo to Zion and Churchical Chants of the Nyabinghi* (Heartbeat, US). Traditional rasta music from nyabinghi ceremonies.

**Various** *Jamaican Roots: Bongo, Baccra and Coolie, Volumes 1 & 2* (Folkways, US). The first volume includes more or less the only kumina music on record, plus Indian Hindu (baccra) music; the second has Revival Zion plus carnival music.

### Ska and Rocksteady

**Alton Ellis** *Cry Tough* (Heartbeat, US). Alton invented the sound of rocksteady, and the name – with his song "Get Ready to Rock Steady".

**Ethiopians** *The World Goes Ska* (Jetstar, UK). Classic 1960s ska, with songs full of ghetto life in Kingston.

*Continues opposite...*

**Skatalites** *Music is my Occupation* (Trojan, UK) and *Hog in a Cocoa* (Esoldun, France). Led by trombonist Don Drummond, the Skatalites had an all-star musical cast, and produced simply the greatest ska sounds. The first disc here is a showcase for Drummond, Tommy McCook and Baba Brooks; the second has them backing the best singers of the 1960s at Duke Reid's studio.

**The Techniques** *Run Come Celebrate* (Heartbeat, US). Classic rocksteady from one of the great vocal trios.

**Various** *Duke Reid's Treasure Chest* (Heartbeat, US). Rocksteady gems from the producer who ruled the sound.

## Reggae

**Abyssinians** *Satta Massagana* (Heartbeat, US). A legendary dread album.

Big Youth *Hit the Road Jack* (Trojan, UK). This was one of the great toaster records of the 1970s.

**Dennis Brown** *The Dennis Brown Collection* (Jetstar, UK). A fine, wide-ranging hits compilation from 1993.

**Burning Spear** *Marcus Garvey* and *Garvey's Ghost* (Mango, UK). Spear's 1976 Marcus Garvey tribute was full of exquisite vocals and horns, and given a sublime dub treatment on *Garvey's Ghost*, packaged with it on this bumper CD. Spear's 1990 album, *Mek We Dweet* (Mango, UK), marked a return to form, updating his sound with heavy guitar hooks.

**Jimmy Cliff** *The Harder they Come* (Mango, UK). No reggae collection is complete without this 1972 movie soundtrack, combining early reggae standards with Cliff songs like the title track and "Many Rivers to Cross".

**Culture** *Two Sevens Clash* (Blue Moon, UK/Shanachie, US). The band never equalled this debut with its gorgeous vocals.

**Eek-a-Mouse** *Wa Do Dem* (Greensleeves, UK/Shanachie, US). One of the wittiest, most imitated 1980s toasting discs.

**Marcia Griffiths** *Naturally* (Sky Note, Jamaica). Greatest hits compilation from Jamaica's top woman singer, and former leader of the I-Threes, Bob Marley's backing trio.

Ijahman *Haile I Hymn* (Mango, UK). Ijahman Levi's unique, soulful, meditative brand of reggae at its (1978) best.

**Gregory Isaacs** *Nightnurse* (Mango, UK). Isaacs has been releasing Jamaica's best love songs for the past thirty years. This set, from 1983, is the finest of the lot to date.

**King Tubby and Yabby You** *Time to Remember* (Yabby You, Jamaica). Ethereal and heavy dub – just as it should be.

**Bob Marley and the Wailers** highlights include:

*Songs of Freedom: the Complete Bob Marley Collection* (Tuff Gong/Island, UK). The definitive Bob anthology: four CDs and 78 songs, dating from 1962 to his death in 1980, including virtually all the classics, plus lots of rare treasures.

*Legend* (Island, UK). If you want just a single disc, this is a near-faultless "best of" selection.

*Burnin'* (Island, UK). The sound of the original Wailers in 1973 with Marley and Tosh at their songwriting best on "Get Up, Stand Up" and "I Shot the Sheriff".

*The Lee Perry Sessions* (Charly, UK). Many consider these the greatest of all Bob's recordings: songs include "Lively up Yourself", "Sun is Shining" and "Kaya".

**Mighty Diamonds** *Mighty Diamonds* (Mango, UK). Fine selection from one of reggae's best vocal harmony groups.

**Junior Murvin** *Police and Thieves* (Mango, UK). The title song, inspired by election violence in Jamaica, was a massive hit on the island and in Britain in 1977. Lee Perry produced and shared writing credits.

**Augustus Pablo** *King Tubby Meets Rockers Uptown* (Jetstar, UK). Pablo and producer King Tubby (the Upsetters' keyboard player, Glen Adams) invented dub in the early 1970s and perfected things on this wonderful and innovative album.

**Frankie Paul** *20 Massive Hits* (Sonic Sounds, UK). One of the best – of innumerable – Frankie Paul compilations.

**Lee "Scratch" Perry and the Upsetters** *Reggae Greats* (Mango, UK). Jamaica's greatest

*Continues over...*

*Continued...*

and craziest arranger is responsible for too many classic reggae albums to mention. This compilation has generous doses of his 1970s "Super Ape" outings, with wild dub. For true devotees, Greensleeves have released three triple-CD sets which pull in most of Perry's greatest moments, with the Upsetters and as arranger. These are titled: *The Upsetter Compact Set, Open the Gate,* and *Build the Ark.*

**Sly and Robbie** *Reggae Greats* (Mango, UK). This drums and bass duo are even more prodigious producers than Lee Perry. This is their own stuff – dub at its most sophisticated.

**Mikey Smith** *Mi C-yaan Believe It* (Island, UK). An album of powerful dub poetry from a radical exponent, Mikey Smith, murdered by JLP gunmen shortly after its release.

**Third World** *Reggae Greats* (Island, UK). Third World were often too slick for their own good, but their late 1970s songs like "96 Degrees in the Shade" and "Now That we Found Love" are pop reggae at its sweetest.

**Toots and the Maytals** *Reggae Got Soul* (Mango, UK). The title says it all – Toots Hibbert is the man who put soul together with reggae.

**Twinkle Brothers** *Twinkle Inna Poland Style* (Twinkle, UK). And if Toots put soul into reggae, the Twinkles' Norman Grant was the man who put Polish folk into the genre, on this, the latest of a series of recordings with the Trebunia family. Strangely enough, it works brilliantly.

**Peter Tosh** *Legalise It* and *Equal Rights* (Virgin Frontline, UK). These two records were recorded after Tosh split from the Wailers, with most of the band along. They're militant songs with razor-sharp backing.

**Yellowman** *Reggae on the Move* (Ras, US). Yellowman was the biggest toaster of the 1980s, and his slack lyrics, full of crudity and anti-feminist and anti-gay raps, were a precursor of the more offensive contemporary ragga habits. This is one of his better outings.

**Various** *Chatty Chatty Mouth Versions* (Greensleeves, UK). Twelve cuts of this hugely popular rhythm.

**Various** *If deejay was your trade: the Dreads at King Tubby's 1974–77* (Blood & Fire, UK). Sixteen dynamite tracks from Kingston's premier DJs of the 1970s – U Roy, Dr Alimantado, Dillinger, Tapper Zukie and others – produced by Bunny Lee.

**Various** *Solid Gold, Coxsone Style* (Heartbeat, US). The likes of John Holt, the Abyssinians and Dennis Brown singing their hearts out for Studio One.

## Dancehall and Ragga

**Bounty Killer** *My Xperience* (VP, US). Double album by this hardcore ragga DJ, with a generous portion of major reggae hits alongside some scintillating fresh material.

**Buju Banton** *Voice of Jamaica* (Polygram, UK) and *'Til Shiloh* (Loose Cannon, UK). The first album has bad-boy Buju at his baddest, the latter sees him in more reflective cultural mood.

**Cocoa Tea** *Kingston Hot* (Ras, US). A silky-smooth dancehall voice, produced by Henry "Junjo" Lawes.

**Chaka Demus and Pliers** *Tease Me* (Mango, UK). Mid-1990s ragga, mixing in Curtis Mayfield soul and hip-hop rhythms, and produced by the ever-inventive Sly and Robbie.

**Lovindeer** *One Day Christian* (TSOJ, UK). Dancehall, poco-style, from its finest exponent.

**Sugar Minott** *Slice of the Cake* (Heartbeat, US). Sweet sounds from "Sugar Sugar", including the great "No Vacancy".

**Shabba Ranks** *As Raw as Ever* (CBS, US). Hip-hop meets reggae in this pioneering ragga album from 1991.

**Garnett Silk** *It's Growing* (Vine Yard, UK; VP,US). The album that established the late Garnett Silk as one of the prime vocalists of the 1990s – a celebration of physical and spiritual love.

**Various** *Reggae Hits – Volumes 1–16* (Jetstar, UK). Essential dancehall and lovers' rock compilations from 1984 on.

# Jamaican art

Though the island has a centuries-old artistic tradition, interesting Jamaican art is very much a modern phenomenon. Before the 1920s, Jamaicans were, on the whole, simply too busy making ends meet to turn to art. Today, however, the island is considered one of the artistic centres of the Caribbean.

The earliest Jamaican art was the work of the Amerindian Tainos, who lived on the island prior to the arrival of Columbus in 1494. A few relics of their art remain – **cave paintings**, for example, at Mountain River Cave, near Spanish Town – and suggest that they were rather primitive wood-carvers and painters. The Spanish, who controlled the island from 1513 to 1655, imported artisans from Spain to produce **limestone carvings**, notably for the now-destroyed governor's castle at Sevilla Nueva on the north coast, and these carvings incorporated Jamaican subject matter such as the figures of Taino women. In contrast, the dominant features of art in Jamaica during the period of British rule were **commemorative sculpture** – produced in Britain by British sculptors – and **portrait and landscape paintings** by British artists who paid occasional visits to the island.

Some of Britain's finest sculptors had their work commissioned for the Jamaican market. **John Bacon** (1740–99) produced the Spanish Town memorial to Admiral Rodney and the smaller but more impressive monument to John Wolmer in the Kingston Parish Church. **John Flaxman** (1755–82), probably the finest English sculptor before Henry Moore, carved the monument to planter Simon Clarke that sits in the church at Lucea. More interesting is the "documentation" of eighteenth- and nineteenth-century Jamaica in the landscape paintings of **George Robertson** and **Joseph Bartholomew Kidd**, who paid visits to Jamaica during the 1770s and the 1830s respectively, and the nineteenth-century photographic records of **Adolphe Duperly** and **V.P. Parkhurst**. A more voluminous artistic legacy of the period is a series of portraits of governors and wealthy planters and their families painted, again, by itinerant British artists like **Philip Wickstead** who was in Jamaica in the 1770s.

## A new art movement

Even after the abolition of slavery, it inevitably took three or four generations before a true Jamaican art began to flourish. Ironically, the prime mover in the new phase was an English sculptor – **Edna Manley** – who had married prime minister-to-be Norman Manley and moved to Jamaica in 1921. Several of her sculptures may be seen as turning points in Jamaican art. *Beadseller*, from 1922, is the small wood figure of a Jamaican street vendor, carved in a way that echoes European cubist and art deco movements of the period; her 1935 *Negro Aroused* – a black body uncoiling out of bondage – depicts early enthusiasm for national independence in art form.

In 1939, around forty artists in Manley's circle stormed into the annual meeting of the island's main (and rather sedate) art museum, the Institute of Jamaica. They demanded an end to the domination of Anglophile attitudes to art and the replacement of the colonial portraits that hung in the art galleries with works by local artists. The event was more symbolic than revolutionary, marking a new departure point for Jamaican painters and sculptors; classes began at the Institute in 1940, organized initially by Manley, and helped to give direction to a new wave of Jamaican artists.

For several decades the primary aim of these pioneers of the island's new art movement – painters like **Albert Huie** (born 1920), **Carl Abrahams** (born 1913) and **Gloria Escoffery** (born 1923) – was to represent Jamaican people and their surroundings. Whereas earlier painters had focused on the simple beauty of nature, ignoring the native people, artists now showed the landscape as a place where people lived and worked. Paintings like *Crop Time* by Albert Huie, for example, showed the sugar plantations in action, with workers cutting, bundling and loading the cane, while in *Constant Spring Road*, his citizens go about their daily business on the streets of Kingston - chatting, selling and reading newspapers.

There were two distinct artistic styles in the work of this new wave of painters and sculptors. The predominant style was **European-influenced**, following twentieth-century trends in European art. Plenty of Jamaicans studied in Britain on British Council scholarships during the 1940s and 1950s, and an exposure to foreign art trends is reflected in much of their work. Most followed a classical approach, with artists like Huie and **Barrington Watson** (born 1931) using natural forms and landscapes as reference points, though Watson's later paintings, like *The Banana Loaders*, show the influence of post-impressionism. Of the early European-influenced painters, Escoffery shows the greatest interest in abstract art, stretching her figures along wide, panoramic canvases which depict a range of subjects from quiet pastoral scenes to the traditional Saturday market.

More distinctive, the **Afro-Caribbean approach** was characterized by the paintings of the self-taught, "intuitive" artists. One of the first, and most unusual, of these intuitives was the prodigious **John Dunkley** (1891–1947). Dunkley was a barber in Kingston, famous for covering every square inch of his shop with pictures of trees, vines and flowers; his later paintings continued his obsession with dark, brooding scenes from nature. Though scorned by the critics during his lifetime, Dunkley's work has become far more appreciated and sought after in recent years, and is excellently represented at the National Gallery in Kingston.

As you would expect in an island where religion plays such a large role, many of the island's other successful intuitive artists have focused their art around **religious imagery**. **Mallica Reynolds** (born 1911) – the shepherd (head) of a Revivalist group in Kingston, better known as Shepherd Kapo – is the best known of these artists; during the 1950s he became the first self-taught Jamaican painter to be fully accepted by local and foreign viewers and is still the island's foremost intuitive sculptor and painter today. Other intuitives such as **Albert Artwell** (born 1942) and **Everald Brown** (born 1917) – a priest in the Ethiopian Coptic Church – concentrate on Rasta beliefs, their paintings rich in religious symbolism and Rasta colours, showing kings and queens living an idyllic existence in heaven (Zion).

Jamaican artists grew in confidence during the 1960s and 1970s, many of them spurred by the promises and hopes of nationalism and independence. **Black iconography** was prominent in the work of artists like **Osmund Watson** (born 1934), who painted miniature portraits of a black Christ and black madonnas, as well as large, spiritual African archetypes. At the same time Jamaican art became more experimental, most noticeably in a specifically Jamaican surrealism, represented by the work of **David Boxer** (born 1946) and Australian-born **Colin Garland** (born 1935). Garland's paintings, inspired by the works of Haitian intuitives, seem to tell a story but instead dissolve into bizarre fantasy – his triptych, *In the Beautiful Caribbean*, for example, appears to be a familiar summary of the island with its jumble of birds, fish and religious figures, until you spot the incongruous parachutist and the soldier with a seashell on his head.

Today, Jamaica's art scene continues its diversity. At the bottom end, it is dominated by the huge carving and painting industry which has grown up around mass tourism and, although much of it is relentlessly mediocre, there is some reasonable quality art at the craft markets in Kingston and across the north coast. At the higher end of the market, the tourist industry helps to expose artists to an audience they would otherwise struggle to reach, and some hotels – like *Mockingbird Hill* in Port Antonio, co-owned by local artist Barbara Walker – have set up exhibition areas for top-quality work. More importantly, the establishment of the National Gallery in Kingston in 1974 has given the island's art an important institutional infrastructure, and its regular exhibitions of the best of Jamaican art continue to encourage the development of young painters and sculptors, as witnessed by the proliferation of studios and galleries island-wide.

# Language

Jamaicans enjoy nothing better than a good debate – you can join in at any rum shop or simply switch on the radio. They take great delight in outwitting each other in verbal battles that Anancy (the sharp-brained spider who's a favourite Jamaican folk hero – see box) would be proud of.

Although Jamaica's official language is English, **patois** is the working mode of expression for most Jamaicans. Its validity as a legitimate language or corrupted slang continues to provoke much debate on the island, fired up in 1996 by proposals to print a patois bible.

Jamaican patois is an incredibly creative and constantly evolving idiom; new words are coined almost daily to suit every development and fall into common use with astonishing speed while older phrases – yesterday's "buzzwords" – disappear without trace. Sex and related topics are generously covered in the patois lexicon; there are no less than four names for the penis in its various stages from boyhood ("pem pem") to teenage years ("tutu"), and countless names for the female genitalia.

An explanation of some of the more obvious idiosyncrasies will go some way to unravelling the labyrinth of patois. If you want to delve deeper, consult the books listed on p.363.

## Rasta linguistics

The Rasta challenge to all things Babylonian includes an assault upon all that "downpresses" the black man in the English language. As a means of resistance, Rastas have embarked on a new classification of words that attempt to correct what is seen as bias against their experiences, perceptions, personal choices and world view as black people. While this may sometimes seem pedantic (greeting a Rasta with "hello" may illicit the cool response "We're not in hell and I'm not low"), language does have a strong effect upon the formation of hierarchies and prejudices, and Rasta linguistics is one of the most creative elements of Jamaican patois. Rastas generally counteract negatives with positives and vice versa, breaking down each word and analysing its syllabic connotations, often reading significance into every nuance; hence cigarette (see-garette) becomes **blind-jah-rette**, understand becomes **over-stand**, oppress (up-press) becomes **downpress**, and Selassie I is interpreted as proof of the deity's omnipresence; **Sela*see eye***. It isn't difficult to see why there are so many cryptic messages embedded in 1970s roots reggae lyrics. The most recognizable aspect of Rasta linguistics is the use of "I" to emphasize unity (Inity) and positivity as well as to protest against the coercive control of language. Hence create becomes **I-rate**, continually becomes **I-tinually**, creation is **I-ration**.

Rasta linguistics are not restricted to the Rastafarian community; the Rasta greetings "hail", "yes Rasta" or the acknowledgement of understanding in "seen Iyah" have become normal phrases for Jamaican (particularly male) youth. Rasta words that have slipped into daily usage are listed below. For a full description of the Rasta lexicon read Velma Pollard's *Dread Talk*.

• Whether male or female, you will commonly be referred to as him: "Wha! Shelley pregnant! (H)im never tell me!"

• "H" is often not voiced, but makes up for the discrepancy by adding itself to plenty of other words. Hence "So yu is 'Enry from Hin-glan, don't?" ("don't" is used to mean "aren't you", or "isn't it?").

• There are plenty more inexplicable additions and absences: "shrimp" is often "swimp", "spliff" is "scliff", "vex" is "bex", "little" is "likkle", "ask" is "aks".

• Plurals are either ignored or conveyed by adding "dem"; hence "two feet" becomes "two foot", and "the girls are cooking for me" is "de gyal dem a cook fe de I".

• If somebody calls you "fatty", "whitey" or "big batty gyal", they are simply being direct rather than attempting to insult. Follow Jamaicans in their directness and convey your meaning as simply as possible. Do not waste time with endless unnecessary pleasantries – please and thank you will suffice.

## Anancy

The Twi word for spider, **Anancy** is a Jamaican hero and the principal character of most of the island's traditional folk stories; even tales without him are often referred to as "Nansi stories". Living by intellect rather than substance, the half-man, half-spider Brer Anancy always outwits his adversaries in a triumph of cunning over force – an allegory of the historical and contemporary struggles of black Jamaicans.

Anancy's Machiavellian use of deception and cunning in his triumphs mean each story has to end with the words "Jack Mandora, me no choose none" – Mandora is the keeper of heaven's gates, and the narrator has to disassociate him or herself from Anancy's wicked ways. Anancy stories are best told in Louise Bennett's *Anancy and Miss Lou* (see "Books", p.359).

## Patois glossary

Jamaican pronunciation presents difficulties with listing words that start with "h". Hence "h" has been put in brackets where applicable ([h]erb). The words have been written semi-phonetically, a sometimes clumsy medium but the only way in which to convey their sound in the available space. Some common phrases are included.

**Ago** Verb meaning will or going to do something; "Me ago kill dat bway".

**Arms house** Militant or negative behaviour, a favourite attitude during sound-system clashes.

**Arnold** Pork meat.

**Atops** Red Stripe beer.

**Babylon** Government or the established and oppressive social system; also an insulting title for police.

**Baggy** Female underwear.

**Baldhead** Non-Rasta, or person of unsound views.

**Bandulu** Trickery or a swindle.

**Bangarang** Noise or disruptive commotion, often used by rival sound systems; "Pack up yu old time bangarang".

**Bakra** White man, traditionally a slave-owner, derived from the Ibo "mbaraka".

**Bare** Only; as in "she ave bare plantain fi sell".

**Bashment** A huge and popular party or dance.

**Batty** Backside/bottom, also used as as an expression of surprise or disbelief.

**Batty riders** Tight lycra hot-pants worn by dancehall queens for maximum buttock exposure.

**Bawl** Cry out or call, particularly to register anguish; "Him a bawl out over the taxi fare".

**Beenie** Small or diminutive; "Me buy a likkle beenie amplifier".

**Big bout yah** Respected, famous.

**Big Up** Boost yourself up (verb); "Big up yu chest" or "Big up yu status/yuself".

**Bly** An opportunity, chance or escape from an unwanted chore; "De rain gimme a bly – me nah haffe go a wuk".

**Blood** Principally a swear word used with claat and hole. Can also be used as a respectful greeting signifying unity; as in "Wh'appen, blood?".

**Bombo** Offensive expletive meaning backside, usually used in conjunction with claat or hole; "Move yu bombo-claat face from me".

**Bow** Verb meaning to indulge in oral sex; "**bow cat**" is a participant.

**Breddah** Friend, usually male; "You a mi breddah". **Bredren** is the plural form, used both as a noun and as an adjective.

**Buck** To meet somebody; "Me will buck up wid yu later".

**Bumper** Backside/bottom.

**Bun** or **burn** To smoke, usually ganja.

**Charged** Intoxicated, stoned; "Me get charge pon dat indica las' night".

**Check** Pay a visit; "Me ago check yu tomorrow". Also a term of platonic or sexual appreciation, as in "me check fe di man's argument" and as a term for sexual advances; "De young bway try check big ooman".

**Clean de rifle** Perform fellatio.

**Copasetic** Cool, good; "Everyting copasetic".

**Cork** Full, as in "the dance cork tonight".

**Cotch** Rest up, chill out; "Sit dung and cotch with me". Also a verb to mean where a person sleeps; "Me a cotch by Evelyn's". Also used to denote bracing something; "Cotch de wheel wid' a rock".

**Craven** Greedy, desperate.

**Criss** Attractive, beautiful; "She a criss, criss gyal".

**Criss-biscuit** Anything of excellence.

**Crub** Dance with a partner slowly and suggestively.

**Dally** To go; "Me mus dally now".

**Dawta** Respectful term for a young woman, interchangeable with **sistah**.

**Dead-stock** Quiet, a non-event; "Dem promote pure dead-stock dance".

**Degeh** Adjective meaning small or measly; "She ave one degeh piece o' yam".

**Deh-deh** Be somewhere; "Me deh-deh" (I am here).

**Don** Respected male; "Him a de don". Also used in conjunction with gorgon or dada to mean the best or the toughest; "Me a di don gorgon/don dada". **Donovan** is an apprentice (or "prenta") don; **donette** is the feminine version.

**Dread** A Rastafarian person, or an adjective used to describe a bad situation; "De times dread, mon".

**Eat under a table** A man performing oral sex on a woman.

**Facety** Impertinent, rude; "De touris' facety to rass".

**Flex** To let loose or party intensively. Also used as an adjective to connote readiness for sexual intercourse.

**Ganja** Marijuana.

**Ginnal** Con man or trickster.

**Gravalicious** Greedy or avaricious.

**Grind** To make love.

**Guidance** An inspirational goodbye meaning "Let God be with you".

**Gwan** Go on or carry on (verb). Also used to mean "go away" or "going to".

**Gweh** Go away. Can also be used as an affectionate retort to foolish actions or speech.

**Gyal** Girl or woman.

**(H)eartical** Conscious esteemed person; "You are mi heartical bredren".

**(H)erb** Ganja, herbal marijuana.

**(H)ol' it dung** Be cool, to be on a low profile or stay quiet; "Me ago hol' it dung, me nah wan bax yu tonight".

**(H)ood** Penis, also called a **wood**.

**Hottie-hottie** An attractive female; "She one hottie-hottie gyal".

**I an' I** Me, I, we, mine, myself. **I-man** equally applies.

**Idren** Used by Rastas to mean friends or bredren.

**Irie** Adjective meaning fine or good; "You lookin' irie tonight". Also used as a greeting.

**Iron bird/fish** Airplane or boat; used mostly by Rastas.

**Ital** Anything natural (an Ital car wash is a river) or pure (a spliff without tobacco). Also describes Rastafarian meatless food cooked without salt.

**Iyah** Greeting to a friend; "What a gwan Iyah".

**Jamdung** Jamaica. **JA** is also frequently used, as is **Jah-mek-ya** by Rastas.

**Jook** Stab or pierce; "De rass fish hook jook me".

**Labrish** Gossip, small talk.

*Continues over...*

**Leggo beast** Wild and undisciplined creature or person.

**Let off** Give something; "She nah let off she tings".

**Lick** To strike a blow; "(H)im a lick dung the pear tree". Also to smoke; "Me a lick de chalice Iyah". Also an adjective meaning hot; "Buju a de lick fe 97!".

**Lick shot** Literally or figuratively firing a gun to demonstrate appreciation in the dancehall.

**Maaga** Thin, scrawny; "You sorry fe a maaga dog, maaga dog turn roun' an bite you".

**Mampy** Fat woman, not necessarily derogatory.

**Mantel** Good-looking but promiscuous man.

**Massive** Crowd of friends or people; "Me play music strictly fe de massive".

**Matey** Girlfriend, often used to denote one of several sexual partners.

**Men** Used in the singular to denote a homosexual man.

**Mule** Woman without children, usually incapable of conceiving. Also a person that smuggles cocaine internally.

**Natty** Used as an adjective or adverb to describe dreadlocks, also a greeting to a Rasta; "Wh'appen, Natty?".

**Nuff** Abundant or copious; "Me have nuff gyal". Often twinned with respect as a courteous greeting; "Nuff respect me breddah".

**Nyam** To eat, from the Hausa word "nyamnyam".

**One love** Greeting or farewell salutation. "Love" is used in the same way; "Love Iyah".

**Pikney** Child.

**Pum pum** Vagina.

**Pon** On or upon.

**Prentice** Apprentice or protégé, usually young man; "Im ah de prentice lifeguard pon Cornwall beach".

**Punanni** Vagina – again.

**Pussy or punny printers** Shorts even tighter than the batty rider.

**Queen** Respectful title for a woman, usually a Rastaman's partner.

**Ragamuffin** Respected and wily sufferah, often used in a musical context.

**Rahtid** Mild expletive or an expression of surprise.

**Rass** An expletive when used with claat or hole; "Wha de rass claat man a deal wid?". Can also express surprise or emphasize a point.

**Reason** Discuss and debate a subject; "Me a reason wid mi bredren".

**Red-eye** Greedy, envious.

**Renk** Extreme insolence or rudeness; "De man talk to me so renk it is a shame". Also foul-smelling.

**Respect** Perhaps the most commonly used greeting or farewell in Jamaica.

**Roughneck** Ragamuffin rascal.

**Runnings** Happenings, things that are going on; "Bway, runnings hard dis year".

**Rush** Assail or be the centre of attention; "De man dem will rush me when me wear dis dress".

**Ramp** Usually used as "ramp wid", meaning to interfere with something or irritate somebody.

**Screw** Be annoyed; "She a screw wid me". A "**screw face**" is a miserable character.

**Seen** Understand or comprehend what someone is saying. Usually used as a reply to a statement.

**Shine** Perform oral sex. Also used as an adjective ("She gimme a shiner") or a noun to describe the participant.

**Shock-out** Looking good; "Me ago shock-out tonight ina mi criss new Clarkes booties".

**Sketel** Term for a promiscuous but glamorous and attractive woman.

**Skin-out** Abandoned dancing or enjoyment, usually with sexual connotations.

**Spar** Friend.

**Spliff** Marijuana joint.

**Star** Used as a salutation or qualifier in greetings; "Wh'appen, star".

**Stoosh** Snooty, condescending from a position of assumed superiority.

**Structure** The body; "Min' you structure" (get out of the way).

**Sufferah** Poor but righteous ghetto-dweller.

**Talawah** Small but strong, applied to Jamaica; itself in the motto "She little but she talawah".

**Tan** Stay or stand; "Tan so back" (hold back).

**Ting** Thing or woman; "A my ting dat" (that's my girlfriend). "Tings" can be male and female genitalia.

**Trace** To curse somebody.

**Trash** Well turned out; "Trash and ready".

**Vex(ed)** Irritated or annoyed.

**Wine** Dance closely and suggestively.

**Wuk** Regular work or sex.

**Yush** Hush or be quiet, also used as a greeting.

# Books

The following books should be readily available in the US, UK and/or Jamaica. We have given the publishers for most of the in-print titles: the US publisher first, separated where applicable from the UK, and then from the Jamaican. Where a book is only published in one country, we have specified which. Most of the titles listed as being out of print (o/p) should be easy enough to find in secondhand bookstores.

## Travel and diaries

**Steve Cohen** *Adventure Guide to Jamaica* (US/UK Hunter). Dated but entertaining look at Jamaica's "adventure tourism" possibilities.

**Patrick Leigh Fermor** *The Traveller's Tree* (UK Penguin). The classic Caribbean travelogue describing Leigh Fermor's visit in the late 1940s, before tourism had really started in the region, though only the last chapter covers his time in Jamaica, with specific reference to the developing Rastafari movement in west Kingston.

**Margaret Hodges (ed)** *Blue Mountain Guide* (JA Pear Tree Press). Useful little guide to the peak trail, with sketch map of the stages up and accounts of the surrounding environment, geology, fauna and flora and human impact.

**Matthew Lewis** *Journal of a West Indian Planter* (o/p). Fascinating diaries of Lewis, an early nineteenth-century English novelist, describing his brief visits to his Jamaican estates and cataloguing the lifestyle and living conditions of the island's slaves.

**Margaret Morris** *Tour Jamaica* (JA Gleaner). A Jamaican's view of Jamaica, recommending sev-

enteen different driving tours around the island, with various big-wigs contributing a brief section on their own favourite places.

**Lady Maria Nugent** *Journal of Residence in Jamaica 1801–5* (JA Institute of Jamaica). Lady Nugent was the wife of Jamaica's governor, and her diary, though often naive and patronizing, paints an interesting picture of how the island's rulers lived.

**Anthony Winkler** *Coming Home to Teach* (o/p). Engaging story of novelist Winkler's own experience, as a white Jamaican, returning to live on his native island during the "anti-white" climate of the late 1970s. Very good on the politics and atmosphere of the period.

**Paul Zach (ed)** *Jamaica: Insight Guides* (US Houghton Mifflin/UK APA). Glossy guide, short on practical information but long on colour photographs, and a decent souvenir book.

## Fiction

**Louise Bennett** *Anancy and Miss Lou* (JA Sangster's). Jamaica's oral tradition of storytelling may be fading, but these are the classic folk-tales – from the greatest of modern Jamaican storytellers – told in patois and including the story of the crafty spider Anancy.

**Herbert de Lisser** *The White Witch of Rose Hall* (UK Macmillan). Richly embellished account of the island's best-known ghost story, a blend of Gothic horror and purple prose, that sticks pretty closely to the generally accepted history of Annie Palmer, mistress of Rose Hall Great House, whose three husbands all died in suspicious circumstances.

**Lorna Goodison** *Baby Mother and the King of Swords* (UK Longman). Rather dark collection of contemporary short stories set in Jamaica.

**Victor Headley** *Yardie* and *Excess* (UK Pan/JA X-Press). Easy-reading, thought-provoking tale of a drug-running "mule" who rises to the top of a UK-based drugs racket, shedding light on the whole sordid business along the way. *Excess* is the sequel.

■

**Perry Henzell** *Power Game* (UK AOIA/JA Ventana). Long, entertaining story of power-seekers at different levels in Jamaican society – politics, the army, the banks, the drug traders. Henzell catches local language and atmosphere with the same skill he used in his movie *The Harder They Come.*

**Evan Jones** *Stone Haven* (JA Institute of Jamaica). Long-winded but readable historical novel that picks its way through modern issues, from 1920s attitudes to colour to the problems of post-independence.

**Roger Mais** *The Hills Were Joyful Together* and *Black Lightning* (US/UK Heinemann). *Hills* is a bleak, compelling picture of life in a Kingston ghetto in the 1950s, with a harsh look at law and order Jamaica-style, by one of the country's earliest novelists. *Black Lightning* is an intense and atmospheric account of the life of a brooding sculptor living in the Jamaican bush.

**Terry McMillan**, *How Stella Got Her Groove Back* (US/UK Doubleday). In the tone of the movie *Waiting to Exhale,* this semi-autobiographical tale tells the story of a holiday romance that turns serious, written as a result of the author's experiences during Jamaican holidays.

**Colin Moone** *Obeah* (JA X-Press). Fascinating and sinister fictional introduction to the world of Jamaican witchcraft.

**Orlando Patterson** *The Children of Sisyphus* (UK Longman). Famous, uncompromising picture of the poorest of Kingston's poor, fighting for survival on the margins of society, and of Dinah, a prostitute who tries to leave them behind and move up in the world. One of the first novels to try to present a fair picture of the Rasta community.

**V.S. Reid** *The Jamaicans* (JA Institute of Jamaica). Juan de Bolas was a slave liberated by the Spanish when the English captured the island in 1655; Reid's fictionalized account tells of his life in hiding and struggle against the English.

**Jean Rhys** *Wide Sargasso Sea* (US Norton/UK Penguin). A view of post-emancipation Jamaica, with Antoinette, a young creole girl, and Rochester, her English boyfriend, trapped by declining financial circumstances and his inability to understand the realities of local life. Written as a "predecessor" to Bronte's *Jane Eyre.*

**Kim Robinson and Leeta Hearn** (ed), *Twenty-two Jamaican Short Stories* (UK/JA Kingston

Publishers). Excellent short story book that covers some of the more chilling psychological aspects of Jamaican life. Venerable authors include Olive Senior, Dennis Scott, Hazel Campbell and Trevor Fearon.

**Tony Sewell** *Jamaica Inc* (UK/JA X-Press). Gripping and intelligent fictional history of a strangely familiar political family dynasty.

**Vanessa Spence** *The Roads Are Down* (US/UK Heinemann). Excellent and amusing first novel of a cross-cultural love affair, set in modern-day Kingston and the Blue Mountains.

**Michael Thewell** *The Harder They Come* (US Grove Atlantic/UK/JA X-Press). Novel inspired by Perry Henzell's brilliant movie, telling the story of Rhygin – country boy turned rude boy – who comes to Kingston and gets caught up in gangs and ganja.

**Anthony Winkler** *The Great Yacht Race* and *The Lunatic* (UK/JA Kingston Publishers). Set just before independence, *The Great Yacht Race* is a hilarious look at the lifestyle of Montego Bay's erstwhile "ruling class" as the lawyers, journalists and hotel-owners go through scandal after scandal in preparation for their annual boat race. *The Lunatic* is the more poignant but equally amusing tale of a Jamaican madman, who wanders the island talking with the trees and bushes, and his encounter with Inge, a sexually voracious German tourist.

## History and politics

**Warren Alleyne** *Caribbean Pirates* (UK Macmillan). Alleyne debunks the myths about the region's leading pirates – from Blackbeard to Henry Morgan – in a series of brief portraits.

**Clinton Black** *Port Royal* and *Tales of Old Jamaica* (UK Longman). *Port Royal* is a solid history of the city once known as the "wickedest place on earth"; *Tales* has brief accounts of some of the key events in the island's past, recalling the capture of Jamaica by the British, the story of "Three Fingered" Jack Mansong, and the women pirates, Anne Bonney and Mary Read.

**Mavis Campbell** *The Maroons of Jamaica 1655–1796* (US/UK Africa World Press). Scholarly work that traces the origins of the Maroons during the English invasion of Jamaica in 1655 and follows their development as a community up to the Trelawny war of the late eighteenth century.

**Gad Heuman** *The Killing Time: The Morant Bay Rebellion* (US University of Tenessee Press/UK

Macmillan). Detailed and articulate study of the 1865 rebellion, its causes and the aftermath, and a review of the tradition of protest in Jamaica.

**Darrell Levy** *Michael Manley: The Making of a Leader* (US University of Georgia Press). Detailed biography of the controversial leader, though it never really captures Manley's sparkle, and Levy lets him off rather lightly on some of his acknowledged errors.

**Rupert Lewis & Patrick Bryan (ed)** *Garvey: His Work and Impact* (US/UK Africa World Press). Twenty-one articles on the historical background to Garveyism, his influence on Jamaica and his worldwide legacy.

**Michael Manley** *The Politics of Change – A Jamaican Testament* (UK Andre Deutsch). Interesting overview of the proposed transformation of the island under Manley's PNP government, written as it got underway in the early 1970s.

**JP Parry, Philip Sherlock & Anthony Maingot** *A Short History of the West Indies* (UK Macmillan). The best concise history of the region, taking the story up to the mid-1980s, and good on general issues such as regional co-operation and debt crisis.

**Carey Robinson** *The Fighting Maroons of Jamaica* (JA Sangster's). Accessible, general history of the Maroons up to 1800.

**Andrew Salkey** *Jamaica* (JA Bogle-L'Ouverture). Short, epic poem narrating Jamaican history from pre-Columbus to today in a punchy patois.

**Olive Senior** *The A-Z of Jamaican Heritage* (JA Heinemann). Concise but useful dictionary, with brief entries on everything from Garvey to Manley, Rastas to Pocomania.

**Tony Sewall** *Garvey's children: The legacy of Marcus Garvey* (US Africa World/UK Macmillan). Readable account of Garvey's black power movement and the inspiration it has provided for black nationalists in Jamaica and abroad.

**Verene Shepherd** *The Experience of Indians in Jamaica, 1845–1950* (JA Peepal Tree). Short, scholarly look at Indian indentured labour and its social and economic consequences.

**John Stewart (ed)** *In Old St James* (JA Sangster's). Small collection of stories of the early English settlers, focusing particularly on the ancestors of Elizabeth Barrett Browning.

## Religion, culture and society

**Mervyn Alleyne**, *Roots of Jamaican Culture* (US Routledge). Academic but fascinating exploration of African-Jamaican culture and society covering history, language, music and religion.

**Marcel Bayer** *In Focus Jamaica: A Guide to the People, Politics and Culture* (US Monthly Review/UK Latin America Bureau). Excellent little handbook, with lucid and relevant sections on history, politics, the economy, society and culture.

**Leonard Barrett** *The Rastafarians* (US/UK Beacon Press) and *The Sun and the Drum* (UK Heinemann/JA Sangster's). The former is one of the most comprehensive accounts of the movement, explaining its origins and politics, and looking at related religious movements like the Twelve Tribes of Israel sect. The latter is an in-depth look at the influence of African traditions in Jamaican culture, including language, witchcraft and folk medicine.

**Derek Bishton** *Black Heart Man – A Journey into Rasta* (o/p). Succinct, well-researched foray into the origins and development of the Rastafarian movement in Jamaica, with discussion of Garvey and a host of less known black theorists.

**Adrian Boot and Michael Thomas** *Babylon on a Thin Wire* (UK Thames and Hudson). Evocative photographic portraits of 1970s Kingston, backed up by cynical and informed text.

**Edward Kamau Braithwaite** *Folk Culture of the Slaves in Jamaica* (JA New Beacon). Fact-packed mini-book with an excellent introduction to black culture under slavery as seen through the eyes of a contemporary black Jamaican university professor. Detailed descriptions of the customs among slave societies, including death rituals, religion, music and dance, dress, entertainment tastes, language and even household decor.

**Horace Campbell** *Rasta and Resistance from Marcus Garvey to Walter Rodney* (US Africa World/UK Hansib). Academic but militant discussion of the development and influence of the Rasta religion and philosophy.

**Laurie Gunst** *Born Fe Dead* (USHolt/UK Payback Press). Gripping account of the dark side of political and drug-related violence in Jamaica. Ably researched with the help of Jamaicans in Kingston and New York, this traces the development of Jamaican posses from political lackeys to drug-trafficking gangsters.

**Polly Patullo** *Last Resorts – The Cost of Tourism in the Caribbean* (UK Cassell). Important, well-researched critique of the tourist industry and its impact on the islands.

**Joseph Owens** *Dread: The Rastafarians of Jamaica* (US Heinemann/JA Sangster's). The author worked and taught in the Rasta community, and this is an interesting and sympathetic account.

**Edward Seaga** *Revival Cults in Jamaica* (JA Jamaica Journal Publications). Anthropological descriptions of the beliefs, rituals and practices within Pocomania, Kumina and Zion religions by former prime minister Seaga.

**M.G. Smith, Roy Augier and Rex Nettleford** *Report on the Rastafari Movement* (JA UWI Press). Published in 1960, the first academic study of Rastafari. Dated but accurate description of the contemporary make-up, history, beliefs and rituals of Rasta.

**Andrea Taylor** *Baby Mother* (JA X-Press) One mother's journey through single parenthood – Jamaican style. Also published by X-Press, Patrick Augustus's *Baby Father* and *Baby Father 2* provide the male point of view.

**Anita Waters**, *Race, Class and Political Symbols – Rastafari and Reggae in Jamaican Politics* (US/UK Transatlantic Publications). Academic but thought-provoking study of the manipulation of Rasta and reggae by Jamaican politicians, with a thorough discussion of shenanigans around the volatile 1976 and 1980 elections.

## Music, art and sport

**Petrine Archer Straw & Kim Robinson** *Jamaican Art* (UK/JA Kingston Publishers Limited). Comprehensive account of the development of modern Jamaican art, well-illustrated with examples of all of the major painters and sculptors, from Edna Marley to Kapo.

**Steve Barrow and Peter Dalton** *The Rough Guide to Reggae* (US/UK Rough Guides). Comprehensive, definitive handbook on reggae music.

**Cedella Booker** *Bob Marley* (UK Penguin). Very personal account of Marley's life and death written by his mother, light on the music but heavy on family anecdotes.

**Stephen Davis** *Bob Marley – Conquering Lion of Reggae* (UK Plexus). Businesslike and exhaustive

examination of Marley's life and work, with lots of gossip thrown in.

**Claire Forrester** *Merlene Otte – Unyielding spirit* (JA West Indies Publishing). Enthusiastic biography of Jamaica's greatest present-day sporting hero.

**Dermot Hussey & Malika Lee Whitney** *Bob Marley* (UK/JA Kingston Publishers). Coffee-table heavyweight, with lavish illustrations, interviews with all the principal characters and text by Jamaicans who were part of the unfolding scene.

**Brian Jahn and Tom Weber** *Reggae Island* (UK/JA Kingston Publishers). The story of reggae told mainly through interviews with all of the key players, from the young Garnet Silk to Buju Banton, Bunny Wailer, Ken Booth and Mykal Rose.

**Howard Johnson & Jim Pines** *Reggae – Deep Roots Music* (US/UK o/p). Penetrative exploration of the development of the national music from Kumina through Rasta drumming, mento, ska, rocksteady and roots reggae.

**Bruce King (ed)** *West Indian Literature* (US Shoe String Press o/p/UK Macmillan). Historical survey of West Indian writing, followed by analysis of individual authors, including Jamaica's Edward Brathwaite and playwright Trevor Rhone.

**Michael Manley** *A History of West Indies Cricket* (UK Deutsch). The late prime minister's superb history of the Caribbean contribution to the world's greatest game.

**Anton Marks** *Dancehall* (JA X-Press). A slippery slide into the steamy world of the dancehall, bringing the familiar players to life and providing an informed slant on ghetto politics.

**Louis Marriot** *Who's Who and What's What in Jamaican Art and Entertainment* (JA Paublo Books). Short biographical entries on all the island's well-known singers, visual artists and dancers, with background pieces on sport, food, dance and theatre.

**Don Taylor** *Marley and Me* (UK/JA Kingston Publishers). Taylor was Bob Marley's manager, and his chatty if rather badly written account – focusing on girlfriends, politics and controversy – is more sensationalist than White's (below).

**Timothy White** *Catch a Fire* (US Holt/UK Omnibus). Exhaustive and loving biography of Bob Marley (including a superb discography), with a detailed look at the early Jamaican music scene and plenty of obeah and superstition.

## Language and humour

**L. Emile Adams** *Understanding Jamaican Patois* (UK/JA Kingston Publishers). User-friendly and intelligent description of patois grammar and language use, with a small dictionary.

**F.G. Cassidy and R.B. LePage**, *Dictionary of Jamaican English* (US/UK Cambridge University Press). Definitive and well-established glossary of Jamaican patois.

**Carolyn Cooper** *Noises in the Blood* (US Duke University Press/UK Macmillan). Provocative study of Jamaican popular culture, particularly the use of language, that looks at Marley's lyrics, the "slackness" of the sexually-explicit DJs and the Jamaican "oral tradition".

**Chester Francis Jackson** *The Dancehall Dictionary* (UK/JA Kingston Publishers). Informed lexicon of dancehall buzzwords and phrases, with sections on Jamaican expletives, dancehall crews and various elements of this vibrant subculture.

**S. Knight and T. Lowrie** *Hustling Jamaican Style* (JA Jamrite Publications). Light-hearted and sarcastically incisive trip through the familiar tourist town hustlers.

**Kim Robinson, Harclyde Walcott & Trevor Fearon**, *The How To Be Jamaican Handbook* (JA Jamrite Publications). Humorous lessons on appropriate behaviour in the resorts and beyond, with painfully accurate tourist caricatures.

## Flora and fauna

**C. Dennis Adams** *Flowering Plants of Jamaica* (US Natural History Publications/UK/JA UWI). Useful introductory guide to Jamaican flora.

**James Bond** *Field Guide to Birds of the West Indies* (US Houghton Mifflin/UK HarperCollins). The classic bird book, from which Ian Fleming took the name of his fictional hero, though generally considered to have been supplanted by the Downer/Sutton book.

**Audrey Downer & Robert Sutton** *Birds of Jamaica: A Photographic Field Guide* (US/UK Cambridge University Press). The definitive field guide on the island's birds, with handy sections on the island's principal habitats and birding "hot spots".

**Philip Gosse** *Gosse's Jamaica 1844–45: Excerpts from a Naturalist's Sojourn in Jamaica* (o/p). Entertaining details of Gosse's trawl across Jamaica, dining on manatee and spotting rare birds.

**Eugene Kaplan** *A Field Guide to the Coral Reefs of the Caribbean and Florida* (US/UK Houghton Mifflin). Attractive guide to the region's reefs.

**G.W. Lennox & S.A. Seddon** *Flowers of the Caribbean; Trees of the Caribbean; Fruits and Vegetables of the Caribbean* (UK Macmillan). Handy pocket-sized books, with glossy, sharp, coloured pictures, and a good general introduction to the region's flora.

**Diane Robertson** *Jamaican Herbs* (JA De Sola Press). Thorough description of the medicinal properties of commonly used herbs, roots, fruits and vegetables, with advice on preparation.

## Food and drink

**Norma Benghiat** *Traditional Jamaican cookery* (UK Penguin). Handy and engagingly written guide to the island's traditional dishes, from ackee and saltfish to curried goat and rice and peas, with all of the classic recipes and a lot more.

**Mike Henry**, *Caribbean Cocktails and Mixed Drinks* (UK/JA Kingston Publishers). All of the classic recipes based mostly around rums and fresh juices.

**Laura Osbourne** *The Rasta Cookbook* (US Africa World/UK Antillean Paperbacks). The low-down on classic Ital cooking with main courses, puddings and (of course) blended health drinks.

**Caroline Sullivan** *Classic Jamaican Cooking* (US/UK Serif). The Jamaican version of Mrs Beeton, little changed since its first publication in 1896. Excellent recipes, anecdotes and the essential "Herbal Remedies and Household Hints".

**Helen Willinsky** *Jerk – Barbecue from Jamaica* (US/UK Crossing Press). DIY jerk manual.

# Index

# the perfect getaway vehicle

## low-price holiday car rental.

rent a car from holiday autos and you'll give yourself real freedom to explore your holiday destination. with great-value, fully-inclusive rates in over 4,000 locations worldwide, wherever you're escaping to, we're there to make sure you get excellent prices and superb service.

what's more, you can book now with complete confidence. our £5 undercut* ensures that you are guaranteed the best value for money in holiday destinations right around the globe.

drive away with a great deal, call holiday autos now on **0990 300 400** and quote ref RG.

# holiday autos
miles ahead

*in the unlikely event that you should see a cheaper like for like pre-paid rental rate offered by any other independent uk car rental company before or after booking but prior to departure, holiday autos will undercut that price by a full £5. we truly believe we cannot be beaten on price.